THE ARMENIAN VERSION OF DANIEL

University of Pennsylvania
Armenian Texts and Studies

SERIES EDITOR
Michael E. Stone

THE ARMENIAN VERSION
OF DANIEL

by
S. Peter Cowe

Scholars Press
Atlanta, Georgia

THE ARMENIAN VERSION
OF DANIEL

BS
1554
.A7
C 68
1992

by

S. Peter Cowe

Published with subventions from the Alex Manoogian Cultural Fund
and the Suren D. Fesjian Endowment for Academic Publications

Library of Congress Cataloging in Publication Data

Cowe, S. Peter.
    The Armenian version of Daniel / by S. Peter Cowe.
    p. cm. — (University of Pennsylvania Armenian texts and
    studies ; no. 9)
    Includes bibliographical references and indexes.
    ISBN 1-55540-687-4 (alk. paper)
    1. Bible. O.T. Daniel—Manuscripts, Armenian. 2. Bible. O.T.
Daniel. Armenian—Versions. I. Bible. O.T. Daniel. Armenian,
1992. II. Title. III. Series.
BS1554.A7C68 1992
224'.5049—dc20
                                    91-48110
                                    CIP

Printed in the United States of America
on acid-free paper

This book is dedicated to
S.P.B.
M.E.S.
J.W.W.
in
gratitude

PREFACE

The last few decades of this century have experienced re-newed interest in the critical study of the Armenian version of the Bible, the establishmen: of an improved textual basis and more detailed examination of its textual affinities and value as a witness to Scripture. This book developed out of that process. It presents the results of a doctoral thesis, subsequently re-vised and expanded, partly with the needs of the non-specialist reader in mind. Both the introduction and general conclusion seek to contextualize the discussion within the wider parame-ters of biblical translation. They also focus attention on the version's contribution to the investigation of Armenia's intel-lectual and cultural history as on its significance as an embodi-ment of political and religious trends of the time.

I should like to take this opportunity to express my warm gratitude to my supervisor, Prof. Michael E. Stone for oversee-ing its primary stage and, in his capacity as general editor of the series, for graciously accepting its publication in this cur-rent form. His advice and encouragement throughout have been much valued and appreciated. I am also beholden to Prof. Emmanuel Tov, also of the Hebrew University of Jerusalem, who, through his seminar in Septuagintal Studies and related computer textual alignment programme, provided an invalu-able introduction to the discipline of researching translation technique. His training in methodological principles did much to sharpen my text-critical judgement.

The kind offices of librarians and other staff at the various Armenian manuscript collections greatly facilitated the task of collating witnesses. I wish to thank particularly His Grace Archbishop Norair Bogharian of the Armenian Patriarchate of Jerusalem for his indulgence of my many queries and readiness to share his unrivalled knowledge of medieval Armenian literature and paleography, also His Grace Archbishop Shahe Ajamian for generously putting his entensive microfilm collection at my disposal and Mr. Sahag Kalaidjian, a true pillar of the patriarchate, for his constant assistance in providing access to rare volumes at the Gulbenkian library. In addition, I am indebted to Fr. Nerses Ter-Nersessian of the Mxit'arist community of Venice, Fr. Grigoris Manian, Generalabt of the congregation in Vienna, the Armenian Catholic Patriarch of Beirut and Abbot of the Monastery of Our Lady at Bzommar for their hospitality during a stay in 1981. At the Matenadaran Institute of Manuscripts in Erevan I am grateful for the general supervision of Dr. Babgen L. Čugaszyan, the codicological information supplied by the late Dr. O. Eganyan and for comparison of notes with my text-critic colleagues Drs. Andranik Zeyt'unyan and Hayk Amalyan. In Britain I am obliged to the curators of oriental manuscripts at the British Library, British and Foreign Bible Society, to the librarian of Lambeth Palace as well as to Sir Harold Bailey for permission to use one of his manuscripts containing the Susanna episode.

These research visits would not have been possible save with the assistance of various foundations which I gladly acknowledge herewith: the board of the Leverhulme Trust Fund for the award of an Overseas Studentship for the years 1978-80, British Council sponsorship of a student exchange with the Soviet Union (1980-81), the Calouste Gulbenkian Foundation for a research grant (1981-82) and the board of managers of the Nubar Pasha Fund of the University of Oxford for welcome support towards microfilm purchase and sundry travel expenses.

I am especially beholden to the trustees of the Alex Manoogian Cultural Fund and the Suren D. Fesjian Endowment for Academic Publications for subventions to defray publication costs and to Mrs. Arpie Balian for her alacrity and precision in preparing the final text.

Above all I am grateful to my examiners, to whom the book is dedicated, for their critical reading of the text and detailed suggestions as to how it might be improved. Finally, I must recall the practical counsels of the Apulian bard which have lost none of their pertinence for the would-be author:

Si quid tamen olim
Scripseris, in Maeci descendat judicis aures,
Et patris, et nostras, nonumque prematur in annum,
Membranis intus positis: delere licebit,
Quod non edideris; nescit vox missa reverti.

CONTENTS

ABBREVIATIONS

a) Texts

Arm the Armenian Version of Daniel. It can be subdivided into an earlier phase (Arm1) and subsequent revision (Arm2).

Geo the Georgian Version of Daniel. It is subdivided according to the MSS employed in the present study: Geo^J=the Jerusalem MS of the Prophets; Geo^O=the Ośki Bible.

Gk the Greek tradition of Daniel. It is subdivided into OG, the 'Old Greek' translation and Th, the version traditionally ascribed to Theodotion.

Luc the Lucianic recension of Th

MT the Massoretic Text, cited according to *Biblia Hebraica Stuttgartensia,* R. Kittel (ed.), Stuttgart, Deutsche Bibelstiftung: 1967-77.

NT the New Testament

OL the Old Latin Version

OT the Old Testament

P the Peshitta Syriac Version

Z the base text of Zohrab's edition of the Armenian Bible: *Astuacašunč̣ hin ew nor ktakaranac̣* [Sacred Scriptures of the Old and New Testaments] Venice: St. Lazar's Press, 1805.

b) Secondary sources frequently referred to

Deut C.E. Cox, *The Armenian Translation of Deuteronomy,* UPATS 2, Chico CA, Scholars Press: 1981.

IV Ezra M.E. Stone, *The Armenian Version of IV Ezra,* UPATS 1, Chico CA, Scholars Press: 1979.

1 Sam   Bo Johnson, *Die armenische Bibelübersetzung als hexaplarischer Zeuge im 1 Samuelbuch.* (C.H. Sjöberg trans.) Coniectanea Biblica OT Series 2. Lund: CWK Gleerup, 1968.

Les origines   S. Lyonnet, *Les origines de la Version arménienne et le Diatessaron.* Biblica et Orientalia 13. Rome, Pontificio Instituto Biblico: 1950.

Jensen: H. Jensen, *Altarmenische Grammatik* Indogermanische Bibliothek 1. Heidelberg, Carl Winter: 1959.

Meillet: A. Meillet, *Altarmenisches Elementarbuch* Indogermanische Bibliothek, Erste Reihe Grammatiken, Band 10. Heidelberg, Carl Winter: 1913.

Ziegler: J. Ziegler, *Susanna. Daniel. Bel et Draco* Septuaginta Vetus Testamentum Graecum Auctoritate Societatis Gottingensis editum Vol. XVI Pars 2. Göttingen, Vandenhoeck & Ruprecht: 1954.

c) Other publications[1]

AB   Analecta Bollandiana

AHUBP   Annual of the Hebrew University Bible Project

AIEA   Association internationale des études arméniennes

AKGW   Gött. Abhandlungen der Königlichen Gesellschaft der Wissenschaften zu Göttingen

Anj B   H. Ačaṙean, *Hayocʿ anjnanunneri baṙaran* [Armenian Prosopographical Dictionery] 5 vols. Erevan, Erevan State University: 1942-62.

Arm B   Id., *Hayeren armatakan baṙaran* [Armenian Etymological Dictionary] 4 vols. Erevan, Erevan State University: 1971-79.

---

[1] Most of these abbreviations and those of books of the Bible conform to the "Instructions for Contributors," *JBL* 99 (1980), pp.83-97.

Bib Biblica
BIOSCS Bulletin of the International Organization for Septuagint and Cognate Studies
BK Bedi Kartlisa
B Mat Banber Matenadarani
B Mus Bibliothèque du Muséon
CATSS Computer assisted tools for Septuagint Studies
CBQMS Catholic Biblical Quarterly: Monograph Series
CHB The Cambridge History of the Bible
CMH The Cambridge Medieval History
CSCO Corpus Scriptorum Christianorum Orientalium
Ejm Ejmiacin
HA Handes Amsoreay
HIS Harvard Iranian Series
HO Handbuch der Orientalistik
HR Hatch, E. and H.A. Redpath, *A Concordance to the Septuagint and the Other Greek Versions of the OT* vols.1-3. Oxford, Clarendon Press: 1892-1906; reprinted Graz 1954.
HTR Harvard Theological Journal
IASHP Israel Academy of Sciences and Humanities Proceedings
ICC International Critical Commentary
IDB The Interpreter's Dictionary to the Bible
IEJ Israel Exploration Journal
ITQ Irish Theological Quarterly
JBL Journal of Biblical Literature
JBS Jerusalem Biblical Studies
JJS Journal of Jewish Studies
JQR Jewish Quarterly Review
JSAS Journal of the Society for Armenian Studies
Mus Le Muséon

MSU	Mitteilungen der Septuaginta Unternehmens der Akademie der Wissenschaften in Göttingen
NAW	Gött. Nachrichten der Akademie der Wissenschaften in Göttingen
NBH	*Nor Baïgirk Haykazean Lezui* [New Dictionery of the Armenian Language]
NGW	Gött. Nachrichten von der (kgl.) Gesellschaft der Wissenschaften zu Göttingen
OBO	Orbis Biblicus et Orientalis
OC	Orientalia Christiana
OLP	Orientalia Lovaniensia Periodica
Or Chr	Oriens Christianus
OTS	Oudtestamentische Studien
PBH	Patmabanasirakan Handēs [Historico-philological Journal]
PETSE	Papers of the Estonian Theological Society in Exile
PG	Patrologia Graeca
PIC	Peshitta Institute Communication
PO	Patrologia Orientalis
PTA	Papyrologische Texte und Abhandlungen
RB	Revue Biblique
REA	Revue des études arméniennes
REB	Revue des études byzantines
RSR	Recherches de science religieuse
SBLTT	Society of Biblical Texts and Translations
SC	Sources chrétiennes
Sef	Sefarad
SeT	Studi e Testi
SJOT	Scandinavian Journal of the Old Testament
SP-B	Studia Post-Biblica
SSN	Studia Semitica Neerlandica

TECC   Textos y Estudios <<Cardenal Cisneros>>
UPATS   University of Pennsylvania Armenian Texts and
        Studies
VT   Vetus Testamentum
WZKM   Wiener Zeitschrift für die Kunde des Morgenlandes
ZAW   Zeitschrift für die alttestamenttiche Wissenschaft

Ziegler's Classification of Th Witnesses

B-26-46-130-239	La Sa Aeth Hippol
A-106-584	(A'=A-106; A'=A-584;
	A''=A-106-584)
Q-230-233-541	(Aeth) (230'=230-233;
	230'=230-541;
	230''=230-233-541)
46-130-534	Aeth Arab (46'=46-130;
	46'=46-534; 46''=46-130-534)
O=V-62-147	Origenic Recension (62'=62-147)
L=22-36-48-51-96-231-763	Lucianic Recension
11=311-538	111=88-449-770 (11+ 111 = 11')
	(L'=L+11; L'=L+111; L''=L+11+111)
	Zᵛⁱ Chr Tht
C=87-91-490	Catena Group
c=49-90-405-764	(C'=C+c)
Aeth=Ethiopic Version	Arm=Armenian Version
La=Latin Versions	Arab=Arabic Version
Laᶜ=Cod. Constantiensis	Laˢ=fragmenta Sangallensia
Laᵛ=Vulgata (ed. Hetzenbauer)	zu Susanna, Canticum Trium
	Puerorum, Bel et Draco
Laʷ=Cod. Wirceburgensis	
Bo=Bohairic Version	Sa=Sahidic Version
Fa=Fayumic Version	Co=Bo+Sa (+Fa)

Sy=Syriac Versions

Syh=Syrohexaplaric Version Syp=Palestinian Syriac Version

Sy^L=Syriac text published by P.A. de Lagarde, *Libri Veteris Testamenti* Apocryphi Syriace, Lipsae-Londinii,

F.A. Brockhaus: 1861, pp.126-138.

Sy^W=Syriac text published by Brian Walton, *Biblia Sacra poly - glotta,* Londini, 1657.

The present study distinguishes the two Syriac texts of Susanna evinced by Sy^W in Biblia Sacra Polyglotta, vol. iv as follows:

MSa=the upper text

MSb=the lower text ('altera versio')

TRANSLITERATION

Armenian transliterations follow the Hübschmann-Meillet-Benveniste system with the following exceptions:

i) names of wellknown historical figures with a widespread traditional spelling.

ii) names of writers who have regularly employed another form of transliteration in Latin characters.

iii) the character *ը* is rendered by *ë.*

Georgian transliterations follow the system recommended by the *Revue des études géorgiennes et caucasiennes* with similar exceptions.

INTRODUCTION

Enigmatic in authorship, date,[1] composition,[2] language[3] and interpretation, the book of Daniel has exerted an insatiable fascination for the most heterogeneous circle of readers of any part of scripture. Armed with incurable curiosity or a flamboyant flair for inductive reasoning, exegetes have not infrequently employed the greatest ingenuity in wresting meaning from its symbolic mysteries.[4] Originating out of traditions perhaps remounting several centuries,[5] its central figure not only attracted secondary narratives to the work in its canonical form, but was seminal in the production of further materials from the same cycle such as the Prayer of Nabonidus extant at Qumran.[6] Radiating his influence directly over the undulating currents of apocalyptic,[7] the seer has sustained his role as literary model for other genres also down the modern times.[8]

Consequently, it is natural to expect that the writing would stimulate the Armenian imagination upon encounter. Moreover, it is likely that the process predates the invention of an alphabet at the beginning of the fifth century A.D. which permitted a written acquaintance with the work. With the establishment of Christianity in Armenia during the previous

1

century, congregations would have gained familiarity with portions of it from the divine office. Institutionalized with the
translation of the Jerusalem lectionary in the mid century,
Daniel's status was solemnized by association with the holiest
festivals of the Christian year, Easter and Theophany.[9]
Furthermore, Armenia's clerical literati were in daily contact
with the book from worship at matins.[10]

Their overall impression of the seer was informed by exposure to secondary reflections on his significance from texts
like the *Vitae Prophetarum*[11] which regularly accompany the
book in medieval manuscripts.[12] Additionally, there exists a
legend regarding the invention of the relics of Daniel's three
companions in Babylon which has been traced to the reign of
the Persian king Bahram V (421-439).[13] It appears that the account entered Armenian via Syriac;[14] however, according to an
indigenous branch of the tradition, the relics found their final
resting place in the region of Gołtn.[15] Thus Armenian receptivity to Danielic materials continued until a relatively late period
borrowing now from Latin,[16] now from Greek sources. A striking instance which may derive from the latter is offered by
"Daniel's Seventh Vision", a seventh century *vaticinium post
eventum*[17] which its author regarded as supplementing and
consummating the revelation of the first six visions into which
the biblical prophecies had been divided.[18]

It is also likely that Daniel provided the visionary paraphernalia for the predictions attributed to Armenia's early hi-
erarchs from the line of St. Gregory the Illuminator. Thus his
grandson Yusik was vouchsafed the appearance of an angel to
reveal the character of his descendants on the catholicosal
throne.[19] Similarly, after his murder, the chorepiscopus Daniel
warns the nobles their action was to precipitate the collapse of
both the temporal and spiritual authority.[20] Finally,[21] the last
scion of the dynasty, St. Sahak (d. 439), under whose direction
Daniel's prophecies were rendered into Armenian, is disclosed
an apparition of the "end times" redolent with number symbol-
ism and featuring the abomination of desolation which is

specifically equated with the prophet's vision.[22] Moreover, it is said to resemble the spectacle witnessed by his forebear Gregory.[23]

The latter's apostolate in Armenia too bore sufficient similarity to Daniel's activity at the Persian court for certain biblical motifs to be applied by the compilers of lives of the saint.[24] In essence, they depict the man of God admonishing a pagan king (Trdat III) for his idolatry and thus undergoing torture and imprisonment in a pit until ultimately vindicated and released. Meanwhile, the monarch is subjected to humiliation in bestial form[25] until he repents and is restored to humanity by the saint's intercession. Subsequently, Gregory experiences a vision embodying the foundation charter for what became Armenia's principal cathedral and forewarning of a period of bitter dissension within the church.[26]

Many would fall away from the 'holy covenant' and persecute those who remained faithful to it. Here parallels with St. Sahak's vision become apparent, where the martyr's death of a catholicos is prefigured after a time of great hardship.[27] The historical situation both seem to envisage is the attempt by the Persian king Yazdgard II to reintroduce Zoroastrianism as state religion in Caucasia. In the ensuing Armenian revolt which led to the martyrdom of the primate and several high ranking clergy as well as the commander Vardan Mamikonean, a faction of the nobility deserted to the enemy under the governor, Vasak Siwni. However, appreciating the impracticability of implementing such a policy, the Iranians agreed to a settlement. Nevertheless, this occurred not before they had razed a number of churches and erected a fire temple in the capital Dwin, deeds which obviously reminded the authors of Antiochus Epiphanes' desecration of the Jerusalem Temple (Dan 11:31).

Hence Etišē, one of the main sources for these cataclysmic events once more appeals to Daniel's model, particularly in his characterization of the protagonists.[28] Yazdgard is portrayed as a Nebuchadnezzar bestialized by his megalomania until, humbled by adversity, he acknowledges God's power and permits freedom of worship. Likewise, Vasak assumes some of Belshazzar's traits in persisting on the 'wrong' course when he should have known better and is therefore a victim of the same summary judgement. There is no one Daniel figure, but rather a composite of all the martyrs, confessors and others enduring suffering for their faith who, like the seer and his companions (Dan 2:48-49), are devoted to the king's service in all respects other than religion.

Consequently, we observe the centrality of the book of Daniel for early Armenian Christianity. The two major foci of the period, the conversion of the court and its official promulgation as well as its baptism of fire in the proscription of the 440's and 450's are both represented by means of imagery heavily dependent on that work. Its continuing popularity is indicated by the large number of manuscripts to adduce it, many of which are here investigated textually for the first time. Previously research focused on what was available in print and publication policy in turn preserved considerable continuity with contemporary scribal conventions.

Although Armenian printing was inaugurated at the beginning of the sixteenth century[30] and the first Psalter was made available in 1565-66,[31] as the Bible was not *per se* a liturgical book, but rather a vehicle for study and reflection,[32] Daniel did not appear in print until 1666-68.[33] The event is to be interpreted against the background of an important cultural revival within the catholicate at Ejmiacin and in the prosperous merchant colony of New Julfa. The undertaking was directed by the enterprising primate Yakob Jułayeci (1655-80) who had already appreciated the significance of the medium from his teacher Xačatur Kesaraci who had established a press at New Julfa in 1639. However, despite the novel format, the overall process remained the same, the work being based on the text of one manuscript, the Het'um Bible of 1295 (M180).[34]

The choice of exemplar mirrors the vogue for copying fine Cilician codices which is manifested earlier in the century at

Istanbul and New Julfa.[35] At the same time the editor Oskan Erewanc'i's commission had been to harmonize the traditional Armenian numeration system with that of the Vulgate and complete its concordance of parallel passages.[36] Discovering in the course of this a number of discrepancies, he informs us that he retranslated the books of Sirach and IV Ezra from Latin.[37] What he fails to disclose to his readership is the fact that he also assimilated his exemplar to the Vulgate in numerous other passages,[38] as his later Georgian counterparts were to 'correct' their text to the standard of the Slavonic before the Moscow printing of 1743.[39]

His action testifies at once to the vitality of the impact of the Counter-Reformation on the east[40] and Armenian readiness to avail themselves of European science and scholarship.[41] While at Ejmiacin Oskan had studied with the Dominican Paulo Piromalli at the catholicos' invitation. Moreover, the latter was in correspondence with Pope Alexander VII and ultimately accepted papal supremacy. Oskan too received a small subvention from the Holy See for his translation activity.[42]

His harmonization to the Vulgate primarily concerned the Gospels. In contrast, my sample collations of Daniel attested his fidelity to his base manuscript. Apart from various minor alterations to bring unusual forms into conformity with the norm, the substance of the original is maintained.[43]

The second printing of this Bible in 1733-35 at Venice heralded a notable methodological advance.[44] Though founding his monastic brotherhood under papal auspices, Mxit'ar Sebastac'i (1676-1749) reveals none of Oskan's extratextual preoccupations. With the monumental industry and encyclopaedic breadth which was to typify his order he set about comparing the existing Armenian edition with the Paris polyglot of 1645 in order to ascertain whether textual unclarities derived from the translators or subsequent copyists. Exploiting the manpower provided by his novices, he completed this prolegomenon to the edition in three years. Of the seven languages represented in the polyglot special attention was accorded the Greek and Syriac as being the most probable *Vorlage* of the Armenian version.[46] Where it was determined that the printed text had suffered scribal corruption, corrections were suggested in the margin which corresponded more closely with the other versions. Perceiving the significance of corroborating his hypothetical reconstructions, he consulted a number of older lectionaries and gospelbooks and records a fair degree of agreement. Unfortunately, he does not specify his results to assist the reader in appraising his proposed improvements.

This deficiency stimulated the vardapet Sargis Malean to broach a comprehensive collation of the edition with the biblical witnesses available to him at the Armenian patriarchal library in Jerusalem. He exposed his findings in a work of 1773 which reveals his sound grasp of textual and editorial principles. Realizing the effect of repeated copying on the text, he reserved special treatment for the older copies and also shows awareness of the evolution of local texts. Pursuing Mxit'ar's axiom concerning the significance of the Greek version, he suggests that in future editions the verse alignment should be accommodated to that standard rather then the Vulgate to facilitate comparison, a proposition adopted in the present edition. Another major advance he introduced was the elaboration of a system of *sigla* to designate the various witnesses, thus permitting the compilation of a general profile of a given exemplar as well as the investigation of possible group affinities among the available manuscripts.[47]

The next major milestone in the history of the Armenian text is formed by the edition of 1805 by another Mxitarist, Yovhannēs Zohrapean (1756-1829 ; hereafter Zohrab) who (independently) incorporated certain of Malean's proposals. Breaking with the tradition of the Het'um Bible, Zohrab preferred the oldest complete biblical codex accessible in the Venice collection (V1508 of 1319 A.D.)[48] as base manuscript for his diplomatic edition. Departing from it only in cases of manifest error, he indicates the corrupt reading in a footnote. He also supplements this by offering selected variants culled from a further eight witnesses[49] in the OT and an indeterminately larger number for the NT. Fundamentally the same text was republished at Venice in 1860[50] and has continued to function as the prime resource for scholarly inquiry into the Armenian version until the recent past.

Appreciable as Zohrab's achievement is in light of the editorial standards of daughter versions of the Greek available in his day, its appropriateness as a tool for textual research has been increasingly undermined. Age and comprehensiveness, the two main criteria for the selection of the base manuscript, similarly determined acceptance of the Codex Ambrosianus for a parallel role in the Peshitta Institute of Leiden's edition of the Syriac OT. However, as the editors readily acknowledge, such a manuscript may be far from preserving the best recoverable text in any particular book.[51]

With the increased accessibility of data relating to the holdings of Armenian biblical manuscripts in collections worldwide through the publication of catalogues[52] and compilation of more specialized listings,[53] several earlier witnesses have been intimated. More importantly, the facilitation of taking collation samples from a larger range of codices has revealed the existence of even certain later manuscripts which are consistently of a higher textual calibre than V1508. In comparison, the latter has been evaluated as secondary and developed. It follows that Zohrab's edition offers the critic a misleading image of the version, obscuring many of its primitive readings.

Obviously the central objective of a diplomatic text is to present a conspectus of the material without necessarily claiming priority for any witness or variant. Hence, the role of the apparatus is crucial. Yet Zohrab's notes are of limited usefulness, since unclarity surrounds its composition and layout. Not only are the data provided not comprehensive, but there is no explanation of the selection procedure of what evidence is included. Moreover, as he did not follow Malean's example in assigning his manuscripts *sigla*, but cites them by vague terms ("many", "few", "one copy") it is impossible to trace the characteristics of a specific manuscript or study relations between witnesses and progress towards a rudimentary stemma. Since the key factor influencing the choice of codices was accessibility, one would be justified in harbouring reservations about the representative nature of an apparatus compiled under such conditions in providing a cross section of the extant evidence. Rather, it is arguable that for the result to be a faithful reflection of the whole it should spring from prior knowledge of the main contours of the manuscript tradition and be executed according to clearly formulated principles. Consequently, under scrutiny most of Zohrab's OT manuscripts which can be identified in fact exhibit a late, secondary text reminiscent of V1508.[54]

Thus, the first part of the present study, embracing chapters one to three, is devoted to the enunciation and implementation of principles designed to isolate a base text closer to the hypothetical autograph of the version and an apparatus more representative of the major textual forms in which the book circulated in medieval Armenia.

Chapter one analyzes the manuscript tradition with a view to uncovering its internal structure. Taken singly codices are of debatable textual value. Only after their position within the on-going copying process is properly grasped can they be used intelligently. The manuscript tradition of a work is never quite a monolithic block, but can be differentiated into component groups by conjunctive error, the particular pattern of departures (deliberate or inadvertent) from the original text by the scribe of the archetype which is retained by the copyists of later members of the group and thus constitutive of group membership. It must be admitted that the editions in circulation have exercised a baneful influence on researchers by conveying the false impression that greater uniformity obtains. To offset this three sample collations were taken from all available manuscripts, the analysis of which established the existence of five main groups, some comprising subordinate sub-groups.

These groupings determined by internal evidence of readings imply a documentary relationship between the various members which should hold stable throughout the compass of the archetype. As the one volume Bible was a relatively late invention in Armenia,[55] the original units of copying were much smaller. Consequently, consistency or variation in group affiliation from book to book has important ramifications for an attempt to reconstruct the version's transmission.[56] As a contribution towards this in the final part of the chapter the manuscript groupings distinguished in Daniel are compared with those emerging from full or partial collations of other books of the OT. With the data provided by future studies it may ultimately be possible to produce a reasonably full account of the version's documentary history, albeit it would preclude a rigorous application of stemmatics because of the loss of too many of the intermediary links.

Obviously, these constellations of inner-Armenian convergence imply a complex network of scribal involvement without, however, leaving any clue as to the specifics of the process. Nevertheless we have access to other data which can assist in offering a historical explanation of the textual phenomenon. As it was traditional for Armenian copyists to insert colophons detailing the circumstances of their commission, chapter two utilizes this material of provenance and date along with documentary type to map out the broad contours of the local texts that seem to have come into existence by the fourteenth century and trace the concomitant development from part-Bibles to complete Bible codices.

Building on the foregoing scrutiny of witnesses by internal and external criteria, a selection of fifteen manuscripts was made in chapter three for full collation towards the edition. They were chosen for their representativeness within their assigned group, exhibiting few eccentricities in either substantive or orthographic variants. Thereafter the method of setting out the evidence is outlined and lists of recurrent orthographical variants appended so as not to burden the apparatus unduly.[57]

In the resulting diplomatic edition the printed text is that of a manuscript representing the best early group, while the variants exposed in the apparatus offer a profile of the whole version in microcosm.

Equipped with the textual raw materials, the second part of the study sketches the model to be observed in reconstructing the version's primitive form, focusing on the identity of Arm's *Vorlage*. In pursuing this end the Greek, Syriac and Georgian versions of the book are consulted. Questions regarding the mode of reconstruction are discussed in connection with the translation technique which Arm reflects. By recovering the principles which informed the translation process and the consistency with which they were applied, it is possible to establish a far higher degree of accuracy in determining how Arm may be retroverted and what contacts it evinces with outside sources. This in turn facilitates decisions on the priority of variant readings in Armenian.

As colophons document manuscript production, so a number of historical works sketch the background and course of events which generated the Armenian version in the first half of the fifth century. Much textcritical attention has been devoted to their interpretation as a means of determining the *Vorlage* from which it derived. However, their conflicting conclusions are a clear indication of the obscurity and contradictory nature of the accounts. The four prime sources which relate these events are subjected to careful scrutiny at the beginning of chapter four.[58]

The only means of testing the veracity of such records is a close analysis of the version's textual affinities book by book. Accordingly, a pioneering study of Daniel appeared in the early part of this century[59] which, though hampered by the inadequacy and unreliability of its bases for comparison,[60] reached the conclusion that Th constituted Arm's primary parent text, despite some agreements noted with OG. In cases where Arm≠Gk the readings were checked against P[61] with positive results in a number of instances.[62] The potential significance of this finding was enhanced by the subsequent discovery that the earliest stratum of the Armenian gospels was rendered from Syriac.[63] Moreover, it was argued that in addition to diverse Armenian sources, this texttype was partially preserved in the Old Georgian version which had absorbed these readings from an Armenian intermediary.[64] Taking into account the abundance of manuscript evidence which current editions of these versions embrace, it was deemed necessary to broach the issue afresh. Accordingly chapter four surveys the possible interrelationships between Arm, P and Geo where Arm≠Gk. From this emerge various similarities with findings in the gospels, including the bipartite division of the version into an earlier (Arm1) and secondary phase (Arm2) and Geo's dependence on the former.

Having established Arm's contact with P, the question of the version's Gk affinities is investigated in chapter five. In contrast to the relatively uniform transmission history characterizing P,[65] Th witnesses can be classified unto several categories more or less affected by various types of recensional activity. After outlining the key points of Gk's textual development Arm's textual orientation is plotted against that general framework.[66] The presence of consistent textual variation and appearance of doublets in Armenian witnesses confirm the existence of two independent points of contact with divergent Gk texttypes.

The precise delineation of Arm's parent texts and assessment of its reliability as a witness to certain textual standards can only be ascertained by a detailed alignment of the versions.[67] Moving beyond the rather broad, impressionistic application of such categories as "literal" and "free" a more nuanced approach to Arm's morphological, syntactic and semantic analysis is required. This procedure would elucidate more precisely the version's allegiance in many instances of textual variation. Moreover, its comprehensive employment would reduce the element of subjectivity which was always present to a noticeable degree when concern for translation technique concentrated atomistically on readings considered as singular and lacking in outside support.[68]

This principle has automatic implications for the mode in which Armenian evidence should be cited in editions of Gk or P. The sort of issues involved may be illustrated by some of the Z retroversions effected in Ziegler's apparatus.

5:21 Th ἡ καρδία αὐτοῦ μετὰ τῶν θηρίων ἐδόθη (=MT)

Z   սիրտ   ընդ գազանս տուաւ նմա (=Geo)
αὐτοῦ 1°] > Arm

Although in gneral retroversions are made with imagination and sensitivity, the above does not allow for Arm's regular tendency to avoid semitisms.[69] Thus no textual variation from the majority text on the part of Arm's *Vorlage* need be presumed.

6:7 Thᵛὅπως ὃς ἂν αἰτήσῃ   αἴτημα

Z   զի   եթէ խնդրեսցէ ոք խնդրուածս

ἄν] εαν L C' alii: + τις C' Sa ոք/խնդրուածս] tr M287 et al
αἴτημα] +τις L; pr τις 26 233' ; pr τι 11 Laˢ (vid) Arm

Here the Armenian indefinite pronoun designating persons (ոք) and therefore equivalent to τις[70] has been wrongly aligned with the corresponding form denoting objects (τι) for which the normal Armenian equivalent would be ինչ.[71] From the perspective of the textual examination in chapter five of the present work the impact of this misrepresentation is to detach Arm2 (Z reading) from some of the extant witnesses closest to its *Vorlage*.[72] In addition, the transposition by M287 etc. exactly parallels the Lucianic recension which is the main translation base of Arm1.[73]

The retroversion at Bel:8 (αὐτά] haec omnia Arm) rightly observes the disjunction between Greek and Armenian idiom in rendering indefinite expressions, the latter preferring the singular number (զայն ամենայն) over against the Greek neuter plural.[74] However, the treatment of v.21 seems to have been misled by Arm's rearrangement of the Gk word order.

Th ὀργισθεὶς ὁ βασιλεὺς *τότε* συνέλαβε τοὺς ἱερεῖς

Z *յայժմամ́ բարկացեալ թագաւորն կալաւ զքրւրմ́ն*

    om τότε 230 Bo Arm

Instead of leaving the temporal adverb unrepresented the Arm translators merely relocated it at the beginning of the phrase.

As we have already observed, the process of retroversion is complicated by Arm's dual contact with Gk witnesses. Another facet of the same problem is its affinity with P, which impinges on the following variant at 4:12:

Th μετὰ τῶν θηρίων ἡ μερὶς αὐτοῦ

Z *րնդ զազանս անապատի բաժին նորա*

    τῶν θηρίων] + αγριων Q-230'' Aeth^P Arm^P Hippol

    (*զազանս*] + *անապատի* M2585 M2627' M182'')

The normal translation of ἄγριος is *վայրի*,[75] however Z reads *անապատի* (=ἔρημος [76]). At v.18 where the reading is paralleled the main Syriac text reads ‫ܒܪܐ‬,, as opposed to ‫ܒܪ‬, at v.12. While it is true that both terms appear in the sense of 'plain, field', only the former denotes 'desert'.[77] Hence it appears more likely that the Armenian rendering is dependent on P's interpretation of Th in v.18. Returning to our consideration of v.12, we note from Ziegler that Armenian witnesses are divided in attesting the plus. From the survey of the manuscript tradition in chapter one it emerges that it is adduced by representatives of groups B3, C3 and D-E only.[78] There it is also demonstrated that this type of constellation usually arises from secondary conflation of sub-groups B3 and C3 to a D standard.[79] This in turn cogently suggests the variant's secondary character within Arm's transmission history. Consequently, it would seem that both the reading of Gk MS Q and satellites and that of the Armenian codices derive from independent assimilation to the parallel passage in v.18. Hence it is misleading to present the traditions as if they were in direct relation.

Another aspect of the multifaceted issue of retroversion concerns the differentiation of semantic levels in a given lexeme, which may be exemplified by a reading from 4:10 (cf. also vv. 14, 20):

Th   ἰδοὺ ιρ καὶ ἅγιος ἀπ᾽ οὐρανοῦ κατέβη
OG   ἰδοὺ ἄγγελος ἀπεστάλη ... ἐκ τοῦ οὐρανοῦ
Z   ահա qnιωրթուն և սուրբ իջանէր յերկնից
vigil Arab=Vulg et P; angelus Arm

Instead of transliterating the semitic root ιρ in company with Th, several other versions provide a translation. However, these in turn differ among themzelves in rendering either 'alert' according to the etymological denotation (P, Vulg, Arab) or 'angel' according to the generic connotation (OG). The impression given by Ziegler's Latin translation of the Armenian evidence is that it falls within the latter category, leaving open the possibility of interpreting it as an instance of OG influence such as has been discovered in other parts of the book.[80] Yet, not only would we have expected the term հրեշտակ in that case as the most common equivalent of ἄγγελος,[81] but the necessity of construing the Arm reading in this way is removed when we note that the root meaning of qnιωրթուն also is 'alert'.[82] Con-sequently, it is more plausible that the translators' exegesis was guided by P and in turn influenced the Georgian rendering ოჳობჲოჳო (vigil). Accordingly, the Arm testimony should be presented along with the other versions noted in the apparatus.

Establishing the character of Arm's translation technique is a major determinant of priority among the version's manuscript variants. However, as the earliest witnesses remount only to the thirteenth century and are thus separated from the origin by a 'dark age' spanning some eight centuries, it is in order to query how far they preserve Arm's pristine form. As a result, the attempt is made in chapter seven to verify this by comparison with two independent streams of tradition. Passages from Daniel have found a place in three liturgical books, the breviary (ժամագիրք), lectionary (ճաշng) and ritual (մաշtnng). Moreover, as has already been indicated, the book exerted a profound fascination for several Armenian writers. Their compositions offer unparalleled access to the earliest period of copying when handled with due regard to the purpose and method of citation.

The General Conclusion provides a synthesis of the work as a whole, setting out the main results of the study and sketching their implications for future research on the Armenian Bible. In particular, it probes the relation of the translation process to contemporary exegetical trends and contextualizes its role within the development of Armenian translation technique in terms of similar undertakings by neighbouring cultures in ancient and medieval times. Tracing the plausible manuscript units and local text-forms in which the book circulated in medieval Armenia, it attempts to elucidate the popularity of the main Cilician text which determined the previous course of investigation of the version through the medium of the printed editions. Finally, it explores the way forward to a fully critical edition of Arm, outlining the criteria by which this may be achieved through separation of the strata.

NOTES

1. Debate continues between conservative scholars adopting a sixth century date and others regarding the work as a pseudonymous composition of the second century B.C. Nor is it clear that all elements of the book derive from the same time and milieu.

2. It continues to be disputed whether the work represents an integral whole or compilation of disparate elements, the court narratives of chapters one to six and visions of seven to twelve. The question of the *Urtext* has also been posed by OG. Previously considered a rather free reworking in chapters four to six, it has more recently been proposed as the faithful reflection of a different semitic *Vorlage.*

3. The transition from Hebrew to Aramaic in 2:4b-7:28 has long puzzled interpreters. There has also been vigorous discussion about the nature of the semitic *Vorlage* of the additional materials found in the Greek text (Susanna, 3:25-90 and Bel and the Dragon).

4. For a recent example of the politicizing trend of interpretation see H. Lindsay and G.C. Carlson, *Late Great Planet Earth,* Zondervan, 1976.

5. It has been suggested that facets of Daniel's characterization derive from the prototypical wise man Danel mentioned in Ezek 14:14, 28:3.

6. See F.M. Cross, "The Contribution of the Qumran Discoveries to the Study of the Biblical Text", *IEJ* xvi (1966), pp.81-95 and M. McNamara, "Nabonidus and the Book of Daniel", *ITQ* xxxvii (1970), pp.131-149. In cave 4 three pseudo-Daniel Aramaic fragments have also been found.

7. Beyond the biblical purview of Mark 13 and Revelation, the work's continuing influence may be observed on texts redefining the calamity in terms of the threat of Islam on Christianity. See *inter alia* K. Berger (ed.), *Die griechische Danieldiegese,* SP 27, Leiden, E.J. Brill: 1976.

8. See especially S.D. Baris, "The American Daniel as Seen in Hawthorne's The Scarlet Letter", *Biblical Patterns in Modern Literature,* D.H. Hirsch and N. Aschkenasy (eds.), Chico, CA, Scholars Press: 1984, pp.173-185 and J. Fruchtman, *The Apocalyptic Politics of Richard Price and Joseph Priestley,* American Philosophical Soc., 1983.

9. For details of the development of the rite and its translation see A. Renoux, *Le codex arménien Jérusalem 121.* For the Daniel passages see particularly pp.75-77, 167-169.

10. For a brief description of the Armenian office see R. Taft, S.J., *The Liturgy of the Hours in East and West,* Collegeville, MN, The Liturgical Press: 1986, pp.219-224, especially p.222 for the canticles from Dan 3. The breadth of impact this afforded the text is well testified by the application of the Song of the Three to Adam's situation on his expulsion from paradise. The youths' invocation of all the natural forces to praise their creator is transmuted into the protoplast's appeal to the same phenomena to commiserate with him in his wretchedness. This dramatic monologue forms part of the medieval Armenian text *Patmuṙiwn apašxaruṙean Adamay ew Ewayi* [History of the Repentance of Adam and Eve]. See W.L. Lipscomb, *The Armenian Apocryphal Adam Literature* UPATS 8, Scholars Press, Atlanta, GA: 1990, p.212.

11. For the Greek text see Th. Schermann (ed.), *Prophetarum vitae fabulosae,* Leipzig, Teubner: 1907 and the Armenian S. Yovsep'eanc *Ankanon girk' hin ktakaranac* [Uncanonical Books of the Old Testament], Venice, St. Lazar's Press: 1896, pp.207-227 and for a study of the metamorphoses of character see D. Satran, "Daniel: Seer, Philosopher, Holy Man", *Ideal Figures in Ancient Jusaism,* G.W.E. Nickelsburg and J.J. Collins (eds.), Chico, CA, Scholars Press: 1980, pp.33-48. Consonant with this interpretation, the Armenian scholar Yohannęs Sarkawag (d.1129) exalts Daniel and his companions as paragons of moral purity for young people to emulate. See A.G. Abrahamyan.

Hovhannes Imastaseri Matenagrutyunë [The Complete Works of Yovhannēs the Philosopher] Erevan, State University Press: 1956, pp.308-9.

12. See M.E. Stone, *The Apocryphal Literature in the Armenian Tradition,* Jerusalem, IASHP 4/4: 1969, pp.72-77.

13. G. Garitte (ed.), "Le texte arménien de l'Invention des Trois Enfants de Babylone", *Mus* 74 (1961), pp.91-108.

14. For subsidiary details see id., "L'Invention géorgienne des Trois Enfants de Babylone", *Mus* 72 (1959), pp.69-100.

15. On this see M.E. Stone, "An Armenian Tradition Relating to the Death of the Three Companions of Daniel", *Mus* 86 (1973), pp.111-123.

16. One such work is included in the corpus "The Names, Works and Deaths of the Holy Prophets", which is preserved in two manuscripts probably of the late seventeenth or early eighteenth centuries. In view of the volume of material entering Armenian from Latin in the seventeenth century, it is quite likely this rendering derives from the same period. For the data on Daniel see M.E. Stone (ed.), *Armenian Apocrypha Relating to the Patriarchs and Prophets,* Jerusalem, IASH: 1982, p.164. On apocalyptic texts extant in Armenian see M.E. Stone, "Jewish Apocryphal Literature in the Armenian Church", *Mus* 95 (1982), p.306.

17. See G. Kalemkiar, "Die siebente Vision Daniels", *WZKM* 6 (1892) pp.109-135 for a preliminary study and edition and pp.227-240 for German translation. In his dissertation ("Die Schrift 'Vom Jungen Daniel' und 'Daniels letzte Vision'", Hamburg, 1972) H. Schmeldt demonstrates that the latter text (which he edits) is not directly affiliated with the Armenian work just cited.

18. See General Conclusion, note 19, p.444.

19. See N.G. Garsoïan, *The Epic Histories,* 3, v, pp.70-72.

20. Ibid., 3, xiv, pp.88-90.

21. A similar vision is also attributed to Sahak's father Nersēs

by the tenth century writer Mesrop Erēc̣. See Sop̣'erḳ'
haykakanḳ VI, Venice, St. Lazar's Press: 1853.

22. Lazar P'arpec̣i, *Patmagirḳ' Hayoc̣,* §17, pp.29-37. On the debate concerning the vision's authenticity and that of book
one of the history see S.P. Cowe, "An Armenian Job
Fragment from Sinai and its Implications".

23. Lazar P'arpec̣i, *Patmagirḳ' Hayoc̣,* §16, p.28.

24. See R.W. Thomson, *Agathangelos History of the
Armenians,* p.lxxxi for the Armenian recension (Aa).
Certain facets of Trdat's modelling are even more explicit
in the Syriac recension (Vs) which probably dates from the
first decade of the seventh century and is also witnessed
by a Karshuni version of 1732. See M. van Esbroeck, "Un
nouveau témoin du livre d'Agathange", *RÉA* NS 8(1971),
p.130. The same is also true of the V recension (in its present form probably from the second half of the sixth century) which survives in Greek and Arabic Versions in
which the Danielic formula 'living God' recurs as a leitmotif
of St. Gregory's teaching. See G. Garitte, *Documents pour
l'étude du livre d'Agathange,* SeT 127, Vatican City,
Bibliotheca Apostolica Vaticana: 1946, §6, 7, 42, 65 etc.

25. On the transformation of the Danielic ox into a wild boar
(varaz) see N.G. Garsoïan, "The Iranian Substratum of the
Agat'angelos' Cycle", *East of Byzantium: Syria and
Armenia in the Formative Period,* N.G. Garsoïan, T.F.
Matthews and R.W. Thomson (eds.), Washington, D.C.
Dumbarton Oaks: 1982, pp.151-172.

26. See R.W. Thomson, *Agathangelos History of the Armenians,* §731-756, pp.272-296.

27. Lazar P'arpec̣i, *Patmagirḳ' Hayoc̣,* p.35.

28. See the discussion of Ełišē's citations in chapter seven and
for further details R.W. Thomson, *Elishε History of
Vardan and the Armenian War* and *Yeghishe: History of
Vardan and the Armenian War.* A photographic reproduc-
tion of the Erevan edition with an introduction by S. Peter
Cowe, Delmar, NY, Caravan Books (forthcoming).

29. Interestingly, the image of the handwriting on the wall (Dan 5:5) which spelled divine judgement on the Babylonian king is utilized by Movsēs Xorenaći in his dramatically heightened depiction of Maštoć's invention of the Armenian alphabet. In a direct citation of the Armenian scriptural text he indicates the forms were vouchsafed the scholar in a vision (*Patmagirk'Hayoc;* III, 53, p.327).

30. The traditional date accepted is 1512.

31. For details see N. Oskanyan et al, *Hay Girkë 1512-1800 t'vakannerin,* pp.8-9.

32. For a discussion of this issue see S.P. Cowe, "A Typology of Armenian Biblical Manuscripts", pp.51-53. The point is underlined by Oskan in his note to readers in which he stresses the impulse moving three New Julfa merchants to offer their financial support to the undertaking was the awareness that there was a paucity of exemplars among Armenians, particularly in the hands of "vardapets, monks and students of the Bible" (N. Oskanyan et al, *Hay Girkë 1512-1800 t'vakannerin,* p.49).

33. N. Oskanyan et al, ibid., pp.44-51.

34. For a description see O. Eganyan et al *Mayr c'uc'ak hayerēn je'agrac;* cols. 729-742. Note especially the remarks on various marginalia concerning chapter and verse numeration which are plausibly regarded as Oskan's work (col.734). In keeping with representatives of the 'Cilician Vulgate', this MS contains Gēorg Skewṙaći's synopses of the various books and was copied by one of the latter's most talented pupils, Step'annos Goyneric'anc', who is known to have executed several other royal commissions. See further General Conclusion, pp.437-8.

35. For details see chapter two, pp.67-8 and the literature cited there.

36. The ardure of this task occupies most of Oskan's dedication to his patron (N. Oskanyan et al, *Hay Girkë 512-1800 t'vakannerin,* pp.49-50). There he notes that the previous efforts to achieve this by Łazar Baberdaći had been nullified

by the inadvertence of copyists (ibid., p.48). For details see chapter two, pp.71-74 and S.P. Cowe, "Armenian Sidelights on Torah Study in 17th Century Poland", *JJS* xxxvii (1986), pp.94-97.

37. Although we are not so informed, his translation activity also extended to the Epistle of Jeremiah, Armenian codices of which are very rare.

38. See further S.P. Cowe, "Problematics".

39. See M. Šanize, "Remarques au sujet de la Bible Géorgienne", pp.105-106.

40. This was particularly advanced by the foundation of the Sacred Congregation de Propaganda Fide and establishment of an Armenian college in 1650 as well as provincial missions in Naxijewan (1630) and New Julfa (1640).

41. Political factors also played a part in this orientation. Mindful of the legacy on the crusades, Catholicos Yakob wished to elicit the pope's support in mounting a western coalition to effect Armenian liberation.

42. For the background to this see A.C. de Veer, "Rome et la Bible arménienne d'Uscan d'après la correspondance de J.-B. van Neercassel", *REB* 16 (1958), pp.172-182.

43. See also H.S. Gehman, "The Armenian Version of the Book of Daniel", p.95.

44. For a description see N. Oskanyan et al, *Hay Girkë 1512-1800 t'vakannerin*, pp.311-333.

45. *Biblia Hebraica, Samaritana, Chaldaica, Graeca, Syriaca, Latina, Arabica,* G.M. Le Joy (ed.), Lutetiae Parisiorum, excludebat A. Vitré: 1645.

46. See N. Oskanyan et al *Hay Girkë 1512-1800 t'vakannerin*, p.312.

47. For an appraisal and translation of the introduction to this work see S.P. Cowe, "An 18th Century Armenian Textual Critic and His Continuing Importance".

48. For a description see B. Sargisean, *Mayr c'uc'ak hayerēn jeŕagrac'*, vol.1, cols.1-20.

49. For the identification of seven of these and a discussion of

their textual witness see General Conclusion, p.439.

50. In this edition the refinement of a critical apparatus has been dispensed with. However, the text has been improved in places by substituting preferred readings of the other witnesses for those of the base manuscript judged to be secondary. Unfortunately, no indication is given of when and why this resort has been made.

51. See P.A.H. de Boer's preface to *The Old Testament in Syriac Genesis-Exodus.* Part 1, fasc.1, Leiden, E.J. Brill: 1977, pp.vii-viii.

52. See further section three of the bibliography.

53. E.g. E.F. Rhodes, *An Annotated List of Armenian New Testament Manuscripts,* Ikebukuro, Tokyo: 1959 and A. Zeyt'unyan, "Astuacašnč̣i hayeren t'argmanut'yan jeṙagrakan miavorneri dasakargman masin" which contains a chronological listing of 228 manuscripts containing at least two books of the Old Testament, (in which V1508 ranks as no.57) supplemented by the continuation in id., *Girk Cnndoc'* p.86 which brings the total to 245.

54. For details see General Conclusion, p.439.

55. See further General Conclusion, pp.435-8.

56. Despite the occurrence of variation in exemplar within a single book in manuscripts of the Gk Bible which necessitated the precaution of multiple collation samples in this study, results indicated complete consistency among the Arm witnesses. The findings of the comparison with other books also suggests that scribes did not deviate from an exemplar in mid course.

57. For the background to this see S.P. Cowe, "Problematics".

58. See pp.229-37.

59. H.S. Gehman, "The Armenian Version of the Book of Daniel and its Affinities".

60. Gehman initially employed the edition of Mxit'ar Sebastac'i and that of Bagratuni (1860), only gaining access to Z after completing the greater part of his research. Hence he tends to emphasize the unity of the manuscript tradition

and underestimate the implications of the variants, particularly those with Greek support which call into question his designation of Arm's texttype. His access to the Gk traditions was provided by H.B. Swete (*The Old Testament in Greek according to the Septuagint in* 3 vols. Cambridge, The University Press: 1895) and R. Holmes and J. Parsons, *Vetus Testamentum Graece cum Variis Lectionibus,* Oxford: 1798-1827. The former thus enabled him to monitor the readings of MSS BAQ and OG while the collations presented in the latter are of uneven quality, not all being equally trustworthy.

61. Probably Walton's polyglott was used for this purpose, though this is not expressly stated.

62. See H.S. Gehman, "The Armenian Version of the Book of Daniel", pp.94-95.

63. *Les origines,* p.270-271.

64. Ibid., pp.144-165.

65. However, as scholars examine the P manuscript tradition in more detail it becomes increasingly apparent that more significant variation is a feature of the earliest witnesses before the establishment of a normative text in the ninth-tenth centuries. See M.D. Koster, *The Peshitta of Exodus,* pp.164-214 and A. Gelston, *The Peshitta of the Twelve Prophets,* pp.26-91.

66. For a full conspectus of Ziegler's presentation of Th's manuscript tradition see pp.xvi-xvii.

67. For an exposition of the method see E. Tov, "The Use of a computerized data base for Septuagint research; the Greek-Hebrew parallel alignment", *BIOSCS* 17 (1984), pp.36-47 and for a practical demonstration R.A. Kraft and E. Tov, *Ruth,* CATSS 1, Atlanta, GA, Scholars Press: 1986.

68. See H.S. Gehman, "The Armenian Version of the Book of Daniel", esp. pp.98-99.

69. For a discussion see chapter six, p.371.

70. For this translation equivalence see B.O. Künzle, *Das altarmenische Evangelium,* Bern, Peter Lang: 1984, vol.2,

p.572.

71. Ibid., p.295.

72. See chapter five, pp.342-52.

73. Ibid., pp.312-24.

74. For examples see chapter six, pp.360-1. Hence on excessively literal rendering 'hoc omne' would have been inappropriate.

75. B.O. Künzle, *Das altarmenische Evangelium*, vol.2, p.629.

76. Ibid., p.41.

77. See R. Payne Smith, *Thesaurus Syriacus*, pp.814, 816.

78. See chapter one, pp.36-39, 41-2.

79. Ibid., pp.45-6.

80. See further chapter five, pp.322-25.

81. B.O. Künzle, *Das altarmenische Evangelium*, vol.2, p.424.

82. It may be that Ziegler was misled by dictionary entries offering 'angel' as the equivalent for the substantival use of զուարթունն (e.g. M. Bedrossian, *New Dictionary Armenian-English*, Venice, St. Lazar's Press, 1875-1879.)

CHAPTER 1

MANUSCRIPT TRADITION

Manuscripts Consulted*

U.S.S.R.: Erevan, Maštoc̆ Matenadaran (M)

73	144	147	177	178	179
180	182	183	184	186	187
188	189	190	191	199	200
201	202	203	204	205	206
207	287	345	346	347	348
349	350	351	352	353	354
1500	2585	2587	2627	2628	2705
2706	2732	3545	3705	4070	4113
4114	4429	4834	4905	5508	5560
5603	5608	5809	6230	6281	6569
6640	7623	9100	9116		

Leningrad, Oriental Institute (LO):B1

Israel, Jerusalem: Armenian Patriarchate (J)

297	304	306	428	501	542
797	1127	1232	1323	1925	1926
1927	1928	1929	1931	1932	1933
1934	2558	2669	3043	3438	

25

Italy: Venice Mxitarists (V)

229(4)[1]	280(10)	623(3)	841(5)	897(15)
935(8)	1006(6)	1007(12)	1182(7)	1258(14)
1270(9)	1482(18)	1507(13)	1508(1)	1634(2)

Kurdian Collection (VK)[2]:(37)
Rome: Collegio Leoniano (RL):2(40)
Rome: Vatican (RV): Cod.Arm 1

Austria: Vienna Mxitarists (W)

| 55(14) | 71(29)[3] | 274(39) |

Austrian National Library (WN): Cod. Arm 11
Great Britain: Cambridge, Sir Harold Bailey's Collection
(CHB)[5]
Cambridge, British and Foreign Bible Society (CBF)
London, British Library (LB) Or 8833
London, Lambeth Palace (LL):Cod. Vet. Test.1209

Eire, Dublin: Chester Beatty Library (DCB) 552.

Holland: Leiden (LR):5504 (Cod. Arm.25)

Iran: New Julfa (NJ):23(336), 1(15)

Further information concerning these MSS may be obtained from the catalogues of the collections listed in the appropriate section of the bibliography.

Manuscripts Unavailable for Consultation

Israel, Jerusalem: Armenian Patriarchate (J):2557, 2559

Iran: New Julfa (NJ): 2(16), 9(71), 34(162)

Lebanon, Bzommar (Z):2(26)

The last manuscript listed is no longer in the possession of the monastery, having been sold about the time of the

Second World War. It may be worth noting that it bears the same contents, is of the same provenance and date and commissioned and copied by the same persons as DCB552. As it is doubtful whether there was a multiplicity of text types circulating contemporaneously in a small, provincial town, it is not unlikely that the two MSS belong to the same textual group.

U.S.S.R., Leningrad: Hermitage Museum (LH): V-P 1011

Leningrad: Oriental Institute (LO):B31, C29

Bulgaria, Plovdiv: MS listed as in the possession of Yovhannes Aramean earlier this century (description by Oskean in *HA*(1937) pp.570-573). As the MS contains the colophon, numeration and miniature motifs of Lazar Baberdaci's Bible (M351) it is extremely likely that textually it belongs to the close-knit E2 sub-group, so that its collation would not require any substantive modification to the present study.

Classification into Groups

Due to the large numbers of manuscripts involved (120) and the uncertainty regarding their relative value as textual witnesses, it was felt to be desirable as a first step to achieve a profile of the whole tradition. This would distinguish the groups and individual witnesses which are textually significant from those whose testimony is of secondary importance, such as epigraphs or other closely related manuscripts.

In order not to impair the comprehensiveness of the survey, it was decided to select three passages to be collated against Z from near the beginning, middle and end of the book. This was to obtain an overview of the manuscript's exemplar. Any change in copying base introduced by the scribe in midcourse would be reflected in the type of variant offered from the Z standard and in the group affiliation it adduced from one collation sample to another.

The main criterion for identifying manuscript groupings is conjunctive error arising from mistakes both perpetrated and perpetuated within the process of copying. They are there-

fore inner-Armenian by definition. As it is presumed that they
were not present in the autograph of the translation, such
readings when not the result of independent coincidence, enter
a given witness through contact with its exemplar. Moreover,
since it is to be expected that the extent of this secondary material expands in direct proportion to the amount of times a book
is copied, documents evincing a larger number of these readings must generally be considered stemmatically later. The
process thus determines not only which manuscript belongs
to which group but also defines where it is to be placed in the
development of that group; for establishing textual chronology
purely on the date of copying is fallacious. We know for a fact
that many seventeenth century scribes copied from choice exemplars of the thirteenth century.[4] Their witness therefore
takes precedence over others emanating from a school of the
fifteenth or sixteenth century at the end of an intense period of
continuous productivity.

In contrast, points at which each of the variants appears
to have support from Greek texts only confuse the issue if allowed to obtrude untowardly at this stage. Before the main
outline of the manuscript tradition has been grasped, it is impossible to decide with precision which reading stems from the
autograph and which has been engendered by secondary factors, perhaps as the result of subsequent contact with a Greek
base.

In order to combine the maximum of inner-Armenian errors with the minimum of possible Greek readings, collation
samples were not selected at random but from sections where a
paucity of variants in Ziegler's apparatus coincided with a high
incidence in that of Z. This fixed the choice on (a) Susanna 44-
64; (b) Chapter 4: 27 -5:7; and (c) Chapter 11: 11-35.

Manuscript Tradition

As a result of our analysis of the variants collected in collating the manuscripts against Z, five main textual groups were
identified. Each of these in turn is composed of a number of

sub-groups whose internal agreements generally mark them off from the others as forming a more homogeneous unit. On occasion one can even detect a sibling relationship between certain members of the sub-group.

Before exposing these findings in detail it is necessary to say a word about a manuscript which has recently come to light in Soviet Armenia. Along with a Gospel also of the seventeenth century this full Bible (AAH1) is the family heirloom of Aršak Haroyan of the village of Areg in the Talin region. The manuscript which is fairly legible but poorly bound and in a bad state of preservation, was copied by the scribe Awet in 1631 A.D. for Aristakēs Vardapet.

With the owner's kind permission I examined the manuscript and collated its text of Susanna 44-64. On that basis it may be confidently classed as essentially of the same type as Z from which it evinces six significant variants, four with some support from the C group and one in the company of group B. In addition, it has five singular readings which are all scribal errors. It was decided not to assign it finally to one or another of the sub-group of D until its performance in the two remaining collation sections could be assessed.

Another unexpected find was recently to discover an almost complete text of Daniel in Union Theological Seminary, New York (NYU4).[5] The codex (dated 15th-16th centuries) is a miscellany encompassing the poetic works of Nersēs Šnorhali and a series of sermons. The final item commences with Vardan Arewelci's commentary on the preface to Daniel, however the continuation presents the biblical book itself, though unheralded by the usual paraphernalia of headpiece, superscription etc. which has allowed it to escape detection. The text commences on p.558, but is interrupted at 5:4 due to a leaf having fallen out, resuming at 5:25 on p.573. Another lacuna occurs after Sus:53 on p.596. The text type it adduces is basically early, generally agreeing with representatives of groups A and B, but without specific allegiance to either. It presents an appreciable number of unique readings, some of which are manifestly secondary, while others may be of value in reconstituting the original text in places.[6]

Arm's Manuscript Groups -
Their Composition and Character

　　　　The format of this section which is applied to each of the five textual groups in turn is first to list the group members according to their breakdown into sub-groups. Then follows a series of variants illustrating how the group hangs together and the relationship its members share over against the rest of the manuscript tradition. The same process is similarly repeated for each of the constituent sub-groups. Finally, where individual MSS exhibit peculiarities of interest, e.g. particular affinity to another member of their sub-group or to a MS from another group, this is noted before moving on to consideration of the text group.

Group A:

A1a　M287-M5560-M5603-M207-M144
A1b　J304-M73-LR25-J297-LL1209-J3438
A2　　M4834-V280-M5809-J2558

Readings which corroborate A's existence as a group:

Sus:55 գլուխդ] գլուխ	A1-J297 J3438 A2　J306
-61 չարութիւն/ի մահի] tr	A B1-M352 B2-W55
11:11 om եւ 2°	A1-J304 J3438 A2-M4834　J797
-20 բնաղատեցից]	A1-J3438 E
բնաւորես	
-24 om եւ 5°	A1-M207 J3438 A2　C1 M178　M352
-31 պղծութիւն] գպղծութիւն	
(-թիւնս 36 232 95 116)	A1-LR25 M207 J297

A1a:M287-M5560-M5603-M207-M144
Readings which distinguish A1a as a closely-knit sub-group.

Sus:47 om դուդ	A1a M199　M147 M204
-55 ստեցեր] + եւ դու	A1a

-63 omնորա 3°   A1ªM73 C1 M2669

4:30 om եւ 1°   A1ª

5:4 զերկաթիս] երկաթիս   A1ª - M207 5:5 գրեր]+ մանէ

        Թեկեղ փարեւ   A1ª

-5 բնելոյ որմնոյ] tr   A1ª W55

11:18 զիշխանն] զիշխանս   A1ª-M144 A2-M5809 J304 NR25

-27 խoutեցին] իռուսիցին   A1ª B1 B2

-30 եւ խոնարհեցին]

        խոնարիին pr   A1ª

-33 իմիք] ի իք   A1ª

-34 տկարանալ] կատարելն   A1ª-M144 J297 C1 M178

                       M199 J306 V1482 B1b-W55

                       M184 M348 M202 M147

A1ª + A2: 4:32 համարեցան]+ նմա   A1ªA2 B1-M178 M352 B2

A1b: J304-M173-LR25-J297-LL1209-J3438

Readings which reveal A1b as a rather looser association. The fact that they share even their most distinctive agreements with members of other groups implies that their relationship is more generic than specific. They all witness to a good early text but clearly do not come from the same textual stream like the members of A1ª.

4:28 բերան] բերանն   A1b-J304 LL1209   B1B2-W55 V280

                                             M5809

5:3 գոսկեղէս եւ   A1b-J304 LL1209   B

    գարծ.] tr

-4 օրհնեցին]   A1b-LR25 J3438   B M2627 M5603

    օրհնէին   M5809 M4905

                                       J797 DCB552

11:13 մտանել] pr ի   A1b-J292 J3438   C2C3 M4834-

                                       M5809

A2 M4834-V280-M5809-J2558

Readings marking off A2 as a distinct sub-group:

Sus:56 զառակ] +դառնացող	A2-M5809	
-57 այդպէս] այսպէս	A2 LL1209	
-57 յուղայ] յուղայի (-ախ	A2 J304 L!B1 V935 W55 J297	
M4834+այսաւր	M187	
M5809)		
4:33 ժամանակի] ժամնւ	A2	
5:2 զապառ] զապասն	A2 M1500 J304 LR25	
11:11 զօր բազում] զօրս		
բազումն	A2 M73	
-18 զնուա] զնա	A2 J304 M184 LR25	
-20 տունկ] տունդ (տուն		
M4834 M1500)	A2-M5809 C1	
-20 բնագատեցին]		
-ցին (-ցեն M5809)	A2	
-30 դարձգի] բարձրացի	A2-M4834	
-32 զած] զտէր աստուած	A2	

V280-J2558 are sisters sharing many readings which diverge from Z, e.g.

Sus:61 արարին] արար

5:4 ունէր] տուիչն է բարեաց եւ (+ որ V280) ունի

11:32 աձգեն] pr հզor

-33 զատուրս] + բազում

Of the two V280 is the more divergent, e.g.

Sus:58 om արդ

-60 om ամենայն

N.B. an uncial variant Ս/Ս between V280-J2558 and M4834 implies that the split in the tradition represented by these MSS took place at a relatively early stage.

1:3 ատիանեզ M4834   ամիւանէ V280-J2558

M5809 has a number of singular readings

Sus:51 զդրոսա] զձերս

-58 նա] ծերն

4:29 հալածեցեն] հալածեցին

-30 վարսք] մազ

5:5 ելին] + երեւելին

Members of the group share several variants with C1

Sus:51 մեկնեցան] -ցին   M4834-M5809   C1

-53 ուր] որ   M5809   C1

-61 նոցին] նոցունց   V280-J2558   C1 M73

4:33 իմ 5°]իմոյ   M5809 (իմն M1500)

5:2 արծաթոյ] գրակւոյ   V280-J2558

                                                 ուկւոյ J1925 ուկո M1500

Group B

B1a   M178-J306-M352-V1258-M5508

B1b   NJ23-WN11 M346-M354

B2   LOB1-M4429-V935-W55-M184-M187

B3   M199-V1482-W71-M2585-M202-M147-M3705

The folowing readings indicate that B is a textual group:

Sus:53 ուր] որում (յորում WN11)		B-M147 A1a LR25 J297
-53 զանմեղն եւ	B1-J306 V1258 M5508	B2B3-M199 C1
զարդարն] tr		
4:32 գոր] որ	B	A1a M2627 M73 J297
-34 նարուբողոննոսր] +	B1-M178 M352	B2B3-M2585 M202
արքայ		
5:3 գրակեղէնս եւ զար-		
ծաթեղէնս] tr	B-WN11	A1b-LL1209
-4 զերկաթիս] -թեղէնս	B1-M352 W55 M5508	B2 B3-M147
-7 զգեցցի] զգեցուցից	B-M346 M354 J297 LL1209	
-7 իւր] իւրում	B-V1482	V280 J297 J2558
11:12ոչ զորացի] զզօրաւորս	B1-M178 M352	
	B2-WN11 B3 M144 J3438	
-20 պատերազմաւ] ոչ	B1 B2-WN11 B3-M202 M5603	
պատարագաւք	M144 J297	
-31 նմանէ] նմանէն	B1-M352 B2-M346 WN11 B3-J297 M4834	

B1: M178-J306-M352-V1258-M5508;   NJ23-WN11-M346-
M354Readings showing that B1 is a sub-group:

Sus:47 դարձառ ամենայն ժողո-	
վուրդն] ամ. ժող. դարձան	B1-M178 M352
-49 բանգի]գի	B1-M352LR25
-59 սուսեր] սուր	B1
-59 առէ] pr եւ	B1-M352 M287 M183 LR25
4:34 իրաւունք] իրաւամբք	B1 V1482 J297 M3705 J3438
5:7 առէ] pr եւ	B1-M352 M183 LR25

Within the cluster a particular affinity exists between M306-
V1258-5508

4:27 ի 1°] om	M306-V1258-M5508 V841 M73
	M354
-27 բարեն] -լնն	V1258-M5508 M354
-30 նորա] իւր	M306-V1258-M5508 B1ᵇ V1482
	M3705
-30 իբրեւ գթնչնոց] որպէս	
գթնչնոց երկնից	M306-V1258 B1ᵇ V1482 M3705

B1ᵃ M178-J306-M352-V1258-M5508
Reading indicating that B1ᵃ is a sub-group:
11:30 դարձցի] -ցին B1ᵃ B3-M202 M354
B1ᵇ 67-113 73-81

Readings corroborating the existence of B1ᵇ as a sub-group:

Sus:45 մինյ տղայոյ] tr	B1ᵇ-M354
-53 գլ նասատկարս]-կարսն	B1ᵇ-M354 M73 LR25 J297
-53 այ] աստուած	
(այ as marginal note)	B1ᵇ-WN11 J306
-56 գմեւս] եւ գմիւս	B1ᵇ-M346 M202 M3705
-61 բերանոց] -ոյ	B1ᵇ M184 M350
4:31 յաւիտենական]	B1ᵇ-M354 M207
յաւիտենից	
11:22 եւ բազուկք] բազումք	B1ᵇ-WN11

Within the sub-group MSS NJ23-WN11 and M346-M354 generally move in pairs, but agreements across the split demonstrate that the division is not absolute and all the MSS are of mixed text.

Readings shared by NJ23-WN11:

Sus:49 om յառեան

-49 վկայեցին] վկայեն   NJ23-WN11 V1865

-49 դարձայք] դարձիք դարձիք

-50 եո ած] tr

-52 om եւ ասէ

11:14 յայնոսիկ] ընդ այնոսիկ

Readings shared by M346-M354:

Sus:52 հասին] + քեզ   M346-M354 M5560 J304 M5508

-54 գղուսա] գղա ասա   B-NJ23 WN11 A1-M5603

Reading highlighting the split:

11:29 ի ժամանակի] -կին   NJ23-WN11 M306 V1482 V1258
                                  (+ եւ M346-M354 M3705 M5508)

Conflate readings across the split:

Sus:53 վնասակարս]-կարսն M346-WN11 LOB1 M352 M187
                                  M5508

4:33 մեծութիւն] +իմ   M346-WN11 M5508 CBF

-33 թագաւորութիւն] -թեան   NJ23-M346 M1500 M73 J297
                                  M5809 J3043 RVI M2669 J1927
                                  DCB552

B2:LOB1-M4429-V935-W55-M184-M187

Readings confirming that B2 is a sub-group:

Sus:53 սպանանիցես]   B2-M4429 M184 V280 J297 WN11
       սպանաներ

-58 ասա] + դու   B2-M4429 M184 J297

-61 ընդ] om   B2B3-V1482 M3705 A2 M2627
                                  LR25   LL1209

4:33 առաւել յաւելաւ]   B2 B1ᵇ J306 V280 J2558
      առաւելաւ
     բաբախէին] բախբախէին   B2⁻ᴹ⁴⁴²⁹ M1500 V1482 M2705
                                       M190 M202 J3438
11:15 իգէ] է   B2⁻ᵂ⁵⁵ M5608
-23 նա] նոսա   B2⁻ᴸᴼᴮ¹ ᵂ⁵⁵
-26 անկ] անդ   B2⁻ᴸᴼᴮ¹ ᵂ⁵⁵ M178 W71 J297
-27 թագաւորացն] -րաց   B2
-30 մացեն] մացէ   B2 M352
-30 ոյք] որք   B2⁻ᴹ¹⁸⁴ M4834 J1925
-30 սուրբ] աստուծոյ   B2 J297
-34 գայթագղութեամբք]   B2 NJ23
        -թիւնք
-35 յայտնել] -նեալ   B2⁻ᵂ⁵⁵ B1ᵇ

Within the sub-group the cluster LOB1-V935-M184-M187 is
particularly close.
Sus:47 խոսեցար] առացեր   LOB1-V935-M184-M187 J297
-48 մէշ] միշի   LOB1-V935-M184-M187
                                           A1ᵃ LR25 J297 M5809 LL1209

A number of readings demonstrate that B1 and B2 have closer
affinities than either has with B3 independently.
Sus:53 դատէիր]առնէիր   B1⁻ᴹ¹⁸⁷ B2 J1930 LR25 J297
-53 գանիմեղս] -մեղսն   B1⁻ᴹ⁵⁵⁰⁸ B2 LR25
-61 վկայս] վկայիցն   B1 B2 LR25 J297
4:29 իբրեւ] որպէս   B1 B2 V1482 M73 LR25 J297
                                       M3705

B3: M199-M1482-W71-M2585-M202-M147-M3705
The following readings corroborate that B3 is a sub-group.
Sus:47 դարձաւ/ամենայն ժողո-
      վուրդ] tr   B³
-55 ապտասիկ] prqh   B3⁻ᴹ¹⁹⁹ ᴹ¹⁴⁷
-61 չարութիւն/ի մտի] tr   B3

11:24 ժամանակ] -նակս   B3B 1b-WN11 J306 V280 M144
                         M5508 J3438

Group C

C 1   J 1925-M 1500
C 2ª M345-M 180-V841-V1006-M6230-W274-M4113-
      M2705-M9116-M7623-M190-M2706-M66406-M9100
C 2b M179-M177-M186-J428-V1182-M350-M205-LB8833
C 3ª M183-M353-M4114
C 3b M2627-J797

The following readings establish C as a textual group.

Sus:53 զղատատանս]   C-M2627 J797 V1258 J3438
       դատատան
4:32 դառնայցէ] դառնայ   C-M2627 J797 M73 V280 J3438
5:4 nqւng] hnqւng   C-M2627 J797
-13 մտանել] pr ի   C-J1925 M1500 M73 LR25
                         M5809   LL1209 M4834
11:15 om nչ 1°   C-M183 M353 V1182 J304 M2627 M73
                         LR25 J1932 M2669 J1927 M348
-16 omեւ 3°   C
-24 զորp] զորս   C-M2627 M9116 M4114 J428 M350 M205
                         J3438 M4834
-24 omնորա 1°   C-M183 M353 M4114 M186 J428

C1: 13-28
Readings demonstrating that C 1 is a sub-group:
Sus:50 վաղվաղակի] pr անդրէն
-5 1 մեկնեցէք] մեկուսեցէք
4:29 թագաւորութեան] ի վերայ թագաւորութեանց
5: 1 բաղտասար] + արքայ
-4 օրինեցին] եստուն փառս

(N.B. the readings shared with A2)

That these MSS' connection is of long standing is revealed by the presence of an uncial variant S/Ս at 4:27.

ի տունե] իմում   J1925-M1500

C2

Readings indicating that C2 is a sub-group:

Sus:49 անդրէն] om	C2
-49 դոբալ] om	C2-M179 M2627 J797
-54 հատեր առ] տեսեր	C2-M345 M179 J428
4:28 ատեմ] ատեն	C2-M179 M180 M177 M287 J304 LR25
	J3438
-34 է] եւ	C2-M179 V1006 V1182 M353 M4114
5:5 տածարի] -րին	C2-M345 V1006 J428 V1182 M205
	RVI J1923 LL1209
11:20 եւ 4°] om	C2-V841 V1006 M190 M2627 J797

C2ᵃ: M345-M180-V841-V1006-M6230-W274-M4113-M2705-M9116-M7623-M190-M2706-M6640-M9100[7]

Readings that delimit C2ᵃ:

Sus:59 մերկ] om   C2ᵃ   M287 M5560 M207 M144
                                                 M5809 LL1209 M4834
-59 եւ 1°] om   C2ᵃ-M6640   V280 M5809 J2558
-62 արդար] -րոյ   C2ᵃ-W274
4:17 իւրով] om   C2ᵃ-V1006 M6640   A2 J1925 M177 J304
                                                 M73 LR25 J797 LL1209
-27 վախձանն ի ժամա-
      նակ] վախձան ի   C2ᵃ-M345   M177 M2627 M73 LR25
      ժամանակ   J797 LL1209 J3438
-30 գողոյ] -գող   C2ᵃ-M345 M180 V841 W274   M5603
-30 բանակր]բնակր   C2ᵃ-W274   M2627 J797

M190-M2706 are sisters.

Sus:46 առէ] + գձողովուրդն	M190-M2706
-48 վերալ] pr ի	M190-M2706
-55 հերձգէ] եւ հերձեսգէ	M190-M2706

5:3 om էր   M190-M2706

11:20 om եւ 1°   M190-M2706

N.B. Their close connection to MSS M2705 and M7623

Sus:45 om զնա   M2705-M7623-M190-M2706
                              W55 M184

11:17 նորա] նմա   M4113-M2705-M7623-M190-
                              M2706-M6640

-31 om եւ 1°   M4113-M2705-M7623-M190-
                              M2706

C2b: M179-M177-M186-J428-V1182-M350-M205-LB8833

Readings that delimit C2b:

5:2 նորof] -բուլ p   C2b-M350 M205   M345 M5560 M180
                                            V841 V1006 M353
                                            M2705 M9116 M144
                                            M4114

-3 նորof] -բուլ p   C2b-M350   M345 M180 V841
                                            V1006 M9116

-4 իշխանութիւն]
   զիշխանութիւնս C2b-M177   V1482 J3438

11:20 յարմատոյ]   C2b-M177
           -տոng

C3: M183-M353-M4114   M2627-J797

C3 is formed of two loosely connected clusters: M4114 is the main liaison between the two. These MSS agree with both sections of C2, though mainly with C2a which implies that their textual branch separated from C2 at some point before the main division (C2a/b) took place.

Readings across the split.

4:27 հաստատութեամբ]-թեան   C3-M183 M353 C1 LL1209

5:1 եռուր] մտին   C3-M183 M353 C1

-1 զինիս] զինի   C3-M183 M353 LR25

5:2 quպաս] quպաս'ն   C3-M4114

-2 hարծը] +'նորա   C3-M183 M353   M352 M2705 M190
M2706 M205

-2 om իւր 2°   C3-M183 M353

11:18 qիշխա'նու'ն]   qիշխա'ն'ն   C3-M183 C2a-W274 M177

Readings delimiting C3ᵃ:

Sus:48 մէջ] միշի   C3ᵃ C2

4:27 om իմnյ   C3ᵃ   C2-V1006 J428 V1182 LB8833
M1500 M184 M354 J3438

-32 nը] pr nը   C3ᵃ M345 M177 W55 M73 LR25
LL1209 M4834

-32 om ի 2°   C3ᵃ C2 M352 M2732 J3438

C3ᵇ: M2627 J797

Readings delimiting C3ᵇ:

Sus:53 qա'նմ'եդu] -մ'եդ'ն   C3ᵇ   M5508

-61շարnւթիւ'ն] շարախ'ousnւթիւ'ն C3ᵇ

5:2 quպաս] quպասu'ն   C3ᵇ

-3 էը] om   C3ᵇ   D-M2587 M189 J1927 M191 V1006
W274 M73 J297 J797 M190

11:24 'նnրա 1°] om   C3ᵇ   C2-M186 J428 C 1

[11:30 pա'նակը] p'նակը   C3ᵇ C2a-W274]

-34 ա'կարա'ն'ա'դ] -'ն'ա'ղnյ   C3ᵇ M345

-36 ժամա'ն'ակ է] ժամա'ն'ակի'ն   C3ᵇ

C3 (particularly C3ᵃ) sometimes supports groups D-E against
the majority of group C, e.g.

Sus:52 ա'հ'ա   D E-CHB5 J1232 C3ᵃ LR25 V280
M187

11:15 ա'ր'քա'յի'ն] + hա'ра'տnյ rel D E C3-M2627 J1925 M179 M180
M177 V1006 M73 V1182

Group D

D 1   M182-J1931-M206-M5608-M4905-M3545
D 2   V1007-M2628-J1932-M348-M2732
D 3   J1926-V1508-J1930-M6569-V1507-J1127-VK37-
V1634-M188-J542-M203-M349-J501-J1929-RL2-
DCB552-V1865

Readings corroborating the existence of D as a textual group:[8]

11:14 յայնոսիկ] om   D1   J1927
-25 խմբեցէ] բղխեցէ   D-J1931 M206 M8569 J1932 M203 DCB552

D1: M182-J1931-M206-M5608-M4905-M3545
Readings marking off D1 as a sub-group:

11:20 պատերազմման] pr ոչ   D 1-J1931 A-M73 M5603 M144 J297 V280 J2558
                               C-V1006 J797 V1182
                               E-J3043 J1934 J1928 J189

-28 ուխտի] -տին   D 1 A-J304 M73 B-J306 C-LB8833
                               E-J1927

-30 յարմարոյ] -տոյն   D 1-M206 E-M2587 M200 V897 M178
                               M352 B 1b-WN11

D2: V1007-M2628-J1932-M349-M2732
Readings marking off D2 as a sub-group:

4:32 ի 1°] om   D2 B3 C-M2627 J797 V1182 LR25
                               J542 J3438 CBF

5:3 զապատան] զապաան   D2-J1932 M2732 A 1a-M5603
                               A 1b-J304 M73 LR25 A 2-V280 J2558
                               C3-M4114 E 1a-V1270 M6281 V897

-7 զզենս] զզենս   D2-V1007 M348 VK37 J501 V1865

D:3   J1926-V1508-J1930-M6569-V1507-J1127-VK37-
V1634-M188-J542-M203-M349-J501-J1929-RL2-
DCB552-V1865

Members of D3 are very close in their common agreements, so
that when they depart from the main D text they do so singly
or in small groups. Normally their strength lies in what they

share, while their aberrations are insignificant. MS RL2 forms an exception to the general rule by evincing a number of interesting agreements with Group A and M5809 in particular, especially in Chapter 11, e.g.

11:17 յամրաացի] յարմարեացի M287 RL2
-18 գնուաա] գնա   A2 J304 M184 LR25 RL2
-21 գայթագղութեամբք]
 -Թակղութեամբ   M5809 WN11 RL2
-25 խորհեցգին] խորհիցին M5809 RL2
-27 երկողցունց] երկունցուն M287 M5560 M4834 M5809
            LL1209

Group E

E 1ᵃ V1270-J3043-RV1-M2669-J1928-M6281-V897
E 1ᵇ M4070-V838 CHB5-J1232[9]
E2 M351-J1934-J1933-M2587-V263-J1928-M189-M200-
  V229-M347-M201-NJ1-M191-M204-CBF

Readings corroborating the existence of E as a textual group:

Sus:49 դոբա] նոբա	E-J3043 M351 J1933 M347 M191
	M179 M144 M2585 M202 M2706
-55 հրեշտակի] -տակ	E-J3043 V623 M189 A2 B1ᵇ C 1
4:33 յաելա] -լան	E-M191 CBF
5:5 ձեռինն] - րին	E-V1270 V623 J1928 M2705 M7623
	M190 M202 M2706
-7 գուցանէ] գուցգէ	E-V623 M1927 A2 B C D1-M5608
11:18 նախատեցին] -տէին	E-V1270 M6281 V897 A-J297
	B2-W55 M184
-20 յարմատոյ] -տոյն	E-M2587 V623 M200 V897
	M178 M182 M1931 M5608 M352
	M4905 M3545
[11:28 ուխտի] -տին	E-V623 J1927 A-J304 M73 B-J306
	C -LB8833 D1]

E1: V1270-J3043-RV1-M2669-J1927-M6281-V897;
  M4070-V838 CHB5-J123

Readings indicating that E1 is a sub-group:

Sus:48 դատապարտեցէք] -պարտէք   E^{a}-J3043 M287 M4834

-49 յստեան] -տեն   E1-J1232 V1865 M1500

E1^{a}: V1270-J3043-RV1-M2669-J1927-M6281-V897

Readings delimiting E1^{a}:

4:33 Թագաւորութիւն] -թեան E1^{a}-V1270 M6281 V897 M1500 NJ23

                             M346 J297 M5809 DCB552

5:3 գապասան] գապասն   E1^{a}-V1270 M6281 V897 A1^{a}-M5603

                             A1^{b}-J304 M73 LR25 A2-V280 J2558

                             B1^{a}(J306 M352 M5508)

                             B1^{b}(NJ23 M346) B3-V1482 M3705

                             C3-M4114 D2-J1932 M2732 M2587

                             M7623 M347 M190

-6 ձունկը] ձունգը   E1^{a} E2-J1934 M2587 M347 M201

                             D1-M182 M4905 M3545

                             D3-J1127 VK37 V1634 J501 J1929

                             RL2 DCB552 V1865

A special relationship subsists between RV1 and J3043, e.g.

5:6 ձունկը] ձնունդը   RV1-J3043

-7 գմոգս] գմոգը   RV1-J3043

-7 ձիրանիս] -նիք   RV1-J3043

E1^{b}: M4070-V838   CHB5-J1232

Readings delimiting E1^{b}:

Sus:52 եկին] եկեալ   E1^{b}

-58 խոսէին] pr կային եւ   E1^{b}

The sub-group is composed of an earlier pair (M4070-V838)
and a later one (CHB5-J1232). MSS M4070 and V838 both
have 7 substantive variants from Z and share several orthographic variants. However, M4070 sometimes agrees with
CHB5-J1232 over against V838, e.g.

Sus:56 om եւ 3°   M4070-CHB5-J1232   RV1 M2669

-59 գնա/դանիէլ] tr   M4070-CHB5-J1232

and with J1232 alone, e.g.

Sus:51 om ի 1°   M4070-J1232

Readings shared by CHB5-J1232:

Sus:52 այ] ի հա

-52 առութք] pr ձեր

-59 om կայ

-60 ամենայն ժողովուրդն/ի ձայն մեծ] tr

-63 զարշութեան] + նորա

The projected inner development of the group can be seen from the folowing complex of variants:

Sus:53 զանմեղն եւ զարդարն]

    զանմեղ եւ զարդարն   M4070-V838

    զանմեղս եւ զարդարն   J1232

    զանմեղս եւ զարդարս   CHB5

E2:   M351-J1934-J1933-M2587-V623-J1928-M189-M200-
        V229-M347-M201-NJ1-M191-M204-CBF

E2 is delimited from the rest of the group by its lack of conjunctive error; however, the following readings show that J1933-M191-M204 and J1928-V229-CBF form related clusters within E2.

Sus:45 ազայոյ]-ng	J1928-V229
-49 դարձայք]-ձաք	J1928-V229
5:2 որ] աստուծոյ	J1933-M204 J1928-V229-CBF
11:14 յայնոսիկ] այն.	J1933-M191-M204 J1928-V229-CBF
-25 om նորա	J1933-M191-M204 J297

GROUP INTER-RELATIONS

A very significant feature of group A is the number of variants it shares separately now with group B, now with group C.

Readings shared by groups A and B:

Sus:49 դարբայք] -ձիք   A1-M287 J304 M207 J297

                              A2-M4834 M5809 B-M352 C1

-54 գղուա] գղատատ   A1-M5603 B-NJ23 WN11

-54 մինչ] մինչդեռ   A-M73 B C1 M183

4:33 իմ] om   A1-M207 J3438 B-W55

Readings shared by A1ᵃ A2 and B:

5:4 ապնձիս] զպղնձեղէնս   A1ᵃ B

11:17 թազատորութիւնս] -թիւն

   (-թեան A2 96)   A1ᵃ J297 LL1209 B-M352 M354

-28 եւ 3°] om   A1 A2-M4834 B-V935 J304 J297

                                                LL1209

Readings shared by groups A1ᵃ A2 and C (mostly - C2ᵇ):

Sus:47 այդ] om   A1ᵃ A2 B3 C-M183 M353 M2627

                             J304 M73 LL1209 M4114 J797

-59 մերկ] om   A1ᵃ-M5603 A2-V280 J2558

                             C1 C2ᵃ M177 LL1209

11:16 սարիմայ] -բիրայ   A1-M207 J3438 A2 C1

                             C2ᵃ-V1006 W274 C3ᵇ

-18 զնախատինս] -տանս   A1ᵃ-M5603 C-V1006 J428 V1182 J304 M4834

Similarly there are several cases where D and E agree against the rest of the manuscript tradition, e.g.

Sus:53 զղատատատանս D-M4905 E B3 J304 V280 J2558] -տան rel

-61 om եւ 3°   A B-J306 C-J1925 V1006 M183 M353

                                    M4114 J428 M190

-63 նորա 3° D E-J2669 CHB5 V897 B3 C3-M183]   om rel

4:28 եւ ասէ   D E B3-V1482 M3705

                           C3ᵇ M73 M187

-31 ատերութիւն D E C2 C3ᵃ NJ23 V280 WN11 J2558 J3438]

                                   արբայութիւն rel

-33 խնդրեցին D E J1925 V1006 M7623 J3438] -րեհն rel

-34 փառաւոր առնեմ]   A 1b- J304 A2-M5809 B 1-M178 M346

   փառաւորեմ   C -M2627 J797 M350 W55 M144

11:24 բազում] pr եւ   A -M207 B-M178 M199 J306 W71V935 M352

                         M202 C-M2627 J797 M350

-27 շարունեան] -թիւն   A 1-J304 A2-M4834 M5809

                         B 1-WN11 V1258 B2-V935

                         B3-M202 M147 C1

                         C2a-M180 V1006 M7623 C3b

-32 ճանաչէ D E   C M73 M201 M5508 J3438] -շեր rel

Comparison of the Composition of the Textual Groups with the Classification Effected in Other Books

1 Samuel[10] On analysis of collations of sixteen manuscripts in five chapters (1, 10, 17, 18, 31) Johnson produced the following schema:

1) J1925-M345-M1500-M1927-V841-V935-W55
2) J1928-J1934-OB41-RV1-WN11
3) M179-M180-M353-W71

Four units of his first group (J1925-M1500 M345-V841) belong to the respective sub-groups C1 and C2a in Daniel, although there the closest relationship is between J1925-M1500, not M345-M1500 as Johnson finds in 1 Samuel. The agreement between V935-W55 is also borne out though they form part of sub-group B2 in Daniel. In comparison with the overall alignment of the others, MS J1927 appears somewhat eccentric viewed from the perspective of Daniel. However, Johnson notes that this MS is rather isolated, since it also has agreements with the second group.

MS OB41 does not contain Daniel and therefore must be excluded from comparison. The remainder of group 2 (+J1927 from group 1) belong to the E Group in Daniel except WN11 which has been located in B1b. Similarly, three of Johnson's third group stem from the C Group in Daniel while the fourth

(W71) is from the sub-group B3 which sometimes unites with C Group witnesses in supporting D E against A + B (1 + 2). The result is therefore that many of the codices maintain the same textual type in both books. In other cases, the congeneric relationship of the witnesses is corroborated all the more by the fact that their textual character varies in the same way from book to book, something far more difficult to attribute to chance.

Testaments of the XII Patriarchs:[11]
Group Alpha　1) M1500
　　　　　　　2) J1925-M353
　　　　　　　3) J2557-J2560

Group Beta　1) (thirty-one MSS are here presented according to the agreements with the Daniel classification)
　　　　　　　M354-WN11　(B1^b)
　　　　　　　M2706　(C2^a)
　　　　　　　J428-M205-LB8833　(C2^b)
　　　　　　　M348-M2732　(D2)
　　　　　　　M188-M203-M349-J501　(D3)
　　　　　　　V1270-RV1-M2669-J1927　(E1^a)
　　　　　　　M351-J1934-J1933-M2587-V623-M200-
　　　　　　　V229-M347-M201-M204-CBF　(E2)
　　　　　　　J2561-NJ2-NJ3
　　　　　　　2) M346-V280-J2558

Several of the MSS containing the Testaments were miscellanies and have been excluded from the present comparison. MSS J2560-J2557 and J2561-NJ2-NJ3 either do not possess Daniel or were not available and must also be excluded. Of the remainder it is notable that three MSS from the C group in Daniel belong to Group Alpha here, although the link between J1925 and M1500 is more attenuated. As in Daniel, V280-J2558 are likely to share a common ancestor. This affinity is further extended to M346 which is classed in Daniel's B1ᵇ sub-group. Nevertheless, it is clear from the apparatus of the present edition that M346-V280 agree not infrequently with only little outside support. Once again the close-knit relationship between the members of the sub-groups E1ᵃ and E2 becomes apparent.

IV Ezra   1) M1500
               2a) J2558
               2b) M354-V1270-M351-RV1-J1934-J1933-
                   V623-J1928-J1927-M200-V229-V1182-
                   M201-NJ1-M205-M2732-J2561-NJ2-
                   LB8833-CBF

Special relationships exist between the following:
               V1270-M351-J1928-V229
               V623-M200
               M354-CBF
               RV1-J1927-V1182-NJ1-M205-M2732-
               J2561-LB8833

MSS J2561-NJ2 must again be excluded from consideration. The position of J2558 equidistant from M1500 and the rest of the tradition finds at least a partial echo in the series of readings where C1 agrees with members of A2 in Daniel without outside support.[12] The first two sub-groups of 2ᵇ listed immediately above belong to Group E in Daniel and with the exception of V1270 derive from the sub-group E2. The association of M354 with CBF does not reflect its status in Daniel: we have already observed the same phenomenon in 1 Samuel where M354's partner WN11 is found in the second group accompanied by MSS whose group allegiance in Daniel is to E2. Of the MSS of 2ᵇ presently under discussion, the majority (10) is assigned to E2 in Daniel, therefore it is noteworthy that Stone's final sub-group contains the remainder, i.e. those which do not belong to E2 in Daniel (excluding M354 and

V1270 which we have dealt with). MS NJ1 forms a special case in that although classed with E2 it lacks the marginal notes which link the other members of the sub-group.[13]

Deuteronomy

a1:   V1311-M178-V1312-J1925-J353-M1500-V1007-
       M352-W55-M184-V280-M207-J2558-J542-LL1209

a11: M354-J1933-V229-M201-M191-NJ3-CBF

b1:   M345-M177-V841-J3043

b11: LH1011-M186-J428-V1507-J1932-M2669-M348-
       M202-M2658-M2732-J2561

c1:   M179-M180-V1006-M182-M6230-M353-M206-
       M2627-V935-M159-Z1-M4114-J2560-M349-J2557-
       DCB552

c11: W71-V1508-LOB1-M2585-J1127-M187-V1634-
       M4905-NJ1-J3438

d: NJ23-M346-M6569-J297-WN11-M351-RV1-J1934-
       M2587-V623-J1928-M189-M200-M347-M6281-
       M204-M3705-NJ2-OB41

e1:   M2628-VK37-M188-V1182-M203-J1929

e11: J1927-M350-M205-LB8833

e111: M2705-M7623-M190-M2706-J501

Neither *Deut* nor the present study consulted Z2 and LOC29. Moreover, MSS LHVP-1011, J2557 and NJ2 must be excluded as appearing there but not here. A further ten MSS have been excluded as they do not contain Daniel (V1311, V1312, J353, Z1, J2560, M2658, J2561, NJ17, OB14, DCB553) and thirty-four MSS which lack Deuteronomy (M287, M199, J306, M5560, J304, V1842, M183, J1926, J1931, J1323, W274, M4429, M5608, M73, M5603, M9116, LR25, M144, M4070, M5809, J797, V1258, M3545, CHB5, M9100, M147, M5508, M6640, J501, J1232, V897, RL2, V838, V1865, M4834). There remain eighty-seven witnesses in the common pool.

Given the affinities that Daniel's A group shows with members of the B group and C1, the combination of M178-M352 from B1ᵃ and W55-M184 from B2 as well as J1925-M1500 along with M207-LL1209 of A1ᵃ and V280-J2558 of A2 in *Deut'* s a1 sub-group is understandable. Of the six witnesses under consideration from sub-group all five have close-knit links within the E2 sub-group in Daniel (J1933-V229-M201-M191-CBF). Once again contact between the documents can be established by attesting the same type of textual variation. The likely explanation is that the group archetype had been copied from more than one MS and thereby diversified its textual complexion. As in IV Ezra MS M354 appeared in concert with CBF, so also in *Deut* while its three fellows from Daniel's B1ᵇ, NJ23 M346-WN11 appear in *Deut'* s d group, surrounded mainly by MSS which also belong to Daniel's E group, indicating a complex background to the composition of the Daniel B1ᵇ sub-group.

The majority of the MSS in *Deut'* s b group reflect Daniel's C group followed by the D group. It is not surprising that J3043 from Daniel's E 1ᵃ sub-group joins them since from the scribe's description of his itinerant existence while engaged in copying the manuscript one may infer the possibility of diverse exemplars.[14] Similarly the presence of M202, a member of the B3 sub-group in Daniel, is explicable on the grounds that it is the most developed element of that group. Thus three of the other members (W71-M2585-J1127) fall within the confines of *Deut'*s c11 and the final one (M3705) in *Deut'*s d group.

The majority of *Deut'*s c1 sub-group is constituted by MSS from the C2+3 sub-groups of Daniel. The support these formations give there to the Z type of text serves to elucidate their accompaniment here by representatives from Daniel's D Group which contains Zohrab's base text. V1508 appears in *Deut'*s c11 sub-group which is formed accordingly by MSS of Daniel's B3 and D groups along with NJ1, the rather isolated member of E2 and J3438 which belongs to the loose grouping of A1^b in Daniel. (The third underlines the lack of any close congeneric relationship between them by supporting *Deut'* s d group.)

*Deut'*s d group is largely composed of E Group MSS from Daniel and, among them the E1 members (M351-J1934-M2587-V623-J1928-M189-M200-M347-M204) are once more distinctive by their agreement, suggesting that stemmatic review would not have far to go to reach the archetype of the subgroup. The same also applies to the combination V1270-RV1 from Daniel's E1 sub-group whose close ties are also testified by the Testaments and IV Ezra. Another unexpected member of *Deut'*s d group is M3705 from Daniel's B3 group. The diverse classification of the four members of that group extant in Deut contrasted with their relative gregariousness (M202 in B11, W71-M2585 in c11 and M3705 in d) in Daniel suggests that, whilst their contact is more than merely generic, as documents, they are of composite origin and coincide in only part of their compass.

*Deut'*s E1 sub-group is formed principally by MSS from Daniel's D group, especially the D3 sub-group, while MS V1182 of sub-group C2^b is not really out of place in their company. The *Deut* e sub-groups 11 and 111 likewise feature mainly MSS from Daniel's C2^b and 2^a sub-groups respectively. As the extremely developed nature of the e group text type hardly matches that of the C Group in Daniel, the implication here must also be that the MSS M350-M205-LB8833 from C2^b and M2705-M7623-M190-M2706 from C2^a owe their form to an exemplar of mixed quality. This result is particularly convincing for the MSS from C2^a as *Deut'*s findings serve further to strengthen the links between them which were already noted in Daniel.

Job[15]

a: J1925-M1500-NJ34-V1258-V1007-V935-J3438-
NJ23-J2557-W55-W316-J297-J3043-V1336-CBF

b: V841-V376-V1006-W71-W274-M2705-J428-V1182-
M350-LB8833
c: V1270-RV1-J1934-J1933-M2587-V623-J1928-J1927-
V229-NJ16-NJ17
d: M179-V1508-V280-NJ96-V1507-J1127-J1932-V1634-
J542-NJ15-J501-J1929-J2561

Of the fifty witnesses included in this partial survey of
Job ten must be discounted from our present investigation on
the grounds that either they do not adduce Daniel or were un-
available for collation (NJ34, V1258, J2557, W316, V1336,
V376, NJ16, NJ17, NJ96, J2561). As out of the remainder
there are no representatives of the Daniel sub-groups A1, B1,
C3, D1 and E1, there is no basis for comparison. Significantly,
only a few witnesses are included from the A and B groups in
Daniel. Continuity is observed in assigning the two members of
the Dan A1 sub-group (J297, J3438) to group *a*[16] In contrast,
V280 which attests a remarkably pure text in Daniel (A2), *Deut*
(a1) and 1-2 kgdms[17] is classified in group *d.* From this we
may plausibly surmise that it derives from part-bibles like its
close counterpart J2558.[18]

Of the four representatives from the B group in Daniel MS
W29 (B3) maintains a comparable complexion in Job, the other
three (NJ23 and V935-W55) are assigned to the *a* group. Of
these the last two also appear together in 1 Sam in a group of
similar text type, although they diverge noticeably in *Deut*
where W55 features in sub-group a1 and V935 in c1. The implication is thus that one (or both) was constructed from part-
bibles. Hence the textual diversity in V935 is probably to be explained by the division of labour in copying the OT between two
scribes.[19]

The C group is fundamentally to be identified with Job's
b group, especially the C2 sub-group. Of the latter the only exception is presented by M179 which is also in D and 1 Sam. As
a scribal colophon records utilizing more than one exemplar,
this would seem to confirm the textual data.[20] The Dan C1 sub-

group comprising J1925-M1500 already indicates its textual calibre by shared readings with groups A and B,[21] a trait even more developed in other books, which led to its classification in the a1 sub-group of both Deut and Job.

There is outstanding continuity between the Dan B group and the corresponding group in Job. The one case of divergence constituted by V1007 is readily explicable in terms of a colophon to the effect that the books Jer-Dan-Ezek derive from a different exemplar.[22] The superior quality of its text in Job is maintained in *Deut* where it is allocated in the a1 sub-group.

Similarly, the Dan E group largely comprises Job's *c* group, with three exceptions. MS J3043 from sub-group E1[a] was copied in several places over a number of years,[23] a situation reflected by its variation in affiliation, being assigned to b1 in *Deut* and *a* in Job. Moreover, the rather peripheral status of NJ1 and CBF within sub-group E2 is indicated by their lack of certain marginalia attested by most of the rest,[24] as we have already observed.

From the above we can conclude a relatively stable relationship between the manuscript groupings in Daniel and Job with the former's A+B groups predominating in *a,* C in *b,* D in *d* and E in *c.* Furthermore, external data concerning the exemplar and circumstances of copying often serve to clarify variations from this norm in individual cases.

CONCLUSION

The foregoing survey has provided a brief insight into the kaleidoscopic patterns of convergence and diversity which are inherent to the manuscript tradition of any version of the Bible. More specifically, it has revealed that, despite the complex interweaving of lost strands which have created the texture of our extant documents, some fairly firm stemmatic inferences may be drawn as a result. One of the most striking is that in general where strong links are forged between documents in Daniel these frequently hold true for other books, even though the text types they witness may not be consistent. However, where their text bears a more unitary character, the implication is that this is the result of a period of direct copying and particularly in the case of the older witnesses, may help underpin a hypothesis of local texts.

Those groups or individual units, on the contrary, which betray only tenuous links in Daniel, usually splinter to form part of new clusters in other books and are therefore destined to remain on the sidelines of any attempt to determine the broad development of the version's transmission history. It is likely that they will demand more detailed attention in order to account for all their varied phenomena. Nevertheless, apart from glaring exceptions (such as the representatives of Daniel's E2 occurring in *Deut*'s all sub-group) which are themselves open to satisfactory explanation as the product of a composite base, the main dispersion of A and B at the top of the tree matched by a concentration of D and E at the bottom persists throughout all the books treated so far.[25]

NOTES

[*] The lack of a systematic approach to the assigning of manuscript *sigla* has given rise to a rather confused situation in recent editions of books of the Armenian Bible. Thus M.E. Stone designated his witnesses by various letters of the alphabet (e.g. H = Erevan Matenadaran no. 1500: *The Armenian Version of IV Ezra,* 1979). Having to deal with a considerably larger number of witnesses, C.E. Cox utilized instead the numbers on the far left-hand column of Zeyt'unyan's listing of manuscripts of the Armenian OT (e.g. 28 = Erevan Matenadaran no. 1500: *Deut,* pp. 15-16, 1981) and this format was followed by me in "The Armenian Version of Daniel" (1983). However, A.S. Zeyt'unyan preferred the mixed *sigla* he had allotted the manuscripts in the next column of his listing which define witnesses by both letter and number (e.g. C_8 = Erevan Matenadaran no. 1500: *Girk Cnndoc,* p. 101: 1985).

Zeyt'unyan's formulation had the initial advantage of its chronological structuring of the evidence. However, this has been undermined by supplements of additional manuscripts as these came to light (*Girk Cnndoc,* pp. 85-86). Moreover, at the Sandbjerg Workshop of 1989 (Priorities, Problems and Techniques of Text Editions) organized under the auspices of the Association Internationale des Etudes Arméniennes, it was felt desirable to create a comprehensive system of manuscript *sigla* to apply in every branch of Armenian Studies. The principle which is here employed for the first time designates all codices by library and catalogue number (e.g. M1500 = Erevan Matenadaran no. 1500). Because of the special nature of the catalogue of the Venice Mxitarist collection, there the shelflist number has been substituted.

1. The number in brackets refers to the numeration accorded the manuscripts in vol. 1 of the Venice catalogue.

2. The manuscript collection of Harry Kurdian of Wichita was bequeathed to the Venice Mxitarists and has been accorded a distinct numeration. Unfortunately, a full catalogue of the holdings has not yet been published.

3. The number in brackets refers to the shelflist, while the main number is taken from the catalogue.

4. E.g. S. Der Nersessian, *Chester Beatty Catalogue,* vol.1, p.xlii.

5. For a description of the manuscript see A.K. Sanjian, *A Catalogue of Medieval Armenian Manuscripts in the United States;* Berkeley: University of California Press, 1976, pp.636-640.

6. See further pp.381-2.

7. M9100 contains only the Susanna episode from Daniel.

8. In both cases Zohrab acknowledges in his apparatus that he does not follow his base manuscript.

9. These four manuscripts only preserve the Susanna episode from Daniel.

10. B. Johnson, "Fünf armenische Bibelhandschriften aus Erevan" *Wort, Lied, und Gottesspruch,* Festschrift for Josef Ziegler, J. Schreiner (ed.), Würzburg: 1972. See also C.E. Cox, "Manuscript Groupings of the Armenian Bible", pp.70-71.

11. M.E. Stone, "The Armenian Version of the Testaments of the Twelve Patriarchs: Selection of Manuscripts", *Sion* 49 (1975), pp.207-214. See also C.E. Cox, "Manuscript Groupings of the Armenian Bible", pp.74-75.

12. For examples see p.48.

13. For details see chapter two p.71.

14. Ibid., p.69.

15. For a preliminary classification see C.E. Cox, "Manuscript Groupings of the Armenian Bible", pp.71-74. The present exposition of the evidence is based on the same author's revised formulation in his paper "Text Forms and Stemmatics in the Armenian Text of Job" circulated at the Sandbjerg Workshop referred to above.

16. The discontinuity of the witnesses in Deut (J297 belongs to the d group, while J3438 is assigned to cII) seems to suggest that although they are codicologically related in the second part of the OT, their text of the first part of the corpus derives from different types of exemplar.

17. See S.P. Cowe, "La versión armenia", p.lxxvii.

18. For details see chapter two, note 10, p.79.

19. Ibid., p.65.

20. O. Eganyan et al (eds.), *Mayr c'uc'ak hayerēn jeṛagrac'*, vol.1, col.728.

21. For examples see p.45.

22. For precise details see B. Sargisean (ed.), *Mayr c'uc'ak hayerēn jeṛagrac'*, vol.1, col.127.

23. See further chapter two, p.69.

24. Ibid., p.71.

25. Unfortunately no comparison could be made with Genesis as no sustained analysis of manuscript groupings was offered. For reviews of A. Zeyt'unyan's *Girk' Cnndoc'* see S.P. Cowe, *JTS* 39 (1988), pp.180-182 and C.E. Cox, *REA* N.S.21.

CHAPTER 2

TRANSMISSION HISTORY

Although deciding between readings may appear the same sort of detached cerebral activity as proving mathematical theorems, ultimately the discipline cannot be divorced from history.[1] The fact that the Armenian Bible was subject to the vagaries of copying from the fifth century till the spread of printed texts in the eighteenth has necessarily left its mark upon the textual tradition as was demonstrated in chapter one. There, on a basis of internal evidence, the MSS were assigned to various groups. The purpose of the present chapter is to investigate the historical dimension of that framework. By probing the external data it is hoped to indicate what contact existed between the documents and thereby to trace the major lines of development which Arm underwent. This type of information can then be fed back into the task of evaluating variants in accordance with Westcott and Hort's famous dictum that final decision on documents should precede final decision on readings.[2]

It may be appropriate at the outset to say something about the chronology of the witnesses.[3] Although Daniel must have been copied many times in the intervening centuries, no evidence survives until the second half of the thirteenth century, the oldest dated witness being MS 8 copied in 1253-55. Excluding the undated MS 229 we obtain the following tables of distribution:

century	no. of MSS containing Arm
13th	17
14th	30
15th	4
16th	3
17th	63
18th	2

In analyzing the data we observe flourishing scribal activity during the thirteenth and fourteenth centuries under the favourable conditions provided by the Cilician monarchy. After its collapse in 1375, Armenia fell prey to a succession of foreign incursions which completely interrupted copying in most centres for two whole centuries. With the improvement of Armenian fortunes in the seventeenth century, scriptoria experienced a revival particularly in the capitals of the Ottoman and Safavid empires. This period yields more extant witnesses than all the rest combined, before giving way to the printing press.

Complementary to its textual homogeneity is the tight chronological span enclosing sub-group A1[a] stretching from its first member M287 of 1258 A.D. to its last M144 of the fifteenth century. This suggests an unbroken tradition of copying until the demise of the scribal schools after which it played no part in the seventeenth century revival.

Details of the provenance of M287 are lacking though Hṙomklay, seat of the Catholicos lying on the east bank of the Euphrates has been proposed.[4] MS V1312 from Anarzabus testifies to the presence of the text in central Cilicia in the final quarter of the thirteenth century. It later appears in M207 in Varag, one of the main centres of fifteenth century Van, the region of Western Armenia which, as we shall see, became the custodian of the A group as a whole where it may have been the local text at an earlier period too. It is also very probably the provenance of MS M144. Protected by its natural mountain barriers it was one of the few areas which offered the necessary stability for copying to continue during the 'time of troubles', so much so that it is the only known source of MSS of Arm during the fifteenth-sixteenth centuries.[5] An outstanding tribute to the way in which early traditions could survive there is the oral tradition which kept alive the folk epic "Sasunc'i Dawit'" throughout the Middle Ages until it was committed to writing last century.[6]

As internal evidence indicated that M5603 stood somewhat on the edge of the group, external considerations also mark it out from the rest. It is the only member from the fourteenth century and was copied in the Crimea. Further investigation may uncover what sort of conflation its exemplar may have been subject to from the other text types circulating there.

The unity of the sub-group is further corroborated by the fact that apart from M207 (whose primitive text is noted in *Deut)* it is composed of partial OTs. No full Armenian Bible exists before the second half of the thirteenth century. Previously it was copied in various units one of the most common of which was either the full corpus of wisdom books and prophets or selections from these. Thus not only must A1[a] be classed as early in terms of text type, but also in document type.[7]

Sub-group A1[b] has a longer span from the second half of the thirteenth century until 1640 A.D. (J3438), while virtually no external data are available for LL1209. Its geographical extent parallels that of A1[b] commencing with J304 which was commissioned by Sosthenes vardapet, abbot of the Monastery of the Holy Spirit in Sis, Cilicia. M73, copied prior to 1361, is probably from the region surrounding Lake Van, since the colophon refers to events in Manazkert. Sure contact with Van is established with LR25 whose scribe Barseł hailed from the village of Gawas. As was the custom of pilgrims, it is likely that he brought his own exemplar to Jerusalem, where he copied the Bible. J297 from the fifteenth century was completed in Xlatʿ, a town on the northern shore of Lake Van, by Priest Karapet, probably to be identified with the well-known exponent of the Van School, Karapet of Berkri. The final member of the sub-group, J3438, was copied in Sebastia, to the north-west, where the work of the Van School continued.[8]

MS J304 once more represents a partial OT containing only the books of Solomon and the prophets as is M73. LR25 contains the full NT, followed by the wisdom books and Isaiah, the Minor Prophets and Daniel. The colophon of J297, more-over, informs us that as a full Bible was not to be found, the scribe pieced one together from several exemplars. Daniel was again taken from one containing wisdom books and prophets. The age of this particular exemplar is testified in a colophon in Baruch (folio 451w) «Ով եղբարք, սպալանագս անմեղադիր լերուք, զի օրինակն հին է և խառնակ և գիրս վատ» (Brothers, don't scold me for my writing mistakes, as the exemplar is old and disordered and writing bad.) MS LL1209 is a partial OT of a different composition. It may have been copied from different exemplars.[9] The only Bible in the sub-group is thus J3438. Its appearance in *Deut's* c11 sub-group may suggest that it has a composite base.

A2, like Al[a], had a short lifespan of three centuries from the end of the thirteenth (M4834) to the end of the sixteenth (J2558) and is even more localized within the Van region. M4834 was copied at Erznka, V280 at Xlatʿ and J2558 in Mokkʿ and Van. None of the three sixteenth century witnesses of Daniel (M4070, M2585 and M5809) is of known provenance but due to the limited geographical spread of the other mem-bers of A2, M5809's close textual affinities and the dearth of scriptoria in the other Armenian provinces at that time, it seems logical to suppose that it had its textual origin in Van even granting the possibility that it happened to be copied somewhere else.

MSS M4834 and M5809 are ժողովածու (miscellany) collections having only Daniel in common. The remaining pair are both Bibles. It is clear that J2558 is composite from the order of books and apportionment between two scribes, the first taking the OT as far as Job, while the second begins with the Gospels and Sirach before the Prophets and finally the rest of NT. Therefore the basis of the text of Daniel must have been a MS of the prophets. It is also arguable that the same applies to MS V280. Its scribe Karapet may have once more been compelled to put together a Bible since a complete text was lacking in the town. This is partially confirmed by the unevenness of the text of the various component parts.[10]

The copying life of sub-group B1ᵃ lasted from 1253-55 (M178) till 1652-53 (V1258).[11] However, its geographical span is comparable with those preceding. The location of Erkaynmawruk' Monastery being uncertain, our survey must begin with MS J306 of Meck'ar Monastery near Sis. The text reaches Crimea for M352 to be copied there in 1367-71, then appears in the Van region near Mokk, home of the scribe of M5508, Awetis Daštec'i. The provenance of V1258 is very probably Ejmiacin since the first scribe is styled 'Aleksiane secretary to Lord P'ilippos, Catholicos of the Armenians, while the copyist of the Apocalypse and Dormition of John as Priest Abraham of Bjni. Further corroboration is offered by the binder's remark that this work was the first Bible to be found in the reign of Catholicos Yakob (1658 A.D.). Perhaps the presence of members of the sub-group in the provinces of Van and Ayrarat may imply that this type of text circulated in Greater Armenia in the preceding period also, though owing to the scale of the destruction there, which has left us no earlier OT material, this is difficult to substantiate.

The documentary basis of the sub-group is also old in type. M178 comprises the historical books followed by Job, Daniel, Isaiah and the Minor Prophets. J306 contains the books of Solomon and the Prophets: the scribe, Toros dpir, further observes in a colophon «արդ գրեցաւ սա ի ստոյգ և յրնտիր աւրինակէ» 'this has now been copied from a precise, choice exemplar'. V1258 similarly possesses only the second half of the OT, while M352 and M5508 are Bibles. The latter at any rate may also be of composite origin.

B1b like the A sub-groups has a short historical span. Three members (NJ336 M346 M354) are from the fourteenth century with WN11 an isolated follower in the sixteenth (pre-1608 A.D.). The possibility that the latter represents a direct copy of an older MS similar to the others may be suggested by the plea the scribe addresses to future readers in the margin of Esther to fill in the portion he has left blank due to the illegibility of his exemplar.

MS NJ336 derives from Marata in N.W. Iran (South of Tabriz and East of Urmia) while M346 was commissioned by Yovhannes Rabuni of the Catholicate of Aḥt̕amar and completed in Xizan. The amount of support it lends MSS V280-J2558, especially in preserving Arm1[12] readings is thus explicable in terms of geographical proximity. Moreover, a scribal colophon informs us that it had been copied from a reliable old exemplar. M354 was copied at Aparaner in the greater Armenian province of Siwnik̕ for Fra Mxit̕arič̕ vardapet, presumably a member of the Catholic "Order of Preachers" which had one of its main centres there.[13] The final witness, MS WN11, is from Poland, which was a growth point for Armenian colonization at that time. The scribe's information that he had searched for an OT to copy for ten years may imply that his exemplar had been brought by one of the new settlers.

The fourteenth century MSS are all Bibles. The fact that three scribes worked on M346 in different centres suggests that it is composite, as is borne out by its uneven showing in the textual classification of different books. WN11 contains OT only.

The attempt to locate the origin of the B Group in Greater Armenia gains in plausibility from a consideration of its second sub-group. Like B1[b] it comprises a closely-knit group of the fourteenth century, with one later follower (M187 of 1640 A.D.).[14] Apart from the earliest witness which is Cilician, the others are from E. Turkey and N.W. Iran, having probably followed the normal trade route from Dwin via Naxiǰewan to Tabriz and Baghdad. MSS M4429 and V935 are from Sultaniya, capital of the Ilkhans, V14 from Ani probably, M18415 from Tabriz and M187 from Amida.

With regard to form, LOB1 is a partial OT. The OT text of V935 may not have been unitary since two scribes were involved and is certainly different from that of the NT which was copied by a third scribe years later in Baghdad. The other witnesses are Bibles.

B's third sub-group is unusual in having a relatively continuous tradition of copying from the second half of the thirteenthth to the second half of the seventeenth century. It is difficult to link it to any geographical region since the provenance of four (W71, M147, M3705) is not known. The first witnesses appear in Cilicia (M199, V1482) and one of the seventeenth century MSS (M202) is from Istanbul. It may be that the final witnesses (M147, M3705) were also copied there: unfortunately details of scribe, patron, etc., which might assist in confirming this are not available. Three of the MSS (M199, V1482, M147) are partial OTs containing the books of Solomon and the Prophets while the remainder consist of full Bibles (MS V29 lacks the Gospels).

Sub-group C1 is the smallest and shortest-lived, being formed by two MSS of the thirteenth century. Their provenance connects them with Greater Armenia, MS J1925 coming from Erznka, and M1500 from the Monastery of Geṫard near Erevan. However, their form binds them more to Cilicia, since J1925 (of 1269 A.D.) is the oldest extant complete Armenian Bible with M1500 following close behind. This form becomes standard for the majority of units in the remaining groups C-E. Nevertheless, as we have observed already, J1925 at any rate is composite. Indeed it is striking that although one of the scribes engaged in copying OT seems to be familiar with the arrangement of the NT that became the norm, that actually found in the MS is highly idiosyncratic. Taking over from his two colleagues after the Test XII Patr., the third scribe copies Isaiah and Jeremiah, the books of Solomon and only then Daniel and Ezekiel which may imply that the latter two books were obtained from a ժողովածու (miscellany) in which they were circulating separately. This might then go some way to account for the agreements between M4834-J1925 in the edition. This type of origin is also highly probably for the group Esther-Judith-Tobit [16] with which the OT section comes to a close. Finally it should be said that the character of the patrons of these works, Bishop Sargis of Erznka and his son Parᵊn Yovhann ᵊs and the famous abbot and pedagogue Mxit'ar Ayrivaneci (who is also the scribe of 28) must in part have been responsible for the fine quality of their text.

Sub-group C2ᵃ is the first we have investigated in which the break in copying between the early period and the seventeenth century reprise is clear cut. A similar geographical cleavage is discernible. The thirteenth and fourteenth century MSS of known origin arise from Cilicia, the final one (M9116 of 1379 A.D.) hailing from Cyprus where the Lusignan dynasty had appropriated the title of the Cilician monarchy after the fall of the Het'umids. The seventeenth century MSS for which data exist (M7623 and M2706) are both from Kafa on the Crimea. Nevertheless a link can be found between the two segments of the tradition, namely M2705 of 1368 A.D. A colophon notes that the OT was written «յաշխարհն Ֆռանկաց... ի քաղաքն Պալունիա» (in the land of the Franks... in the town of Pᵊlonia [Bologna]). The NT was added in the Crimea. The contact between MSS M2705-M7623-M2706 which this information supports is also sanctioned by their close agreement in Daniel as well as *Deut* and Ruth too. In both these cases the formation is joined by MS M190 which may in turn be suggested to originate in the Crimea. In keeping with C1 the vast majority of C2ᵃ is composed of full Bibles: three are partial Bibles

(V39, M9116, M6640) and one is a ժողովածու (miscellany) in which the only Biblical item is the Susanna episode.

Sub-group C2^b reveals an even more extreme cleft in its tradition, being composed of two MSS from the end of the thirteenth century (M179-M177) followed by six seventeenth century witnesses. As we should expect by now, the tradition begins in Cilicia. The three later MSS of known origin (M186, J428, M350) were copied in Istanbul. Moreover, Stone[17] is of the opinion that M205 and LB8833 may have been copied there, a suggestion which is similarly compatible with *Deut* and Ruth's manuscript classification. On the grounds that scribe Yovannes of V1182 describes himself as Լհուգհ ('from Poland') Sargisean conjectures that the MS may have been copied there. Stone does not find this convincing,[18] and certainly judging by textual affinity it would be more plausible to propose Istanbul instead. The magnetism of the great capital lured many copyists from far-flung places.[19]

Again, the simplest method of bridging the gap between the two parts of the sub-group is to postulate the direct copying of Cilicia originals in the Istanbul scriptoria, a practice for which much evidence is available. Now that prosperity had returned to the communities they were no longer satisfied with the technically inferior products of the preceding two hundred years and turned back rather to the richness and subtlety of the Cilician masterpieces for their inspiration. Considerations of text type probably yielded priority to the quality of the illustrative miniatures in stimulating this move.

Both sections of the C3 sub-group reveal the same split in tradition, being composed of a fourteenth century base followed by renewed copying in the seventeenth century. Like the preceding sub-group, all the members are full Bibles except J797, which is also of composite origin. There Daniel is sandwiched between Tobit and Esther and Ruth and Judith. M353 was copied at the prestigious Armenian monastery of Glajor which attracted students from both Greater Armenia and Cilicia and thus brought about a synthesis of texts and styles. J797 derives from Trebizond, which having fallen from its former glory, may not have held a full Armenian Bible, thus necessitating the construction of the MS from such portions as were accessible.

With the commencement of discussion of Group D, we have already left the thirteenth century behind, which seems to justify the impression that it is a developed text. D1 is composed of four witnesses of the fourteenth century, followed by two of the seventeenth which were copied in quick succession (M4905 in 1649 A.D., M3545 in 1667-68). The pattern of a Cilician text (M182, J1931) moving to Glajor (M206) is duplicated, while a further branch reached Jerusalem (M5608). A brief revival was experienced in Šarot (M4905, M3545). The majority are again full Bibles while J1931 lacks the first half of OT and M5608 is also partial.

D2 begins in Glajor with V1007 of 1332 A.D. before starting to be recopied in Istanbul (J1932, M348) in the seventeenth century. The provenance of M2628 and M2732 is uncertain. All are full Bibles.

D3 was in circulation in Cilicia during the fourteenth century. It is marked out from all Arm's other sub-groups by the diversity of scriptoria in which it was copied during the seventeenth century revival, encompassing Istanbul (M188, M349), Zeytun (DCB552), Amida (J1127) and Bethlehem (J542) even though the remaining six members have insufficient evidence to be placed. The spread of witnesses coupled with the numerical superiority it possesses over the others testifies to the wide popularity it enjoyed, which it is probably justified to project back to the fourteenth century, the major source of exemplars from which these late copies were drawn. The overwhelming majority are full Bibles: 160 contains the OT (except Psalter) while J1926 has the second half of the OT, as does J1930 to which the NT was then added.

With Group E we may also have left behind the fourteenth century, since MS V1270 is undated and has been designated a borderline case between the fourteenth and fifteenth. More importantly, that and M4070 apart, all the rest stem from the seventeenth and eighteenth centuries. Three such MSS from sub-group E1ª were definitely copied in Istanbul (RV1, M2669, J1927) with the further tie linking the latter two in that they are probably by the same scribe Astuacatur dpir. MS J3043 took seventeen years to copy and was added to in Egypt, Jerusalem and other places until its completion. Nevertheless, the indications are that the part containing Daniel was written in 1622 at Istanbul where the Gospels were completed in the following year. A later branch appears in New Julfa (M6281, V897) in the second half of the century, such cultural interchange being a regular feature of the life of the Armenian communities of the two capitals.

A subsequent colophon in V1270 indicates that the document was presented to the Mxitarist vardapet Minas Bžškean at Lvov in Poland in 1820. Yet being copied in the fourteenth-fifteenth century before the migration there it is unlikely to have originated there. It seems, rather, to have been brought there in the sixteenth century when much of the movement took place.[20]

Once more the vast majority are full Bibles while V1270 extends only to OT and V897 to the wisdom books and Prophets.

Sub-group E1ᵇ is even more chronologically circumscribed, spanning little more than a century from M4070 of 1550-53 A.D. to CHB5 of 1674-76 (J1232 is undated). The documents are also at one in belonging to the category ժողով մատ (miscellany) though of quite varied contents. While MS V1865 places Ruth before the block Esther Judith Tobit Susanna, CHB5 and J1232 attest it after these books, underlining their frequent textual agreement in the sample collation. We encountered this sort of collection when describing J1925 in which the whole book of Daniel was present. These in contrast contain only the Susanna pericope, with the result that the compilation somewhat resembles the regular Syriac "Book of the Women", though there is no reason to suppose direct dependence on that tradition. The similarity of the heroines and narrative style of the stories is probably sufficient to explain their mutual gravitation. With no details available of the provenance of MSS V1865 and J1232, the two fixed points, as in the case of E1ª, are Ilov and Istanbul, thus strengthening the impression that the development of the whole group involves the existence of the text in sixteenth century Poland followed by its transference to and establishment at Istanbul in the next century.

The E2 sub-group's duration was only of about half a century from M351 (of 1616-19 A.D.) to CBF (of 1667). The close textual affinity we have noted among the members is evidenced in the previous studies compared in the last chapter. Nevertheless, although all are full Bibles, not all possess Test XII Patr. and thus are not so likely to be epigraphs of one exemplar. Moreover, *Deut* revealed a cleft in the tradition by which MSS J1933-V229-M201-M7093-CBF attested a significantly better text form than the others whose standard was more comparable to that characterizing the whole sub-group in Daniel.[21] The clear suggestion is that the aberrant group originates directly or indirectly from a composite MS.

The Eastern spread of the manuscript tradition, familiar from the preceding sub-groups, is again apparent, only this time the destination is Persia and more particularly New Julfa, the Armenian town across the river from the then capital of Isfahan.[22] Sargisean is inclined to assign MS V229 to Poland on account of the Ilov colophon it has duplicated, but this must be rejected as the document shares the same scribe with MS J1928 of Persian provenance, namely Deacon Markos, son of Priest Yovhannes. The second owner, moreover, is styled Pawłos of (New) Julfa and close contact between the two MSS is postulated in *IV Ezra* too. A further problem lies in trying to locate MS CBF. Both date and place are uncertain: the only sure evidence we have is the scribe's name Astuacatur.[23] Considering that textually it belongs to the New Julfa "family", among which the scribe of MS M201 shares the same name, and both these MSS are classed together in *Deut*'s all sub-group and Ruth's D2 sub-group, it seems more reasonable to trace CBF there rather than Cilicia with which the E group in general has no contract.

The majority of the sub-group is also united in re-copying Lazar Baberdaci's colophon which is original to MS M351, as well as his introduction, and the verse numeration in gold letters he introduced as a reader's aid, complemented by the Latin system in black (chapters) and red (verses). It is interesting that two of the five MSS from this sub-group classified in *Deut*'s all set (M191-CBF) lack these items. This may be interpreted as a sign of their comparative isolation from the main body but the fact that they are found in the remaining three witnesses should serve as a check against pressing this too far.

The other MS to omit the above material (NJ1) is certainly to be taken separately since it diverges dramatically from the formation's textual norm in other books and lacks the marginalia which are a feature of the majority of the sub-group in Daniel. One of the clearest examples is at Susanna 62 where the reader is referred to Deuteronomy ԺԹ.Ժ in all the witnesses except V623, M347, NJ1 and CBF. Another occurs at 4:31 հ ւ եր ն. 100 in MSS M351-J1934-J1933-M2587-M200-M191-M204.

CONCLUSION

Although textual groupings are constituted solely on grounds of internal evidence of readings and cannot be undone by historical criticism, the aim of the foregoing survey has been to examine the plausibility of the process by which these groups took shape. Its point of departure was the assumption that as text types propagated themselves by physical contact between documents and details of the circumstances are accessible by means of colophons, etc., the process should not be consigned to inscrutable chance but to a degree was capable of hypothetical reconstruction. Indeed correlation between the internal and external approaches logically confirms their mutual verisimilitude.

Historical investigation has illuminated certain general features of the manuscript classification. As one might have expected, sub-groups with superior readings are principally composed of early witnesses and thus largely represent a unitary transmission, capped by one or two late copies. Sub-group C2ª marks the mid-point of the development, in that it evinces a unilinear development from Cilicia to the Crimea with an almost equal number of units from either centre. C2ᵇ sets a binary trend which applies throughout the D group of a brief Cilician period followed by a prolific revival after a hiatus of two to three centuries. With the E group we have come full circle: the tradition is unitary once more. A slightly earlier unit precedes the main body, whose potential for expansion has been cut short by the spread of the printed word. Its derivative textual character is thus explained by its shallow historical roots.

The investigation has uncovered a certain number of possible local texts, though not all are of equal definitiveness or significance. If the main Persian text-type of the seventeenth century is that witnessed by the E2 sub-group we should not overlook the two-carriers of E1ª type (M6281-V897) and those of D1ª (M4905-M3545). A similar situation existed in sixteenth century Poland where E-group members circulated with B1ᵇ (WN11). Crimea received members of A1ª, B1ª and C2ª, while the density thickens when we focus attention on Istanbul where exemplars of B3, C2ᵇ, D2 and D3 were being copied concurrently.

Nevertheless we encounter the most complex concentration of types in Cilicia of the thirteenth and fourteenth century. Nine varieties of text are found, two from each of the groups A C D and three from B. In works treating the Armenian Bible the phrase "Cilician Vulgate" often recurs. In the eighteenth century discussion of the issue this was understood to mean a revision harmonizing the traditional Armenian text with the Latin Vulgate.[24] However, this has largely been discounted now.[25]

More recently the term has been employed to denote the text type prevalent in the Cilician realm[26] and, more particularly, the one mediated by MSS M180 and V1508, base manuscripts of the editions of Oskan and Zohrab respectively. Correspondingly, in Daniel that accolade belongs to C2[a] which spans a full century from M345 (1270 A.D.) to M9116 (1379 A.D.), is witnessed in sites extending throughout mainland Cilicia as well as Cyprus and is preserved in six witnesses of the period.

What distinguishes D3 (to which V1508 belongs) is the range and number of its seventeenth century MSS from which we can deduce that, originating in Cilicia at the very end of the thirteenth or beginning of the fourteenth century, it soon commended itself widely among scriptoria in such a way that sufficient copies endured the disruption of the intervening two centuries to exert an influence on the revival.[27] This developmental model is corroborated by the lack of any significant variants between the earlier and later strata, a phenomenon general to the groups C, D and E.

The more noticeable divergence to be observed among the witnesses of A B must be attributed to their position at the end of eight centuries of continuous copying from the fifth century autograph onwards. In that sort of time scale it is understandable that the exemplars of the present sub-groups, taken from different points of the formation's pre-history, would already have drifted so far apart that the distance separating their earliest extant members becomes automatic

When we compare the early witnesses of A sub-groups with those of B the distance between their text types is even more palpable, implying that what they read in common generally must be attributed to their most primitive stage. Subsequently, the traditions moved further and further apart with decreasing contact between them. The situation regarding groups D E is completely the reverse; in fact a close accord exists between them, often displayed over against the other text types. Granting that E has no advocate before MS 93 we are probably justified in concluding that the group evolved from

a D matrix and achieved its particular identity by further scribal error compounded with a certain amount of conflation from
MSS of the other textual groups;[28] for it evinces no readings
with an a priori case to be regarded as early without outside
support.

Unfortunately, historical data do not allow us to pinpoint
the locus of the activity with absolute precision. Nevertheless,
according to the testimony of M4070 it was fully formed in its
essentials in mid-sixteenth century Poland, while the scholarly interests of the local community are highlighted by the
scribal 'correspondence' in the margins of WN11's text of
Sirach (folio 407a).[29] Moreover, Lvov was an important mer-
cantile and ecclesiastical centre and already seat of the archbishop of the Armenians of Eastern Europe since the second
half of the fourteenth century.

The same is true of the systematic correction the
manuscript underwent. Lazar Baberdaći similarly displayed
his erudition by inserting the Vulgate chapter divisions into his
copy. Thus, I am inclined tentatively to suggest this as the region in which the group acquired its distinctive character.

As no pre-Cilician manuscripts of Arm have survived,
nothing can be said with certainty about which sort of text was
traditionally transmitted at which scriptorium in Greater
Armenia. Nevertheless the indications are that the surest
ground for attempting such a reconstruction is presented by A
B 1+2 and C1. Their primitive text and the early date of the majority of their witnesses both support this. Moreover, the unitary nature of their transmission history which continues to
the end of the Van school but plays no part in the seventeenth
century renascence suggests that these texts were highly localized and had little opportunity for conflation with C2+3 and
D. These factors permit us to project this situation back into
the final centuries preceding our written sources and postulate
B as the ancestral text of the E. and S.E. provinces of Greater
Armenia (Siwniҟ), A of the S.W. (Vaspurakan) and C1 of the
N.W.

With the gradual exodus of Armenians to Cilicia towards the end of the tenth century, a movement which steadily gathered momentum in the course of the following century, exemplars of various sorts of Biblical text found their way there in the wake of their local communities. One of the main causes of dispersion was the cession of Kars and Ani to the Byzantines and resulting disaffection at their rule, this complex of events being brought to a head by the resounding defeat the latter sustained at Manazkert from the advancing Seljuk forces under Alp Arslan (1071). Therefore it should come as no surprise that manuscripts related to the C1 sub-group which, according to our speculative reconstruction, was the main type of the region, became established in Cilicia at an early date.[30] It then consolidated its position to such an extent that contact with precursors of the B3 sub-group resulted not in cross-fertilisation but in the displacement of many characteristically B group readings and impregnation of the witnesses with the C type text. The effect of this is observable in our extant members of B3, as indicated in the previous chapter.

This framework is similarly reinforced by our analysis of the content of the documents. From an analysis of the data we are able to conclude that the regular standard for groups A and B was the partial Bible and more particularly a collection of the wisdom books (usually excluding Sirach and sometimes Job as not being of Solomonic authorship) and prophets. These corpora normally follow the Psalter and form the second half of the Armenian OT canon.[31] The significance of this phenomenon emerged when these witnesses had to be excluded from the comparison with *Deut*. Conversely, ten of *Deut*'s witnesses were excluded, including three of the earliest members of the most preferred sub-group a1 (V1311, V1312, J353), indicating that other parts of OT also circulated independently. Such types of Biblical manuscript are not foreign to Greek, Syriac and Georgian traditions also.

One of the reasons why no pre-Cilician MSS of Arm have survived is that OT *per se* was not a liturgical book and therefore not an essential possession of every monastery and parish.[32] As is apparent from the age and extent of available evidence, apart from the Gospels and Psalter, Biblical readings for use in services were excerpted in lectionaries, the only partial exception being MSS of Isaiah and the Pauline Epistles, books from which the majority of readings were taken. Manuscripts containing other parts of scripture were designated for individual study and class instruction with the result that their future depended on the economic resources of patrons and the growth and systematization of monastic life in Armenia. Both reached their apogee in Cilicia.

In considering the origin of the full Bible we must add the factor of script. As convention governing the transmission of scripture was conservative, uncial letters continued to be used even after minuscule had become the rule in certain other types of document.[33] The larger size of the characters compounded with the very restricted use of abbreviations meant that it was more convenient to bind as a series of volumes. That a one volume minuscule copy was still a rather unusual event in the mid-thirteenth century is testified by the ascription of the patron's intent to divine inspiration. «Շարժեալ եղև ի Հոգւոյն Սրբոյ հոգիրնկալ միաս սրրա ժողովել ի մի վայր գամենայն սատս հոգիանունագ մարգարէից, և զքի ... քարոզութիւնն ... և զսրբոց առաքելոցն գործսն...» (his [i.e. Bishop Sargis of Erznka] spiritually-receptive mind was moved by the Holy Spirit to collect in one place all the books of the Spirit - playing prophets [Old Testament], the teaching... of Christ [Gospels] ... and the Acts of the holy Apostles...).[34]

The implication of the preceding argument for our textual classification is that the D group which (along with E) frequently supports C group readings, has no witnesses earlier than the fourteenth century and is largely composed of whole Bibles, evolved in Cilicia from a developed form of C text. In this way it represents an extension of the organic development whereby C2 seems to have arisen from a type more resembling C1, though the scale of the variation has passed the point at which it can be regarded as a sub-group.

Drawing together the main stages of Arm's transmission history which have been elucidated and tentatively reconstructed in the course of the chapter, we arrive at the following overview. After a certain period of copying, three text types distinguish themselves in the North and North-West, East, South-East and South-West of Greater Armenia. As a result of a population drift to Cilicia primarily from Kars-Ani the first text (c) becomes established there and exerts an influence on units of the other types when they appear also. A particular branch of this group is singled out and develops into the D group which spreads to other centres before the collapse of the Cilician Kingdom. A further emigration ensues carrying a variety of exemplars to the Crimea and so to Poland where the D group undergoes a certain amount of conflation which ends in the formation of group E. When social and economic conditions improve in the seventeenth century, D and E along with C 2^b become the staple models of the scriptoria of Istanbul and New Julfa before being overtaken by Oskan's printed edition.

NOTES

1. E.g. the historical crux posed by M.D. Koster's reconstruction of the manuscript tradition of Pešitta Exodus whereby a Nestorian manuscript became increasingly influential within the Jacobite community. See *The Peshitta of Exodus.* The Development of its Text in the Course of Fifteen Centuries, SSN 19, Assen/Amsterdam: Van Gorcum, 1977, p.535. The issue is further elucidated in P.B. Dirksen, "The Relation", pp.167-171 and K.D. Jenner, "Some IntroductoryRemarks Concerning the Study of 8a1", in *The Peshitta: Its Early Text and History,* P.B. Dirksen and M.J. Mulder (eds.), Leiden: E.J. Brill: 1988, pp.200-224.

2. B.F. Westcott and F.J.A. Hort, *The New Testament in the Original Greek* vol.2. Cambridge: Cambridge University Press, 1881, p.31.

3. To outline their geographical spread is to chart the wanderings of the Armenian people and is best reserved for the detailed discussion of each sub-group.

4. See the description of the manuscript in chapter four.

5. On the possible significance of the relative distribution of manuscripts chronologically see D. Kouymjian, "Dated Armenian Manuscripts as a Statistical Tool for Armenian History", *Medieval Armenian Culture,* T.J. Samuelian and M.E. Stone (eds.), UPATS 6, Chico, Ca: Scholars Press, 1984, pp.425-438.

6. For the principal collection of variant forms of the narrative see M. Abełyan and K. Melik-ōhanjanyan (eds.), *Sasna crer*[Daredevils of Sasun] vols.1-3, Erevan: Academy of Sciences 1936-1951. The wider Van region also maintained certain traditions of scholarship up to the time of Srapēon Uřhayeci (d. 1606), a lively cultivation of the poetic genre of *tał* (ode) and inspired two contrasting schools of miniature illumination. On the last point see S. Der Nersessian, *L'art arménien,* pp.227-233.

7. For further details see S.P. Cowe, "A Typology of Armenian Biblical Manuscripts".
8. S. Der Nersessian, *L'art arménien*, p.233.
9. See *Deut*, p.16.
10. See the appropriate entry in the Venice Mxitarist Catalogue.
11. Although M5508 appears as a seventeenth century witness in Zeyt'unyan's list, the Matenadaran catalogue reports the manuscript as from the fifteenth century, which date is also more compatible with its provenance.
12. For details see chapter five.
13. For the background to the movement see M.A. van den Oudenrijn, "Uniteurs et Dominicains d'Arménie", *Or Chr* N.S. IV 40 (1956), pp.94-112; VI 42 (1958), pp.110-133; VII 43 (1959), pp.110-119; IX 45 (1961), pp.95-108; X 46 (1962), pp.99-116.
14. The particular agreement of LOB1 and M187 carried over into *Deut* may be the result of the known policy of the seventeenth century school of Amida to copy earlier Cilician MSS. See S. Der Nersessian, *Chester Beatty*, p.xli.
15. Dashian's suggestion is likely based on the provenance of the scribe Yovhannes — yet since patrons frequently supplied the exemplar to be copied, it might have come from further East as it was commissioned by Samuel, bishop of Bǰni.
16. See discussion of sub-group E1.
17. *IV Ezra*, p.16.
18. Ibid.
19. S. Der Nersessian, *Chester Beatty*, p.xlii. N.B. the original colophon mentions the young Turkish Sultan Ahmet and a later owner who adds no new date (and thus allows us to surmise that only a short time had expired from the copying) writes that he transferred the MS from Istanbul to Venice.
20. See the discussion of WN11.
21. Cf. the similar results arrived at in Ruth where MSS

J1933-M191-CBF were assigned to the A2 sub-group (V229 did not form part of the collation sample), while M201 aligned itself to the D2 sub-group (S.P. Cowe, "The Armenian Version of Ruth and its Textual Affinities", p.190).

22. For the commercial and cultural importance of the Armenian colony there see V. Gregorian, "Minorities of Isfahan: The Armenian Community of Isfahan 1587-1722", *Iranian Studies* 8(198), pp.652-680.

23. See M.E. Stone, *The Testament of Levi,* pp.9f.

24. For a synopsis of the hypothesis see Johnson, "Armenian Biblical Tradition", pp.357-360.

25. Alexanian ("Armenian Gospel Text", pp.387-387) argues for a limited influence in the inclusion of certain gospel lections.

26. C.E. Cox, "Concerning a Cilician Revision of the Armenian Bible", *De Septuaginta,* pp.209-222.

27. We can assert indirectly that the text had also reached Poland as where the corrector of WN11 is not simply righting scribal blunders, his changes transform the manuscript's allegiance from sub-group B1 to D3. This is clearly discernible from the regularity with which his readings support M182 in the apparatus to the edition. Moreover, an identical tendency is shown by the corrector of M177 in the three sample collations made, as outlined in chapter two.

28. This is observable in the edition in the few cases where E's main representative M351 leaves the company of M182-V1508 from D for that of other groups.

29. The first notes that much of what the Latin text reads in full is lacking, while a second 'replies' that on comparing another copy of the Armenian, he finds that the MS contains all that is found in the Armenian translation of the book. The non-representation of large textual blocks current in Gk is characteriztic of the Z edition of Armenian Sirach, though the Bagratuni edition is not complete ei-

ther. See J. Ziegler, *Sapientia Jesu Filii Sirach*, Septuaginta vol.xii,2 Göttingen: Vandenhoeck and Ruprecht, 1965, pp.33-35.

30. No such violence or abruptness marked the transfer of sovereignty in the provinces where A and B circulated. Recognition of Seljuk supremacy allowed the local dynasties of Siwnik to remain in power till 1166, while the Arcrunis and Mamikonids held out until 1189-1190. In the absence of major demographic disruption, it is logical that these texts arrived late in Cilicia and in fewer numbers. For details see C. Toumanoff, "Armenia and Georgia", *CMH* (ed.) J.M. Hussey, vol. IV, Part 1, chapter xiv, Cambridge: The University Press, 1966 and the ample bibliography cited there.

31. See S.P. Cowe, "A Typology of Armenian Biblical Manuscripts", p.60.

32. Ibid., pp.51-53.

33. See Ch. Mercier, "Notes de paléographie arménienne", *REA* N.S. 13 (1978-1979), pp.51-58.

34. MS 13, folio 810. The originality of conception and execution of the narrative cycle in this codex eloquently confirms the impression formed from other data as to the manuscript's uniqueness. See S. Der Nersessian, *Etudes byzantines et arméniennes*, Louvain: 1973, pp.603-609.

CHAPTER 3

BACKGROUND TO THE EDITION

In the absence of detailed investigations of patristic citations and commentaries it was felt that the groundwork was insufficient as yet to support an eclectic critical edition. Therefore, it was determined that the most appropriate method of presenting the evidence was via the diplomatic format.

Once the various manuscript groups had crystallized, the second stage of the process consisted of selecting representatives from each of them to go forward for full collation in the edition in accordance with the Claremont Profile Method.[1] The choice was informed by two principles which directly affected the procedure to be followed. The first was the desire to display the version in all its rich diversity of forms. The type of witness best suited to satisfy this criterion is not the most outstanding one but the most average, one which possesses little material not shared by the majority of the group. Solecistic MSS evincing a large amount of singular readings, on the contrary, are undesirable as they only give a false impression of the character of the group they are supposed to represent. Singular orthographic variants in particular tend to be secondary corruptions caused by similarity of sound or written form and therefore not of direct relevance to the textual critic. As a result, their presence would needlessly clutter up the apparatus.

In order to avoid this eventuality tests were conducted independently of singular substantive and orthographic variants the results of which are tabulated below. The MSS are set out according to their textual classification opposite which is given the number of variants they adduce in the three collation samples individually, followed by the overall total. MSS scoring low on both counts (substantive and orthographic) were most eligible for a place in the edition. Those prefixed by an asterisk proved the final choice.

SINGULAR SUBSTANTIVE VARIANTS

Chapter	Sus	4	11	Total	Chapter	Sus	4	11	Total
A1ª *M287	0	0	1	1	B2 LOB1	0	0	1	1
M5560	1	0	0	1	M4429	0	0	1	1
M5603	1	0	5	6	V935	0	0	0	0
M207	2	2	3	7	W55	1	2	4	7
M144	0	0	2	2	M184	0	4	0	4
					M187	0	1	1	2
A1ᵇ J304	0	1	4	5					
M173	5	5	19	29	B3 M199	0	0	0	0
LR25	1	4	8	13	V1482	3	0	1	4
J297	5	4	8	17	W71	5	1	3	9
LL1209	3	7	7	17	*M2585	0	0	0	0
J3438	2	1	1	4	M202	0	1	0	1
					M147	1	1	1	3
A2 *M4834	2	1	2	5	M3705	2	3	3	8
*V280	0	1	1	2					
M5809	6	14	19	39	C1 *J1925	5	2	7	14
J2558	1	1	2	4	M1500	2	2	5	9
B1ª *M178	0	0	0	0	C2ªM345	0	0	1	1
J306	2	0	0	2	M180	0	0	0	0
M352	2	6	5	13	V841	0	0	0	0
V1258	0	0	0	0	V1006	3	0	0	3
M5508	4	3	2	9	M6230	0	0	0	0
					W274	0	1	4	5
B1ᵇ NJ23	2	2	1	5	M4113	0	0	0	0
*WN11	2	4	4	10	M2705	0	0	1	1
*M346	0	0	0	0	*M9116	0	0	0	0
M354	0	0	1	1	M7623	1	0	3	4

Chapter	Sus	4	11	Total	Chapter	Sus	4	11	Total
C2ªM190	1	0	0	1	D3 M349	0	0	1	1
M2706	0	4	4	8	J501	0	1	0	1
M6640	1	0	0	1	J1929	0	0	0	0
M9100	4	-	-	4	RL2	2	8	7	17
					DCB552	3	1	2	6
C2b M179	0	0	0	0	V1865	0	0	1	1
M177	1	0	0	1					
M186	0	0	0	0	E1ªV1270	0	0	0	0
J428	3	0	0	3	J3043	9	7	4	20
V1182	1	0	2	3	RV1	0	2	0	2
M350	0	3	2	5	M2669	2	2	3	7
M205	0	0	0	0	J1927	2	1	0	3
LB8833	0	0	0	0	M6281	0	2	2	4
					V897	2	1	1	4
C3ª M183	0	1	1	2					
M353	2	1	2	5	E1bM4070	1	-	-	1
*M4114	0	0	0	0	V83	12	-	-	12
					*CHB5	5	-	-	5
C3b *M2627	0	0	2	2	J1232	1	-	-	1
J797	1	5	5	11					
					E2 *M351	0	0	0	0
D1 *M182	0	0	1	1	J1934	1	0	2	3
J1931	0	0	0	0	J1933	0	0	1	1
M206	0	0	0	0	M2587	4	1	0	5
M5608	0	1	0	1	V623	0	0	0	0
M4905	0	0	1	1	J1928	0	2	2	4
M3545	0	3	2	5	M189	0	1	2	3
					M200	0	0	1	1
D2 V1007	2	0	1	3	V229	1	0	0	1
M2628	0	0	0	0	M347	0	2	0	2
J1932	0	0	0	0	M201	1	0	0	1
M348	1	0	6	7	NJ1	0	1	2	3
M2732	1	1	3	5	M191	1	1	2	4
					M204	1	1	1	3
D3 J1926	0	0	1	1	CBF	0	1	0	1
*V1508	0	0	0	0					
J1930	0	0	0	0					
M6569	0	1	0	1					
V1507	0	0	0	0					
J1127	1	0	1	2					
VK37	0	1	1	2					
V1634	1	3	0	4					
M188	0	0	0	0					
J542	1	2	1	4					
M203	0	0	3	3					

SINGULAR ORTHOGRAPHIC VARIANTS

Chapter	Sus	4	11	Total	Chapter	Sus	4	11	Total
A1a*M287	3	5	2	10	C1 *J1925	1	1	2	4
M5560	1	2	0	3	M1500	16	20	13	49
M5603	2	3	8	13					
M207	2	7	4	13	C2aM345	0	1	1	2
M144	3	6	2	11	M180	0	2	2	4
					V841	0	0	0	0
A1b J304	2	4	1	7	V100	0	2	1	3
M73	1	6	3	10	M6230	1	1	0	2
LR25	1	8	2	11	W274	1	3	2	6
J297	0	3	2	5	M4113	0	0	0	0
LL1209	3	5	1	9	M2705	1	1	1	3
J3488	0	2	1	3	*M9116	0	0	0	0
					M7623	1	2	1	4
A2 *M4834	9	5	8	22	M190	0	1	1	2
*V280	0	0	1	1	M2706	2	2	2	6
M5809	5	10	18	33	M6640	0	1	0	1
J2558	2	3	4	9	M9100	1	-	-	1
B1a*M178	1	0	0	1	C2b M179	0	0	0	0
J306	0	0	0	0	M1770	0	0	0	0
M352	0	0	2	2	M186	0	0	0	0
V1258	0	1	0	1	J428	0	0	0	0
M5508	2	5	4	11	V1182	0	0	0	0
					M3501	1	1	1	3
B1b NJ23	2	1	0	3	M2050	0	2	0	2
*WN11	6	7	5	18	LB8833	0	0	0	0
*M346	2	5	0	7					
M354	6	3	5	14	C3a M183	3	0	0	3
					M353	2	5	1	8
B2 LOB1	1	0	2	3	*M4114	0	1	0	1
M4429	0	0	1	1					
V935	0	0	0	0	C3b *M2627	0	3	0	3
W55	5	0	4	9	J797	0	4	4	8
M184	3	7	4	14					
M187	2	1	3	6	D1*M182	0	0	0	0
					J1931	0	0	0	0
B3 M199	0	0	0	0	M206	1	1	0	2
V1482	1	4	3	8	M5608	4	1	0	5
W71	2	0	1	3	M4905	1	0	0	1
*M2585	0	0	2	2	M3545	0	1	0	1
M202	2	1	0	3					
M147	0	3	2	5	D2V1007	2	1	1	4
M3705	2	6	3	11	M2628	0	0	0	0

Chapter	Sus	4	11	Total	Chapter	Sus	4	11	Total
D2 J1932	0	3	0	3	E1ª J1927	0	0	0	0
M348	0	3	0	3	M6281	0	0	0	0
M2732	0	2	0	2	V897	2	2	0	4
					E1ᵇ M4070	10	-	-	10
D3 J1926	0	0	0	0	V838	5	-	-	5
*V1508	0	0	0	0	*CHB5	4	-	-	4
J1930	0	0	0	0	J1232	1	-	-	1
V1507	1	0	0	1					
J112	1	0	0	1	E2 *M351	0	0	0	0
VK37	1	1	0	2	M6569	1	3	0	4
V1634	0	0	3	3	J1934	0	1	1	2
M188	0	0	0	0	J1933	0	0	1	1
J542	0	2	0	2	M2587	0	4	1	5
M203	2	0	5	7	V623	0	0	0	0
M349	1	1	0	2	J1928	1	1	0	2
J501	0	0	0	0	M189	0	0	1	1
J1929	0	1	0	1	M200	0	0	0	0
RL2	2	2	4	8	V229	0	0	0	0
DCB	2	4	1	7	M347	0	1	0	1
V1865	0	0	0	0	M201	0	0	0	0
					NJ1	0	0	0	0
E1ª V1270	1	0	1	2	M191	0	0	0	0
J3043	13	15	4	32	M204	0	0	0	0
RV1	0	3	1	4	CBF	0	0	1	1
M2669	1	5	0	6					

At the same time, the edition was designated for collation against the Greek, Syriac and Georgian versions to elucidate the nature of Arm's primitive textual colouring and hence that of its *Vorlage*. This undertaking demanded representatives from the earliest recoverable stratum of the groups, possessing as few secondary changes and mistakes as possible. The key position of base manuscript of the edition was to be attributed to a representative of Group A as the group most closely approximating to the original.

In order to isolate witnesses of the required type the manuscripts' performance was monitored in cases of substantive variation and their readings were graded as either preferred (+) or inferior (-) in comparison to Z. Cases where both readings appeared to have outside support or where it was difficult on other grounds to give a +/- judgment were given a zero grading (0). Orthographical variants were deliberately excluded from the survey as being of lesser importance.

Examples of typical readings falling within the parameters of the three categories outlined above include the following:

+ (Preferred)

Sus:61 և 3°] om. There is no equivalent for this element in either Gk or P and, if original, there is no clear reason why it should have been omitted by so many earlier witnesses. Moreover, և is often found after որպէս to lend a slight emphasis to the feature being compared, so that it seems to have been inserted here too almost unconsciously by a copyist.

Sus:63 նորա 3°] om. The possessive pronoun is not represented in either Greek or Syriac and is most plausibly explained as the result of parallelism with the preceding phrases կին նորա and արամբ նորա, while the rather balder form ազգականաւնաւք(ն) constitutes the *lectio difficilior.* It should further be noted that repetition of the possessive pronoun runs contrary to the translator's general practice. So far is he from adding an extra instance that where his source repeats the form after every item in a list, he regularly omits all but the final occurrence.[2]

11:15 արքային] + հարաւոյ. The king's dominion is specified in both Gk and P and was probably omitted as being inconsistent with the reference to the king of the South at the beginning of the same verse. Clearly two protagonists are required and therefore the omission is to be regarded as a secondary attempt at correction. In Gk and P the difficulty does not arise as the first king is described as coming from the North.

- (Inferior)

Sus:59 կայ] վկայ Both Gk and P support the Z reading while the orthographical similarity of the two forms coupled with their wide difference in meaning confirms the inner-Armenian origin of the variant. The genuine occurrence of the word in v.61 may have facilitated its entry into some witnesses at this point.

Sus:50 վադվադակի] pr անդրէն. There is no external support for the variant. It seems rather the result of contextual harmonization paralleling Daniel's command (v.49) դարձայք անդրէն and echoing the narrative of the elders' return v.14. դարձեալ անդրէն եկին.

Sus:62 արդար] -ոյ. Once more there is no external support for the variant. It seems to have originated from dittography of *J* from the following յաւուր real (in an exemplar) or imagined (a copyist's hasty impression). The probable source is an old uncial manuscript from the period before word division was introduced.

0 (Indeterminate)
Sus:49 բանզի] զի. Both causal conjunctions are appropriate in context. Since the translator's technique regarding such "function" words is inconsistent, it is difficult to decide between the variants purely on internal evidence of readings.

Sus:55 հերձէ] հերձնցէ. The variants represent the aorist conjunctive forms of the cognate verbs հերձանել and հերձել respectively. As the verb only occurs here in Daniel we cannot recover the translator's general preference and since the variation in meaning is so slight we must conclude that both have the possibility of being original.

Sus:54 հասեր ատ] տեսեր. In this case both readings have support: the latter follows the majority of the Gk tradition, whilst Z agrees with A'BoSy[L2]. Thus although it may be claimed that Z results from a harmonistic change rendering the text equivalent to Daniel's question to the second elder in v.58, it cannot be

immediately ruled out that it represents a direct translation
from a witness similar to those cited above.

Sus:58 աստ] + դու. There is no equivalent to the variant in Gk
and it might be interpreted as a scribal addition to inject a little
more liveliness into the dialogue except for the fact that P reads
ԷԼ ս Խ; Խ. Hence, far from being a later incursion into the text,
it is plausible that the reading derived from Arm1 in which pro-
nominal subjects characteristically accompany verbs even
without P support and subsequently dropped out of many
primitive manuscripts in the revision which engendered Arm2.

In the following table the witnesses are again set out in
their pre-arranged groupings. Opposite them in sequence is
given the overall number of preferred, inferior and zero-grade
readings each attests in the collation samples. MSS combining
a high score in the first column with a low rating in the second
(i.e. with a preponderance of valuable, early readings and a minimum of secondary corruptions) were seriously considered for
inclusion in the edition. Those marked with an asterisk were finally selected.

SHARED SUBSTANTIVE VARIANTS

	+	-	0			+	-	0
A1a *M287	13	18	9		C1 *J1925	9	37	18
M5560	13	20	8		M1500	11	41	17
M5603	11	23	11					
M207	10	20	7		C2a M345	11	18	9
M144	12	21	7		M180	10	15	11
					V841	11	17	1
A1b J304	11	19	18		V106	4	16	9
M73	10	16	10		M6230	12	20	12
LR25	9	21	19		W274	13	12	7
J297	12	20	13		M4113	11	20	12
LL1209	14	23	14		M2705	12	24	13
J3438	10	19	10		*M9116	10	14	11
					M7623	8	25	11
A2 *M4834	11	20	11		M190	11	26	12
*V280	10	70	16		M2706	11	30	11
M5809	8	35	12		M6640	11	21	9
J2558	10	69	16		M9100	4	7	3
B1a *M178	12	13	17		C2b M179	8	11	4
J306	10	23	18		M177	7	12	8
M352	10	19	12		M186	10	13	6
V1258	9	12	17		J428	8	16	5
M5508	10	26	17		V1182	6	12	4
					M350	9	24	5
B1b NJ23	10	34	18		M250	9	20	6
*WN11	10	37	15		LB8833	9	13	6
*M346	11	28	19					
M354	11	27	19		C3a M183	5	8	4
					M353	5	10	4
B2 LOB1	12	24	16		M4114	5	8	3
M4429	9	17	8					
V935	9	22	17		C3b *M2627	9	17	8
W55	10	24	17		J797	6	18	6
M184	9	25	11					
M187	7	26	17		D1 *M182	2	3	0
					J1931	0	2	0
B3 M199	9	16	9		J206	2	3	1
V1482	11	28	13		M5608	2	5	0
W71	8	21	9		M4905	2	4	0
*M2585	10	19	9		M3545	1	3	1
M202	8	19	9					
M147	7	21	10		D2 V1007	0	6	2
M3705	10	33	13		M2628	0	5	0

	+	-	0		+	-	0
				E1b M4070	0	5	0
D2 J1932	0	5	2	V838	1	10	0
M348	0	7	2	*CHB5	0	11	0
M2732	0	5	1	J1232	0	10	0
D3 J1926	0	3	1	E2*M351	2	1	2
*V1508	0	3	2	J1934	1	1	1
J1930	0	4	1	J1933	1	4	2
M6569	1	1	1	M2587	2	8	5
V1507	0	2	1	V623	0	2	2
J1127	0	4	1	J1928	1	6	2
VK37	0	3	0	M189	1	4	1
V1634	0	4	1	M200	2	2	3
M188	0	2	1	V229	2	5	2
J542	0	2	0	M347	1	5	2
M203	0	4	0	M201	2	2	2
M349	0	2	1	NJ1	1	4	2
J501	0	3	0	M191	1	4	2
J1929	0	5	1	M204	2	8	2
RL2	4	6	1	CBF	1	3	2
DCB	1	8	1				
V1865	0	3	0				
E1a V1270	2	2	1				
J3043	1	20	0				
RV1	1	17	2				
M2669	3	11	3				
J1927	1	8	2				
M6281	2	6	2				
V897	0	7	2				

In making the final selection of fifteen representatives for full collation preference was given as far as possible to those manuscripts which combined excellence in both areas under investigation, i.e. those which preserved what was typical of their group as well as what was fundamental to the version itself.[3] A further balance was struck in apportioning representatives to the various groups. A larger allotment was granted to the textually superior groups ABC than to DE which are generally derivative. In so doing it was hoped to uncover a wide spread of early readings for analysis. At the same time, the move was sanctioned by the consideration that the sheer amount of variation between the members of ABC is far more extensive and of greater significance than that which obtains in DE. Under those conditions a small number of representatives can still function as adequate spokesmen for the rest, a conclusion which is borne out by the apparatus of the edition. Few indeed are the occasions on which DE's three witnesses have to be specified singly instead of as M182".

Integrating the results from the three tests the following MSS were selected to represent their sub-groups:
A1 (M287: designated base MS) A2 (M4834 V280) B1ᵃ (M178)
B1ᵇ (M346-WN11) B3 (M2585) C1 (J1925) C2 (M9116) C3ᵃ
(M4114) C3ᵇ (M2627) D1 (M182) D3 (V1508) E1 (CHB5) E2
(M351)

Short Physical Description of the MSS
Employed in the Edition

Erevan, Maštoc̆ Matenadaran No.287

Date of Copying: 1258 A.D.
Place of copying: Hŕomklay (probably suggested because of the first major miniaturist school of painting established there by Catholicos Kostandin 1 (1221-67)
Scribe: Priest Kostandin
Commissioned by: Petros[4]
Material: parchment
Dimensions: 21.3 x 15.5; No. of folios: 290
No. of lines per page: 33 in one column
Script: *bolorgir;* Binding: leather on wood
1 colophon by the scribe
Contents: second half of the Old Testament, i.e. Job, Pss, Prov, Eccl, Cant, Wis, Isa, XII Proph, Jer, Bar, Lam, Dan, Ezek.

Additional information: The orthography of the manuscript is in keeping with the quality of its text. The implication is that it was copied from an early exemplar. The letter ō which was introduced after the twelfth century is never used, unhնայն is always written in full and endings of the -թիւն declension are frequently found so. Abbreviations are limited to ած, տր, ար, վ (վասն) and a few numerals. It evinces few effects of the Western sound shift which led to the confusion of voiced and unvoiced stops as pronounciation departed increasingly from the traditional orthography.[5] Moreover, ե is normally retained in եթե and in the first and second persons of the imperfect indicative according to ancient practice. M287 always writes initial յ (ասպարէզ is a recognized variant) and usually inserts final յ where appropriate to the genitive singular (except in the case of foreign names, e.g. Շուշան). It is also lacking from the first person singular of ա - stem aorist indicatives (առձու, լուա etc.). There is evidence of corrections by a contemporary second hand similar in execution to the style of the original scribe. Nevertheless, it is difficult to state categorically that they are identical.

Erevan, Maštoc̆ Matenadaran, no.4834

Date of copying: 1289, 1296 A.D.
Place of copying: a) St. T'oros' Monastery, Čmin;
b) Erznka
Scribe: a) Aŕak̕el; b) Yakob
Commissioned by: Aharon vardapet
Material: paper
Dimensions: 24.5 x 17; No. of folios: 219
No. of lines per page: 25-27 in two columns
Script: *bolorgir;* Binding: stamped leather on wood
1 colophon by each of the scribes
Contents: ժողովածու (miscellany) Yovhannēs Erznkac̆i's excerpt from Nersēs Lambronac̆i's Commentary on Pss, Vardan Arewelc̆i's Commentaries on Cant and Dan, Prophecy of Daniel.

Venice Mkhitarists, no.280(10)

Date of copying: 1418-22 A.D.

Place of copying: X lat

Scribe: Karapet

Commissioned by: Yovhannes vardapet

Material: paper

Dimensions: 28.2 x 16; No. of folios: 778

No. of lines per page: 43 in two columns

Script: *bolorgir;* Binding: leather on wood

Many colophons by the scribe

Contents: Bible (lacking Pss)

Additional information: Sargisean notes that the text of several of the books diverges greatly from Z and suggests that this cannot be attributed to scribal inattentiveness alone. Some of the historical books have a noticeably shorter text.

Erevan, Maštoc Matenadaran, no.178

Date of copying: 1253-55 A.D.

Place of copying: Erkaynmawruk Monastery

Scribe: Priest Mikayel

Commissioned by: Same

Material: paper

Dimensions: 24.8 x 16.4; No. of folios: 281

No. of lines per page: 47 in two columns

Script: *bolorgir;* Binding: stamped leather on wood

3 colophons by the scribe

Contents: Octateuch, Reigns, Job, Dan, 1 Ezra, Neh, Esth, Tob, 3 Macc, 2 Macc (abbreviated), Isa, XII Proph (lacking Mal), Death of the 12 Prophets.

Additional information: The scribe remarks in his colophon on folio 212b «վասն առաւել սիրոյ՝ փոյթ առ փոյթ գրեցի որ ոչ գրի պետս եմ» (though not a skilled scribe I lavished great love and care on copying [this]). Folios 228-55 were inserted by Yakob Lrimeci in 1406, the original having been lost in the interim. Thus he is responsible for copying the chapter on Bel and the Dragon.

Erevan, Maštoċ Matenadaran, no.346

Date of copying: 1390, 1400 A.D.

Place of copying: Norašēn Monastery, Xizan

Scribe: a) Monk Petros, Priest Yovhannēs; b) Melkʿsēd

Commissioned by: Yovhannēs vardapet

Material: paper

Dimensions: 28 x 18.5; No. of folios: 560

No. of lines per page: 47 in two columns

Script: *bolorgir;* Binding: stamped leather on wood

9 colophons by the scribes

Contents: Bible (including Asaneth and T. 12 Patr.), commentaries.

Additional information: On folio 555r the scribe Yovhannēs informs the reader that he had copied «ɿ[ɳ]ṳɰһɿɾ և ի uɰnɿʒɋ ɰɿɿһˈuɰɿɥɛ» ('from a choice, accurate exemplar').

Vienna, Austrian National Library. Cod. Arm11

Date of copying: before 1608 A.D.

Place of copying: perhaps Suczawa, place of origin of the scribe and certainly in Poland, the contemporary monarch of which is noted in the scribe's final colophon

Commissioned by: Priest Yakob

Material: paper

Dimensions: 27 x 20; No. of folios: 541

No. of lines per page: 37 in two columns

Script: *bolorgir;* Binding: leather on wood

5 colophons by the scribe

Contents: OT (including T.12 Patr.)

Additional information: There is evidence of later correction to the standard of sub-group D3.

Erevan, Maštoċ Matenadaran, no. 2585

Date of copying: sixteenth century A.D.

Place of copying: -

Scribe: -

Commissioned by: -
Material: paper
Dimensions: 25 x 18; No. of folios: 475
No. of lines per page: 53 in two columns
Script: *bolorgir;* Binding: stamped leather on wood
1 colophon by the scribe
Contents: Bible and Epiphanius of Salamis on Pss.

Jerusalem, Armenian Patriarchate, no. 1925

Date of copying: 1269 A.D.
Place of copying: Erznka
Scribe: Monk Mxit'ar, Monk Yakob, Scribe Movses
Commissioned by: Paron Yohanes
Material: paper
Dimensions: 36 x 26; No. of folios: ɖ2 + 1190
No. of lines per page: 48 in two columns
Script: *bolorgir;* Binding: stamped leather on wood
23 colophons by the scribes
Contents: Bible (including T. 12 Patr., Joseph and Asaneth)
and related material.

Erevan, Maštoc̆ Matenadaran, no. 2627

Date of copying: 1338 A.D.?
Place of copying: -
Scribes: Yakob, Priest Sargis
Commissioned by: Catholicos Yakob
Material: parchment
Dimensions: 23.4 x 16; No. of folios: 546
No. of lines per page: 52 in two columns
Script: *bolorgir;* Binding: stamped leather on wood
9 colophons by the scribes
Contents: Bible and Nerses Šnorhali's verse colophon on Prov.

Erevan, Maštoc̆ Matenadaran, no. 9116

Date of copying: 1379 A.D.
Place of copying: Cyprus

Scribe: -
Comissioned by: Priest Sargis
Material: parchment
Dimensions: 22.2 x 17; No. of folios: 433
No. of lines per page: 30 in two columns
Script: *bolorgir;* Binding: stamped leather on wood
No colophons by the scribe
Contents: Bible and Nersɛs Šnorhali's verse colophon on Prov and an anonymous poem.

Erevan, Maštoc' Matenadaran, no. 4114
Date of copying: 1609-10 A.D.
Place of copying: Palestine, Cilicia?
Scribe: Monk T'oros
Commissioned by: -
Material: paper
Dimensions: 31 x 19; No. of folios: 819
No. of lines per page: 41 in two columns
Script: *bolorgir;* Binding: stamped leather on wood
8 main colophons by the scribe
Contents: Bible and Vanakan vardapet's Comparison of the Testaments.

Erevan, Maštoc' Matenadaran, no. 182
Date of copying: 1303-04 A.D.
Place of copying: Gɨner, Monastery of Xačatur, Cilicia
Scribe: Martiros vardapet
Commissioned by: -
Material: paper (17 leaves of parchment)
Dimensions: 24.8 x 16.7; No. of folios: 755
No. of lines per page: 42-45 in two columns
Script: *bolorgir;* Binding: stamped leather on wood
4 colophons by the scribe
Contents: Bible, *awetaranac'o c'* and discourses

Venice Mkhitarists, no. 1508 (1)

Date of copying: 1319 A.D.
Place of copying: probably Cilicia
Scribe: Yohanes, son of Priest Yovanes
Commissioned by: same
Material: paper
Dimensions: 26 x 17; No. of folios: 536
No. of lines per page: 53 in two columns
Script: *bolorgir;* Binding: leather on wood
12 colophons by the scribe
Contents: Bible

Erevan, Maštoc' Matenadaran, no. 351

Date of copying: 1619 A.D.
Place of copying: Lvov, Poland
Scribe: T'oros dpir
Commissioned by: Lazar Baberdac'i   Material: parchment
Dimensions: 26.5 x 20.4; No. of folios: 601
No. of lines per page: 53-59 in two columns
Script: *bolorgir;* Binding: stamped leather on wood
8 main colophons by the scribe
Contents: Bible (including T.12 Patr.)

Additional information: It is probable that the manuscript played a major role in disseminating the European style of illumination in New Julfa.[6] In an almost unparalleled case, Lazar's original introduction in which he explains the Latin and Armenian system of verse numeration which he has inserted in his MS appears in most of the members of group E2.

Cambridge, Sir Harold Bailey's collection, no.5

Date of copying: 1674-76 A.D.
Place of copying: Istanbul
Scribes: Step'annos, T'uma tirac'u, Hovanes dpir
Commissioned by: Pilgrim Arut'iwn
Material: paper
Dimensions: 14.4 x 10; No. of folios: 411

No. of lines per page: 20 in one column
Script: *notrgir;* Binding: leather on wood
4 colophons by the scribe
Contents: ժողովածու (miscellany) biblical books: Esth, Jdt, Tob, Sus and Ruth

EDITORIAL POLICY

Text The printed text represents at all times the reading of the first hand of M287 except where this is manifestly in error or its orthography might cause the reader undue confusion. In all such cases the reading substituted from other MSS is enclosed in pointed brackets.

As this proved necessary on only 110 occasions, it was decided not to make any special provision but simply to present the evidence in the main apparatus. The repetition of letters at the line break (Sus: 12 ե/ե, 11:43 եզ/զպատուցւնg) has not been noted. In accordance with normal editorial practice all abbreviations have been resolved and punctuation standardized.

Ziegler's verse numeration has been adopted instead of Z for ease of comparison with Th., except at the following points where it was required by the sense breaks: Sus: 61, 1:17, 5:18 and 7:8. His metrical division of the Song of the Three (3:52-90) has also been followed, involving the full repetition of the refrain. This convention is not observed by M287 or the other witnesses featured in the present edition, but is sanctioned by the lectionary J121. The others instead try as far as possible to devote one line to each verse. As most of them are written in two columns per page this leaves too little space for it to be practicable to include the refrain in full. The amount represented depends on the length of the first line of each couplet. Thus in verses like 3:79 and 86 many witnesses omit the refrain altogether: only such cases of complete omission are noted in the apparatus.

Critical Apparatus: Here are displayed most of the variants from M287 which are cor'~ined in the remaining fourteen manuscripts. If the base MS has been only lightly affected by the Western sound change, it has penetrated deeply into the fabric of others with the result that the same letter variations appear over and over again. Not wishing to overburden the apparatus and conscious that the phenomenon is of at least as much interest (if not more) to the student of historical linguistics as to the textual critic, I have reserved these recurrent variants for separate treatment.[7] In the same place a section is devoted to other recurrent orthographic features characteristic of one particular manuscript, the ubiquitous variation ɲɑɞ/ɞɲɑɞ, -ɪnɹ/nɹ as the genitive singular termination of -ɦ declension nouns and all variation in the use of the article (-u, -ɳ, -ʮ) from that found in M287. Also included is variation in ɹ in medial and final position; as addition of ɹ in initial position could be construed as the prevocalic form of the preposition ɦ, all such cases are noted in the apparatus.

The MSS are always cited in the order of the groups they represent. Where representatives of two sub-groups regularly agree they appear under a composite siglum and are only distinguished where they diverge. A complete list of these follows:

M287' = M287 + V280
M287' = M287 + M4834
M287'' = M287 + V280 + M4834
V280' = V280 + M4834
M346' = M346 + WN11
J1925' = J1925 + M9116
M182' = M182 + V1508
M182' = M182 + M351
M182'' = M182 + V1508 +M351

Recurrent Orthographic Variants: The standard of comparison adhered to in the following tables is that found in Meillet and *NBH* Where several forms are cited by the latter the first is taken. It is this standard which introduces each of the examples. As the point at issue is stated at the head of each table, variants from the standard are referred to only by chapter and verse and the witnesses which evince them there, i.e. the form read by MSS M178 and M351 at Sus:15 is եմնուտ not եմնուտ etc.

Vowel Table 1ᵃ) ե/է
Variation in the aorist augment:

եմնուտ	]	Sus:15 MSS M178 M351; 2:24 MS WN11; 10:3 MS J1925
երաց	]	Sus:25 MSS M178 V280
եհար	]	2:35 MSS WN11 M351; 8:18 MS V280; Bel:26 MSS WN11 J1925; Bel:35 MS M351
ելից	]	2:35 MS WN11
եպազ	]	2:46 MSS WN11 J1925 M351; 3:95 MS WN11
եհան	]	5:2 MS M351
եխից	]	6:22 MSS V280 WN11
եկաց	]	7:4 MS WN11
եկեր	]	Bel:38 MS M9116

Variation in the termination of the imperfect indicative: Since most of the witnesses attest the later form in է it has been more convenient to cite the MSS which maintain the earlier standard in ե (as this is the norm of MS 10 its agreement with the following cases is implicit).

Cases attested by M346:

առնեիր	Sus:52		ապրինեին	3:24; 5:4
գովեին	3:24		խնդրեի	8:15
խնդրեին	6:4		գտանեին	6:4
պաշտեիր	6:20		պաշտեին	7:10
տեսանեի	7:2,9,13; 8:4,7		հայեի	7:4,6 (bis), 8
եի	8:27		եին	4:28
լինեի	9:20		դնեի	8:5
սպասեի	8:27		խաւսեի	9:20,21
արկանեի	9:20		խաւսեին	9:6

M4114   J1925
հայերր   2:34   սպասին   Sus:17
եին   7:20; Bel:31   տեսանեիր 2:41

V280   M9116
տեսանեին Sus:8   ելաներ   Bel:2

Shared readings
գործեիր   Sus:52 MSS M346 M2627
ըմպեիր   1:5 MSS WN11 J1925-M2627
գրեին   5:4 MSS M346 J1925

Miscellaneous
Sus:15 երեկWN11 M9116 M351] երեկ M4834   երեկ rel
-15երանդ] M4834
3:6 անկեալ] M2627
4:9,18 տերե] տեր. WN11
Bel:6կերեալ] կերեալM9116

Vowel Table 1ᵇ) է/ե
3:38 ողջակէզք] M4834;   3:40 գողջակէզս] M4834
9:10 մարգարէից] M346
Bel:6 երբէք] M287 M346 J1925

Vowel Table 2ᵃ) ե
եթանասունե] 9:2 եաւթ.J1925; Bel:9 իւթ. M4834

Vowel Table 2ᵇ) ի/ւ
օրիորդ] 11:6 օրւ.M178

Vowel Table 2ᶜ) իւ/ե
աղբիւրք] 3:77 M287 M178-M346-M2585   J1925-M4114
M182' (իւ > ե V280' WN11)
առիւծ] 6:7 M287 M178-M346'; v.12 M287' M178-M346'
M351; v.16 M287' M178-M346; v.18 M287' M178-M346'; v.19
M287' M178-M346' M4114; v.20 M287' M178-M346; v.22

M287' M178-M346 M2627;   v.24 M287' M178-M346 V1508;
v.24 M287' M178-M346-M2585;   v.27 M287';   7:6 M346; Bel:33
M287 M346 M4114.

(6:24, 27 M4834 առեալ)

եղշիւր] 7:7 M287' M178 M2627' M182';   v.8 1°M287'' M178
M4114 M182', 2° M287' M178 M2627' M182';   v.11 M287'
M178-M2585 M2627' M182';   v.21 M287' M178-M2585
M9116-M2627 V1508;   v.24 M287' M178-M2585 J1925'-
M2627 M182.

(իւ/ե : 7:7 M4834 M9116;   v.8 WN11 M9116-M2627;   v.11
M9116; vv.21,24 WN11)

(իւ/եաւ: M4834 7:8 2°, 11, 21, 24)

երկիւղ] Sus:57 M351

(իւ/ե Sus:57 M4114)

երկիւղած] (իւ/ի: Sus:2 M287 M2627)

իւղ] Sus:17 V280' M346'-M2585 M9116-M2627' M182''; 10:3
M287' M9116-M4114 M351.

(իւ/եա: Sus:17 CHB5)

(իւ/ե: 10:3 M346' J1925)

հիւսիս] (իւ/ւ : the variation mainly affects M287 which witnesses the reading alone in the following cases: 8:9,
11:7,11,40,44. It is joined by M4114 at 11:8 and 11:13, by
M2585 in the two occurrences of the word at 8:4, by M178 at
8:4(2) and 11:6 and by M4834 at 11:6.

միւս] Sus:56 M182'

Vowel Table 3ᵃ)   n/o
The most frequent witness is WN11.

լալով]   Sus:35
ձիւթով   ]   3:46
վալով]   3:46
նուկլով]   11:38 (նակոլ)

CHB5	M182	M4834
հոլանի] Sus:32	երրորդ] 1:21	անկողին] 7:1

Shared readings:
upnηĕաι] Sus:32 WN11 CHB5
կաpnη⁹] 2:10 M2585 M4114 M182"; v.26 M2585 M4114
M182"; 3:17 M2627' M182"; v.96 M182'; 4:15 M182"; 5:16
M2585 M2627 M182'.

Vowel Table 3ᵇ) nվ/n
pրnվ pĕu] 3:54 V280 M346 M351

Vowel Table 3ᶜ) o/n

ծ̈ũoηp	]	Sus:3,30 WN11 J1925'; v.27 M9116
op	]	Sus:64 CHB5
opխnpη	]	11:6 MSS M4834 J1925

Vowel Table 3ᵈ) o/nվ
This variation is not so much phonetic as declensional in nature. Although the original form of the հ-declension instru-
mental-աι is retained in the singular, it is regularly written -op
in the plural before the final consonant. These forms are sometimes assimilated to the corresponding termination of the n-
declension in-nվ(p).

pաqմop	]	11:40 M9116 M4114
opխ̈op	]	9:11 M2627
gաùկաι ĕop	]	11:38 (-oվ p) WN11
աnաշ̈ùnpηաù]		9:26 (-nվ ù) V280

N.B. As was stated in connection with the preservation of the
original spelling of the instrumental singular, o was not inter-
changeable with աι on every occasion. հաιթ is a loan word from
Persian in which the diphthong is retained: however, as such
forms are comparatively rare, scribes are liable inadvertently to
convert the spelling to o as does M346 at 3:46.

Vowel Table 4) nι/pι
The pronunciation of nι in prevocalic position came to resemble the phoneme v. Where they followed phonetic rather

than traditional orthographic spelling scribes resorted to three main forms ռւ, ւ and վ. This practice is most widely employed in V280.

ու/ոււ

ահււան	]	9:6,10,11,14; 10:9; 12:7,8.
գււարակաց	]	3:40
գււարթ	]	4:10 (գււարթււթիււն), 14, 20.
գււարձագեաւ	]	4:1; 6:23
թււեցաււ	]	3:99; 6:1

ււււեաւ in its respective forms Sus:26,44; 3:7,91; 5:16; 8:13; 9:6,10,11,14; 10:9; 12:7,8; Bel:27

ււււանաւ in its respective forms Sus:15,17

նււագարան	]	3:7
նււադեւ	]	3:37
նււերթ	]	9:27
գրււեցեթ	]	9:7
ստււաււ	]	4:13(apparatus), 5:21,28; 7:4,6,11,12,14,27; 8:12,13; 10:1; Bel:25

ոււ/ւ

ահււանս	]	1:7 V280	ահււան] 4:5; 9:17,19 V280
արձււոյ	]	7:4 M287'	
երդււաււ	]	12:7 V280	
թււի	]	Bel:5 V280	
նււերթ	]	9:27 M178	
ստււաււ	]	4:3 M287	
գրււեցեթ	]	4:11 V280	
թււոյ	]	9:2 (թռվn) WN11	
պատււեր	]	6:9 M4834	
պատււիրեւ	]	3:30 WN11c	
ստււաււ	]	7:4,12 WN11; v.14 M346; 8:13 M287	

Consonant Table 1ᵃ) բ/պ[10]

ամբարիշտ	]	12:10 M346-M2585 M2627' M351'
ամբարշտււթիււն		9:24 V280 M346 J1925'-M2627' M351'
ապատամբեցաթ		9:9 M287

թմբկի	]	3:5 M346; v.15 M287 M2585 M4114
ձեռամբ	]	9:15 M287

Consonant Table 1ᵇ)   բ/փ

գուբն	]	M287 6:19,20; Bel:34

Consonant Table 1ᶜ)   պ/բ [10]

ըմպեր	]	1:15 M4834 WN11 J1925-M2627; Bel:5
		WN11*; v.23 M4834
ըմպելոյ	]	1:8 M4834 WN11 J1925; v.16 M4834
		WN11
ըմպէին	]	5:3 M287; v.4 M4834 WN11
ըմպէիք	]	5:23 M4834

Consonant Table 1ᵈ)   փ/բ

փակեցէք	]	Sus:17 CHB5

Consonant Table 2ᵃ)   գ/կ [10]

The main witness is WN11

կանգուն	]	3:11°,2°; v.47
կանգնեցեր	]	3:18
անգամ	]	2:7 M346
կանգնեաց	]	3:1 WN11 J1925; v.2 M187-WN11; v.31°
		M4834 M178-WN11 M2627, 2° V280
		M4834-WN11 J1925; v.5 M4834 WN11;
		v.7 M178 WN11 J1925
կանգնեցեր	]	3:12 M4834 WN11
կանգնեցի	]	3:14 WN11 J1925
հանգուցեալ	]	4:9 J1925
ծունգք	]	5:6 V280' M178-M346'-M2585 M2627'
		M182'
գայթագղութիւն		11:21 M4834; v.32 M4834 WN11-M2585;
		v.34 M4834 WN11-M2585
նենգութիւն		11:23 M9116-M4114
պագանեմք		3:18 M351
սրնգի		3:4 M287' M346'-M2585 J1925'-M2627'

M182"; v.10 M287" M346'-M2585 J1925-
M2627' M182"; v.15 M287" M346'-M2585
M2627' M182'

Consonant Table 2b) զ / բ
գմոգս   2:2,10 M4834

Consonant Table 2c) կ/գ [10]

The main exponent is M4114		WN11	
անկաւ	Sus:37; 2:46	յանկեան	Sus:38
անկանիշիբ	3:45		
անկեալ	3:6	M178	
անկցի	11:19	անկցի	3:6
անկանեին	3:7	ցանկացան	Sus:8
ընկեցի	3:6		
յանկողնի	2:29, 7:1	M346	
		խունկս	1:46

Shared readings: J1925

անկանել	Sus:23 WN11 M4114	անկանեին 7:9
անկան	Sus:26 WN11 M4114	
անկաւ	8:12 10:7,15 M4834 M4114; 8:17,18 M4834 WN11 M4114 M351	
անկցի	3:11, 6:7,12 M4834 M4114; 11:26 M4834 M2585 M4114	
անկեալ	3:11 M4834 M4114	
անկանիցիբ	3:15 M287' J1925-M4114	
ընկեցաց	8:10 M4834 M4114	
ընկեցի	6:24 M4834 M4114	
ընկերի	Sus:61 M4834 J1925	

Consonant Table 2d) բ/գ
թագուցեալ   Sus:16 M287 J1925-M2627 CHB5; v.18 M287'
M346 J1925-M2627 CHB5; v.37 M287' J1925-
M2627 CHB5

Consonant Table 3ᵃ)   դ / տ[10]

անդ	Sus:36 M346; 3:49 M346 J1925; Bel:32 M346-M2585
անդր	Sus:27 M178
անդրէն	Bel:38 V280
խորհուրդ	2:28 J1925
ունդ	1:12 M4834 M2585 M2627 V1508 M182 (supra lin); v.16 M4834 M178-M346-M2585 M182'
երանդ	Sus:15 M2627' M351

A special group is formed by the article (-դ)

գիրդ	12:4 M346
գլուխդ	Sus:55 M178 J1925-M2627; v.59 M178-M346
խորհուրդդ	2:27 J1925; v.28 M346 J1925
հետդ	Bel:18 M346'
ճաշդ	Bel:32 M346; v.36 M4834 J1925
մանկանցդ	1:10 M4834
պահեսդ	9:4 M346
պատկերիդ	3:12 M4834
վիշապդ	Bel:25 M346 M9116
տեսիլդ	8:13 WN11; 8:19, 10:14 M4834

Consonant Table 3ᵇ)   տ / դ[10]

անտի	3:48,49 M4834 WN11; 6:23 M4834 J1925; 7:3 M4834
երտ [11]	5:18 V280; 9:10, Bel:21 M287
ընտանիք	Sus:26 M287' WN11 M2627 CHB5
ընդրեալք	11:15 M4834 WN11; 12:10 M4834 WN11 J1925
հետ	Bel:18 M287

Consonant Table 4ᵃ)   լ / ղ

Most variants in this sphere derive from the transliteration of foreign words where the letter ղ was used to represent
Greek λ. When it became a velar fricative, scribes began to sup-
plant it with լ. It seems that in the resulting confusion, by a

process of hypercorrection, scribes sometimes substitute ղ for
լ in native Armenian words.[12]

փայլուն	10:6 M178-M346	փայլատակունք 3:73 M178
ծուլածոյիւք	11:8 J1925	
այլ	2:11,18; 3:34,39,42,96; 6:17; 8:22 M178	
այլազգունեցան 3:94 M178		
այլակերպ	7:7 M178	

Consonant Table 4ᵇ) խ / ղ

After ղ's sound change when only its voicing distinguished it from խ the two became the frequent cause of variation. The main exponent is WN11.

վախճան	7:28; 8:17,19 bis; 9:26 bis, 27; 11:35,36;
	12:6,8,9,13 bis.
վախճանեաց	5:6; 11:16,36

Shared readings:

| վախճան | 6:26 WN11 J1925 |
| չախշախ | 2:42 M4834 M346 M9116 M351 |

Consonant Table 5ᵃ)   ձ / ծ

իղձք	4:4 M9116
ինձ	7:6 V280' M178-M2585 M9116-M2627' M182''
մերձեալ	10:10 M287
պղինձ	2:35,39,45 V280 M4114; 5:4 V280 J1925; 10:6
	J1925; 5:23; Bel:6,23 V280
պղնձեղէն	5:4 WN11
պղնձապատ	4:20 V280

Consonant Table 6)   ճ / ջ / չ

J1925 consistently represents the ջ of աղջիկ by ճ while
M346 and CHB5 use չ, the latter adding ը in oblique cases,
where the ի drops out due to the changed position of the ac-
cent.

աղշկամբ Sus:15 J1925 M346; v.36 J1925, CHB5
աղշկունս Sus:17,21,26 J1925 CHB5
աղշկունք Sus:19 J1925 M346 CHB5

Variations in medial յ [13]

a) omission

The main witness is WN11

արբայութիւն 3:55,100; 6:26,27
արբայի 1:21, 2:14, 3:1, 8:1
այն 4:27
երեկոյին 9:21
երթայի 10:20
զգնայաք Sus:36
ծառայի 3:35   ծառայից 3:33   կայի 7:16
հայրոյութիւն 3:96 (om յ 1°)
հայէի 7:6
հրամայեաց Sus:18, 2:12, 5:2
տայր 1:3

	M346		M4834
արբայի	2:15,25	գային	Sus:6
մերձենային	Sus:57	հայեաց	Bel:18
վայր	Bel:37	հայոյեաց (յ 2°)	Bel:8
վկայեմբ	Sus:21	տային	Bel:31

M287		M9116		J1925	
երթայի	10:20	վայր	Bel:37	արբայի	2:14
կային	1:19				

բոյին Sus:55 M287'M178-M346' J1925'; v.59 M287'
M187-M346' J1925'

բայց 6:7 V280 M2585 M4114 M182'; v.12 M2585
M182'; Bel:41 V280 M178-M346-WN11*-M2585
M4114 M182''

b) addition

	M4834		J1925
1:12	տացեն] տայցեն	2:16; 4:14	տացէ] տայցէ

6:26 յերեսաց] -սայg
11:31 տացեն] տայgեն M287 WN11
3:35 բաg] բայgM287 WN11

Variations in final յ

a) omission

The word most affected by the variation is վերայ The
variant spelling is generally evinced by the following MSS in
concert: V280 M178-M346'-M2585 M4114 V1508-M351 (+
CHB5 in Susanna).
Sus:19,45,61; 1:11; 2:10,35,46,48,49; 3:12,19,27,45; 4:14,21;
6:4; 7:4,21; 8:12; 9:11,12(1˙),19,24 (1˙)
The same combination + M287: 6:1; 9:12(2˙)+ M4834: 5:5;
6:17; 7:17; 8:6,18(2˙),19; 9:13(1˙),24(2˙),27; 11:4; 12:7
+ M4834 M287: 3:31; 4:25(1˙); 5:11; 8:17
+ J1925: Sus:48; 11:4
+ M182: 11:2; 12:7

The same combination lacking WN11: 4:25 (1˙) lacking M4114:
4:20,22,25(1˙ 2˙),26,29,30; 5:5; 6:2; 11:2
lacking V1508: 4:25(2˙); 6:2; 8:18(2˙); 9:12(2˙),27

M4834 evinces the omission alone at the following points:
9:14(1˙),18; 10:15; 11:24,25(1˙),32,40,43; 12:6(1˙);
Bel:35(1˙)
with M178: 11:23,25(2˙), 30(1˙)
with M2627: 12:1(1˙)
with M4114: 11:28(1˙)
M287 evinces the omission alone at 8:18 (1˙)
with M182 at 12:1(2˙)
V280 M178-M346'-M2585 evince the omission together at
4:13.

Variation from the standard գոյ is mainly restricted to M178-
WN11 at 3:38,92,96; 4:5,6; 5:12
with M4834: 2:10; 3:33; 4:15

M4834, J1925: 10:16

M287: 5:11

M4834, M346, J1925: 2:28

վերոյ 3:55 V280 M178-M346'-M2585 M4114 M182-V1508-M351, M4834 WN11

Variation from the standard արքայ is mostly attested by WN11.

alone: 2:1,27,36 (2˚); 4:15; 7:1

with M287: 3:12,18; 5:1,9,11,31; 6:6,12 (1˚), 15,25

    V280: 3:16

    M4834: 5:10

    M346: 2:30; 3:91; Bel:10(1˚),16

with M287 M4834: 3:8; 6:12(2˚),21(2˚)

    M287 M346: 4:24,28

    M178-M346: 2:28

    M178 J1925: 4:21

    M346 J1925: 2:7

with M287 V280 M178: 6:8(1˚)

with M346-M2585 J1925: 6:2

    M287 V280 J1925: 6:8 (2˚)

    M287-M4834 M346 J1925: 2:4

    M287 M4834 J1925: 4:20

    V280-M4834 M178-M346

    J1925: 1:1; 2:11

    M287 M4834 J1925: 5:12,30

    M287 M346 J1925: 1:2; 5:18

Other MSS yield two examples:

3:17 V280 M2585 J1925'-M2627' M182"; 6:21(1˚) M287 J1925

In the following examples most of which are witnessed by WN11 alone variation concerns the genitive-dative singular of nouns, adjectives, infinitives and participles:

114   *The Armenian Version of Daniel*

աթողոյ 5:20 ամուոյ 4:26 անըոյ 8:25 արձաթոյ 5:2 արմատոյ *2:41;* 4:23 արշատոյ 4:22,29; 5:21 բարբատոյ 7:10 բերանոյ 6:20,27 բորբոքելոյ 3:6,11,15,17,20,21,46,93 բոելոյ *5:5* գբոյ 6:23 գինոյ 1:8 գիշերոյ 2:19 գլխոյ Sus:34; 2:28; 7:1 երկաթոյ 2:41, *42* ըմպելոյ 1:16 թոչնոյ 7:6 իմոյ 4:2,5,15,21, 26,27,33; 5:16; Bel:24 իւրոյ 1:2(2) 5:20; 6:5,10 կալոյ 2:35; 10:17 կատարելոյ 1:15 կենդանւոյ 6:20 հածոյ 3:99; 4:24; 6:1 հարաւոյ 11:15 հողմոյ 2:35 մարդոյ 3:10; 5:3; 6:7, *12;* 7:4,8 մjoy Sus:45 միշոյ Sus:34; *3:88(2);* 5:6 ներքոյ *4:8, 11,*18 նսկոյ 2:32; 11:8,43 որդւոյ 10:16 որմոյ 5:5 որոյ Sus:20; 2:32; 4:17; 5:23; 7:20; 9:18 ուժոյ 8:6 պղնձոյ 10:6 սեղանոյ 1:5,8 սրբեցելոյ 12:7 սրբոյ 2:32; 3:28,35; 9:20 սոոյ Bel:25 տալոյ 3:38 ցաւդոյ 4:30; 5:21 փողոյ 3:5,15; Bel:17

nominative-vocative singular: ծառայ 6:20

Other MSS evince the following examples:
M4834 արմատոյ 2:41 բոելոյ 5:55 իմոյ 5:16; Bel:24 մարդոյ 6:12 միշոյ 3:88(2) ներքոյ 4:8,11 որոյ 7:20 սրբոյ 3:28 սոոյ Bel:25 տալոյ 3:38 ցաւդոյ 5:21 փողոյ 3:5

M346 ծառայ 10:16 մարդոյ 6:12 միշոյ 3:93 սրբեցելոյ 12:7 փողոյ 3:10
M178 ներքոյ 4:8,11; 7:26
M2585 ներքոյ 4:8
M4114 երկաթոյ 2:42

     The last important class of variation is provided by the first person singular form of aorists in -այ: անկայ 8:17 M287 M346-WN11; V.18 M4834 M346-WN11; 10:15 M287-M4834 WN11

առաքեցայ	10:11 M287 M346-WN11
աւծայ	10:3 M287 WN11
գոհացայ	9:4 M287 M346-WN11
լուայ	5:14,16 M287-M4834 WN11 J1925; 8:13

	M287-M4834 M346-WN11 J1925 M351; 16
	M287-V280-M4834 M178 J1925 M182; 10:9
	M287-V280 M346-WN11 J1925 M182; 12:6
	M287-M4834 WN11 J1925; 8 M287 M346-
	WN11
խաւթագաj	8:27 M287 M346-WN11
խաւսեգաj	10:16 M346-WN11 J1925
խոսվեգաj	4:2 V280 M346-M2585 J1925-M9116
	M2627-M4114 M182-V1508
կերաj	10:3 M287 M346-WN11
հաստատեգաj	4:33 M287 M346-WN11 J1925
jարեգաj	8:27 M4834 M2585 M9116-M4114 V1508-
	M351
jիմարեգաj	8:17 M287 M346-WN11; 18 M287 M346-
	WN11 J1925

third person singular of present indicative in -աj

կաj	6:26 M287-V280-M4834 M178 J1925; 12:1
	M4834 M178-WN11
մնաj	4:23 M287 WN11 J1925-M9116
տաj	2:21 V280-M4834 M178-M346

b) addition

The largest single category is provided by the various cases of the demonstrative pronouns.

հա	M4834 at Sus:4,26,58(1˙); 2:21,47; 3:95; 6:6,16;
	7:5; 11:16; Bel:16
	M346 at Sus:35(1˙); 2:47; 3:95; 6:16,23; 8:18;
	11:16,30
	M9116 at Sus:48(1˙)
qհա	M4834 at Sus:8,12,14,56; 1:1; 3:88; 4:14,16,22,29;
	5:21,26; 6:14; 7:7,10,23; 8:7(2˙),14; 10:13; 11:45;
	Bel:29
	M346 at Sus:8,12,14,32(1˙),33,39,45,56; 1:1
	M178 at Bel:24,40
	V1508 at Bel:40
	M287-M4834 M182-V1508 at Bel:21

M178-M2585 M182 at Bel:22

նմա M4834 at Sus:10,12,16,24,63; 1:15;
2:16(1˚),22,41,46,48;4:5,8,13,18; 5:11,12(2˚),19,21;
6:3,23,26; 7:7; 8:11,17; 9:11,26; 10:1; 11:6,17,26
M346 at Sus:63; 6:26; 7:4,7
M178 at 2:22
J1925 at 2:22

նորա M4834 at Sus:3(1˚),4(1˚),63(2); 1:2,8,20; 2:1,4,5(1˚),
6(2˚),9,13,31(2),36,44,45; 3:1,89,90,97,100(2˚);
4:4,6,7,8(1˚),9(2),12,13(2),15,16(3),18(2),20(2),
21,30(3˚),31(2),32,34; 5:3,9,19,20(2),21(2),22,23,
24,29(3); 6:1,18,22,26(2); 7:4,5,8(2˚),9(2˚),10(2),
20(2),25,26,27; 8:3,4(2),5,8(2˚ 3˚),21,22,24(1˚);
9:10,14; 10:6(2˚), 9(2˚),11,15,19; 11:2,4,5(1˚),
6,10,12,15,16(2),17(2),25(2), 40(1˚),41(ult.),45;
Bel:7(1˚),40(1˚)
M346 at Sus:1; 1:20; 4:20(2˚); Bel:40(2˚)
M287 at 2:25; 7:8(2˚)
M2627 at 2:25; 7:27
J1925 at 3:1; 5:23; 10:6(1˚ 2˚); 11:25(2˚),28,41(ult.)
M2585 at 7:1

նոքա M4834 at Sus:6(1˚),57; 8:7(2); Bel:30(1˚)
CHB5 at Sus:57

նոսա M4834 at Sus:6,61(2),62; 1:5(2),14,18(2),19(1˚);
2:3,35; 3:46,50(2),92,94; 6:3; 8:10; 9:7,14; 11:7;
Bel:7
M346 at Sus:51
CHB5 at Sus:61(2˚)
M2627 at 1:6,19(1˚)

նոցա M4834 at Sus:48(1˚); 1:14,16(2),17; 2:35;
3:94(2),93(1˚), 96; 4:4; 5:3; 6:24; 7:8,21; 10:7;
11:8(1˚, 2˚),18,24,34,43; Bel:31,35(2˚)

դա M346 at Sus:36
CHB5 at Sus:36,37

զդա M346 at Sus:40,54; 4:20
CHB5 at Sus:40

	M4834 at Sus:54
դմա	M4834 M346 M9116 at Sus:37
դորա	M4834 at Sus:46,56; 4:11(3),30; 5:7,16
	M346 at Sus:46,56; 4:11(3˙); 5:7
	V280 M9116 at Bel:10
	CHB5 at Sus:46,56
	J1925 at 4:11(1˙)
	M2627-M4114 at 4:11(2˙)
դորբա	M9116 at Sus:49
դոսա	M4834 at Sus:51(2),58
	M346 at Sus:51(2),54(1˙),58
	CHB5 at Sus:38,58
դոցա	M346 at Sus:38

The second major category is provided by **ըո**, genitive singular form of the second person pronoun **դու**[14]. The two main witnesses are M182-V1508:

at 2:28(1˙) with M2585, 30 with V280 M351; 3:34(1˙) with M178-WN11-M2585 M4114; 3:35(2˙) with V280 M4114 M351, (4˙) with V280 M2585 M4114 M351, 53 with V280; 5:11 with M2585, 17 with M178 M9116; 9:17 with M2627-M4114, 18 (ult.) with V280-M4834 M2585 M4114, 24(1˙) with V280 M4114; 10:12(2˙) with M2585 M4114; 11:14 with M4114 M351

2:31 V280 M182; 3:35(3˙) V280 M2585 M4114 M182, 40(2˙) V280 M182, 55 V1508; 4:22 V280; 9:18 J1925; 12:1 M2585 M4114 V1508

Another source of variation is the form of the imperative singular in -**ա**.

The main witness is M9116 which is alone at:

պատմեա Sus:50	վրկեա 3:43	աոա 4:1	կնեա Bel:10
with M4834	հաստատեա 6:8	բաւեա 9:19	
M2627	փակեա 12:4	կնեա 12:4	

CHB5   աաա Sus:58
with V280-M4834 փորձեա 1:12
    M4834 M346 գրեա 6:8
    M4834 M178 J1925 M351 անաա 9:19

There are three cases of variation in the imperative singular in -ո
իմացո   8:17   M287-V280-M4834 M178-WN11
                    J1925-M9116-M4114 M351
երևցո   9:17   M287-V280 M178 J1925-M9116 M4114
                    M351
խոնարհեցո   9:18   M287-V280 M178 J1925-M9116 M4114
                    M351

miscellaneous cases
այո   3:91   M346-WN11-M2585 J1925-M9116
                    M351
ահա   M4834 at 7:6,8; 8:3,15; 9:21; 10:5,10,15;
                    11:12
                    M2627 at 9:21
յապա   2:45 V280-M4834 M346-M2585
                    M9116-M351

Variation ոյ/ոյ
in nouns not belonging to the -ի declension
ամարայնոյ 2:35 V280 M178-WN11 M2627' արմատոյ 4:20
J1925 արծունոյ 7:4 M351 բերանոյ 3:51 V280; 6:20,27 M4114
գետոյն 12:7 V280 գիշերոյ 2:19 V280 M178; 4:10 V280 M178
M9116; 7:2 M178-M346 M4114 M182; 13 M178 M9116
երգոց 3:35 V280 ընպելոյ 1:8 V1508-M351; 16 V1508 կալոյ
2:35 M4114 հիւսխոյ 11:6 J1925 մարդոյ 6:12; 7:4,13; 8:17
M4114 միայնոյ Bel:13 M4834 որթով 3:46 V280 սիրելոյ 3:35
M287-M4834 WN11 J1925-M9116-M4114 տղայոյ Sus:45
M287-M4834 M346-M2585 J1925-M9116 M2627-M4114
M182-V1508-M351-CHB5

Variation ʉɴɾ/ɴɾ

in nouns of the -ի declension

գիւղոյ 1:5 M287-V280-M4834 M346-WN11 M9116-M2627, 8
M287-M4834 M178-M346-WN11-M2585 J1925-M9116
խեցւոյ 2:33 V280-M4834 WN11 J1925-M9116, 41 WN11
J1925-M4114, 42 M287-M4834 WN11 J1925-M9116-M2627
կենդանւոյ 6:20 M287 WN11 J1925-M2627 հոգւովք 3:39
M4834 մանկտւոյ Bel:13 M287-V280-M4834 WN11 J1925-
M9116-M2627, 19 M287-M4834 M178-WN11-M2627 նզւոց
Sus:22 M4834 WN11 M9116 M182-V1508-CHB5; 5:4 M4834
WN11 նակւոյ 3:32 M287-M4834 WN11 M9116-M2627; 3:7
M4834 WN11 J1925, 11 M287-M4834 WN11 M9116, 12
M287-M4834 WN11 J1925-M9116, 14 M287-M4834 WN11,
18 M287-M4834 WN11 J1925-M9116-M4114, 52 M287-
M4834 WN11; 10:5 M287-M4834 M178-WN11-M2585 M351;
11:8 M287-M4834 WN11 M9116-M2627, 38 M287-M4834
WN11 M9116-M2627, 43 M4834 WN11 M2627 որդւոց 1:3
M4834 M346 J1925-M9116, 6 M4834 WN11 M9116-M2627;
2:25 M4834 WN11 M9116-M2627; 5:13 M4834 WN11 M9116;
6:13 M4834-M2627; 9:1 M4834 M346-WN11; 10:16; 11:41;
12:1 M4834 WN11; Bel:14 M4834 WN11 M4114 որդւոյ 3:92
M4834 WN11 տարւոյն Sus:5 M287-V280-M4834 M178-
WN11 M9116-M2627 տեղւոջէ 11:38 M287 WN11 J1925-
M9116

Variation թե/եթե

Where M287 witnesses the monosyllabic form the vowel is always ե, while the majority of the MSS evince the later spelling
թե. In the following cases various MSS support M287's reading
(թե).

Sus:5 V280 WN11-M2585 M2627 M351-CHB5; 14 V280
M178-M346-WN11-M2585 J1925-M9116-M2627 M182-
V1508-M351-CHB5; 23 M351; 4:6 J1925; 12:7 M346 M182;
Bel:7,8 M346

In the following case M4834 counterbalances M287's ɲҍ with the singular reading ҍɲէ: Sus:5,14; 3:15(1˚, 2˚),18; 4:6; 12:7; Bel:5,8

Where M287 reads ɲҍ, others read ҍɲէ in the following cases: Sus:5 M178-M346 J1925-M9116 M182-V1508; 14 M4114, 21 M4834 M178, 23 M178; 2:6 V280-M4834 M178-M346 J1925-M9116-M4114 M182-M351; 3:15(1˚) V280 M178-M346-WN11-M2585 J1925-M9116-M4114 M182-V1508-M351, 18 J1925; 4:14 M182-V1508-M351 WN11ᶜ; 5:21 M178-M346-WN11-M2585; 12:7 M178-M2585-WN11; Bel:5 M346, 7 V280 WN11-M2585, 8 J1925-M9116 M2627-M4114 M182-V1508, 11 M4834 M9116, 28 M4834, 29 V280-M4834 M178-M346-WN11 J1925-M4114 M182-V1508-M351

Where M287 reads ɲҍ, others read ҍɲҍ at: 3:100 J1925; Bel:5 V280, 23 M346

Variation ҍɲҍ/ɲҍ

The orthography of the bisyllabic form witnessed by M287 is always ҍɲҍ. M346 shares this reading at Bel:11. At the following points M4834 reads the form ҍɲէ.

Sus:22(2),54; 2:8,9(2); 5:14; 6:7(2˚),20; 10:20; Bel:5.
At the following points some MSS counterbalance M287's ҍɲҍ with ɲէ: Sus:21(2˚) V280 M346-WN11-M2585 M9116-M2627-M4114 M182-V1508-M351-CHB5, 22(2) WN11, 54 WN11 M9116-M4114; 2:8(2˚) WN11 J1925-M9116 M2627-M4114 M182-V1508-M351, 9(1˚) M178, 9(2˚) M346-WN11-M2585 M2627, 11 WN11, 29 V280-M4834 M2627-M4114 M182-V1508-M351; 5:14 M9116 M182-V1508-M351, 16 M4834 J1925-M9116 M2627-M4114 M182-V1508-M351; 6:5 V280, 7(1˚) M2627-M4114, 7(2˚) M2627, 10 M9116-M4114 M182-M351; 10:20 M9116; Bel:8 M9116-M2627-M4114 M182-V1508-M351 (ɲҍ V280 M346 J1925)

Recurrent Variants of Individual MSS

1. J1925 sometimes tends to use the vowel 'e' where 'a' is the accepted form, e.g. կալոյ] կելոյ 10:17, մազ] մեզ Bel:27. Frequently it evinces ը instead of ա in occurrences of the word անկողին, e.g. 2:28,29; 4:2,10; 7:1.

2. WN11 diverges from the general conventions governing the representation of the vowel 'i' in two particular words. Normally the vowel is present in the nominative-accusative singular form աղջիկ but drops out in all other cases as a result of accentual shift. However, WN11 retains it in these cases also, e.g. Sus:19 աղջիկունս vv.19,36 զաղջիկունս. The opposite phenomenon arises in connection with the form ներքինապետն where ի is usually retained, but WN11 omits in the following instances of the word 1:8,9,10,11,18.

3. The noun աղջիկ leads CHB5 to depart from the orthographical norm. In the above-mentioned cases where ի drops out the vowel is reduced to ը though this does not generally appear in writing. CHB5 on the contrary, makes its presence explicit where the word occurs in Sus:17,19,21,36(2).

4. M4834 frequently doubles the ը of ordinal numbers beyond the two cases երրորդ, չորրորդ where this is accepted as follows: 3:1 ութուտասաներորդի ; 7:1 առաջներորդի (with WN11 J1925) and at 9:1 with J1925 9:27 Լթներորդ, Լթներորդի (with M346) and Լթներորդին; and also alone at 10:2,3; Bel:4; 10:1 superscript. վեցերորդ; 10:3 քաաներորդի.

5. WN11 inclines in the opposite direction, evincing only one of the pair of ը's in the occurrences of չորրորդ at 2:49 superscript; 7:7,19,22(2˚).

6. WN 11 shows a further tendency to introduce a dental stop between a nasal and liquid r in two words:

a) մաներ] մանտրէր   7:7,19

   մանր] մանտրէ   2:40

b) ծուևր] ծուևդր   6:10

Variation in the article (-ս, -դ, -ն)

Sus:2	աևուն] + ն	CHB5
-3	ծևաւդք] + ն	V280' M178 M2627
	զդուստրն] -ն	WN 11 J 1925
-4	յապարանս] + ն	J 1925
-5	ժողովրդենէ] + ն	CHB5
	ծերոց] + ն	M2627' M182''
	դատաւորաց] + ն	M178-M346'-M2585 CHB5
	ժողովրդեանն] -ն	WN 11
-7	աւուրբն 10''] -ն	M178 J 1925
	Շուշան] + ն	V280
-10	երկոքին] + ն	V280 M178-WN 11-M2585
-11	զգանկութիւն] + ն	M9116-M2627 M182''
-14	զգանկութիւնն] -ն	V280' M178-M346'-M2585 J 1925
		CHB5
-15	սպասել] + ն	M4834 M178-M346-M2585
		V1508
	երեքին] -ն	M2585 M9116
	եռանդն] -ն	M4834 M2585
-16	ծերքն] -ն	CHB5
	Թարուցեալք] + ն	M178 M351
-17	բուրաստանիս] -ին	V280 M178-M346'-M2585 J 1925
-18	զծերսն] -ն	WN 11
-20	դուրք] + ն	CHB5
	բուրաստանիս] -ին	J 1925
-21	զաղջկունսն] -ն	WN 11
-25	մին] + ն	V280' M346' J 1925', CHB5
	զդուրս] + ն	V280 M4834 M178-M2585
		J 1925'-M2627' M182

-26 բուրաստանի] + ն   V280'

     կողմն] -ն   M4834 M178-M2585 J1925'-

                          M2627' M182

-28 այր] + ն   V280' M178-M346-M2585

                          M2627' M182'

     մտաւք] + ն   CHB5

-30 ծնաւղք] + ն   CHB5

     ազգականք] + ն   J1925

-36 ծերք] -ն   CHB5

-38 զանաւրէնութիւնն]-ն WN11 CHB5

     զլինելն M287 M2627 M182"] -ն rel

-39 զդուրսն] - ն   M346' J1925

-40 ընբռնեցաք] +դ   M4834 M178 M9116-M2627'

                          M182"

     զայս M287"] զայդ rel

Sus:41 ժողովրդեան] + ն   M178-M346'-M2585 J1925'

                          M9116'

     ատեան] + ն   CHB5

-42 զլինել] + ն   J1925

-45 անուն] + ն   CHB5

-47 -10] դուդ   (-դ M346 M351)

-48 զդուստր] +դ   V280 M2585 M2627 M182"

           +ն   WN11

-49 դոքա] նոքա   M2585 M351

     նմանէ M287' M4114 M182'] + ն J1925'

     դմանէն M4834] դմանէ rel

-50 ժողովուրդն]-ն   CHB5

     երիցութիւն] +դ   V280 M178-M346'-M2585

            + ն   CHB5

-52 զմինն] զմին   M2627-M182"

     զմի   M4834 M178-M346'-M2585

     նոցանէ] + ն   J1925

     մեղք] + ն   J1925

     գործէիր] + ն   J1925

-53 զդատաստան] + ն   M346 J1925-M2627 CHB5
     զանմեղս] + ն   M178-M346' J1925
     զվնասակարս] + ն   M178-M346'
-55 զլուխդ] -դ   M346'-M2585 M9116-M4114
                            M182''
-57 զդստերս M287] -ն   rel
     այդպէս] այսպէս   V280'
     դուստր] + ս   V280
            + դ   M2585 M2627 M182'
     զանաւրէնութիւնդ]-դ M4834 J1925-M2627
            -թիւնս   V280 M4114 M182''
-58 աղոցեան] -ն   CHB5
-59 զլուխ] + դ   M178-M346'-M2585
            + ն   CHB5
     աւադիկ]-սիկ   V1508
-61 վկայս] + ն   J1925
-63 կին] + ն   V280
     դստերն] -ն   CHB5
     արամբ] + ն   M4834
     ազգականաւք] + ն   V280' M178-M346'
-64 ժողովրդեանն]-ն   CHB5
     յաւրէ] + ն   V280 J1925
1:1 Թագաւորութեան M287 M4114]+ ն rel
-2   տանն] -ն   M9116
     տուն] + ն   WN11
-3   ներքինապետ] + ն   V280' WN11 M4114
     գերութեանն] -ն   M4834 M4114
     Պարտնաց] + ն   M178-M346'-M2585
-4   տածարի M287 M9116-M4114] + ն rel
     լեզու + ն   V280
-5   արքայի] + ն   J1925
     զինոյ] + ն   V280
-10 կարգեաց M287'WN11-M2585 M9116-M2627' M182']
                            + ն J1925 + դ rel
     կերակուրդ]-դ   M2627

	զրմպելի] +դ	J1925
	մանկանցդ] -ցն	V280 J1925 -դ M9116-M4114 M182"
	հասակակցաց] + ն	V280 J1925] + դ M178-M346'
-11	կացուցանել] + ն	M178 V1508
-12	ծառայս] + ս	V280 M178-M346-M2585 M4114 M182'
-13	մանկանց	M287 J1925] +ն V280 M346'- M2585 M2627 + դ rel
	ծառայս] + ս	V280' M178-M346-M2585 M9116-M2627
-15	աւուրցն] -ն	M178-M2585 J1925
-16	զրնորիս] + ն	M178-M346 + ս WN11
	գինի] + ն	M178 M182
	մանկանցն] -ն	WN11
-17	տեսլեան] + ն	WN11
-19	յամենեսեան M287]	(յամենայնի) + ն M346'
-20	բանի] + ս	M2585 M2627' M182"
	նոցանէ] + ն	J1925
	Թագաւորութեան] + ն	WN11

Chapter 2

-1	յամի M287 M346'] + ն rel
	Թագաւորութեանն]+ ն V280' M4834-M346-M2585 J1925'
	երազ] + ն WN11
	քուն] + ն V280
	նմանէն M287 M2585 M2627] -ն rel
-2	զերազ] + ն V280
-4	զմեկնութիւնն M287] -ն rel
-6	զմեկնութիւնն M287] -ն rel
-8	արքայն] -ն V280 M9116 V1508
-9	ժամանակն] -ն M346
-10	Թագաւորի] + դ M4834 M2585
	+ ն M178-M346' J1925
2:11	բանդ] -դ M2627 V1508-M351 բանս M346

-12 իմաստունս] + ն M346'
-13 հրամանն] -ն M4834 J1925'-M4114 WN11ᶜ
-14 դահճապետի] + ն WN11 J1925'-M4114 M182"
     զիմաստունս] + ն WN11
     արքային] -ն V280
-15 թագաւորին] արքայի (+ ն M2627)
-16 զարքայն] -ն V280 M2585
-18 բարեկամք] + ն J1925
     իմաստունս] + ն V280 M178-M346'-M2585
-19 տեսլեան] + ն M346'-M2585 J1925
     գիշերոյ] + ն J1925'
-22 զխորհինս] + ն M178
     զգադտնիս] + ն M178-M346
-24 զիմաստունս] + ն V280' M346
     զմեկնութիւնն] -ն M4834 M4114
-25 զերութեանն] -ն M346'
     զմեկնութիւնն] -ն V280 WN11-M2585
     արքայի] + ն WN11 + դ M4834
-26 անուն] + ն V280 M9116-M4114
-28 տեսիլ] + ն J1925
-29 խորհրդոց] + ն M4114
     լինելոց] + ն M4834 M178
-30 զմեկնութիւնն] -ն WN11 J1925
-31 տեսիլ] + ն M178
-32 ձեռք M287 M346'-M2585 M2627] + ն rel
     լանջք] + ն V280' M2627' M182"
     բազուկք] + ն V280'
     մէջքն] -ն J1925 V1508
     բարձքն] -ն J1925-M4114 M351
-33 սրունքն] -ն M4834 J1925
     կէս 1°] + ն V280' M178-M346' V1508
     կէս 2°] + ն V280' M178-M346' J1925 V1508
-34 վեմ] + ն V280 J1925
     ոտիցն] -ն M4834
-35 երկաթն] -ն M9116-M4114 M182"

	արձաթն] -ն	M9116 V1508-M351
-39	Թագաւորութիւն 2°] + ն	M346' M9116-M2627' M182'
	երրորդ] + ն	M2627
	պղինձն] -ն	M351
2:40	Թագաւորութիւնն] -ն	M4834 M346 J1925-M4114
	երկաթ] + ն	M4834 M178-M346 J1925
-41	կողմն] -ն	M9116-M4114
	կէսն M287 M2627] -ն rel
	կողմն 2°] -ն	M2585 M9116-M4114
	Թագաւորութիւն] + ն	M2585 J1925-M4114 M182"
-42	կողմն 1°] -ն	V280'
	կողմն 2°] -ն	V280
	մի 2°] + ն	V280'
	նմանէ] + ն	J1925
	ջախջախն] -ն	M2585 WN11
-43	զաւակէ] + ն	M351
	խեցին] -ն	WN11-M2585 J1925'-M4114
		M182"
	երկաթ] -ն	M4834 WN11-M2585 J1925'-
		M4114 M182"
-45	լեռնէն] -ն	M178-M346'-M2585
	վէմ M287' M9116-M2627] + ն rel
	զերկաթն 1°, 2°] -ն	M9116-M4114 M182"
	զոսկին] -ն	M9116-M4114 M182'
	լինելոց] + ն	V280 J1925
-46	արքայ M287 M2585 M2627] + ն rel
-47	զխորհուրդ] + դ	M4834 WN11 M4114 V1508
		(+տ M346 J1925)
-48	իմաստոցն] -ն	J1925
-49	դրան] + ն	V280 M4114

Chapter 3

3:3	արքայ M287] + ն rel
-4	քարոզ] + ն	M287 M346' M2627
-5	փողոյ] + ն	M178
	արքայ] + ն	WN11

	ոչ] + ն	M4834 M178 V1508
-6	ժամ՛նւ] + ն	M4834
	հնոգ] + ն	M346' M4114 M182"
	հրոյն] -ն	M346
-7	ազգք] + ն	V280 J1925'-M2627-M182''
	փողոյն] -ն	WN11
	զնուագարանագն M287'] -ն rel	
	ազգագ] + ն	V280
	ազգն V287 M346']	om -ն rel
	ազգք + ն	M4834 M2585 M9116-M2627 M182"
	ազինքն] -ն rel	
	լեզուքն M287 J1925] om -ն rel	
-8	զհրէիգն] -ն	V280 J1925'-M2627' M182
-11	ոչ] + ն	V1508
-12	պատկերիղ (-ին M4834)] -ին V280 M346' J1925	
		om -ղ M178
-14	պատկերի] + ղ	M4834 + ն V280 M2585 J1925'-M2627 M182"
-15	փողոյ] + ն	J1925
	արուեստականնագ] + ն J1925	
	պատկերին] -ն	M4114
	հնոգ] + ն	WN11
	հրոյն] -ն	M4114
-16	գարքայ] + ն	M4834 M178-M2585 J1925 M351
-17	աստուած] + ն	M4834
	մեքն] -ն	M346'-M2585
	հնոգէ] + ս	M2627 + ղ M287
	հրոյ M287 M2627] + ն M4834 M346'-M2585 + ղ rel (-V280)	
-18	պատկերիղ] -ին	V280 M346' J1925
-21	հնոգին] (om M287 J1925) -ն V280' M346'] M9116 -M4114 M182''	
	հրոյն] -ն	M2627

-28 ամենայնի] + ն   M4114 M182
-29 լինել] + ն   M9116-M4114 M182"
-38 ժամանակի] + ս   V280
-40 յուսացելոց M287 M9116-M4114] + ն M351, +u rel
-45 փառաւորեալ] + ղ   M178-M346'
-46 սպասաւորք] + ն   V280' M178 J1925' M182
-49 ազարիանս] + ն   V280 M346' J1925'-M4114
-50 հողմ] + ն   M346' J1925-M2627
-51 երեքեան M287" M2627' M182"] + ն rel (- J1925)
-56 նստիս] + ղ   M4834
-84 քահանայք] + ն   M178 J1925
-88 բոցոյ M287' J1925] + u rel
-90 զաստուածն] -ն   M287
-91 մեծամեծս] + ն   M178-M346
-92 որդւոյ] + ն   M346' J1925'
-93 հնցի M287 M2585 M9116] + ն rel
    հրոյն] -ն   M2627'
    բարձրելոյ] + ն   M346'
-94 նախարարքն] -ն   V280
    զաւրավարքն] -ն   M287" WN11 M4114
-95 աստուած] + ն   V280
    զբան] + ն   WN11
    Թագաւորին M287' WN11 M9116-M2627'] -ն rel
    աստուծոյ] + ն   V280 M2627'
-96 զաստուծոյ] + ն   V280
    այնպէս] այսպէս   J1925
-97 Թագաւորութեան] + ն M4834 J1925

Chapter 4

-5 անուն] + ն   V280
-6 երագոյն] -ն   J1925
-9 տերև] + ն   M9116
    պտուղ] + ն   V280 M178 M9116-M2627
    նմանէ] + ն   M9116 M182
-11 զոստս] + ղ   M9116
    գազանք] + ղ   WN11-M2585 M2627' M182"

	+ ն	M9116
	Թոչունք] + դ	WN11-M2585 M9116 M182"
-13	սիրտ] + ն	J1925'
-15	նորա] դորա	M2627
-17	բարձրութիւնն] -ն	V280 WN11 M9116
-19	մեծութիւն] + դ	M4834 M178-M346'
	տէրութիւն] + դ	M178-M2585
-20	նորա] դորա	M346'-M2585
	նորա 2°] դորա	WN11-M2585 (-դայ M346)
-23	ծառռյն] -դյդ	M4834 J1925
	զիշխանութիւն] + ն	M4834 M178 M2627' M351
-26	ամսոյ] + ն	J1925 M182"
	տածարի] + ն	M9116
	Թագաւորութեան] + ն WN11 J1925	
-27	եւ M287 M346' J1925'-M2627'] + ն rel	
-28	բանքն] -ն	M4834
	բերան] + ն	V280 J178
	Թագաւորութիւն] + դ	M178-M346'-M2585

Chapter 5

-2	հարձք] + ն	V280
-3	տածարէ M287] + rel	
-5	տածարի] + ն	V280 M9116
	Թագաւորին] -ն	V280
	ձեռինն] -ն	M2585 M351
-7	զմոգս] + ն	V280 M346'
	զքաղդեայս] + ն	V280
	զգէտս] + ն	V280
	զիմաստունս] + ն	V280 M9116
-9	արքայ] + ն	M4834 J1925
	տածարն] -ն	M4834 M2585 J1925'-M2627'
-11	արքայ] + ն	M4834 J1925
-12	զմեկնութիւն] + ն	M4834 J1925
-18	բարձրեալ M287' M346] -ն rel	
-19	մեկնութիւն] + ն	M178 J1927 V1508

-20 նմանէ] + ն   J 1925-M2627' M182"
-21 բարձրեալն] -ն   M346'-M2585 J1925'-M2627'
                           M182"
-22 գայդ] գայս   V280
-23 տան] + ն   M4834
-24 ձեռին] + ն   V280' WN11 J1925' M182"
      այնորիկ] այս.   V1508
-26 Թագաւորութիւնդ M287' J1925] -դ rel
-28 Թագաւորութիւն   V280
-30 արքայ] + ն   V280

Chapter 6

-1   Թագաւորութիւնն M287'] -ն rel
      մի] + ն   V280
-4   Թագաւորն] -ն   M178-M9116
-7   գուրն M287' M346' M2627] -ն rel
-8   գուխտն] -ն   M346': գուխտդ V280 M178
-10 յաւուրն] -ն   V280 M182"
-12 գուր] + ն   V280 M178-M346-M2585 M2627
-13 յորդւոց] + ն   V280
      գերութեան M287' WN11 + ն rel
-16 գուրն] -ն   WN11 J1925
      արքային] -ն   V280 M9116
      աստուածն] -ն   J1925'
      դու M287' J1925' M2627 M2585] + ն rel
-18 բուն] + ն   V280
      նմանէ] + ն   M178-M346 J1925
-19 արքային] -ն   V280
      գուրն] -ն   M4834 J1925
-20 դուն] -ն   V280 M346'-M2585 M9116-
                           M2627' M182"
      առնձուցդ] -ձուցն   J1925: -դ V280
-21 ցարքայ] + ն   M2627
-24 գուրն] -ն   J1925
      կանայք] + ն   M4834
-25 երկրին M287] -ն   rel

-26 ասաուծոյն] -ն   J 1925
-27 փրկեաց] + ն   M4834 M2585
-28 Թագաւորութեանն] -ն M 178

Chapter 7

-1   արքային M287] -ն   rel
-2   գծով] + ն   V280 M178-M346'-M9116-
                            M2627
-5   երեք] + ն   WN 11
-7   գազան M287] +ն   rel
-8   եղջերս] + ն   J 1925 (-իւրսն)
     յառաջնոցն] -ն   M 35 1
-9   հիննաւուրցն] -ն   M 178-J 1925'-M2627'
-12 գազանաց M287 M346'-M2585 M9116-M4114] + ն rel
     իշխանութիւն] + ն   M4834 J 1925
-16 այնորիկ] այսորիկ   WN 11
     գճշմարտութիւն M287] + ն rel
-17 գազանք] + ն   M 178-M346' M4114
-18 բարձրելոյ M178 M287] + ն rel
-19 գազանսն] -ն   M 287 WN11*
-20 եղջերացն] -ն   WN 11 M 35 1
     տասանցն M287 M346'] -ն om rel
     այլքն] -ն   V280' M2585 M2627'
     բերան] + ն   V280' M178-M346-WN 11*
-21 պատերազմ] + ն   WN 11
     սուրբս] + ն   M4834
-22 սրբոց] + ն   M4834
     բարձրելոյ M287'] + ն rel
     սուրբք] + ն   WN 11 J 1925
-23 Թագաւորութիւն] + ն   J 1925
-25 կես] + ս   M 178
-27 բարձրելոյ] + ն   V280 M346' J 1925' M2627' M 182''
-28 բանին] -իս   M287'' WN 11-M2585 M9116-
                            M2627 M 182''

Chapter 8

- 1   տեսլեանն] -ն   V280
- 2   յայարանսն M287'M2585 J1925-M2627' M182'] -ն rel
- 3   մին M287 M9116-M2627' M182''] + ն rel
- 4   գագանքն] -ն   V280 M2585 J1925-M2627'
                                M182''
- 7   խոյն] -ն   V280 M178
- 8   գաւրանալն M287] -ն rel
- 9   նոցանէ] + ն   J1925
- 10   գաւրութիւն] + ն   M178-M346
- 11   գերութիւնն] -ն   WN11 J1925
- 13   մեղքդ] -դ   V280'
        սրբութիւնդ] -դ   V280' J1925
        գաւրութիւն] + դ   M178-M346'-M2585
- 14   սրբութիւն M287 M346'] + ն rel
- 17   նմա] դմա   M2585 M2627' M182'' WN11ᶜ
        գալն] -ն   V280' M2585 J1925'-M2627
        տեսիլդ] -սիլս   M178 M2627
- 19   լինելոց] + ն   M178-M346' J1925
        վախճանն] -ն   V280 M346'
- 20   Թագաւոր M287 WN11ᶜ] + ն rel (-V280)
- 21   Թագաւոր M287 M178] + ն rel
        Թագաւորն] -ն   M9116
- 22   խորտակելն M287 M2585 M4114 M182''] -ն rel
        եղջերբք] + ն   M2585 J1925-M2627' M182'
- 23   Թագաւորութեան] + ն M4834
        մեղացն M287] -ն   rel
- 24   զիգաւրս] + ն   M2627
- 26   ասացան] -ն   WN11 M9116 M182''
        բազումս] + ն   J1925

Chapter 9

- 1   Թագաւորութեան M287 WN11 M9116] + ն rel
- 4   մեծ 1°] + դ   WN11-M2585 J1925'-M2627
                                M182''
        պահես] + դ   M178-WN11 (-տ M346)

-6   մարգարէից] + ն   V280 J1925'-M4114 M182"
       իշխանսն M287' M346'] -ն rel
       հարսն] -ն   V280' M178 M2627 V1508
-7   առն] + ն   M2627
-8   հարց M287' J1925'-M2627' M351] + ն rel
-11   անէծքն] -ն   V280 WN11 J1925'-M2627
       երդումն] -ն   WN11 M2627
       յաւրենսն M287" M2585 J1925-M2627}-ն rel
-12   եղեն] + ն   M178-M346'-M2585 M2627
-13   հարցն] -ն   M4834
-14   չարեացն] -ն   V280'
-17   սրբութիւնն] -ն   M4834 WN11 J1925
-18   գթութեան] + դ   M2585
-20   ժողովրդեան M287 M2627] + ն rel
-21   յաղաւթսն] -ն   V280
       յառաջնումն M287' WN11 J1925'-M4114 M351] -ն rel
       պատարագին] -ն   M9116
-23   աղաւթից] + ն   J1925
       պատգամ] + ն   V280
-24   մեղաց M287 M9116-M4114 M182"] + ն rel
       անաւրէնութեանց M287' J1925'-M4114 M182'] + ն rel
       անիրաւութեանց] + ն M346'-M2585
       անբարշտութեանց M287' J1925-M4114 M182"]+ն rel
       տեսլեան] + ն   M178-WN11-M2585
       մարգարէի] (-էից)+ ն M4834 J1925
-25   չինելն] -ն   M4834 M178-M346-M2585
                             J1925 M351
       ժամանակքն M287] -ն rel
-26   սրբութիւն M287 WN11] +ն rel (-J1925)
       զապականութիւնն M287] -ն rel
-27   մի] + ն   V280
       եւթներորդի 2°] + ն   V280'
       ապականութեան M287 WN11] + ն rel
       եւթներորդին M287' J1925 M182']-ն rel
       ժամանակի] + ն   V280

Chapter 10

- 1   յամին] -ն   M287'
          բան M287" M2627] + ն rel
- 3   աւուրցն] -ն   M287' M9116-M2627' M182"
- 4   ամսեանն] -ն   WN 11
- 7   իս] + ն   M4834
- 8   զաւրութեան M287' WN11 J1925] + ն rel
- 9   բանից] + ն   M287"
          նորա 2°] + ն   M287' J1925
- 10   Ճայն] (Ճերն) + ն   M4834
- 11   խաւսել ն M287" M346'-M2585] -ն rel
          զբանս] + ն   J1925
- 13   Թագաւորութեանն]-ն WN 11-M346
- 15   խաւսել ն] -ն   M346'-M2585 J1925' M2627'
                               M182"
- 16   կայր] + ն   M287
- 19   խաւսել ն M287" M346'-M2585] -ն rel
- 20   պատերազմն M287 WN11] -ն rel
- 21   Ճշմարտութեան] + ն V280' M2585 J1925
          իշխանն] -ն   J1925

Chapter 11

- 2   Ճշմարտութիւն M287 WN11] + ն rel
- 6   զաւրութեան] + ն   M4114
          աձելիք] + ն   V280' J1925'-M4114 M182"
- 7   զաւրութիւն M287 M2627-M9116 WN11]
                                    + ն rel (-J1925)
- 10   որդիք] + ն   WN 11
- 11   պատերազմ] + ն   WN 11
- 12   սիրտ] + ն   M4834
- 13   ժամանակացն] -ն M4114 M182"
- 14   ժողովրդեան] + ն M4834 J1925
- 16   մտանել ն] -ն   M2585
- 20   Թագաւորութեան] + ն J1925'-M2627 V280
- 23   խտնիցին] -ն   V280 WN11
- 25   պատերազմ] + ն WN 11

-27 վախճանն] -ն   M9116-M2627
-28 ուխտին] -ն   V1508
     ժամանակի] + ն   M346'
-31 նմանէ] + ն   M4834   M178-M346'-M2585
     զսրբութիւնն] -ն   M287
     զհանապագորդու-
         թիւնն] -ն   M287' WN11
     ապականութիւն] + ն   M4834 J1925
-36 բարկութիւն] + ն   J1925'-M2627' M182''
-37 հարց] + ն   M9116-M2627
     ցանկութեան] + ն   M2627
-38 զաստուած] + ն   M178-M346'-M2585
     հարք] + ն   J1925
-43 ցանկալեացն] -ն   J1925
-45 զխորան] + ն   V280
     ծովուցն] -ն   M287'
     լեառն] + ն   M4834
     կողմն] -ն   M2585

Chapter 12

- 1 ժամանակ] + ն   M4834
     նեղութեան] + ն   V280
     ժամանակի M287'M2585] + ն rel
     ննջեցելոց] + ն   V280'
- 2 կեանսն] -ն   M287 M346'
     յաւիտենականս] + ն M287
     յամաւթ] + ն   V280 J1925
- 3 իմաստունք] + ն   M287''
- 4 գիտութիւն] + ն   V280
     զգեցեալ] + ն   M287' J1925 V1508
- 6 զգեցեալ] + ն   M287' J1925 V1508
     զբաղէնն] -ն   V280
- 7 յառնէն] + ն   WN11
     զգեցեալն] -ն   WN11-M2585 M2627-M9116
         M351

ժողովրդեան] + ն   V280' M346'-M2585 J1925-
M4114 V1508- M351

-9   բանքս] բանքդ   V280 J1925

-11 փոփոխման M287' M346' M9116-M2627] + ն rel
յաճախականու-
թեան] + ն   M4834

Bel:1 հարս] + ն   M346

-7   զքուրմս] + ն   M287 M178-M2627' M182''

-9   քուրմք] + ն   V280 J1925

   տուն] + ն   V280

-10 քուրմքն] -ն   M346'-M2585 M182''

   զգինիդ] -դ   M4834

-14 զքուրմքն] -ն   M346' M2627

   սովորութեան] + ն   V280'

-16 կնիքդ] -դ   J1925 M351

-18 ատակդ] -դ   WN 11

-23 գդնամէ] + ն   J1925

   ահաւասիկ] -դիկ   M287'' M9116-M2627' V1508-
M351

   դմա] ամա   V280

-25 զվիշապդ] -պն   M287'

-26 զպաշտամունսդ] -դ   V280' M178-M346 M182:
-սն WN 1 1

-27 քուրմսն] -ն   M346'

-33 հրեշտակ] + ն   M287' M346'-M2585 J1925-
M2627

   ունիս] +դ   M2585

   գուբն] -ն   WN11-M2585 J1925

   առիծուց] + ն   J1925' M182''

-35 հոգւոյ] + ն   V280' J1925

-38 հրեշտակ] + ն   M287' J1925'-M2627 M351

   տեղի] + ն   M178

-40 զվնասակարս] + ն   V280 WN11

   գուբն] -ն   M2585

NOTES

1. See P.R. McReynolds, "The Claremont Profile Method and the Grouping of Byzantine New Testament Manuscripts", (Ph.D. dissertation, Claremont Graduate School, 1968).

2. For the deictic suffix implicity bearing a quasi-possessive sense see S.P. Cowe, "The Two Armenian Versions of Chronicles".

3. The apparent exception to this rule was the inclusion of V280. However, both the quantity and quality of its variants (usually supported by J2558) were such as to suggest that, far from representing a corrupt, secondary aberration from the principal standard, it should be regarded as the faithful witness of a different early text.

4. See H. Ačaŕean, *Anj B*, Vol.4, pp.248-9 for possible identification.

5. The sound change was complete in the eleventh century and is reflected especially in the Middle Armenian literature of Cilicia. See G. Garitte (ed.), *La Narratio de rebus Armeniae* CSCO subsidia t.4, Louvain: L. Durbecq, 1952, pp.399-400 and J. Karst, *Historische Grammatik des Kilikisch-Armenischen*, Strassburg: K. J. Trübner, 1901, pp.29-33.

6. S. Der Nersessian, *The Chester Beatty Library*, p.xli. For further details see also *IV Ezra*, pp.29f., and S.P. Cowe, "Armenian Sidelights on Torah Study in Seventeenth Century Poland", *JJS*37(1986), pp.94-97 for Jewish influence on his Biblical activities.

7. Cf. Ziegler's Orthographica p.68 and M. Goshen-Gottstein's similar suggestion for P in "Prolegomena to a Critical Edition of the Peshitta", *Studia Hierosolymitana* 8(1961), p.36, note 34. An exception has been made in the case of proper nouns, variations in the form of which are given in full in the apparatus and not repeated elsewhere.

8. As CHB5 of Susanna belongs to Group E, its reading is

taken to be implicit in that of M351. Only when it departs from the latter is it recorded in the apparatus.

9. The letter ō was adopted from the Latin alphabet after the twelfth century to represent the diphthong ուլ which had become a monophthong. In manuscripts like M287 with a primitive orthography this letter never appears (except as a numeral = 10,000). The terminations -nη, -oη originally distinct in form and function later converged and were used interchangeably. Nevertheless, a certain pattern of scribal preference emerges from the examples in Daniel. See Meillet, pp.27-28, §31.

10. In cases of juxtaposition of *n* and *m* with stops it is often difficult to decide whether the original form of the latter was voiced or unvoiced (e.g. նկ / նգ, նք / նում, մբ / մփ). See Meillet, p.23, §27.

11. Although the form thus constituted (են) is an independent morpheme with a different meaning, its presence at these points without clear support is better explained as the result of phonetic variation.

12. See Meillet, pp.12-13, §16.

13. (1°) etc. indicates the particular instance of the word in which variation occurs. Where all the instances of a word in any verse are affected, this is noted as (2), (3) etc.

14. Meillet, p.65, §72.

Explanation of Signs and Abbreviations Employed in the Critical Apparatus

A   *   marks the original reading of a MS.

     c   marks the activity of a later corrector.

     s   marks the suppletor of a MS. This sign is used only for MS M178 in the chapter Bel and the Dragon.

B   +   addition to the reading given in the lemma

     ↰   omission through parablepsis from one occurrence of a word to another. The precise occurrence in question is noted thus 1°, 2°, 3°, etc.

C   —   means the lemma includes all the text between the words found at either end of the line.

     ---   means the lemma consists of only the words at either end of the dotted line and not in the intervening text.

D   mg   marginal reading of a MS.

     txt   reading found in the body of a MS' text

E

ante	before	rel	the remainder[1]
cap	chapter	superscript	title
cf	compare	sup lin	above the line
cum cod	with codex	tr	transposes(s)
ditt	dittography	ult	final
fin	end	var	variation(s)
hapl	haplography	vid	apparently,
homoeotel	homoeoteleuton		indicates MS
homoeoarc	homoeoarcton		reading not
init	beginning		clearly legible
min	minor		
om	omit(s)		
omn	every	vid seq	see following
pr	place(s) before		variant
ras	erasure		

---

[1] This always applies to the last of a series of variants and comprises all the manuscripts not previously cited.

Sigla

Sub-group

A 1	M287 (base MS)
A 2	M4834 and V280

$$M287' = M287 + V280$$
$$M287' = M287 + M4834$$
$$M287'' = M287 + V280 + M4834$$

B 1ᵃ	M178
B 1ᵇ	M346 and WN11 M346' = M346 + WN11
B 3	M2585
C 1	J1925
C 2	M9116
C 3ᵃ	M4114
C 3ᵇ	M2627 M2627' = M2627 + M4114
D 1	M182
D 3	V1508
E 1	CHB5
E 2	M351

$$M182' = M182 + V1508$$
$$M182' = M182 + M351$$
$$M182'' = M182 + V1508 + M351$$

ԴԱՆԻԷԼ ԴԱՏԱՍՏԱՆԱ8

[1] Եւ էր այր մի բնակեալ ի Բաբելովն եւ անուն էր նորա Յովակիմ: [2] Եւ առ իւր կին, անուն նորա Շուշան, դուստր Քեղ-կեաս, գեղեցիկ յոյժ երկիւղած ի Տեառնէ: [3] Եւ ծնաւղք նորա ար-դարք եւ ուսուցին զդուստրն իւրեանց ըստ աւրինացն Մովսեսի: [4] Եւ էր Յովակիմ մեծատուն յոյժ եւ էր նորա բուրաստան մերձ յապարանս իւր եւ առ նա ժողովէին հրեայք զի փառաւորագոյն էր քան զամենեսեան: [5] Եւ երեւեցան երկու ծերք ի ժողովրդենէ անդի դատաւորք տարոյն այնմիկ, զորոց խաւսեցաւ Տէր թէ ել անաւրէնութիւն ի Բաբելովնէ ի ծերոց դատաւորաց որ համա-րեին առաջնորդել ժողովրդեանն: [6] Եւ նոքա հանապագորդ էին

superscript.: Գիրգ Դանիէլի մարգարէի V280 մարգա-րէութիւն Դանիեղի (-իէլի: M182 -իէլի V1508) M2627 M182'
superscript. cap.: Դանիէլ (-իէղ M2627') Դատաստանաց M287
M9116-M2627' M182'' Դանիէլի դատաստանաց (+է WN11) M346'
Գիրք դատաստանաց Դանիէլի մարգարէին M4834 Դանիէլի
դատաստան շուշանայ և ծերոց CHB5 |
[1] Եւ 1°◡2° M178 | այր մի էր M346'| Բաբելոն V2180' M346'
M2627 M182' (-լոն M351) | Եւ 2°] pr յորդւոցն խարայէղի V280 | էր
անունն M2585 | էր M287] om rel
[2] Եւ 1°] om J1925 | կին] + Եւ J1925 | քեղկեայ V280' M2585
M9116-M2627' M182' | գեղեցիկ] om V280 | յոյժ M280' M9116-
M4114 M182'] + Եւ rel
[3] ուսուցանէին M178-M346'| մոսխի V280 մովսեսի M4834
մօսխի M4114 մովսիսի M182''
[4] մեծատուն յովակիմ V280 | բուրաստան մի V280 | մերձ]
մեծ CHB5 | ի յապարանս J1925 | հրեայք M9116-M2627 M351]
հրեայքն V280 M178-M346'-M2585 հրեայքն M4834 J1925 |
զամենեսեան M4834
[5] Եւ 1°] ւ CHB5 այնորիկ M178-M346' J1925 | զոր M178 |
անաւրէնութիւնք J1925 անիրաւութիւն V280 բաբելոնէ M4834
M346' M2627 M351 (-լոնէ M4114) | ի 3°] om M351 | որ] Եւ M4114 |
համարէին] արհամարհեին M351 | առաջնորդ (-նորդք V280
J1925) V280' J1925
[6] Յովակիմա M287 WN11 J1925] -մայ rel | ամենեքեան առ
նոսա M346' | ամենեքեան J1925'-M2627 M182''

143

ի տանն Յովակիմա, և գային առ նոսա ամենեքին ի դատաս
տան: ⁷ և լինէր իբրև ժողովն մէկներ զհասարակ աւուրբն, մտա
նէր Շուշան և գնայր ի բուրաստանի առն իւրոյ: ⁸ և տեսանէին
զնա երկոքին ծերքն հանապազ զի մտանէր և զգնայր և ցան
կացան նմա: ⁹ և դարձուցին <զսիրոս> իւրեանց և խոտորե
ցուցին զաչս իւրեանց չհայել յերկինս և չլիշել զարդար դա
տաստանն: ¹⁰ և էին երկոքին <հարեալք> ի նմա. և չպատմէին
միմեանց զգաւսն իւրեանց ¹¹ զի պատկառէին պատմել զգան
կութիւնն իւրեանց, քանզի կամէին լինել ընդ նմա: ¹² և սպա
սէին նմա ատել հանապազ տեսանել զնա ¹³ և ասեն գմիմեանս
«երթիցուք ի տուն քանզի ճաշոյ ժամ է» և ելին մեկնեցան ի
միմեանց: ¹⁴ և դարձեալ անդրէն եկին միւսանգամ առ մի
մեանս և հարցեալ միմեանց զպատճառսն, խոստովան եղեն
զգանկութիւնն իւրեանց. ապա եղեն ժամադիր միմեանց թէ երբ

⁷ ժողովն M287 J1925] ժողովուրդ rel (-վուրդք CHB5) |
աւուրբն M287'' M178] աւուրբք rel | Շուշանն V280 | զնայր M287
WN11 CHB5] զգնայր rel | բուրաստան J1925 | իւրում M178-
WN11 M182

⁸ երկու V280' | զի հանապազ V280 | զնայր J1925 CHB5

⁹ <զսիրոս> V280' M346'-M2585 M9116 M182] զերեսս M287
զմիսս rel | յերկին M346 | արդար CHB5 | դատաստանն M2585
M9116-M2627' V1508

¹⁰ երկոքեան V280' M9116-M2627 M182'' | <հարեալք> V280
M2585 J1925] հարեալք M287 հարեալ rel | ոչ պատմէին V280
WN11

¹¹ զգանկութիւնս V280' M178-M346'-M2585 CHB5 | նմա] նա
M178-M346' (նայ J M4834)

¹³ ասէին V280 M4114 | տունս V280 | քանզի M287' M178-
M346'-M2585] զի rel | ժամ է ճաշոյ J1925 | ճաշու WN11

¹⁴ և 1°] om M9116-M2627' M182'' | դարձեալ –միւսանգամ]
դարձեալ միւսանգամ անդրէն եկին V280 դարձ.եկին անդրէն
միւ. M178-M346'-M2585 | միւսանգամ] om CHB5 | առ միմեանց
CHB5 ի միմեանց V280' M178-M346'-M32585 M4114 | զպատճառն
V280 M2585 J1925 | եղեն 1°] եղան CHB5 | զգանկութիւնս V280
M178-M346'-M2585 J1925 | ապա] pr և CHB5 | ժամադիր եղեն
M178-M346'-M2585 եղեն ժամադիրք V280 | յերբ CHB5 | գտանել
միմեանց զնա միայն CHB5

կարասցեն զնա միայն գտանել: ¹⁵ և եղև ի սպասել նոցա նմա ի
դիպող աւուր, եկն եմուտ երբեմն որպէս յերեկն և յեռանդն
երկուք միայն աղջկամբք և ցանկացաւ լուանալ ի բուրաստանի անդ քանզի տաւթ էր ¹⁶ և չեր ոք անդ բայց միայն երկու
ծերքն <Թաքուցեալք> որ սպասին նմա: ¹⁷ և ասէ ցաղջկունսն
«երթայք բերէք ինձ իւղ և աւծառ և գդուրս բուրաստանիս
փակեցէք զի լուացայց»: ¹⁸ և արարին որպէս ասաց գնոսա,
փակեցին գդուրս բուրաստանին և ելին ի կողմանէ դրացն բերել
զոր ինչ <հրամայեաց > նոցա և չտեսին գծերսն քանզի
<Թաքուցեալք> էին. ¹⁹ և եղև իբրև ելին աղջկունքն, յարեան
երկու ծերքն և դիմեցին ի վերայ նորա: ²⁰ և ասեն «ահա դուրք
բուրաստանի փակեալ են և չիք ոք որ տեսանէ զմեզ և մեք
ցանկացեալ եմք քեզ, վասն որոյ և քո հաւանեալ լեր ընդ մեզ. ²¹
ապա թէ ոչ, վկլայեմք գքեն եթե ումն պատանի էր ընդ քեզ

¹⁵ ի 1°] om WN11 | երբեմն] om WN11* | երեկն M178 երեկն
WN11 | երկուք M287 M346'-M2585 J1925] երկու rel |
յաղջկամբք CHB5 | և ցանկացաւ] մերկացաւ M4834 | լուանիլ
M178-M2585 լուսանալ M4834 | անտ M178-WN11 | էր] + ժամն
V280

¹⁶ ոչ էր ոք CHB5 ոչ ոք էր J1925'-M4114 | անտ M178-M346
անտր J1925 | <Թաքուցեալք>] Թագուցեալք (-եալ J1925) M287
J1925-M2627 Թագ.անդ CHB5: cf v18 | որ] որք CHB5 om M346' |

¹⁷ ինձ] om V280 | աւծառ M4834 M2585 J1925-M2627 M182''

¹⁸ արարին] + այն V280 | որպէս] + և M9116-M4114 (pr
այնպէս M4834) | գնոսա M287 M2585] նոցա rel | բուրաս-
տանին] om WN11 -տան J1925 | ի] om J1925 ընդ M346' | դրացն
M287' M178-WN11 J1925] դրանն V280 դրանց rel | որ M4834 |
<հրամայեաց>] հրամեաց M287 | ոչ տեսին V280 M9116-M4114 |
<Թաքուցեալք> ed] Թագուցեալք M287 -գեալ rel

¹⁹ նորա] չուշանայ V280

²⁰ ասեն] + գնա J1925 | դուրս V280' գդուրքն CHB5 |
փակեալ են բուրաստանիս CHB5 | ոք] om M178-M346 | որ] om
WN11 | եմք] եմ CHB5: hapl | հաւանեալ] + մեզ V280'-M2627''
M182'' + յանձն առ և M178-M346'

²¹ ապա] ապ M178 | էր] կայր ընդ քեզ և CHB5 | և] om M351 |

և վասն այնորիկ արձակեցեր զաղշկունսն ի քէն»: 22 Յոգւոց ե-
հան Շուշան և ասէ «տագնապ <է> ինձ յամենայն կողմանց. եթէ
զայդ գործ գործեցից, մահ <է> ինձ և եթէ ոչ գործեցից, չեմ
ապրելոց ի ձեռաց ձերոց: 23 Բայց լաւ լիցի ինձ չգործել զայդ և
անկանել ի ձեռս ձեր քան թէ մեղայց առաջի Տեառն»: 24 ԵՒ
աղաղակեաց ի ձայն մեծ Շուշան, աղաղակեցին և երկոքին
ծերքն կից նմին. 25 ԵՒ ընթացաւ մին եբաց զդուրս բուրաստանին: 26 իբրև լուան գձայն ճչոյն ի բուրաստանի անդ ընտա-
նիքն անկան ընդ կողմն դրանն ի ներքս տեսանել թէ զինչ իրք
ընդ նա անցեալ իցեն: 27 ԵՒ իբրև ասացին ծերքն զբանս իւր-եանց
զամաւթի հարան ծառայքն յոյժ, զի ոչ երբեք այնպիսի բանք
ասացան զՇուշանայ: 28 ԵՒ եղև ի վաղիւ անդր իբրև եկին
ժողովուրդն առ այր նորա Յովակիմ, եկին և երկու ծերքն
անաւրէն մտաւք զՇուշանա սպանանել զնա, և ասեն առաջի
ժողովրդեանն 29 «յղեցէք և բերէք զՇուշանա այր որ դուստր է

22 գործ M287 M9116-M2627] om rel | <է>] om M287
23 լիցի M287' M178-M346' M9116] է rel| զայդ] pr զգործծդ
V280'| անկանիլ M178| քան] քանզի WN11| Տեառն] աստուծոյ
V280'
24 և 2°] om CHB5 | երկուքին M4834 երկոքեան M2627 երկու
V280 J1925'-M4114 CHB5 | կից] om J1925 | նմին] նմայ M4834
pr ընդ M346' ընդ նմա M178 J1925
25 եբաց] pr և M346'
26 իբրև] pr և V280 M178-M346' M9116| ճչոգն CHB5 | ի 1°] +
մէջ M178-M346' | անն WN11 om V280' | ընտանիքն tr ante ի 1°
J1925 | ընդ 1°] ի J1925 | կողմն M182 կողմանն CHB5 կողմանէ
J1925 | դրանն] om J1925 | ներքոյ J1925 | տեսանեն CHB5 |
նմա M178-M346'-M2585 V1508 նոսա V280 J1925 նցա CHB5 |
անցանիցեն J1925 | իցեն] են V280'
27 և 1°] om M178-M346'| ամօթ CHB5| յոյժ ծնողքն շուշա-
նայ V280| ծառայքն M287 M2627 V1508] ծնաւղքն M4834
M2585 J1925'-M4114 M182 +ծնողքն M346' M9116| յոյժ] om
M2627| երբեք] + լրւան V280| բանս V280| ասացան] om V280|
շուշանա CHB5
28 եղև]om V280 M346'| անտր M178| և 2°]om M4834 CHB5|
երկոքին J1925' om M182| անորէնք M2585| շուշանայ CHB5| ի
սպաննել V280| ասել CHB5| ամենայն ժողովրդեան CHB5
29 յղեցէք] -ցեալ CHB5 | և բերէք M287 sup.lin] om rel | այր

Քեղկեաս, որ է կին Յովակիմա». և նոքա յղեցին: ³⁰ և եկն նա և
ծնաւղք իւր և որդիք իւր և ամենայն ազգականք նորա: ³¹ և
Շուշան էր փափուկ յոյժ և գեղեցիկ տեսլեամբ, ³² և անաւրէնքն
հրամայեցին հոլանի առնել զնա, քանզի սքողեալ էր զի լցցին
գեղով նորա: ³³ և իւրքն լային ամենեքեան որ ճանաչէին զնա:
³⁴ Յարեան ծերքն երկոքեան ի միջոյ ժողովրդեւէն եղին գձեռս
իւրեանց ի վերայ գլխոյ նորա: ³⁵ և նա լալով հայեցաւ յերկինս
քանզի էր սիրտ նորա յուսացեալ ի Տէր: ³⁶ և ասեն ծերքն
երկոքեան «մինչդեռ մեք միայն զգնայաք ի մէջ բուրաստանին,
եմուտ դա անդր երկուք աղջկամբք և փակեաց զդուրս բուրաստանին և արձակեաց զաղջկունսն: ³⁷ և եկն առ նա պատանի
ումն որ <Թաքուցեալ> էր և անկաւ ընդ դմա: ³⁸ և մեք եաք յան-

որ M287] om rel | դուստր է M287] զդustերէ (դստ. M2585 J 1925'-
M2627' M182-CHB5) M178-M2582 J 1925'-M2627'M182'' զդustեր
(դստ. V280) V280 M346' դustերէ դustեր M4834 | կին] om M178
M182
³⁰ և 1°] om CHB5 | եկ J 1925 CHB5: hapl
³² հոլենի M4834ᵗˣᵗ
³³ լային M287] + և rel | ամենեքեան M287 M346'-M2585
M9116 M351 | որք V280' | զնոսա M2627
³⁴ երկոքին ծերքն M178-M346'-M2585 M2627' M182''| եր-
կոքեան M287] -քին V280' J 1925'| մէջ CHB5 |ժողովրդեանն
M4834 M2627 M182''|և եղին V280 M2627 M182'-CHB5 | իւրեանց]
om M178
³⁶ և 1° M287] om rel | երկոքին M178-M346'-M2585 J1925'-
M4114 երկուքին M4834 | միայն մեք J 1925| զնայաք M4834
J 1925-M4114 CHB5 | անդ (անտ M346) M178-M346'-M2585
M9116-M2627' ընդ J 1925 | երկուք M287 (+ միայն M2627)]
երաւք J 1925 -կու rel | աղջկամբք M4834 M346 | և 2°↷3° M2627 |
զաղջկունս արձակեաց M2627 |
³⁷ և 1°] om V1508 | ումն M287'' M346'-M2585] մի rel |
Թաքուցեալ էր M287' M178-M346'] tr rel| <Թաքուցեալ>] Թաq.
M287' J1925-M2627 CHB5 | ընդ]առաջի CHB5
³⁸անկեան CHB5

կեան բուրաստանին: ³⁹ իբրև տեսաք զանաւրէնութիւնն ընթացաք առ դոսա և տեսաք զլինելն դոցա ընդ միմեանս. զնա ոչ կարացաք ունել քանզի բուռն էր քան զմեզ և եթաց դուրսն և փախեաւ արտաքս: ⁴⁰ Զդա որ ըմբռնեցաք հարցաք թէ ո՞վ էր պատանին ⁴¹ և ոչ կամեցաւ պատմել մեզ, զայս վկայեմք». և հաւատաց նոցա ատեանն իբրև ծերոց ժողովրդեան և դատաւորաց և դատեցան զնա մեռանել: ⁴² Աղաղակեաց ի ձայն բարձր Շուշան և ասէ «Աստուած յաւիտենական ծածկագէտ, որ գիտես զամենայն յառաջ քան զլինել նոցա: ⁴³ Դու գիտես զի սուտ վկայեն զինէն. ահա մեռանիմ որ ոչ ինչ գործեցի զոր դոքայդ անաւրինեն զինէն». ⁴⁴ և լուաւ Տէր ձայնի նորա. ⁴⁵ և մինչդեռ տանեին զնա կորուսանել, զարթոյց Աստուած զոգի սուրբ ի վերայ մանկան միոյ տղայ որում անուն էր Դանիէլ: ⁴⁶ և աղաղակեաց ի ձայն բարձր և ասէ «անպարտ եմ ես յարենէ դորա»: ⁴⁷ և դարձաւ ամենայն ժողովուրդն առ նա և ասեն

---

³⁹ զլինել] զլեալ J1925 | ունել] տեսանել CHB5 ըմբռնել M346' J1925: cf v 40 | էր քան] եհար + զմեզ զի զօրաւոր էր քան զմեզ CHB5 | և 2°] om V280 CHB5 |
⁴⁰ որ M287' M9116-M4114] om V280 J1925 զոր rel | և հարցաք V280
⁴¹ և 1°] + դ ա V280 | չկամեցաւ M9116 | զայս M287"] զայդ rel | և 2°] զի J1925 | դատեցին V280 | մեռանիլ M178
⁴² բարձր] մեծ CHB5 | Շուշան] tr ad init vers V280 | զամենայն] om CHB5
⁴³ Դու] pr և M178-M346 M351 pr | զի] զիս CHB5 | վկայեցին J1925 | ահա M287 M351] ի զուր V280 և rel | որ] զոր V280 M178-M346 | ինչ ոչ M4114 | զոր] յոռց J1925 զորդիք CHB5 | դոքայդ] om CHB5 | յանօրէնին CHB5
⁴⁵ ի կորուսանել M178-M346' | արթոյց CHB5 | միոյ մանգան տղայոյ M4834 | տղայոյ միոյ M346' | դանիէլ M178
⁴⁶ և 1°] որ V280 | աղաղակեալ J1925 | և 2°] om J1925 | կան յանպարտ WN11
⁴⁷ դարձաւ առ նա ամէն. ժողովուրդն M178 V280' ամ. ժողով. դարձաւ (-ձան WN11) առ նա M346'-M2585 | բանդ M287'' M2585 J1925'] + այդ rel | զոր M287] + դուդ rel

«զի՞նչ է բանդ գոր խաւսեցար»։ ⁴⁸ և նա եկաց ի մէջի նոցա և ասէ
«այդպէ՞ս անմիտք էք որդիք իսրայէլի. ո՛չ քննեցէք և ո՛չ
յիրաւանց վերայ հասէք և դատապարտեցէք զղուստր իսրա-
յէլի։ ⁴⁹ <Դարձա՛յք> անդրէն յատեան քանզի սուտ վկայեցին
դրքա զնմանէ»։ ⁵⁰ և դարձաւ ժողովուրդն վաղվաղակի և ասեն
ցնա ծերքն «եկ նիստ ի մէջի մերում և պատմեա մեզ, զի քեզ ետ
Աստուած գերիցութիւն»։ ⁵¹ և ասէ ցնոսա Դանիէլ «մեկնեցէք
զդոսա ի միմեանց ի բաց և քննեցուք զդոսա»։ ⁵² և իբրև
մեկնեցան ի միմեանց, կոչեաց զմիհն ի նոցանէ և ասէ ցնա «այ,
հնացեալ աւուրբք չարութեան, այժմ եկին հասին մեղք քո գոր
գործէիր յառաջագոյն. ⁵³ զի դատեիր զդատաստան անիրա-
ւութեամբ, զանմեղս դատապարտեիր և զվնասակարս արձակեիր, որում Աստուծոյ ասացեալ էր թէ զանմեղն և զարդարն

---

⁴⁸ միջի M287 M178 M9116-M4114] մէջ rel ǀ նոցա] om
M9116-M4114 ǀ անմիտ V280 WN11 M9116-M4114 ǀ Իսրայէլի 1°]
-էլի WN11 M9116-M4114 M182'' ǀ ո՛չ 2°] om J1925 ǀ քննէք M4834
J1925 ǀ յիրաւունս J1925 իրաւանց WN11 CHB5 ǀ ի վերայ J1925
CHB5 ǀ անմեղ դատապարտեցիք V280 ǀ դատապարտէք M287*-
M4834 CHB5 ǀ Իսրայէլի 2°] -էլի M9116-M2627' M182''

⁴⁹ <դարձայք>] դարձէք M287 դարձիք M178-M346-M2585
J1925-M2627 (pr և M4834) bis scr WN11 ǀ անդրէն] om M9116 ǀ
յատեան] om WN11*ի յատ. M4834 ǀզի M178-M346-WN11* M2627 ǀ
վկայեն WN11 ǀ դրքա] om M9116-M2627 ǀ ոստ դմանէ CHB5

⁵⁰ վաղվաղակի] pr անդրէն J1925: cf v 49 ǀ երեւտ
աստուած CHB5 աստուած եւ WN11 ǀ զիրիցութիւնն CHB5

⁵¹դանիէդ M178 ǀ մեկուսեցէք J1925 ǀ ի 1°] զի CHB5 ǀ ի բաց]
om V280

⁵² և 1°] om M2627' M182'' ǀ իբր WN11 ǀ մեկնեցին M4834
J1925 ǀ կոչեաց] pr և M4834 ǀ և ասէ] om WN11* ǀ ցնա] om M4834
M346 ǀ այա M346 ի նա CHB5 ǀ հնացեալ] + ծեր CHB5 ǀ աւուրբք
J1925 CHB5 ǀ չարութեամբ V280' ǀ այժմ] + ահա M4114 M182'' ǀ
եկեալ CHB5 ǀ հասին քեզ M346 ǀ գործ J1925

⁵³ դատեիր] առնէիր V280 M178-M346' M4114 ǀ զղատաս-
տանս M182'' դատաստան J1925'-M4114 ǀ անիրաւութեան
M287* J1925 ǀ զանմեղն M2627 ǀ զվնասակար M2627 ǀ որում
M287 M178-M346' M2627] յորում WN11 որ J1925 ուր rel ǀ ասացեալ էր աստուծոյ V280 ǀ զար. և զանմեղն M346'-M2585 J1925 ǀ
զանմեղս M9116 CHB5 ǀ զարդարս CHB5 ǀ սպանիցես J1925 սպա-

մի սպանանիցես: ⁵⁴ բայց արդ եթէ տեսեր զդա աստ ընդ որով ծառով հասեր առ դոսա մինչդեռ խաւսէին ընդ միմեանս». և նա ասէ «ընդ հերձեաւն»: ⁵⁵ և ասէ Դանիէլ «բարիոք ստեցեր ի քոյն գլուխ. ահաւասիկ հրեշտակի Աստուծոյ առեալ հրաման հերձցէ զքեզ ընդ մէջ»: ⁵⁶ և ի բաց մերժեաց զնա, հրամայեաց ածել զմիւսն և ասէ ցնա «զաւակ Քանանու և ոչ Յուդա, գեղ դորա պատրեաց զքեզ և ցանկութիւն շրջեաց զսիրտ քո: ⁵⁷ Այդպէս առնեիք զդստերսն Իսրայէլի, և նոքա առ երկիւղի մերձանային առ ձեզ, այլ և ոչ դուստր Յուդա կալաւ յանձին զանաւրէնութիւնդ ձեր: ⁵⁸ բայց արդ ասէ, ասա ընդ որո՞վ ծառով հասեր առ դոսա մինչդեռ խաւսէին ընդ միմեանս»: ⁵⁹ և նա ասէ «ընդ սղոցեաւն» և ասէ ցնա Դանիէլ «բարիոք ստեցեր և դու ի քոյն գլուխ, զի կա աւադիկ հրեշտակ Աստուծոյ, սուսեր ի

նաներ V280 WN11

⁵⁴ զդա M287 M346'-M2585] զդրսա rel | ասա M287 M346'-M2585] om rel | որուն] որ J1925 | հասեր առ դոսա] տեսեր զդրսա M9116 | մինչ M9116-M2627' M181''| միմեանց CHB5 | M287] om rel
⁵⁵ դանիէղ M178 | բարիոք M287' WN11 CHB5] բարւոք rel | <ստեցեր>] pr և դու M287: cf v 59 | ահաւասիկ] pr զի M2585 | հրեշտակ V280' M346' J1925 M351 | հերձեսցէ J1925 հերձել V280 հերձ CHB5
⁵⁶ և 1°] om M9116 | զնա] + և M178-M346' J1925' | աձել] + և WN11 | զաւակ] + դառնացող V280'| և 4°] om CHB5 | Յուդա M287 WN11] -դայի V280' J1925 CHB5 -դայ rel| գեղ] գեղեցկութիւն J1925 | պարտեաց M4834 CHB5 | շրջեաց] շիշոյց J1925| քո ult] om CHB5
⁵⁷ այսպէս V280' | Իսրայէլի WN11 M9116-M4114 M182''| երկիւդի] + կային և CHB5 | մերձանային M287] -ձենային rel | առ 2°] առ ի J1925 | ոչ և M178-M346-M2585 M9116-M2627 | ոչ] tr ante կալաւ V280 | Յուդա M287' WN11 J1925] -դայի V280'-դայ rel | կալաւ] om J1925 | յանձինս ձեր եղև անարէնութիւն J1925 | զանաւրէնութիւնս V280 M4114 M182''
⁵⁸ արդ] om V280
⁵⁹ և 1° M287 M346'] om rel | դանիէլ ցնա CHB5 | ցնա] om J1925 | դանիէղ M178 | բարիոք M287 M346'] բարեաւք M4834 բարի CHB5 բարւոք rel | և 3°] om V280 | կա] om CHB5 | ահաւադիկ WN11 CHB5 | աստուծոյ] + և V280 | սուսեր] սուր M178-M346' | ի 2° M287' J1925'] pr մերկ rel | ձեռին] + իւրում

ձեռին, սպրգէ զքեզ ընդ մէջ զի սատակեսցէ զքեզ»: ⁶⁰ և աղաղակեաց ամենայն ժողովուրդն ի ձայն մեծ և աւրհնեցին զԱստուած որ ապրեցուցանէ զյուսացեալս իւր: ⁶¹ և յարեան ի վերայ
երկուց ծերոցն քանզի յանդիմանեաց զնոսա Դանիէլ ի նոցին
բերանոց սուտ վկայս և արարին ընդ նոսա որպէս եդին ի մտի
չարութիւն առնել ընդ ընկերի ⁶² ըստ աւրինացն Մովսէսի և
սպանին զնոսա և ապրեցաւ արիւն արդար յաւուր յայնմիկ: ⁶³
իսկ Քեղկեաս և կին նորա աւրհնեցին զԱստուած վասն դստերն
իւրեանց Շուշանա հանդերձ Յովակիմաւ արամբ նորա և ամենայն ազգականաւք զի ոչ գտան իրբ գարշութեան ի նմա: ⁶⁴ և
Դանիէլ եղև մեծ առաջի ժողովրդեանն յաւրէ յայնմանէ և
անդր:

V280 ∣ սղոցէ M287] -գել rel ∣ զքեզ 2°]զձեզ J1925
⁶⁰ ի ձայն մեծ ամ.ժող. CHB5 ∣ ամենայն] om V280
⁶¹ երկուց] երկու V280 - կուս M9116 երկոցունց CHB5 ∣
դանիէդ M178 ∣ նոցունց V280 J1925 ∣ բերանոյ M4834 WN11
CHB5 ∣ զսուտ M4834 M178 ի սուտ V280 ∣ վկայիցն V280 M178-
M346' ∣ արար V280 ∣ որպէս] + և M4114 M182'' ∣ եդին] էր V280 ∣
չարութիւն (չարախաւսութիւն M2627) ի մտի առնել J1925'-
M2627' M182'' ի մտի առնել չարութ. M2585 ∣ առնել] om V280 ∣
ընդ] om V280' M2585 M2627
⁶² մովսիսի V280 M182' ∣ սպանին CHB5 ∣ արդարոյ
M9116
⁶³ քեղկիա V280 M4114 M351 -կիայ M4834 M9116 -կեայ
M346 CHB5 ∣ նորա] իւր V280 ∣ Շուշանա M287 M346' J1925
CHB5] -այ rel ∣ ովակիմաւ WN11 ∣ արեամբ CHB5 ∣ ազգականք
CHB5 ∣ զի] քանզի J1925 pr նորա M2585 M2627' M182'' ∣
գարշութեան] -թեամբ WN11 + նորա CHB5
⁶⁴ դանիէդ M178 ∣ առաջի]+ ամենայն M346' ∣ յաւրէ] որ է
CHB5 յաւուր M346' ∣ և անդր] om V280.

The Armenian Version of Daniel

ՏԵՍԻԼ ԵՐԿՐՈՐԴ

¹ Յամի երրորդի Թագաւորութեան Յովակիմա արքայի Յուդա, եկն Նաբուքոդոնոսոր արքայ <Բաբելացւոց> յերուսաղեմ և պաշարեաց զնա: ² Եւ ետ Տէր ի ձեռն նորա զՅովակիմ արքա Յուդա և ի մանէ սպասուց տանն Աստուծոյ. և տարաւ զայն յերկիրն ի Սենաար ի տուն աստուծոյ իւրոյ, և զսպասն եմոյծ ի տուն գանձի աստուծոյ իւրոյ: ³ Եւ ասէ Թագաւորն ցԱզ- փանեզ ներքինապետ իւր աձել յորդոց գերութեանն Իսրայելդի և ի զաւակէ Թագաւորութեանն և ի Պարտևաց, ⁴ մանկունս անարատս, զեղեցիկս երեսաւք և խելամուտս ամենայն իմաս- տութեան և հմուտս գիտութեան, մտավարդս հանձարով և զաւրաւորս կալ ի տաձարի առաջի Թագաւորին, և ուսուցանել նոցա դպրութիւնս և լեզու Քաղդեացւոց: ⁵ Եւ կարգեաց նոցա

superscript. Գերութիւնն Դանիէլ ի V280
¹ երրորդի M287ᶜ]երկրորդի M287* V280' M2585 J1925-M2627 M182 | Բաբելացւոց M346'-M2585 J1925'-M2627' M182''] om M287
² ձեռն M287] ձեռս rel | Յուդա]-այի M4834 om V280 | մանէ սպասուց] սպասէ մանի ինչ J1925 | սպասուց] om V280 | տանն] ի տանէ J1925 | Աստուծոյ 1°] տեառն M346' | յերկիրն] pr ի M4834 WN11 | ի 3°] om M2585 J1925-M2627' M182' | սենիար V280 սենեար WN11 J1925 սէնէար M346 սենայար M4834 M9116 M182'' | ի 4°] pr և եդ V280 | աստուծոյ 2°] -ng V280' M2585 -ուածոg M4114 | իւրոյ 1°'52° M287*-V280 M9116-M4114 | տուն 2°] տան J1925 | աստուծոյ 3°] -ուածոj M4834 տեառն M346'
³ Ազփանեզ]-նէս WN11 M4114 M182'' ասփ. M4834 ամփանէ V280 | ցներքինապետ V280 | ի յորդոց J1925 որդոց WN11 | Թագաւորութեանն] + յուդայ V280 | և ի 2°] om M2627
⁴ մանկունս] մանուկա WN11| անարատս] + և V280 M2627 | և 1°] om M2627 | իմաստութեամբ J1925' M351 | հմուտ V280' J1925-M4114 | գիտութեան] գերութեանն WN11 + և V280 | հանձարոյ M2627 | զաւրաւորս] + ուժով V280 | ի տաձարի] om V280 om ի WN11* | առաջի Թագաւորին] om M346-WN11*| դպրութիւնս]-թիւն rel | լեզու M287]-զուս J1925 զլեզու rel | քաղդեացոg WN11-gոgն M4834 քաղդեաց. J1925
⁵ նոցա Թագաւորն] tr M4834 | ոոձիկա V280 M2585 J1925-M2627' M182'' | արքայի]Թագաւորին V280 M178-M346' M9116 | ի 2°] om WN11 | սնուցանէր M287] սgուցանել M4114 -նել rel | զնոսա 1°'52° om M351 |

Թագաւորն ոռճիկ աւր րստ աւրէ ի սեղանոյ արքայի, և ի գինոյ զոր ինքն ըմպէր սնուցանէր զնոսա ամս երիս, և ապա կացուցանել զնոսա առաջի Թագաւորին: ⁶ Եւ եին ի նոսա յորդւոցն Յուդա Դանիէլ և Անանիա և Միսայէլ և Ազարիա. ⁷ Եւ եդ նոցա ներքինապետն անուանս, Դանիէլի Բաղտասար և Անանիայ Սեդրաք և Միսայէլի Միսաք և Ազարիայ Աբեդնագով: ⁸ Եւ եդ Դանիէլ ի մտի իւրում չճաշակել ի սեղանոյ Թագաւորին, և ոչ ի գինոյ ըմպելոյ նորա, և աղաչեաց ներքինապետն զի մի ճաշակեսցէ: ⁹ Եւ ետ զԴանիէլ ի շնորհս և յողորմութիւն առաջի ներքինապետին. ¹⁰ Եւ ասէ ներքինապետն զԴանիէլ «երկնչիմ ես ի Տեառնէ <իմմէ> արքայէ որ կարգեաց ձեզ զկերակուրդ ձեր և զըմպելի, գուցէ տեսանիցէ զերեսս ձեր տրտմագոյն քան զայլոց մանկանցդ հասակակցաց ձերոց և առնիցէք զիս գլխապարտ առաջի Թագաւորին»: ¹¹ Եւ ասէ Դանիէլ ցամեղասադ զոր կացու-

ամս] ամիս M182ᵐᵍ ամիսս M178 | ապա] om J1925 | զնոսա M287''] om rel | Թագաւորին]արքային V280

⁶ դանիէդ M178 | Անանա] M4834 M9116-M4114 M351 | ազարիա] և միսայէլ V280 | միսայէդ M178-M2585 V1508 | ազարիա] M4834 M346 M9116

⁷ բաղդասար V280' M178-M346-M2585 M9116-M2627' M182'| Անանիահ M287 J1925] -իա WN11 M2627 -հա] M9116 -հա]ի rel | Սեդրաք M287']-րակ J1925' -րաք rel | միսայելի J1925'-M4114 M182'' -եղի M178 | միսաք M178-WN11-M2585-սակ M9116 | Ազարիա] V280 M9116-M2627 M182 -հա M351 | աբեդնաքով M351աբեթնագով M4834

⁸ դանիէլ եդ V280 | իւրում] om V280 | ոչ ճաշակէլ M178-M346' | ի 3°] om WN11 | նորա] նցա V280 | ճաշակիցէ M4834

⁹ զԴանիէլ ի շնորհս]դանիէլի (-իէդի M346') շնորհս M4834 M178-M346' շնորհս դանիէլի V280 | և յողորմութիւն] om WN11* | ողորմութիւն V280' M178-M346-M2585

¹⁰ցդանիէլ ներք. V280 | ես] om M2627 |<իմմէ>]իմէ M287: hapl | յարքայէ V280 | զկերակուրդ] + զայդ V280' | տրտմագդջն M287' M9116]-գոյնս rel | զհասակակցացն V280 | զլխապարտ] om J1925ᵗˣᵗ | առաջի M287] om rel

¹¹դանիէդ M178 | ցամալասադ WN11ցամադեսադ M9116 | ներքինապետն] -պետին M178-M346-M2585 | դանիելի M346 M4114 M182'' -իեղի M178 | Անանիա - fin]ընկերաց նորին V280 |

ցեալ էր ներքինապետն ի վերայ Դանիէլի և Անանիա և Միսայելի և Ազարիայի ¹² «ադէ, փորձեա զծառայս քո աւուրս տասն և տացեն մեզ ունդս և կերիցուք և ջուր արբցուք. ¹³ և երևեսցին գոյնք մեր առաջի քո և գոյնք մանկանց որ ուտեն զսեղան թագաւորին. և, որպէս տեսանիցես, այնպէս արասջիր ընդ ծառայս քո»: ¹⁴ և անսաց նոցա և փորձեաց զնոսա աւուրս տասն: ¹⁵ և յետ կատարելոյ աւուրցն տասանց երևեցան երեսք նոցա նմա բարիք և հզաւրք մարմնով քան զամենայն մանկունսն որ ուտէին զսեղան թագաւորին: ¹⁶ և առնոյր ամեղասապ զրնթրիս նոցա և զգինի ըմպելոյ նոցա և տայր ունդ չորեցունց մանկանցն: ¹⁷ և ետ նոցա Աստուած իմաստութիւն և հանճար յամենայն դպրութեան և իմաստութեան, և Դանիէլ իխելամուտ էր ամենայն տեսլեան և երազոց: ¹⁸ և յետ կատարածի աւուրցն հրաման ետ թագաւորն ածել զնոսա, և ած

անանիայի M4834 M346-M2585 J1925 M351 | միսայելի M4834 WN11-M2585 M2627 -եղի V280 M178 | ազարիա WN11 J1925 -իայ V280 M178 M9116-M2627' M182'' -հայի M4834 M346-M2585

¹² ադէ]ադեա J M4834 ասէ M346'| ծառայքս V280 | տացեն] տացին V280 տացես M2627 տացգեն M2585: ditt տուր J1925 | կերիցիք J1925 | և 3°⊃13 և 1° V280' | և արբցուք M4114

¹³ գոյնք մեր/առաջի քո M287'] tr rel | գոյնք 2°] գոյն V1508 գոյնքթ M4834 | զսեղան] ի սեղան WN11 ի սեղանոյ M2585 | այնպէս] om V280' J1925'-M2627' M182'' | արասցես M346'-M2585 M2627 | ծառայքս M4834

¹⁴ նոցա] + ամեղասադ V280 | փորձեաց] փորեաց J1925*| յաւուրս M4114

¹⁵ յաւուրցն M4114 | երևեցան] pr և M4834 | բարուք M9116 բարիոք M4834| հզաւր M9116| մարմնով] om V280 -նով p M4834 J1925 | զմանկունս M4834 | զոր M351 | զսեղանս M178-M346 ի սեղանոյ WN11

¹⁶ ամեղասադ M9116 | ունդ M287]ունդս rel pr նոցա V280 M178 (vid) J1925

¹⁷ աստուած նոցա M346 | իննաստութիւն] pr չնորիս և J1925: cf v 9 | դպրութիւն J1925 | իմաստութիւն J1925 | էր իխելամուտ V280 իմնուտ էր J1925 | յամենայն M351 | տեսլեանց J1925 | և ult] om M178-M346' V1508 | երազոյ M346'

¹⁸ կատարածի] կատարման V280 | երից աւուրցն V280 |

զնոսա ներքինապետն առաջի Նաբուքոդոնոսորա: ¹⁹ և իսաւ-
սեցաւ ընդ նոսա արքայն, և ոչ գտան յամենեսեան նման
Դանիէլի և Անանիայի և Միսայէլի և Ազարիայ. և կային առաջի
Թագաւորին: ²⁰ և յամենայնի բանի իմաստութեան և
գիտութեան զոր խնդրէր ի նոցանէ Թագաւորն գտանէր զնոսա
տասնապատիկ առաւել քան զամենայն զգէտս և զմոգս որ էին
ի Թագաւորութեան նորա:

ՏԵՍԻԼ ԵՐՐՈՐԴ

²¹ և եղև Դանիէլ մինչև <յամ մի> Կիւրոսի արքայի:

²:¹Յամի երկրորդի Թագաւորութեան իւրոյ տեսես երազ Նաբուքոդոնոսոր և յիմարեցաւ հոգի նորա և քուն հատաւ ի նմանէ: ² և

Թագաւորն] արքայ V280 | զնոսա 1°↩2° WN11* | առաջի] +
արքային V280

¹⁹արքայն] om V280 | և 2°] om M346' | գտաւ V280 M346' |
յամենեսեան M287] յամենայնի rel | դանիէլի M178-M2585
J1925'-M4114 M182'' | անանիայ M178 M9116-M2627' M182'' -իա
WN11 | ազարիա (-իաի M346) և միսայէլի M346' | միսայէլի
M178-M2585 J1925'-M2627' M182'' | և Ազարիաի] om V280 |
ազարիայ M178 M9116-M2627' M182'' -իայի M4834 M2585
J1925 | կացին WN11

²¹ յամենայնի M287' M182] զամենայն V280 յամենայն rel |
բան M4834 M346' J1925' բանս M2585 M2627' M182' |
գիտութիւն J1925 | Թագաւորն] + M178 | տասնապատիկ
գտանէր զնոսա M178 | զամենայն] om V280 | զգէտս M4834
J1925'-M2627' M182'' | մոգս J1925'-M4114 |

superscript. Տեսիլ երրորդ] + Դանիէլի երազ M4834
²¹ om tot vers V280 | դանիէղ M178 | <յամ մի> ed] յամ ի
M287 M9116 յամին J1925 յամս M4834 M178-M346-M2585
M2627' M182'' ամս WN11 | կիրոսի J1925

¹ pr երազն ահագին V280 | Յամի M287 M346'] և յամին
V280 յամին rel | երրորդի J1925-M2627 երկրորդ M346 |
Թագաւորութեան իւրոյ] om WN11* | Նաբուգոդոնոսոր V280
M346 J1925 | և 1° M287'' J1925-M2627' M182''] pr արքայ rel
²ասաց] ասէ M9116-M4114 M182'' իրաման եւս V280 հրամ-

ասաց Թագաւորն կոչել զգէտս և զմոգս և զկախարդս և զբաղ-
դեայս պատմել Թագաւորին զերազ իւր. և եկին կացին առաջի
Թագաւորին: ³ և ասէ ցնոսա Թագաւորն «երազ տեսի և յիմարեցաւ ոգի իմ խելամուտ լինել երազոյն»: ⁴ և խաւսեցան քաղդեայքն ընդ Թագաւորին ասորերէն «արքա յաւիտեան կեաց.
ասա դու զերազն ծառայից քոց և զմեկնութիւնն նոր ասասցուք»: ⁵ պատասխանի ետ արքա և ասէ ցքաղդեայսն բանն վերացաւ յինէն. արդ եթէ ոչ ցուցանէք ինձ զերազն և զմեկնութիւն նորա, ի կորուստ լինիցիք և <տունք> ձեր յաւար լինիցին:
⁶ Ապա թէ զերազն և զմեկնութիւն նորա ցուցանէք ինձ, պարգևս և տուրս բազումս և պատիւս առնուցուք լինէն, բայց միայն
զերազն և զմեկնութիւնն նորա պատմեցէք ինձ: ⁷ Պատասխանի ետուն կրկին անգամ և ասեն «ասասցէ արքայ
զերազն ծառայից քոց և զմեկնութիւն նորա պատմեսցուք»:
⁸Պատասխանի ետ արքայն և ասէ «ճշմարտիւ գիտեմ եթէ
ժամանակաշ լինիք զի տեսէք եթէ բանն վերացաւ լինէն: ⁹ Արդ,
եթէ զերազն ոչ պատմեցէք ինձ, գիտեմ զի բան սուտ և զեղծու-

մայեաց J1925 |կոչել] կոչեցէք M9116-M4114 M182''|զամենայն
զգէտս (զէտս M346'-M2585) V280 M178-M346'-M2585 M351
զբ_ողեայս M346' M9116-M4114 | Թագաւորին 1°] արքայի V280 |
կային M9116

⁴ քողեայքն WN11 M9116-M4114 քաղդեայն V1508 |
Թագաւորին] Թագաւորն J1925 | ասորերէն] + և ասեն V280 |
արքա-դու] ասասցէ արքայ V280: cf v 7 | ասա] ասու M178 |
զերազն քո M4834 J1925 | քոց]իւրոց V280

⁵ արքա] Թագաւորն V280 | զքաղդեացիսն WN11 | յինին
V280 | ցուցանէք M287''] ցուցանիցէք rel | զերազ իմ ինձ V280 |
<տունք>]տունն M287 | լիցին V280 լինիչիք M346'-M2585

⁶ զերազն 1°] + իմ V280 |ցուցանէք M287 M346-M2585] ցու-
ցէք WN11 ցուցանիցէք rel | և 2°] om WN11 | բազումս] om V280 |
պատիւ M4834

⁷ ետուն] + քաղդեայքն (քողեայքն WN11) M346' | կրկին և
ասեն անգամ WN11* | պատմեսցուք] ասասցուք V280 J1925 |

⁸ լինիցիք V280' | բանս J1925

⁹ զերազն 1°] + իմ V280 | պատմեցէք M4834 M346 M2627

ցանելի միաբանեալ էք ասել առաջի իմ մինչև ժամանակն
անցցէ. ասացէք ինձ զերազն իմ և գիտացից եթէ և զմեկնութիւն
նորա պատմելոց էք ինձ: ¹⁰ Պատասխանի ետուն քաղդեայքն
առաջի Թագաւորին և ասեն «ոչ գոյ մարդ ի վերայ երկրի որ
զբան Թագաւորի կարող է ցուցանել, զի ամենայն Թագաւոր մեծ
և իշխան բան զայդպիսի ոչ հարցանէ զգէտ և գմոգ և զքաղդեայ.
¹¹ զի բանդ զոր արքա հարցանէ ծանր է և այլոք չիք որ պատմիցէ
զայդ առաջի արքայի բայց եթէ դիքն որոց ոչ է բնակութիւն ի
մէջ ամենայն մեղեցաց»: ¹² Յայնժամ Թագաւորն
սրտմտութեամբ և բարկութեամբ բազմաւ ասաց կոտորել
զամենայն իմաստունս Բաբելացւոց: ¹³ և հրաման ել և
իմաստունքն կոտորէին. խնդրեցին զԴանիէլ և զբարեկամս
նորա սպանանել: ¹⁴ Յայնժամ Դանիէլ խաւսեցաւ խորհուրդ և
խրատ ընդ Արիովքա դահճապետի արքային որ ելեալ կոտորէր

պատմէք WN11 M9116-M4114 | և 1°] om M9116-M4114 |
երծանելի V280 անգեղծուցանելի J1925* | արդ ասացէք V280 |
զերազն իմ ինձ V280 | ինձ 2°] om M4114 | իմ 2°] om 346' | եթէ
2°] զի J1925 | և 3°] om V280' WN11 M351

¹⁰ ետուն 1°] + մի անգամ WN11 + միւս անգամ rel (tr post
քաղդեայքն M2627) | քաղդեացիք V1508 | առաջի Թագաւորին]
om J1925: cf v 7 | Թագաւորին] արքայի V280 | կարող է զբան
Թագաւորի J1925 | բան զայդ J1925 զայսպիսի բան V280 | զգէտ
M287 J1925'-M4114 M182''] զգէտս rel | գմոգ M287 J1925'-M4114
M182''] գմոգս rel | զքաղդեայ (զքադեայ M9116) M287 J1925'-
M4114 M182''] զքադդեայս rel

¹¹ զի] om V280 | բանս M346 | պատմեսցէ V280 WN11 J1925
| առաջի] om J1925 | որ ոչ է բնակութիւն նոցա J1925 որոց
բնակութիւն (-թիւնք M346) չէ M178-M346'-M2585 որոյ ոչ է
բնակութիւն J1925

¹² բարկութեամբ և սրտմտութեամբ M9116-M4114 M182''|
ասաց] հրամայեաց V280 M178-M346 | բաբեղացւոց V280 M178
բաբեղացոց WN11

¹³ խնդրեցին] pr և WN11ᶜ և խնդրէին M2627' M182''|
զդանիէդ M178 և զդանիէլ V280 J1925

¹⁴ խօսեցաւ Դանիէլ V280 | խորհուրդ և խրատ] om V280 |
Արիովք ը J1925 -քայ M2585 M9116-M2627' M182''| դահճապետ
V280 | որ—15 ասէ] om V280 | ելեալ (եկեալ M346) էր կոտորել

զիմաստունս Բաբելացւոց: ¹⁵ Եհարց նա և ասէ ցիշխանս Թագաւորին «վասն է՞ր եւ իրամանդ այդ խիստ յերեսաց Թագաւորի» և
յայտնեաց զբանն Արիովք Դանիէլի: ¹⁶ և Դանիէլ եմուտ
աղաչեաց զարքայն զի տացէ նմա ժամ և զմեկնութիւն նորա
պատմեսցէ Թագաւորին: ¹⁷ և եմուտ Դանիէլ ի տուն իւր և
Անանիա և Ազարիա և Միսայէլ և բարեկամաց իւրոց եցոյց
զբանն: ¹⁸ և խնդրեին զգութիւն յԱստուծոյ երկնից զի մի կորի-
ցէ Դանիէլ և բարեկամք իւր ընդ այլ իմաստունս Բաբելացւոց:
¹⁹ Ցայնժամ Դանիէլի ի տեսլեան գիշերոյ յայտնեցաւ խոր-
հուրդն և աւրհնեաց զԱստուած երկնից Դանիէլ ²⁰և ասէ «եղիցի

M346-WN11* J1925 I բաբեղացւոց V280 M178 բաբեւացոց WN11
pr Թագաւորին M347-M2585 I fin M287 M346-WN11*-M2585
M2627]+իշխան Թագաւորին rel
¹⁵ եհարց—ասէ] om J1925' I եհարց M287 M2585 M2627'
M182''] pr և rel I նա M287]զնա rel I Թագաւորին M287 J1925]
արքայի rel I յայտար. դանիէլի զբանն M4834 I զբանն] om
V280 I արիովդ J1925 արիոք M4114 I դանիէլդի M178 -ելի M2585
M9116-M2627' V1508-M351
¹⁶ և 1°] om WN11* I Դանիէլ] om WN11* արիովք V280 pr
ասէ M178-M346-M2585 M2627' M182'' I եմուտ առաչեաց] եմ. և
առաչ. V280' J1925' մուտ և աղաչեա rel I զի] pr բանիւն
դանիէլդի V280 I տաijցեն M4834
¹⁷ և 1°] om M2627 I Անանիա—եցոյց] եցոյց բարեկամաց
իւրոց անանիայի և ազարիայի և միսայէղի V280 I Անանիա
M287 WN11] -հայ M9116-M2627' M182'' -հայի rel I Ազարիա
M287 J1925] -հայ M9116-M4114' M182'' -հայի (-հաի M346) rel I
Միսայէլ M287ᵗˣᵗ] -ելի M4114 M182'-ելի (-աելի M346') rel I և 5°
M287] om rel I եցոյց] յայտնեաց M178-M346'
¹⁸ խնդրեցին M346': cf v 13 I հարցէին V280 I յաստուծոյ
(ատ. WN11) երկնից զգութիւն (զգթ. M2585) M178-M346'-M2585
I զգթութիւն M2627 I յերկնից V280' J1925-M4114 I կորիցի
M178-WN11 I դանիէղ M178 I բարեկամք] եղբարք V280 I
բաբեղացւոց V280 M178-M2585 բաբեւացոց (-էւացոց M2627)
M346' M2627
¹⁹ յայտ. ի տեսլեան գիշերոյ խորհ. դանիէլի V280 I
դանիէղդի M178-M346 -ելի M9116-M4114 M182'' I ի 1°] om WN11*:
hapl I և 1°] om V280 I դանիէլ (-իէդ M178) զած երկ. M178-M346' I
երկնից] om V280 I Դանիէլ] om J1925
²⁰ եղեցի J1925 I ի յաւիտենից M287'] յայաւմհետէ V280

անուն Տեառն աւրհնեալ ի յաւիտենից մինչև յաւիտեանս, զի
իմաստութիւն և հանճար և զաւրութիւն նորա է: 21 և նա փո-
փոխէ զժամանակս և զժամս, կացուցանէ զԹագաւորս և փո-
փոխէ, տա իմաստութիւն իմաստնոց և խորհուրդ խորհրդա-
կանաց: 22 ինքն յայտնէ զխորինս և զզաղտնիս գիտէ որ կա ի
խաւարի, և լոյս ընդ նմա է: 23 Զքէն, Աստուած հարցն մերոց,
գոհանամ և աւրհնեմ, զի իմաստութիւն զաւրութիւն ետուր ինձ.
և ծանուցեր ինձ որ ինչ աղաւթիւք խնդրեցաք մեք ի քէն, և
զտեսիլ Թագաւորին ցուցեր ինձ»: 24 և եմուտ Դանիէլ առ
Արիովք զոր կացուցեալ էր Թագաւորին կորուսանել զիմաստունս Բաբելովնի, և ասէ ցնա «զիմաստունս Բաբելացւոց մի
կոտորեր, բայց զիս տար առաջի Թագաւորին և ես պատմեցից
զմեկնութիւն Թագաւորին»: 25 Յայնժամ Արիովք փութապէս

յաւիտ. rel | յաւիտեան V280ʹ M178-M2585 M9116 (գյաւ. M4834)
| զաւրութիւն և հանճար WN11
21 փոփոխէ 1°] փոփոխեացէ J1925 | զժամս և զժամանակս
V280 J1925-M2627| և զժամս] om WN11* + և M351 | զիմաստու-
թիւնս M178-M346-M2585 | ամենայն իմաստնոց WN11 |
խորհուրդս V280ʹզխորհ. M178-M346ʹ-M2585 M2627
22 զխորս V280 M9116 | զզաղտն. WN11 | որ կա ի խաւարի
գիտէ (գիտեր WN11*) M178-M346-WN11*-M2585 | նմա] նման
M178 | է M287ʹ M346-M2585 M2627ʹ] om rel
23 որ] զոր V280 | խնդրեցաք մեք ի քէն աղաւթիւք V280 |
ցուցեր]ծանուցեր M2627
24 և 1°] om V280 | դանիէդ M178 | արիովդ J1925 արիգովք
WN11* արիօք WN11ᶜ M4114 | զորս J1925 | Թագաւորին 1°] Թա-
գաւորն J1925 արքայի V280 | զիմաստունս 1°] om WN11*զիմաս-
տուն WN11ᶜ պ ր մի կորուսաներ V280 | Բաբելովնի M287 M9116]-
նի M4834 M346 -եղովնի M178-WN11-M2585 -լացւց rel | և 2°-
Բաբելացւց] om V280 J1925 | ասաց V1508 | բաբեղացւց M178-
լացոց WN11 բաբելոնի M4834 | մի կոտորեր] om V280 | այլ
տար զիս V280 | Թագաւորին 2°և3° M9116 | ես] om V280 | զմեկ-
նութիւն երագոյ M4834 | Թագաւորին 2°] արքայի V280 | զմեկ-
նութիւն Թագաւորին] նմա զերազն և զմեկնութիւն նորա V280
25 տարաւ արիովք փութապէս V280 | Թագաւորին]
արքայի V280: cf v 24 | ցնա] om J1925 | իրեաստանի M4114 -իս
V280 | զմեկնութիւնն] + երագոյն V280 զպատմութիւնս J1925 |
պատմեացէ] մեկնէ J1925

տարաւ զԴանիէլ առաջի Թագաւորին. և ասէ ցնա «գտի այր մի
յորդւոց գիտութեանն Հրէաստանի որ զմեկնութիւնն պատմեացէ արքայի»: ²⁶ Պատասխանի ետ Թագաւորն և ասէ ցԴա-
նիէլ որոյ անուն է Բաղտասար եթէ «կարո՞դ ես պատմել զերա-
զըն զոր տեսի և զմեկնութիւն նորա»: ²⁷ Պատասխանի ետ
Դանիէլ առաջի Թագաւորին և ասէ «զխորհուրդ զայդ զոր արքա
հարցանէ ոչ է իմաստնոց և մոգուց և <գիտաց> և <ողձից>
պատմել առաջի արքայի, ²⁸ այլ զոյ Աստուած յերկինս որ յայտնէ զխորհուրդս, և եցոյց Նաբուքոդոնոսորա արքայի որ ինչ
լինելոց է յաւուրս յետինս. երագն և տեսիլ գլխոյ քո յանկողնի
քո այս է: ²⁹ Արքա, խորհուրդք քո մտայոյզ առնեին զքեզ յանկողնի քում եթէ զինչ լինելոց է: ³⁰ և ինձ ոչ առ իմաստութեան
ինչ որ իցէ յիս քան յամենայն կենդանիս յայտնեցաւ խոր-
հուրդն այլ վասն ցուցանելոյ արքայի զմեկնութիւնն զի
ծանիցես զխորհուրդս սրտի քո: ³¹ Դու, արքա տեսանեիր և

---

²⁶ Թագաւորն] արքայ V280 ⏐ զդանիէզդ M178 ⏐ որոյ M178''
M9116'-M4114] որում rel ⏐ է M287] om M9116-M4114 էի rel ⏐
բաղդասար V280 M346 ⏐ եթէ] բա V280 ⏐ ես (+ ինձ M346) M287'
M346] իցես rel ⏐ զերազն M287 M346] + իմ V280 pr ինձ rel
²⁷ առաջի 1°] om J1925 ⏐ զայդ] om V280 ⏐ զոր] որ M4834 ⏐
հարցանէ արքայ V280 ⏐ մոգաց J1925 ⏐ և 3°] om M346'-WN11*⏐
<գիտաց>] զէտաց M287 դիտաց J1925 զիտնոց M178 om M346-
WN11*⏐<ողձից>] դձից M287
²⁸ զխորհուրդս J1925 ⏐ Նաբուքոդոնոսորա M287 WN11]
Նաբուք. M346 (-րայ V280) -սոր J1925 -սորայ rel ⏐ որ 2°] զոր
V280 ⏐ է 1°] էր J1925 ⏐ քո յանկողնի] om M178 ⏐ յանկողնի քո]
om V280 M346-WN11*-M2585 ⏐ քո 2° M287 J1925] քում rel
²⁹ խորհուրդ V280 WN11: hapl ⏐ մտայոյզք M9116 ⏐ առնեին
J1925 ⏐ յնկողնի քո tr ante քո J1925 ⏐ է 1°] իցէ M4834 M178-
M2585 M9116-M2627'⏐է 2°] իցէ M4834 J1925
³⁰ իցէ] ինձ է J1925 ⏐ քան թէ V280'⏐ զմեկնութիւն նորա
V280 ⏐ զխորհուրդ V280 J1925: hapl ⏐ սրտի քո] մտաց քոց M2585
M2627
³¹ մեծ] om M351 ⏐ պատկեր 2° M287' WN11ᵐᵍ M9116-M4114
M182'] om rel ⏐ երեսս J1925 ⏐ յոյժ ահաւոր էր V280 ⏐ յոյժ 2°] om
J1925'

ահա պատկեր մի մեծ պատկեր, և երեսք նորա և տեսիլ նորա
ահագին յոյժ և կայր առաջի քո, ահաւոր էր յոյժ ³² պատկերն
որոյ գլուխն յոսկոյ սրբոյ, ձեռք և լանջք և բազուկք իւր
արձաթիք, մէջք և բարձք պղնձիք ³³ և սրունք երկաթիք և ոտքն
կէս յերկաթոյ և կէս ի խեցոյ: ³⁴ <Հայեիր> մինչև հատաւ վէմ
առանց ձեռին և եհար զպատկերն ի վերայ երկաթեղէն և
խեցեղէն ոտիցն և մանրեաց զնոսա ի սպառ ³⁵ Յայնժամ առ
հասարակ մանրեցան խեցին և երկաթն և պղինձն <և ար-
ձաթն> և ոսկին և եղեն իբրև զփոշի կալոյ ամարային[*ոյ*] և առ
զնոսա սաստկութիւն հողմոյ և տեղի ոչ գտանէր նոցա. և վէմ
որ եհար զպատկերն եղև լեառն մեծ և ելից զամենայն երկիր:
³⁶ Այս է երազն և զմեկնութիւն նորա ասասցուք առաջի արքայի:
³⁷ Դու ես, արքա, արքայից, արքա, որում Աստուած երկնից Թագաւորութիւն հզաւր և հաստատուն և պատուական ետ ³⁸ և ընդ
ամենայն տեղիս որ բնակեալ են որդիք մարդկան, զգազանս
վայրի և զթռչունս երկնից և զձկունս ծովու ետ ի ձեռս քո, և
կացոյց զքեզ Տէր ամենայնի: Դու ես գլուխն ոսկի ³⁹ և զկնի
քո կայցէ այլ Թագաւորութիւն խոնարհագոյն քան զքեզ և

³² յոսկո WN11 | ձեռք] pr և V280 J1925 + իւր M346 | իւր]
om J1925 | մէջք] pr և M346'-M2585 + նորա V1508

³³ ի յերկաթոյ V280 երկաթո WN11

³⁴ init] pr և V280 | <հայեիր>] հայեի M287 | ձեռին] +
մարդոյ M2627 | զնոսա]զնա M4834

³⁵ պղինձէն WN11 | մանրեցաւ J1925|<և արձաթն>] և եր-
կաթն M287*(om M287ᶜ) | և 4°] om V280 |կալոց M287ᶜ M178-WN11
M9116-M2627' |ամարայնոյ]մանրելոյ J1925 | զնոսա]զնա
J1925 տեղի]տեսիլ J1925 | գտանէին V280 | ամենայն WN11

³⁶ երազն արքայի V280 | արքայի քո V280 M346-WN11*

³⁷ Դու] pr արքայ V280 pr գլուխն M4834: ex 38 | զԹա-
գաւորութիւն M346 | հզաւր] om M178-M346'| և 1°] om V280
M178-M346' J1925'-M4114 M182''| հաստատուն]հաստատ M178
om V280 J1925'-M4114 M182''| ետ]tr ante [Թագ. M178-M346' |

³⁸ և 1°]om M346'-M2585 | որ M287'] ուր rel | որդիք] pr ամե-
նայն WN11 ուռք M4114 | վայրի]վայրենիս J1925 | զտէր J1925

³⁹ այլ] om M2627 | պղինձ] + և V280 | երկիր WN11

Թագաւորութիւն երրորդ որ է պղինձ տիրեսցէ ամենայն երկրի
40 և Թագաւորութիւն չորրորդ հզաւր իբրև զերկաթ. զոր արինակ երկաթ մանրէ և մալէ զամենայն, նոյնպէս մանրեսցէ և
մալեսցէ զամենայն: 41 Եւ զի տեսանէիր զոտսն և զմատունսն,
կէս կողմն ի խեցոյ և կէս կողմն յերկաթոյ, Թագաւորութիւն
բաժանեալ լիցի և յարմատոց երկաթոյն եղիցի ի նմա: Զոր
արինակ տեսանէիր զերկաթն ընդ խեցին խառնեալ 42 և
մատունք ոտիցն կողմն մի յերկաթոյ և կողմն մի ի խեցոյ, մի
կողմն Թագաւորութեանն հզաւր կացցէ և ի նմանէ եղիցի
ջախջախին: 43 Եւ զի տեսանէիր զերկաթն ընդ խեցին խառնեալ,
եղիցին խառնեալ ի զաւակէ մարդկան և ի միմեանս ոչ
<խառնեսցին>, զոր արինակ ոչ խառնի երկաթ ընդ խեցի: 44 Եւ
յաւուրս Թագաւորացն այնոցիկ յարուսցէ Աստուած երկնից Թագաւորութիւն որ յաւիտեան ոչ եղծանիցի և Թագաւորութիւն
նորա ազգի այլում ոչ մնասցէ. մանրեսցէ և հոսեսցէ զամենայն
Թագաւորութիւնս և ինքն կացցէ յաւիտեանս: 45 Որպէս տեսա-

40 և 2°→3° V280 | նոյնպէս] այնպէս M346
41 զի] om J1925 | ի խեցոյ] յերկաթոյ (ի յերկ. M4114) ի
խեցւոյ M2585 M2627' M182'' | կողմն 2°] om M2627 | յերկաթոյ] ի
յերկ. M9116 ի խեցոյ M2585 M4114 M182'' | եղեցի J1925 | ի 2°]
om WN11 M9116-M4114 | զոր] pr զի M178-M2585 J1925 pr և
M346' | տեսանէիր 2°] + ի նմայ M4834 | խեցոյն M346' J1925 |
խառնեալ] + ի նմա V280
42 մատունս WN11 | կողմն 1°] կող V280 | ի 1°] ընդ M2627:
cf v 41 | Թագաւորութիւն V280 M346' | կացէ WN11 : hapl | և 3°]
om WN11 + մին M178-M346'-M2585 | եղիցին J1925
43 և 1°] om M9116-M4114 M182'' | եղեցին J1925 եղիցի V280'
M346 | խառն M178 | մարդկանէ M287*-M4834 M178-M2585 |
<խառնեսցին> M178-M346-M2585] յարեսցին (-իցին M9116)
M287'' J1925'-M2627 յարիցեն rel | չխառնի M2585 | խառնիցի
M9116 | խեցի] + ի միմեանս — fin: ditt WN11-M2585 M4114 M182'
44 յաւուր M346-WN11* | Թագաւորացն]-ութեանցն M2585 |
յերկնից V280' WN11 J1925 | Թագաւորութիւն 1°] + նոր M346 +
նորա WN11 | յաւիտեան M287 M346 J1925'-M2627]-տեևական
WN11 -տեևից V280 -տեաևս rel | յայլում M178 | կացցէ] կեցցէ
V280 J1925 | յաւիտեան V280 M351
45 որպէս] pr և V280 | և զպղինձն M4834 WN11-M2585

նեիր զի ի լեռնէ հատաւ վէմ առանց ձեռին և մանրեաց զիւեցի և
զերկաթն, զպղինձն և զարծաթն և զոսկին: Աստուած մեծ եցոյց
արքայի որ ինչ լինելոց էր առ յապա և ճշմարիտ է երազն և
հաւատարիմ մեկնութիւն նորա»: [48] Յայնժամ արքա Նաբուքոդոնոսոր անկաւ ի վերայ երեսաց և երկիր եպագ Դանիէլի և
զոհս և խունկս անոյշութեան հրամայեաց մատուցանել նորա:
[47] Պատասխանի ետ Թագաւորն և ասէ գԴանիէլ «արդարն
Աստուածն ձեր նա է աստուած աստուծոց և տէր տերանց և
Թագաւոր Թագաւորաց որ յայտնէ զխորհուրդս, զի յայտնել
կարացեր զխորհուրդդ զայդ»: [48] Եւ մեծացոյց Թագաւորն զԴանիէլ
և պարգևս մեծամեծս և բազումս ետ նմա և կացոյց զնա ի
վերայ աշխարհին Բաբելացւոց և իշխան նախարարացն և ի
վերայ ամենայն իմաստոցն Բաբելացւոց: [49] Եւ Դանիէլ
խնդրեաց յարքայէն և կացոյց ի վերայ գործոց աշխարհին
Բաբելացւոց զՍեդրաք Միսաք և զԱբեդնագով, և Դանիէլ էր ի
դրան արքային:

M2627 | պղինձն M4114 | աստուած իմ M4834 | մեծ] om M4834
M9116-M2627 | զոր V280 M346 | էր M287]իցէ J1925 է rel | առ ի
յապա J1925 | հաւատարիմ է J1925

[46] նաբուգոդոնոսոր V280 M346 J1925 նաբnք. WN11 |
երեսաց իւրող V280' M346' J1925-M4114 M182'' | դանիէղի M178
-ելի M346 M4114 V1508 | խունկս և M9116

[47] գդանիէղ M178 | արդարն M287] արդար rel | ձեր] քո
V280 | նա] om J1925 | և 2°] om WN11 զխորհուրդս] + սիրողաց
իւրող V280 | և 3°] om WN11

[48] բազում M351 | Բաբելացւոց 1°] բաբեդացւոց V280 M178
-լացւոց WN11 M4114 | նախարարաց իւրող V280 | Բաբելացւոց
2°] բաբեդացւոց V280 M178 -լացոց WN11-M2585 J1925

[49] գործոյ J1925-M2627 | աշխարհին] արքային V280 |
բաբեդացւոց V280 M178 -լացոց WN11 բաբելացւոց M182 Միսաք]
om WN11* զմիսաք V280' M2585 | դանիէղ M178 | էր ի] om M178 |
դրունս WN11 | արքային] արքունի V280' M2585 M2627

³·¹ Յամին ութուտասաներորդի Նաբուքողոնոսոր արքայ արար պատկեր ոսկի. բարձրութիւն նորա վաթսուն կանգուն և լայնութիւն նորա կանգուն վեց և կանգնեաց զնա ի դաշտին Դեհերա յաշխարհին Բաբելացւոց։ ² և արձակեաց ժողովել զաւրավարս և զաւրագլուխս և զկուսակալս, զպետս և զբռնաւորս և զգործակալս և զամենայն իշխանս աշխարհաց գալ ի նաւակատիս պատկերին զոր կանգնեաց արքայն Նաբուքողոնոսոր։ ³ և ժողովեցան կուսակալք, զաւրավարք և զաւրագլուխք, պետք և բռնաւորք, մեծամեծք, գործակալք և ամենայն իշխանք աշխարհաց գալ ի նաւակատիս պատկերին զոր կանգնեաց արքայ Նաբուքողոնոսոր և կային առաջի պատկերին զոր կանգնեաց Նաբուքողոնոսոր։ ⁴ և քարոզն կարդայր զաւրութեամբ և ասէր «ձեզ ասի ազգք և ազինք և լեզուք, ⁵ յորժամ

superscript. Կանգնումն պատկերին կրող V280
3:1 ութնուտասաներորդի M4114 | Նաբուքողոնոսոր M287 WN11]-սորա M178 J1925 -սորայ (Նաբուք. V280 M346) rel | արքայ M287] արքայի (-քայ WN11) rel | վացսուն M178 | կանգուն 1°] -գունք M178 | կանգուն 2°] -գունք M4834 M178 J1925 M2627 -գունս M9116 | ի] om WN11 | Դեհերա M287 WN11] դեերա (-րայ J1925) M4834 J1925 դեհերայ (դահ. V280) V280 M178-M346 M4114 դեերայ rel | բաբելացոց WN11 J1925
² ժողովեաց J1925 | զաւրավարս M287] զգաւր. rel | և 2°] om J1925 | զաւրագլուխս M287] զգաւր. rel | և 3°] om V280 M2585 J1925 | և զպետս V280 | աշխարհին V280 | Նաբուք.→3 Նաբուք. 1° M2627 | նաբրքողոնոսոր WN11 նաբուզ. V280 M346 J1925
³ և զաւրավարք M4834 M346'-M2585 | մեծամեծք] pr և M178-M346 J1925-M2627 M182 | և գործակալ ք V280 M2585 | գալ] om V280 նաբուք. 1°→2° V280 J1925 | Նաբուքողոնոսոր 1°] նաբրք. WN11 նաբուզ. V280 M346 J1925 | կացին M2627 | կանգնեաց M287' M2627] + արքայն rel | Նաբուքողոնոսոր 2°] նաբրք. WN11 նաբուզ. M346 M9116
⁴ ազգ V280' M346'
⁵ լսէք WN11 | տեսանիցէք J1925 | զսրրնկի V280 | զթմբկի V280 J1925 | և 1°] om M2627 | բնարի M178-WN11 M2627' M182'' | տաւղի] զտաւղի V280' M2585 J1925 pr և M4834 V1508 | միաբանութեանց J1925 | անկանիցէք M2627 | արքայ նաբ. M287 J1925] tr rel | նաբուզգողոնոսոր V280 J1925'

լսիցէք զձայն փողոյ, սրնկի, թմբկի, և զքնարի, տաւղի և զեր-
զոց միաբանութեան և զամենայն ազգաց արուեստակա՛նաց,
անկանիչիք և երկիր պագանիչիք պատկերին զոր կանգնեաց
արքայ Նաբուքոդոնոսոր: [6] Եւ որ ոչ անկեալ երկիր պագանիցէ ի
նմին ժամու ընկեսցի ի հնոց հրոյն բորբոքելոյ»: [7] Եւ եղև իբրև
լուան ազգք զձայն փողոյն, զսրնգին և զտաւղին և զնուա-
գարանացն և զամենայն ազգաց արուեստակա՛նաց, անկանէին
ամենայն ազգն և ազինքն և լեզուքն և երկիր պագանէին
պատկերին ոսկոյ զոր կանգնեաց արքա Նաբուքոդոնոսոր:
[8] Յայնժամ մատեան արք Քաղդեացիք և եղեն չարախաւս զՀրե-
իցն [9] առ Նաբուքոդոնոսոր արքա և ասեն «արքա յաւիտեան
կաց: [10] Դու հրաման ետուր ամենայն մարդոյ որ լսիցէ զձայն
փողոյ, սրնկի, զտաւղի և զնուագարանաց և զամենայն ազգաց
արուեստակա՛նաց [11] և որ ոչ անկեալ երկիր պագցէ պատկերին
ոսկոյ անկցի ի հնոց հրոյն բորբոքելոյ: [12] Արդ են ասա արք
Հրեայք զորս կացուցեր ի վերայ գործոց աշխարհիս <Բաբելաց-
ւոց>, Սեդրաք, Միսաք և ԱբեթՆագով որ ոչ հնազանդեցան հրա-

---

[6] անկեալ J1925: bis scr | ժամի WN11* | ընկեսցի] անկա-
նիցի WN11 անկցի V280' M178-M346-M2585 J1925: cf v 11

[7] ազգն M4834 M346' | սրնգի J1925 սըրրնկի WN11 սրնկի
M346 | և 2° M287'] om rel | զտաւղի] տաւղի M346' pr զթմբկի
M2627 + և զքնարին V280 | ամենայն] om V280 | ազգն M287
M346'] ազգքն rel | և ազինք] om WN11* | պատկերին] om J1925:
homoeotel | արքա] om V280 M2627 | Նաբուքոդոնոսոր WN11
Նաբուզ. V280 M346 J1925'

[8] մատեան] om M2585 | Քաղդեացիք M287' WN11 M2627'
M182']-դեացիք rel | չարախաւսք V280 J1925-M2627

[9] Նաբուքոդոնոսոր WN11 Նաբուզ. V280 M346 -սորայ M9116-
M4114 M182'' (-րա M4834) | արքա 1° M287 M2585] om rel | կաց
M287 J1925' M346'] կեաց rel |

[10] զոր WN11 | սրնկի M287 M346'] զսրնկի (pr և M9116 +
զթմբկի V280 M2627) rel | զտաւղի M287] pr զքնարի V280 M178
J1925-M2627 և զքն (քն. WN11) rel | և 1°] om V280 | նուագարա-
նաց V1508

[11] և 1°] զի J1925 | պագցէ M287 M351] -գանիցէ rel |
անկանիցի V280

[12] Հրեայք J1925-M4114 հրէեայք WN11 | զորս] զոր M9116 |

մանի քում, արքա, և գդիս քո ոչ պաշտեն և պատկերիդ ոսկոյ
զոր կանգնեցիր երկիր ոչ պագանեն»։ ¹³ Յայնժամ Նաբուքոդոնոսոր սրտմտութեամբ և բարկութեամբ հրամայեաց ածել
զՍեդրաք, Միսաք և զԱբեդնագով և ածին առաջի թագաւորին։
¹⁴ Պատասխանի ետ Նաբուքոդոնոսոր և ասէ ցնոսա թէ «արդարև Սեդրաք Միսաք և Աբեդնագով գդիս իմ ոչ պաշտիցէք և
պատկերի ոսկոյ զոր կանգնեցի երկիր ոչ պագանէք։ ¹⁵ Բայց արդ
թէ պատրաստ լինիցիք զի յորժամ լսիցէք զձայն փողոյ,
սրնկի և թմբկի և զքնարի և զմիաբանութեան ամենայն ազգաց արուեստականաց, անկանիցիք և երկիր պագանիցիք
պատկերին ոսկոյ զոր արարի, ապա թէ ոչ պագանիցէք երկիր, ի
նմին ժամու <անկանիցիք> ի հնոց հրոյն բորբոքելոյ և ով է
աստուած որ փրկեսցէ զքեզ ի ձեռաց իմոց»։ ¹⁶ Պատասխանի
ետուն Սեդրաք, Միսաք և Աբեդնագով և ասեն ցարքայ Նաբուգոդոնոսոր «ոչ ինչ է պիտոյ վասն բանիդ այդորիկ տալ քեզ պատասխանի ¹⁷ զի <է> մեր Աստուած յերկինս զոր մեք պաշտեմք.
կարող է փրկել զմեզ ի հնոցէդ հրոյ բորբոքելոյ և ի ձեռաց քոց,
արքա, ապրեցուսցէ զմեզ։ ¹⁸ապա թէ ոչ, այս յայտնի լիցի քեզ,
արքա, զի գդիս քո ոչ պաշտեմք և պատկերիդ ոսկոյ զոր կանգ-
նեցեր երկիր ոչ պագանեմք»։ ¹⁹ Յայնժամ Նաբուքոդոնոսոր լի

պագանիցիք M287] -անիչիք J1925 պագէք M2627 -անիցէք rel |
ոսկոյ M287' M2585 J1925] om rel | ապա—երկիր 2°] om J1925 |
<անկանիցիք>] անգանիցի M287 անգցիք M4114 | է] իցէ M2627 |
փրկեսցէ J1925 փրկէ V280 M182'
    ¹⁶ Սեդրաք M287' WN11 J1925'-M4114] -րաք rel | Միսաք
M287] -սաք V280 M346' J1925'-M4114 -սաք rel | Աբեդնագով]
աբեթ. M4834 -քով V280 -գո M4114 | նաբրոքոդոնոսոր WN11
նաբուգ. V280 J1925' | պիտոյ է (+ մեզ M4834) M4834 M178-M346
    ¹⁷ <է>] և M287 էր M4834 | երկինս M346 | հրոյ բորբոքելոյ]
om V280 | քոց] om V280 | արքա] om M4834 M346-WN11* M351 |
ապրեցուցանել M346'-M2585 J1925-M4114 M182''
    ¹⁸ այս M287] + ինչ rel | զի M287 WN11*] + մեք rel
    ¹⁹ նաբուքոդոնոսոր WN11 նաբուգ. V280 J1925' | սրտմտու-
թեամբ] բարկութեամբ V280 +և բարկութեամբ M4834 M178-

եղև սրտմտութեամբ և գոյն երեսաց նորա շրջեցաւ ի վերա
Սեդրագա, Միսաքա և Աբեդնագովի և ասէ «ջեռուցէք զհնոցն
եւթնապատիկ զի մինչև ի վախճան այրեսցին»: ²⁰ և արք հինգ
զաւրաւորք զաւրութեամբ կապեցեն զՍեդրաք, Միսաք և
զԱբեդնագով արկանել ի հնոց հրոյն բորբոքելոյ: ²¹ Յայնժամ
արքն այնորիկ կապեցան պատմուճանաւք վարտաւք և
արտախուրակաւք և զանկապանաւք իւրեանց և ընկեցան ի մէջ
հրոյն բորբոքելոյ: ²² Զի հրաման թագաւորին սաստկանայր և
հնոցն բորբոքէր առաւել եւթնապատիկ յոյժ: ²³ և երեքին նոքա Սեդրաք, Միսաք և Աբեդնագով անկան ի մէջ հնոցին կապեալք ²⁴ և գնային ի մէջ հրոյն, աւրհնէին և գովէին զՏէր
Աստուած: ²⁵ Յարեաւ Ազարիաս և եկաց յաղաւթս. այսպես
եբաց զբերան իւր ի մէջ հրոյն և ասէ: ²⁶ «Աւրհնեալ ես Տէր

M346'-M2585 | ի վերա] om WN11* | Սեդրագա M287] -գաj V280
M9116-M4114 -բա M4834 M346' J1925 -բաj rel | Միսաբա M287
(pr և WN11)| -բեա J1925 -գաj M9116-M4114 -բաj rel | Աբեդնա-
գով[ի]-բով[ի V280 -գоհ M4114 -բով[րա WN11աբեթ. M4834 J1925|
զհնոցն] + մինչև V280 | մինչ V280 | այրեսցի M346-WN11*
J1925-M2627
²⁰ կապեցեն M287 M2627 M182''] -եցին rel | սեդրագ V280
J1925'-M4114 -րակբ M4834 | միսագ V280 M2585 (զմիս. M346
M9116-M4114) | զաբեդնագով] զաբեթ. M4834 J1925 -բով V280
WN11-գоվ M4114
²¹ վարտաւք M287 M346' J1925-M2627] վարտեաւք (pr և
M9116 M182') rel | և 1°] om M4834 M346' M4114 M182''| և 2°
M287 M4114 M182] om rel | ընկեցան]անկան V280 | հրոյն M287
J1925] pr հնոցին rel
²² առաւել] om M346-WN11* tr post եւթնապատիկ M9116-
M4114 M182''
²³ երեքին M287'' M346' J1925'-M4114]-բեան rel | սեդրագ
V280 M2585 M9116|միսագ V280 M346-M2585 M9116-M4114 | և
2°] om M4834 M178 | աբեթնագով M4834 J1925 աբեդնաբով
V280 WN11 M2627 V1508 | անկանէին M2627 անկեալք J1925 |
հնոցին] հրոյն V280
²⁴ և 1°] om M2627 M182'' | զՏէր] om V280 M351
²⁵ Ազարիաս M287]-իաj V280' M346' J1925'-M2627 -իա rel|
և 1°] om M346-M2585 J1925 | կաց յաղоթս M9116-M4114-V1508-
M351(եկաց V280) | հրոյն] հնոցին J1925
²⁶ ես] + դու M2627 | <և >] om M287 | է] om WN11 | առաւել

Աստուած հարցն մերոց, գովեալ <և> փառաւորեալ է անուն քո
յաւիտեան. ²⁷ զի արդար ես յամենայնի զոր ածեր ի վերայ մեր և
ամենայն գործք քո ճշմարիտ են, և <ուղիղ> են ճանապարհք քո
և ամենայն դատաստանք քո ճշմարտութիւն: ²⁸ և իրաւունս
ճշմարտութեան արարեր ըստ ամենայնի զոր արարեր մեզ և
քաղաքի սրբոյ հարցն մերոյ երուսաղեմի, զի ճշմարտութեամբ
և յիրաւի ածեր զայս ամենայն վասն մեղաց մերոց: ²⁹ Զի մեղաք և անաւրինեցաք <ապստամբ> լինել ի քէն և առաւել մեղաք յամենայնի: ³⁰ և պատուիրանաց քոց ոչ անսացաք, ոչ պա-
հեցաք և ոչ արարաք որպէս պատուիրեցեր մեզ զի բարի լինիցի
մեզ: ³¹ և զամենայն զոր ածեր ի վերա մեր և զամենայն զոր
արարեր մեզ, արդար դատաստանաւ արարեր: ³² և մատնեցեր
զմեզ ի ձեռս թշնամեաց մերոց անաւրինաց, խստաց և
<ապստամբողաց> և թագաւորի անաւրինի և չարի քան զամե-
նայն երկիր: ³³ և արդ ոչ գոյ մեզ բանալ զբերանս մեր զի ամաւթ
և նախատինք եղաք ծառայից քոց և պաշտաւնեից: ³⁴ Այլ
մի մատներ զմեզ ի սպառ վասն անուան քո և մի ցրեր

փառաւորեալ J1925 | յաւիտեանս V280' M2585 M4114 V1508
²⁷ զի] ի M178 M182 | յամենայնի] ամեն. WN11 -նայն
M351 | և 2°—քո 2°] ճանապարհք քո ուղիղ են J1925 | ամենայն 1°]
om V280 |<ուղիղ>]ուղիղ M287 -դեղ M4834 | ճանապարհք]
դատաստանք M178 | և 3°] om J1925 | դատաստանք] -տան
WN11 | ճանապարհք M4834 J1925| ճշմարտութիւն] ճշմարիտ
են M2627
²⁸ ճշմարտութիւն V280 | ըստ ամենայնի J1925 bis scr |
սրբոյ] om M178 | ամենայն]+ ի վերայ մեր V280' J1925
²⁹ և 1°] om M346' J1925 | <ապստամբ>]ապաստամբ M287ᶜ
(pr և M287*) յապստամբ M9116-M4114 M182''
³⁰ քոց 1°] + մեք M4834 | պատուիրեցեր] + դու (պատիրեաց
WN11*) V280' M346' J1925 | լիցի WN11 M2627
³² և 1°] om M346 | մերոց] om J1925 | յանաւրինաց J1925
| խստից WN11 |<ապստամբողաց >] ամբստամբողաց M287
ապաս-տամբ. J1925 | և 3°] + ի ձեռն M2585 | անաւրինի |
անիրաւի J1925'-M4114 M182''
³³ մեզ] + ժամ V280 M346' | մեր] om J1925' | եղաք]եղեն
V280 M9116 | քոց] om M182'
³⁴ և 1° M287' M4114 M182''] om rel | մատնեցեր M351 |

զուխտաս քո: ³⁵ Մի ի <բացէ> <առներ> գողորմութիւն քո ի մէնջ
խասն Աբրահամու սիրելոյ քո և վասն Սահակա ծառայի քո և
Իսրայելի սրբոյ քո, ³⁶ որոց խաւեցաւ բազմացուցանել զաւակ
նորա որպէս զաստեղս երկնից և որպէս զաւազ առ ափն ծովու:
³⁷ և արդ Տէր նուաղեցաք քան զամենայն ազգս և եմք տառա-
պեալք յամենայն երկրի այսաւր վասն մեղաց մերոց. ³⁸ և ոչ
գոյ ի ժամանակի յայսմիկ իշխան, մարգարէ և առաջնորդ, ոչ
ողջակէզք և ոչ զոհք և ոչ պատարագք և ոչ խունկք, և ոչ տեղի
տալոյ երախայրիս առաջի քո և գտանել ողորմութիւն: ³⁹ Այլ
անձամբք բեկելովք և ոգւով տառապանաց ընդունելի լիցուք
⁴⁰ իբրև զողջակէզս խոյոց և զուարակաց և զբիւրաւորս գա-
ռանց պարարտաց, այնպէս եղիցի պատարագս մեր այսաւր
առաջի քո լինել կատարեալ զկնի քո, զի չիք ամաւթ յուսացելոց

գրուեր WN 11 | զուխտ M4834 M2627' M182''
³⁵ մի M287] pr և rel | <բացէ>] բայցէ M287 J1925 |
<առներ>] առնել M287 | գողորմութիւն M287 M178-M346] -
թիւնս rel | աբրահամու M351 | և 1°] om M4834 M351 | վասն 2°]
om M4834 M2585 M346 M351 | Սահակա M287] խսահակայ V280
M346-M2585 M9116-M2627' M182'' (-կա rel) | քո 3°] om J1925 | և
2°] + վասն իսրայէլի V280 M346' M9116-M4114 M182''
³⁶ բազմացուցել WN 11* | զաւակ M287] զզաւակ (-ակս V280)
rel որպէս 1°] իբրև M4834 M2585 M9116-M4114 M182'| և 1°] om
M178 | որպէս 2°] իբրև V280' J1925'-M2627' M182''
³⁷ նուաղեցաք M287'' J1925-M4114] նուազ. rel | քան] pr
մեք V280 M178-M346'-M2585 M9116 | տառապեալ V280 M346'
J1925'-M2627' | յամենայն երկրի] om M346-WN 11* | այսաւր]
այս է J1925
³⁸ ժամանի M2627 | ողջակէզք V280: ditt | և 6°] om V280' |
տալով J1925 | երախայրի WN 11 | ողորմութիւն M287]գողորմ.
rel +ի քէն M178-M346-WN 11*
³⁹ բեկելաւք M9116-M4114 | խոնարհեալ WN 11* | ոգւով
M287]հոգւովք rel | տառապանաւք V280 | լիցուք մեք V280'
⁴⁰ իբրև] որպէս M4834 M178-M346'-M2585 | խուլց M4834 |
և 2°] om M178 J1925 + իբրև M4834 M2585 J1925'-M2627' M182'' +
որպէս V280 M278-M346'| զբիւրաւորս] բիւր. M4834 J1925'-
M2627 M182''| պարարտից M346' J1925'| եղիցի]-ցին V280' pr ըն-
դունելի WN 11*J1925 ընդունելի լիցի M346-M2585| պատարագք
V280' M178 | այսաւր] om M287* M2627 | զի]և M346' J1925

The Armenian Version of Daniel

ի քեզ: ⁴¹ Արդ գամք զհետ քո ամենայն սրտիւք մերով՝ք և երկրնչիմք ի քէն ⁴² և խնդրեմք զերեսս քո. մի յամաւթ առներ զմեզ,
այլ արայ ընդ մեզ ըստ հեզութեան քում և ըստ բազում
ողորմութեան քում: ⁴³ և փրկեա զմեզ վասն սքանչելեաց քոց և
տուր փառս անուան քում, Տէր: ⁴⁴ և յամաւթ լիցին ամենեքեան որ ցուցանեն չարիս ծառայից քոց և ամաչեսցեն յամենայն բնութենէ իւրեանց և զաւրութիւն նոցա խորտակեսցի:
⁴⁵ և ծանիցին զի դու ես Տէր Աստուած միայն և փառաւորեալ ի
վերայ ամենայն տիեզերաց: ⁴⁶ և ոչ դադարեին որք արկին
զնոսա սպասաւորք Թագաւորին ի հնոցն բորբոքելոյ նաւթիւ և
ճիթով և վշով և որթով: ⁴⁷ և ելանէր դիզանէր բոցն ի վերոյ
քան զհնոցն ի քառասուն և ինն կանգուն. ⁴⁸ և շրշէր պատեր

---

⁴¹ արդ] pr և rel ǀ սրտոք M4114 ǀ մերաւք M9116-M4114 ǀ և
1° M287 M9116-M4114 M182''] om rel ǀ երկրնչիմք M287' WN11
M9116] + մեք rel
⁴² և 1° M287' M9116-M4114 M182''] om rel ǀ խնդրել J1925 ǀ
քո] + տեր M4834 M178-M346' J1925 ǀ ընդ] առ V280 M346' M2627
ǀ քում 1°] քոյ V280 ǀ քում 1°→2° M182 ǀ և 2°] om J1925
⁴³ և 1° M287'' M4114 M182''] om rel ǀ Տէր om M178-M346-
M2585
⁴⁴ և 1°] om M178-M346 ǀ ամենեքին M4114 ǀ որ M287'
J1925-M2627] ոյք rel ǀ և 2°] om J1925 ǀ բնութենէ M287'' WN11
J1925-M2627] -թեան rel ǀ զաւրութիւն M287 J1925- M2627'
M182''] -թիւնք (pr ամենայն V280) rel ǀ խորտակեսցի M287
M2627' M182']-ցին rel
⁴⁵ և 2°] om M287ᶜ որ V280 M346' ǀ փառաւորեալ] + ես V280
M178-M346'-M2585 M2627
⁴⁶ որք արկին] om M178: homoeotel ǀ արկին] արկանէին
WN11 ǀ զնոսա] + ի հնոցն V280 ǀ ի հնոցն M287 WN11 M9116]
զհնոցն rel ǀ ի բորբոքելոյ M4834 M9116 ǀ նաւթo M346 ǀ և 3°] om
V280 M2585 J1925
⁴⁷ դիզանար M4834 -նայր V280 M346 J1925-M2627' M182''ǀ
վերոյ] վերա M178 վեր J1925 ǀ ի 2°] om V280 WN11 J1925-
M2627 ǀ և 2°] om M178 ǀ ջինն]ինն J1925-M2627
⁴⁸ շրշապատեր V280 շրշեալ պատեր M178-M346' ǀ
զհնոցաւն M287'' J1925] pr շուրջ rel ǀ զորս] զոր ինչ J1925 ǀ ի]
om WN11 ǀ Քաղդեացւոց] -եացոց M2585 J1925-M4114 -ցից
M4834 -ցոց WN11

զինցաւն և այլեր զորս գտանէր ի Քաղդէացւոց անտի: ⁴⁹ և
իրեշտակ Աստուծոյ էջ եկաց ընդ Ագարիանս ի հնցի անդ և
Թաւթափեաց զբոց հրոյն ի հնցէ անտի: ⁵⁰ և արար ի մէջ հնոցին իբրև զհողմ որ ցաւղագին շնչիցէ և ոչ մերձանայր ամենևին հուրն ի նոսա և ոչ տրտմեցուցանէր և ոչ նեղէր զնոսա:
⁵¹ Յայնժամ երեքեան իբրև ի միոջէ բերանոյ աւրհնէին գովէին և
փառաւոր առնէին զԱստուած ի մէջ հնցին և ասէին: ⁵² Աւրհնեալ ես Տէր Աստուած հարցն մերոց գովեալ և առաւել բարձրացեալ յաւիտեանս և աւրհնեալ է անուն սուրբ փառաց քոց.

< գովեալ և առաւել բարցրացեալ յաւիտեանս: >

⁵³ Աւրհնեալ ես ի տաճարի փառաց սրբութեան քո.

< գովեալ և առաւել բարցրացեալ յաւիտեանս: >

⁵⁴ Աւրհնեալ ես որ հայիս յանդունդս և նստիս ի քրովբէս.

< գովեալ և առաւել բարցրացեալ յաւիտեանս: >

⁵⁵ Աւրհնեալ ես ի վերայ աթոռոյ արքայութեան քո.

< գովեալ և առաւել բարցրացեալ յաւիտեանս: >

⁴⁹ Աստուծոյ] om V280 | ազարիեանս M4834 | անտ M346
J1925 | զբոց] om WN11* | հնցէ անտի] նոցանէ V280 նոցանէ
անտի (անդի M4834) M4834 J1925

⁵⁰ հնոցին 1°] նոցա J1925 | իբրև] որպէս M178-M346'-M2585
| ցաւղագին որ շնչիցէ M178-M346' ցաւղ. զի շնչ. J1925 | և 3°
M287] om rel | տրտմեցուցանէր ... նեղէր] tr V280

⁵¹ երեքեան (երեքին J1925) նոքա V280 J1925 | իբրև]
որպէս M178-M346'-M2585 | բերանէ WN11 | աւրհնէին] om
M178-M346'-M2585 + և J1925 | և 1°] om M4834 | փառաւորէին
V280' M178-M346-M2585 J1925-M2627 | ի մէջ հնցին] om
M9116| հնցի հրոյն M178-M346'-M2585 M2627

⁵² ես դու V280' M346' M351| բարձրացեալ ես V280| յաւի-
տեանս M287 M9116 V1508]-տեան rel | և 2°] om M4834 J1925

⁵³ om tot vers WN11*

⁵⁴ 54 tr post 55] V280 M346'-M2585 V1508-M351 | ես 2°] +
տէր M178-M2585 J1925' M182| նստիս ի Քրովբէս (քրոբ. V280) և
հայիս յանդունդս V280 J1925 | քրովբէս] քեր. M4834 M9116
քրոբ. V280 M346 M9116

⁵⁵ om tot vers M182 | աթոռոյ] -ng M2627' V1508 -ռոյ V280 |
քո] + երկնից V280

⁵⁶ Ալրինեալ եւ որ նստիս ի խառտատուԹեան երկնից.

< գովեալ և առաւել բարցրացեալ յաւիտեանս: >

⁵⁷ Ալրինեցէք ամենայն գործք Տեառն զՏէր.

< աւրինեցէք և բարձր արարէք զնա յաւիտեան: >

⁵⁸ Ալրինեցէք երկինք զՏէր.

< աւրինեցէք և բարձր արարէք զնա յաւիտեան: >

⁵⁹ Ալրինեցէք հրեշտակք Տեառն զՏէր.

< աւրինեցէք և բարձր արարէք զնա յաւիտեան: >

⁶⁰ Ալրինեցէք ջուրք ամենայն որ ի վերոյ քան զերկինս զՏէր.

< աւրինեցէք և բարձր արարէք զնա յաւիտեան: >

⁶¹ Ալրինեցէք ամենայն զաւրուԹիւնք Տեառն զՏէր.

< աւրինեցէք և բարձր արարէք զնա յաւիտեան: >

⁶² Ալրինեցէք արև և լոյս զՏէր.

< աւրինեցէք և բարձր արարէք զնա յաւիտեան: >

⁶³ Ալրինեցէք ամենայն աստեղք զՏէր.

< աւրինեցէք և բարձր արարէք զնա յաւիտեան: >

⁶⁴ Ալրինեցէք ամենայն անձրևք և ցաւղք զ<Տէր>:

< աւրինեցէք և բարձր արարէք զնա յաւիտեան: >

⁶⁵ Ալրինեցէք հողմք զՏէր.

---

⁵⁶ ի] om WN11* + վերայ M4834 J1925
⁵⁸ աւրինեցէք 2°—fin] om M178-M346-M2585 J1925'-M2627
⁵⁹ հրեշտակք] -տակ V280 M9116 | աւրինեցէք 2°—fin] om M287 M178-M346 J1925'
⁶⁰ ամենայն] om V280 M346-WN11* M182 | որ] om M351 | զՏէր] om V1508 աւրինեցէք 2°—fin] om V280 M178-M346 J1925 V1508-M351
⁶¹ ամենայն] om V280 WN11* Տեառն] om WN11* | աւրինեցէք 2°—fin] om M287 M178-M346 J1925' V1508
⁶² արև] արեգակն V280' J1925 | լոյս M287] լուսին rel | աւրինեցէք 2°—fin] om M178-M346 J1925'
⁶³ ամենայն] om V280 | աստեղք M287] + երկնից rel | աւրինեցէք 2°—fin] om M287 M178-M346 J1925'
⁶⁴ om tot vers M178 | զ<Տէր>] զ M287' | աւրինեցէք 2°—fin] om M287 M346 J1925'
⁶⁵ հողմք M287 J1925] pr ամենայն rel (հողմնք WN11) |

⁶⁶ Աւրհնեցէք հուր և տապ զՏէր.

< աւրհնեցէք և բարձր արարէք զնա յաւիտեան: >

⁷¹ Աւրհնեցէք տիւք և գիշեր զՏէր.

< աւրհնեցէք և բարձր արարէք զնա յաւիտեան: >

⁷² Աւրհնեցէք լոյս և խաւար զՏէր.

< աւրհնեցէք և բարձր արարէք զնա յաւիտեան: >

⁶⁷ Աւրհնեցէք ցուրտ և տաւթ զտեր

< աւրհնեցէք և բարձր արարէք զնա յաւիտեան: >

⁷⁰ Աւրհնեցէք եղեմն և ճիւն զՏէր.

< աւրհնեցէք և բարձր արարէք զնա յաւիտեան: >

⁷³ Աւրհնեցէք ամպք և փայլատակունք <զՏէր>.

< աւրհնեցէք և բարձր արարէք զնա յաւիտեան: >

⁷⁴ Աւրհնեցէք երկիր զՏէր.

< աւրհնեցէք և բարձր արարէք զնա յաւիտեան: >

⁷⁵ Աւրհնեցէք լերինք և բարձունք զՏէր.

< աւրհնեցէք և բարձր արարէք զնա յաւիտեան: >

⁷⁶ Աւրհնեցէք ամենայն բոյսք երկրի զՏէր.

աւրհնեցէք 2°—fin] om M178-M346' J1925 | vv. 66-73 order 66 71 72 67 70 73] M287'' J1925-M2627; 66 67 68 69 70 71 72 73] M178; 66 67 70 71 72 73] rel

⁶⁶ տապ] չեր M4834 J1925-M2627' | զՏէր] om V280 | աւրհ-նեցէք 2°—fin] om M178-M346 J1925' 71 տիւք] տիւ M346 M351 | գիշեր M287 M351] -երք rel | աւրհնեցէք 2°—fin] om M178-M346' J1925'-M4114 72 աւրհնեցէք 2°—fin] om M178-M346' J1925'-M4114

⁶⁷ ցուրտ և տաւթ] տաւթ և տապ M4834 J1925 | տաւթ] սառն M9116-M4114 M182'' WN11ᶜ| աւրհնեցէք 2°—fin] om M287 M178-M346' J1925'

⁷⁰ եղեմն M287 J1925] եղեամն rel | աւրհնեցէք 2°—fin] om M178-M346' J1925'-M4114

⁷³ <զՏէր>] om M287 | աւրհնեցէք 2°—fin] om M287' M178-M346' J1925'-M4114

⁷⁴ աւրհնեցէք 2°—fin] om M178-M346 J1925'

⁷⁵ բարձունք] բլուրք M178-M346' | աւրհնեցէք 2°—fin] om M287' M178-M346' J1925'-M4114

⁷⁶ ամենայն] om J1925 | զՏէր] om V280 | աւրհնեցէք 2°—fin] om M287 M178-M346' J1925'-M4114

< աւրհնեցէք և բարձր արարէք զնա յաւիտեան: >
78 Աւրհնեցէք ծովք և գետք զՏէր.

< աւրհնեցէք և բարձր արարէք զնա յաւիտեան: >
77 Աւրհնեցէք աղբերք զՏէր.

< աւրհնեցէք և բարձր արարէք զնա յաւիտեան: >
79 Աւրհնեցէք կետք և ամենայն կայտառք որ ի ջուրս զՏէր.

< աւրհնեցէք և բարձր արարէք զնա յաւիտեան: >
80 Աւրհնեցէք ամենայն Թոչունք երկնից զ<Տէր>.

< աւրհնեցէք և բարձր արարէք զնա յաւիտեան: >
81 Աւրհնեցէք ամենայն գազան և անասուն զ<Տէր>.

< աւրհնեցէք և բարձր արարէք զնա յաւիտեան: >
82 Աւրհնեցէք որդիք մարդկան զՏէր.

< աւրհնեցէք և բարձր արարէք զնա յաւիտեան: >
83 Աւրհնեցէք Իսրայէղ զՏէր.

< աւրհնեցէք և բարձր արարէք զնա յաւիտեան: >
84 Աւրհնեցէք քահանայք զՏէր.

---

78 78 tr ante 77 M287'' WN11* J1925'-M2627' ծովք] ծով
M4834 M178-M346'-M2585 J1925 M182''| աւրհնեցէք 2°—fin] om
M178-M346' J1925'
77 աղբերք] + երկրի M2585 | աւրհնեցէք 2°—fin] om M178-
M346' J1925'
79 կետք և] om WN11* J1925 | ամենայն] om M178-WN11*
J1925 | որ ի ջուրս] om WN11* | աւրհնեցէք 2°—fin] om M287
M178-M346'-M2585 J1925'-M2627 M351
80 ամենայն M287' J1925'-M2627'] om rel | q<Տէր>] q M287 |
աւրհնեցէք 2°—fin] om M287' M178-M346' J1925'
81 ամենայն] om V280 M178-M346-WN11*-M2585 | qգազան]
-անք M346-M2585 M9116-M2627' M182''| անասուն] -ունք M346-
M2585 M2627 M351 | q<Տէր>] q M287 | աւրհնեցէք 2°—fin] om
M287 M178-M346' J1925'
82 աւրհնեցէք 2°—fin] om M287 M178-M346' J1925'-M4114
83 Իսրայէղ]-այէլ V280 WN11 M9116-M2627' M182''|
աւրհնեցէք 2°—fin] om M287 M178-M346 J1925'
84 քահանայք] + տեառն M178-M2585 | աւրհնեցէք 2°—fin]
om M287 M178-M346' J1925'

< աւրինեցէք և բարձր արարէք զնա յաւիտեան:>
⁸⁵Աւրինեցէք ծառայք Տեառն զՏէր.

< աւրինեցէք և բարձր արարէք զնա յաւիտեան:>
⁸⁶Աւրինեցէք ոգիք և շունչք արդարոց զ<Տէր>.

< աւրինեցէք և բարձր արարէք զնա յաւիտեան:>
⁸⁷Աւրինեցէք սուրբք և խոնարհ սրտիւք զՏէր.

< աւրինեցէք և բարձր արարէք զնա յաւիտեան:>
⁸⁸ Աւրինեցէք Անանիա Ազարիա և Միսայէլ զ<Տէր>.

< աւրինեցէք և բարձր արարէք զնա յաւիտեան:>
Զի փրկեաց զմեզ ի դժոխոց և ի ձեռաց մահու ապրեցոյց զմեզ և
փրկեաց զմեզ ի հնգէս և ի միջոյ բորբոքեալ բոցոյ և ի միջոյ
հրոյ փրկեաց զմեզ: ⁸⁹Գոհացարուք զՏեառնէ զի քաղցր է, զի յաւիտեան է ողորմ նորա: ⁹⁰Աւրինեցէք ամենայն պաշտաւնեայք
Տեառն զԱստուած աստուծոց, աւրինեցէք և գոհացարուք զի
քաղցր է, զի յաւիտեան է ողորմ նորա»:
⁹¹Ը Նաքուքողոնոսոր իբրև լուաւ զաւրինութիւն նոցա և զար-

⁸⁵ Տեառն] om WN11* | աւրինեցէք 2°—fin] om M178-M346'
J1925'

⁸⁶ Աւրինեցէք 1°] + անձինք և M178-M346-M2585 | ոգիք
M287'' M2627'] om M346-M2585 հոգիք rel| և 1°] om M346 | զ<Տէր>
զ M287| աւրինեցէք 2°—fin] om M287' M178-M346' J1925'-M2627
M351

⁸⁷ սուրբք] սուրբ WN11 | խոնարհի] -արիք M4834 M346-
M2585 J1925-M2627' M182'| սրտիւք] -տիւ M182'-WN11°|
աւրինեցէք 2°—fin] om M287 M346' J1925'| յաւիտեան→88 յաւի-
տեան V280

⁸⁸ Անանիա M287 M346'-M2585 M182''] -հայ rel | Ազարիա] -
հայ M4834 M346-M2585 J1925'-M351| զ<Տէր >] զ M287 |
աւրինեցէք 2°—յաւիտեան] om M287 J1925 | յաւիտեան] -տեանս
M2585 M9116| և 4°] om M4834 WN11* M4114 | հրոյ] հրոյսն |
փրկեաց 2°] ապրեցոյց J1925

⁸⁹է 1°] om M182 | ողորմ] ողորմութիւն M4834 M346' M2627'

⁹⁰ զի քաղցր է M287 M2585] om rel | ողորմ] ողորմութիւն
V280' M178-M346' V1508-M351

⁹¹ Նաքուգողոնոսոր M287' M346 J1925] նաբոք. WN11 նա-
բուք. rel | զաւրինութիւն M287 M9116-M2627'] -թիւնս rel| և 2°]

The Armenian Version of Daniel

մացաւ, յարեաւ տագնապաւ և ասէ գմեծամեծս իւր «ո՞չ արս
երիս կապեալս արկաք ի հնոցն» և ասեն գթագաւորն «այոյ,
արդար ասես, արքայ»: ⁹²և ասէ Թագաւորն «այլ ես տեսանեմ
արս չորս արձակս և գնան ի մէջ հրոյն և ապականութիւն
ոչ գոյ ի նոսա և տեսիլ չորրորդին նման է որդւոյ Աստուծոյ»:
⁹³Յայնժամ մատեաւ Նաբուգոդոնոսոր ի դուռն հնոցի հրոյն
բորբոքելոյ և ասէ «Սեդրաք, Միսաք և Աբեդնագով, ծառայք
Աստուծոյ բարձրելոյ, ելէք և եկայք» և ելին Սեդրաք, Միսաք և
Աբեթնագով ի միջոյ հրոյն: ⁹⁴և ժողովեցան նախարարքն և
զաւրաւարք և կուսակալք և զաւրաւորք Թագաւորին և տեսանեին զարսն զի ոչ տիրեաց հուրն ի մարմինս նոցա և հեր գլխոյ
նոցա ոչ խանձատեցաւ և վարտիք նոցա ոչ այլագունեցան, և
հուր հրոյ ոչ գոյր ի նոսա և երկիր եպագ Թագաւորն առաջի նոցա Տեառն: ⁹⁵և պատասխանի ետ Նաբուգոդոնոսոր և ասէ
«աւրհնեալ է Աստուած Սեդրագա, Միսաքա և Աբեդնագովի որ

om rel ։ ոչ ապաքէն V280 ։ արկաք կապեալս V280 ։ հնոցն
M287] մէջ հրոյն rel ։ գթագաւորն] om V280 ։ ասեն] ես V280'
M178 J1925
    ⁹²այլ]ախա V280 ։ չորք M2627' ։ գոյր J1925 ։չորրորդ
M178 ։ է] om J1925
    ⁹³Նաբ. մատեաւ V280' M2585 M2627'։ Նաբուգոդոնոսոր
M287' M346' J1925] Նաբոր. WN11 նաբուգ. rel։ դուրս J1925 ։
հրոյն] om J1925 ։ Սեդրաք 1° M287' M2585 J1925'] -րաք rel ։
Միսաք 1°] -սաք V280 M346-M2585 J1925'։ Աբեդնագով] աբեթ.
M4834 J1925 -քով V280 ։ տեառն աստուծոյ V280 ։ բարձրելոյ]
om V280 M178 ։ եկայք արտաքս V280 ։ և 4°] om WN11*։ Սեդրաք
2°] -րաք V280 M2585 J1925'։ Միսաք 2°] -սաք V280 M346 J1925'։
Աբեթնագով M287' J1925] աբեդնագով (-քով V280) rel ։ մէջ V280
    ⁹⁴նախարարքն] om J1925 և 2°] om J1925 ։ կուսակալք ...
զաւրաւարք] tr M182''։ կուսակալք] զօրագլուխք M2585 J1925-
M2627 ։ զաւրաւորք] pr և կուսակալք J1925 զօրագլուխք M4114 ։
և 3°] om V280 ։ տեսանեին M346'։ և 5°] om J1925 ։ գլխոյ] -խու
M178 ։ ոչ 2°]որչ J1925 ։ խանձատեցաւ]-ձոտեցաւ J1925 խա-
ձատ. M9116 խանձեցաւ M4834 ։ վարտիք] վարսք M280 ։ այլա-
գունեցաւ J1925։ հրոյ] om WN11 ։ Տեառն] om WN11 + աստուծոյ
V280
    ⁹⁵Նաբուգոդոնոսոր M287' M346 J1925'] նաբոր. WN11

առաքեաց գիրեշտակ իւր փրկեաց գծառայս իւր զի յուսացան ի
նա և զբան Թագաւորին անարգեցին և մատնեցին զմարմինս
իւրեանց ի հուր զի մի պաշտեսցին և մի երկիր պագցեն
ամենայն աստուծոց բայց միայն Աստուծոյ իւրեանց: ⁹⁶ և արդ
ես տամ հրաման ամենայն <ազգք> և ազինք և լեզուք որ
խաւսիցին հայհոյութիւն զԱստուծոյ Սեդրաքա Միսաքա և
Աբեդնագովլի ի կորուստ մատնեցին և տունք նոցա
յափշտակութիւն զի ոչ գոյ այլ Աստուած որ կարող իցէ այնպէս
փրկել»: ⁹⁷ Յայնժամ Թագաւորն առաւել շքեղացոյց զՍեդրաք,
Միսաք և զԱբեդնագով. յերկրին Բաբելացւոց և բարձրացոյց
զնոսա, և աղաչեաց զնոսա լինել իշխան Հրեիցն որ էին ի
Թագաւորութեան նորա:

Նաբուք. rel | է] om M9116 | Սեդրագա M287] սեդրագայ V280
M2585 M9116 սեդրաքայ (-քա M4834 WN11 J1925) rel | Միսաքա]
pr և WN11 -գայ V280 M2585 M9116 -քայ M4834 M346 M2627'
M182'' | աբեթնագովլի M4834 J1925 | զբանս J1925 | պաշտիցեն
J1925 | պագանիցեն V280 WN11-M2585 J1925-M2627' V1508 |
աստուծոց] + օտարաց V280 M346' աստուածոց WN11 M9116-
M2627'| միայն] om M2627'
    ⁹⁶ <ազգք>]ազգ M287' M346 M2627' | և լեզուք] om V280 |
խաւսիցեն M178-M2585 M4114 -սեացին M4834 խօսին M346' |
սեդրաքայ M2627' M182'' -րագայ V280 M2585 M9116 | միսագա
M2585 M9116 -քայ V280' M2585 M2627' M182'' | Աբեդնագովլի
M287 M346 J1925'-M2627 M351] զաբեթ. M4834 J1925 զաբեդ. (-
քովլի V280) rel | մատնիցին J1925 -նեսցի M178 |
յափշտակութիւն M287''] pr ի rel | կարող իցէ | կարիցէ V280 |
իցէ] է J1925 | այսպէս J1925
    ⁹⁷ զՍեդրաք M287 WN11] զսեդրաք (-րագ M2585 M9116)
rel| միսագ M2585 M9116 զՄիսաք V280' M178 | զԱբեթնագով
M287' J1925]զաբեդ. rel | բաբելացոց WN11 բաբեդացոյց M178 |
զնոսա 1°]+ յոյժ M4834 J1925 | զնոսա լինել M287' J1925]լինել
նոցա rel | իշխանս M2585 M2627 | հրեիցն M287] հրէիցն (-էից
M4834) rel

ՏԵՍԻԼ ՀԻՆԳԵՐՈՐԴ

⁹⁸ Նաբուքոդոնոսոր արքա առ ամենայն ազգս և ազինս և լեզուս որ բնակեալ են յամենայն երկրի, խաղաղութիւն բազմասցի ձեզ: ⁹⁹ զնշանս և զարուեստս զոր արար ընդ իս բարձրեալն հաճոյ Թուեցաւ առաջի իմ պատմել ձեզ ¹⁰⁰ թէ որպէս մեծամեծք և զաւրաւորք են. արքայութիւն նորա արքայութիւն յաւիտենից և իշխանութիւն նորա ազգաց յազգս:

⁴⁑¹ Ես Նաբուքոդոնոսոր ուրախ էի ի տան իմում և զուարճացեալ. ² երազ տեսի և զարհուրեցոյց զիս, և խռովեցա յանկողնի իմում և տեսիլ գլխոյ իմոյ տագնապեաց զիս: ³ և <տուաւ> հրաման յինէն ածել առաջի իմ զամենայն իմաստունս Բաբելացւոց զի զմեկնութիւն երազոյն ցուցցեն ինձ: ⁴ և մտին առաջի իմ <զէնք> և մոգք, եղձք և քաղդեայք և զերազն ասացի առաջի նոցա, և զմեկնութիւն նորա ոչ ցուցցին ինձ ⁵ մինչև եկն Դանիէլ որում անուն էր Բաղտասար, ըստ անուան աստուծոյ իմոյ, զի հոգի սուրբ Աստուծոյ գոյ ի նմա, զոր ասացի թէ

---

⁹⁸ init] pr Վասն ահաւոր ձառոյ V280 + Ես M4834 | նաբորոդոնոսոր WN11 նաբուգ. V280 M346 J1925 | արքա] om V280' M178-M346 | և ազինս M287 M346'] om rel | ամենայն WN11| բազմացի M4834 | ձեզ] om V280

⁹⁹ Զնշանս] զշնորհս V280'

¹⁰⁰ յազգս] ազգս WN11

⁴⁑¹ Ես] և ս WN11 | նաբուգոդոնոսոր V280 M346 J1925 նաբոք. WN11 | Էի] եղէ WN11 | տանի WN11: ditt | զուարձացայ J1925

³ <տուաւ>] ուաւ M287 | յինէն հրաման առաւ V280 յինէն հրամանք M346' | բաբեղացւոց M178 բաբելացոց WN11 | երազոյ իմոյ J1925 | ցուցէն M287' J1925 M351]ցուցցէն rel

⁴ <զէնք>] զէտ M287 զէնք J1925 | մոգք M287 J1925] + և rel | եղձք M287 M346] իղձք M9116 իղձք rel | քաղդեայք M287 M351] քաւղեայք V280 քաղդեայք WN11 քաղդեայք rel | զերազն իմ WN11-M2585 M182ᵐᵍ V1508 | առաջի 2°] om V280

⁵ դանիէղ M178 | որում] որոյ V280 M9116 | էր] է V280 | բաղդասար V280 բալտ. M2627' | աստուծոյ V280 աստուածոյ M9116 M351 | իմոյ] -ng V280 | սուրբ] om V280 | գոյր M4834 | գոր] յոր J1925 + և M2585 M2627' M182''

⁶ «Բաղտասար, իշխան գիտաց, զոր ես գիտեմ թէ հոգի սուրբ Աստուծոյ գոյ ի քեզ և ամենայն խորհուրդ ոչ ծածկի ի քէն, արդ
լուր դու գտեսիլ երազոյն իմոյ զոր տեսի և զմեկնութիւն
նորա ասացես ինձ: ⁷ Տեսանէի յանկողնի իմում և ահա ծառ
մի ի մէջ երկրի, և բարձրութիւն նորա բազում յոյժ: ⁸ Մեծացաւ
ծառն և զաւրացաւ և բարձրութիւն նորա եհաս մինչև յերկինս, և լայնութիւն նորա ի ծագս ամենայն երկրի, ⁹ տերև նորա
գեղեցիկ և պտուղ նորա բազում և կերակուր ամենայնի ի նմա.
ի ներքոյ նորա բնակեալ են գազանք վայրի և յոստս նորա
հանգուցեալ են թռչունք երկնից. ի նմանէ կերակրեր
ամենայն մարմին: ¹⁰ Տեսանէի ի տեսլեան գիշերոյ յանկողնի
իմում և ահա զուարթուն և սուրբ իջանէր յերկնից ¹¹ և բարբա-
ռէր զաւրութեամբ և ասէր այսպէս «հատէք զծառդ և քշտեցէք

⁶ բաղդասար V280 բալտ. M2627' | գիտաց] գիտա V280
M2627' գիտեա M346' M2585 M182'' | զոր] զի M346 | ես] + տեսի
(+զի M2627' M351) M2627' M182'' | թէ] զի M178 WN11*-M346 |
սուրբ] om V280 | խորհուրդք ծածկին V280' J1925-M9116 M182'' |
դու] om M346-WN11* | ասացես] պատմեցես M346' | ինձ] om
M2627'

⁷ տեսանէի ես M4834 տեսի ես J1925 | իմոյմ M178 | մի]
om M351 | բարձրութիւն] բազմութիւն V280 | նորա] om M346' |
նորա 8➔նորա 1° M178 | բազում] om V280

⁸ ծառն] + և բարձրացաւ V280 | բարձրութիւն նորա] om
V280 | մինչև յերկինս հասանէր J1925

⁹ բազում] + յոյժ M346'-M2585: cf v 7 | ամենայնի]
ամենայն M4834 WN11 J1925-M9116 (tr ante կերակուր V280) | են
1° M287] էին rel | վայրի] om V280 վայրենիք M4834 J1925 |
հանգուցեալ են M287] հանգչէին V280 հանգուցեալ էին rel |
ամենայն թռչունք M2585 M2627'| երկնից] + և V280' M178-
M346'-M2585 J1925'-M2627' M182'| ի 3°—fin] om M351 | նմանէ]
նման V280 նմա են J1925 | կերակուր ամ. մարմնոյ J1925

¹⁰ տեսանէին M351 | ի տես. գիշ./յանկողնի իմում] tr
V280 | զուարթութիւն V280 | և 2°] om M4834 J1925-M2627'|
զծառդ] + այդ WN11 զծառոդ M2627'

¹¹ և 1°] om J1925 | քշտեցէք] կարեցէք J1925 | դորա 1°] + և
M2627 | ցրուեցէք զպտուղ դորա M2585 M2627'| զպտուղս V280|
ցրուիցէք J1925 | թռչունք] + որ M2627'| ի յոստոց V280' յոստոյ
M178 յոստս M2627' M182' ի յոստս WN11 J1925 V1508 յոստոդ
M351

The Armenian Version of Daniel

qnumu նորա, Թալ Թափեցէք զտերև նորա և զպտուղ նորա
ցրուեցէք. շարժեսցին գազանք ի ներքոյ դորա և Թոչունք յու-
unng նորա. ¹² բայց զշարաւիղ դորա Թողէք յերկրի երկաԹակապ
և պղնձապատ ի դալարի վայրի. և ի ցաղ երկնից դադարեսցէ և
ընդ գազանս բաժին նորա և ի խոտ երկրի: ¹³ սիրտ նորա ի
մարդկանէ փոփոխեսցի և սիրտ գազանաց տացի նմա, և և Թն
ժամանակք փոփոխեսցին ի վերայ նորա: ¹⁴ ՄեկնուԹեամբ
զուարԹնոց է բանս և պատգամ սրբոց է հարցուածս, զի ծանի-
ցեն կենդանիք Թե տէր է բարձրեալն ԹագաւորուԹեան մարդկան, և ում կամի տացէ զնա և զարհամարհին ի մարդկանէ
յարուցէ ի վերայ նորա» ¹⁵ Այս է երագն գոր տեսի ես Նաբուքոդոնոսոր արքայ, և դու, Բաղտասար, ասա ինձ զմեկնուԹիւն
նորա, զի ամենայն իմաստունք ԹագաւորուԹեան իմոյ ոչ կարացին զմեկնուԹիւն նորա ցուցանել ինձ. այլ դու, Դանիէլ, կարող ես զի հոգի Սուրբ Աստուծոյ գոյ ի քեզ»: ¹⁶ Յայնժամ Դանիէլ,

¹² զշարաւեղ M4834 M346 J1925'-M2627 M182' -եդս WN11-
M2585 զարմատս M287^mg | դորա] pr արմատոց M178-WN11-
M2585   M9116 -ոյ V280' M346 J1925-M2627'-M182''| երկաԹա-
կապ M287] երկաԹապատ rel| դալար M9116-M2627' M182''|
վայր M9116| ցաւղոյ V280 M178-WN11-M2585 M182'': cf v 20, 30 |
դադարեսցէ] հանգիցէ M2627' M182'': cf v 20| գազանս] +
անապատի M2585 M2627' M182''| երկրի] + դադարեսցէ և ընդ
գազանս բաժին և ի խոտոյ երկրի V280: ditt
¹³ փոփոխեսցի M287] փոխիցի V280 փախեսցի J1925
փոխեսցի rel| տացի] որլաւ V280| ժամանակ WN11| փոփո-
խեսցին M287 WN11| փոխ. rel
¹⁴ զուարԹնոց M287' J1925| -նոյ rel|սրբոց] զուարԹնոց
M178 | հարուածս M2627 | տէր է M287' J1925'] տիրէ rel|
ԹագաւորուԹեանց M4834 J1925| զարհամարիանս V280|
յարուցանէ V280' J1925 M182'| նորա| նոցայ M4834
¹⁵ տեսանէի V280 տեսանէ J1925| եսol om J1825| Նաբո-
քոդոնոսոր WN11 նաբուգ. V280 M346 J1926| բաղդասար V280|
ասա] տաս V280| իմաստուԹիւնք V280| ցուցանել զմեկնու-
Թիւն նորա J1925' V1508-M351 (M182 vid seq)| ինձ] tr ante
զմեկն. M182
¹⁶ որո J M287 M9116] որում rel | բալտասար M2627' բաղդ.
V280 | խռովեցուցին V280' J1925 | ասէ] + զնա V280 WN11 sup lin
M2585 M2627' M182''| բաղտասար V280 բալ տ. M2627'| մի]+ և ու

որոյ անուն էր Բաղտասար, հիացաւ իբրև ժամ մի և խորհուրդք նորա խռովեցուցանեին զնա։ Պատասխանի ետ Թագաւորն և ասէ «Բաղտասար, երազն և զմեկնութիւն նորա մի
տագնապեցուցացէ զքեզ»։ Ետ պատասխանի Բաղտասար և ասէ
«տէր, երազն ատելեաց քոց և մեկնութիւն նորա թշնամեաց քոց։
[17] <ծառն> զոր տեսանեիր մեծացեալ և զաւրացեալ. որոյ
բարձրութիւնն հասանէր մինչև յերկինս և լայնութիւն նորա
յամենայն երկրի, [18] տերև նորա գեղեցիկ և պտուղ նորա բազում և կերակուր ամենայնի ի նմա, ի ներքոյ նորա բնակեալ
էին գազանք անապատի և յուստ նորա հանգուցեալ էին
թոչունք երկնից, [19] դու ես, արքա, զի մեծացար և զաւրացար և
մեծութիւն քո բարձրացաւ յոյժ և եհաս յերկինս և տերութիւն
քո ի ծագս ամենայն երկրի. [20] և զի տեսանեիր, արքա, զգուար-
թունն և զսուրբ զի իջանէր յերկնից և ասէր կտրեցէք զծառդ և
ապականեցէք զդա, բայց զշառաւիղս արմատոց դորա թողէք
յերկրի երկաթակապ և պղնձապատ և ի դալարի վայրի. և ի
ցաւղ երկնի հանգիցէ և ընդ գազանս անապատի բաժին նորա

M4834 J1925 | տագնապեցուցեն M4834 WN11 J1925' -ցուցանէ
M178-M346 M2627 -ցուցանեն V1508 | բալտասար M2627'
դանիէլ V280 | տէր] + արքայ V280 om M2627 | քog 1°→քog 2° V280

[17] <ծառն>] առն M287 M178 pr զի V280 | տեսեր J1925 |
զաւրացեալ] բարձրացեալ M2585 | որոց J1925 յորոյ WN11 |
բարձրութիւն նորա V280 | մինչև M287'' M2627'] om rel |
յամենայն] ի ծագս ամ. M2585 M2627' ամ. WN11 | երկիր M4834
J1925' M182'' յերկիր WN11

[18] գեղեցիկ] գեցիկ M178 | ամենայն M4834 J1925: hapl cf v
9 | նմա] + և M2627'' | բնակեալ էին] om V280 բն. են J1925 | ի
յուստ M4834 | են հանգուցեալ V280 | էին] om M4834 M9116
M182'' են J1925

[19] զի-զաւրացար] om M178 | զի]որ V280' | քո 1°] om M351 |
յոյժ M287] tr ante և 2° V280 om rel | և 3°] om M178 M182' | եհաս]
om M178 + մինչև (մինն.ի V280) V280 M346'-M2585 M2627' M182'':
cf v 8

[20] և 1°] om V280 | արքա] om J1925' | զգուարթունն] pr
զինքն M4834զնոյն ինքն զուարթ. V280 զի զուարթ. M178-WN11-

մինչև եթն ժամանակք փոխեցին ի վերայ նորա: ²¹ Այս <է>
մեկնութիւն նորա, արքայ, և դատաստանք բարձրելոյ են հասե
ալ ի վերայ տեառն իմոյ արքայի. ²² և զքեզ հալածեսցեն ի
մարդկանէ, և ընդ գազանս անապատի եղիցի բնակութիւն քո և
խոտ իբրև արջառոյ ջամբեսցեն քեզ և ցաւղոյ երկնից հանգիցես
և եթն <ժամանակք> փոխեցին ի վերայ քո մինչև ծանիցես թէ
տիրէ բարձրեալ ն Թագաւորութեան մարդկան, և ում կամի
տացէ զնա: ²³ և զի ասաց թէ Թողէք զշառաւեղ արմատոյ
ծառոյն, Թագաւորութիւն քո քեզ մնա մինչև ծանիցես
զիշխանութիւն երկնաւոր: ²⁴ Վասն այդորիկ, արքա, խրատիմ
հաճոյ Թուեսցի քեզ. և զմեղս քո ողորմութեամբ քաւեսչիր

M2585 M2627' M182''| և 2°] om M4834 J1925-M2627'| ՍՈւրբ
J1925-M2627' M182'' զսրբութիւնն V280 | յերկնից զի իշանէր
J1925| զի 2°] om M9116 M182''| q2առաւիղս] -իղ M2627' V1508
-եղս M178-M346'-M2585 -եղ V280 J1925' M182' q2աւիղ M4834|
արմատոց] -ոյ M4834 J1925 M182''| երկաթակապ M287'] -
ապատ rel | ի 1°] om J1925 | դալար M2627' M182''| ցաւղոյ V280
WN11ᶜ-M2585 M4114 M182'': cf v 12,30 | երկնի M287] յերկնից
M4834 J1925: cf v 12,30 երկնից rel | ընդ]ի V280 | գազան J1925|
<ժամանակք>] ժամանակ M287
²¹ <է> 1°] om M287 | արքա յ] om M9116 | և–բարձր>] om
V280 | և] om WN11*-M346 J1925 | են] om V1508 tr post հասեալ
V280' M2585 J1925-M2627' M182''| իմում M9116 | արքայի]
արքա յ +ի ձեռն Տեառն ամենակալ ի V280
²² զքեզ հալածեսցեն] հալածեսցիս V280 | յանապատի
WN11 | եղիցի] om M4834 M346-WN11*| ջամբ.քեզ խոտ իբրև արջ.
V280 | իբրև] որպէս M178-M346'-M2585 |<ժամանակք >]
ժամանակ M287 | տիրէ] տէր է M4834 J1925: cf v 14 | Թագաւո
րութեան] pr ամենայն V280 -թեանց M4834 J1925
²³ Թէ] om 4834 | Թողէք] պահեցէք M346'| q2առաւեղս
M346' -իղ M2627' M182' -իղս M178 M2585: cf v 12 | արմատոց
M2585 M2627'| երկնաւոր M287* M178-M346' J1925'] -որին
(զերկ. M4834) rel
²⁴ այդորիկ] որ WN11 | Թուեսցին V280 Թոյ Թուեսցի
J1925 | և 1°] om M346-WN11* M2627'| քաւեսչիր M287 J1925'
M182''] -եսցես rel | տրաւք M287ᵐᵍ V280] om M287ᵗˣᵗ qԹով M178-
M346' J1925-M2627' qԹով p rel |<տնանկաց>]-qաց M287 M178 |
Թերևս] prqի V280 |լիցի] tr post քոց V280 լինիցի M178-M2585

և զանիրաւութիւնս քո տրաւք <տնանկաց>, թերևս երկայնա-
միտ լիցի ի վերա յանցանաց քոց Աստուած: 25 Այս ամենայն
եկն եհաս ի վերայ Նաբուքոդոնոսրա արքայի»: 26 Յետ երկու-
տասան ամսոյ մինչդեռ ի <վերայ տաճարի> Թագաւորութեան
իւրոյ ճեմէր ի Բաբելովն, 27 խաւսել սկսաւ Թագաւորն և ասէ «ո՞չ
այս այն մեծ Բաբելոն է զոր ես շինեցի ի տուն Թագաւորութեան
հաստատութեամբ զաւրութեան իմոյ, ի պատիւ փառաց իմոց»:
28 և մինչդեռ բանքն ի բերան էին Թագաւորին, ճայն եղև յերկնից «քեզ, ասեն, Նաբուքոդոնոսոր արքա, Թագաւորութիւն քո
անցեալ է ի քէն 29 և ի մարդկանէ հալածեսցեն զքեզ և ընդ գազանս անապատի բնակութիւն քո և խոտ իբրև արջառոյ ջամբեսցեն քեզ և եւթն ժամանակք փոխեսցին ի վերայ քո մինչև
ծանիցես թէ տիրէ բարձրեալն Թագաւորութեան մարդկան և
ում կամի տացէ զնա»: 30 ի նմին ժամու բանն կատարեցաւ ի վե-

---

25 Այս] pr և V280 | եկն] om M178 | Նաբուքոդոնոսրա
M287] -սոր (նաբուզ. J1925) WN11* J1925-M2627' -սորայ
(նաբուզ. V280 M346) rel

26 մինչդեռ] + էր V280 |<վերայ տաճարի>] վերնատան
M287 | ճեմէր] om V280 | բաբելոն V280' M346' M2627' M182'

37 բաբելովն M4834 M178-M2585 M9116 | ի տուն] իմում
J1925 | Թագաւորութեան իմոյ M346'| հաստատութեան J1925-
M2627'| զաւրութեամբ V280 J1925 | իմոյ]-ով V280 om J1925'

38 քեզ] pr և ասէ (-սէր V280) V280 M2585 M2627' M182'' |
ասեն M287] ասեմ rel | Նաբուգոդոնոսոր V280 M346 J1925'
նաբոք. WN11

29 յանապատի WN11: cf v 22 | իբրև] որպէս M178-M346': cf v
22 | և 4°] om M178: hapl | ժամանակ V280 WN11 | ծանիցեն
J1925 | Թագաւորութեանց (pr ի վերայ J1925) M4834 J1925 | և
5°–fin] om V280

30 կատարեցաւ բանն V280 | Նաբուքոդոնոսրա M287]
նաբոք. WN11 -սորայ rel(նաբուզ. V280 M178-M346 J1925) | <և>
1°] om M287 | հալ. ի մարդկանէ V280 | ուտէր խոտ իբրև զարջառ
M4834 | իբրև 1°] որպէս M178-M346'-M2585 | արջառ V280
J1925'-M2627' M182''| մարմին նորա ներկեաւ ի ցաւղոյ երկնից
V280 | ցաւղ M9116: cf v 12,20 | յերկնից WN11: cf v 12, 20|
ներկեաւ մարմին նորա M4834 J1925 | մարմինք M346' |
ներկեաւ WN11 | մինչև] և M346-WN11* | նորա 2°]իւր M346'|

 բայ նաբուքդոդոնոսրա <և> ի մարդկանէ հալածեցաւ և խոտ
իբրև զարջառ ուտէր. և ի ցաւղոյ երկնից մարմին նորա ներ-
կաւ, մինչև վարսք նորա իբրև զառևծուց մեծացան և եղեն
գունք նորա իբրև զթռչնոց երկնից։ ³¹ և յետ կատարածի
աւուրցն ես Նաբուքդոդոնոսր զաչս յերկինս համբարձի և միտք
իմ առ իս դարձան, և զբարձրեալն աւրինեցի զկենդանին
յաւիտենից գովեցի և փառաւորեցի, զի իշխանութիւն նորա իշխանութիւն յաւիտենական և արքայութիւն նորա ազգաց
յազգս։ ³² և ամենայն բնակիչք երկրի իբրև ոչ ինչ համարեցան
նմա. ըստ կամաց իւրոց առնէ ի զաւրութիւն երկնից և ի բնա-
կութեան երկրի և չիք որ ընդ դեմ դառնայցէ ձեռին նորա և
ասիցէ թէ «զինչ գործեցեր»։ ³³ ի նմին ժամանակի միտք իմ առ
իս դարձան և ի պատիւ Թագաւորութեան իմոյ եկի. և կերպարանք իմ առ իս դարձան և իշխանք իմ և մեծամեծք խնդրէին
զիս և անդրէն ի Թագաւորութիւն իմ հաստատեցա և մեծութիւն առաւել յաւելաւ ինձ։ ³⁴ Արդ ես Նաբուքդոդոնոսր աւրի-

իբրև 2°] որպէս M178 | զառիւծու J1925 | եղենգունք M287
M9116] եղ[Թ]նգ. M178-M346 M182'(-կունք V280)ողունկունք WN11
եղնգ. M4834 M2627' V1508 (-կունք J1925)| իբրև 3°] որպէս M178-
M346' (pr եղեն V280) | Թռչնոց M178-M346'-M2585 M2627
զ[Թռչնո] J1925 | երկնից (երկնի M346) M287 M346'-M2585] om rel
³¹ յետ] եղև WN11 | աւուրն J1925 | Նաբուգոդոնոսոր M287'
M346 J1925] նաբրք. WN11 Նաբուք. rel| ի յերկինս M9116 |
աւրինեցի] գովեցի V280 | գովեցի և] om V280 | զի իշխան.]
զիշխան. WN11: hapl| յաւիտենից M346' | արքայութիւն]
տէրութիւն M9116 M182'°
³² երկրի 1°] om J1925 | զոչ ինչ V280' J1925' M182''| նմա
M287'' M2585] om rel | առներ V280 | ի 1°] om V280' J1925'|
զզաւրութիւնս M4834 J1925| և 3°] om WN11 | ի 2°] om V280| որ]
pr որ V280' J1925 WN11| դառնայ V280 J1925'| ձեռին]
զաւրութեան V280 | [Թե]բայ V280
³³ ժամանակի] ժամու V280'| իմ 1°] om M346| մեծամեծք
M287 M178-M346-M2585] + իմ rel| խնդրեցին J1925 M182'|
[Թագաւորութեան M346| իմ 3°]om V280 | մեծութիւն] + իմ WN11
| առաւել յաւելաւ] առաւելաւ V280 M346'
³⁴ Նաբուգոդոնոսոր V280 M178 J1925 նաբրք. WN11|
աւրինեմ] pr արքա M4834 M178-M346'-M2585 M9116-M2627' | և

նեմ և առաւել բարձրացուցանեմ և փառաւոր առնեմ զարքայն
երկնից զի ամենայն գործք նորա ճշմարիտ են, և շառաւիղք
նորա իրաւունք և զամենեսեան որ գնան ամբարտաւա-
նութեամբ կարող է խոնարհեցուցանել:

5:1 Բաղտասար արքա արար ընթրիս մեծամեծաց իւրոց
հազար առն և ըստ հազարացն նոյնպէս և գինի: ² Եւ իբրև ընդ
գինիս եմուտ Բաղտասար, հրամայեաց բերել զսպաս զարձա-
թոյ և զոսկոյ զոր եհան Նաբուքոդոնոսոր, հայր նորա, ի տաճա-
րէն որ յերուսաղեմ զի արբցեն նոքաւք թագաւորն և մեծամեծք
իւր և հարճք և կանայք իւր: ³ Եւ բերին զսպասն զոսկեղէնս և
զարձաթեղէնս զոր բերեալ էր ի տաճարէ Աստուծոյ որ էր յերու-
սաղէմ. և ‹ըմպէին› նոքաւք թագաւորն և մեծամեծք իւր և
հարճք նորա և կանայք: ⁴ Եւ ‹ըմպէին› գինի և աւրհնեին

1°] om WN11 | բարձր առնեմ M178-M346'-M2585 | փառաւորեմ
V280' M346' J1925 | զի 1°] om J1925 | շառաւիղք] շառաւիղք V280 |
իրաւամբք M178-M346' | զամենեսին V280' J1925'-M2627 M182'' |
որ M287'' WN11   J1925] nյք rel | ամբարտաւանութեամբ]
ամբասատանութեամբ J1925 | է] ես M9116
5:1 pr Վասն Ընթրեաց Արքայիկ V280 | բաղտասար V280
բալտ. M2627' | արքա] + որդի նաբուգողոնոսորաj V280 |
մեծանեծաց WN11 | և ըստ հազարացն] om V280
² եմուտ] մտին J1925-M4114 | Բաղտասար] բաղդ. V280
բալտ. M2627' + արքաj J1925 | զսպաս M178-M2585 J1925'-
M2627' | զարձաթոյ M287ᶜ] արձ. M287* WN11 M9116-M2627'
M182'' | զոսկւոյ (ոսկ. J1925) V280 J1925 | զոսկոյ] ոսկ. M2627'
զարձաթոյ (արձ. J1925) V280 J1925 | հան J1925 | նաբուգողո-
նոսոր V280 M346 J1925 նաբքռ. WN11 | հայր նորա tr ante նաբ.
V280 J1925 | նորովք M9116 | հարճք մորա M4114 | կանայք➔3
կանայք V280 | իւր 2°] om M4114
³ զսպասն V280 M178-M346 J1925' M182'' | զոսկ. և զարձ.
M287'' M2627' M182''] ոսկ. և արձ. J1925' զարձ. և զոսկ. rel |
Աստուծոյ] om M178-M2585 | էր 2° M287'' M9116 M182'] om rel |
‹ըմպէին›] ըմբէին M287 | նորովք M9116 | յարճ WN11
⁴ Եւ 1° M287] om rel | ըմպէին գինի և] om J1925 |
‹ըմպէին›] ըմբէին M287' WN11 | զոսկեղէնս M9116 M182'' |
արձաթեղէնս M287*-V280 J1925-M2627' | զպղնձեղէնս M287ᶜ
M178-M346'-M2585] պղնձ. M287* զպղինձս V280   M9116

զաստուածս ոսկեղէնս և զարծաթեղէնս և զպղնձեղէնս և
զերկաթիս և զփայտեղէնս և զքարեղէնս, և զԱստուած յաւիտենից ոչ աւրհնեցին որ ունէր զիշխանութիւն ողւցն նոցա: 5 Ի
նմին ժամու ելին մատունք ձեռին մարդոյ և գրեին հանդէպ
զենդին ի վերայ <բռելոյ որմոյ> տաճարի Թագաւորին. և Թագաւորն տեսանէր զԹաթ ձեռինն որ <գրէր>: 6 Յայնժամ հատան
գոյնք Թագաւորին և խորհուրդք նորա խռովեին զնա և յաւդք
միջոյ նորա լուծանեին և <ծունկք> նորա զմիմեանս բախա-
խէին: 7 և աղաղակեաց Թագաւորն զաւրութեամբ աձել զմոգս և
զքաղդեայս և զգէտս. և ասէ ցիմաստունս Բաբելացոց «որ
ընթերցի զգիրդ զայդ և զմեկնութիւն դորա ցուցցէ ինձ ծիրանիս զգեցցի, և մանեակ ոսկի ի պարանոց իւր և երրորդ ի
Թագաւորութեան իմում տիրեսցէ»: 8 և մտանեին ամենայն
իմաստունք Թագաւորին և ոչ կարեին <զգիրն> ընթեռնուլ և ոչ
զմեկնութիւն նորա ցուցանել Թագաւորին: 9 և արքա Բաղտա-

զպղնձիս (պղ. V1508) rel I զերկաթիս M287ᶜ-V280' J1925'-M2627'
M182''] երկ. M287* զերկաթեղէնս rel I զԱստուածն ... աւրհնե-
ցին] աստուածոյ ... եսուն փառս J1925 I աւրհնեցին M287'' M9116
M182''] աւրհնէին rel I որ] + տրւիչն է բարեաց և որ V280 I
զիշխանութիւն M287' M346' J1925'] իշխ. rel
    5 <բռելոյ որմոյ>] tr M287 բռեալ որմ. V280 J1925 I <գրէր>]
+ մանէ Թեկեղ փարէս M287: ex v 25
    6 խռովեցուցանէին M2585-WN11 M2627'M182''I <ծունկք>]
ծունք M287 J1925 I զմիմեամբք V280 I բախբախէին M287]
բախէին V280' WN11 J1925 բախախ. rel
    7 զքաղդեայս M9116 I Բաբեղացոց M178 -ցոց WN11 I որ
M287'' J1925'] +ոք rel I ընթերցի M287' WN11]-ggի rel I զգիրադ
V280 I ցուցանէ M178 J1925 V1508 I ինձ] om M2627'I զգեցուցից
(+ նմա M346) M178-M346-M2585 I մանեակա V280 I ի պարանոց
իւր] պարանոցի իւրոյ J1925 ի պարանոցս իւրում M4834 M178-
M346'-M2585 I երկրորդ V280 M178-WN11 I իմոյ V280'
    8 Թագաւորին 1° M287'' M178 J1925'] բաբելացոց rel I
<զգիրն>] om M287 զգիրս M178-M346 I Թագաւորին 2°] արքայի
V280
    9 բաղդասար V280 բալտ. M2627'I և 3° M287] om rel I ընդ
նմա] om M178

սար խոռվեցաւ և գոյն երեսաց նորա շրջեցաւ, և խոռվեցան մեծամեծք նորա ընդ նմա: ¹⁰ և եմուտ տիկինն ի տաճարն խրախխութեան և ասէ «արքա, յախտեան կաց. մի խոռվեցուցեն քեզ խորհուրդք քո և գոյն երեսաց քո մի եղծցի, ¹¹ զի է այր մի ի Թագաւորութեան քում յորում գո հոգի սուրբ Աստուծոյ և յաւուրս հաւր քո զաւրութիւնք և իմաստութիւնք գտան ի նմա և արքա Նաբուքոդոնոսոր հայր քո իշխան կացոյց զնա ի վերա <գիտաց> և մոգուց և քաղդէից և <ըղձից> ¹² զի հոգի առաւել գոյ ի նմա, իմաստութիւն և հանճար. մեկնէ զերազս և պատմէ զառակս և լուծանէ զիրս կապեալս, Դանիէլ էր և արքա Բաղտասար անուն եղ նմա: արդ կոչեսցի և զմեկնութիւն դորա պատմէ»: ¹³ Յայնժամ աձին ի ներքս զԴանիէլ առաջի Թագաւորին, և ասէ Թագաւորն զԴանիէլ «յորդւոց գերութեանն Հրեաստանի զոր աձ Նաբուքոդոնոսոր հայր իմ: ¹⁴ Լուա զքէն եթէ հոգի Աստուծոյ է ի քեզ և զուարթութիւն և հանճար և իմաստութիւն առաւել

---

¹⁰ և 1°] om M2627' | խրախութեամբ V280 խրախուսու-թեան M178 J1925 | և ասէ] om M346 | կաց M287 M346' J1925] կեաց rel | խոռվեցուցանեն զքեզ M346 խոռվեցցին V280 | գոյնք եղծցին V280

¹¹ ի 1°] om WN11 | Աստուծոյ] յաստ. M287* | զուարթու-թիւնք M4834 M9116 | իմաստունք M9116 | գտանէին M4834 J1925' M182'' | նմա] նա M351 | Նաբուգոդոնոսոր V280 M346 J1925' նաբոք. WN11 | կացոյց զնա իշխան V280 | <գիտաց>] գէ-տաց M287 | մոգաց J1925 | քաւդէայց M9116 | <ըղձից>]-դձից M287

¹² իմաստութեան առաւել գոյ ի նմա J1925 | ինաստու-թիւն M287' M178-M346 M9116] pr և V280 -թեան rel | հանձարոյ WN11-M2585 M2627' M182'' | դանիէլ M178 | էր] om V280' J1925'-M2627' M182'' | և 4°] om M178 | անուն նորա M287ᵐᵍ M346'-M2585 | արքա] + հայր քո V280: cf v 11 | բալտասար M2627' բաղդ. V280 | նա պատմեսցէ զմեկնութիւնն M4834 J1925 | պատմեսցէ M346'-M2585 (+ արքայի V280)

¹³ աձեն M4114 | զդանիէլ M178 | Թագաւորն] արքա V280 | գդանիէլ M178 | դանիէլ M178 | նաբուգոդոնոսոր V280 M346 J1925 նաբոք. WN11

¹⁴ հոգի] + սուրբ V280 M2585 M2627' M182'' | Աստուծոյ] om

գտաւ ի քեզ: ¹⁵ և արդ աւադիկ մտին առաջի իմ իմաստունք մոգք, իղձք զի զգիրդ զայդ ընթեռնուցուն, և զմեկնութիւն դորա ցուցցեն ինձ, և ոչ կարացին պատմել ինձ: ¹⁶ և ես լուա զքեն եթէ կարող ես մեկնել մեկնութիւնս և արդ եթէ կարիցես զգիրդ ընթեռնուլ և զմեկնութիւն դորա ցուցանել ինձ, ծիրանիս զգեցցիս և մանեակ ոսկի ի պարանոցի քում և երրորդ ի թագաւորութեան իմում տիրեսցես»: ¹⁷ և աս Դանիէլ առաջի Թագաւորին «պարգևք քո քեզ լիցին և զպատիւ տան քո այլում տուր, բայց զգիրդ ես ընթերցայց և զմեկնութիւն դորա ցուցից քեզ: ¹⁸ Արքա, Աստուած բարձրեալն զմեկնութիւն և զԹագաւորութիւն և զպատիւ և զփառս ետ Նաբուքոդոնոսորա հաւր քում: ¹⁹ Ի մեծութենէ զոր ետ նմա ամենայն ազգք և ազինք և լեզուք զարհուրեալ դողային յերեսաց նորա. <զորս> կամէր, հարկաներ և զորս կամէր սպանաներ, զորս կամէր ինքն բարձ-

J1925 | զուարթութիւն M287 M9116] զուարթունն J1925 զաւրթ. M178 զօրութ. rel | առաւել] om V280 |
¹⁵ աւադիկ M287*-V280 M2627'] om M287ᶜ ահաւադիկ M178-M2585 ահաւասիկ M346' աւասիկ rel | իմ 1°] om WN11: hapl | ցուցանեն J1925
¹⁶ և 1°] om M346 | մեկնել] պատմել V280 | զմեկնութիւնս (-թիւն V280 WN11 J1925) V280' WN11 J1925-M2627' | զգիրդ] + զայդ J1925 | ոսկի] + լիցի M4834 M178-M346' | ի 1°] om WN11 | երրորդ M351: hapl | իմում] om M2585 իմոյ V280' M346' | տիրից-ցես J1925
¹⁷ Դանիէլ M178 | պարգև V280'| լիցին] om V280 |<զպա-տիւ>] զպատիւս M287 քո 2°] քում V280 M2585 J1925| զգիրս M346
¹⁸ արքա] om M2627'| բարձրեալ ն աստուած WN11* | և 2°] om WN11 | ետ] եդ V280 | նաբուգոդոնոսորա J V280 M346 V1508 (-րոյ J1925) նաբոք. WN11
¹⁹ ազգ M346 M2627'| և լեզուք] om V280: homoeoarc | դողացին J1925 |<զորս>] զոր M287 M346 pr զի V280 | հարկաներ ... սպասաներ] tr WN11 | կամէր 1°→2° M178 | և 3°—սպանաներ] om M346 | և 4°] om M2585 M9116 M182'| բարձրացուցանէր ... խոնարհեցուցանէր] tr M2627'| և 4°—խոնարհեցուցանէր V280 bis scr | ինքն 2°] om M346' | խոնարհեցուցանէր] կեցուցանէր M346|

րացուցանէր և զորս կամէր, ինքն խոնարհեցուցանէր: ²⁰ և յորժամ բարձրացաւ սիրտ նորա և ոգի նորա զաւրացաւ յամ-
բարտաւանել, անկաւ յաթոռոյ Թագաւորութեան իւրոյ և պա-
տիւն բարձաւ ի նմանէ: ²¹ և ի մարդկանէ հալածեցաւ և սիրտ
ընդ գազանս տուաւ նմա և ընդ ցիռս բնակութիւն նորա և խոտ
իբրև զարջառոյ ջամբեին նմա, և ի ցաւղոյ երկնից մարմին
նորա <ներկաւ> մինչև ծանեաւ թէ տէր է Աստուած բարձրեալ
Թագաւորութեան մարդկան և ում կամի տացէ զնա: ²² և արդ.
դու, որդի նորա Բաղտասար, ոչ խոնարհեցուցեր զսիրտ քո
առաջի Աստուծոյ, ուստի զայդ ամենայն գիտեիր. ²³ և ընդդէմ
Աստուծոյ երկնից հպարտացար և զսպաս տան նորա բերին
առաջի քո, և դու և մեծամեծք քո, հարճք քո և կանայք քո
ըմպէին նոքաւք գինի և զաստուածս զոսկեղէնս և զարծաթեղէնս, զպղընձիս և զերկաթիս և զփայտեղէնս և զքարեղէնս
որ ոչ տեսանեն և ոչ լսեն և ոչ իմանան, աւրհնեիր. և զԱստուած որոյ շունչ քո ի ձեռին նորա է և ամենայն ճանապարհք քո,
զնա ոչ փառաւորեցեր: ²⁴ վասն այնորիկ յերեսաց նորա

²⁰ յամբարտաւանութիւն M287* | յաթոռոյ] -ng V280 աթոռ.
WN11 | բարձաւ ի նմանէ պատիւն V280 | պատիւ նորա M4834
²¹ իբրև] որպէս M178-M346'-M2585 | զարջառոյ M287''] արջ.
rel | ցաւղ M346 | ներկեաւ մարմին նորա J1925 | <ներ-կաւ>]
ներկան M287 -կեաւ V280 M346'| տէր է M287'] տիրէ rel |
Թագաւորութեան մարդկան աստուած V280 | Աստուած] om
J1925 M182''| բարձրեալ] om V280'| Թագաւորութեանց J1925
²² արդ] om M2627' V1508-M351 | բաղդասար V280 բալ.տ.
M2627'| զայս V280 | զտեր WN11 M2627' M182''
²³ երկնից աստուծոյ J1925 | հարճք] pr և V280 J1925 | ըմ-
պէիք J1925-M2627' | նոքովք M9116 | զոսկեղէնս M287' M9116
M182''] ոսկ. rel | արծաթեղէնս J1925 M2627'| զպղնձեղէնս
M2585 | ոչ 1°] + ինչ են և ոչ M4834 | տեսանեն] + և ոչ զնան.
M287ᵐᵍ M178-M346'-M2585: ex Ps II3 v 7 | աւհնեիք M4834 J1925|
յամենայն WN11|ճանապարհս J1925 | քո 6°] + առաջի աչաց
նորա V280| զնա] pr և M178
²⁴ այսորիկ V1508 | նորա] նորին M2585 | գրեաց զգիրդ
զայդ V280 | ի գիրդ M4114 |

առաբեցաւ թաթ ձեռին և զգիրդ զայդ գրեաց: 25 և այս ինչ է
գիրդ որ գրեալ է մանէ, Թեկեղ, փարէս: 26 և այս է մեկնութիւն
բանիդ, մանէ չափեաց Աստուած զթագաւորութիւնդ քո և վախճանեաց զնա: 27 Թեկեղ, կշռեցաւ ի կշիռս և գտաւ պակասեալ:
28 Փարէս, բաժանեցաւ թագաւորութիւն քո և տուաւ Մարաց և
Պարսից»: 29 և հրաման ետ Բաղտասար և զգեցուցին նմա ծիրանիս և մանեակ ոսկի ի պարանոց նորա և քարոզ կարդայր
առաջի նորա լինել իշխան երրորդ ի թագաւորութեան նորա:
30 և ի նմին գիշերի սպանաւ Բաղտասար արքա Քաղդէացի 31 և
Դարեհ արքա առ զթագաւորութիւնն, որ էր ամաց վաթսուն և
երկուց:

6:1 և հաձոյ Թուեցաւ առաջի Դարեհի և կացոյց ի վերա
թագաւորութեանն նախարարս <հարիւր> և քսան զի իցեն յամենայն թագաւորութեանն նորա 2 և ի նոսա վերայ երիս հրա-

25 թէթեղ M2585 V1508-M351 (-կեղ M9116) թէկել (-ել
M4114) M2627' թակեղ M4834 J1925
26 բանիցդ V280 | մանէ M178 M9116
27 թեկել WN11 M4114 թէկեղ M346-M2585 V1508-M351 (-էլ
M2627) թակեղ V280' թէկեղ M178 | կշռեցաւ] ետ M2627' | ի] om
J1925 | կշիռ V280
29 բաղդասար V280 բալ տ. M2627' | զգեցուցին] ազգուցին
J1925 | ի պարանոց նորա] om նորա J1925' ի պարանոցի նորա
M178-M2585 V1508 pr արկին M346'-M2585 M2627' + արկին
M4834 ի պարանոցն արկին V280 | երրորդ M346: hapl երկրորդ
V280
30 բաղդասար V280 բալ տ. M2627' | քաղդէացի M287 WN11]-
դեացի V280 M178-M346 քաղդէացիոց (-դեացւոց M4834 J1925'
M182'') rel + Վասն Արկմանն Դանիէլի ի Գուբն V280
31 առ զթագաւորութիւն նորա դարեհ արբայ V280 | արբա]
մար M2627 | թագաւորութիւնն WN11 | և 2°] om V280 | երկուց]
չորից M346'
6:1 հաձոյ Թուեցաւ] հաձեցաւ M2585 | Դարեհի] իւր V280 |
թագաւորութեանն 1°] + իւրոյ V280 | նախարարաւն J1925 |
<հարիւր>] հարոյր M287 | և 3°] om V280 M2627 | ամենայն WN11
2 ի նոսա վերայ M287' M9116-M4114 ի նոսա ի վերայ J1925
ի վերայ նոսա rel | դանիէլ M178 | հրաման նախարարացն
V280 | մի ինչ V280 | լինիցի M287'' M178-WN11] լիցի rel

մանատարս, և մի ի նոցանէ էր Դանիէլ, տալ նոցա նախարարացն հրաման, զի արքա աշխատ ինչ մի լինիցի: ³ Եւ Դանիէլ
առաւել էր քան զնոսա զի հոգի առաւել գոյր ի նմա. եւ թագաւորն կացոյց զնա ի վերայ ամենայն արքայութեան իւրոյ: ⁴ Եւ
հրամանատարքն և նախարարքն նախանձէին և խնդրէին
պատճառս զԴանիէլէ. եւ ամենին պատճառս և յանցանս եւ
բաղբաղանս ոչ գտանէին զնմանէ քանզի հաւատարիմ էր: ⁵ Եւ
ասեն հրամանատարքն «չգտանեմք ուստեք պատճառս զԴանիէլէ բայց եթէ յաւրէնս Աստուծոյ իւրոյ»: ⁶ Յայնժամ հրամանատարքն եւ նախարարքն կացին առաջի Թագաւորին և ասեն
ցնա. «Դարեհ արքա, յաւիտեան կեաց ⁷ Խորհուրդ արարին ամենեքեան որ են ի Թագաւորութեան քում զաւրաւարք և նախա-
րարք, իշխանք և կուսակալք հաստատել արքունի հաստատութեամբ և զաւրացուցանել ուխտ մի զի եթէ խնդրեսցէ
խնդրուածս ոք յամենայն աստուծոյ կամ ի մարդոյ մինչև յաւուրս երեսուն բայց եթէ ի քէն, ‹արքայ›, անկցի ի գուբն առ-

---

³ դանիէդ M178 I հոգի սուրբ M178 I արքայութեանն M287
J1925-M2627 M182''] Թագաւորութեան rel
⁴ Եւ 1°] վասն որոյ V280 I նախանձէին] + ընդ նմա (նայ
M346) V280 M346'I պատճառս 1°→2° V280 I զԴանիէլէ →5
զԴանիէլէ J1925 զԴանիէլէ M346 M2627-M9116 M182' -իեղէ
M178 I բաղբաղանս M287'']-դայju rel
⁵ զԴանիէլէ M287' WN11-M2585] -լեղէ M178 -իելե M4834
-իելէ rel I
⁶ ցնա Դարեհ] om J1925-M2627I կեաց M287' M2585 M9116-
M2627 M182] կաց rel
⁷ ամենեքին M4834 M4114 I են M287' M2627 M182'] om
M178-M346' M351 էին rel I իշխանք] om M2627 I ‹հաստատել›]-
տեալ M287'' (-եալք M346) I Եւ 3°] om M346 M2627 I մի զի] մեզ
J1925 I խնդրեսցէ M287' J1925-M4114 M182' -րիցէ rel I ոք
խնդրուածս V280' M2585 M9116 M2627' M182''I ոք] om J1925 I
աստուածոյ (-ծոց WN11) WN11 M4114 աստուծոց V280
ստացուածոց M4834 I մինչեւ] om V280 I եթէ 2°] om J1925'-
M4114 M182''I ‹արքայ›] -քայէ M287 M178-M346'-M2585
առնձուց →12 առնձուց V280 I առնձող WN11

ծուց: ⁸ Արդ հաստատեա, արքա, զուխտն և գրեա գիր զի մի եղ
ծանիցի իրաման Պարսից և Մարաց»: ⁹ Յայնժամ Դարեհ արքա
պատուէր ետ գրել զիրամանն: ¹⁰ և Դանիէլ, իբրև գիտաց եթե
կարգեցաւ իրամանն, եմուտ ի տուն իւր և պատուհանք բաց էին
նմա ի վերնատունս իւր ընդ դեմ Երուսաղեմի և երիս ժամս
յաւուրն դներ ծունր և կայր յաղաւթս և գոհանայր առաջի
Աստուծոյ իւրոյ որպես առներ յառաջագոյն: ¹¹ Յայնժամ արքն
այնոքիկ գիտացին և գտին զԴանիէլ զի կայր յաղաւթս և
աղաչէր զԱստուած իւր: ¹² Մատեան և ասեն զթագաւորն «ար
քա, ո՞չ ուխտ մի կարգեցեր զի ամենայն մարդ որ խնդրիցէ
խնդրուածս յամենայն աստուծոյ կամ ի մարդոյ մինչև յա
ւուրս երեսունս բայց եթե ի քէն, <արքայ> անկցի ի գուբ առն
ծուց»: և ասէ արքա «ճշմարիտ է բանդ և իրաման Մարաց և
Պարսից չէ աւրէն շրջել»: ¹³ Յայնժամ պատասխանի ետուն ար
քայի և ասեն «Դանիէլ որ յորդւոց գերութեան Հրէաստանի ոչ
հնազանդեցաւ իրամանի Թագաւորիդ և երիս ժամս խնդրէ
խնդրուածս յԱստուծոյ իւրմէ»: ¹⁴ Յայնժամ Թագաւորն, իբրև

⁸ եղծի J1925 | Պարսից ... Մարաց M287' J1925] tr rel
¹⁰ յաւուրն] ի յաւուր M4834 | դներ M287]դնել J1925 դներ
rel | առաջի Աստուծոյ] զաստուծոյ M2627 | որպէս և M346'|
յառաջագոյն] առաջ. WN11 -գոյնս J1925
¹¹ գիտացին M287 M9116-M4114] դիտեցին M4834 M2585
J1925-M2627 M182 գիտեցին rel] զդանիէլ V280 M178
¹² արքա 1°] om J1925| զի] Թէ J1925| խնդրեացէ M4834 |
խնդրուածս] pr յաստուծոյ J1925| յամենայնի J1925 ամենայն
WN11 | յաստուծոյ J1925 աստուծոց (ուածոց WN11) V280 M178-
WN11 M2627 M351 ստացուածոց M4834 | ի 1° M287] om rel|
<արքայ> J1925-M2627] -բայէ rel | գուբին WN11 | և 3°] om
J1925'-M4114 | իրամանն M287] զիրամանն (-մանս V280) rel |
Պարսից M287' M346' J1925']զպարս. rel
¹³ դանիէլ M178 | գերութեան M287' J1925' M182']+ էր rel |
իրեաստանի M4114 | ոչ]prէ J1925 | Թագաւորիդ M287]քում (+
արքայ M2585 M2627 M182') rel | երիս | pr աւուրն V280 | ժամս]
ժամ V280 V1508 + յաւուր M2585 J1925 | աստուծոյ WN11 |
իւրոյ J1925-M2627
¹⁴ Յայնժամ] + և M2627 | Թագաւորն tr post լուաւ V280'

լուաւ զբանն, տրտմեցաւ յոյժ և վասն Դանիէլի ջանայր փրկել
զնա, և մինչև ցընդերեկս ջանագաւ փրկել զնա: ¹⁵ Յայնժամ
արքն այնոքիկ ասեն ցԹագաւորն «գիտասջիր, արքա, զի հրամանի Մարաց և Պարսից և ամենայն ուխտի և հաստատութեան զոր արքա հաստատիցէ, ոչ է աւրէն շրջել»: ¹⁶ Յայնժամ
հրաման ետ Թագաւորն և ածին զԴանիէլ և արկին զնա ի գուբն
առևծուց և ասէ արքայն զԴանիէլ «Աստուածն զոր դու պաշտես
յաճախ, նա փրկեսցէ զքեզ»: ¹⁷ և բերին վէմ մի և եդին ի
վերայ զբոյն և կնքեաց Թագաւորն մատանեաւ իւրով և մա-
տանեաւք մեծամեծացն, զի մի այլազգ ինչ իրք շրջեսցին զԴանիէլէ: ¹⁸ և գնաց Թագաւորն ի տուն իւր և ննջեաց առանց
ընթրեաց, և խորտիկս ոչ մուծին առաջի նորա, և քուն հատաւ ի
նմանէ. և եկից Աստուած զքերանս առևծուցն և ոչ լլկեցին
զԴանիէլ: ¹⁹ Յայնժամ յարեաւ արքա ընդ առաւաւտս լուսով և

M2627 | իբր M4114 | զբանն] om V280 M2627 | սրտմեեցաւ V280 |
և 1°] tr ante ջանայր M4834 J1925 M182' | դանիեղի M178 -իելի
M346-M2585 M9116-M2627' M182' | ջանայր] pr և M2627 M351 |
զնա 1°→2° M9116-M4114 | զնա 1°] + և ընդ երեկս ջանագաւ փրկել
զնա V280: ditt | ցընդերեկս M287 M2627] յընդ. V280' ընդ երեկսն
J1925 ցերեկս (ցյեր. WN11) M346' ցընթրեկերս rel
¹⁵ հրաման M4834 J1925 -նաց V280 | հաստատեսցէ արքայ
V280 | հաստատեսցէ M4834 J1925 -տեաց M2585 M2627 | ոչ է]չէ
M2585 M2627 | շրջիլ M178-M346-M2585 M4114
¹⁶ զԴանիէլ] -իեղ M178 | ի] om M351 | զԴանիէլ] -իեղ
M178| Աստուած քո M4834 J1925 | յաճախ] om M9116 tr ante
պաշտես M2627: cf v 20 | փրկէ V280
¹⁷ մի] մեծ V280 | վերայ] om V280 | զքին V280| մատա-
նեաւք]-նեաւ V280 M346 | մեծամեծաց իւրոց V280'| այլ ինչ
ազգ V280 | այլազգ]-ազգք M4834 WN11 M9116-M2627'| ինչ] om
M351 tr post իրք M182 | իրք] om M178-M346-M2585 J1925 M182'
tr post շրջեսցին V280 | շրջիցին M4834 J1925'| զԴանիէլէ M287]
վասն դանիէլի (-իեղի M178 -իէլի M346 M9116-M4114 M182'') rel
¹⁸ խորտիկս M287' M346'-M2585 J1925-M2627]-տիկ rel |
եկից] խցեաց J1925 | զքերան J1925 | առևծոցն WN11 |
զդանիէդ M178
¹⁹ առաւաւտն լուսոյն M4834 J1925 առ. լուսով M346'-M2585
M2627 լուսանալ առաւաւտուն V280 | եկն փուԹանակի V280 |

փութով եկն ի <գուբն> առնձուց: ²⁰ և իբրև մերձեցաւ ի
<գուբն> ապաղակեաց ի ձայն մեծ և ասէ «Դանիէլ, ծառայ
Աստուծոյ կենդանւոյ, Աստուածն զոր դուն յածախ պաշտեիր
եթե կարա՞ց փրկել զքեզ ի բերանոյ առնձուցդ»: ²¹ և ասէ
Դանիէլ ցարքա «արքա, յաւիտեան կեաց. ²² Աստուած իմ առաքեաց զհրեշտակ իւր և եփից զքերանս առնձուցս և ոչ ապականեցին զիս, զի առաջի նորա ուղղութիւն գտաւ իմ և առաջի
քո, արքա, վնաս ինչ ոչ արարի»: ²³ Յայնժամ թագաւորն զւար-
ձացաւ յանձն իւր յոյժ և հրաման ետ հանել զԴանիէլ ի գբոյ
անտի. հանաւ Դանիէլ ի գբոյ անտի և ամենին ապականութիւն ոչ գտաւ ի նմա զի հաւատաց յԱստուած իւր: ²⁴ և հրաման
ետ թագաւորն և աձին զարսն զչարախաւսս զԴանիէլէ և ի
գուբն առնձուց ընկեցան ինքնեանք և որդիք իւրեանց և կանայք
նոցա և չէին յատակս գբոյն հասեալ մինչև տիրեցին նոցա
առնձքն և զամենայն ոսկերս նոցա մանրեցին: ²⁵ Յայն-

գուբն→20 գուբն V280 | <գուբն>]գուփն M287 | առնձոցն WN11
²⁰ և 1°] M9116-M4114 M182'|<գուբն > գուփն M287 |
Դանիէլ]- իէղ M178 V280: bis scr | Աստուածն] +քո M4834 J1925'-
M4114 M182'' | դուն] om J1925
²¹ արքա] յարք. M182 | կաց WN11 J1925
²² եփից J1925 | զքերան J1925-M2627 | նորա] աստուծոյ
M2627 | գտաւ ուղղութիւն իմ J1925 | վնաս ինչ արքայ J1925 |
արքա] om M2627
²³ յոյժ M287' WN11-M2585 J1925-M2627] om rel | հրաման
ետ] հրամայեաց J1925 | զԴանիէլ] tr postանդի V280-իէղ M178
om M346-WN11* | անդի 1°→2° M4834 M2627 | անդի 1° M287
M9116 M182''] + և rel | դանիէղ M178 | ամենևիմբ պակասու-
թիւն V280 | ոչ] pr ինչ M9116-M4114 | ի նմա] tr ante ոչ J1925 |
նմա] նա M346' | յԱստուած] աստ. WN11
²⁴ և աձին]և աձեն M346 աձել V280 | զարսն] om J1925 |
զչարախաւսս M287' M346'-M2585] զչարախոսուս J1925 չար. rel |
զԴանիէլէ M287' WN11 M351] դանիէլի V280 J1925 -իէլէ rel
(-իէղէ M178)| ընկեցան] tr ante ի M2585 M2627 M182''(ընկ. ինքն.
ante ի V280) ընկեցինն J1925 | չէին M287] չև ես էին V280 չև էին
rel | յատակ J1925 | հասեալ tr ante յատակս V280 | մինչ V280
J1925
²⁵ գրեաց դարեի արքա V280 | և 1°→2° V280'| եին M287'

ժամ Դարեհ արքա գրեաց առ ամենայն ազգս և ազինս և լեզուս
որ բնակեալ էին յամենայն երկրին. խաղաղութիւն ձեզ
բազմասցի: ²⁶ Ցերեսաց իմոց եդաւ հրաման այս յամենայն իշ-
խանութեան Թագաւորութեան իմում զի երկնչիցեն և դողայ-
ցեն յերեսաց Աստուծոյն Դանիէլի, զի նա է Աստուած կենդանի
և կա յաւիտեան և արքայութիւն նորա ոչ եղծանի և տերութիւն
նորա մինչև գլախճան: ²⁷ Ալզնական լինի և փրկէ և առնէ
նշանս յերկինս և յերկիր որ փրկեաց զԴանիէլ ի բերանոյ
առնձուցն: ²⁸ և Դանիէլի աջողէր ի Թագաւորութեանն Դարեհի և
Կիւրոսի Պարսկի:

⁷:¹ Ցամին առաջներորդի Բաղտասարա արքային Քաղդեացւց երագ ետես Դանիէլ և տեսիլ գլխոյ նորա յանկողնի
իւրում և զերազն գրեաց: ² Ես Դանիէլ տեսանէի ի տեսլեան զի-

M9116 V1508] էք V280 M178-M346' են rel ǀ յամենայն] om M351 ǀ
յերկրի WN11 M351 ǀ ի խաղաղութիւն ձեր WN11 ǀ ընդ ձեզ
M4834
²⁶ իմոց] դարեհ արքայի V280 ǀ եդաւ] է V280-M4834ᵗˣᵗ ǀ
այս] om M9116 ǀ ընդ ամենայն WN11ᶜ-M2585 M2627' M182'' ǀ
իշխանութեան] + և V280 -թիւն WN11-M2585 M2627' V1508-M351
ǀ իմոյ J1925 ǀ երկնչիցեն M287 WN11 M9116-M4114] -իցին rel ǀ
դողան V280 -ասցին M4834 J1925 (-ցեն WN11) ǀ յերեսաց] -սայց
M4834 երես. M2585 ǀ Դանիէլի M287'' WN11-M2585 J1925-M2627
M351] -իելի rel (-իեղի M178)ǀ Աստուած] om M178 ǀ կա] կեա
V280 ǀ յաւիտեան M287] -տեանս rel ǀ եղծանին J1925 ǀ մինչ
V280' M178-WN11-M2585 M4114 V1508
²⁷ յերկինս] երկրի WN11* ǀ և յերկիր]ի վերև յերկրի M4834
J1925 ǀ յերկիր M287] -կրի զդանիէլ M178
²⁸ Դանիէլի M287' M346-M2585 M182'] -իէլ V280 WN11*
J1925 -իելի (-իեղի M178) rel ǀ յաջողէր V280 ǀ Թագաւորութե-
նէն M9116 ǀ կիւրոս M4834 ǀ Պարսկի] om J1925'-M4114
⁷:¹ init] pr Վասն ապագին գազանացն և ներինն և
գալստեանն Քրիստոսի V280 ǀ առաջնորդի M9116 ǀ Բաղտասարա M287' WN11ᶜ J1925] -սար (բալ. M2627) M178-M346'-M2585
M2627 -րայ (բաղդ. V280) rel ǀ Քաղդեացւց M287 M2627]
քաղդեաց. (-ցւց WN11) rel ǀ դանիէդ M178 ǀ իւրում] իւր M346-
WN11* +տագնապեաց զնա V280
² Հողմք] կողմք M9116 ǀ յերկնից V280

շերոյ և ահա չորք հողմք երկնից բախէին գձով մեծ: ³ և չորք
գազանք մեծամեծք ելանէին ի ծովէ անտի այլակերպք ի միմեանց, ⁴ առաջինն իբրև մատակ առիւծ թևաւոր, և թևք նորա
իբրև գարձուլ. հայէի մինչև թափեցան թևք նորա և չնչեցաւ
յերկրէ և եկաց իբրև ի վերայ ոտից մարդոյ և սիրտ մարդոյ
տուաւ նմա: ⁵ և ահա երկրորդ գազանն նման արջոյ և եկաց ի
կողմն մի և կողք երեք ի բերան նորա ի մէջ ժանեաց նորա և
այսպէս ասէին ցնա «արի, կեր զմարմինս բազմաց»: ⁶ և զկնի
նորա հայէի և ահա այլ գազան ելանէր իբրև զինձ, և չորք
<թևք> թռչնոց ի վերայ նորա և չորք գլուխ գազանին և իշ-
խանութիւն տուաւ նմա: ⁷ և զկնի նորա հայէի և ահա գազան
չորրորդ ահեղ և զարմանալի և հզաւր առաւել և ժանիք նորա
երկաթիք և մագիլք նորա պղնձիք, ուտեր և մանրեր և զմնա-
ցորդսն առ րան կոտորեր և ինքն առաւել այլակերպ քան գամենայն որ յառաջ քան զնա և եղջևրք տասն ի նմա: ⁸ Պշու-
ցեալ հայէի ընդ եղջևրս նորա և ահա այլ եղջևր փոքրիկ ելա-

---

³ Ի 2°] om M346' V1508

⁴ իբրև 1°] որպէս M178 | մատակ M287] զմատ. rel |
թևաւորս M4834 | իբրև 2°] որպէս M346'-M2585 | գարձւոյ M287']
գարձուի WN11 արձւոյ (-ձւլոյ M351: ditt) M178 M9116-M4114
M182' զարձւոյ rel | հայէի] pr և WN11 | մինչև M287' WN11
J1925'-M2627] մինչ rel | չնչեցան V280 | և 3°] om M2627 |
եկաց] եկեաց M2627

⁵ կաց V280 | մի կողմն M178

⁶ այլ] om V280 | գազան] om M178 | ելանէր M287 M178-
WN11-M2585] էր M346 om rel | զինձ] զառձ M346: cf v 4 | չորք
1°] չորս WN11 | <թևք>] թև M287 թևս WN11 | թռչնոց M287'
M346 J1925] -նոյ rel | նորա 2°] om M287-WN11 | գլուխ M287' M2627]
զգլուխք rel | տուաւ] om M178

⁷ ահեղ յոյժ M4834 | և հզաւր] tr V280 om J1925 | առաւել
om J1925 | և 5°] om M178-M346 J1925' | և 6°—պղնձիք M287'
M178-M346'] om rel | զմնացորդն M346 | տասն V280 WN11
J1925 | այլակերպ էր առաւել J1925 | քան] pr էր V280' M2585 |
զայլ գազանն ամենայն V280 | եղջիւր M351

⁸ Պշուցեալ] pr և WN11 | որ M287 M4114 M182' WN11°]
նորա rel | մեծամեծս M287] զմեծ.rel

ներ ի մէջ նոցա և երեք եղջևրք յառաջնոցն ի բաց խլեին յերեսաց նորա. և ահա աչք իբրև գաչս մարդոյ յեղջևրն յայնմիկ և
բերան որ խաւսէր մեծամեծս: ⁹ Տեսանեի մինչև աթոռք <ան-
կանեին> և հին աւուրցն նստէր. հանդերձ նորա իբրև գձիւն
սպիտակ և հեր գլխոյ նորա իբրև զասր սուրբ, աթոռ նորա իբրև
զբոց հրոյ, անիւք նորա իբրև հուր բորբոքեալ: ¹⁰ և գետ հրոյ
յորդեալ ելանէր առաջի նորա. հազարք հազարաց պաշտէին
զնա և բիւրք բիւրուց կային առաջի նորա, ատեան նստաւ և
դպրութիւնք բացան: ¹¹ Տեսանեի յայնժամ ի բարբառոյ մեծամեծ բանիցն զոր եղջևրն այն խաւսէր մինչև բարձաւ գազանն և կորեաւ և մարմին նորա տուաւ յայրումն հրոյ: ¹² և
այլոց գազանաց իշխանութիւն փոխեցաւ և երկայնութիւն
կենաց տուաւ նոցա մինչև ի ժամանակ: ¹³ Տեսանեի ի տեսլեան
գիշերոյ և ահա ընդ ամպս երկնից իբրև որդի մարդոյ գայր և
հասանէր մինչև ի հինաւուրցն և մատուցաւ առաջի նորա: ¹⁴ և
նմա տուաւ իշխանութիւն և պատիւ և արքայութիւն և ամենայն ազգք և ազինք և լեզուք նմա ծառայեսցեն. իշխանութիւն նորա իշխանութիւն յաւիտենական որ ոչ անցանիցէ, և
թագաւորութիւն նորա ոչ եղծանիցի: ¹⁵ Սոսկացաւ մարմին իմ

---

⁹ յաթոռք M351 | <անկանեին>] անզ. M287 J1925 | իբրև 1°]
որպէս M178 | սպիտակ M287'] tr ante իբրև 1° rel | իբրև 2°] որպէս
V280 M178 | իբրև 3°] որպէս M178-M346' | անիւք] pr և M4834
J1925 | իբրև 4°] որպէս M346' | հուր M287 M9116-M4114] զբոց
V280 զհուր rel
¹⁰ և 1°] om M9116 V1508 | բիւրոց M4834 WN11 M2627 |
դպրութիւն M346
¹¹ բարբառ M4834 | մեծ V280 | բանիցն այնոցիկ M2585
M2627 | գազանն այն WN11
¹² փոփոխեցաւ V1508 | նոցա] նմա V280 | ժամանակս
V280 WN11 J1925
¹⁴ ազգք] ազգ J1925-M2627 | իշխանութիւն 2°] pr և M182' |
յաւիտենից M2627 | անցանիցէ M287 J1925] անցանէ rel | Թա-
գաւորութիւն նորա V280: bis scr | Թագաւորութեան M9116
¹⁵ դանիեղ M178 | և 1°] pr տեսիլ WN11* | խռովեցոյց] զար-
հուրեցոյց V280

յանձին իմում, ես Դանիէլ և տեսիլ գլխոյ իմոյ խռովեցոյց զիս: ¹⁶ և մատեա առ մի ումն որ կային անդ և զճշմարտութիւն կա-մեի ուսանել վասն ամենայնի այնորիկ և ասաց ինձ զճշմար-տութիւն և զմեկնութիւն բանիցն եցոյց ինձ: ¹⁷ Արդ գազանք մեծամեծք չորք Թագաւորութիւնք յարիցեն ի վերայ երկրի, բարձին ¹⁸ և առցեն զԹագաւորութիւնս սուրբք բարձրելոյ և կալցեն զնա մինչև յաւիտեանս յաւիտենից: ¹⁹ և քննեի <ճշմարտիւ> վասն գազանին չորրորդի զի առաւել այլակերպ <էր> քան զամենայն գազանս և ահագին յոյժ, և ժանիք նորա երկաթիք և մագիլք նորա պղնձիք, ուտէր և մանրէր և զմնա-ցորդսն առ ոտն կոտորէր: ²⁰ և վասն եղջերացն տասանցն որ ի գլուխ նորա և վասն միւսոյն որ ելանէր և զերիսն ի բաց Թաւթափէր որոյ աչքն էին և բերան նորա խաւսէր զմեծամեծս, և տեսիլ նորա առաւել քան զայլոցն: ²¹ և տեսանեի և եղջերն այն տայր պատերազմ ընդ սուրբս և զարրանայր ի վերայ նո-ցա ²² մինչև եկն հինաւուրցն և ետ իրաւունս սրբոց բարձրելոյ. ժամանակ եհաս և զարքայութիւն նորա սուրբք ընբռնեցին:

¹⁶ և 1°] om M9116 | որ] թr առ WN11 | զճշմարտութիւն 1°] զստուգութիւնն V280 | կամեի M287' M178] կամեցայ M4834 խնդրեի rel | ուսանել] + ի նմանէ M4834 J1925 | այսորիկ M346
¹⁷ արդ M287 M178-M346-WN11* M4114] այդ rel | Թագաւո-րութիւնք] Թագաւորք (-որ WN11*) M178-M346' | բարձին] բարցին M4834 -ցեն M346 բարձրացին J1925 pr և V280
¹⁸ Թագաւորութիւնս M287 J1925] -թիւնն rel | կալցեն M287'] -ցին rel | յաւիտեանս] om WN11* homoeoarc
¹⁹ <ճշմարտիւ>] ճշմարիտ M287 | <էր>] եր M287 om M351 | գագանս] + որ յառաջ քան զնա M2585 M2627' M182''| և 3°➔4° M2627 | և 3°] om M178-M346' | ոտանն V280 J1925
²⁰ վասն 1°] om M178 J1925 | որ 1°] + էին M346' էր M2585 M2627' M182''| միւսոյն] միոյն J1925 | Թաւթափէր M178 Թափէր J1925' M182''| և 4°] ի M351 | նորա 2° M287'' M2585 J1925'-M2627] om M178-M346-WN11* որ rel | քան M287'] pr էր rel
²¹ և 1° M287] om rel | և 2°] om M9116-M4114 զի WN11 + ահա V280' M287-M346' + որ M9116-M4114
²² սրբոյն V280 | ժամանակք V280

²³ Եւ ասէ գազանն չորրորդ Թագաւորութիւն <չորրորդ> կայցէ
յերկրի, որ առաւել իցէ քան զամենայն Թագաւորութիւնս և
կերիցէ զամենայն երկիր և կոխեսցէ և հարցէ զնա: ²⁴ Եւ տասն
եղջևր նորա տասն Թագաւորք յարիցեն, և զկնի նոցա յարիցէ
այլ որ առաւել իցէ չարիւք քան զամենայն առաջինսն և երիս
Թագաւորս խոնարհեցուցէ: ²⁵ Եւ զբանս առ բարձրեալն խաւ-
սեցի և զսուրբս բարձրելոյն մոլորեցուցէ և <կարծեսցէ >
զժամանակս և զաւրէնս փոփոխել և տացի ի ձեռս նորա մինչև ի
ժամանակ և ի ժամանակս և ի կէս ժամանակի: ²⁶ Ատեան նստցի
և զիշխանութիւն նորա փոխեսցեն յապականել և ի կորուսանել
մինչև ի սպառ: ²⁷ Եւ Թագաւորութիւն և իշխանութիւն և
մեծութիւն Թագաւորաց որ ի ներքոյ ամենայն երկնից տուաւ
սրբոց բարձրելոյ և արքայութիւն նորա արքայութիւն յաւիտենական և ամենայն իշխանութիւնք նմա ծառայեսցեն և
հնազանդեսցին մինչև ցայս վայր է վախճան բանիս: ²⁸ Ես
Դանիէլ և խորհուրդք իմ յոյժ խոովեցուցանէին զիս և գոյն
երեսաց իմոց շրշեցաւ և զբանն ի սրտի իմում պահեի:

²³ ասէ] այս է M178-M346 J1925 | <չորրորդ>] չորրոր M287 |
յերկրի] pr ի M178 M2627 ի վերայ երկրի V280 | Թագաւորու-
թիւնս] -թիւն M2627'-M9116 | կոխեսցէ M287' M2585 J1925-
M2627] կոխիցէ rel
²⁴ եղջևրք V280 M2585 M9116-M4114 M182'' | Թագաւորք] -
լոր J1925 | յարիցեն] + յետ նորա M4834 J1925 | նոցա M287''
M2585 M2627 M182'] նորա rel | իցէ] է J1925 | չարիւք M287]
չարեօք rel | առաջինն WN11
²⁵ զբանս M287] բանս rel | խոսիցի M182' | <կարծեսցէ >
M178-M346-M2585 J1925'-M2627 V1508] կարծեսցէ rel | ի 1°] om
WN11* | ի ժամանակ] om M4834 M178 J1925 M351 ի ժամանակս
V280 | կէս M178 | ժամանակի M287 M2585] կաց rel
²⁶ փոփոխեցեն V280 | և ի կորուսանել] om J1925'-M4114
M351: homoeotel | ի 1°] om WN11
²⁷ և 2°➜3° J1925'-M4114 M182'' | ամենայն 1°] om M9116-
M2627' M182'' | սրբոյ V280 | և 4°] om V280' | արքայութիւն նո-
րա] om M351: homoeoarc | յաւիտենական] -տենից WN11 |
ամենայն 2°] om M2627 | հնազանդեսցեն WN11
²⁸ խորհուրդ V280 | երեսաց իմոց] իմ M287*-V280' J1925' |

The Armenian Version of Daniel

8:1 Յամին երրորդի Բաղտասարա <արքայի> տեսիլ երևեցաւ ինձ. Ես Դանիէլ յետ տեսլեանն առաջնոյ ² էի ի Շաւշա ապարանս, որ է յերկրին Ելամա, և կայի ի վերայ Ուբաղա: ³ Ամբարձի զաչս իմ և տեսի և ահա խոյ մի <կայր> հանդեպ Ուբաղա և եղջիւրք նորա բարձունք. և մին բարձրագոյն էր քան զմիւսն և որ բարձրն էր յետոյ ելանէր: ⁴ Տեսանեի զխոյն զի ոգորէր ընդ ծով և ընդ <հիւսիսի> և ընդ հարաւ, և ամենայն գազանքն ոչ կային առաջի նորա, և չէր որ ապրէր ի ձեռաց նորա. և առներ ըստ կամաց իւրոց և մեծանայր: ⁵ և ես միտ դնեի, և ահա քաւշ մի այծեաց գայր յարևմտից ընդ երեսս երկրի և յերկիր ոչ մերձանայր և քաւշին եղջեր մի էր ի մէջ աչաց նորա: ⁶ և եկաս մինչև ի խոյն եղջերաւոր գոր տեսանեի զի <կայր> հանդեպ Ուբաղա և յար ձակեցաւ ի վերայ նորա

զբանն M178 M351 | պահէի ի սիրտ իմ V280 | պահեցի M346'

8:1 pr Վասն Խոյին Քաւշին V280 | երրորդի M287' M346-WN11*] + Թագաւորութեանն rel | Բաղտասարայ M287 J1925] -րայ (բաղդ. V280 բալտ. M2627) rel | <արքայի >] արքայութեանն M287 | դանիէլ M178

² Շաւշա M287 WN11*] շաւշայ M4834 շաւշ (+ քաղաքի V280) V280 M2585-WN11ᶜ M4114 M182'' շոշայ (շոշա M346) rel | ապարանսն M287' J1925-M2627] ի յաալ. V280 յաալ. rel | է] էր M178 | Ելամա M287' WN11] ելամայ (եղ. M4834) M4834 M9116 էլամա (-մայ M178-M2585) M178-M346-M2585 էլամայ rel | Ուբաղա M287 WN11-M2585 (pr J1925)]ուբալայ M2627 ուբաղայ (յուբ. M9116)rel

³ <կայր>] գայր M287 M178-M346 | Ուբաղա M287 M346'] սիբեղայ (-լայ M4834) M4834 J1925 -ղայ rel | բարձունք] բարձրագոյնք V280 | էր] om WN11*

⁴ <հիւսիսի >] հւսսի M287 M178-M2585 հիւսիսի M346 J1925 հիւսիւսի M4834 | նչ] om V280 | կացին J1925 | չէր] նչ էր M346 | որ] om WN11*| նորա 2°] pr առաջ WN11* | կամս իւր M2627

⁵ ի մոի M9116 | այծեաց] om J1925 յաածեաց V280' M178-M346'-M2585 | յարևմտից գայր J1925 | յարեիմտից] om M9116| երեսս երեսս M346: ditt

⁶ գխոյն M9116 M351 |<կայր>] գայր M287 | Ուբաղա M287 M346'] ուբալայ M2627 ուբեղայ J1925 ուբաղայ rel | յուծոյ WN11

զաւրութեամբ ուժով իւրոյ: ⁷ ԵՒ տեսանեի <զնա> հասեալ մինչև ցխոյն. զայրացաւ և եհար զխոյն և խորտակեաց զերկուսին զեղջևրս նորա, և ոչ գոյր զաւրութիւն խոյին ունել զդեմ նորա. արկ զնա յերկիր և ոտից իւրոց կոխան արար զնա և ոչ ոք էր որ թափէր զխոյն ի ձեռաց նորա: ⁸ ԵՒ քաւշն այծեաց մեծացաւ յոյժ, և ի զաւրանալն նորա խորտակեցաւ եղջևր նորա. մեծ. և ելին չորք եղջևրք ի ներքոյ նորա ընդ չորս հողմս երկնից. ⁹ ԵՒ ի միոջէ ի նոցանէ ել եղջևր մի հզաւր: ¹⁰ ԵՒ մեծացաւ առաւել ընդ <հիւսիսի> և առ զաւրութիւն և բարձրացաւ մինչև ի զաւրութիւն երկնից, և <ընկեաց> յերկիր ի զաւրութենէ երկնից և յաստեղեաց և կոխեաց զնոսա ¹¹ մինչև զաւրաւարն փրկեացէ զզերութիւնն և նովաւ պատարագք խռովեցան. և եղև և յաջողեցաւ նմա և սրբութիւն նորա աւրեացի: ¹² ԵՒ տուան ի վերայ պատարագացն մեղք և անկաւ յերկիր արդարութիւն, և արար և յաջողեցաւ: ¹³ ԵՒ լուա ի միոջէ սրբոյ որ խաւսէր ցիս և

⁷ <զնա>] զի նա M287 զի (+զնա M4834 sup. lin) M4834 J1925 | հասեալ] եհաս J1925| ցխոյն 1°→2°] om V280 | զայրացաւ] զօր. M346 | երկուսին M287] երկուսեան M346' M9116 -կուսին rel | եղջևրս V280' M346'-M2585 M9116-M2627' M182' եղջևր V1508 | ունել] առնել V280| ոտից] կոխից M2627 | առնէր V280' M178 J1925' M182'| նորա] քաւշին M2585 M2627' M182' (pr M178) նոխազին V280

⁸ յայծեաց V280 M346'| յոյժ] pr մեծութիւն M178-M2585 M2627' M182''| եղջևր] աղջեաւր M4834 | չորս] om M346-WN11*| հողմոց J1925 |

⁹ միոջէ] միոյ M9116 միջէ M351 միջոյ V280 M346 J1925 | ի նոցանէ] նոցա V280'| ել] om V280 M178-WN11-M2585 M9116 M351: homoeoarc

¹⁰ առաւել] om WN11*| <հիւսիսի>] հւսսի M287 M2585 հիսիսի J1925 M351 հիւսիսի M9116 հիսիսի WN11 | մինչև] om V280 | և 3° M287ᶜ M2585 J1925-M2627' M182''] om rel | զաւրութիւն M287] -թիւնն M178 -թիւնս rel | երկնից] om V280 յերկ. WN11 | <ընկեաց> J1925] -եց rel | ի յերկիր J1925 | աստեղաց M4114 | զնա J1925

¹¹ նովաւ] նորա V280 | պատարագ WN11 | և 3°] om WN11*| նորա M287 M178] om rel | աւերեցաւ V280

¹³ մի M178-M346'| ցիս M287 M346'-M2585| զի M178 om rel |

ասէր սուրբ մի գփիլմնիհս որ խաւսէր «մինչև ցե՞րբ տեսիլդ այդ <կացցէ > պատարագք բարձեալք և մեղբդ աւերածի <տունեալք> և սրբութիւնդ և զաւրութիւն կոխեցին»: 14 և ասէ ցնա «մինչև յերեկոյ և ի վաղորդեայն աւուրս երկու հազարս երեք հարիւր և սրբեսցի սրբութիւն»: 15 և եղև տեսի ես Դանիէլ զտեսիլն և խնդրեի խելամուտ լինել. և ահա առաջի իմ եկաց իբրև զտեսիլ մարդոյ. 16 և լուա բարբառ մարդոյ ի միջոյ Ուբադա, և կոչեաց և ասէ «Գաբրիէլ, իմացոյ նմա զտեսիլդ»: 17 և եկն եկաց ուր եսն կայի, և ի գալն նորա յիմարեցա և անկա ի վերայ երեսաց իմոց. և ասէ ցիս «ի միտ առ, որդի մարդոյ. զի տակաւին ի ժամանակ վախճանի է տեսիլդ»: 18 և մինչդեռ խաւսէր նա ընդ իս յիմարեցա և անկա ի վերա երեսաց իմոց յերկիր և բունն եհար զինեն և կացոյց ի վերայ ոտից իմոց: 19 և ասէ ցիս «աւասիկ, ես ցուցից քեզ որ ինչ լինելոց է ի

և 2°] om M178 | ասէ V280' J1925'-M2627' | ցուրբ M346-M2585 | գփեղմնիհս (pr սա գնա M4834 pr գնա V280) V280' M178 M9116 V1508 գփել. M182' գփեղ. J1925-M4114 գփելմովնին M2585 M2627 փիլիմնիհս (փել. WN11) M346' | խաւսէր] + գնա M178-M346'-M2585 | յերբ M346' J1925'-M4114 M351: cf v 12 |<կացցէ>] կայցցէ M287* | <տունեալք> ed] տվեալք M287 տրւեալք V280 տունեալբդ WN11 տեսեալք rel | սրբութիւնբ J1925 | և զաւրութիւն] om M9116 | զաւրութիւնբ կոխեցին J1925

14 և 1°] om M346' | ցերեկոյ J1925 | ի 1°] om WN11 | վաղոր-դայն M2585 M4114 M182 | աւուր M178 | երկուս M4834 J1925'-M2627 | երեք] pr և V280' M178 J1925'-M2627 | երեկիւր եօթանա-սուն և ութ M351 | հազար երեկերիւր և վաշսուն և ութ V1508 հազար երեկիւր եօթանասուն և ութ M2585 M4114 M182 հազար երեք հարիւր և եօթանասուն և ութ WN11 հազար և երկու հարիւր և եթանասուն M346 հազար երեկերիւր և թնասուն և թն M4834mg

15 դանիէղ M178 | եկաց առաջի իմ M2627 | իբրև] որպէս M178 | մարդոյ ➜16 մարդոյ V280

16 մարդոյ] om M2627 | Ուբադա M287 M346'] ուբալաj M2627 ուբադայ rel | զաբրիէղ M178 | նմա] om J1925

17 ուր եսն] ուրեմն J1925 | իմոց➜18 իմոց M2627 | ի 4°] om V280 WN11 | ժամանակս M4834 M346'-M2585 J1925'-M4114 M182': cf v 19

18 յերկիր] om M346' | հար J1925

19 աւասիկ M287] ահաւասիկ rel | ես] om V280 | զոր V280'

վախճանի ի վերայ երկրի, քանզի տակաւին ի ժամանակս է
վախճանն: 20 Խոյն զոր տեսանէիր եղջերաւոր Թագաւոր Պար–
սից և Մարաց է, 21 և քաւշն այծեաց Թագաւոր Յունաց, և
եղջերն մեծ որ էր ի մէջ աչաց նորա նոյն ինքն է Թագաւորն
առաջին: 22 և ի խորտակելն նորա ընդ որով էին այլ եղջերք,
չորք Թագաւորք յազգէ նորա յարիցեն և ոչ իւրեանց զաւ–
րութեամբ: 23 և յետ Թագաւորութեան նոցա ի կատարել մեղացն
նորա յարիցէ Թագաւոր ժպիրհ երեսաւք, յառակս խորհրդական
24 և հզաւր <զաւրութիւն> նորա, և զքանչելիսն ապականեցէ.
և յաջողեցի և արասցէ և ապականեցէ հզաւր և զժողովուրդն
սուրբ: 25 և լուծ անրոյ նորա յաջողեցի և <նենգութիւն> ի ձեռս
նորա և ի սրտի իւրում մեծամտեցէ և նենգութեամբ
ապականեցէ զբազումս և կորստեան բազմաց կայցէ, և իբրև
զձուս ի ձեռին մանրեցէ: 26 և զտեսիլն երեկորին և առա–
լաւատին որ ասացաւն ճշմարիտ է. և դու, կնքեա զտեսիլդ զի յա–

M346' J1925 | է 1°] իցէ M2585 | վախճանն] տեսիլ վախճանի
J1925 տեսիլ ւո ի վախճանի M4834
20 եղջեաւրաւոր M4834 | Թագաւոր] Թագաւորութիւն V280
21 յայծեաց M346' M9116 | Յունաց M287' M2627] + է rel | և
2°] om M351 | եղջեաւրն M4834
22 և 1°] om M9116 | խորտակեալ ն M4834 | ընդ] om V280 |
եղջերք] + չորք M346' | իւրեանց] իւրով V280
23 Թագաւորութեանց J1925 | նորա] նոցա V280 M346'-
M2585 M2627' M182'
24 <զաւրութիւն >] -թեամբ M287 | և 3°—fin] հզաւրս և
զժողովուրդն սուրբ և արասցէ և աջողեցէ J1925 | յաջողեցէ
M4834 | և 5°] om WN11*| զժողովուրդսն WN11 | սուրբ] +
ծառայեցուցէ M2627
25 անրոյ] անւոյ V280 | յաջողեցի] ծանրասցի M4834
J1925 | և 2°] om M346'| <նենգութիւն>] կենդանութիւն M287*-
V280 նենգութիւն V287ᶜ| մեծամտեցէ M287ᶜ M178-M346' J1925'
M351] մտեցէ M287* -տեսցի rel | ի կորստեան M287ᶜ V280'
WN11 J1925-M2627'] կոր. rel | և ult→26 և 1° M9116 | իբրև] որպէս
M178-M346' M351 | ձեռին իւրում V280 | մանրեսցի J1925
26 առաւատուն և երեկորին J1925 | յերեկորին WN11 երե–
կոյին V280 M2585 | կնքեա] գրեա M178

լուրս բազումս է»։ ²⁷ Եւ ես Դանիէլ ննջեցի եւ խաւթացա եւ յարեա
եւ գործեի զգործ արքունի եւ զարմացեալ էի ընդ տեսիլն, եւ ոչ ոք
էր որ իմացուցանէր։

⁹:¹ Յամին առաջներորդի Դարեհի, որդւոյ Արշորա, ի զաւակէ Մարաց, որ Թագաւորեաց ի Թագաւորութեան Քաղդէացւոց
² ես Դանիէլ խելամուտ եղէ ի գրոց Թուոյ ամացն որ եղև բան
Տեառն առ երեմիա մարգարէ ի կատարումն աւերածոյն
երուսաղէմի յամս եօթանասուն։ ³ Եւ դարձուցի զերեսս իմ առ
Տէր Աստուած իմ խնդրել խնդրուածաք եւ աղաւթիք, պահաք
եւ խորգով. ⁴ Եւ կացի յաղաւթս առ Տէր Աստուած, զոհացա եւ
ասեմ «Տէր Աստուած մեծ եւ սքանչելի որ պահես զուխտ քո եւ
զողորմութիւն սիրելեաց քոց եւ որոց պահեն զպատուիրանս
քո։⁵ Մեղաք, անաւրինեցաք, անիրաւեցաք եւ ապստամբեցաք եւ
խոտորեցաք ի պատուիրանաց քոց եւ յիրաւանց քոց. ⁶ Եւ ոչ

²⁷ դանիէդ M178 | գործեի M287' M346 M2627] գործեցի rel |
արքունի] արքայի J1925
⁹:¹ pr Աղօթք դանիէլի եւ երևումն գաբրիէլի եւ մեկնութիւն
եաւթներորդաց V280 | առաջներորդի] երկրորդի M2585
առաջնորդի M9116-M2627' M182''| արշորա M287] -շօրա WN11
-շաւուրայ M178 աշօրեայ (-րայ M4834) V280' աշուրայ J1925
արշաւրայ rel | որ] ուր WN11 | Թագաւորութիւնն V280 |
քաղդեացւոց M346 J1925 V1508 քաղդէացոց WN11
² եղայ M9116 եղեա J1925 | Թունց M4834 J1925 | եղեն
V280 | բան Տեառն] om V280 | յերեմիա (-եմիա M2585) M178-
M2585 երեմիայ V280' M346 M9116-M2627' | աւերածոցն M346
³ զերես M2627 | խնդրուածաւք ... աղաւթիք M287] tr rel |
խնդրուածաւք M287 M9116-M4114 M351] om V280 -ծովք rel |
պահաք եւ աղաւթիք V280 | աղաւթաք M9116 | խորգով]
խորիրդով M2585
⁴ Եւ 1° M287] om rel | կայի M4834 M9116-M4114 M351 | առ
Տէր Աստուած] om WN11 | Տէր 2°] om M178 | քո 1° M287'] om rel |
Եւ 4°] om V1508 | որ J1925 ոյք M2627 | զպատիրանս WN11
⁵ անիրաւեցաք] om M2627 WN11*: homoeotel | Եւ 1°] om V280
M178-M346' M2627 | պատիրանաց WN11 | քոց 2°] om M2627
⁶ քոց] քո V280 | որ] որք V280 M178-M2585 M9116 |
խոսեցան J1925-M2627' M182''| Թագաւորն V280 M178 J1925 |
առ 2°] om M2627 M182 | մեր 2°] om WN11* M2627 | առ 3°] om

լուաք ծառայից քոց մարգարէից որ խաւսեին յանուն քո առ
թագաւորսն մեր և առ իշխանսն մեր և առ հարսն մեր և առ
ամենայն ժողովուրդ երկրին: 7 Քո, Տէր, արդարութիւն և մեր ա-
մաւթ երեսաց իբրև յաւուր յայսմիկ առն Յուդա և բնակչաց
Երուսաղեմի և ամենայնի Իսրայէղի մերձաւորաց և հեռաւո-
րաց յամենայն երկրի ուր ցրուեցեր զնոսա անդր վասն անհր-
նազանդութեան իւրեանց զոր աննազանդեցան քեզ: 8 Տէր, մեզ
ամաւթ երեսաց և թագաւորաց մերոց և իշխանաց մերոց և
հարց մերոց որք մեղաք: 9 և Տեառն Աստուծոյ մերոյ գթութիւնք և քաւութիւնք զի <ապստամբեցաք> ի Տեառնէ 10 և ոչ
լուաք ձայնի Տեառն Աստուծոյ մերոյ գնալ յաւրէնս նորա զոր
<եւ> առաջի մեր ի ձեռն ծառայից իւրոց մարգարէից: 11 և ամե-
նայն Իսրայէղ անցին զաւրինաւք քովք և խոտորեցան զի մի
լուիցեն ձայնի քում և եկին ի վերայ մեր անէծքն և երդումն
որ գրեալ յաւրէնսն Մովսէսի ծառային քո, զի մեղաք նմա: 12 և

WN11* | ժողովուրդս V280 M4114 M182'' WN11ᶜ

7 յամօթ M4114 M351 | յերեսաց M351 | յաւուրս V280
M178-M346-M2585 J1925 աւուրս մեր WN11 | Յուդա M287 M346'
J1925] յուդայի V280 -դայ rel | ամենայն բնակչաց V280 |
Իսրայէղի M287'' M346 J1925] իսրայէղի (+ և WN11) rel |
մերձաւորաց ... հեռաւորաց] tr V280' M178-M346'-M2585 |
յամենայն] prև J1925 | յերկրի M4834 երկիր M346 J1925-M4114
M351 | անդ V280

8 մեզ M287' M9116-M2627] մեր rel | երեսաց M287'] + մերոց
rel | և 1°➙2° M178 | մեղան M346'

9 զթութիւն և ողորմութիւն V280 | և 2°] om V280 | քաւու-
թիւն և թողութիւն V280 | <ապստամբեցաք>] ամպատամպեցաք
M287

10 ոչ] om M351 | զոր] om V280 | <եւ>] եղ M287

11 Իսրայէղ M287 M2627] -էլ rel | անց M178-M346' M2627
M182'| զօրինովք M2627 զպատուիրանաւ V280 | քովք] քո V280
M346'| մեր] om M9116 | անէծն V1508 | որ] om V280' J1925'
M4114 M182''| գրեալ] + է M178-M346'-M2585 էր M2627 |
մովսիսի V280 M346 M182'| քո M287ᵗˣᵗ] աստուծոյ M287ᵐᵍ V280'
+ Տէր rel

12 հաստատեցաք M4834 J1925 | զբան V280' M346'-M2585
J1925-M2627' M351 | ի 1°➙2° om M178 | ի վերայ 1°] վասն WN11 |

խատտատեաց զքանս իւր զոր խաւսեցաւ ի վերայ մեր և ի վերայ
դատաւորաց մերոց որ դատեին զմեզ ածել ի վերա մեր չարիս
մեծամեծս որ ոչ եղեն ի ներքոյ ամենայն երկնից ըստ այնմ որ
եղեն յերուսաղեմ: ¹³ Որպէս և գրեալ է յաւրէնսն Մովսէսի, այն
ամենայն չարիք եկին ի վերայ մեր և ոչ աղաչեցաք զերեսս
Տեառն Աստուծոյ մերոյ դառնալ յանիրաւութեանց հարցն մերոց և խելամուտ լինել ամենայն ճշմարտութեան քում: ¹⁴ և
զարթեաւ Տէր Աստուած մեր ի վերայ չարեացն մերոց և ած
զնոսա ի վերայ մեր, զի արդար է Տէր Աստուած մեր ի վերայ
ամենայն գործոց իւրոց զոր արար ընդ մեզ զի ոչ լուաք ձայնի
նորա: ¹⁵ և արդ Տէր Աստուած մեր որ հաներ զժողովուրդ քո յեր-
կրէն Եգիպտացւոց հզաւր <ձեռամբ> և արարեր քեզ անուն որպէս յաւուր յայսմիկ, մեղաք, անաւրինեցաք: ¹⁶ Տէր, ամենայն
ողորմութեամբ քո դարձցի սրտմտութիւն քո և բարկութիւն քո
ի քաղաքէ քումմէ յերուսաղեմէ և ի լեառնէ սրբոյ քո, զի մեղաք
և առ անաւրէնութեան մերում և հարցն մերոց երուսաղեմ և

մերոց] մեր և ի վերայ M9116 M182' | զչարիս V280 | մեծս M346-
WN11* | եղեն] +ի վերայ երկրի V280: ex 12:1
¹³ մովսիսի V280 M182' մօսէսի M346 M4114 | այն ամե-
նայն] այնպէս WN11 | եկին հասին V280 | յանիրաւութեան
M4834 անիրաւ. WN11 յանաւրէնութեանց J1925 | ամենայն 2°]
om V280
¹⁴ զարթաւ M4114 | մեր 1°] om V280 J1925 | վերայ 1°] +
ամենայն M4834 J1925 | ընդ մեզ] ի վերայ մեր V280 | ընդ] om
M346-WN11* | զի] և M178-M2627 V1508
¹⁵ եգիպտացւոց M287] եգիպտացւոց rel (-gng M4834 WN11)
հզաւր ձեռամբ] om J1925 | <ձեռամբ>] -ամպ M287 + և բարձր
բազկաւ V280 | որպէս M287' M2585] + և (pr նոր M9116: ditt) rel |
յաւուր M287 M9116-M4114 M182'] յաւուրս (աւ. WN11) rel | և
մեք մեղաք V280 | անաւրինեցաք M287 WN11* J1925] pr և rel
¹⁶ քո 1°→3° M178 | քո 1°] քով V280' WN11 J1925'-M4114
M182'' | դարձի M346' M2627' M182'' | սրտմտութիւն] om M2585 |
քո 2°] om V280 M2585 | և 1°] om M2585 + բարձգի M346' M2627'
M182'' | յերուսաղեմէ-քո 4°] om V280 | քո 4°] քումմէ M4834 | և
3°] om V280 M346-WN11* | առ] om WN11* | անաւրէնութեան] pr
ամենայն (-թեանց J1925) V280 J1925 անիրաւութեան M4834 |

ամենայն ժողովուրդ քո և ի նախատինս ամենեցուն որ շուրջ
<զմեաւք> էին: ¹⁷ Եւ արդ լուր, Տէր Աստուած մեր, աղաւթից ծա-
ռայից քոց և խնդրուածոց, և երևցոյ զերեսս քո վասն քո ի
սրբութիւնն որ աւերեցաւ: ¹⁸ Խոնարհեցոյ, Աստուած իմ, զունկն
քո և լուր ինձ, բաց զաչս քո և տես զապականութիւն մեր. և
զքաղաքին քո յորոյ վերայ կոչեցեալ է անուն քո, զի ոչ առ
արդարութեանց մերոց արկանեմք զգուծս մեր առաջի քո, այլ
վասն բազում գթութեան քո, Տէր: ¹⁹ Լուր. Տէր, քաւեա Տէր, անսա
Տէր, և մի յամենար վասն քո, Աստուած իմ, զի անուն քո կոչեցեալ է ի վերայ քաղաքին քո»: ²⁰ Եւ մինչդեռ ես խաւսեի և յաղաւթս կայի և խոստովան լինեի զմեղս իմ և զմեղս ժողովըր-
դեան Իսրայէղի և արկանեի զգուծս իմ առաջի Տեառն Աստուծոյ իմոյ վասն լերինն սրբոյ, ²¹ և մինչդեռ խաւսեի յաղաւթս,
ահա այրն Գաբրիէլ զոր տեսանեի յառաջնումն տեսլեանն

մերում] մերոց J1925 om M346 ǀ մերոց] + և մեր և M346' ǀ
ամենայն] այն V280 ǀ ամենեցուն] om V280 ǀ<զմեաւք> V280'
J1925] զմիաւք M287 զմնք rel ǀ էին] իցեն V280 են J1925'-M4114
M351

¹⁷ մեր 1°] om V280 ǀ ծառայից քոց M287' WN11-M2585
J1925] ծառայի քո (քոց M4834) rel ǀ խնդրուածոց J1925 ǀ քո 1°→2°
M4834 J1925 ǀ վասն անուան V280 ǀ սրբութիւն քո J1925 + վասն
անուան քո M4834

¹⁸ իմ M287'' J1925-M4114 M182''] om rel ǀ զապականու-
թիւնս V280' J1925 ǀ որոյ M178-WN11 J1925 որոց M4834 ǀ կոչե-
ցեալ] om J1925'ǀ առ] om WN11 ǀ արդարութեան մերոյ V280 ǀ
զգուծ M9116 M351 ǀ բազում] om V280 ǀ գթութեանց քոց M4834
J1925 ǀ քո ult] + և ողորմութեան քոյ V280 ǀ Տէր 3°] om M346-
WN11* M2627

¹⁹ յամենար M287] յամեր rel ǀ վասն] + անուան V280' ǀ
իմ] մեր M4834 J1925 ǀ վերայ] +մեր WN11

²⁰ և 1°] om M9116 ǀ ես] om WN11 ǀ խաւսեի և] om J1925 ǀ
Իսրայէղի M287'' M346 J1925] իմոյ M2627 -իէլի rel ǀ և 5°] om
M9116 ǀ զգուծ V280 J1925 ǀ իմ 2°] om M346'ǀ վասն—fin] om
J1925'

²¹ և 1°—յաղաւթսն] om J1925 ǀ ի յաղօթս V280 ǀ ահա M287]
և ահա rel ǀ այր V280 ǀ տեսանեի] տեսի M2627 ǀ Թոււցեալ]+
գայր V287ᵐᵍ-M4834ǀ երեկոյին M178-WN11-M2585 M2627

Թողցեալ և մերձեցաւ առ իս իբրև ի ժամ երեկորին պատարագին: ²² Եւ խելամուտ արար զիս և խաւսեցաւ ընդ իս և ասէ «Դանիէլ, այժմ ելի խելամուտ առնել զքեզ: ²³ ի սկզբան աղաւ-թից քոց ել պատգամ և ես ելի պատմել քեզ, զի այր ցանկալի ես դու. արդ աձ զմտաւ զբանդ և ի մխ առ զտեսիլդ: ²⁴ Եւթա-նասուն Եւթներորդք համառաւտեցան ի վերայ ժողովրդեան քո և ի վերայ քաղաքին սրբոյ ի վախճանել մեղաց և ի կնքել անաւրէնութեանց և ի չնչել անիրաւութեանց և ի քաւել ամ-բարշտութեանց և ի գալ յաւիտենական արդարութեանն և ի կնքել տեսլեանն մարգարէի և յաւձանել սրբութեան սրբու-թեանցն: ²⁵ Եւ գիտասցես և խելամուտ լիցհս յելից բանին տալ պատասխանի և ի չինելն երուսաղէմի մինչև ցաւձեալն առաջնորդ <եւթներորդք> եւթն և եւթներորդք վաթսուն և երկու և դարձցին և չինեցին հրապարակքն և պարիսպքն և նորոգեցին ժամանակքն: ²⁶ Եւ յետ վաթսուն և երկուց եւթնե-

²² և 2°] om V280 | դանիէղ M178 դանիէլ դանիէլ V280: ditt | այժմ] այլժմ J1925 այժ M4834
²³ զի ի սկիզբն J1925 | քոց 1°] քո J1925 | պատմել] pr խելա-մրտել V280 | այր մի M4834 M178 | զբանդ—առ] om M192' | ի 2°] om WN11
²⁴ Եւթներորդք] և Եւթներորդ (-րրդք M4834) M4834 J1925 | համառաւտեցան] համարեցան M4834ᵗˣᵗ J1925 | և 3°→4° V280 M2627 | չնչիլ M346 | ի 6°] om J1925 | անբարշտութեամբ M4834 WN11-M2585 J1925 M351 | արդարութիւնն J1925 - թեանցն V280'| կնքել 2°] -քիլ M346 | տեսլեանց M4834 J1925 | մարգարէի M287] -էից V280' J1925 pr և rel | սրբութեան] om J1925': hapl
²⁵ և 1°] om M9116-M2627 | լինիցիս J1925 լիցից WN11 | չինիլ M178 M351 | յոձեալ ն V280' | և առաջնորդ M178 |<եւթ-ներորդք>] եւթներորդ M287 | եւթներորդք 2°] -րրդ M9116-M4114 M182' | և 5°] om V280 | չինեցեն J1925 չինիցին M178 | հրապարակքն ... պարիսպքն] tr M4834 M178 | ժամանակ M346
²⁶ Եւ յետ M2627 | և 2°] om V280 M178 | երկու M4834 M2627 | բարձցի] pr սպանցի աւձեալ ն և (բարձցին V280) V280' | <աւձութիւնն>] -թիւնք M287' | քաղաքք M178 J1925-M2627 | սրբութիւնք J1925 | ապականեցցի V280 | առաջնորդով ն V280 | կայցէ M2627 | չնչեցին WN11 | և ult] om M346' | ի 2°] om WN11

որդաց բարձցի աւձութիւնն և իրաւունք ոչ իցեն ի նմա, և
քաղաքն և սրբութիւն ապականեցին առաջնորդաւն հանդերձ
որ գայցէ, և չնչեսցին հեղեղաւ և մինչև ի վախձան պա-
տերազմին համառաւտելոյ կարգեսցէ զապականութիւնն: 27 և
զաւրացուցէ զուխտ բազմաց ևթներորդ մի և կես ևթներորդի
դադարեցուսցէ զսեղանս և զպատարագս և մինչև ի ձայր ան-
կեանն ապականութիւն, և մինչև գվախձան և <գտագնապ>
կարգեսցէ ի վերայ ապականութեան և զաւրացուսցէ զուխտ
բազմաց ևթներորդ մի և կես ևթներորդին բարձցին գոհք և
<նուէրք> և ի վերայ տաձարին պղծութիւն աւերածոյն կացցէ և
մինչև գվախձան ժամանակի կատարած տացի ի վերայ
աւերածին»:

ՏԵՍԻԼ ՎԵՑԵՐՈՐԴ

10:1 Յամի երրորդի Կիւրոսի արքայի Պարսից բան յայտնեցաւ Դանիէլի, որոյ անուն կոչեցաւ Բաղտասար, և ճշմարիտ է
բանն, և զաւրութիւն մեծ և հանձար տուաւ ի նմա ի տեսլեանն: 2 Յաւուրսն յայնսիկ ես Դանիէլ եղէ ի սուգ երիս ևթնե-
րորդս աւուրց. 3 հաց ցանկութեան ոչ կերա և միս և գինի ոչ
եմուտ ի բերան իմ և եղով ոչ աւծա մինչև ի կատարել երից

---

27 ևթներորդ] յևթներորդ V280 -երրորսն J1925 | մի] om
J1925 ամի M4834 | ի կես կես V280' | ևթներորդի→ևթներորդին
V280 | դադարեցուսցէ M287 J1925' V1508] pr և rel | և 4° om
J1925-M2627 | <գտագնապ>] տագնապ M287* M2627 | կարգես-
ցի M346' | <նուէրք>] նւերք M287 M178 M2627 | պղծութեան
V280 M346 | աւերածոյն J1925 | և ult] om M178 J1925 | գվախձան
2° M287] ի վախ. rel | ժամանակի] + և M4834 J1925
10:1 երրորդի M287*] երկրորդի M287ᶜ ութերորդի J1925 |
կիւրոսի J1925 | պարսից արքային M4834 | Դանիէլի M178 -ելի
M346 M9116-M2627' M182'| որում V280 | կոչեցաւ] էր J1925 |
բաղդասար V280 բալտ. M2627 | ի 1° M287] om rel
2 դանիէղ M178 | սուգ]սւ V280 | ևթներորդ V280 M346'

նթներորդաց աւուրց: ⁴ <Յաւուրն> քսաններորդի և չորրորդի
ամսեանն առաջնոյ կայի ես առ ափն գետոյն մեծի որ է Դկղաթ:
⁵ Ամբարձի զաչս իմ և ահա այր մի զգեցեալ բադեան, և ընդ մէջ
իւր աձեալ կամար յոսկոյն ոփազա. ⁶ և մարմին նորա ծո-
վազգոյն, երեսք նորա իբրև զտեսիլ փայլատակական և աչք նորա
իբրև զձառագայթք հրոյ, և բազուկք և բարձք նորա իբրև զտեսիլ
փայլուն պղնձոյ և բարբառ բանից նորա իբրև զբարբառ
զաւրու: ⁷ և տեսի ես Դանիէլ միայն զտեսիլն և արքն որ ընդ իս
էին ոչ տեսին այլ ահ մեծ անկաւ ի վերայ նոցա, և փախեան
զարհուրեալք: ⁸ և ես միայն մնացի և տեսի զտեսիլն զայն
մեծ. և ոչ մնաց յիս զաւրութիւն և փառք իմ յապականութիւն դարձան, և ոչ հանդարտեցի զաւրութեան: ⁹ և լուա
զբարբառ բանից նորա և ի լսելն իմում զբարբառ բանիցն կայի
հիացեալ և երեսք իմ յերկիր խոնարհեալ: ¹⁰ և ահա <ձեռն>

---

³ oծեցայ V280
⁴ <Յաւուրն> յաւուրս M287 | և 1°] om M178-M346'-M2585
M2627 V1508 | յափն M346'| որ է] om M346'| է] կոչի V280 +
տիգրիս M178 J1925'-M2627 M182''| դկլաթ V280 M346'-M2585
M9116-M2627 M182''
⁵ բադեան M287] բադեն M346 բադեն (-էն V280) փառս
V280' M2585 փառս rel | ընդ—fin] կամար յոսկոյն աձեալ ընդ
մէջ իւրն ափագայ V280 | ոսկոյն WN11 | ոփազա M287] -զայ
(ափ. V280) V280 M9116-M4114 M182'' ովփազայ M178-M2585
M2627 ովփադեա M346' կափիզայ J1925
⁶ ծովազգոյն —փայլատակական] om M178 | երեսք] երես
J1925 pr և V280' M346'-M2585 J1925'-M2627' M182''| փայլա-
տակական] փայլուն WN11 | և 2°] om V1508 | ձառագայթք M178-
M346-M2585 J1925'-M2627 M182' -զայք V280'| բարձք և բազ.
V280 | բազուկ M9116 | զտեսիլ 2°] om V280 M178-M346-WN11*|
փայլուն] զփայլիւն V280 | ի բանից V280 M178-M2585: cf v 9
⁷ դանիէլ M178-M346 om V280 | տեսին M287] տեսանէին
V280 | տեսին M287]+զտեսիլն rel
⁸ չմնաց M178 M2627 M182'| ի յիս M4834 J1925 | դարձաւ
J1925 | ոչ հանդարտեցի M287] չհանդ. rel
⁹ բանիցն M287'' J1925]բանից նորա rel
¹⁰ <ձեռն>] ձայն M287 զձեռն J1925 | մերձեցեալ M287'] -
եցաւ M346' մերձեալ M4834 M178-M2585 M2627 ձրզեալ (ձզեալ

մերձեցեալ առ իս կանգնեաց զիս ի ծունկս իմ և ի թաթս ձեռաց
իմոց: ¹¹ և ասէ ցիս «Դանիէլ, այր ցանկալի, խելամուտ լեր բանիցս զոր ես խաւսեցայց առ քեզ և կաց ի կայի քում, զի այժմ
առաքեցա առ քեզ». և ի խաւսելն նորա ընդ իս զբանս զայս կացի յոտն դողութեամբ: ¹² և ասէ ցիս «մի երկնչիր, Դանիէլ, զի
յաւրէ յորմէ եւտուր զսիրտ քո խելամուտ լինել և վշտանալ
առաջի Աստուծոյ քո, լսելի եղեն բանք քո, և ես եկի ընդ բանից
քոց. ¹³ և իշխան Թագաւորութեան Պարսից կայր հակառակ ինձ
զքսան և <զմի> աւր և ահա Միքայէլ, մի յառաջին իշխանացն,
եկն աւգնել ինձ, և Թողի զնա անդ ընդ իշխանի Թագաւորութեանն Պարսից ¹⁴ և եկի խելամուտ առնել զքեզ որչափ ինչ
անցք անցանիցեն ընդ ժողովուրդ քո յաւուրս յետինս, զի տեսիլդ յաւուրս է»: ¹⁵ և ի խաւսելն նորա ընդ իս ըստ բանիցս
այսոցիկ, անկա ի վերայ երեսաց իմոց յերկիր և կայի հիացեալ:
¹⁶ և ահա իբրև նմանութիւն որդւոյ մարդոյ մերձենայր ի
շրթունս իմ. բացի զքերան իմ և խաւսեցա և ասեմ ցայրն որ

M35 1) rel I իմ] om J1925 I Թաթ M346 Թաթաց V280 I ձեռաց] om
V280

¹¹ դանիէդ M178 I եւս M287' J1925ᶜ-M2627 M182'] om rel I
խաւսեցա յ V280 I առ V287'' M351] ընդ rel I կաց—քում] կացի
առաջի քո V280 I կայի] om J1925: homoeoarc I ի 2°] om J1925 I
ընդ իս om J1925 I յոտն կացի V280' M9116-M4114 M182''I ոտն
WN11

¹² դանիէդ M178 I Աստուծոյ] pr Տեառն M9116: ex 9:20 I
եղև բան V280 I եկից WN11

¹³ Պարսից 1°] om V280 I ինձ հակառակ V280 I ինձ 1°] om
J1925 WN11*I զաւուրս քսան մի V280 I<զմի>] մի V280 I միքա-
յէդ M178 I ինձ 2°] մեզ V280 I անդ] անտ M178 անդր V280 I
իշխանս M1925

¹⁴ անցանիցեն M287'' J1925'] անցանելոց իցեն rel I ժողո-
վուրդքն J1925 -վուրդս WN11 -վրդեան V280 M2627 I քո] om
J1925 I<յաւուրս>] + յետինս M287: ditt I է] om J1925

¹⁵ երեսաց իմոց] երեսագս V280

¹⁶ ի նման. V280 J1925'-M2627 M182'' որդւոյ] om J1925 I
մերձեցաւ M4834 J1925 I զայրն] զայն V280 I երնելդ WN11 I քո]
+ ինձ M4114 M351 I զոյր V280

կայրն յանդիման ինձ «տէր, յերևելդ քո խոռովեցաւ փոր իմ յիս,
և ոչ գոյ յիս զաւրութիւն. [17] և զիա՞րդ կարիցէ ծառայ քո, տէր,
խաւսել ընդ տեառն իմում. և ոչ եւս է յիս զաւրութիւն կալոյ և
շունչ ոչ մնաց յիս». [18] և յաւել եւս մերձեցաւ յիս իբրև զտեսիլ
մարդոյ և զաւրացոյց զիս [19] և ասէ «մի երկնչիր, այր ցանկալի,
խաղաղութիւն ընդ քեզ, զաւրացիր <և> քաջ լեր» և ի խաւսելն
նորա ընդ իս զաւրացա և ասեմ» խաւսեցաց տէր իմ, զի զաւրա-
ցուցեր զիս». [20] և ասէ եթէ «գիտեցես վասն է՞ր եկի եւս առ քեզ.
և արդ դառնամ անդրէն տալ <պատերազմ> ընդ իշխանին
Պարսից. և եւս երթալի և իշխանն Յունաց գայր: [21] բայց պատմեցից քեզ զինչ կարգեալ է ի գիրս ճշմարտութեան և ոչ ոք է ինձ
աւգնական այսոնցիկ, բայց Միքայէլ իշխանն ձեր».

[11:1] և եւս յառաջնումն ամին Կիւրոսի կացի ի հաստատութեան և ի զաւրութեան: [2] և արդ պատմեցից քեզ զճշմարտութիւն. ահա երեք Թագաւորք յարիցեն յերկրի Պարսից և չոր-
րորդն մեծասցի մեծութիւն մեծ քան զամենեսեան և յետ զաւրանալոյ նորա ի մեծութեան իւրում, յարիցէ ի վերայ Թագաւ-

---

[17] կարիցէ—խաւսել] կարասցէ խաւսել ծառայ քո V280 | քո]
ո M4834 և.ս] և M9116 | է] իցէ J1925 | ի յիս M4834 | կելոյ J1925
[18] և.ս M287 M346'-M2585 V1508] և rel | ի յիս M4834 J1925 |
տեսիլ J1925 | զիս] յիս WN11
[19] քեզ] + և WN11 |<և.>] om M287 | ի] om M2627 | իս] իմ
M346 | խաւսեցացի]-եաց J1925 | իմ M287'' M346'-M2585] om rel
[20] ասէ] + զիս V280 M346'-M2585 | գիտիցես եթէ V280 | եւս 1°
M287'] om rel | <պատերազմ >] պատերազմն M287 WN11 |
իշխանս J1925 | Պարսից]մարաց V280
[21] կարգեալ] գրեալ M287-M2585 M2627 | ի] om WN11 |
աւգն. ինձ M346 | այսոնցիկ] om V280 | միքայէդ M178 -աւել
M4834
[11:1] առաջնումն WN11 յառաջին V280 | կիւրոսի J1925 | կայի
V280' M2627 V1508-M351 կարգեցի J1925 | ի 1°] om M4834: hapl
[2] քեզ] om V280 | երեք] om M346 | մեծութիւն մեծ/քան
զամենեսեան] tr (զամենեսին M4114) J1925'-M4114 | զամենե-
սին M4834 | Թագաւորութեանն M287' J1925-M2627] -թեանցն
rel | յունանց WN11

րութեանն Ցունաց։ ³ Եւ յարիգէ Թագաւոր հզաւր եւ տիրեաց ատ-
րութեամբ բազմաւ եւ արասցէ ըստ կամս իւր։ ⁴ Եւ իբրև յարիգէ
Թագաւորութիւն նորա փշրեսցի եւ բաժանեսցի ի չորս հողմս
երկնից, եւ ոչ ըստ տերութեան նորա զոր տիրեաց, զի խլեսցի
Թագաւորութիւն նորա եւ այլոց Թողէ զնոցայն։ ⁵ Եւ զաւրասցի
Թագաւորն հարաւոյ եւ մի յիշխանացն զաւրասցի ի վերայ նոցա եւ տիրեսցէ տերութիւն մեծ։ ⁶ Եւ յետամաքն իւրեանց խառ-
նակեսցին ընդ մեմեանս եւ դուստր արքային հարաւոյ մտցէ առ
արքայն <հիւսւսոյ> առնել ընդ նմա դաշինս եւ չհանդարտեսցէ
զաւրութեան բազկին, եւ ոչ կայցէ զաւակ նորա, եւ մատնեսցի
ինքն եւ <ածելիք> իւր, եւ աւրիորդքն եւ որ զաւրացուցանիցէ զնա
ի ժամանակին։ ⁷ Եւ յարիգէ ի ծաղկէ արմատոյ նորա ի վերայ
պատրաստութեան իւրոյ և եկեսցէ առ զաւրութիւն եւ մտցէ ի
հաստատութիւնս Թագաւորին <հիւսւսոյ> եւ արասցէ ընդ նոսա
եւ զաւրասցի։ ⁸ Եւ զաստուածս նոցա կործանեսցէ հանդերձ
<ձուլածոյիւքն > նոցա եւ զամենայն սպաս ցանկալի նոցա
զոսկոյ եւ զարծաթոյ գերի առեալ բերիցէ յեգպտոս եւ

³ տերութեամբ] զօրութեամբ V280 | զկամս WN11
⁴ փշրեսցի] փլեսցի WN11 | ի] om WN11 | եւ 4°] om WN11* |
նորա 3°→ 4° | Թողէ M287] Թող rel
⁵ նոցա M287″ J1925] նորա rel
⁶ <հիւսւսոյ >] հւսւսոյ M287′ M178 | ընդ նմա/դաշինս
M287] tr rel | չհանդարտեսցէ M287] ոչ հանդ. rel | զաւրութիւն
J1925 | ոչ] om M4834 J1925 |<ածելիք>] ածտելիք M287 ածիք
WN11ᵗˣᵗ| աւրիորդքն M287 WN11] օրիորդն (որի. M4834) V280′
M346 M9116-M2627′ որորդն J1925 օրւորդն rel | զաւրացուցէ
V280 -ցուցանեն M178-M346-ցուցանէր (-ներն WN11 J1925) rel
⁷ ծաղկեսցէ WN11 | իւրոյ] նորա WN11 J1925 om V280 |
զաւրութիւնս J1925 | հաստատութիւն V280′| առ Թագաւորին
WN11 | Թագաւորին] Թագաւորութեան J1925′-M4114 V1508-
M351 | <հիւսւսոյ>] հւսւսոյ M287
⁸ հանդերձ] om M351| ձուլածոյիւք] ձուլ. J1925 ձուլա-
ծոյք M287 -ձիւք M346′ M9116-M4114 -ձուիւք M178 ձիւլայծ.
V280| սպաս ցանկալի] սպասակալի V280| ցանկալի V280′] -լիս
rel| <նոցա> 3°] նոցա ա V287: ditt | բերիցէ V280 M178-M346-M2585
M2627 | եւ 4°] om WN11 |<հիւսւսոյ>] հւսւսոյ M287 M4114 |

ինքն հաստատեցի քան զԹագաւորն <հիւսւսոյ>: ⁹ Եւ մնցէ Թագաւորութիւն արքային հարաւոյ եւ դարձցի անդրէն յերկիր իւր:
¹⁰ Եւ որդիք նորա ծողովեսցեն ամբոխ զաւրաց բազմաց եւ մնցէ
դիմեալ եւ հեղեղատեցէ եւ անցցէ եւ դաղարեսցէ եւ գրգռեսցի
մինչեւ ի զաւրութիւն նորա: ¹¹ Եւ գազանասցի Թագաւորն
հարաւոյ, եւ ելցէ եւ տացէ պատերազմ ընդ Թագաւորին
<հիւսւսոյ> եւ գումարեսցէ զաւր բազում մատնեսցի զաւրն ի
ձեռս նորա: ¹² Եւ առցէ զամբոխն եւ բարձրասցի սիրտ նորա, եւ
կործանեսցէ զբիւրաւորս եւ ոչ զաւրասցի: ¹³ Եւ դարձցի արքայն
<հիւսւսոյ> եւ ածցէ զաւր բազում քան զառաջինն եւ ի վախճանի
ժամանակացն եկեսցէ մտանել զաւրաւ մեծաւ եւ բազում
ստացուածովք: ¹⁴ Եւ ի ժամանակին յայնոսիկ բազումք յարիցեն
ի վերայ Թագաւորին հարաւոյ եւ որդիք մնացելոց ժողովրդեան
քո բարձրասցին հաստատել զտեսիլն եւ տկարասցին: ¹⁵ Եւ մնցէ
Թագաւորն հարաւոյ եւ կուտեցէ հող եւ առցէ զքաղաքս ամուրս
եւ բազուկք արքային հարաւոյ ոչ հաստատեցին, եւ յարիցեն
ընտրեալք նորա եւ ոչ իցէ զաւրութիւն կալոյ: ¹⁶ Եւ արասցէ ի
մտանել իւրում առ նա զկամս իւր, եւ ոչ ոք իցէ որ ունիցի զդէմ
նորա, եւ կայցէ յերկրին Սաբիրա եւ վախճանեցցի ի ձեռս նորա:

⁹ մնցէ] մաց M178 +ի M4834 M346 J1925-M2627ʹ M182ʹʹ
¹⁰ դիմեալ մնցէ V280 անցէ WN11: hapl | եւ 5°] om WN11 |
դաղարեսցի M346 | գրգռեցցէ V280 M4114 | զօրութիւնս J1925
¹¹ ելցէ] om V280 M346ʹ pr եւ M4834 M178-M2585 J1925ʹ-
M4114 M182ʹʹ | <հիւսւսոյ>] հւսւսոյ M287 | գումարեսցի J1925 |
զօրս բազումʼս V280ʹ | ձեռն V280
¹² զամբոխ նորա V280 | եւ ոչ զաւրասցի] եւ զզօրաւորս
M346-M2585
¹³ <հիւսւսոյ> հւսւսոյ M287 M4114 | ի մտանել M4834
M2627ʹ | զաւրաւ] զօրու V280
¹⁴ յայնոսիկ] ընդ այն. WN11 om M182 | բարձրասցին] բազ-
մասցին M2627 | ի հաստատել M178-M2585 M9116-M2627ʹ M182ʹʹ
¹⁵ հարաւոյ 2°] M4114 M182ʹʹ| ոչ 1°] om J1925ʹ-M2627ʹ
M182ᵗˣᵗ-V1508ᵗˣᵗ-WN11ᶜ| յարիցեն] յարեն WN11*
¹⁶ զկամս] om V280 | ունիցէ J1925 | եւ 3°→4° om V280 | եւ 3°]
om J1925ʹ-M2627| ի յերկրին M9116 յերկիրն WN11 | Սաբիրա

¹⁷ Եւ դիցէ զերեսս իւր մտանել զաւրութեամբ իւրով յամենայն Թագաւորութիւն նորա եւ զամենայն ուղղութիւնս առնիցէ ընդ նմա, եւ զդուստր կանանց տացէ նմա յապականութիւն եւ մի <յամրացի> եւ մի եղիցի նա նորա: ¹⁸ Եւ դարձուսցէ զերեսս իւր ի կղզիս եւ առցէ զբազումս եւ այրեսցէ զիշխանս որ նախատէին զնոսա եւ զնախատանս նոցա: ¹⁹ դարձուսցէ յերեսս նոցա, եւ դարձցի զաւրութեամբ յերկիր իւր եւ տկարասցի եւ անկցի եւ ոչ գտանիցի: ²⁰ Եւ յարիցէ յարմատոյ նորա տունկ Թագաւորու-թեան ի վերա պատրաստութեան նորա եւ բռնադատիցէ առնել շուք Թագաւորութեան, եւ յաւուրսն յայնոսիկ խորտակեսցի, եւ ոչ <երեսաւք> եւ ոչ պատերազմաւ ²¹ կայցէ ի վերայ պատրաս-տութեան իւրոյ, զի արհամարհեցաւ եւ ոչ եստուն նմա փառս Թագաւորութեան եւ եկեսցէ յաշողութեամբ եւ բռնաւորեսցի Թագաւորութեանց գայթագղութեամբբ: ²² Եւ բազուկք այլեր որ հեղեղատիցեն եւ <հեղեղատեսցին> յերեսաց նորա եւ խորտա-կեսցի առաջնորդ ուխտին: ²³ Եւ այնոցիկ որ խառնիցինն ի նա արասցէ նենգութիւն, եւ ելցէ եւ զաւրասցի ի վերայ նոցա սակաւ

M287] -ռաj M4834 J1925'-M2627 ասբաjիմ M2585 սաբիմաj (-մա M178) rel

¹⁷ ի մտանել J1925: cf v 13 | իւրով WN11* | եղիցի—fin] յեր-կարեսցի V280 | եղիցի J1925

¹⁸ զիշխանն M9116-M2627' | նախատեցին M178-M346'-M2585 M4114 M182'' | զնոսա] զնա V280' | զնախատանս M287 J1925 M2627'] -տիսս rel

²⁰ տունկ] տունդ (տուն M4834) V280' J1925 | պատրրստու-թեան WN11* | բռնադատեսցէ M4834 M178-M346'-M2585 -եսցի V280 | եւ 4°] om M9116 |<երեսաւք>] երեսաւր M287 | ոչ 2°] om V1508 | պատերազմաւ] պատարագաւք V287ᵐᵍ M178-M346-M2585

²¹ կաj J1925 | նմա] om V280 M346-WN11* | եւ 3°] om WN11* | բռնաւորեսցի M287 J1925-M2627] բռնադատեսցի (-ցին V280') rel

²² եւ 1°] om M346-WN11* | աjնր] աjն V280 | հեղեղատիցեն]-տեսցեն V280' J1925'-M2627 |<հեղեղատեսցին>]-եսցեն M287 om WN11* | եւ 3°] om V280'| առաջնորդ M287 M346'] pr եւ rel

²³ եւ 1°] om WN11 | խառնեսցինն M4834 | նոցա] նորա V280

The Armenian Version of Daniel

ազգաւ: ²⁴ և յաջողութեամբ և բազում աշխարհաւք եկեսցէ և արասցէ զոր ոչ արարին հարք նորա և ոչ հարք հարց նորա, զաւար և զկապուտ և զստացուածս բաշխեսցէ նոցա և ի վերայ եգւպտացւոց խորհուրդ խորհեսցի մինչև ի ժամանակ: ²⁵ և զարթիցէ զաւրութիւն նորա և սիրտ նորա ի վերայ Թագաւորին հարաւոյ զաւրութեամբ մեծաւ և Թագաւորն հարաւոյ խմբեսցէ պատերազմ զաւրաւ մեծաւ և հզաւրաւ յոյժ. և ոչ հանդարտեսցէ զի խորհեսցին զնա և զզաւրսն այրեսցեն և անկցին վիրաւորք բազումք: ²⁶ և կերիցեն որ ինչ նմա անկ իցէ. և խորտակեսցեն զնա, և զզաւրսն այրեսցեն, և անկցին վիրաւորք բազումք: ²⁷ և երկուցուն Թագաւորացն սիրտք իւրեանց ի չարութիւն և ի միում սեղան սուտ խաւսեցին, և մի յաջողեսցի զի վախճանն ի ժամանակս է: ²⁸ և դարձցի յերկիր իւր մեծութեամբ բազմաւ և սիրտ նորա ի վերայ ուխտին սրբոյ. արասցէ և դարձցի յերկիր իւր: ²⁹ ի ժամանակի դարձցի <և> եկեսցէ ի

²⁴ և 2°] om M178-M346 M182'' | զորս M4834 J1925'-M2627 |
հարքն նոցա V280 | նորա 1°] om J1925'-M2627 | և 3°—նորա 2°]
om V280 | հարց] om M2627 | զաւար M387' M178 J1925] pr և rel
| խորհուրդս V280 | ժամանակս V280 M346-M2585
²⁵ զարթիցի WN11 | հարաւոյ 1°→2° M178 | խմբեսցէ]
բդխեսցէ M182'| մեծաւ զաւրաւ WN11 | հզաւր J1925 | խորհեն
V280 խորհեսցի նաj M4834
²⁶ կերիցէ նա M4834 J1925 | ի նմա M346 | անկ] անդ
M178 | խորտակեսցէ M178 -գէն M4834 | զօրսն WN11
²⁷ երկուցուն M287' J1925] երկոցունց rel | Թագ.—իւրեանց
սիրտք Թագաւորացն J1925 | չարութիւն] -Թեան J1925-M4114
M182'' | սեղանի M4834 J1925 | խաւսիցին M287 M2585]-սեսցին
rel| յաջողեսցին J1925 | զի—fin] ի ժամանակին վախճանին
J1925 | ժամանակի V280 ժամանակ M9116-M2627
²⁸ և 1°] om M346-WN11* J1925| արասցէ] pr և M4834 J1925'-
M2627' M182''
²⁹ ի 1°] pr և M346-M2585 | դարձցին M346'| <և>] om M287|
եկեսցեն M346'| և 2° M287] + ոչ rel| եղեց J1925| վերջինն) om
V280: homoeotel
³⁰ բանակք] բնակք M9116-M2627 | կիտացոց M178-WN11
J1925 | <խոնարհեսցին> խոնարհին V287 | դարձցի] դարձցին

վերայ հարաւոյ, և եղիցի իբրև զառաջինն վերջինն։ ³⁰ և մրա
ցեն ի նա բանակք կիտացւոց, <խոնարհեցին> և դարձցի և
բարկացցի ի վերայ ուխտին սրբոյ, և առասցէ և դարձցի և գու
մարեսցի ի վերայ այնոցիկ ոյք Թողին զուխտն սուրբ։ ³¹ և յա
րիցեն զաւակք ի նմանէ և պղծեսցեն զսրբութիւն բռնութեամբ և
փոխեսցեն զհանապազորդութիւն և տայցեն զպղծութիւն
ապականութեան։ ³² և ապականիչք ուխտին աճցեն ի վերայ
իւրեանց զգայթակղութիւն, և ժողովուրդ որ ճանաչէր զԱստ
ուած իւր զաւրասցին և արասցեն։ ³³ <և> հանճարեղք ժողովր
դեանն բազում իւիք խելամուտ եղիցին և տկարասցին սրով և
հրով և գերութեամբ և յափշտակութեամբ զաւուրս։ ³⁴ և ի
տկարանալն նոցա աւգնականութիւն ինչ սակաւ գտցեն և յա
ւելցին ի նոսա բազումք գայթագղութեամբք։ ³⁵ և ի հանճարե
դացն <տկարասցին> փորձել զնոսա և <ընտրել> և յայտնել
մինչև ի վախճան ժամանակի, զի տակաւին ժամանակ է։ ³⁶ և
առասցէ ըստ կամաց իւրոց և բարձրասցի Թագաւորն և հպար
տասցի ի վերայ ամենայն աստուծոյ և ի վերայ աստուծոյն
աստուծոց խաւսեցցի ամբարտաւանս և <յաջողեսցի> մինչև
վախճանեսցի բարկութիւնն, քանզի ի վախճանի լինելոց է։

M2585 բարձրասցին V280 J1925 | ոյք] որք M4834 J1925 որ V280
   ³¹ պղծիցեն M178 M182'' | զպղծութիւն M287' J1925] պղծ.
rel
   ³² ապականիչ J1925 | աճցեն] pr հզոր V280 | ճանաչէ
J1925'-M2627' M182'' (pr ոչ M346) | զտէր աստուած V280'
   ³³ <և>] om M287 | հանճարողք V280| իւիք M287] իմիք rel |
եղեցին J1925 | հրով և սրով V280 | զաւուրս] + բազում V280
   ³⁴ տկարանալոյ M2627 կատարելն M178-WN11 J1925 |
oգնութիւն V280 M4114 M182 | ոչ ինչ V280 | նոսա] նա J1925 |
գայթագղութեամբ V280
   ³⁵ հանճարողացն V280 |<տկարասցին>]-gի M287 | փորձել
M287'] ի փորձ. rel | զնոսա] om V280 | <ընտրել >] խնդրել M287
WN11 | մինչև] pr և V280 | ժամանակ է] ժամանակին M2627
   ³⁶ աստուծոյ M287 M9116-M2627]-ծող rel| և 4°] om M346-
WN11* | աստուծոյն ամենայն M287 M9116| աստուածոց
WN11| ամբարտաւանութեամբ V280 |<յաջողեսցի>] յաճողեսցի
M287| վախճանի M287' WN11 J1925'-M2627]-ճան rel

The Armenian Version of Daniel

³⁷ և ի վերայ ամենայն աստուծոց հարց իւրոց զմտաւ ոչ ածիցէ և վասն ցանկութեան կանանց և զամենայն դիս զմտաւ ոչ ածիցէ, և ի վերայ ամենայնի հպարտասցի: ³⁸ և զաստուած իգաւր ի տեղւոջէ իւրմէ փառաւորեսցէ և զաստուած զոր ոչ ծանեան հարք նորա փառաւորեսցէ ոսկով և արծաթով և ականբք պատուականաւք և ցանկալեաւք: ³⁹ և անցցէ յամուրս փախստականաց ընդ աստուծոյ աւտարի և յաճախեսցէ փառս և հնազանդեցուսցէ նոցա զբաղումս, և զերկիրն բաժանեսցի ի պարգևի: ⁴⁰ և ի ժամանակի վախճանի ոգորեսցի ընդ նմա արքայն հարաւոյ և զաւրաժողով լիցի ի վերայ նորա արքայն <հիւսւսոյ> կառաւք և հեծելաւք և նաւաւք բազմաւք: ⁴¹ և մտցէ յերկիրն Սաբաիմ և բազումբք տկարասցին և սոքա իցեն որ ապրիցեն ի ձեռաց նորա եդովմ և Մովաբ և իշխանութիւն որդւոցն Ամոնա: ⁴² և ձգեսցէ զձեռն իւր յերկիրն և երկիրն

³⁷ և 1°] om V280 | ամենայն M287' M346'-M2585] om rel | աստուածոց M2585 M4114 M182'-ւծոյն J1925'-M2627 | իւրոց] իւրեանց M9116-M2627 V1508 | ածիցէ 1°] ածցէ V280' M9116-M2627' M182''| ցանկութեան] pr յանդգնութեան J1925 | բազում M178-M346'-M2585 | զդիս J1925] ածիցէ 2°] ածցէ V280' V1508

³⁸ իգաւր] մաղ WN11 + մաւղզին V280'| զոր M287'' M9116-M2627' M351] որ rel | և ցանկալեաւք] om V280: homoeotel | ցանկալովք WN11

³⁹ անցէ WN11: hapl | ընդ ամուրս V280 յաւուրս M4834 J1925'-M2627 | ընդ M287' M2585 M4114] ոստ rel | օտարոտի V280 | հնազանդացուսցէ J1925 | նոցա M287' J1925'-M2627] նմա rel | <բաժանեսցէ>]-եսցի M287-նիցէ M178-M2585

⁴⁰ վախճանի ժամանակի V280 | որոգեսցի M178 | նմա արքայն M287'] նմա և Թագաւորն V280 արքայն J1925 արքային rel | լինի J1925* | նորա] նոցա V280* J1925'| <հիւսւսոյ >] հւսւսոյ M287 | հեծելովք WN11-M2585 M182'| նաւք M9116: hapl | բազմովք M9116-M4114

⁴¹ Սաբաիմ M287 WN11]-այիմ rel | սոքա իցեն] այս որ ի կեն J1925 | ապրիցին M346-եսցին V280 J1925 | եդոմ V280 M346 M182' եդով WN11 M4114 | և 7°] om WN11* | որդւոյն J1925| Ամոնա M287 M346']-նաJ V280 M351 ամօնաJ M4114 անով նաJ (-նա M4834) rel

⁴² յերկիրն] երկ. WN11 +եզիպտացւոց (եզւպտ. WN11) M346' -M2585 | եզւտացւոց M287] եզպտ. WN11 եզիպտ. rel| եղեցի J1925

Text   219

եզպատացող ոչ եղիցի ի փրկութիւն։ ⁴³ Եւ տիրեսցէ ի վերայ գաղտնեաց ոսկոյ և արծաթոյ և ի վերայ ամենայն ցանգալեացն Եգիպտացող և Լիբեացող և եթենվպացող ամուրս նոցա։ ⁴⁴ Եւ ապա համբառք և տագնապ ճեպեսցեն զնա յարևելից և ի <հիւսուսոյ> եկեսցէ <սրտմտութեամբ> բազմաւ ապականել զբազումս։ ⁴⁵ Եւ հարցէ զխորան իւր յապարանս Յեփանդրն ի մէջ ծովուց ի լեառն Սաբային սուրբ և եկեսցէ մինչև ի կողմն մի նորա և ոչ ոք իցէ որ փրկիցէ զնոսա։

¹²∶¹ Եւ ի ժամանակի յայնմիկ յարիցէ Միքայէլ, իշխան մեծ որ կայ ի վերայ որդւոց ժողովրդեան քո և եղիցի ժամանակ նեղութեան, նեղութիւն որպիսի ոչ եղև յորմէ հետե եղև ազգ ի վերայ երկրի մինչև ի ժամանակն յայն և ի ժամանակի յայնմիկ ապրեսցի ժողովուրդ քո, ամենայն որ գտցի գրեալ ի դպրութեան։ ² Եւ բազումք ի ննջեցելոց ի հող երկրի յարիցեն. ումանք ի

⁴³ գաղտնեաց M287¹' WN11 M2627] գազանեաց rel | <ցանկալեացն>] ցանգ. M287 | եզպատացող M287] եզիպտացոց (-ցոցն WN11) M4834 WN11 M4114 եզիպալ. rel | Լիբեացող M287¹' M182¹] -եացող M2585 M9116-M2627 M351 -իացող M4834 -բացոց WN11 -բացող rel | եթենվպացող M287] եթով. M351 եթեսպ. M4114 եթնովպ. J1925 M182¹ եթինովպ. (-ցոց WN11) M346¹ եթէովպ. rel | յամուրս] prև M346-M2585 յաւուրս M2585 M2627

⁴⁴ ապա] ահա V280 | <տագնապք>] տագնապ M287 | ճեմեսցեն M2585 | և ի] om WN11* | <հիւսուսոյ>] հւսւսոյ M287 | եկեսցէ] pr և M178-M346¹-M2585 M2627 | <սրտմտութեամբ>] -թիւն M287

⁴⁵ յապարանս M287 M346¹-M2585 M4114ᵐᵍ M182ᵐᵍ] om rel | Յեփանդրն M287 M346] յեփրադնոն WN11 -ադնովն M178-M2585 J1925 -անովն V280¹ -ադովն M9116-M2627 -ադնոն M4114ᵗˣᵗ M182ᵗˣᵗ-V1508-M351 | ծովին M346¹ Սաբայինի (-ախինի M4834) M287¹] սաբայ M178 M9116 -այիմ V280 -ային (-ախին WN11) rel | ոք] om V280 | փրկեսցէ M4834 | զնոսա M287] om M182¹ զնա rel

¹²∶¹ յայնմիկ 1°] om M346 | միքայէղ M178 միքայէլ WN11 | մեծ] om V280¹ | որդւոյ J1925 | եղեցի J1925 | ժամանակք V280 | ազգ] այս V280 +(ի M4834) մարդկան M4834 J1925

² ննջելոց J1925 M351 | հողդ M4834 J1925 | յարիցեն] om M346-WN11* | յամ°թս M346-M2585 | յաւիտենականս M178 M346¹-M2585 M4114

կեանս յաւիտեանսն և ոմանք ի նախատինս և յամառթ յաւի-
տենականն: ³ և իմաստունքն ծագեսցեն իբրև լուսաւորութիւն ի
հաստատութեան և բազումք յարդարող իբրև զաստեղս
յաւիտեանս և ևս: ⁴ և դու, Դանիէլ, փակեա <զբանսդ> և կրն-
քեա զգիրդ մինչև ի ժամանակ վախճանի մինչև սրբեսցին բազումք և բազմասցի գիտութիւն»: ⁵ և տեսի ես Դանիէլ և ահա
երկու կային յայս կոյս և յայն կոյս գետոյն: ⁶ և ասեն ցայր որ.
զգեցեալ էր զբադենն և կայր ի վերայ ջուրց գետոյն «մինչև
գե՞րբ իցէ վախճան սքանչելեացդ զոր ասացեր» ⁷ և լուա յառնէն որ զգեցեալն էր զբադենն և կայր ի վերայ ջուրց գետոյն
ամբարձ զաջ իւր և զձախ իւր յերկինս և երդուաւ ի կենդանին
յաւիտենից թէ ի ժամանակ և ի <ժամանակս> և ի կէս ժամանակի ի կատարել լրման ձեռին ժողովրդեան սրբեցելոյ ծանի-
ցեն զայս ամենայն: ⁸ և ես լուա և ոչ առի ի միտ և ասեմ «տէր,
զի՞նչ է վախճան այդոցիկք»: ⁹ և ասէ «երթ, Դանիէլ, զի արգել-

³ և 1°] om M4834 | ծագեսցեն M287' M9116-M4114 M182'']-
եսցին rel | լուսաւորութիւն M287] -թիւնք M178-M346' J1925
լուսաւորքը M2585 զլուս. rel | ի] om WN11 | յաւիտենականն]-
կանս V280' M346'-M2585 J1925 (ի յւ. M4834)

⁴ դանիէլ M178 |<զբանսդ> M4834 J1925'-M2627' V1508-
M351] զբանդս M287 զբանդ rel | զգիրսդ M9116 | ժամանակս
M4834 J1925'-M2627 | սրբեսցին] ուսցին V280' J1925-M2627 |
<գիտութիւն>]-թիւնք M287ᶜ (զթուp. M287*)

⁵ դանիէլ M178 | երկուք M346'-M2585 | կացին M178-
M346-M2585 M9116 | և յայնկոյսյ] om M178 | և 3°] om WN11

⁶ ասեմ M4834 J1925'-M4114 WN11ᶜ| ցայրն] ցայն V280 |
որոյ J1925 | զբադէն V280 զբադեանն J1925'-M2627: cf v 7 | յերբ
M4834 M346 J1925 M182| վախճան] + ժամանակի M346'-
M2585 | որ J1925

⁷ զբադեանն J1925'-M2627: cf v 6 | զաջ] զաչս J1925: cf 8:3|
երդուաւ] երդաւ M178 | ի ժամանակ և] om: homoeoarc | ի 3°] pրև
V280 J1925 | և 5°] om V280 J1925 |<ժամանակս>] pr կէս WN11
ժամանս M287 | ժամանակի] -կաց M4834 M178-M346' J1925-
M2627 | ի 6° M287 M346'] pr և rel

⁸ ես] + դանիէլ M346'-M2585 |<է վախճան>] վախճան է
M287

⁹ դանիէլ M178 | և կնքեալ] om M178: homoeotel | և 2°] om

եալ և կնքեալ են բանքս մինչև գժամանակ վախճանի: ¹⁰ ընտ-
րեսցին և սպիտակեսցին և փորեսցին և սրբեսցին բազումք. և
անաւրինեսցին անաւրէնք և ոչ առնուցուն ի միտ ամբարիշտք,
և իմաստունք իմասցին: ¹¹ և ի ժամանակ <է> փոփոխման յա-
ճախութեան և տացի պղծութիւն աւերածին աւուրս հազար և
երեք հարիւր եկ երեսուն և հինգ: ¹² և երանի որ համբերիցէ և
հասցէ յաւուրսն հազար և երեք հարիւր և երեսուն և հինգ: ¹³ և
դու, եկ հանգիր, զի տակաւին են աւուրք և ժամանակք ի
կատարումն վախճանի. և հանգիցես և յարիցես ի ժամանակի
քում վախճանի աւուրց»:

ᴮᵉˡ:¹ և Թագաւորն Աստիադդես յաւելաւ առ հարս իւր և առ
Կիւրոս Պարսիկ զԹագաւորութիւն նորա: ²և Դանիէլ էր կենաց կցորդ Թագաւորին և փառաւոր քան զամենայն բարեկամս

M346' | են] է M346'| գվախճան ժամանակի M346'| գժամանակ]
ի ժամանակս J1925
¹⁰ ընտրեսցեն M346'| սպիտակեսցին M287'] -եսցեն M346
M351 խորտակեսցին V280 -կացին rel | ի միտ առնուցուն
M2585 | ամբարիշչտք] tr ante ոչ M346' անք. M178-M2585
¹¹ և 1°] om M178-M346'-M2585 M182''| ի] om WN11 |
<ժամանակ է>] -ակի M287 J1925 | փոխման V280 M2627 |
յաճախականութիւն M4114 | և 2°] om V280 | յաւուրս J1925-
M4114 | և 3°, 4° M287] om rel | երեք հարիւր] երեկերիւր M2585
M4114 M182' երեկիւր M351 | և 5°] om M178-M346 | հինգ] և Թն
M4114
¹² tot vers] om M4834 M178 M2627 | և 3°, 4° M287] om rel |
երեք] երկու M4114 | և 5°] om V280 M346' | հինգ] և Թն M4114
¹³ եկ] + և V280' M346-M2585 J1925'-M2627'| և 2°] om
WN11*| ժամանակք M287 WN11 J1925] ժամք rel | վախճանի]
ժամանակի V280 | և յարիցես] om M178: homoeotel
Bel superscript. վասն Բելայ և կործանման նորա V280
Պատմութիւն դանիէլի մարգարէի վասն կռոցս Բելա WN11ᶜ
(կռոցն բելայ M4114)
¹ Աստիադդես M287] -իադես M2585 M351 -իազէս J1925'-
M4114 M182 աստեզէս J1925 աստիյագէս WN11 -իադէս rel |
կիրոս J1925 | իւր M287 M178ᵉ M9116 M351] նորա rel
² կցորդ կենաց V280 | նորա] իւր WN11

նորա: ³ և եին կուրք մի Բաբելացւոց, անուն Բէլ և ելանէր նմա
ոռօիկ աւուր միոջ նաշիի երկոտասան արդու և քառասուն ոչ-
իսար և գինի վեց մար: ⁴ և Թագաւորն պաշտէր զնա և երթայր
հանապազ երկիր պագանէր նմա, բայց Դանիէլ երկիր պագանէր
Աստուծոյ իւրոյ. և ասէ ցնա Թագաւորն «դու, ընդէ՞ր ոչ պագա-
նես երկիր Բէլա»: ⁵ և նա ասէ «քանզի ոչ պաշտեմ զկուռս ձեռա-
գործս, այլ զԱստուած կենդանի, զարարիչն երկնի և երկրի որ
ունի իշխանութիւն ամենայն մարմնոյ»: ⁶ և ասէ ցնա Թագաւորն «իսկ Բէլ ոչ Թուի՞ քեզ Թէ իցէ աստուած կենդանի եթէ ոչ
տեսանես որչափ ուտէ և ըմպէ հանապազ»: ⁷ և ասէ Դանիէլ
ծիծաղելով «մի իսաբիր, արքայ, զի դա ի ներքոյ կաւեա և ար-
տաքոյ պղնձի, ոչ կերեալ դորա երբեք և ոչ ըմպեալ»: ⁸ և բարկացեալ Թագաւորն կոչեաց զքումանն նորա և ասէ ցնոսա Թագաւորն եթէ ոչ ասիցէք ինձ ով ուտէ զսեղանն զայն մահու վախ-
ճանեցից. ⁹ապա Թէ յայտ առնիցէք եթէ զայն ամենայն Բէլ

³ բաբելացւոց M178ˢ-լացւոցն M4834 J1925 | անուն նորա
V280 | բեղ M178ˢ M4834 բէլ M2585 M4114 om J1925 | ի նմա
V1508 | աւուր միոջ] յաւուրն V280 | նաշեի J1925 նաշի M4834 |
երկուտասան J1925 | և 4°] om V280 | գինի tr ad fin V280
⁴ պագանէր 1°] -նել V280' M178ˢ-M346'-M2585 | դանիէղ
M178ˢ| երկիր/պագանէր M287'' WN11-M2585] tr rel | տեառն
աստուծոյ V280' M2585 J1925 | իւրոյ -ում M4834 M178ˢ-M2585|
չպագանեա J1925 | երկիրպագանեա M4834 M9116-M4114
M182'' | բէլա M346(-աJ M351) բելա WN11բեղաJ M4834 M178ˢ
⁵ արարիչն V280 | երկնից M4834 | մարմնոյ նարդոյ V280
⁶ բեղ M178ˢ| Թուիցս M2585 M9116-M2627' M182'| Թե իցէ]
om M9116-M2627'| եթե—ըմպէ] om V280| տեսանիցես M9116 (+
Թէ M2585) տեսիցես V1508 | և 2°] om WN11*| հանապագ] հագար
J1925
⁷ դանիէղ M178ˢ| դա M287]+ է rel | կաւէ J1925| արտաքոյ]
ի ներքոյ J1925: ditt| պղինձ M2585 | ըմպեալ M287 M9116] ար-
բեալ rel
⁸ և 1°] + ըստ այն V280 | Թագաւորն 2°] om V280 | ասիցէք]
ասէք WN11 | ինձ] om V280 J1925 + եթէ V280 WN11-M2585 (Թե
M346) | ով] ն°ոք V280 | ուտիցէ V280' J1925'-M2627'| վախճա-
նեցից M287]- եսցից V280 մեռանիցիք (-նիք M9116-M2627) rel
⁹ առնէք V280 | ուտիցէ M287]ուտէ rel | մեռանիցի V1508 |

ուտիցէ, մեզցի Դանիէլ զի հայրոյեաց զԲէլ. և ասէ Դանիէլ զթագաւորն «եղիցի ըստ բանի քում»: [10] և եին քուրմքս Բելա ևթա-
նասուն թող զկանայս և զմանկտիս և եկն Թագաւորն Դանիէլիւ հանդերձ ի տուն Բելա: [11] և ասեն քուրմքն Բելա «ահաւասիկ
մեք արտաքս ելցուք, և դու արքայ դիր առաջի դորա զկերակու-
րող և զգինիդ խառնեալ դիցես, և փակեա զդուրսդ և կնքեա
մատանեաւ քով: [12] և եկեալ ընդ առաւաւտս եթե ոչ գտցի այդ
ամենայն կերեալ ի Բելայ, մեռցուք մեք, ապա թե ոչ Դանիէլ որ
սուտ խաւսեցաւ զմէնջ»: [13] և նոքա վստահ եին զի արարեալ էր
ընդ սեղանովն մուտ անյայտ և ընդ այն մտանեին հանապազ
և ուտեին զայն: [14] և եղև իբրև ելին նոքա արտաքս և Թագաւորն եդ զկերակուրն առաջի Բելա. և հրամառ ետ Դանիէլ իւրում մանկտոյ բերին մոխիր և ցանեցին ընդ ամենայն մեհեանն առաջի Թագաւորին միայնոյ. ելեալ արտաքս փակե-

---

և] om WN11 | եղեցի J1925
[10] եին] om M346-WN11* | Բելա M287 WN11] բելայ V280
J1925 (-լա M346') բեղա M4834 բելայ rel |<նԹանասուն>] Թա-
նասուն M287 | զմանկտիս M287' J1925] -տի rel | հանդերձ դա-
նիէլիւ J1925 | դանիէլիւ M287' WN11] -ելիւ rel | Բելա M287(-աJ
V280 J1925)] բեղայ M4834 բերելայ M182 բելայ (-լա M346') rel
[11] Բելա M287 M346] բեղայ M4834 բելայ (-լա WN11) rel |
արքաJ—առաջի] գիստաշիր J1925 | զդորա J1925 | զկերակուրդ
M287''] կեր. J1925 զկերակուրսդ rel | և 3°→4° M9116-M2627
M182'| փակեսցես V280 | զդուրսդ J1925
[12] առաւաւտն V280 J1925 առաւտս M4834: hapl | գացես
M178-M346'-M2585 | զայդ M346'-M2585 | Բելայ M287' (-լա
M346')] բեղա M4834 բելա WN11 բելայ rel
[13] էր M287' J1925'-M2627] էին rel | մուտս անյայտս M4834
J1925 անյայտ մուտ V280 | մտանին J1925 | ուտին | M4114
[14] նոքա] om M9116-M2627' M182'' | Թագաւորն] դանիէլ
M178ᵍ | զկերակուրն M287' M346'-M2585 J1925] -կուրս rel | Բելա
M287 M346 (-լաJ V280 M351)] բեղայ M4834 բելայ (-լա WN11)
rel| հրամառ ետ] հրամայեաց V280 | Դանիէլ] om V280 | մանկ-
տող իւրոց V280 | բերին M287 M9116-M2627] pr և rel| ամենայն]
յատակաւ V280| մեհեանն J1925 մեհենին V280 | միայնոյ] om
V280 | զդուրսն (զդուռսն M178ᵍ) V280-M178ᵍ-M346'

ցին գզուռն և կնքեցին մատանեաւ Թագաւորին և գնացին:[15] և
քուրմքն գիշերի մտին ըստ սովորութեան իւրեանց կանամբք և
որդւովք իւրեանց. և կերան և արբին գամենայն և <ոչ> ինչ
Թողին: [16] և կանխեաց Թագաւորն Դանիելիւ հանդերձ [17] և ասէ
«ողջ ե՞ն կնիքդ, Դանիէլ» և նա ասէ «ողջ են, արքայ»: [18] և եղև
ընդ բանալ դրացն հայեցեալ Թագաւորն ի սեղանն, ի ձայն մեծ
աղաղակեաց և ասէ « մեծ ես, Բէլ, և ոչ գոյ նենգութիւն ի քեզ և
ոչ մի»: [19] և ծիծաղեցաւ Դանիէլ և կալաւ զԹագաւորն զի մի
մտանիցէ ի ներքս և ասէ «ահէ, հայեաց ընդ յատակոդ և տես
ո՞յր է <հետ> այդ»: [20] և ասէ Թագաւորն «տեսանեմ հետս արանց,
կանանց, մանկտոյ»: [21] Յայնժամ բարկացաւ Թագաւորն, կալաւ
զքուրմսն և զկանայս և զորդիս նոցա և ցուցին նմա
զգաղտնի դուրսն ընդ որ մտանէին և ծախէին զսեղանն: [22] և

[15] և 1°] om WN11 | գիշերի մտին M287] tr rel | ի գիշերի
M346' J1925 M351 | իւրեանց 1°→2° V280 | և 3° M287'] om rel | գա-
մենայն M287'] tr post կերան rel | <ինչ>] om M287 | Թողեն M178ˢ
[16] կանխեալ V280 | Թագաւորն M287] + ընդ առաւաւտն
(-աւտս M4834) rel | հանդերձ դանիելիւ M178ˢ-M346-M2585
M2627 | հանդերձ] om WN11* | դանիելիւ M4114
[17] են 1°] է M178ˢ J1925 V1508 | նա] om V280 M346' | են 2°] է
M346'-M2585 J1925
[18] դրանցն M346'-M2585 M4114 M182' դրանն J1925 | հայե-
ցաւ V280 J1925 V1508 | Թագաւորին M178ˢ-M346'-M2585 M9116-
M2627' | ընդ սեղանն M178ˢ-M346'-M2585 | ի 1°] pr և V280 |
աղաղ. ի ձայն մեծ J1925 | և ասէ] om V280 | և ոչ մի ի քեզ M178ˢ
[19] և 1°] յայնժամ V280 | և 2°] om WN11 | մՙոցէ V280-J1925-
M4114 M182' | ահէ] ահեա M4834 om V280 | <յատակոդ >]
ատակոդ M287 M178ˢ-M2585 J1925' V1508-M351 յատակդ V280 |
է] om M4834 M178ˢ-M346 M2627' V1508 tr post հետ V280 |
<հետ>] հեղ M287
[20] տեսանեմ ես M346' | հետս M287'' J1925] հետ rel | արանց
M287 M2627 M182'] + և rel | կանանց M287 WN11] + և rel |
մանգոյ M4834 մանկանց J1925 տղայոց V280
[21] Յայնժամ] pr և M4114 | Թագաւորն բարկացեալ M4834 |
բարկացաւ M287] -ցեալ rel | զգաղտն WN11 | դրունս V1508
(-ունս M4834) դուրնն J1925
[22] <հետ>] եղ M287 | Դանիէլի M287' WN11 M9116 M351]

կոտորեաց զնոսա Թագաւորն, և զբԷլ եռ ի ձեռս ԴանիԷլի, և
կործանեաց զնա և զմեհեան նորա: ²³ Լ Էր վիշապ մի մեծ և
պաշտԷին զնա Բաբելացիքն: ²⁴ Լ ասԷ Թագաւորն գԴանիԷլ
«միթԷ՞ և զդմանԷ ասիցես Թէ պղնձի Է. ահաւադիկ կենդանի Է,
ուտէ և ըմպԷ, և ո՛չ կարես ասել թէ չէ դա աստուած կենդանի.
արդ եկ պագ դմա երկիր»: ²⁵ Լ ասԷ ցնա ԴանիԷլ «ես Տեառն Աստուծոյ իմոյ երկիր պագից զի նա Է Աստուած կենդանի: ²⁶ բայց
դու, արքայ, տուր ինձ իշխանութիւն և սպանից զվիշապն
առաջի քո առանց սրոյ և գաւազանի». և ասԷ Թագաւորն
«տուեալ Է քեզ»: ²⁷ Լ առ ԴանիԷլ ճիւթ և ճարպ և մազ, եփեաց ի
մասին և արար գնդակ և եհար ի բերան վիշապին, և իբրև
եկեր, պայթեաց վիշապն և ասԷ «տեսԷք զպաշտամունսդ ձեր»:
²⁸ Լ եղև իբրև լուան Բաբելացիքն բարկացան յոյժ և կու-
տեցան ի վերայ Թագաւորին և ասեն «ՀրԷայ եղև Թագաւորն.
զբԷլ կործանեաց և զվիշապն սպան և զքուրմսն կոտորեաց»:
²⁹ Լ իբրև եկին ասեն ցԹագաւորն «տուր մեզ ի ձեռս զԴանիԷլ,

-իելի rel | զմեհեանս V280 J1923 | superscript. Վասն Վիշապին
V280
  ²³ Էր] om WN11*| բաբելացիքն M351
  ²⁴ ասիցես] ասես M351 | թէ 2°] om M178ˢ-WN11 M4114 |
պղնձի M346' M9116-M2627 | ահաւասիկ M178ˢ-M346'-M2585
J1925 M182 | ուտէ] pr և V280 J1925 | կարիցես M346'-M2585 |
դա չէ V280 | չէ M287']ոչ իցե M9116 չիցէ rel | դ ա] om M346'
  ²⁵ ցնա] om M346 | երկիր պագից տեառն աստուծոյ իմոյ
V280 | պագից M287' M9116-M2627] պագանեմ rel | Է] pr մ իայն
V280
  ²⁶ ինձ] om V1508 | իշխանութիւն] հրամ ան M346'-M2585 |
և 1°] + ես V280 | առաջի քո] om V280' J1925' M2627' | Է] om
M4834 J1925-M2627 M182| քեզ] + իշխանութիւն M4834 J1925
  ²⁷ ճիւթ] pr և ղ M9116-M2627' M182'' WN11ᵐᵍ | մազ] մեզ
J1925 | եփեաց M287] pr և rel | գնդակ M287] զողդուկա J1925
գնդակս rel | բերանս J1925 | եկեր M287] կերաւ rel | ասէ] +
դանիէլ V280 | տեսանէք M4834
  ²⁸ հրեա WN11 | եղև] om WN11*| եսպան (էսպ. WN11)
M346'| և 5°—կոտորեաց] tr post կործանեաց V280 | և 5°] om
M2627 M351
  ²⁹ և 1°] om M346 | ձեռն M346-WN11*| սպանցուք V280

ապա թե ոչ սպանանեմք զքեզ և զտուն քո»: ³⁰ և իբրև եւեւս
Թագաւորն թե կարի տագնապեն զնա, հարկաւ ի ձեռս եւ նոցա
զԴանիէլ: ³¹ և նոքա արկին զնա ի գուբն առևձուց և անդ էր
զվեց աւր: ³² և եին ի գուբն եւթն առևձք. և տային նոցա հանապազ երկուս մարդս և երկուս պատրուճակս, բայց յայնժամ ոչ
ինչ արկին նոցա զի վաղվաղակի կերիցեն զԴանիէլ: ³³ և էր
Ամբակում մարգարէ ի Հրեաստանի և եփեաց Թան և բրդեաց
հաց ի <կուր> և երթայր յանդ տանել մշակաց իւրոց: ³⁴ և ասէ
հրեշտակն Տեառն զԱմբակում «տար զճաշդ զոր ունիս ի Բաբելոն Դանիէլի ի <գուբն> առևձուց»: ³⁵ և ասէ Ամբակում «Տեր
իմ, զԲաբելոն չիք տեսեալ և զգուբն ոչ գիտեմ ուր իցէ»: ³⁶ և
բուռն եհար հրեշտակն զգագաթանէ նորա և կալաւ զվարսից
գլխոյ նորա և եդ զնա ի Բաբելոն ի վերայ գբոյն սասկտու-
թեամբ ոգւոյ իւրոյ: ³⁷ և աղաղակեաց Ամբակում և ասէ «Դանիէլ, Դանիէլ, առ զճաշդ զոր առաքեաց քեզ Աստուած»: ³⁸ և

---

³⁰ և 1°] om   M346-WN11*I կիւրոս Թագաւորն V280 I
տագնապէին M351 I եւս ի ձեռս M9116-M2627 M351 I ձեռս] +
նոցա M4114*
³¹ ի] om V280 M178ˢ M9116 M182 I անդ WN11 I վեց M178ˢ-
WN11 M182
³² առեաւձք և եւթն M2585 I առևձք M287' V1508] -իւծ rel I
հանապազաւր M287ˢ-M2585 I յայնժամ] յայնմ աւուրսն V280
³³ ամբակումն J1925 անպակ. WN11 ամպակ. M178ˢ M4114 I
մարգարէ] om V280 I հրեսաստանի M4114 I և 2°] om V280 I
Թան] om M178ˢ I <կուր>]կերակուր M287'' I յանդ V280
³⁴ ցամբակումն J1925 I ցանպակ. WN11 ցամպակ. M178ˢ
M4114 I տար] տէր J1925 I Բաբելոն]-լոն M4114 -լովն M2585
M9116 + տար J1925 I Դանիէլի M287'' WN11 J1925] -իելի rel I
<գուբն>] գուբին M287 I առիւձողն WN11
³⁵ անպակում WN11 ամպակ. M4114 I իմ 1°] tr ante չիք rel I
զբաբելоն M4114 -լովն M2585 J1925 I չիք] չէ J1925
³⁶ հար J1925 I հրեշտակն] om V280 I զգագաթէ V280
M178ˢ I բաբելոնի V280: ditt -լоն M4114 -լովն M2585 J1925 I
վերայ] om M4114 I գբին V280 M346'
³⁷ ամբակումբ (-կումն M4834) M4834 M9116 ամբակում
M4114 անպակում WN11 I դանիէդ M4834 I առ] pr արի J1925'-
M2627' M182'' WN11ᶜ I տէր աստուած M4834 J1925

ասէ Դանիէլ «յիշեցեր զիս, Աստուած, և ոչ ընդ վայր հարեր
զսիրելիս քո»: ³⁹ և յարեաւ Դանիէլ և եկեր, և հրեշտակն Աստուծոյ տարաւ զԱմբակում նոյնժամայն ի տեղի իւր: ⁴⁰ և Թագաւորն եկն յաւուրն եւթներորդի աշխարել զԴանիէլ և եկն ի
բերան գբոյն և հայեցաւ և եւեւս զի նստէր Դանիէլ: ⁴¹ և
աղաղակեաց ի ձայն մեծ և ասէ «մեծ ես, Տէր Աստուած Դանիէլի, և չիք այլ ոք բայց ի քէն»: ⁴² և առ զնա ի վեր և զվնասակարս կորստեան նորա արկին ի գուբն, և գէշ գէշ պատառեցան
նոյնժամայն առաջի նորա:

³⁹ եկեր] + գձաշն M 178ˢ-M346'-M2585 M 182 | Աստ.
—նոյնժամայն] om WN11ᵗˣᵗ | Աստուծոյ] om V280 տեառն M178ˢ-
M346 | նոյնժամայն զամբակում V280 | զԱմբակում] զանպ.
M4114 -կունբ M9116 -կումն J1925 | ի M287 J1925] pr անդրէն
(անտ. V280) rel | տեղ WN11*
⁴⁰ եկն 2° M287' J1925-M2627'] pr իբրև rel | հայեցաւ M287'
J1925' M2627' M182''] հայեցեալ V280 om rel | և 4° M287 M4114]
om rel | զդանիէլ զի նստէր J1925'-M2627 M351
⁴¹ և 1° M287' J1925-M2627 M351 | om rel | ես] + դու M2627 |
Դանիէլի M287 M346' J1925 M351]-իեդի M4834 -իելի rel
⁴² արկ M178ˢ-M346-M2585 M4114 V1508 | զուբն] pr նոյն
M178ˢ-M346'-M2585 M4114 V1508 | պատառեցին նոյնժամայն
զնոսայ առիւծբն M4834 | պատառեցան] պատառեցին զնոսա
V280 հանին զնոսա առևծբն J1925 | նոյնժամայն] om M4114 tr
ante գէշ 1° V280 J1925 | նորա 2°] նոցա M4834 J1925 | արքային
և դանիէլի V280 | subscript. կատարեցաւ մարգարէութիւն
դանիէլի WN11 (-թիւնն M182) կատ. մարգ. դանիէլի (+ ի փառս
Աստուծոյ Տունք ոլի M2585) M346-M2585 M9116

CHAPTER 4

THE EARLIEST STRATUM OF
THE ARMENIAN VERSION AND
ITS AFFINITIES TO THE
GEORGIAN VERSION AND PESHITTA

In preparing the edition all variants with possible external contact were zero-graded and questions touching on Arm's
Vorlage deliberately side-stepped as inappropriate to the present purpose.[1] On the basis of the textual data assembled in
the preceding edition, we are better equipped to set about a detailed study of the issue. By a natural extension of the process
we applied to the individual MSS in order to define their position on the organic line of tradition connecting the translator
with the final copyist, we must now consider the place occupied
by the version within the wider context of the work's transmission history. This line of development, if retraced far enough,
arrives at a point where textual and literary criticism converge
in their investigation of the original composition of the material
in book form. Employing the same methodology of comparing
readings contained in our text and apparatus, representing
Arm's tradition as a whole, with those of related versions we
shall investigate its genealogical affinities in the attempt to
clarify its textual witness, beginning with P.

Ancient Traditions: Arm's translation is set against the historical backcloth of a country divided between Byzantium and Iran most recently by the peace of 387 A.D.[2] Ecclesiastically too Armenia had long been under the influence of the culturally diverse centres of Caesarea and Edessa. St. Gregory the Illuminator, official founder of Armenian Christianity and first hierarch had been consecrated in the former metropolis in 314[3] and it remained closely associated with his dynasty until the time of St. Sahak with whom the line came to a close.[4] Conversely, there is much mention of Syrian missionary activities in the fourth century, particularly in the southern provinces, by figures such as Daniel and Šaŧitay[5] which was canonized by the Armenian appropriation of the Abgar legend of Edessa and apostolic visit by St. Thaddeus.[6] Thus, in the absence of an indigenous alphabet, worship and instruction were based on texts in Greek and Syriac[7] mediated by oral translation,[8] with the result that religious terminology derived from both languages.[9] Moreover, references have been perceived in later sources to the effect that both acted as parent texts for the Armenian translation of the Bible.[10]

It has become conventional to commence one's treatment of the version with speculation on the nature of its *Vorlage,* appealing to the historical data to support the approved conclusion often arrived at through internal evidence of readings. The result of such attempts at harmonizing the disparate material is at times disconcerting. Lyonnet draws an investigation to a close with the following remark:[11]

> "Cette parfaite concordance entre la critique interne (i.e. textual criticism of the Armenian Version) et la critique externe (examination of the traditions) paraît, à tout prendre, un des meilleurs arguments en faveur de la traduction de la Bible arménienne sur un modele grec."

Fifteen years later he expresses himself in a rather different vein at the beginning of his weighty monograph:[12]

"si l'on examine les détails ... on doit avouer que, sans le dire ouvertement - en disant même le contraire et beaucoup mieux peut-être qu'en l'affirmant explicitement - ils laissent entendre que l'entreprise a commencé sous l'influence du syriaque."

The possibility of such a *volte face* should alert us to the potential ambiguity of the historical records as well as the shortcomings in critical methodology for evaluating them. Clearly before discussing the specifics of their account of the translation of the Bible, one must take into consideration the character of the historiographic tradition to which the authors belong and contextualize this particular episode within their wider purview. As with scrutinizing the bearing of the Letter of Aristeas[13] on the origin of the Septuagint, it is imperative to ascertain how trustworthy the sources are, how unitary their testimony is and what limitations they may reveal.

The four extant narratives relating to the invention of the script and scriptural rendering betray the panegyrical hallmarks of early Armenian history, celebrating the exploits of Catholicos Sahak and the monk Maštoc[14] for the advancement of Christianity and national culture. Congruent with this, it is almost axiomatic that all the writers were ecclesiastics and that the earlier ones, at least, were ardent protégés of the Gregorid tradition with its pro-Byzantine orientation. The first of these, Koriwn, is proud to acknowledge being a pupil of Maštoc and to have studied Greek in Constantinople.[15] Moreover, he is commissioned by another pupil Yovsep who succeeded Sahak as *locum tenens,* being refused full ratification by the Persian shah Yazdgard II, and suffered martyrdom in 454. Although not susceptible to exact dating, the work was written either during or immediately following a period in which church administration was firmly in the hands of Persian nominees or sympathizers.[16] Consequently, by selective coverage and intermittent distortion he seeks to shield his protagonists at the expense of their opponents.[17] Chronologically the second author,[18] Lazar Parpeci, writing at the turn of the sixth century, enjoyed a Greek education in Byzantine territory and spent a period of exile in Amida, according to an early account.[19] He is thus virulently anti-Syriac in attitude, the acerbity perhaps in part due to personal circumstances.[20]

Apart from the general question of ideological commitment, we have to recognize that, far from working independently from one another, the authors derive the core of their information from the same matrix which each redacted and embellished as appropriate. Essentially they all therefore retell the same story as Koriwn without significant factual variation. Despite a widespread tendency among Armenian historians not to disclose their sources, it is noteworthy that Łazar states he has read his predecessor's account several times and encourages his audience to consult it for fuller details.[21] A reference on the part of Movsēs Xorenac̣i, the third author, seems calculated to lend versimilitude to the latter's claim to a mid fifth century ambiance.[22] However, no acknowledgement is made of familiarity with his hagiographical activity as of Łazar's history on which he also relies. The fourth text is a synopsis presumably designated for the school curriculum, epitomizing Koriwn's narrative with certain interpolations from Xorenac̣i, which will be cited as Koriwn II.

In view of the importance of Koriwn's record for an investigation of the translation process, it is disconcerting that the evidence is so late, the earliest witness being dated 1672. The main features of the account, as it has been preserved, which are germane to our concerns are as follows.[23] After discerning the inadequacy of Bishop Daniel's letters as a vehicle for representing Armenian phonology, Maštoc̣ descended upon the Syrian cities of Edessa[24] and Amida with his pupils and proceeded to divide them into two contingents.[25] One was to stay in Edessa and apparently occupy itself with Syriac, while the other would continue to Samosata, former capital of the Hellenistic kingdom of Commagene, for instruction in Greek. While still in Edessa Maštoc̣ produced a rough draft of the alphabet which was refined in the latter locality by the scribe Rufinus[26] who penned the initial passages of the Bible translation at Maštoc's dictation. No direct reference is made to the language of the *Vorlage* or the provenance of the exemplar employed, but the first book to be rendered is stated to have been Proverbs.[27]

Returning thereafter to Vałaršapat via Edessa amid great rejoicing, Maštoc continued the task of translation along with Sahak until all the Old and New Testaments were available in Armenian. If we accept the timespan of about a year which Koriwn allots the entire journey, it is highly likely that the team would require an additional period to complete their task.[28] The author alludes to Sahak's role in the process in connection with the revision, noting that he had previously translated 'the assemblage of church books' from Greek.[29] Although the passage is hardly pellucid, a quality for which Koriwn is not renowned, it seems to imply this term includes the Bible; for the next sentence relates Sahak's correction of the original rendering, with Eznik's assistance, to the standard of the exemplars brought from Constantinople, among which the Bible features prominently. If one can rely on this, it suggests the *Vorlage* of at least some parts of scripture was Greek as, one may assume, were the copies from the Byzantine capital which formed the basis for the revision.[30]

The background to this second phase in the process is presented as a new initiative to expand the corpus of Armenian literature through translations from Syriac also to be conducted in Edessa by two of the pupils.[31] Dispatching their work to Armenia they proceeded to Constantinople where they studied Greek with a view to translating from that medium. Subsequently they were joined there by another delegation involving Koriwn himself.[32] Finally, they returned home with 'reliable' (հաստատուն) scriptural codices, the canons of the Council of Ephesus (431) and a number of patristic writings.[33]

Forming only one episode out of his history spanning the years 387-485, Łazar's presentation of events is greatly telescoped, omitting mention of the various journeys and therefore of the revision. Apart from practical considerations of space, this is probably also conditioned by his anti-Syrian bias. Another aspect of the issue is the enhanced emphasis on Catholicos Sahak. Although the latter's spiritual authority pervades Koriwn's composition, Maštoc̣ is naturally presented as the indefatigable champion and model for emulation. Here, as Lazar devotes his third book to his patron Vahan Mamikonean, governor of Armenia, his second extols the prowess of the latter's uncle Vardan who was martyred at the battle of Avarayr in 451.

Forming only one episode out of his history spanning the years 387-485, Lazar's presentation of events is greatly telescoped, omitting mention of the various journeys and therefore of the revision. Apart from practical considerations of space, this is probably also conditioned by his anti-Syrian bias. Another aspect of the issue is the heightened emphasis on Catholicos Sahak. Although the latter's spiritual authority pervades Koriwn's composition. Maštoc̣ is naturally presented as the indefatigable champion and model for emulation. Here, as Lazar devotes the third book to his patron Vahan Mamikonean, governor of Armenia, his second extols the prowess of the latter's uncle Vardan who was martyred at the battle of Avarayr in 451. The first accordingly focuses on Catholicos Sahak as the martyr's grandfather, frequently comparing his virtues with those of his forebear Gregory, thus enhancing the lustre of his patron's ancestry.[34]

In keeping with this, Lazar portrays Maštoc̣ consulting with Sahak continually on devising the new alphabet and, lacking confidence in his command of Greek, joining the nobles and clergy in beseeching the hierarch to consummate his ancestor's illumination of the country by undertaking to translate scripture.[35] Sparing no effort, Sahak accepts the challenge and sees the project to its successful conclusion. Clearly the historian's approach was to appropriate his predecessoe's brief reference to the catholicos' part in the overall activity and expand it tendentiously without apparently adducing any supplementary source material. In consequence, he interprets the very translation process as a means of releasing the Armenian church from dependence on Syrian scholarship,[36] thereby anticipating the state of affairs which, according to Koriwn, resulted only with the revision two decades later. In view of this we are surely justified in setting aside Łazar's account as offering no dependable data unattested by Koriwn.

The third author to treat these events, Movsēs Xorenaci, displays the influence of both his predecessors, as has been noted. Contrary to Łazar's proclivity to abbreviate, however, Movsēs elaborates the basic narrative with embellishments of his own, drawn ostensibly from his recollections as one of Maštoc's disciples. Nevertheless, apart from one occasion, he is accustomed to style his master Mesrop, a practice unparalleled among early writers.[37] Another significant contrast over his sources is the absence of any anti-Syrian animus. Not only does Mesrop have indirect contact with the Syrian bishop Daniel in connection with his attempt to adapt an alphabet for Armenian, but actually visits him on his way to Edessa.[38] Moreover, whereas Koriwn, followed by Łazar, reports Sahak performed various translations from Greek, Xorenaci depicts him rendering unspecified books from Syriac, arguing that Greek study was banned in Persarmenia and all available texts destroyed.[39]

At the same time the historian attributes supervision of the Bible translation completely to Mesrop during his Mesopotamian journey which is replete with new circumstantial detail explaining his movements to the various centres and dramatising their effect. Xorenaci frequently records his reliance on various city and temple archives,[40] in the light of which it is appropriate that he presents the Armenian contingent in dialogue with the Edessene archivist Plato. The latter is also a pagan rhetor of the type under which the author himself purportedly studied during his visit to Alexandria.[41] As tension mounts over the invention of the script, Plato in turn directs Mesrop to his teacher Epiphanius who had moved to other parts. This too proves ineffectual because of the latter's death, yet the investigation leads us to Rufinus, already familiar from Koriwn. Here too our expectations are deceived. In the ensuing impasse divine intervention rescues the situation by revealing the forms of the characters to Mesrop in a vision. Only then is Rufinus of service in effecting the slight refinements necessary. Omitting any reference to the division of Mesrop's pupils between the two cities, Xorenaći enlarges on other aspects of the translation process, noting that after Proverbs they rendered the rest of the OT and then turned their attention to the NT. However he neglects to comment on the nature of the *Vorlage.*

His handling of the circumstances surrounding the revision follows Koriwn's account even more closely, apart from minor additions such as the topos of the translators receiving an honourable reception from the patriarch on their arrival in Constantinople.[42] However, where his predecessor describes the revision in terms of confirming (հաստատէր) the original version, Xorenaći views the process as a retranslation by both Sahak and Mesrop (դարձեալ Թարգմանեցին … վերստին յորջ-նեալ նորոգմամբ). Granted his general policy of redacting Koriwn on the basis of almost no fresh material, it is uncertain whether this last point too is other than a mere stylistic variation.

As an epitome, Koriwn II follows the *Vark' Maštoci* even more closely in most facets of the narrative, simplifying and attempting to clarify the obscurities of the original text.[43] The writer's temporal distance from the events described manifests itself in heightened reverence towards the protagonists; Sahak, in particular, is regularly referred to as a saint.

The material held in common with Xorenaći points in the same direction. It is far more plausible that Koriwn II borrowed from Xorenaći than vice versa in consideration of the former's usual practice of copying sources almost verbatim, whereas the latter harmonizes them into his own fabric. Thus, the epitomator adopts Xorenaći's version of Mesrop's Mesopotamian visit, though with a number of omissions.[44] Perhaps the redactor judged it inappropriate that the blessed Mesrop should have consulted with a pagan on the creation of an Armenian alphabet. At all events, the Plato episode is not represented and consequently the later mention of Epiphanius is highly abrupt and ill-prepared. Similarly, in describing the initial version, Koriwn II rightly glosses Xorenac̆i's reference to the twenty-two books as applying to the OT, yet is totally silent on the NT.[45]

Although his treatment of the revision is largely that of Koriwn, the redactor affords a unique interpretation of Eznik and Yovsep's journey to Edessa. Alone of all the sources, he states the purpose was to produce a new translation of scripture from Syriac, thereby introducing a third stratum to the process.[46] Yet this appears to rest on a misconstruction of Koriwn's rather inclusive phrase 'traditions of the holy fathers',[47] perhaps guided by Xorenac̆i's rendering 'books of the first holy fathers'[48] not on any external source.

Hence, this serves to reinforce our previous conclusions concerning the secondary character of the later authors who deal with the version's inception. All are closely dependent on Koriwn whom they redact in accordance with their overarching literary purpose, adding little of substance. Similarly, Koriwn's intention was to celebrate the figure responsible for Armenizing scripture and to extol the fruit of his labours. In his preoccupation with the result of the process, he almost completely ignores the source. The only dependable details he provides relate to the two strata of translation and revision executed on the basis of different exemplars. From the context of the revision it is plausible to assume a Greek text is intended. With regard to the initial version nothing can be deduced with assurance, though it may be surmised that at least part of it also derives from a Greek *Vorlage.* In view of the remaining uncertainty, one must acknowledge the impossibility of employing the historical records as a shortcut to determining the character and value of the Armenian version, which can only be achieved through textcritical analysis of its component parts.

STRATIFICATION: Textual investigations of several books have confirmed Koriwn's data concerning a duality of strata in the Armenian Version, though their argumentation is not uniformly convincing.[49] Some of these also indicate the second stratum (Arm2) to be a revision of the first (Arm1) (e.g. Ruth,[50] 1-2 Kgdms[51]), though in at least one case (Chron) it has been shown that Arm2 represents a distinct version which not only derives from a divergent text type, but embodies a different translation technique.[52] Moreover, traces of an earlier translation have been postulated in 2 Macc where the Armenian version evinces even more doublets than the other textual witnesses. Levy accordingly explicates the phenomenon as a sign of an incomplete revision of the first attempt at rendering the book.[53] Similarly, Baumstark finds the agreements of the Armenian Psalter with P so convincing in quality and extent that he regards it as proof of the Syriac basis of the Armenian translation. Greek support for some of Zohrab's variants is then taken as evidence of revision to a Greek standard.[54] Cases where Armenian evidence is divided in its support of two contrasting Greek text types may also be best explained on this hypothesis.[55]

PATRISTIC CITATIONS: Research has uncovered a body of readings attested by early Armenian writers which diverges from Z while disclosing agreements with Syriac versions. Some affinities have been detected between the text type they cite and that of early Syrian Fathers. As their formulations vary notably from P, they have been regarded as evidence for the existence of a *Vetus Syra* to the Pentateuch which both antidated P and approximated more closely to the Palestinian Targums.[56]

Such readings do not automatically presuppose a full translation since many of the early authors were conversant with Syriac and Greek and were thus capable of rendering themselves the phrase they quote. However, drawing on the rich indirect textual tradition for the gospels, it has been demonstrated that Arm1 must have arisen from a Syriac original resembling the Diatessaron. The MSS, although most-ly witnesses to Arm2 executed in conformity to a Greek stan-dard, still retained elements of the unrevised text.[57] A more de-tailed investigation of this type of evidence follows in chapter seven.

GEORGIAN VERSION: The testimony of this witness has proved of great value in reconstructing aspects of Arm1 in vari-ous books of the Bible. Its translation seems largely a product of the fifth century and hence not only predates most extant Armenian documentation, but is considered to derive from a text type approximating to the original Armenian rendering. Although much research is still required to clarify the various stages of revision it subsequently underwent in order to isolate the early stratum in composite manuscripts, its study is at a more advanced level than that of the Armenian (partly through being less hampered by *embarras de richesse* in primary sources).[58]

NT investigations have suggested that the base of the Georgian version of Acts was an Old Syriac text diverging from P which was mediated by an Armenian redering radically dif-ferent from Z.[59] Parallel results are forthcoming from an exam-ination of James[60] and seems to hold true also for the other Catholic and Pauline Epistles.[61]

Blake's pioneering surveys of OT manuscripts reveal that the earliest of them betray Armenian loan words, construc-tions and metaphrastic errors which may best be explained by reference to an Armenian *Vorlage.*[62] More detailed research on the Psalter also seems to indicate an ultimate Syriac origin communicated via and Armenian intermediary of a type more primitive than Z.[63] Similarly, investigation of Jeremiah has un-covered a certain degree of affinity with Z, though it is proposed that the percentage would be higher if an earlier text type were to be consulted.[64] The question of Syriac contact remains in-conclusive though an independent study of the oldest palimpsest evidence for Jeremiah implies that the answer may be positive.

As the above indications intimated that collation of the Georgian version of Daniel might yield valuable information about the primitive aspect of the Armenian and help define whether it had had any dependence on P, it was decided to compare the versions in the corpus of readings where Arm≠Gk. This precaution was necessary as not even the two earliest MSS (Geo⁰ and Geoᴵ) have escaped Greek revision, so that where all three sources converge, ambiguity might arise as to whether the Georgian reading is of Armenian or Greek provenance.

The witnesses utilized for the comparison, in addition to being the oldest and the most accessible,[66] are generally regarded as the best representatives of the first recension of the Georgian Bible. The Oški MS of 978 A.D.[67] was copied in one of the monasteries of the large complex in the West Georgian provinces of Tao-klarjeti which owes its foundation to the initiative of St. Grigol Xanzteli in the late 8th/early 9th century. The Jerusalem MS of the Prophets[68] was copied in the eleventh century for P'roxore, abbot of the Monastery of the Cross in Jerusalem, himself a native of the Oški region. The correspondence between this historical circumstance and the close internal affinity the documents possess impels Blake to pronounce them "kindred representatives of the Tao-Klardjet'ian text."[69]

First we shall consider certain linguistic criteria which suggest that the earliest Georgian translation originated from Armenian and then the results of our survey of shared substantive variants which has been divided into three sections:

a. agreements with V280-J2558;
b. agreements with other individual witnesses and small groups;
c. agreements with Arm as a whole.

The accompanying Latin translation is that of Blake and Brière, except in cases where a more literal rendering was required to highlight a feature of the morphology or syntax of the original which had a bearing on the thesis of dependence on Armenian sources. Such cases are marked by an asterisk.

1a) Agreements in the form of Proper Names

Sus:1 Յովակիմ   ომჳაჳად   Geo°   (Iovak'im)

The use of the combination ու (ov) to represent the Greek letter ω in transliterations is a characteristic peculiar to Classical Armenian[70] (cf. Geo[I] ომაჳად Ioak'im=Gk Ιωακιμ).

3:97 Բաբելացւոյ	ბაბილონელთასა (Βαβυλῶνος)	(Babyloniorum)
8:2 Շաւշա (շոշ V280) ᲨᲝᲨ	(Σούσοις)	(šoš)
-13 փելմոնիս	ჴელმონის (φελμουνι)	(pelmonis)
9:15 Եգիպտացւոց	ეგჳპტელთაჳთ (Αἰγύπτου)	(Aegyptiorum)

While reference to peoples is Arm's almost ubiquitous practice, in Gk and P (often followed by Geo) the name of the country (e.g. Babylon, Egypt) is generally found. It is therefore suggested that the above cases may represent isolated remains of the old Georgian text which have survived the Greek revision.

1b) Occurrence of Armenian cognates and loan words

1:5	ռոճիկ	როჭიკი	(ročiki)[71]	(τὸ τῆς ἡμέρας)
5:18	պատիւ	პატივი	(pativi)[72]	(τὴν τιμήν)
9:26	քաղաք	ქალაქ	(kalak)[73]	(τὴν πόλιν)
Bel:19	յատակ	ევატაკი	(evataki)[74]	(τὸ ἔδαφος)
Bel:21	քուրմն	ქურუმნი	(kurumni)[75]	(τοὺς ἱερεῖς)

However, this phenomenon should be interpreted with caution as they are by no means an infallible guide to the Armenian provenance of a particular text. Thus although Georgian ებრ (ebr) is cognate with Armenian իբրև, Tsindeliani notes that it is precisely in that section of the Georgian version of Kingdoms which has been most revised to Gk that the term is most prevalent.[76]

Thus ჭეშმარიტად (češmarit'ad: vere)* parallels ճշմարտիւ at 2:8. Yet while Geo repeats this form in 2:47 and 3:14, Arm reads արդարև in company with P (ܒܐ̈ܫܪܐ). Similarly ტაძარი (t'adzari: templum) parallels տաճար at 3:53, 4:26, 5:3 yet when the same Georgian term recurs at Bel:22, Arm uses մեհեան.[77] Both versions describe Bel as a վիշապ (ვეშაპი vešapi) yet although Geo employs the Armenian loan word at 3:79,[78] Arm reads կետք, itself the result of borrowing from Greek (κῆτος).[79] The witness of the Jerusalem lectionary confirms this as the original reading of the version. Therefore the appearance of վիշապ in Eznik[80] must be deem-ed a free rendering in keeping with the character of the citation as a whole. Nevertheless, as we noted, Blake's observation that Geo° frequently replaces loan words with native equivalents, means that the above examples are not devoid of interest.

2a)   **V280 (+ J2558 = Geo ≠ (Gk + P)**

Sus:18	դրացն] դրանն	კარსა	(ostium)
-41	ոչ] pr դա	მაგან	(ista)
1:12	տացեն] -ցին	მოცქედეც	(dentur)
2:6	զերազն] +իմ	ჩუენებაჲ ჩემი	(somnium meum)
-11	omզի	= Geo	
-25	զմեկնութիւնն]	შეყყუებაჲ იგი	(interpreta tionem
	+ երազոյն	ჩუენებათაჲ	illam somnio rum)
3:44	զաւրութիւնք]	ყოვჯელი	(omnis potentia)
	+ ամենայն	ძლოჲრებაჲ	
-91	om gթագաւորն[81]	= Geo^I	
4:5	om սուրբ	= Geo°	(cf. Chr^lem)
-22	հալածեցեն]-ցին Geo°	განიჯკეჼ	(eieceris)
-32	ձեռին] զորութեան Geo^I	ვჯრძმრთებასა	(potestati)
5:17	om լիցին[82]	= Geo	

6:1 Դարեհ] իւր   წინაჰჲ მისსა   (illi:lit. coram eo)

-24 չև] + և́ս   ვიდრე არღარა   (antequam non-
                                                                   dum)

7:1 իւրում] +   Geo°   შეაძრწნებდა   (conturbabat)
    տագնապեաց զնա

-7 զայլ զագանսն   სხუათა მათ   (aliae illae bes-
                                       მკეცთა   tiae)

-25 ի ժամանակ]-նակս V280   ჟამთა   (ad tempora)

8:16 om և լուայ   =Geo°
    բարբառ մարդոյ

9:13 եկին] + հասին   Geo¹   მოვიდა და მიიწია   (venit et pervenit)

(-15 ձեռամբ] + և   Geo°   და მკლავითა   (et in bracchio
    բարձր բագկաւ   მაღლითა   excelso) (cf. OG)

-15 մեղաք] pr մեք   Geo¹   ვცოდეთ ჩუენ   (peccavimus nos)

10:20 գիտիցես եթէ   Geo°   იწყი უკუე   (scito igitur)

W.O.

Sus:14 միւսանգամ   Geo¹   მერმე მუნვე   (rursus eodem
    անդրէն եկին[83]   მოვიდეს   venerunt)

MS Groupings including V280-J2558=Geo≠(Gk+P)

Sus:11 ցանկութիւնս   Geo¹   გულისთქუმათა   (concupiscentias
    V280' M178-M346'-   მათ   illas)
    M2585 CHB5

1:19 գտաւ V280 M346'   არავინ იპოვა   (nemo inventus
                                                             est)

2:2 հրաման ետ   Geo°   ბრძანა   (praecepit)
    V280' J1925

3:30 պատուիրեցեր] +դու   შენ მამცენ   (tu mandasti)
    V280' M346' J1925

-37 նուաղեցաք] +մեք   შევმცირდით   (imminuti
    V280 M178-M346'   ჩუენ   sumus nos)
    -M2585 M9116

-39 լիցուք] + մեք V280'   შეკცავიორუო   (suscipiamur
                                           ვართ ჩუენ   nos)

-91 զաւրհնութիւնս]-թիւն გალობაჲ იგი   (canticum illud)

4:6 դու   Geoᴵ   შენ   (tu)

8:1 om թագաւորութեանն = Geo
     M287' M346-WN11*

11:1 կայի V280' M2627   დავდეგ   (stabam)
     V1508-M351

Bel:11 կերակուր M287" J1925   საჭმელი   (escam)

2b) MS Groupings excluding V280-J2558=Geo≠(Gk+P)

Sus:5 այնմիկ]այնորիկ   წელიწადისა მის   (anni illius)
     M178-M346' J1925

-7 ժողով M287 J1925 Geoᴵ   კრებული იგი   (congregatio)

-20 ասեն]+ցնա J1925   ჰრქუეს მას   (dixerunt ei)

-49 վկայեն WN11   შევამცბენ   (testantur)

-52 մեկնեցին J1925   განაშორვნეს   (separassent
                                    იგინი   illos)

-53 արդար և անմեղ Geoᵒ   მართალი და   (iustum et
     M346'-M2585 J1925   უბრალოე   innocentem)

-59 սղոցել] -ցէ M287   განგხერხონ   (secabit)

-64 ժողովուրդն]pr (Geoᵒ)   ყოვლისა მის   (omni illo
     ամենային M346'   ერისა   populo)

2:5 տունն ձեր M287 Geoᵒ   სახლი თქუენი   (domus vestra)

-9 որ]qh⁸⁴ J1925   ვითარმედ   (quoniam)

-17 և Անանիա ...   Geoᵒ   ანანია-მოყუასითა...   (cum Anania ...
     և բարեկամաց իւրոց   მისთურთ და   sociis suis et
     եցոյց զբանն M287   სიტყუაჲ იგი   verbun illud
                                    აუწყა მათ   indicaverit eis)

-27 առաջի] om J1925 Geoᵒ om   წინაშ   (om coram)

-34 հայեի M287⁸⁵   Geoᵀ ვხედევდ   (videbam)

3:32 Ի ձեռն թագաւորի Geoᵒ   ჴელთა მეფისა   (in manibus
     M2585   regis)

-40 ընդունելի լինել   შევიწყნარებ   (susceptum sit)
     M346'-M2585 J1925

-41 երկնչիմք]+ մեք rel   მეშინის ჩუენ   (timemus nos)
     M287'-WN11 M9116

-98	init] pr ես M4834	მე	(ego)
4:7	տեսանէի] + ես M4834 (J1925)	Geo° მე ვხედევდ	(ego videbam)
-14	յարուցանէ	აღადგინის	(consituit)
8:13	փիլիմոնին M346'[86]	Geo° პილემონი	(Pilemoni)
9:24	տեսլեան] -լեանց M4834 J1925	ხილვათა	(visiones)
11:6	զաւրացուցանէր WN11 -M2585 J1925'-M2627 M182"	განაძლიერა	(confortavit)
-24	om հարց M2627	Geo° om მამითა	(om patrum)
-33	init M287] pr եւ rel	=Geo°	
12:1	ազգ] +մարդկանց M4834 J1925	Geo° ნათესავი კაცთაჲ	(gens* hominum)
Bel:21	դուռնն J1925	Geo° კარი	(ostium)
-40	ես] + դու M2627	Geo° ხარ შენ	(es tu)
WO 11:6	ընդ նմա դաշինս M287	მის თანა აღთქუმისა	(cum eo pactum)

The variant **քո հաւանեալ յանձն առ** read by M178-M346' at Sus:20 seems to be a *lectio duplex* which has been taken over by Geo: თავს იდევ ჩუენ თანა და ნება მეც ჩუენ (assentire nobis et licentiam da nobis). It is possible that the active form აღადგინოს (suscitabit) found in Geo° at 11:25 resulted from a misinterpretation of the Armenian verb **զարթիցէ** which though intransitive has an active form of aorist conjunctive.[87] The Gk and P variants in contrast are patently middle/passive. Similarly, it may be the case that Geo°'s reading ყოველსა სიტყუასა და სიბრძნესა და მეცნიერებასა (in omni verbo et sapienta et scienta) at 1:20 is dependent on a variant such as that of J1925 *in loco* **յամենայն բան և իմաստութեան և գիտութեան**. Perhaps the first was added to balance the two genitives dependent on **բան**. However, the Georgian translator seems to have construed all three nouns as locatives connected with the preposition **ի** and translated accordingly.

Arm as a whole =Geo≠(Gk+P)

Sus:12 սպասէին նմա Geo¹ უმზირდეს მას   (observabant
                                         eam)

-24 կից նմին] ընդ նմա მის თანა   (cum ea)
     J 1925

1:10 կարգեաց ձեզ զկե- რომელმან დაგა-   (qui constituit
      րակուրդ ձեր և ⴂესა თⴈⴗენ ზედა   vobis cibum
      զըմպելի საზრდელი თⴈⴗე-   vestrum et
                              ნი და სასⴑⴂელი   potum)

2:27 զխորհուրդ զայդ საიდⴂⴃⴔოⴑსა მას   (mysterium illud)

3:95 միայն მხⴐⴑⴐⴑსა   (solum) (588)

4:6 արդ լուր դու Geo¹ აⴂ ისმინე შეն   (nunc audi tu)

-20 և զի   Geoᵒ და რამეთⴃ   (et quia)

-28 յերկնից] + և ասէ და თⴈⴗა   (et dixit)
     (ասէր V280 M2585
      M2627' M182'')

5:7 ցուցից քեզ მაⴂⴂⴗოⴑ მე   (indicaverit mihi)

-9 գոյն երեսաց նորա ⴔⴈⴐⴈ პⴈრისა   (color faciei eius*)
                                 მისისაⴃ

-17 ցուցից քեզ გაⴂⴂⴗო შენ   (indicabo tibi)

6:4 խնդրեին ⴄⴃⴈⴂⴔⴃⴔⴑ   (quaerebant)

-20 պաշտեիր   Geo¹ ⴈⴃⴑახⴃⴐⴄⴃⴔⴃ   (serviebas)
     (-V280 WN11 J1925

7:7 առ ոտն ⴔⴈⴐⴈⴃⴑⴈⴑⴔ ⴔⴃⴑⴈⴑⴔ   (pede suo)*

-13 հասանէր მⴔⴈⴒⴃ   (pervenit)
     (-V280 J1925)

-19 առ ոտն ⴔⴈⴐⴈⴃⴑⴈⴑⴔ ⴔⴃⴑⴈⴑⴔ   (pede suo)*

8:23 յետ ⴃⴌⴃⴃⴌⴃⴑⴔⴈⴂⴄⴚ   (post)

9:8 մեզ ամաւթ երեսաց ⴈⴃⴂⴄⴃⴃⴃ ⴑⴈⴐⴚⴈⴑⴂⴚⴈ   (nobis confusio
      մերոց և հարց մե- პⴈⴐⴈⴑⴃ (ⴈⴃⴂⴃⴈⴑⴃⴃ   faciei nostrae et
      րոց որ մեղաք om Geoᵒ) და მⴃ-   patribus nos-
      (om մերոց 1˚ M287') მⴃთⴃ ⴈⴃⴂⴃⴃⴃ რⴐ-   tris qui pecca-
                               მⴄⴂⴃⴃ შⴄⴚⴂⴃⴃⴃⴄⴔ   vimus)(Bo Aeth)

-11 ծառայ քո Geo¹ მⴐⴌⴈⴑⴃ შⴄⴌⴈⴑⴃⴑⴃ   (servi tui)

-16 ամենայն ժողովուրդ Geoᵒ ⴗⴐⴂⴄⴃⴈ ⴄⴐⴈ   (omnis populus)

-18 յորոյ վերայ կոչե-ցեալ է	Geo° ռոմელსա ზედა წოდებულ არს	(super quam vocatum est)
-19 ի վերայ քաղաքի քո	Geo° ზედა ქალაქსა ამის შენსა	(super civitatem hanc tuam)
-23 արդ	აწ	(nunc)
10:9 յերկիր խոնարհեալ	დამეღრიკო ქუეყანად	(inclinata est ad terram)
-11 զբանս զայս (-V280)	სიტყუათა მათ	(sermones illos)
11:24 խորհուրդ	ზრახვაა	(cogitationem)
11:29 առաջինն Geo°	პირველი	(primum)
-32 աձցեն ... զզայթաց-ղութիւն	მოაწიონ შეკკოლებაა	(afferrent offen-diculum)
-40 ի ժամանակի վախ-ճանի	ჟამსა დასასრულისასა	(in tempore finis)
Bel:9 զայն ամենայն	ესოდენსა ამას რომიკსა	(tantum hunc victum)

In addition, it appears that Geo[r]'s reading აღიხუნეს (suscepe-runt) at 7:17 is the result of scribal error by which բարձգին was read as բարձին (either on the part of the Georgian transla-tor or his exemplar). This particular variant is not attested in any of the fifteen final witnesses collated. Instead, two MSS omit the other consonant to produce the forms բարգին M4834, բարգեն M346. Nevertheless, as the Georgian reading cannot so adequately be explained in terms of Gk or P, the reading is probably of Armenian origin.

It may be useful to draw attention at this point to several trends which emerge from the foregoing presentation. The type of reading supported by Geo is generally substantive (plus, minus or one involving semantic variation), while WO does not feature at all prominently. Many of them are typical of Arm's translation technique (particularly Arm1) - insertion of direct and indirect object as well as pronoun subject, the asyndetic juxtaposition of two verbs, preference for the singu-lar of the demonstrative pronoun այս. Moreover, Geo, like

Arm, usually adds the copula foreign to the semitic idiom of P and Th's more literal technique. As this last move could easily be interpreted as an inner Georgian phenomenon no examples have been cited. However, cases of metaphrastic mistakes are particularly important as this forms one of the most incontravertible criteria for direct contact between versions.

Regarding the testimony of the witnesses, in cases where Geo divides, it is normally Geo° which accompanies Arm (as one might expect of its greater age). However the position is reversed in Susanna and Chapter 9 where Geoᴵ's text is closer. On the Armenian side, although a number of agreements are attested by all the MSS, the majority are found in only a small group (mainly V280-J2558, then M346' J1925 and M287). The implication is that Arm's transmission has not been unilinear. The early date of the Georgian Version as well as the primitive text type generally evinced by the Armenian witnesses whose readings it reflects suggest that the majority are the product of a recension. Moreover, one of its principles must have been to heighten the version's literalism and suppress the earlier accommodation to Armenian idiom exhibited by the minority of MSS in common with Geo.[88]

The three following tables relating to aspects of Arm's rendering of its *Vorlage* underline Geo's dependence which was established from a consideration of cases where Arm diverged from Gk and P. As Lyonnet demonstrated in the Gospels, the sources of Arm readings supported by Geo are provided by both Gk and P. Due to the fact that Gk represents a Hebraizing recension, a third category has had to be instituted in Daniel to deal with those instances where either of the sources could have served as the basis of Arm's reading.

a) Geo dependent on Arm's rendering of Gk

Sus:	18 πλαγίας	ի կողմանէ	Geoᴵ ჯიფოთ	(a latere)
-22	ἀνεστέναξε	յոգւոց եհան	ხუთა თითუნსა	(ingemuit)
-57	ὑπέμεινε	կալաւ յանձին	თავს იდვა	(sustinuit)

1:4 ἐν πάσῃ σοφίᾳ	ամենայն իմաս-տութեամբ (J1925' M351)	Geo¹ ყოვკლსა საბრძნესა	(in omni sapientia)
2:1 ἐγένετο ἀπό	հատաւ	განეჭრჰა	(recessit)
3:18 γνωστόν	յայտնի	უწყებულ	(notum)[89]
-90 οἱ σεβόμενοι τὸν κύριον	պաշտաւնեայք[90] Stառն	მსახურნი უფლისანი	(ministri domini)
5:21 ἡ καρδία αὐτοῦ ἐδόθη	սիրտ տուաւ նմա	გული... მოცა მას	(cor datum est ei)
-29 ἐκήρυξε	քարոզ կարդայր (cf. 3:4)	Geo° ჴალაგი იგი ჴმობდა	(praeco clamabat)
6:2 μὴ ἐνοχλῆται	աշխատ ինչ մի լիցի	არა რათ უცალო იყოს	(ne ... ullis negotiis impedire-tur)
8:6 ὁρμῇ	զաւրութեամբ	სიმჰაგრითა	(vi)*
-17 ἦλθε	եկն եկաց	მოვიდა და დადგა	(venit et stetit)
9:16 τοῖς περικύκλῳ ἡμῶν	են J1925'-M4114 M351	Geo° არიან	(sunt)
10:11 ἔντρομος (ἐν τρόμῳ 534)	դողութեամբ	ძრწოლით	(cum tremore)
11:32 ἐπάξουσιν ἐν ὀλισθρήμασι	ածցեն ի վերայ իւրեանց զգայ-թագղութիւն	მოაწიან შეკრულებად	(offerent offendicu-lum)
12:8 τὰ ἔσχατα	վախճան	აღსასრული	(finis)
Bel:6 ὅσα	որչափ	რავღენსა	(quan-tum)*
-12 πάντα βεβρωμένα	այդ ամենայն կերեալ	ყოველი შეჭამული	(omne comes-tum)*

Geo dependent on Arm's rendering of P

Sus:4 ⲟⲕⲟ   յապարանս   Geoᴵ ṭɑdɑ́ṁoɑ   (aedes)
Although Gk and the available Syriac witnesses here read
'house' the Armenian rendering reflects 'palace'. This plausibly derives from the graphically similar Syriac form ⲓⲗ̄ⲓ̈ⲟ,
though whether this represents a manuscript variant or simply the reading of the Armenian translator cannnot be determined. At all events the Armenian morpheme is a *pluralis tantum* which has resulted in an unnatural plural form in Geoᴵ.

Sus:21 ⲕⲟ̄ ⲩ		nuʼu	ȝ06ⴃⴄ ... ⴛɑ̇ⴃ̇ⴈȝ0	(quidam
(MSS a + 7a1)	պատանի			iuvenis)
3:37 ⲕⲉⲩⲁ ⲟⲅⲟ		ⲗ ⲁⲣⲇ	ⴐⲟ ɑⴖ	(et nunc)
4:5 ⲟ (cf. Gk ὅς)	qⲏ		ⴌɑⴛ̇ⴑⴍⴈ	(quia)

As the Syriac conjunction , can introduce both relative and ca-
sual clauses it is the most likely basis of Arm's interpretation
which has been carried into Geo also.

9:21 ⲓⲟⲩⲟ		յառաշնուⲙ	Geoᴵ ⴊⲟ̇ⴐȝⴈⴈⴖⴑɑ	(in prima
ⲣ̄ⲟⲩⲟ ⲟ	տⲉⲩⲗ ⲉⲁⲛ̄ⲛ̄		ⴛɑⴑ ⴐ̇ⴈȝ6ⴈⴃɑⴑɑ ⴐ̇ⴈⴛⴑɑ	illa visione
				mea)

Arm's reading is dependent on the Syriac similarity between
ⲣ̄ⲟⲩⲟ ⲟ 'of old' and ⲟⲩⲟⲟ which means both 'first' and 'early'.

-23 ⲅⲓⲟⲟⲟ̣	ⲁⲣⲁⲩⲑⲏⲥ	Geoᴵ ⴇⴍⴌ̇ȝ3ɑⴍɑ	(precum)

The Georgian plural seems clearly to have arisen from the
Armenian rendering which is another *pluralis tantum* and as
such presents an exact translation of P.

9:24   ⲏ qⲁⲗ   ⴛⴍⴖ̇ȝ36ɑⴓ   (ut adveniat)
Gk reads τοῦ ἀγαγεῖν which is paralleled by P ⲟⲕⲟⲟⲕ. However
as the *P̄eal* infinitive of the same root is graphically close ⲓⲗ̄ⲕⲟ
Arm's interpretation seems to have arisen from Syriac.

Geo dependent on Arm's rendering (from G or P)

1:2	զայն	იგი	(id)*
2:11	մնեղեաg	კორცილოსა	(carnali)
3:12	դիս	ღმერთთა	(diis)

Yet again Arm's *pluralis tantum* is rendered by a Georgian plural.

3:92	ապականութիւն ինչ	განრყუნილებაჲ ... რაჲ	(corrupionis ... quid)*
6:4	ամենևին պատճառս Geo°	ყოვვლად მიზეზი	(omnino causam)
-23	ամենևին ապակա- Geo° նութիւն	ყოვვლად გან- რყუნილებაჲ	(omnino laesio)
4:5	զոր ասագի թե Բաղտասար իշխան գիտաg զոր ես գիտեմ թե ...		
	Geo¹ ბალტასარ მთავარმან უწოდა რომელ ეკა მე კიკი უწყი რაჲეთუ		
	(Baltasar princeps vocavit tu quem ego *novi scio* quod ...)		

As we saw earlier, Agathangelos cited a rather confused version of this sentence. Geo has likewise taken Բաղտասար as Nebuchadnezzar's son who therefore befits the title իշխան. Construing him as the subject has meant additional rearrangement of WO. However, the double appearance of the verb 'to know' can only be accounted for with reference to Arm. գիտաg genitive plural of գէտ 'wise man', had somehow to be given a place in the translation. As it is only one letter short of becoming գիտացի, normal equivalent of კიკი (novi), it seems that this gave the translator sufficient cause to render it as above.

The demonstration of Geo's reliance both on material peculiar to Arm and on the latter's representation of readings from Gk and P establishes as a corollary the validity of Geo's witness to the textual character of an early phase of Arm's transmission. However before proceeding to an exposition of the evidence we have gathered in support of this statement it is necessary to review Gehman's treatment of Arm's relation to P.

Gehman's Study: After stating that Arm's main allegiance is with Th Gehman subjects all readings diverging from this norm to comparison with P using Lee's edition. He then sets out a list of nine cases of agreement between Arm and P, although he acknowledges that some of them may be the result of coincidence. His examples repay detailed scrutiny as they raise in nucleus all the questions we shall have to deal with, i.e. Arm's affinities with P, OG, Th and MT.

The more extensive collations Ziegler puts at our disposal require us to suspend judgement over three of the instances in that they are shared by other Th witnessees. Thus in the minus at 6:(14)13 of τῆς ἡμέρας Arm is joined by 87* La^s (vid.). The same OL witness accords with Arm at 9:16 in the plus 'et a' before *'monte sancto'.* Concerning Arm's rendering զզեղեալ բարեանն at 10:5 Gehman admits the possibility of Th influence via two MSS 26 89.[91] At the same time he proposes P (ܠܒ݂ܫ ܠܒ݂ܘܫ̈ܐ ܝܠܝܢ) as an alternative. However the absence of an equivalent for ܠܒ݂ܘܫ̈ܐ 'garments' in Arm and the stereotyping of փառք - δόξα պատիւ - τιμήν militate against the acceptance of the second possibility. This conclusion is further corroborated by the incidence of պատիւ (not փառք) at 5:17 where Th reads δωρεάν and P ܝܒ݂ܠ.

In the minus of αὐτοῦ 1° at 7:20 Arm is supported by La^s and follows MT with the result that we cannot rule out Arm's having been influenced by a Lucianic or Hexaplaric Greek MS. The origin of the Armenian variants քոշին M2585 M2627 M182" նոխազին V280 and քոշին նոքա M178 at 8:7 is postulated as P (ܝܡ, ܠܝܓ) yet OG variant απο του τραγου approximates to Arm even more exactly.

The remaining four cases can be advanced as examples of P influence with more justification. Arm's reading անցգէ at

11:39 is clearly ascribable to what must be assumed to have been an early copyist's mistake which altered the position of the diacritical point distinguishing *dolat* and *riš* P's present text is ובו but its original form was most probably גבּ, = MT עשׂה. Two other readings result from Arm's translation of semitic words simply transliterated in Th. Thus ապարանն corresponds to τῇ βάρει at 8:2 and hqատր to μαωζειν at 11:38. In the second of these especially the proximity of Arm and P over against the various interpretations suggested for MT suggests that Arm derived it from P rather than an anonymous marginal gloss. Some reserve might be expressed about the final example which concerns the case of a personal pronoun (סוהם = նղշիրք նորա) which might have arisen from Arm's translation technique from Th. Yet though not constitutive of a relation between Arm and P, now that the previous readings have gone some way to proving that it provides additional confirmation.

P=Arm=Geo: Taking into account the issues which have just been raised about Arm's hybrid origins, although following basically the same schema as before, our presentation of P=Arm=Geo agreements will note those cases where P=MT and devote a separate table to readings which are supported by OG or one or two Th witnesses. Despite the fact that P=Arm contact has been demonstrated and parallels in other witnesses are often likely to be fortuitous, these cases must be viewed more sceptically than the majority where P is the sole source.

With regard to agreements with MT, only those instances are signified where its meaning is unequivocable in absolute terms and has then been rendered more adequately by Arm=P than by Th. For it is precisely those cases where MT is unclear or capable of diverse construction that are so regularly a cause of bifurcation in the subsequent textual tradition as P and Gk opt for different interpretations. Thus in treating the phrase נגע אל in 9:21 Th's literalist tendency favours the usual translation equivalent ἥψατο whereas P (+OG) takes account

of the setting in which the word appears and renders ܕܝܠܗ which
is also Arm's basis (մերձեցաւ). Although MT is regarded as P's
main source, the value of isolating those cases where a direct
line of continuity exists (MT=P=Arm) is that it enables us to
measure the extent to which MT influence was communicated
to Arm via P (which is probably pre-hexaplaric) as opposed to
Gk.

A further distinction has been introduced to separate
out readings according to their value in determining a chain of
textual dependence. Even accepting that P is the only extant
source to attest the precise nuance of Arm, there is still another factor to be considered, especially if the feature is syntactic
or morphological, namely the craftmanship of the translator.
As their representation in translation is bound up with that of
the surrounding context, much depends on the way he frames
the whole sentence structure. As the common witness of P and
Arm in such cases may amount to no more than shared interpretation arrived at independently, they have been set out at
the end.

1a)   **V280-J2558=P=Geo**

=MT   3:13 աձիՆ] + զնոսա ܘܢ ܐܬܝ   Geo[I] მოჰყვანნებს კაცნი ესე
                                        (adduxerunt viros hos)

       -63 om ամենայն   P[txt]ܟܘܟܒ   ვარსკულავნი
                                        (stellae)

=MT   4:17 բարձրութիւն] +   ܪܘܡܗ   Geo°სიმაღლე მისი
             Նորա   (altitudo eius)

       9:18 արդարութեանց] ܙܕܩ̈ܘ   სიმართლეთა
             -թեան   (iustitiam)

       -19 վասն] + անուան ܡܛܠ ܫܡܟ   სახელისა (შენისა) თვს
             (քո)   (propter nomen tuum)

       -24 մարգարէ]-էից   ܢܒܝ   წინაწარმეტყუელებათა
                                        (prophetiae)

       -26 ապականեսցին] ܢܬܚܒܠ   Geo[I] განირყუნეს
             -եսցի   (destruetur)

10:16 գայրն] գայն　　(,) օﬔ　ﬗ (illi)

Bel:26 սպանից] pr եսﬖﬖﬖ Geo°ﬗ ﬗﬗﬗﬗﬗ
　　　　　　　　　　　　　　　(ego interficiam)

1b)　Additional examples with some outside support

Sus:51 om ի բաց[92] (=MS b)　=　Geo[l] (584 Bo Ps Chr
　　　　　　　　　　　　　　　Lucif)

=MT　2:11 որոց բնակու-　　ﬔﬖ,　Geo°ﬗﬗﬗﬗﬗﬗﬗ ﬗﬗﬗﬗﬗﬗﬗ
　　　　թիւն չէ] որ　　ﬗﬗﬗﬗ　　ﬗﬗ ﬗﬗﬖ
　　　　ոչ է բնակ. նոցա　　　　　(quorum habitatio eo-
　　　　　　　　　　　　　　　rum non est) (88 Aeth)

N.B.　The Syriac origin of V280's reading is emphasized by the
neat, but unidiomatic use of որ to represent the conjunction ,.

　　　3:92 այլ] + ահա　　　ﬗﬔ　　Geo°　ﬗﬗﬗﬗ
　　　　　　　　　　　　　　　　　(ecce) (OG)

WO　Sus:57 ոչ կալաւ յան-ﬗﬗﬖﬖ ﬖ　ﬗﬗ ﬗﬖﬖ ﬗﬗﬖ
　　　　δին　　　(MS a)　　(non sustinuit)

2a)　Small groupings including V280-J2558=P=Geo

Sus:5 առաջնորդել] ﬔﬖ, ﬗﬗﬔ;　Geo° ﬗﬗﬗﬗﬗﬗﬗ
　　　-նորդ(ք)　　(MS b)　　(curator)*
　　　V280' J1925

3:51 երեքեանն]　　ﬗﬖﬖﬖﬗ　ﬗﬗﬗﬗﬗ ﬗﬗﬗ
　　　+ նորա　　　　　　　(tres iidem illi)
　　　V280' J1925

6:24 զԴանիելէ]　　ﬖﬖﬔ,,　ﬗﬗﬗﬗﬗﬗﬗﬗ
　　　դանիելի　　　　　　　(Danieli)*
　　　V280 J1925

11:7 ի հաստատութիւնս] ﬔﬗﬗﬖﬖ　Geo° ﬗﬗﬗﬗﬗﬗﬗﬗ
　　　-թիւն(ն)　　　　　　(munimento)
　　　V280

Bel:18 huyɡɡɡɡuıɡ]   اره   მიხედნი
        -ɡguıɭ   (intuitus est)
        V280 J1925 V1508

   -41 qɡɡ 1˚]   اححہ حد   მეყსუელად
        pr unjh ժամայh   (confestim)
        V280 J1925

WO 3:55 huyɧhu juɡn ...uuuɧu ɧ ɡpnuɡpɡu

          ܒܘܥܘܙ ܟܐ ܠܡܘ ܒܘܬܘ ܟܙ ܟܐ ܙܟ   (P MS 1114)

          (3)ზი ქერაბინთა და ჴედავ უფსკრულთა

          (qui sedes super Cherubim ... aspicis abyssos)

2b) Examples with outside support

=MT 2:46 ɧ uɡpuy ɡpɡuug]   اقة ܗ\   პირსა თჳსსა ზედა
           + ɧunɡ   (in faciem suam)
           V280 J1925   (62' verses)

WO=MT 5:2 quɡɡuɡɡnɡ ... qnuɡɡnɡ]tr V280 J1925

            ܒܘܠܘ،ܘ ܒܘ܂،،

            ოქროისაჲ ... ვეცხლისაჲ

            (auri ... argenti) (311)

It may be appropriate to add here the agreements of M287''
J1925-M2627 with P and Geo in the succession of verses in
chapter three. P's order is 66 86 71 72 67 70 73 which is duplicated by Geo and Arm's units with the exception of v. 86 which
they place in the expected order.

3a) Small groupings excluding V280–J2558=P=Geo

        1:15 quɡɡuɡ] ɧ   ܟܳܒ܂ ܪ   ჲაბლისა მისგან
              uɡɡuɡnɡ WN 11   (de mensa)
         -17 uɡɡuɡ ɡuɡ]   ܪܘܡ Geo°ხილჳითა
              -ɡuɡg J1925   (visiones)
        2:49 qnɡɡɡg] -ɡnɡ   ا،حد   საქმეს მას
              J1925-M2627   (super *opus*)*
=MT 3:12 qnɡɡɡg] -ɡnɡ   ܠܐܘܙ   საქმესა
              J1925-M2627   MS 6h10   (super *opus*)*

-26 եւ] + դու   ܐܢܬ   ხარ შენ
     M2627   (es tu)

-41 fin] + Տէր   ܡܪܝܐ   უფალო
     M4834 M346'   (V.42 init)   (domine)
     -M2585 J1925

Bel: 18   դրացն] դրանն   ܒܝܠ   Geo° კარი
     J1925   (ostium)

-20 տեսանեմ] + եւ   ܐܢ ܐܦ   Geo° ვხედავ მე
     M346'   (video ego)

-21 բարկացաւ   ܐܬܚܡܬ   განრისხნა
     M287   (iratus est)

(3:20) կապեսցեն M287 ܠܡܐܣܪ,   შეჰკრვათ
     M2627 M182'   (ut ligarent)

As Nebuchadnezzar's bully boys are instructed a) to bind the Three and b) to throw them into the furnace, both Greek versions subordinate the former command hypotactically by means of a participle. Thus perhaps Arm's translator had a hand in the restoration of balance between the commands. Conversely Arm's reading might be regarded as a direct translation of P. One might also combine the two conjectures, in which case P guided the translator's hand in rendering the Gk.

7:20 միւսյն] միոյն J1925   ერთისა (uno)

P's Leiden text reads ܐܚܪܢ in concert with Arm majority. Nevertheless, it may be that the variant found its way into Geo via Arm once more by confusion of *dalat* and *riš* either in Syriac or perhaps in Hebrew where the two forms אהד / אהר are even closer. Thus the basis of the reading may have been a P variant not now attested.

3b) Supplementary examples with outside support

1:13 զսեղան] ի   ܠܚܡ ܕ   ტაბლისა მისგან
սեղանոյ   (de mensa) (584
M2585   verssᴾ
         Hi. ep. 100, 7)

3:52 om և 3˚   =P   =Geo   (410 Arab)
M4834 J1925

4:9 թոչունք] pr   ܒܗܘ ܐܠ   ყოველნი მფრინველნი
ամենայն   (omnes volucres)
M2585 M2627'   (Aethᴾ)

-11 թալթափեցէք]   ܐܘܥܨܘ   და დაჰყარეთ
pr և M2627   (et excutite)(231
         Aeth)

-16 տագնապեցուցէ] ܣܘܐܕܝ   გან̇წრაფებ
-գեն M4834   (premant) (311)
J1925'

7:9 անիւք] pr և   ܘܓܠܓܘܗܝ   Geoˢდა ̇გ̇ბლის ̇უ̇ლ̇ნი
M4834 J1925   (et rotae) (22 26 Bo
         Aeth Arab)

=MT -17 թագաւորութիւնք] ܡܠܟܐ   მეფენი
թագաւորք M178-   (reges) (62' 230 410
M346-WN11*   Aeth)

9:18 Տէր ult] om   =P   =Geo   (V Aug)
M346-WN11*-
M2585 M2627

Bel:27 գնդակ M287]   ܐܡܣܝ   გრგოლ̇ად
-դակ u rel   (MS 6h10   (in massam) (410
         and un-   OG)
         specified
         later MSS)

Many of the above cases are less significant than the foregoing. One third consists of variation in the copula, while "all" (4:9) is frequently subject to the caprice of individual scribes. Moreover, the subject of the verb in 4:16 is compound so that independent attempts to 'improve' the grammar in various languages would hardly be surprising. The close affinity between Th MS 410 and P marked here in three places is observable throughout the book and is the focus of discussion in the appendix to this chapter. The only reading in which a strong case could be made for Th influence on Arm is 7:17 where the hexaplaric MSS 62' and others coincide with P in championing MT.

4) **Arm as a whole =P=Geo**

Sus: 1 աևուև ևորա   ܘܡܗ   სახელი მისი
            (MSS ab7a1)   (nomen eius)

-2 իւր կիև   ܘܠܬܝ ܘܠ   თავისა თჳსისა ცოლი
            (MSS a7a1)   (sibimetipsi uxorem)

-8 գաևկագաև   ܘܗܝ   Geo¹ ჰჶაღოჶდა მისი
    ևմա   (MSS a7a1)   (concupiscebant de
                                 illa)

-9 դատաստաև (ܘܠܝ,) ܘܝ,   Geo¹ სამჴჯლისა
            (MS b)   (iudicii)

-18 զոր իևչ հրա-   ܠܙܠܝ, ܡܪܡ   რომელი იგი უბრძანა
     մայեաց ևոցա (MS b)   მათ
                                 (quod praeceperat-
                                 eis)

-37 պատաևի մի   ܚܠܡܐ ܗܘ   ჭაბუკი ვინმე
            (MSS ab7a1)   (iuvenis quidam)

-39 և եբաց   ܗܝܠ ܘܠܗܘ   Geo¹ და განახენა კარნი
     զդուրսև և   (ܘܗܙܝܠ)   სამოთხისანი და
     փախեաւ   (ܘܗ ܘ)   განივლტოდა
            (MSS a7a1)   (et aperuit ostia
                                 horti
                                 et effugiebat)

-45 միևչդեռ տա-   ܘܗܘܙܝ, ܗܪ   ვითარცა
     ևեիև զևա   (MS a)   ჶაჳყჳჶანდა
                  ܗܗ ܝܙܪ, ܗܙ ܘܠ   (cum abducerent
                  (ܘܪܝܒ)   illam)
                  (MS b)

	-57	առ երկիւղի	ܒܪܬܝܬܐ (MS 7a1)	მოშიშებით (in timore)
=MT (-M287)	1:4	դպրութիւն[93] M182	ܣܦܪܐ	წიგნი (librum)*
	-8	ի սեղանոյ	ܡܢ ܦܬܘܪܗ	ტაბლისა მისგან (de mensa)
	-15	երեսք	ܐܦܝܗܘܢ	პირნი (facies
=MT	-15	մարմնով (-M4834 J1925)	ܒܣܪܗܘܢ	ჴორცითა (carne)
	-13,15	հրաման (Th 13 δόγμα; 15 γνώμη)	ܦܘܩܕܢܐ	ბრძანებაჲ (praeceptum)
=MT	-35	առ	ܫܩܠܬ	აღიღო (rapuit)
	-35	սաստկութիւն հողմոյ	ܚܣܢ ܕܥܠܥܠܐ	სიმძაფრემან ქარისამან (violentia venti)
=MT	3:6	հնոց հրոյն բորբոքելոյ	ܐܬܘܢ ܢܘܪܐ ܝܩܕܬܐ	საჴუმილსა მას ცეცხლისა (fornacem illam ignis ardentis)
	-19	գոյն	ܓܘܢܐ	ფერი (color)*
	3:27,28,29	ամենայն (գամ.31) =P	ܟܠ =Geo	ყოვლისა (omne)
	-33	ոչ գոյ մեզ բանալ (ժամ բանալ V280 M346')	ܠܝܬ ܠܢ ܡܦܬܚ	არა არს აღებად (non est aperire)*
	-33	զի ամաւթ	ܡܛܠ ܕܒܗܬܬܐ	რამეთუ სირცხვლი (quia pudor)*
	-42	բազում ողորմութեան	ܪ̈ܚܡܝܟ ܣܓܝܐܐ	მრავალითა წყალობითა (multam misericordiam)
	-50	ի մէջ	ܒܡܨܥܬܗ	შორის (in medio)
	-51	ի մէջ հնոցի	ܡܢ ܓܘ ܐܬܘܢܐ	შორის საჴუმილსა მას (fornacis in medio)
	-76	բոյսք երկրի	ܥܣܒܐ ܕܐܪܥܐ	მცენარჱ ქუეყანისაჲ (germinantia terrae illius)
	-79	կայտառք	ܙܪܝܙܐ	ირძჳსნი (agiles)*

		Armenian	Syriac	Georgian (Latin)
	-88	ապրեցոյց	اسى	მაცხოვნნა (salvos fecit)
	-89	քաղցր	ܒ.ܚܕ	ტკბილი (dulcis)*
	4:5	գոյ ի նմա	اܠ ܒ ܗܕ	არს მის თანა
				(est apud eum)
	-6	ծածկի(ն) ի քէն	اܠܗ ܡܢ ܡܗܕ	დაეფარების შენგან
				(abscondatur a te)
	-8	ի ծագս	(ܠܚܐ) ܡܘܓܘ	Geo¹ კიდეთა (terminos)
=MT	-9,18	գեղեցիկ	بلمؤ	შუენიერ (pulchrum)*
				(Th9 ὡραῖα;
				18 εὐθαλῆ)
=MT	-10	զուարթուն	ܗ˜ܫ	იღოისტაკი (vigil)
=MT	-12,20	զշառաւիղ(ու)	ܗ˜ܗ	მორჩი (surculum)
=MT	-20	կտրեցէք	ܗܘܘܡܓ	მოკაფეთით
				(praecidite)
	5:11	յորում	ܡ ܗ اܠ ... ;	რომლისა თანა არს
				(apud quem est)
=MT	-14	առաւել	اܠܚ	უმეტესი (amplior)*
	6:3	Դանիէլ	ܗ˜ܡ ܗ اܠܒ,	იყო დანიელ
		առաւել էր	ܗܡܚ ܗ ܡ اܘܗ	უფროის მათა
		քան զնոսա		(erat Daniel maior
				illis)
=MT	7:7	առաւել	ܒ˜ܡ	უმეტეს (amplius)*
=MT	7:8	զմեծամեծս	اܚ˜ܘܢ	დიდდიდსა (grandia)
	8:1	յետ տեսլեանն	; ܗ ܒ ܗ	შემდგომად ჩუენებისა
		առաջնոյ	ܠ˜ܡ ܡ اܘ˜ܗ	მის ჩემისა პირველისა
				(post visionem illam
				meam primam)
=MT	-2	յապարանս	اܚܒ	ციხე (castro)
	-2	կայի	ܠا քܡ	ვდეგ (stabam)
	-6	եհաս	اܠ ܡ˜ܗ	მოიწია (pervenit)
		(om ܡ˜ܗ 1111)		
(-J1925)	9:16	առ անաւրէ-նութեան	ܠܐܕܗ	უმჯელობით (iniquitate)
	10:2	ի սուգ	ܠܐܕ	გლოვანა შინა (in luctu)

12:6 ի վերայ ⟨Syriac⟩ ⟨Syriac⟩ ზედა მცინარებსა მას

ჭურց գետոյն ⟨Syriac⟩ წყალთასა (super flu-
men illud aquarum)

Bel:8 ոյ ուտէ ⟨Syriac⟩ ვინ ჭამს (quis come-
dat)

-12 մեք ⟨Syriac⟩ ჩუენ (nos)

-13 ուտէին ⟨Syriac⟩ ჭამადოან (comedunt)

-27 մազ (մէզ J 1925) ⟨Syriac⟩ თმაჲ (pilum)*

The question of the identity of the clothes the Three
were wearing when thrown into the furnace and the order in
which they are described is rather complex. The simplest approach will be to analyze the evidence in stages.

1) In P the order of MT's final two elements is inverted. Thus
   their headgear ⟨Syriac⟩ is mentioned after ⟨Syriac⟩ which
   represents MT's לבושׁיהון.

2) The meaning of לבושׁ in Aramaic is general ('garments,
   clothes') while its Syriac equivalent can also denote a specific article of dress, 'cloak, long tunic'.

3) It is in this specific sense that Arm interprets P, rendering
   it by պատմունճանաւր.

4) This item (which is absent from Th) heads Arm's list, the
   remaining three terms following in the order adopted by Th
   (i.e. σαράβαρα, τιάραι, περικνημίδες).

5) Geo then inverts the order of Arm's first two terms and
   cites all the clothes in the singular, probably on the grounds
   that each of the three had only one. In addition Geo[1] has a
   plus "and with all their garments", analogous to that of
   Lucian whose basis is once more the Aramaic of 2).

3:21 պատմուճանաւ վարտաւք և արտախուրակաւք և
զանկապանաւք իւրեանց

ნიცხაჳ კუართით ურთ მათით და ვარშემანგით და საწმართუღით

(cum braca tunicaque sua et tiara et tibialibus)

P ܘܒܣܪܒܠܝܗܘܢ ܘܟܪܒܠܬܗܘܢ ܘܦܛܝܫܝܗܘܢ ܘܠܒܘܫܝܗܘܢ

(MT: בסרבליהון פטישיהון וכרבתהון ולבושיהון)

Most of the points emerging from the previous examination of
Geo dependence on Arm are reinforced by analysis of their
common agreements with P. This therefore gives grounds to
suppose that the Arm readings which form the hub from
which the lines of textual affinity were seen to radiate in both
tests belong to basically the same early stratum of the version's transmission. Once more the witness of V280-J2558 is
paramount, closely followed by M4834 and J1925 (often accompanied by M2627) then M346' M287 at some remove, all of
them MSS with a low rate of secondary accretions.

Characteristics of Arm's translation technique are also
abundantly represented, though here the contention is that
they emanate directly from P (e.g. clarification of direct and indirect object, pronoun object, etc.). A further indication of the
age of the readings attested by this group is the two instances
where its representatives support MS 6h10, the oldest dated
MS of the Leiden Peshitta. One case involves a closer approxi-
mation to MT than the reading of the majority of P MSS (3:12,
table 3a) while the other (Bel:27, table 3b) has also a chance of
being P's original rendering, being read by Th MS 410, OG and
several later P witnesses (see p.v. of the Leiden edition).

The categories of variant dominating the tables were
again substantive, comprising plus, minus and especially differences in semantic expression with WO adopting a largely
subsidiary role, notwithstanding some notable exceptions (e.g.
3:55 in table 2a). Of the P agreements witnessed by Arm as a
whole, the most remarkable variety consisted of simple,
straightforward equivalents counterpoised by more unusual or

elevated expressions in Th. Thus, at Sus:8 they match ἐγένοντο ἐν ἐπιθυμίᾳ with the simple verb "they desired" (cf. OG ἐπιθυμήσαντες). Instead of the violent energy of ἐκπεδᾶν at Sus:39 'bolted' they read 'fled' (cf. OG ἔφυγεν). In the same way, the more concrete term 'face' contrasts with 'form' at 1:15, 'took' with 'raised up and away' at 2:35, 'plants' with 'things that grow' at 3:76, 'prayer' with 'supplication' at 9:23, 'who eats' with 'the devourer' at Bel:8 and 'used to eat' with 'used to consume' at Bel:13. A similar tendency was also apparent in other minor cases where the same underlying meaning was assured by their common patrimony from MT yet the precise mode of expression employed by P-Arm-Geo differed from that of Th.

With regard to the certainty with which Arm's source is ascribed to P, linguistic evidence is decisive in favour of the proposition in several instances. This applies first to the readings qnιωηβηιь (4:10) and յաιщարωьս (8:2) where Th only transliterates. Greek does not possess a reduplicated form like ١ﻛﯾﻭ (7:8) which has been so skilfully imitated by Arm and Geo in turn. The plural rendering ριιρg at 12:6 which is unidiomatic to Armenian as to Greek presupposes a semitic prototype, while the use of qnյ in various places corresponds to ﻛﯽ where Th like MT leaves this implicit. Moreover, the dichotomy between Th and Arm is only resolved by postulating Arm contact with the Syriac ﻡﻗﻡ which can mean 'first' as well as 'former, ancient'. P similarly transmits to Arm the correct interpretation of a MT phrase which recurs throughout chapter 3 concerning the furnace of fire whereby the epithet 'burning' is construed with the feminine noun fire and not furnace as in Th (ﺍﻟﻣﯿﻝ ﻭﺍﯾﻝ ﻭﻟﻝ). Without wishing to be as categorical about the validity of the etymological argument as Molitor[94] it is certainly worth noting the coincidence of P-Arm-Geo at 3:88 in employing a verb compounded from the root 'life' to render 'save' (cf. Th ἔσωσεν).

A further argument is provided by P's uniqueness as a possible source of Arm. In the canonical part of Daniel it is always feasible that a Hexaplaric MS of a type not preserved may have communicated a reading instead of P where this is also read by MT. However, as the following data show, this supposition, which is at all events *argumentum ex silentio,* has little effect on our results since the number involved is less than a third of the total. Similarly, in the deuterocanonical sections the Gk-supported readings amount to less than 1/6th of the whole. An interesting feature of the table is the unprecedentedly high concentration of examples in the latter section. Nevertheless, granted that Th betrays a noticeable 'Hebraizing' tendency in addition to the fact that MT is the matrix of P and Gk, the possibility of variation is severely curtailed in the main body of the text. Without that unifying influence, disparity multiplies and manifests itself especially in the form of P plusses over against Gk, several of which have been communicated to Arm-Geo.

TABLE	=MT	≠MT	Deuterocanonical=Gk	≠Gk
1	3	6	2	2
2	2	2	0	5
3	2	11	2	5
4	20	40	5	35
Individual Totals	27	59	9	47
Final Total		86		56

Given the lack of firm linguistic evidence in various cases where Arm=P=Geo variants are also evinced by extant witnesses of Th and OG, the issue of Arm's parentage is difficult to decide. As indicated in a previous paragraph, the explanation of many of the coincidences with OG may well be parallel traditions for interpreting MT. Since the balance of probability cannot be assessed on the basis of isolated readings but requires systematic treatment throughout the book, we shall leave the detailed discussion until chapter five.

Concurrences with Th were both fewer and less significant in kind. However, the readings shared with Luc witnesses and OL are worth further comment as they may be associated with P through their mutual relation to the local text of Syria. It seems that this branch separated from the mainstream c. 100 A.D. with the result that it preserves much old material which dropped out of general circulation.[95] Thus if P made use of Th as we suggest, the likelihood is that the text was of the type locally available. Textual and chronological antiquity is also the hallmark of OL yet it is more difficult to identify its precise point of contact with this tradition, especially as the version is not a homogeneous entity, but embraces a range of standards in Europe and North Africa. It appears that the ancestor of one of these had been brought from Asia Minor. That some such specific contact rather than merely generic similarity lies behind their agreement is further suggested by the close companionship of OL and Old Syriac witnesses of the Gospels.[96]

Unfortunately the Leiden edition has not found place for an analysis of the disparate text types represented by the MSS collated and their interrelationships.[97] Therefore it is not possible to penetrate far into Arm's support for particular units or groups. We have already remarked upon two agreements with MS 6h10. In addition V280-J2558 read with the Malkite lectionaries 1114 and 1115 at 3:55, while out of 22 cases of Arm agreement in Susanna the three P witnesses read as follows: together thrice, MSS a 7a1 six times, and individually: MS a twice, MS 7a1 thrice, MS b seven times. The textual complexion of the two Geo MSS was very reminiscent of the previous test. Their affinity is proved by the majority of cases where their testimony is united. When they diverge Geo° preserves Arm ties marginally better than Geoᴵ throughout the book (16 cases) except in Susanna where 6 (as opposed to 1 of Geo°) of Geoʳs 11 independent agreements with Arm are located.

P=Arm≠Geo: Nevertheless, as we had occasion to remark, Geo's witness to Arm=P readings is compromised by the effects of subsequent Greek revision which has left its mark on even the version's oldest and best representatives. In view of this circumstance we set forth a second set of tables in which Arm's P-centered orientation finds no reflection in Geo. All the examples are taken to derive from Arm's earliest stratum.

1a) V280-J2558=P≠Geo

	Sus:64	om և անդր	(MS a)	ܡܢ ܗܘ ܝܘܡܐ
	1:4	զաւրաւորս] + ուժով		ܡܢ ܒܚܝܠܐ
	-18	նաբուքոդոնոսորա] pr արքայի		ܒܬܘܪܓܡܢ ܡܠܟܐ
	4:8	մեծացաւ ծառն] + և բարձրացաւ		ܘܐܬܬܩܦ ܐܝܠܢܐ
=MT	8:11	աւերեսցի] աւերեցաւ		ܬܪܐ
=MT	9:13	om ամենայն		= P
	-17	վասն քո] վասն անուան քո		ܡܛܠ ܥܕܢ
	Bel:3	անուն] + նորա		ܫܡܗ
	-8	ով] եթե ո՞ոք[98]		ܡܢܘ
	-16	կանխեաց] -եալ (pres. participle)		ܩܐܡ
	-19	և] յայնժամ		ܗܝܕܝܢ
	-32	յայնժամ] յայնմ աւուրս		ܒܗܘܢ ܘܩܛܠܐ
	-42	առաջի նորա] առ. արքային		ܩܕܡܘܗܝ ܕܡܠܟܐ
		և դանիէլի		ܘܩܕܡ ܕܢܝܐܝܠ

1b) Supplementary examples of less moment

Sus:27	ծառայքն] ծնաւղքն շուշանայ	(MS a)	ܐܬܒܗܬܘ ܥܒ̈ܕܝܗ
		(MS b)	ܒܥܒ̈ܕܘܗܝ ܘܐܬܒܗܬܘ ܥܒ̈ܕܝܗ
-27	այնպիսի ասացան] լըւան զայդպիսի բանս	(MS b)	ܐܬܟܡܟܡ ܐܝܟ ܗܠܝܢ
-48	դատապարտեցէք] + անմեղ[99]	(MS b)	ܠܫܒܩܘܢ ܕܝܢܐ
-58	om արդ[100]	(MS b)	ܐܬܐ ܕܝܢ ܐܡܪ
-59	սուսեր ի ձեռին] և սուսեր ի ձեռին իւրում	(MS a)	ܘܣܝܦܗ ܚܪܒܗ ܕܝܠܗ
2:34	հայեիր] pr և		ܘܚܙܝܬ
6:15	արքա հաստատիցէ] հաստատես-ցէ արքայ		ܢܩܝܡ ܡܠܟܐ

8:19 om եւ   (MS 7a1)   om ել2˚

11:33 tr սրով և հրով   (MS 12d1)   ܚܘܙܒܐ ܘ ܚܘܙܐܐ

-34 զայթագդուբեամբք] -բեամբ   ܠܐܘܦܚ

-39 ընդ աստուծոյ] ընդ աստուածս   ܠܠ ܐܠܘܦ

12:10 սպիտակեցեն] խորտակեցեն

Perhaps the prototype of this reading was ܢܘܒܙܐ instead of
ܢܘܐܙܐ. It may be that the process was influenced by the following verb which has the necessary consonants arranged in a
different order (ܢܘܙܒܐ).[101]

2)   Small groupings including V280-J2558=P≠Geo

2:37	om և հաստատուն	V280 J1925'-M4114 M182''	= P
3:35	Իսրայէղի] pr վասն	V280 M346' M9116-ܠܝܡܐ ܘܩܩ M4114 M182''	
4:12	ի գաւղ] -ղոյ	V280 M178-WN11-M2585 M182''	ܣܩ ܦܝ
=MT-19	զի] որ	V280 M2585 M4114 M182''-WN11c	ܪܣܝܐ
-20	ի գաւղ] -ղոյ	V280'	ܣܩ ܦܝ
-32	համարեցան նմա	M287'' M2585	ܘܗܘܘ ܚܝܫܒ
=MT7:27	և 4˚] om	V280'	ܘܠܣܘܣ
=MT9:18	զապականութիւն] -թիւնս	V280' J1925	ܣܒܠܐ
-27	պղծութիւն] -թեան	V280 M346	ܠܐܘܒܟ,
Bel:19	հետ] հետս	V280' J1925	ܠܩܚܣ
WO 7:9	tr սպիտակ/իբրև գծիւն	M287'	ܠܝܘ ܠܟܠ ܐܪܒ
9:7	մերձաւորաց և հեռաւորաց] tr	V280' M178-M346'-M2585	

P MSS 6hl 8a1c 10d1 12d1.2 and ܢܙܣܡܝ ܘܝܡܙܚܝ and
unspecified post 12th century MSS.

3)   **Small groupings excluding V280-J2558=P≠Geo**

Sus:53 qqшипшıнил M287   (MS 7a1)   ܡܿܚ, ܠܝ,
        шücpuınnıpfbuıli

3:5   մհաբանութեան] J1925   (MS 1114)   ܠܐܩܝ
        -թեանց

-51   հնոցին] + հրոյն   M178-   ܠܝܐ, ܐܟܠ|
        M346'-M2585 M2627

-90   qh puınqn է   M287   ܪܡܚ,
                M2585

4:12   quınüuınu   M287ᵐᵍ   ܠܘܐܦܬ

=MT   MSS-17 jшüüüшjü]   M2585   (ܠܝܠ,) ܠܚܐ ܗܡܩܩܘ
        h ծшqu шübü.   M2627'

=MT   -22   uihnt]uitn է   M4834 J1925   ܠܚܟ

        -27   թшqшинnnı-   M346'   ܟܠܘܠܐܘ
        թեшü]+ hünj

=MT   8:11   шppnıpfhü ünnш   M287 M178   ܡܡܪ,ܘ

        -13   unınp] gunınp   M346-M2585   (MS 6h10)ܟܢ ܡܪܟ|ܠ

=MT   -25   üшünpüog] -üog   J1925   ܠܟܝܙ

=MT   9:6   խшınıbhü]   J1925-M2627' M182''   ܐܚܠܠ
        խшınıbouü

        -20   om խшınıbh k   J1925   = P

        11:6   шınhnnnpü   M287 WN11   ܘܠܚܡܚ

        -6   qшınшonıgшüh-   M178-M346   ܗܘ;ܗܡܚ
        gt] -onıgшüü

=MT   -18   qhշխшüu] -խшü   M9116-M2627'   ܠܚܝܟ

        -27   jшշnnbnog] -ghü   J1925   ,ܗܐܝ;

        -29   om nշ   M287   = P

        -45   ծnı[nıg] ծnı[hü   M346'   ܠܗ

        12:8   bu] + qшühbL   M346'-M2585   ܠܚܝ, ܠܝ

        Bel:13   шnшnbшL tn   M287' J1925-M2627 ܠܘܘ ;ܚܕܣ¹⁰²

4)   **Arm as a whole =P≠Geo**

Sus:15   h uıuıuıbLü   (MSS a 7a1)   ܩܘܘ ;ܐܝܟܠ ܕܪ
        ünguı üüuı   ܗܠ

	-17	երթայք բերէք	(MSS ab 7a1)	ܪ̈ܗܛܝ ܐܝܬܝܢ ܠܝ
	-21	վկայեմք	(MSS ab 7a1)	ܡܣܗܕܝܢ
	-22	տագնապ	(MSSa 7a1)	ܐܘܠܨܢܐ
	-23	լաւ լիցի ինձ	(MS b)	ܛܒ ܠܝ
	-46	ի ձայն բարձր	(MSS a 7a1)	ܒܩܠܐ ܪܡܐ
	-52	*այ* հնացեալ	(MS a)	*o* ܐܠܬܝ
	-56	գեղ դորա	(MSS b 7a1)	ܫܘܦܪܗ
	-59	զի աւադիկ	(MSS 7a1)	ܗܐ ܓܝܪ
			(MSS ab)	ܗܐܟܝܪ
	-60	որ ապրեցուցանէ	(MSS b 7a1)	ܕܐܚܝ
	-62	ապրեցաւ	(MSS b 7a1)	ܚܝܐ
	-63	գտան	(MS a)	ܐܫܟܚܘ
	1:3	Պարտեւաց		ܦܪܛܘܢܐ
=MT	-4	ի տաճարի		ܒܗܝܟܠܐ
	-5	զոր ինքն ըմպէր		ܕܫܬܐ
=MT	-12	ունդս		ܙܪ̈ܥܘܢܐ

The Armenian Version generally differentiates between animal progeny (զաւակ) and plant (սերմն). Thus the latter would have been expected here if the reading had been based on Th (σπέρμα) which is an interpretation of MT's זרעים in terms of the more common pointing and not according to the massoretic tradition which renders it a *hapax legomenon*. In the event, Arm belongs to the interpretation MT-P which is also sanctioned by OG in taking the word as a kind of vegetable.

	1:13	գոյնք	ܓܘܢ̈ܝ
	2:46	մատուցանել	ܠܡܩܪܒܘ
=MT	-47 and 3:14	արդարև	ܒܩܘܫܬܐ

(Gk at this point reads ἐπ᾽ ἀληθείας as at 2:8 where Arm again accompanies P (ܫܪܝܪܐܝܬ) in evincing ճշմարտիւ).

3:4	և ասէր		ܘܐܡܪ
-10	և զնուագարանաց	(MS11d11)	ܘܣ̈ܝܦܘܢܝܐ
		(MS 1114)	ܘܣ̈ܦܘܢܝܐ

	-12	աստ	ܠܟܝ
	-18	մեք (- M287 WN11*)	ܚܢܢ
	-22	բորբոքէր	ܫܓܝܪ ܗܘܐ
	-24	հրոյն	ܕܢܘܪܐ
	-31	արդար դատաստանաւ	ܒܕܝܢܐ ܟܐܢܐ
	-41	մեք (- M287' WN11 M9116)	ܚܢܢ
	-50	մերձանայր ի նոսա	ܡܩܪܒ ܠܗܘܢ
	-51	և ասէին	ܘܐܡܪܝܢ
	-81	գազան և անաւրէն(- M346-M2585 M2627 M351)	ܚܘܛܐ ܘܡܥܒܪܐ
	-91	այր արդար ասես (ես)[103]	ܐܝ ܒܩܘܫܬܐ
	-100	յաւիտենից (- M287 WN11*)	ܠܥܠܡ
(Qure in some MSS of MT)			
	4:16	մեկնութիւն դորա	ܦܫܪܗ
	-18	անապատի	ܕܕܒܪܐ
	-20	զի իջանէր	ܕܢܚܬ
=MT	-23	մնայ	ܥܩܪܐ
	5:2	զի արբցեն	ܕܢܫܬܘܢ
	-3	բերին	ܐܝܬܝܘ
=MT	-5	տաճարի	ܒܗܝܟܠܐ
=MT	-5	զթաթ	ܦܣܬܐ
=MT	-6	գոյնք	ܙܝܘܗ
=MT	-6	միջոյ նորա	ܚܨܘܗܝ
=MT	-12	զառակս	ܐܚܘܝ
=MT	-12	զիրս կապեալս	ܡܫܪܐ
	-17	զպատիւս	ܐܝܩܪܐ
	-20	անկաւ	ܢܚܬ
	-26	վախճանեաց	ܐܫܠܡܗ
	6:8	գրեա (6:9)	ܠܟܬܘܒ
=MT	-18	առաջի նորա (6:19)	ܩܕܡܘܗܝ
=MT	7:3	մեծամեծք	ܪ̈ܘܪܒܢ
	-4	իբրև ի վերայ ոտից մարդոյ (- M287 M4114 M182''-WN11c)	ܥܠ ܪ̈ܓܠܝܗ ܐܝܟ ܐܢܫܐ
	-8	բերան նորա խաւսէր (- M287 J1925)	ܦܘܡܗ ܡܡܠܠ

-14 անցանէ (present participle) ܥܒܪ

-20 և վասն միւսոյն ܘܥܠ ܐܚܪܬܐ

8:3 եղջերք նորա ܩܪܢܬܗ

-6 զի կայր ܕܩܐܡ

-10 առաւել ܠܬܪܬܐ

-10 զաւրութիւնս երկնից (- M287 M178) ܠܚܝܠܐ ܕܫܡܝܐ

-15 իբրև տեսի ես ܡܕ ܚܙܝܬ ܐܢܐ

-17 ուր եսն կայի ܐܬܪ ܕܩܐܡ ܐܢܐ

-18 մինչդեռ խաւսեր ܟܕ ܡܡܠܠ

9:3 աղաւթիւք ܒܨܠܘܬܐ

=MT 9:10 առաջի մեր ܩܕܡܝܢ

=MT -14 ի վերայ ամենայն գործոց իւրոց ܒܟܠܗܘܢ
ܒܥܒܕܘܗܝ

-23 պատգամ ܦܬܓܡܐ

10:3 ցանկութեան ܕܪܓܬܐ

-11 ընդ քեզ ܥܡܟ

=MT 11:2 Թագաւորութեանն (MS 7a1) ܡܠܟܘܬܗܘܢ

-4 ըստ վախճանի ܐܝܟ ܣܘܦܗ

-6 ի ժամանակին ܒܙܒܢܐ

=MT -17 դիցէ ܢܣܝܡ

-17 նորա 2° ܕܝܠܗ

-23 այնոցիկ որ խառնիցինն ܐܝܠܝܢ ܕܡܫܬܘܬܦܝܢ

-35 փորձել ܠܡܒܚܪ

-35 ժամանակ է ܐܝܟ ܢܛܪܐ (ܠܙܒܢܐ)

-38 ակամբք պատուականաւք ܣܘܡܪܐ ܛܒܬܐ

-38 զԱստուած հզաւր (զաստ. մարզ. WN11) ܠܐܠܗܐ ܥܫܝܢܐ

-39 անցցէ ܢܥܒܪ

-41 ի ձեռաց նորա ܡܢ ܐܝܕܘܗܝ

(-11 գալ) ܥܠ

cf. v. 12 where P repeats the above reading but Arm (ամբոխ) supports Th = MT).

Bel:13 վստահ էին ܬܟܝܠܝܢ ܗܘܘ

-25 ես Տեառն ܐܢܐ ܠܡܪܝܐ

-29 սպանանեմք ܡܩܛܠܝܢ

-39 նոյնժամայն ܒܗ ܒܫܥܬܐ [104]

ANALYSIS: Again the early nature of the stratum preserving P contact is underlined by the quality of the witnesses. MSS V280-J2558 appear an even richer repository of readings of Syriac origin than before. Moreover, as these mainly involve objective variations in the length of the text, for which P in the overwhelming number of cases offers the only other attestation, its ascription as their source is established on an even more irrefutable basis. As before, the protagonists are attended by M4834 J1925 M346 and M287 (though these play a comparatively minor role here since they are not so differentiated from the majority of MSS). Agreement with the early P MS 6h10 is maintained at 8:13 (table 3), while three cases are shared with MS 7a1 in the main body of the book, a further two with the Malkite lectionary 11I4, one with 11d1 at 3:10 (table 4). This, however, may not be of any consequence since its addition of *seyame* there is unique[105] and one with 12d1. The significance of the b text in Susanna has been intensified by 10 shared readings with Arm (sometimes in conjunction with 7a1). MS A has 9, 7a1 - 5, a + 7a1 only 3, while their combined testimony of all three witnesses accounts for 2.

Commensurate with the high ratio of plus-minus readings V280-J2558 share with P is the rise in the occurrence of this type in the version as a whole (N.B. the plus to prepare the way for indirect speech introduced at 2:4 (+Լ ասեն) and 3:4 (+Լ ասէր). Also interesting is the tendency to cite people by name (e.g. addition of Daniel at 12:8, Susanna at Sus:27 and "the king and Daniel" at Bel:42). The phenomenon is of further significance in the appendix to this chapter. The penchant for plainer renderings in P's vein as opposed to Th's use of a more abstract or elevated stylistic register (often closer to the letter of MT) is again discernible. Thus in describing the wine the king had allotted to his trainee administrators Arm reads "which he himself drank", contrasting with "of his imbibing", similarly 'middle' stands over against 'loins' at 5:6, 'write' against 'publish' at 6:8, 'where I was standing' against 'my station' at 8:17, 'fear' against 'ecstasy' at 10:7 and 'set' against 'align, order' at 11:17.

Other examples adumbrate features of Arm's translation technique to be discussed in chapter six. Two instances of an active verb counterpoising a passive construction in Th are noted (Sus:63 զտան and 5:3 բերին). Repetition of a preposition occurs at 7:20 while other plusses are intended to enliven the dialogue (Sus:52 այ, 3:91 այն). P is further responsible for a certain percentage of Arm's use of the present tense where Th evinces the future (e.g. Sus:21 վկայեմք, 4:23 մնայ, 7:14 անցանէ, Bel:25 պազանեմ and v.29 սպանանեմք). Moreover, the tables are replete with examples of expressed pronoun subjects, direct and indirect objects in keeping with the data provided by the previous set with Geo support.

Linguistic considerations enable us to decide in favour of a semitic source at various points, which in the absence of any known targum to the book and the frequent disparity of MT must be acknowledged as P (though sometimes Arm's form requires us to postulate that its exemplar included readings not found in extant MSS of P). One such consideration is the name շուշան (= ܫܘܫܢ)[106] which could not have been transmitted from Greek since the sibilant lies outside its sound system. In addition, a further two cases of translation, where Th is content to transliterate must be mentioned, 'Parthians' for φορθομ–μιν (an interpretation shared by Chysostom and Theodoret)[107] and 'strong' for μαωζιν at 11:38.

Similarly, in contrast to Greek the semantic range of the Armenian term տաճար corresponds to that of ܗܝܟܠܐ in that it denotes to a large hall or building, which usually refers to a temple but can indicate a royal palace, in which sense it appears at 1:4 and 5:5. The basis of the variant տէր է at 4:22 must likewise be Aramaic-Syriac in which the form ܫܠܝܛ as well as its function as present participle (cf. Th κυριεύει) by extention also refers to the official occupying such a position, i.e. ruler. Two additional incidences of ապրել/ապրեցուցանել representing P verbs from the cognate root "life" may be noted at Sus:60 and 62 while at 9:23 both Arm and P read the respective forms of their common borrowing from Persian պատգամ/ ܦܬܓܡܐ.[108]

The small number of times MT=P=Arm in the canonical and Gk=P=Arm in the apocryphal sections as the following digest of the results of the test show, confirms our previous impression that in the overwhelming majority of cases P is the only source which can be predicated for the readings.

TABLE	=MT	≠MT	Deuterocanonical=GK	≠Gk
1	4	15	5	12
2	3	6	0	2
3	9	19	2	3
4	19	59	3	28
Sectional Totals	34	99	10	45
Final Total	134		55	

The distribution of this type of agreement between P and Arm may have interesting implications for the method by which the Georgian revision was carried out. Although the situation obtaining in the deuterocanonical section is remarkably stable both in extent and relative balance between the three "additions" in both tests, the data are rather different in the main body of the work. It is true that the MT figure is relatively static yet the non-MT column has taken a sharp rise. If the earliest Geo stratum possessed the sort of textual affiliation we are positing for Arm, then the clear suggestion is that the effect of the Hellenizing recension was more appreciable in the core of the book than its additions, even allowing for the shorter compass of the latter. One factor which may have inhibited change in the Prayer of Azariah and Song of the Three was their familiarity as liturgical readings. The fact that many of the variants of P=Arm≠Geo featuring in the present test were more substantial and therefore obtrusive goes far to explain why they may have been supplanted by the Georgian revisers when the examples in our former table (P=Arm=Geo) were allowed to remain.

Of the cases where Th MSS=P=Arm the most part can be regarded as coincidental since they were embodied in a variety of individual witnesses for which no clear pattern of affinity to Arm was observed. The exceptions to this rule were again units of the Lucianic recension and OL (which *inter alia* twice joins P-Arm in reading 'angel' without further specifications at 3:49 and Bel:39). The several cases of agreement with the Ethiopic Version are probably to be explained by the latter's dependence on P via an Arabic translation which formed the basis of the version's thirteenth century revision. Ethiopic's access to P is clear from the reading Israel at 11:16, 'strong' at v. 38 and "in the level place" at v. 45. OG in contrast offers important confirmation of the antiquity of some of P's readings. Though its candidacy for having transmitted certain readings to Arm cannot be immediately rejected, the existence of other cases where the relationship to P-Arm was still parallel but sufficiently distanced for contact to be out of the question, may imply that the main link between the traditions was dependence on a pre-massoretic text type. This proposition might still stand, even although isolated OG readings incorporated in Th MSS entered Arm directly.

Granted the ragged edges skirting every revision and the remarkable resilience shown by early translations in persisting however thorough the redactional process has been, it is not in the least surprising that Geo preserves P agreements which find no place in Arm MSS. We have argued Geo's reliance on Arm mediation of Greek and Syriac readings from metaphrastic and linguistic evidence including cases of a hypothetical Syriac original. As a result our *a priori* assumption must be that the following cases were communicated by the same means. Without compelling proof it is ill-advised to multiply the stages of any given line of transmission. If more detailed scrutiny upholds the view expressed here, then this set of readings will conversely throw light on the path taken by the

Greek revision Arm underwent. Indeed the process may already have been partly complete by the time of Geo's translation with the result that traces of it may be present in the Greek-based readings we mentioned above as having emanated from Arm. The instances cited below are intended purely as a sample.

P=Geo≠Arm

	Sus:15 ܝ ܠܗܐ MS b(v. 12)	დღესა ერთსა
		(diem unam)
=MT	1:5 ܠܡܠܟ ܩܕܡ ܝܗܘܢ	რათთა დგენ იგინი წინაშე მეფისა
		(ut starent illi coram rege)
	2:15 ܠܡ ܠܐ Geo°	მთავარი რაისა თუ̈ს
	(cf. B-26-239 Hippol (vid)	(princeps, quare)
=MT	3:23 ܠܝܘ, ܒܓܘ ܐܬܘܢ	შორის საჴუმილსა მას ცეცხლისა
	ܢܘܪܐ	(in medium fornacis
	(cf. Th rel.=MT)	illius ignis ardentis)
	-24 ܠܫܠܗܒܝܬ	შორის ალსა მას ცეცხლისასა
	ܠܝܘ,	(inmedio flammae illius ignis)

-94 the origin of Geo reading სული (spiritus) may stem from a Syriac variant. The usual equivalent is ܠܘܗ; which seems to have been read here either by a translator or exemplar for the MSS reading ܠܘܝ= Arm.

=MT-94	ܒܗܘܢ	მათ თანა
		(apud eos)

(+և երկիր եպագ Թագաւորն առաջի նորա Sեառն Arm)
(P-Geo = Bˡˣˡ62' L⁻³⁶⁻311 Hippol)

=MT5:1	ܠܚܡܐ	პური
		(panem) (Arm ընթրիս)
=MT7:24	ܢܩܘܡܘܢ Geoˡ	დგენ
		(stabunt) (cf. OG
8:17	ܕܬܗܘܐ	აღსასრულსა იყოს ხილვაჲ ესე
	ܚܙܘ ܗܕ	(in fine erit visio haec)
=MT8:19	ܚܡܬܐ ܒܚܪ	უკუანაჲსკნელსა რისხვასა
		(in novissima ira)

The gap between P's noun 'end' and Geo's adjective 'final' may be bridged by positing an Armenian intermediary since there the difference consists of only two letters from the noun վերջ to the adjective վերջին. On the other hand the reading may stem from Gk since several MSS read ἐπ᾽ ἐσχατοῦ/ –τω for ἐπ᾽ ἐσχάτων Bel:42 ܘܡܢ ܐ 12d1 (and post 12th cent. MSS) Geoᴵ აღმოჰაჯეს (eripuerunt) ܝܠܝܕ 6h10 (and post 12th cent. MSS) დანიელ (Danielem (Aethᴾ OG) ܒܗ ܘ ჯურღმულისა მასგან (de laco illo) (11-770 230 590 Laᵛ + leonum/OG).

The examples in this motley assortment demonstrate the key facets of the earlier sets of tables. Frequently P is the undisputed source of the readings, as is underlined by the presence of linguistic factors, though sometimes a parallel vein is found in OG and the Lucianic recension. At other times one might argue the variant entered Geo from Gk at the time of the revision. Links with the earliest P MS 6h10 were maintained at Bel:42 as well as MS 12d1. The distribution of the examples is also noteworthy in confirming our view of the comparative lightness of the revision in the apocryphal part, for all three sections are represented here.

Comparison with Lyonnet: During the examination of past research on the question of early Armenian contact with Syriac, we saw the most complete study to achieve positive results was that conducted by Lyonnet on the gospels. In differentiating his Syriac-related Arm1 from the subsequent recension, Arm2, the product of a Greek revision, he not only produced evidence from variant readings, but was able to draw the data together systematically so as to delineate some of the central features of their respective vocabulary and translation technique. In view of the fact that the foregoing tables have established Arm's earliest stratum had a significant degree of contact with P it is important to compare his findings with those available in Daniel in order to determine whether both translation units formed part of the same process.

Lyonnet enumerates eleven characteristics of Arm1 the tenth of which is not relevant for it deals with quotations from OT by NT writers. What is significant is his remark under this heading that OT and the Epistles have preserved more of their original form. The statement gains credence from the greater unanimity shown by Z and the MSS of early text type in tending towards Arm1 readings. Consequently, the contrasting Arm2 standard is often better represented by direct reference to the Greek.

Thus variation between the locative adverb and the demonstrative particle in defining substantives does not arise in Daniel, and the former though definitely the minority is quite widespread. However the frequent (pleonastic) incidence of the model verb (կարեⱂ) in the Gospels finds no parallel here. On the contrary its occurrence always mirrors the corresponding form of P and Th. Of the remaining aspects three have produced a positive result which we have sufficiently illustrated already, namely the repetition of prepositions, periphrastic designations of countries, etc. and Syriac forms of proper names. The final five items are as follows:

1) variation in translation equivalent
2) Periphrastic rendering of the Greek participle
3) insertion of pronoun subject
4) citations regularly introduced by եթե
5) fondness for the indefinite particle ինչ

1.   This section is composed of three cases, the first of which is not immediately applicable, since it refers to the replacement of Arm1's արդարև by transliteration in representing ἀμήν. Still, if we are justified in making the generalization that priority resides with translation rather than transliteration, this principle may be of assistance in constructing a stratification of text types later in the chapter.

In the second instance կատարեⱂ not լնուⱂ renders πληροῦν. Of the three occurrences of the word in Daniel the first at 2:35 is not appropriate since the sense required is not "fulfill" but "fill" (describing the wondrous growth of the stone till it encompassed the earth) which can only be expressed by the latter term. The second incidence at 5:26 describing God's judgement upon Belshazzar's kingly rule is appositely rendered by վախճանեաց (=P) since fulfilling in the event meant bringing abruptly to an end. However կատարել is found at 8:23 relating to committing sin, as well as in two further cases of fulfillment at 9:2 (կատարումն) and 10:3 where Th employs the cognate nouns πλήρωσις and συμπλήρωσις. Thus in a suitable semantic context կատարել appears to be the preferred translation equivalent in Daniel also.

The third variation involves յաւիտենից, the genitive case of the substantive being later supplanted by the adjective յաւիտենական to render αἰώνιος. In contrast to the correspondence evinced with Lyonnet's findings in the previous paragraph, at seven out of eight points cited by *HR,* MS M287, the base of our edition, supports Arm2. However, two incidences of dissent from the apparatus uphold the other reading, perhaps as remnants of an earlier level of tradition where its usage was more general (4:31 by MSS M346' and 7:27 MS WN11).

2.   In Arm1 the participle is used extremely sparingly in Lyonnet's submission, while its frequency in Arm2 is conditioned by the desire to capture the Greek form as closely as possible. A detailed analysis of the diverse modes the translator of Daniel has recourse to is presented in chapter six, in which it is demonstrated that the most simple and usual solution suggested to the problem was to render by finite forms. However, there are certain cases where these are found as variants of participial constructions in MS 287, and may actually have more claim to originality, e.g.

3:48	շրջէր պատէր] շրջեալ պատէր	M 178-M346'
8:7	զնա հասեալ] զի եհաս	J 1925
10:10	մերձեցեալ] մերձեգուն	M346' (= P = OG)

Bel: 18 հայեցեալ] -եցաւ   V280 J1925 V1508 (=P)
-21   բարկացաւ M287 = P] -գեալ   rel.

3.   We have had occasion to note Arm's inclusion of pronoun subjects both before but normally after the verb in company with P and independently.[109] The antiquity of the practice and its connection with translation from Syriac is neatly
demonstrated by the fact that it is precisely those MSS which
distinguish themselves as witnesses to P readings which score
high on this count.

4.   Lyonnet's fourth point is the greater regularity with
which եթե introduces citations in Arm1 than in Z. In the absence of citations in Daniel, there are nevertheless a few examples of MSS of early text type reading the particle to introduce
direct speech,[110] e.g.

Bel:8   ով] եթե ո՞վ   V280   (=P)

5.   The final category concerns Arm1's penchant for the
indefinite particle ինչ which is widely represented in Daniel,
e.g. Sus:18 զոր ինչ, 1:2 (MS J1925) մասն ինչ 2:23 որ ինչ, v. 29
իմաստութիւն ինչ, 3:18 այս ինչ, v. 92 ապականութիւն ինչ also
at 5:25, 6:2 աշխատ ինչ, v. 17 այլազգ ինչ.
        In conclusion we can state that most of the traits
Lyonnet discovered in the Arm1 layer of the Gospels are amply
documented in Daniel in varying degrees, the greatest harvest
being reaped from those witnesses most consistently offering
P readings. This kinship further implies that by embodying
the same translation procedure, though partly obliterated by
the activity of redactors, they belong to the same early phase of
the process. That OT may have been less affected by the revision is suggested by the amount of this material to be found in
Z.[111] This is also plausible historically since the difference between the standard of the original translation and revision is
far less than that between a text influenced by the Diatessaron
and canonical gospels.

Nevertheless, if change there was, the operation must have left some trace by which it can be identified. Since we opened the chapter by asserting that Th is the main *Vorlage* of Arm's extant disparate translation bases, Syriac and Greek. Two additional kinds of evidence reinforce this conclusion.

Variants consisting of synonyms or terms of closely related meaning occur sporadically in the manuscript tradition of many ancient texts in a variety of languages. In Daniel there are several instances of զի/բանզի which may often be attributed to scribal inattentiveness and unconscious change. Where there is a lack of stereotyping so that two words are used almost interchangeably now this, now the other without a consistent policy, the second alternative frequently appears as a variant, e.g.

արբայ/թագաւոր and արբայութիւն/թագաւորութիւն

A third type, however, seems to have arisen from a dual standard of translation both in terms of prototype and technique.

Difference in *Vorlage* is evident from the following instances. At the second stage of the process where stereotyping of translation equivalents was more prevalent, a linkage was established between γνωρίζειν and ցուցանել, which is maintained throughout the book and as such is the constant here. The variant from this in both cases is an apposite rendering of P.

2:17   եգոյց] յայտնեաց M178-M346'   (- իլ)
-23   ցուցեր] ծանուցերM286 M2627   (= ܐܠܝܘ)

The second renews the old debate about the seat of the affections. Thus while at Sus:9 MSS M280' M346'-M2585 M182 witness the Th standard stereotype զսիրասա, the others evince զմիասա in support of P (MS 7a1 ܗܘܢܗ). The priority of the latter is confirmed by Geo"s testimony (გონება : intellectum*). At 1:8 the united force of the version is set behind P

(ܡܫܝܚ) in reading ի մահ. However the balance of probability on the original reading at 2:30 is more debatable since Th P MT and Arm majority attest սրտի over against մնաց in MSS M2585 M2627. The final example is more clear-cut: Arm majority is ranged with P (ܠܒ݂ܝ) in բարձունք which is also etymologically cognate (բարձր = բ), while MSS M178-M346' evince բլուրք in agreement with Th's βουνοί.

Distinction in translation technique allows us to categorize the aspiration of the early phase as the communication of the meaning of the *Vorlage* according to the given context as simply and directly as possible. Untrammelled by any consideration of providing a read-back to the translation base, their approach was extremely flexible but unsystematic when compared to the network of equivalents set up in Arm2 usually on the basis of the prime usage of the word.

The variants at 4:24 present an interesting insight into the nature of the change սրայք M287ᵐᵍ V280 զթով M178-M346' J1925-M2627' զթովք rel. As the context speaks of atoning for sin by one's behaviour towards the poor, the required sense is alms as found in M287-M280. Yet this is a secondary use of οἰκτιρμός. The revisers' strategy being to employ the root meaning where possible, զթովք was substituted here.

The collapse of the statue described at 2:35 was so total that the various parts vanished without trace. Arm majority join P and Th in witnessing to the passive form զտաևէր 'a place was not found for them'. However, V280-J2558 contain what must be construed as the corresponding active զտանէին 'they did not find a place for them'. Since Arm often avoids the passive voice, sometimes with P support, the minority reading may be that of Arm1 with Arm2's increased literalism then being responsible for the change.

The variation at Bel:26 largely concerns level of discourse. According to the majority reading իշխանութիւն (=Th=P), Daniel requests the monarch's 'authorization' to slay Bel while M346'-M2585 read հրաման 'order' which belongs to the register of everyday speech, so that the phrase might be paraphrased 'just say the word'. Renderings which retain close contact with colloquial usage over against literary convention are appropriate to the undertaking which produced the first Armenian book.

In keeping with this observation it is instructive to note that one aspect of the revisers' literality was their heightened awareness of the figures of speech occurring in their exemplar and their desire to do them justice when rendering into Armenian. Whereas the translators had regarded the expression առնել դատաստան as an adequate representation of their exemplar (P MSS b 7a1]ας, ա, Նοα Ն ; Th κρίνων κρίσεις) at Sus:53, their successors perceived a further dimension in the phrase, that of the device *figura etymologica.* Rectifying the omission, therefore, they replaced the reading առնէիր preserved in MSS M178-M346' with դատէիր, in order that both verb and noun should recall the same root.

The following examples further illustrate the way in which word choices diverging from the later standard have been brought into line. The first reading in each instance is that of the majority.

եթե]բա V280-J2558 at 2:24 and 4:32
5:29 զգեցուցին] ագուցին   J1925 (ἐνέδυσαν)
Bel:8 մեռանիցիք]վախճանիցիք M287 վախճանեսջիք V280
              (ἀποθανεῖσθε)

Doublets: Doublet translations can likewise arise from a number of different reasons. The probability is that the two cases found in MS CHB5 were interlinear glosses which at some point were incorporated into the text. Both offer a commonplace equivalent of the original. At Sus:39 բանգի բուռն էր is explained by զի զօրաւոր էր and similarly at v. 52 հնացեալ by ծեր. If some scribes were interested in textual interpretation all were committed by the very nature of their profession to the preservation of the works they took in hand to copy. Particularly when that book formed part of sacred scripture their conservation often prompted them to include rather than reject material in case of doubt. In this way certain MSS have come to possess the original and the revised reading sometimes juxtaposed paratactically, sometimes joined by the copula. This will now be illustrated by a few examples:

Sus:20Arm maj.   քո հաւանեալ   լեր ընդ մեզ = Th
M178-M346'   քո հաւանեալ յանձն առ և լեր ընդ մեզ

The plus may be derived from a P source like Walton's b text which has ܝܗ ܘܗܒ ܠ ܝܣܒ . Its antiquity is vouched for by its inclusion in Geo (თა3ნ ოღ33 ჩ-ჯ6 თა6ა ღა 6ჯბა ძ33 ჩ-ჯ6: assentire nobis et licentiam da nobis).

Sus:24 Arm maj. կից նմին   MS J1925   ընդ նմա
MSS M346'   կից ընդ նմին   MS M178   կից ընդ նմա

Elucidating the stages by which the above situation was produced we must postulate J1925's reading as a straightforward rendering of an examplar like MS b (ܝܒܣܡ ܝܪܒܣ) which then passed into Geo (ძონ თა6ა: cum ea). Later կից was instated to render Th κατέναντι which led to the conflation of the two in different combinations as revealed by M178 and M346'.

8:7 Arm maj.   ի ձեռաց նորա   = Th
                       (ἐκ χειρὸς αὐτοῦ)
     M2585 M2627' M182'   ի ձեռաց քո2ին   = P
     M178   ի ձեռաց քո2ին նորա

The second reading which agrees with P (ܝܢ, ܟܝ3, ܝܣܘܗܠ ܡ) is probably original, being later transformed into the Th form witnessed by the majority. Some early MSS then made their own harmonization of the variants.

As we might expect, several examples are available from V280-J2558 too, e.g.

4:8　 մեծացաւ] + և բարձրացաւ

The second verb which corresponds to P (ܪ݂ܒܠܠܗ) is likely to have been the one read by Arm1 before being ousted from the majority of witnesses in favour of the Th equivalent.

9:9　գթութիւնք]գթութիւն և ողորմութիւն

գթութիւնք is the stereotype equivalent of Th's οἰκτιρμοί and is therefore secondary. The other component coincides with P's ܚܣܕ; as also at v. 18 and so has a greater claim to priority over the majority reading գթութեան there also. Later in v. 9 a similar situation confronts us:

բաւութիւնք] բաւութիւն և թողութիւն

Once again V280's second component must be deemed the original reading (= P ܫܘܒܩ , while the first is the accepted rendering of Th ἱλασμός.

9:23　պատմել] խելամուտել (խելամուտ առնել J2558) եւ պատմել regularly translates Th ἀναγγείλαι. Of the other forms the one supported by J2558, made up of compound adjective and auxiliary verb is frequently encountered in Arm, typical of Classical Armenian in general and therefore to be preferred. Moreover it probably represents the Arm1 text in dependence on P (ܐܣܬܟܠ).

12:7　յաւիտեանս]յաւիտենից V280; + յաւիտենից J2558

Indicative of the unforeseen significance seemingly minor variations sometimes conceal, the change from genitive to accusative case marks an important shift in textual allegiance. The reading of MS V280 represents the construct relationship of P (ܥܠ ܥܠܡ), while that of the majority follows a distinct branch of the Th tradition which includes V230 239 Hippol[J Met.].

In this case the desire to conserve both in doublet form may have been influenced by the presence of the compound formula at the conclusion of liturgical doxologies.

11:38 hqɯıɲ] ɗɯnq J1925; + ɗɯınqhʹu V280'

This instance is particularly instructive in showing that the revisers' changes were not always adopted. The majority consensus echoes P ᴜᴀ which must also have precedence according to our earlier conclusion that translations usually antedate transliterations.[112] The earlier term was probably retained since it was perfectly comprehensible whereas the other was not.

CONCLUSION

In the preamble to his list of P agreements Gehman raised the issue of modality. Granted that some sort of connection existed between Arm and P, did this come about through the translator's introduction of P elements with which he was familiar a) simply from memory; b) from a codex; or c) is this evidence of a prior translation from Syriac? The results of our study enable us to decide firmly in favour of the final alternative, thereby adding Daniel to the list of hybrid books exhibiting an earlier P-oriented phase subsequently revised to a Greek text type.

The ascription of P as a translation base is founded upon multiple examples of agreement distributed throughout the book and mostly of a substantive nature, whether plus, minus or semantic variant which preclude their being assigned to chance or coincidence. The majority of these readings are to be found in all fifteen MSS chosen for their ability to represent the version as a whole. Additional and often more significant agreements are attested by a few witnesses belonging to groups of proven textual purity. Moreover linguistic arguments frequently demanded a Syriac exemplar, while in most cases variation in MT and Gk left no other source which might be held responsible for Arm's formulation. Often approximate rather than identical, OG parallels in addition to P's Gk dependence were sometimes considered to reflect shared exegetical traditions of MT and perhaps common reliance on a pre-massoretic *Vorlage* at other points. The latter contention is reinforced by the fact that all the examples were read by the pre-hexaplaric Chester Beatty Papyrus 967 except for 3 cases where it is not extant (11:27, Bel:4 and 27), one where it is fragmentary (10:17) and a further case (1:9) of agreement with MT which the editor, W. Hamm regards as secondary to the reading of 88-Syh. Th support was sporadic and peripheral apart from OL and Luc. The latter form a textual complex with P based on the local text of Antioch and Syria from which one branch of OL was translated, which was used as a standard of comparison by P and acted as the raw material of Lucian's revision.

In establishing a stratification of the stages the Georgian Version proved a useful auxiliary, as Lyonnet had found in the Gospels and Georgian scholars predict for other books. Linguistic and metaphrastic material enabled us to identify Arm as its earliest *Vorlage.* Moreover its Armenian base text had substantial contact with P. Indeed Geo preserves P readings no longer extant in Armenian MSS. However, there is evidence (e.g. doublets) to suggest that the recensional process towards Th had already begun by the time Geo's exemplar broke off from the Armenian tradition, while Geo itself was subject to a medieval revision which therefore limits its capacity to reflect Arm1.

The context-related, variable translation technique posited for Arm1 is no isolated phenomenon, but in accordance with Baumstark's findings in the Psalter and Lyonnet's from the Gospels typifies a primitive stage of translation which is gradually systematized as more experience is gained in the art and a greater desire for literalist accuracy and consistency manifests itself. A similar progression marks the development of Greek and Syriac biblical translation from the Pentateuch and Old Syriac through to Aquila and the Syrohexapla. Furthermore, like OL Arm1 does not have a separate existence. Painted over by a recensional veneer it only shows through at some points. Again it is significant that it is MSS of early text type which lend most assistance in reconstructing it.

Variation in translation equivalents and doublets spotlight the transitional phase which led to the increasing substitution of Arm1 readings by those of Arm2. Nevertheless, it would be inappropriate to describe this as a wholescale obliteration of the former order; for it was not always Th readings which won final acceptance. This factor must be borne in mind when assessing the character of representatives of groups A, B and C. Although normally the majority exhibit the influence of the later text, there are occasions in which it espouses Arm1 with the result that the minority, when not in error, read a proposed revision which did not commend itself to the version's tradents.

NOTES

1. See chapter three, pp.89-90.
2. For a discussion of the dating see C. Toumanoff, "Armenia and Georgia", *CMH* iv, i, J.M. Hussey (ed.), Cambridge, The University Press: 1966, note 1.
3. See P. Ananian, "La data e le circostanze della consecrazione di S. Gregorio Illuminatore", *Mus* 84 (1961), pp.43-73, 319-360.
4. For the record of the consecration there of St. Gregory's successors by the historian P'awstos see N. Garsoian, *The Epic Histories*, III, 12 Yusik I (p.82), III, 16 P'arēn (p.91), IV, 4 Nersēs (p.111).
5. Ibid., p.367 (Daniel) and p.405 (Šaḷitay).
6. For details see R.W. Thomson (trans.), *Moses Khorenats'i*, pp.163-176. Ultimately the two traditions were united by the legend that St. Gregory was conceived at Artaz on the site of St. Thaddaeus' martyrdom. See M. van Esbroeck, "Le résumé syriaque de l'Agathange", *AB* 95 (1977), p.295.
7. For sources indicating that Syriac was more prevalent in Persarmenia see General Conclusion, pp.421-2.
8. On the background to this practice see S.P. Cowe, "The Two Armenian Versions of Chronicles".
9. A handy conspectus of the material is provided by H. Hübschmann, *Armenische Grammatik*, Leipzig, Breitkopf and Härtel: 1897, pp.322-89 for Greek derivations and 281-321 for Syriac.
10. For a concise presentation of the antithetical scholarly viewpoints on the subject see B.M. Metzger, *The Early Versions of the New Testament*, pp.164-165. For a more detailed discussion see H. Ačaṙyan, *Hayo c' Grer ē* [Armenian Letters] Erevan, Erevan State University Press: 1984.
11. S. Lyonnet, "Aux origines de l'église arménienne. La traduction de la Bible et le témoignage des historiens ar-

méniens", *RSR* XXV (1935), p.187.

12. *Les origines,* p.9.

13. See A. Pelletier (ed.), *Lettre d'Aristée à Philocrate,* SC 89, Paris, Cerf: 1962 for a critical edition of the work.

14. The earliest of these devotes a large portion of his brief account to the justification of writing the life of someone who had not died a martyr's death. See Koriwn, *Vark Maštoci* §2, pp.72-84.

15. Ibid., §1, pp.70-72 and §19, p.122.

16. The last reference is to the erection of a baldachin over Maštoc's grave, which is dated 443 (K.H. Maksoudian, "Introduction", pp.x-xi). *The terminus ante quem* is provided by his laudatory references to Vasak, prince of Siwnik', (Koriwn, *Vark' Maštoci* §14, p.110) whose complicity in Yazdgard II's reintroduction of Zoroastrianism into Armenia would have rendered it obsolete. For the conduct of ecclesiastical affairs see G. Winkler, "An Obscure Chapter", pp.94-109.

17. For the significance of the prior Syrian initiative of bishop Daniel to accommodate an alphabet for Armenian see S.P. Cowe, "Literary and Theological considerations Governing the Strata of the Armenian Version of Scripture", *Translation of Scripture JQR* Supplement, Philadelphia, Annenberg Research Institute: 1990, pp.29-46. Similarly, Koriwn makes no allusion to Sahak's deposition in 428 and diminished jurisdiction after 432. Moreover, he seems to imply the pro-Persian catholicoi are responsible for the introduction of the works of Theodore of Mopsuestia when these had already become doctrinally suspect. For a recent study of these issues see G. Winker, "Die spätere Überarbeitung", pp.143-180.

18. One might mention in passing an intermediate champion of the Gregorid tradition in the person of Agathangelos, the illuminator's hagiographer. The fictional claim to be a secretary hailing from the city of Rome is already a sufficient indication of his inclinations. Although his life of St.

Gregory is now viewed as a composite work, it appears that the nucleus of its present form dates to the 460's (R.W. Thomson (trans.), *Agathangelos History of the Armenians,* p.xc). It thus follows the hierarchy of Melitē and Movsēs, two representatives of the house of Ałbianos in Manazkert, which was traditionally pro-Persian. Therefore, the work's original purpose may have been a re-affirmation of the Byzantine perspective which would have been more conducive to the new incumbent Giwt. It is significant that Łazar depicts the inception of his reign "according to God's governance" and after summarily dismissing the predecessors, dilates on the abundance of his Greek learning (*Patmagirk' Hayoc',* §62, p.110).

19.   See Łazar P'arpeċi, *Patmagirk' Hayoc',* p.186, from the famous introductory note accompanying his famous letter.

20.   In his letter to his patron Vahan Mamikonean he remarks that he had been accused of some sort of sectarianism and seeks to defend his conduct by reference to the standards he imbibed during his study abroad (ibid., p.193).   Hence, since his traducers are presented as unsympathetic to this, it may be that their formation was more Syrian.

21.   Ibid., §10, p.13.

22.   See R.W. Thomson, *Moses Khorenats'i,* p.48.

23.   Koriwn, *Vark' Maštoc'i,* §§vi-xi, pp.90-104.

24.   The MSS witness the bishop's name as Babilas, elsewhere unattested in connection with the see, yet in light of the long transmission history and general tendency for foreign names to suffer scribal corruption. Peeter's emendation to Rabbula seems eminently plausible.   The form seems already to have been familiar to Movsēs Xorenaċi. See *Patmuṭiwn Hayoc',* III,53 p.327. The graphic similarity of ṗ and p is such that the former might easily be assimilated to the following p. The opposite seems to have occurred in Xorenaċi's transmission history whereby some of the later MSS adduce the dissimulated corrup-

tion ṗարnuէ. As Rabbula's episcopal tensure dates from 411/2, Peeters dates Maštoc̣'s journey to c.414 ("Pour l'histoire des origines", pp.204-211).

25. For one possible result of this division of labour see General Conclusion, p.436.

26. It has sometimes been inferred that Rufinus himself was Greek (e.g. B.M. Metzger, *The Early Versions of the New Testament* p.155), though the assumption goes beyond textual warrant. The epithet հելլենական unequivocally relates to the scribe's literary training, not his ethnic background (cf. the description of Maštoc̣'s Greek formation at §3, p.84), for which in any case յոյն would be the normal term. No occasion is given for assuming he was anything but a native of the region where his name was not uncommon. The historian Rufinus was born at Concordia near Aquileia in the mid fourth century.

27. For the possible codicological significance of this datum see General Conclusion, p.435 and note 88, p.450.

28. For a brief discussion of the dating problems see Koriwn, *Vark̇ Maštoc̣i* p.310, note 59.

29. Ibid., §xix, p.124. That the *Vorlage* of at least part of the original Armenian version of the Bible was Greek is proved by chapter four of the present work as well as a number of studies of OT books.

30. In this connection it is noteworthy that in the long preamble to his work Koriwn refers specifically to St. Paul's fourteen epistles which manifestly indicates the Greek corpus, not the Syriac which included the apocryphal third letter to the Corinthians (*Vark̇ Maštoc̣i*, §2, p.80).

31. For the proposal that the mission to Edessa was instigated by the Syrian catholicoi whom the Persian shah had appointed in Armenia see G. Winkler, "An Obscure Chapter", pp.107-10. There is suggested that this took place in early 432.

32. Winkler argues the second embassy was sent by Sahak to

gain information on doctrinal developments in the Empire ibid., pp.111-113.)

33. Winkler places the return in 435 (ibid., p.115).

34. On Łazar's first book see further Introduction, p.18, note 22.

35. Łazar P'arpec'i, *Patmagirk' Hayoc',* §10, 11, p.6.

36. Ibid., §11, p.6.

37. II, 10. For details see R.W. Thomson, *Movsēs Xorenac'i,* p.146, note 7.

38. Movsēs Xorenac'i, *Patmut'iwn Hayoc',* III,53, p.326.

39. Ibid., III,54, p.329.

40. For a discussion of this see R.W. Thomson, *Movsēs Xorenac'i,* pp.12-13.

41. Movsēs Xorenac'i, *Patmut'iwn Hayoc',* III,53, p.326. For the Alexandrian visit see III, 61-62. On the basis of Xorenac'i's disparagement of the style of the Sahak-Mesrop translation it has been argued that the object of the historian's studies was a further scriptural revision, introducing a third stratum into the process. Yet the thesis outstrips the data and has found no support from textual analysis. See *Deut,* p.11.

42. Movsēs Xorenac'i, ibid., III, 60, p.341. His treatment of the first contingent's mission to Constantinople seems to betray dependence on Eznik's letter (G. Winkler, "An Obscure Chapter", pp.113-115).

43. For Koriwn's secondary features see K.H. Maksoudian, "Introduction", p.xiii. Archbishop Norair Bogharian would identify him with the epitomator of the Armenian version of the ecclesiastical history of Socrates Scholasticus ("p'okr Koriwni hetinakē" [The Author of the Lesser Koriwn] *Sion* (1959) 7-8, pp.167-168).

44. *Patmut'iwn srboyn Mesrovbay,* pp.10-11. The same interpolation appears in some late manuscripts of Łazar. G. Tēr-Mkrtč'ean has demonstrated that it derives from the Amsterdam edition of Xorenac'i. For details see Łazar P'arpec'i, *Patmagirk' Hayoc',* p.15, note 3.

45. *Patmutʻiwn srboyn Mesrovbay,* p.11.

46. Ibid., p.16.

47. Koriwn, *Varkʻ Maštocʻi,* §19, p.122.

48. Movsēs Xorenacʻi, *Patmutʻiwn Hayocʻ* III,60, p.341.

49. For a review of the thesis regarding Chron. Eccles, Cant, Sir, Wisd and Prov see S.P. Cowe, "Problematics".

50. Id., "The Armenian Version of Ruth and its Textual Affinities", p.184, note 6.

51. Id., "La versión armenia", pp.lxxi-lxxviii.

52. Id., "The Two Armenian Versions of Chronicles".

53. Quoted by W. Kappler in *Maccabaeorum liber I,* Septuaginta IX, 1, Göttingen, Vandenhoeck and Rupprecht: 1967, p.21.

54. A. Baumstark, "Der armenische Psaltertext. Sein Verhältnis zum syrischen der Peschitta und seine Bedeutung für die LXX-Forschung", *Or Chr* 22 (1922-24), pp.180-213; 23 (1926/27), pp.158-169, 319-333; 24 (1927) 146-159.

55. See, for example, J. Ziegler, *Duodecim prophetae,* Septuaginta XIII, Göttingen, Vandenhoeck & Ruprecht: 1943, p.81.

56. A. Vööbus, *Peschitta und Targumim des Pentateuches, Neues Licht zur Frage der Herkunft der Peshitta aus dem altpalästinischer Targum.* PETSE vol.9, Stockholm, 1958. For a refutation of Vööbus's interpretation of the data see p.447.

57. S. Lyonnet, *Les origines,* pp.181.

58. For a recent survey of the state of research see M. Šanize, "Remarques au sujet de la Bible géorgienne", *BK* XLI (1983), pp.105-122.

59. G. Garitte, *Lʻancienne version géorgienne des Actes des Apôtres dʻaprès deux manuscrits du Sinai,* B Mus 38, Louvain, Publ. Univ.-Inst. Orient: 1955. More recently J.N. Birdsall has pointed out that the Sinai MSS represent a distinct recension of two pre-existing texts and rightly cautions against theorizing on an insufficient

foundation. However, one should encourage more intense investigation of the Armenian transmission history before proposing that the agreements between the Armenian and Georgian versions may derive from comparable Greek exemplars of similar provenance. See "The Georgian versions of the Acts of the Apostles", *Text and Testimony* (in honour of A.F.J. Klijn), T. Baarda et al (eds.), Kampsen, Kok: 1988, pp.39-45.

60. J. Molitor, "Zum Textcharakter der altgeorgischen katolischen Briefe", *Or Chr* LI (1967), pp.51-66.

61. Id., "Das altgeorgische Corpus Paulinum der neuen Tifliser Ausgabe und sein Textcharakter", *BK* XXXIV (1976), pp.190-198.

62. See R.P. Blake, "Ancient Georgian Versions of the OT", *HTR* 19 (1926), pp.271-297. He also notes that later codices show the much more widespread impact of various Greek text types, e.g. the Octateuch of the twelfth century Gelati Bible: MS Q-1108 of the Manuscript Institute, Tbilisi, which displays the influence of the contemporary Grecophile movement. Nevertheless, Blake argues it frequently retains words of Armenian origin which have been replaced by native Georgian terms in the Oški MS.

63. M. Šanize, *Psalmunta cignis zveli kartuli targmanebi* [Ancient Georgian Translations of the Psalter] Tbilisi, Mecniereba: 1979.

64. K.D. Danelia, *The Ancient Georgian Versions of the Prophecies of Jeremiah and the Question of their Origins* (Georgian) Tbilisi: (résumé in *BK* XIX-XX (1965), pp.215-216).

65. J. Molitor, "Spuren altsyrischer Bibelübersetzung in den Chanmeti-Palimpsesten aus Jeremias", *BK* 15-16 (1963), pp.99-102.

66. "The Old Georgian Version of the Prophets", Critical Edition with a Latin translation by R.P. Blake and M. Brière.

67. For a full description see R.P. Blake, "The Athos Codex of

the Georgian Old Testament", *HTR* XXII (1929), pp.39-53 and O. Wardrop, "Georgian Manuscripts at the Iberian Monastery on Mount Athos", *JTS* XII (1910-11), pp.593-597.

68. For a description see R.P. Blake, "The Georgian Version of Fourth Esdras from the Jerusalem Manuscript", *HTR* XIX (1926), pp.300-302.

69. Ibid., p.304.

70. See Meillet, §22, p.16.

71. According to *Arm B* (vol.IV, pp.145-146) this Pahlavi term entered Georgian via Armenian.

72. According to *Arm B* (vol.IV, p.43) this Pahlavi term entered Georgian via Armenian.

73. According to *Arm B* (vol.IV, p.543) this term derived from an Akkadian original entered Georgian via Armenian.

74. According to *Arm B* (vol.III, pp.386-387) this is an Armenian word which was borrowed by Georgian. A variant form *iataki* appears in IV Ezra 2.2.2. Blake remarks that it is seldom encountered in Old Georgian (*HTR* XIX (1926), p.308).

75. According to *Arm B* (vol.IV, p.596) this Syriac term entered Georgian via Armenian.

76. Ou. Tsindeliani, "Equivalents of κατά in the Georgian version of kingdoms", *Mravaltavi,* vol.V, Tbilisi, Mecniereba: 1976.

77. See chapter six, p.367 for the theological significance of this reading.

78. According to *Arm B* (vol.IV, pp.341-2).

79. According ro *Arm B* (vol.II, pp.582-4)

80. For a discussion of the citation see chapter seven, pp.391-2.

81. MS J2558 reads գնա.

82. MS J2558 reads լիցի.

83. MS J2558 reads անդրէն միւսանգամ եկին.

84. The Greek conjunction ὅτι regularly introduces both indirect statements and clauses of purpose. Although its

Armenian counterpart զի appears in both capacities, որ far more frequently performs the first function. Therefore զի would be more open to misinterpretation here as fulfilling its more common causal role.

85. This reading appears to be an early Armenian error which has also slipped into the Georgian version.

86. This reading is similarly an early mistake confusing the unfamiliar form փիլիմոնի with the addressee of one of the Pauline epistles.

87. See Meillet, §106, p.95.

88. For details see General Conclusion, pp.430-2.

89. Geo's reading can best be explained by Arm which alone possesses the two senses required ('worshipper' and 'servant').

90. See *NBH,* vol.2, p.599.

91. In Ziegler, p.193, MS 239 appears instead of 89.

92. For a full discussion of the relationship between P and Th, in the deuterocanonical sections of the book, see the appendix to this chapter. As regards the source of Arm's agreements with P there, although we cannot rule out the possibility that the former had access to a Greek text analogous to P of a type which is no longer extant, since Syriac contact is indicated by the examples hinging on linguistic criteria, P must be considered having prior claim to be Arm's source in these cases.

93. Arm and P's renderings can mean (a) literature and (b) its concrete manifestation, i.e. book. It is in the latter sense that Arm has been interpreted by Geo.

94. J. Molitor, "Altgeorgische Evangelienübersetzung als Hüter Syrischer Tradition," *BK* XXIII-XXIV (1967), pp.136-ff.

95. S.P. Brock, "A Doublet and its Ramifications", *Biblica* 56 (1975) pp.550-553.

96. For additional examples from 1/2 Samuel illustrating the complex P-Lucian-Old Latin see T. Stockmeyer, "Hat Lukian zu seiner LXX-Rev. die Peschitto benützt ?" *ZAW*

12 (1892), pp.218-223.

97. See Introduction, p.iv.

98. MS J2558 reads թէ.

99. MS J2558 reads անմեղ դատ.

100. MS J2558 reads արդ.

101. For supplementary examples with outside support see S.P. Cowe, "Armenian Daniel," pp.270-271.

102. For supplementary examples with outside support see S.P. Cowe, "Armenian Daniel," pp.272-273.

103. As P here repeats 2:47, 3:14 Arm's original rendering may well have been արդարեւ which later developed into արդար *hu* and its variant *wuhu.*

104. For supplementary examples see S.P. Cowe, "Armenian Daniel," pp.276-277.

105. See p.278.

106. The form of the name Աբեդնագով is similarly close to both P and MT and is also supported by the Lucianic recension and see also MS M287's reading at 3:35 which contrasts with Arm majority=Gk.

107. See J.A. Montgomery, *A Critical and Exegetical Commentary on the Book of Daniel,* p.125.

108. For the same occurrence in Ps 32:4 see A. Baumstark, "Der armenische Psaltertext," note 10, p. 195.

109. Leloir does a disservice to Lyonnet in his synopsis of the latter's conclusions by inserting the explanatory phrase "comme le syriaque" at this point in his article "Orientales de la Bible (Versions): arméniennes," coll.810-818. Lyonnet, however, does not express the opinion that the trait is an exclusive Syriac preserve and indeed P's actual procedure in Daniel is quite the reverse.

110. A. Baumstark records 14 examples in the first forty psalms using Z ("Der armenische Psaltertext," p.193).

111. Also Z in Psalms and in *Deut* where the editor discounts substantive Syriac contact.

112. For the same development in technique on the part of the original translators of OG over against its later revisers

see E. Tov, "Transliterations of Hebrew Words in the Greek Versions of the Old Testament," *Textus* 8 (1973), p.83.

APPENDIX

P's affinities with the Lucianic Text
with special reference to
the studies of Kallarakkal and Wyngarden

The extent to which Arm=P readings were paralleled by Greek witnesses in the foregoing tables seems hardly coincidental and therefore requires a more comprehensive investigation. It is also desirable as a transition to our consideration of Arm's direct association with Gk which occupies the next chapter.

The kernel of Kallarakkal's[1] argument (with a certain reserve on some points) may be stated as follows: P Daniel was translated from a semitic base (of which the deuterocanonical sections formed an integral part) in the first century A.D. by the Jewish community of Edessa. Since the version is held to antedate Th, agreements arise either through the latter's dependence on P or their common adherence to a text type purer than that represented by MT.

Recent research[2] into the origins of Th taking into account its use in citations in NT and near contemporary writers, its literalism and distinctive vocabulary[3], makes it more plausible to suppose that it may contain elements in common with P since it is suggested that it came into existence in Palestine or Syria about the turn of the eras. However it does not seem possible to include all the types of agreement within the categories of a shared consonantal text differing from MT or shared exegetical traditions of a *Vorlage* resembling MT. Moreover, granted that the whole attention of Th's translator was focused upon rendering his Hebrew-Aramaic exemplar with rigorous fidelity, it is not at all clear why he would have had recourse to P nor is it self-evident that he was even conversant with Syriac. At the same time Kallarakkal candidly admits that "the exact date of the translation is difficult to arrive at"[4] while his evidence regarding use of the construct case of the substantive is not sufficiently specific to warrant placing P so early, particularly as his only fixed historical co-ordinates are Edessene inscriptions of 6 A.D. and the fourth century fathers Afrahat and Efrem.

His exclusion of Susanna from treatment of the apocryphal sections on the grounds that it exhibits a different translation technique and is usually found separately in the Syriac Bible requires further justification. P's main feature here is the same as in the additions to chapter 3 and Bel and the Dragon, i.e. the number of plusses it evinces over the Greek text. Similarly 6h10[5], the oldest dated MS of P Daniel, adduces the episode immediately after the Dragon as is also the norm among the Massora MSS while 8a1 introduces it immediately before the main book as is customary in Greek. Thus it is at least arguable that the Syrian convention of segregating Susanna with the other OT heroines Esther and Judith in the collection "Books of Women" is a secondary development.

The contention that the other deuterocanonical portions stem from a semitic original is only supported by generalizations about style although it is usually accepted that all the Syriac apocrypha with the exception of Sirach emanated from Greek. Moreover, the absence of fragments of this part of Daniel from Qumran[6] as well as its absence from discussion at Jamnia may be taken to suggest that the conjectural *Vorlage,* if indeed it existed, must have been something of a rarity and increasingly so as time went on.

Recognizing similarities between P and Th, Kallarakkal asserts that since the former possesses the longer text it is free of Th influence. Not only that, his value judgement on these plusses is that they reflect the primitive standard whereas "it is very likely that Ψ has shortened a longer text."[7] However, there is no discussion of how the abbreviation posited is compatible with the literalism which Th consistently applies elsewhere. On occasion the author himself is inclined paradoxically to ascribe such unique readings to the *Tendenz* of P's translator as for example ܐܟܠ ܩܪܨ 'slanderers', qualifying Chaldaeans at 3:48.

Summing up, we may say that Kallarakkal's views on such key areas as P's dating, the source of its deuterocanonical sections and its relationship to Th are not argued with the necessary thoroughness to be compelling. The facts are capable of diverse interpretation as is shown by Wyngarden.[8]

In his submission, P Daniel was translated by Christians and coloured by Th although primarily based on a semitic original. The *terminus ad quem* is provided by citations in Afrahat and St. Efrem[9] while the lack of influence on quotations in the Old Syriac gospels is taken as evidence for their priority with the result that he dates P within the span 200-250 A.D.

He reinforces this dating by his negative conclusions regarding possible contact with the Origenic and Lucianic recensions (implying thereby that it antedates them). However, his handling of Greek sources is rather wooden and misleading in so far as he employs mainly B to represent Th, A for the Hexapla along with Q and considers these and the Lucianic text type as fixed, discrete entities when in fact the textual situation is far more fluid and individual witnesses are contaminated by readings from different streams. Moreover, he sometimes inserts the same examples in different lists. While these are seen as convincing in relation to Th, their effect in other cases is curiously negligible, e.g. his comments on a reading at 11:15.[10]

> "Though the last instance is rather striking, it is not sufficient to prove dependence of S upon A or Q, since AQ differ from Th here only by a καί. And it has been proved, in Section V, that S is dependent upon Th."

Nor is it apparent precisely what affinity Wyngarden postulates between P and OG. In addition to the examples afforded on pp. 18-19 he notes OG's close parallelism to some of the A readings cited on p. 21 and a further five are listed in concurrence with Lucian on p. 23. In his conclusions he does not absolutely reject the possibility of some form of contact, yet he has previously acknowledged that though "there are some correspondences between S and G (i.e. OG), the differences are much greater."[11] What the writer envisages as actually having happened is left somewhat nebulous. Thus the question remains whether a more inclusive thesis can be formed to encompass the varied data Wyngarden presents.

Considering the geographical location of Edessa, where in the joint opinion of the foregoing scholars P Daniel first saw light, one is tempted to suggest that if any contact with Gk is mooted, the most likely candidate is the local text of Antioch. This must have served as the basis of the recensional activity of Lucian (himself a Syrian probably hailing from Samosata) and figures in that later form in the commentaries of St. Chrysostom, Theodoret of Cyrrhus, Theodore of Mopsuestia and his brother, Polychronius of Apamea.

Since Wyngarden holds the translation to be the work of Christians, it is surprising that he limited his study to the Hebrew-Aramaic section of Daniel, since the remainder was accepted by the church and regularly copied in the Greek Bible. It is significant that Ziegler[12] classifies P as a witness to the Lucianic text of Baruch and the Epistle of Jeremiah and by the mere fact of including P in his apparatus to the apocryphal additions in Daniel tacitly indicates his conviction that its exemplar was not semitic. Indeed, even a cursory glance at its showing there is enough to demonstrate its distinctly Lucianic colouring.

In particular, it manifests a number of agreements with MS 410 which Ziegler relegates to his "codices mixti"[13] with no clear affiliation. The consistency of the mixture in this MS of the prophets is usually different types of Alexandrian text. However its character is markedly Lucianic in the Dodekapropheton[14] and there are unmistakable signs that it is so in Daniel. Thus it reads the atticistic form εἶπον over against the Hellenistic at Sus:35, 36, 50 and Bel:28, 29, etc., and frequently accompanies Lucianic witnesses. A similar judgement seems warranted to a lesser degree for MS 588, which only contains Daniel (e.g. Sus:61 τῷ πλησίον tr post ποιῆσαι (v. 62) Q L-311-88

410 588).

The following examples display several typical Lucianic features:

1)   Expression of subject and object

Sus: 17 εἶπε]	+ σωσαννα	588 Sy
3:21	ἐπεδήθησαν] επεδησαν	311 87ᵗˣᵗ-490 410
		(+αυτους =P)
Bel: 17 δέ]	+ δανιηλ	410 Sy
-27	εἶπε] + δανιηλ	L-88 230" 584 Bo Sy Aethᴾ

2)   Explanatory additions to smooth the sense

Sus: 18 κεκρυμμένοι] εγκ. εκει		L' 534 Sy
-21	κοράσια] + σου	VL' 588 Sy Aeth Hippol
-48	ἀνακρίναντες] +το δικαιον	230" 588 Sy
Bel: 42 + εκ του λακκου		ΙΙ-770 230 590 Laᵛ
		(+leonum) Sy: ex OG

3)   Intensifying Additions

Sus: 28 ὁ λαός] pr πας		L s y
-61	ἀνέστησαν] + πας ο λαος	233 Syᴸ²

4)   Influence of Parallel Passages

3:90   ὑμνεῖτε] + και υπερυφουτε   410 Sy   αυτον εις τους αιωνας

If we accept that P's deuterocanonical additions arose from the Lucianic text of Th it is already more understandable that the same text was consulted during the rest of the translation process. Returning to Wyngarden's list of Th agreements we observe several instances where Lucianic witnesses have a better claim to have acted as the intermediary than B, e.g. 2:35 where it is the majority text which evinces P's doublet

ܠܘܙ ܠܘܐ and 5:22 ܟܘܕܟ ܕܗ, 7:6 ܠܠܝܐ ܠܠܘ where they share P's WO. The most convincing example is the confusion of κλῆρον/καιρόν at 12:13 arguing persuasively for P dependence on the latter (ܗܕܣܝ) since it is hard to visualize how the variant might have come about in Hebrew or Syriac. Here B reads the former variant demonstrating P's affiliation with L⁻³⁶ 230 584 Arm HippolᴹᵉᵗChr Thtⁱᵉᵐ in support of the second.

On the contrary, there are certain cases where the main Lucianic text has adopted Hexaplaric revisions of Th towards MT which find no echo in P. At such times it is in the regular company of the Old Latin translation which, though a frequent satellite of B, betrays a deep strain of pre-Hexaplaric Lucianic readings,[15] as in other books of the OT. Stockmeyer[16] has presented an important collection of triple agreements of Lucian P and OL for 1 Samuel which Johnson[17] believes could easily be multiplied. A similar state of affairs obtains in NT also, especially in the gospels. Corraboratory examples can be afforded from the deuterocanonical sections of Daniel:

Sus:41 ἡ ουναγωγή] pr omnis Laˢ(vid.) Bo Sy Lucif; + πασα 588
        = OG
-50   δέδωκεν/ὁ θεός] tr 534 Laᵛ Sy.
Bel:32 ἑπτὰ λέοντες] tr 763 584 Laᵛ Sy.
-39   om τοῦ θεοῦ Laˢ Sy.

Lucianic witnesses support most of Wyngarden's instances of agreement with A and Q as well as with OG, a trait discernible in some of the deuterocanonical examples already cited. Once more OL exhibits the same propensity,[18] allowing us to infer that where such cases are not original to Th an early process of conflation and particularly the augmentation of Th by OG probably without reference to MT must have taken place. In this way we can account for P's partial exposure to OG readings, and more numerous contacts with Th.

Reverting to P's unique plusses in the deuterocanonical sections we may be justified in maintaining that several of these also existed in Greek and that it is purely accidental that no such MS has survived. That characteristic Lucianic readings have been preserved only in OL of Kgdms has been cogently demonstrated by Fischer[19] and parallels can be adduced in Daniel too, e.g. Bel:15 ἐξέπιον] pr vinum La^s:ex OG, v. 10 τέκνων] παιδιων A 11 90 230"; parvulis et filiis La^v (doublet), v. 22 ἔδωκε] + rex La^s, v. 22 καθημενος] + in medio leonum La^v.

Thus, if neither P nor OL reveals any trace of Lucian's doublet additions, those they witness have every likelihood of being traditional to his recensional base text and therefore deserve the term "proto-Lucianic." Since in the Prayer of Azariah and Song of the Three the relationship between OG and Th is extremely close,[20] it is far more logical to regard P's plusses there not as a conservative rendering of a full semitic exemplar of the B.C.era,[21] but as the product of a "progressive" exegetical movement active in the early centuries of our era, further examples of which are retained only in Arm.

a) doublets: ܝܐܚܒ݈ܩ̈ܘ ܣܡܬܪ; at 3:35 and 42
    ܠܐܘܝܘ ܠܘ and ܐ݈ܟܢܐ / ܐܝ; at 3:38
b) parallels ܐܝܘ ܐܢ̈ܒܘܐܟ (+ Th MS 410) 3:24 cf. 3:49, 7:9:
    + ܠܝܣ :42 cf. 3:43
c) intensifying additions: ܝܘܢܒ at 3:58, 63, 77, 84, 86, 87
    ܠ݈ܙܗܐ ܐܢ̈ܪܒ, ܝܘܢܒ 3:83 (ܐ݈ܟܡܒ݈ܘ, at 3:36 cf. Gk ἐλάλησας).

Thus P emerges as a significant secondary witness to the proto-Lucianic text[22] of Daniel which can enrich our garner of readings from this stratum provided by OL. Regardless of whether some of these are held to be original to Th in the final analysis, they give an insight into the methodology by which the Antiochian local text developed. Their primary utility is that of distinguishing Lucian's foundation from the structure he erected upon it. According to the present study the major dividing line is marked by extensive early OG conflation which then seems to have gone out of fashion amid growing doubts about the version's reliability. This reappraisal was probably hastened by the advent of the Hexapla which replaces OG as the dominant source of external readings. Their introduction into the traditional text to bring it into greater conformity with MT is seen as one of the hallmarks of Lucian's own activity.

NOTES

1.   A.G. Kallarakkal, *The Peshitto Version of Daniel - A Comparison with the Massoretic Text, the Septuagint and Theodotion.*

2.   For details see *inter alia* the works of Barthélemy, McCrystall, Pace and Busto Saiz cited in the bibliography.

3.   Klaus Koch, "Die Herkunft der Proto-Theodotion-übersetzung des Danielbuches," *VT* XXIII (1973), pp.362-365.

4.   A.G. Kallarakkal, *The Peshitto Version of Daniel,*p.225.

5.   See *List of Old Testament Peshitta Manuscripts,*preliminary issue ed. Peshitta Institute, Leiden: E.J. Brill, 1961.

6.   A. Mertens, *Das Buch Daniel im Lichte der Texte vom Toten Meer.* Stuttgarter biblische Monographien, 12. Würzburg. Echer: 1971.

7.   A.G. Kallarakkal, *The Peshitto Version of Daniel,*p.223.

8.   M.J. Wyngarden, *The Syriac version of the book of Daniel.*

9.   This work appears to have been compiled by a ninth century Jacobite author. See I. Ortiz De Urbina, *Patrologia Syriaca* 2nd. ed. Rome: Pont. Institutum Prientalium Studiorum, 1965, p. 73.

10. M.J. Wyngarden,*The Syriac Version of the Book of Daniel,* p. 22. The same reading appears on p. 20, this time referred to Th.

11. Ibid., p. 18.

12. J. Ziegler, *Ieremias Baruch. Threni. Epistula Ieremiae.* Septuaginta Vetus Testamentum Graecum Auctoritate Societatis Litterarum Gottingensis editum Vol. XV. Göttingen: Vandenhoeck and Ruprecht, 1957, pp. 84-85. P's Lucianic affiliation is similarly noted by the editors of the Göttingen Septuagint Volumes of 1-3 Maccabees and 1 Esdras. N.B. the existence of a Syrolucian version also.

13. Ziegler, p.60.

14. Ziegler, p.78.

15. J.A. Montgomery, *A Critical and Exegetical Commentary*

on the *Book of Daniel,* p. 43.

16. Th. Stockmeyer, "Hat Lucian zu seiner Septuaginta revision die Peschitto benützt?" *ZA W* 12 (1892), pp. 218-223.

17. *1 Samuel,* p. 73.

18. Ziegler, p. 27; J.A. Montgomery, *A Critical and Exegetical Commentary on the Book of Daniel,* p. 40.

19. B. Fischer, "Lukian-Lesarten in der VL der vier Königsbücher."

20. F.F. Bruce, "The Oldest Greek Version of Daniel," *OTS* XX (1977), pp. 22-40.

21. A.G. Kallarakkal, The Peshitto Version of Daniel, p. 171.

22. Cf. E. Tov, "Lucian and Proto-Lucian. Toward a New Solution of the Problem," *RB* 79 (1972), pp. 101-113.

CHAPTER 5

THE TWO STRATA OF ARMENIAN DANIEL AND THEIR AFFINITIES WITH THE GREEK TRADITION

We stated at the outset of the last chapter that Arm's main allegiance was found to lie with Gk and consequently the scope of the investigation of Syriac agreements was conditioned by the formula Arm≠Gk=P. Since the links established by the tables were only partial, the question of the original extent of P contact in Arm1 was raised: did it amount to a full translation or was it combined with Greek elements from the first?

The phenomenon of Armenian versional variants in which both readings have support from Greek witnesses with some consistency in text type leads us to posit two separate phases in Arm's contact with Gk. The implication is therefore that the interweaving of threads of Gk and P was already a feature of Arm1. This may be neatly illustrated by an example which is noteworthy in several respects.

11:45 εφαδανω] εν απαδανω (αποδ. 231) L - 88 Tht
    in loco pulchro Aeth Arab=P
յապարանս M287 M346'-M2585 M4114ᵐᵍ M182ᵐᵍ] om rel
յեփանդրն omn cod cum var min

311

Arm's reading is clearly a doublet the second portion of which can be directly retroverted into a Greek form resembling that of the *lemma* excepting that if յ, the prevocalic form of the preposition հ, is not rejected as a secondary corruption, the likelihood is that its Greek exemplar prefixed ἐν cf. the Lucianic variant. Arm cannot be dependent on P here which offers a completely different interpretation of the Hebrew *hapax legomenon*. Its rendering, ܟܐܐ ܒܠܝܐ 'in a smooth, level place' (not *beautiful* as implied in Ziegler's Latin translation which would derive from ܐܐܒ) construes פדן as 'field'.

In fact, apart from Aquila[1], with which it is probably unconnected, Arm is the sole witness to offer a suitable translation according to the derivation of the term. The latter arises from the Persian *apadana* which is also a loan word in Aramaic-Syriac. Thus the Armenian translators who belonged to the Eastern provinces under Persian sovereignty would have easily recognized the meaning 'palace, great hall' which is the first component of the doublet. Moreover, as we observed that translation as a technique preceded transliteration, this must be regarded as the text of Arm1 to which the revisers of Arm2 juxtaposed յեփասդոն. The fact that the original contours of the Persian borrowing are best preserved by the Lucianic recension[2] argues strongly for its inception with P as the joint matrix from which Arm1 emerged. This conclusion is corroborated by the same witnesses of early text type (M287, V280, J1925, etc.) which generally support P.

Arm did not need to resort to a Greek codex to secure a complete translation as P had done in the deuterocanonical sections where there was probably no available semitic exemplar.[3] Nevertheless, granted that the step was taken, it is fully consonant with the traditional setting of the translation in Mesopotamia that the standard employed was the local Antiochian text which had already been of assistance to the translators of P. Nevertheless, some two centuries had passed during which that basis had been transformed by Lucian both stylistically and textually in which developed form it had served as the basis of the Gothic Version in the fourth century. In comparing the character and support of the examples of Lucianic influence in the tables that follow we shall endeavor to identify the nature of Arm's *Vorlage.* In several instances where Arm=Luc=P, it cannot be decided with certainty whether the reading entered Arm directly from Greek or via Syriac.

Table 1a: V280[4] = Luc

Bel: 14 om ւքհայնոյ   om μόνου Q-230''62 L'[1-36] 410
590 742 La[sv] Bo Sy[4]

WO 2:14 Դանիէլ խաւնե-   Δαν. ἀπεκρίθη] tr L[-311] Bo
գաւ]tr

Table 1b: V280 = diverse Lucianic witnesses

3:49 om Աստուծոյ   κυρίου] > La[w]
4:16 ատր] + արբայ   κύριε] +μου βασιλευ 588 Tht
-31 om և փառաւորեցի   om καὶ ἐδόξασα   106 La[s] Tht
5:3 om tot vers   Qtxt 22-51''764
742 Hippol[AS*]
-14 om Աստուծոյ   om θεοῦ   Tht
-31 qԹագաւորութիւն]   βασιλείαν] +   230 Aeth Hippol[s]
+ նորա   αυτου
6:1 Թագաւորութեանն]   βασιλείας] +   311 230 584 La[s]
իւրոյ   αυτου   Aeth Tht (=P)
-17 ւքի] + ւքեծ   λίθον] + μεγαν   11-449 106 742
(=P 7al)
9:1 title Աղոթք   προσευχη δανιηλ   410
Դանիէլի
Bel:1 title Վասն Բելայ   περι του βηλ   410 541
-23 title Վասն Վիշապին περι του δρακοντος   36 410 541
-39 om Տէառն   θεοῦ] >   La[s](=P)
WO Sus:42 ի ձայն   φ. μεγάλη /   26 588 verss
բարձր/ծուշան]tr Σουσ.] tr   Lucif. Or[lat]XVII 73
Lo.

1:6 Միսայել ...   Μισαήλ...   88 87 46 393? Aeth
      Ազարիա]tr   Αζαρίας] tr   Hippol Chr Tht
4:30 բանն կատարե-   ὁ λόγος/   Q-541 11   Chr Tht
          գաւ]tr   συνετελ.] tr
-30 ի մարդկանէ   ἀπὸ τῶν   588 Hippol cf 230
      հալածեցաւ]tr   ἀνθρώπων/ἐξεδ.] tr Tht[p]

Table 2a: groups of witnesses including V280 = Luc

Sus: 47 om այդ   M287'' om   οὗτος   538 (=P)
                            M2585   J1925˙
1:5 կացուցանել] +qնոսա   στῆναι] + αυτους L' - 88 46 Tht
                            M287˙
3:28 ամենայն] +   πάντα ταῦτα] +   L''c 233 239 588
      ի վերայ մեր   εφ ημας   Co Aeth[p]Arab
                   V280˙   J1925   Tht (=P)
-84 բահանայք   ἱερεῖs   B-46˙ 62 L-36 88
                   M287'   J1925'-410 Fa
                   M2627   M182''
5:14 հոգի] +սուրբ V280   ἐν σοί I˙] pr αγιον Q-541 L-88 534
                   M2585   M2627˙   Aeth[p] Arab Chr
                   M182'   Tht (=P)
-16 զմեկնութիւն V280   συγκρίματα   Q[mg]=233 L-36 88
WN11 J1925   410 742 Chr
11:18 զնոսա]զնա V280˙ αὐτῶν] - του   L-770 46 Aeth
                                             Tht (=P= MT)
-40 ոգորեցի ընդ նմա և συγκερα-   Q L 46'' 106 239
         Թագաւորն M287'[a] τισθήσεται μετ'   410 584 Bo Tht
                            αὐτοῦ βασιλεὺs   (=P)
WO 8:20 Պարսից ...   περσῶν...   Q-230'62'L'' C'
         Մարաց]tr   Μήδων] tr   534 Bo Arab
                   V280 M2627   (=P= MT)
(3:54 tr post V55 V280˙ M346'-M2585   V-62 L-3 11-88'
                   V1508 - M351   La[v] Tht (=OG)

Table 2b: supplementary examples of agreement with Luc witnesses

3:95 աստուծոյ]+ousարագ θεῷ] + αλλστριω V280 M346'		11
5:17 պարգևք] a պարգևք (-զ M4834) V280'	τὰ δόματα] το δομα	584 Chr
7:7 om և hզաւր V280 J1925	καὶ ἰσχυρόν] >	HippolA p.194 5 et 204, 7 Tht
-7 և 6° -պղնծիք M287' M178-M346	superadd. και οι ονυχες αυτοι χαλκοι	Hippol ThtP Prisc.
9:24 om և ի շնչել անիրաւութեանց M280' M2627	om καὶ τοῦ ἐξιλ. ἀδικίας	410 Chr 1. 898 Thttem Tert (=P)
11:32 զԱստուած] զաէր աստուած V280' (doublet)	θεόν] τον κυριον	11
WO 5:2 զարծաթոյ ... զոսկւոյ]tr V280 J1925	χρυσᾶ ... ἀργυρᾶ] tr	311 (=P)

Table 3a: individual MSS and smaller groups excluding 95 = Luc

2:32 ձեռք] + իւր M346	χεῖρες] + αυτης	L' verssP Chr (=MT)
-35 մանրեցան] - գաւ J1925	ἐλεπτύνθησαν] - θ η	Chr
-39 om այլ M287 M2627	om ἑτέρα	L-36(51*)-311 590 (=OG)
3:27 ձշմարտութիւն] ձշմարիտ են M2627	ἀλήθεια] αλιθιναι	Q-541 L'-311 c 407 ThtP (=OG)

4:30 զառիւծուց] - ծու   λεόντων] λεοντος   L'49-90-405 410
   J1925   588 (=OG)

5:2 Բագտասար] + արքայ βαλτ.] ο βασιλευς   L'Chr
   J1925

-7 պարանոց] - նոցի   τὸν τράχ.] του   L-88 (=P)
   M178 J1925   τραχηλου

9:14 և M178-M2585   καί ult] διοτι   L" Tht
   J1925-M2627
   V1508] զի rel

11:42 յերկրին] +   γῆν] + αιγυπτου   L(48ᵐᵍ) 46 Tht
   եգպտացւոց
   M346' M2585

-43 յամուրս] pr և   Αἰθιόπων] +και   L'410 Tht
   M346-M2585

(12:9 ἕως καιροῦ πέρας | ε.κ. περατος L-88 Chr (=1895) Tht

Gramatically the meaning of the phrase 'until the time of the end' is unaffected by the morphological variation, the majority adducing the indeclinable form which Lucian has adjusted. However, it may have given rise to the variant մինչև վախճանի ժամանակի 'until the end of time' evinced by M346'-M2585 which have been adduced in support of several other Lucianic readings.)

Table 3b: supplementary examples of agreement with Luc witnesses of individual MSS and smaller groups excluding 95

1:2 Աստուծոյ] տեառն   τοῦ θεοῦ 1°]κυριου   311 ϲ Lᵃᵉ BoAeth
   M346'   Hippol (= P = OG)

2:32 om իւր J1925   om αὐτῆς   538 (OG)

3:19 այրեցին] - զի   ἐκκαῆ] εκκαυθη   Q* 538 410 (=P)
   M346'J1925-
   M2627

-38 ողորմութիւն] +   ἔλεος] + σου   Laᵛʷ Aeth
   ի քէն M178-M346-WN11*   + a te Cypr.

-78 ծով[ք] ծով   θάλασσαι] -σα   V* 36ᶜ-538-449
    M178-M346'-
    M2585 J1925 M182"

4:8 եհաս] հասանէր   ἔφθασεν] εφθανεν   Thtᴾ
    J1925

-33 խնդրէին] - րեցին   ἐζήτουν] εζητησαν Chrˡᵉᵐ(=P)
    J1925 M182'

6:18 զբերանս] - րան   τὰ στόματα]   V 311 261 130
    J1925 M351   το στομα

-22 զբերանս] - րան   τὰ στόμ.]   Aeth Tht (=P=
    J1925-M2627   το στομα   MT)

9:2 [թուոյ] - ng   τὸν / ἀρ.]   62 36-88
    M4834 J1925   των αριθμων

-19 իմ] մեր   μου] ημων   36-538 490 239
    M4834 J1925   Aeth

-20 վասն լերինն սրբոյ om περί - fin   11 230' 584 Tht
    om J1925

11:37 ի վերայ ամենայն π. τους θεους   36-11-88 534
    աստուծոց
    M287' M346'-M2585

WO 4:20 զի իջանէր/   tr ἀπ᾽ οὐρανοῦ ante L-311
    յերկնից]tr J1925   καταβαίνοντα

Table 4a: Arm majority = proto (pre-hexa-plaric)
Luc witnesses

2:13 սպանանել   ἀνελεῖν]αποκτειναι   L'Chr (=P)

3:3 գալ   εἰς τὸν ἐγκαιν.] pr   O L"-zᵛⁱ 410 534
               του ελθειν   588 Arab

-16 և ասեն   λέγοντες]   L¹ (=P=MT)
               και λεγουσι

-38 ողջակէզք   ὁλοκαύτωσις]   Laʷ Verˡᵉᵐ
               holocautomata

-41 զհետ քո   ἐξακολουθοῦμεν] +   L-⁴⁸-88 verssᴾ
               σοι   Thtᴾ Cypr.
                                      test.3,20 (=P)

-74 արհնեցէք և բարձր արարէք	υμνειτε και υπερυψουτε	62 96 405 410 534 Tht^p(=P)
5:8 Թագաւորին] բաբելացւոց M346' -M2585 M2627˙ M182''	τοῦ βασ.] βαβυλωνος	11 La^sAeth
6:7 կամ ի մարդոյ	καὶ ἀνθρ.] η ανθρωπου	L^-36-88 Hippol p.88. 18 Chr Tht
7:16 գճշմարտութիւն	ἀκρίβειαν 2°] αληθειαν	Chr (=P)
-20 եղջերացն	κεράτων La^s] + αυτου rel	La^s (=P =MT)
-23 հարցէ զնա	κατακόψει Aug. civ. 20,23]+ αυτην	62'L''590Bo Aeth Arab Chr Tht (=P =MT)
-26 զիշխանութիւն նորա	τὴν ἀρχήν] + αυτου	L'' 46 Chr Tht (=P=MT)
9:4 զուխտ (+քn M287')	διαθήκην Q L''Aeth^pTht^p] + σου rel	(=P=MT)
-6 առ 2°	ἄρχοντας] pr προs	L''-48Aeth Tht (=P)
-10 ի ձեռն	χερσί] χειρι	L'' Sa Aeth Tht (=P=MT)
-25 պարիսպք	τεῖχοs Clem. Ps Cypr.] περιτειχοs	A'' L'-88 87^c- 49^c -405 46 Sa Chr^lemTht Tert
-27 աւերածոյն	τῶν ἐρημώσεων] τηs ερημωσεωs	L-88-770 Co Arab Hippol^sChr (=1.899)Tht Tert Ir^latx1.78 (=P)
10:12 om πρώτηs		Chr 1.723 (=P7a1)
12:11 տացի	δοθήσεται	B ThtII 1432^p (=P)

Table 4b: Arm Majority = (later)ᵖLuc. witnesses

1:8	ոչ ձաշակել	ὡς οὐ μὴ ἀλισγηθῇ	L'-88 46 Chr (om
		1'] του μη	τοῦ Tht)
		αλισγηθηναι	
3:5	om τῇ χρυσῇ		Aᵗˣᵗ ThtP
-33	եղաբ	ἐγενήθη] εγενηθημεν	VL' -³⁶87-490
	(-V280 M9116)		46 106
4:23	մինչև ծանիցես	ἀφ᾽ ἧς ἂν γνῷς]	11 Bo Arm.
		εως ου γνως	
5:15	և արդ	νῦν οὖν] και νυν	L' verssᴾ (=MT)
6:27	om καὶ πέρατα		Tht
7:7	om αὐτοῦ 2˙		46 Chrˡᵉᵐ
-8	ելանէր	ἀνέβη] - βαινεν	O L'' Chr
			Polychrᶜᵒᵐᵐ Tht
8:7	om πρὸς αὐτόν		147 Chrᶜⁱᵗ˙
11:21	նմա	ἐπ᾽ αὐτόν] αυτω	11 verssᴾ
Bel:11	զդուրս	τὴν θ.] τας θυρας	L
-41	ապապակեաց ...	ἀναβοήσας] -βοησεν	88 534
	և ասէ		

Table 4c: Arm majority = Luc in WO

Sus 61	առնել ընդ	τῷ πλησίον] tr post	L-311-88 410
	ընկերի	ποιῆσαι (v. 62)	588
2:5	վերացաւ յինէն	ἀπ᾽ ἐμοῦ /ἀπέστη] tr	L'-88 verssᴾTht
-8	վերացաւ յինէն	ἀπ᾽ ἐμοῦ /τὸ	L-311
		ῥῆμα] tr	
4:5	գոյ ի նմա	ἐν ἑ. / ἔχει] tr	L-88 Hippol Chr
			Tht (=P)
-26	ձեմէր ի բարելովն	ἐν βαβ. περιπατῶν]	L
		περιπ. ην εν βαβ.	
9:23	ես դու	σὺ εἶ] tr	Q-230''L''87-91
			26 393 410 534
			584 HippolᴬChr

11:2 բեզ գՁշմարտու-   ἀλήθειαν/ἀναγγελῶ   L' verss[P]Chr Tht
    թիւն   σοι] tr

Supplementary agreements with Luc witnesses

2:7 ասացէ արքայ   ὁ βασιλεὺς/ἐιπάτω]   Arab Chr VI. 213
                          tr
-25 գմեկնութիւն պատ-   τὸ σύγκριμα τῷ
    մեցէ արքայի   βασ. ἀναγγελεῖ] το
                          συγκρ. αναγγ.
                          τω βασ.   Chr
-30 ծանիցես գխոր-   τοὺς διαλ. τῆς καρδ. 88 verss[P] Chr
    հուրդս սրտի քո   σου / γνῷς] tr   Tht
3:12 հրամանի քում   βασιλεῦ] tr post   538-88-Z[vi]588
    արքայ   σου 1˚   verss Tht
                                               (=P=MT)
-40 այսաւր առաջի քո   ἐνώπιόν σου /   88
                          σήμερον] tr
4:29 հալածեցեն գբեզ   σε / ἐκδιώξουσι] tr   verss[P] Chr (=P)
6:14 տրտմեցաւ   πολὺ / ἐλυπήθη] tr   1I
-19 յարեաւ արքա   ὁ βασ./ἀνέστη] tr   36-763 verss[P]

Analysis: As the first three tables show, Lucianic affiliation
was much more pronounced in Arm1, although some significant readings have survived the revision. One type which did
not was the larger minus whether preserving the original Th
text against OG encroachment at 9:24 or as the result of secondary *homoeoteleuton* as at 9:20. Other characteristics include the familiar addition of pronoun objects and possessive
pronouns as well as explanatory plusses e.g. արքայ 5:2 and
եզատաց ng 11:42. The titles to the various pericopes, if original to Armenian, should be included in the same category of
readers' aids. Influence of parallels is also noted at 7:7 in table
2b from V. 19 and at 5:8 in table 4a from V.7.

Among the Lucianic witnesses the greatest number of agreements is evinced with the first sub-group (ll) comprising MSS 311-538, while MS 410, whose proximity to P was noted in the appendix to Chapter 4, maintains a similar relationship here. Moreover, Ziegler remarks that Arm often accompanies the Catena sub-group c (49-90-405-764).[7] This link is demonstrated in the foregoing tables. However, in the seven or so instances where the sub-group or its individual members are cited it is usually joined by 311-538.

In his volume on the Dodekapropheton Ziegler classifies the latter as a Catena sub-group with which the Armenian Version is often identified,[8] while 311 especially is regularly Lucianic in the other prophetic books.[9] Moreover, both in the Dodekapropheton and Ezekiel the editor regards the Catena MSS as partly dependent on the Lucianic recension. Thus without wishing to exaggerate the affinities or take them out of context, the ties discernible between Arm c and ll are not without precedent.

The frequent support offered by the Ethiopic Version is probably due to indirect P contact during the version's medieval revision. In addition, there are some interesting cases of agreement with Hippolytus without support from Q-230 (with which his text is closely aligned). At the same time some of these may be due to later scribal correction and not to the patristic commentator.[10]

Arm=Luc=OG: We have observed something of the procedure by which the Antiochian text filled out Th's narrative by borrowing from OG and then transmitted some of these to P. Now we shall consider examples of the same process at work in respect to Arm.

Table 1: Arm = proto-Luc witnesses = OG

2:8 om ἐγώ

62'88 670 verss[P]
Hippol[A] Tht[P]

-10 երկրի	ξηρᾶς] γης	L' verssᴾ Hippol (vid.) (=P)
-17 Ազարիա ... Միսայէլ	Μισαηλ ... Αζαρία] tr	88 C'230 Bo Aeth Hippolˢ Tht
6:2 և 2˙	ὅς] και	L' -538 130 LæˢSa Aeth Arab Tht (=P)
7:17 մեծամեծք	τὰ τέσσαρα] τα μεγαλα	HippolᴬChr
8:4 ի ձեռաց	χειρός] plur.	Laˢ Bo (=P)
-8 այլ չորք եղջիւրք	κέρατα τέσσαρα] ετερα τεσσ. κερ.	538 Bo Or XXXV 208 Lo. Chr
9:26 ոչ իցեն ի նմա	οὐκ ἔστιν ἐν αὐτῷ] ουκ εσται εν αυτω 1.899	ΙΙ C' LaᶜˢArab Chr
11:25 հանդարտեսցէ	στήσονται] στήσεται	V L' C' 46 AethᴾTht (=P=MT)
-32 որ ճանաչէ(ր)	γινωσκοντες] ο γινωσκων	ΙΙ 230" Bo Aethᴾ Arab Chrᶜⁱᵗ

Table 2: Arm=(later) Luc witnesses = OG

Sus:32 հոլանի առնել	ἀποκαλυφθῆναι] αποκαλυψαι	62' L' -311 26 46' (=Pab)
2:40 om ἔσται		c Polychr
3:96 և արդ եւ	καὶ ἐγώ] και νυν (+ ιδου Tht) εγω	Thtᴾ
6:17 մատանեաւ ք	ἐν τῷ δακτυλίῳ] εν τοις δακτυλιους	311 ΙΙ
9:27 բարձցին	ἀρθήσεται	Chr 1.899

Arm also contains a number of OG additions which have, to a varying degree, become the common property of most Th MSS although absent from P. As Lucianic witnesses are usually included in that majority they are the most probable source. However, some of the readings may have entered at Arm2 stage. The major instances are the following:

2:15 Եհարց նա և ասէ   init] pr και   (B-26-239
                               επυνθανετο αυτου   Hippol vid)[12]
                               λεγων

-38 և գձիւնս ծովու   ουρανου] +και τους   (BQ[txt]Q Hippol
                               ιχθυας θαλασσης   Chr Tht)

3:22 Լթնապատիկ   εκ περισσου]+   =36 C'46"106
                              επταπλασιως   230' 407 410 742
                                         Aeth[P] Arab

-61 աղինեցէք ամե-   ευλ. π. η δυναμις]
     նայն զաւրութիւնք   ευλογειτε πασαι αι   (B Clem.)
     Տեառն   δυναμεις κυριου

5:4 և զԱստուածն յա-   fin] +και τον θεον   =B[mg]46" 239 A"
     լիտենիցոչ աղի-   του αιωνος ουκ   11- 88 230" 407
     նեցին որ ունէր   ευλογησαν τον εχον-   410 590 742
     զիշխանու-   τα την εξουσιαν   La[s][13]
     թիւն ոգւոց նոցա   του πνευματος αυτων.

6:18 և եհից Աստուած   fin] + και απεκλει-   (62'L[-36]-499 230
     զբերանս առ-   σεν ο θεος τα στο-   La[s] Hippol (vid.)
     ծուցն և ոչ լլկեցին   ματα των λεοντων   Chr Tht)
     զԴանիէլ   και ου παρηνωχλησαν
                               τω δανιηλ.

11:8 կործանեսցէ   αυτων 1°] +   =B[c]-26-46"-239
                               καταστρεψει   A" 230" Aeth
                                         Arab PolyChr

-20 յարմատոյ նորա   επι] pr εκ της ριζης   (La[cs])
     տունկ   αυτου φυτον

12:10 և սրբեսցին   πολλοι] pr και   =B[c]-26-130-
                               αγιαισθωσι(ν)   239-534 A" 36-
                                         311-770 C' 233'
                                         393 Aeth Arab

-13 զի տակաւին են   αναπαυου] + ετι γαρ   (Ir[lat]Hi.)
     աւուրք և ժամա-   ημεραι και ωραι εις
     նակք ի կատարումն   αναπληρωσιν συντε-
     վախճանի   λειας.

Bel:24 մի թե և զղնամէ   ου δυνασαι] pr μη   (B[txt])
     ասիցես թե պղնձի է,   και τουτον ερεις οτι

ահատասիկ կենդա-   χαλκους εστιν ιδου
նի է, ուտէ և ըմպէ   ζη εσθιει και πινει
-35 ուր իցէ   fin] + που εστι(ν)   (BQ 62 L' ⁻³⁶590
                                              921 Laˢᵛ Bo)

In addition, Arm evinces certain affinities with OG which
are not shared by any extant source.[13] The fact that one of the
most striking examples at Sus:56 բանանու] pr դատնագոդ is
only adduced by V280', prime witnesses to Arm1, strongly
suggests that the following readings of the majority text derive
from the same early stratum.

1:4 անարատու[14]   = ἀμώμους (cf. Th οἷς
                           οὐκ ἔστιν ἐν αὐτοῖς μῶμος)
-4   զաւրաւորս[14]   = ἰσχύοντας (cf. Th οἷς
                           οὐκ ἔστιν ἰσχὺς ἐν αὐτοῖς)
8:5 բաւշին եղջևր մի էր   ἦν τοῦ τράγου κέρας ἕν
                           (Th τῷ τράγῳ κέρας)
-27 արքունի (-J1925)   βασιλικά
     cf. 2:49 where this is the text of MSS V280' M2585 M2627
9:24 անաարէնութեանց   ἀδικίας (Th ἁμαρτίας)
-26 բարձցի   ἀποσταθήσεται
                           (Th ἐξολεθρευθήσεται)
10:4 առ ափն գետոյն   ἐπὶ τοῦ χείλους τοῦ ποταμοῦ
                           (Th ἐχόμενα τοῦ ποταμοῦ)
-4   որ է   ὅς ἐστι (Th αὐτός ἐστιν)

Further possible examples of OG Influence

1:10 զայլոց մանկանցդ   παρὰ τούς ... νεανίας τῶν ἀλλο-
                           γενῶν (Th παρὰ τὰ παιδάρια)
                           cf. v.13 παρὰ τοὺς ἄλλους
                           νεανίσκους
2:14 խաւսեցաւ   εἶπε (Th ἀπεκρίθη)
-43 ի միմեանս   ἀλλήλοις (Th οὗτος μετὰ τούτου)

6:4 զսասնէին	ηὕρισκον (Th εὗρον)
7:6 om αὐτή	
-19 om αὐτοῦ ult.	
10:3 իւղով ոչ աւծայ	ἔλαιον οὐκ ἠλειψάμην
11:2 ի մեծութեան իւրում	ἐν τῷ πλούτῳ αὐτοῦ
-15 ոչ որք իցէ որ ունիցի	οὐκ ἔσται ἰσχὺς εἰς τὸ ἀντιστῆναι
զդեմ նորա	αὐτῷ (Th καὶ οὐκ ἔσται ἰσχὺς τοῦ στῆναι)
-24 և ոչ հարբ	οὐδὲ οἱ πατέρες
	(Th καὶ οἱ πατέρες)
-39 ի պարգևի	εἰς δωρεάν

Commands

1:18 հրամանն եաս[15]	ἐπέταξεν (Th εἶπεν)
2:12 հրամայեաց	προσέταξεν (Th εἶπεν)
-46 հրամայեաց	ἐπέταξε (Th εἶπε)
3:13 հրամայեաց	προσέταξεν (Th εἶπεν)
-22 հրամանն	τὸ πρόσταγμα (Th τὸ ῥῆμα)

The extent and quality of the preceding examples is not such as to justify postulating the regular employment of OG as a translation base for Arm 1. The virtual absence of readings from Chapters 4-6, where OG is so idiosyncratic is of particular significance.[16] Moreover, as much of the material in the second list relates to questions of translation technique, some of its agreements may be coincidental. The remainder were probably conveyed to Arm via an Antiochian codex either as part of the text or in some cases as a marginal note. The greater preoccupation of Lucian with correcting Th towards MT suggests that the OG layer of readings passed into the textual stream at the proto-Lucianic phase.

A further aspect of the proto-Lucianic character of Arm's *Vorlage* is its lack of the major doublets listed by Montgomery. If it shares this feature with OL and P, it also resembles them in witnessing a number of characteristic Lucianic readings without support. As Fischer remarks, the OL in Kgdms

"ist also teilweisen <<lukianischer>> als L, auch wenn
sie andererseits nur etwas über die Hälfte der
Sonderlesen von L enthält."[17]

Of the eight categories Fischer enumerates in his article, seven
can be exemplified in Arm also.[18] Moreover, since they are
mostly preserved only in V280-J2558 and a few other MSS
against the consensus of the majority, the likelihood is that
they represent a facet of Arm1 which has been suppressed in
the revision.

a)   Translation instead of transliteration:
11:45 յապարանս, the example with which we broached the
subject of Lucianic contact.[19]

b)   Influence of Parallels:
1:18 առուրցն] pr երից V280 (երից ամացն J2558) cf. 1:5
2:4 արքայ յաւիտեան կեաց ասա դու] ասասցէ արքայ[20] cf. 2:7
2:47 գխորհուրդս] + սիրողաց իւրոց
                cf. Wisdom 6:13 Դիւրաւ երևի սիրողաց իւրոց
5:23 և ոչ գնան M287[mg] M178 -M346'-M2585
                cf. Ps.113:7 (v.15 in Gk) ոսս ունին, և ոչ գնան
Bel:14 ամենայն մեհեանն] յատակատ մեհենին   cf. v.19

c)   Subject/Object expressed:
Sus:23 գայդ] + զգործդ M287"
1:14 նոցա] + ամեղասադ   (Aeth[P])

d)   Proper name instead of a pronoun:
Sus:19 նորա] շուշանայ   see also v. 27

e)   Explanatory additions to smooth the sense:
Sus:1և 2'] pr յորդւոցն իսրայէլի
-15 էր ult] + ժամն
2:36 երագն] pr արքայի
-37 դու] + արքայ
-41 խառնեալ] + ի նմա
4:21 արքայի] + ի ձեռն տեառն ամենակալի
-28 յերկնից] + և աւեր

5:1 արքայ] որդին նաբուքոդոնոսորայ

-4 ունէր] տրւիչն է բարեաց և որ ունի V280 (և ունի J2558)

-23 ձանապարհ քո] + առաջի աչաց նորա

-26 իմ ng] + դարեհ արքայի

7:1 իւրում] + տագնապեաց զնա

Bel:30 թագաւորն] pr կիւրոս

f)   Intensifying additions:

Sus:43 ապա] + ի զուր

4:22 թագաւորութեան] pr ամենայն

9:9 բնակչաg] pr ամենայն

11:32 ածեն] pr hqop

-33 զաւուրս] + բազում

Bel:25 է] pr միայն

g)   Stylistic improvements:

1)   Omission of tedious repetitions:

1:11 Անանիա և Միսայելի և Ազարիայի] ընկերաց նորին

The existence of a Greek *Vorlage* for these singular read-ings, as for their P and OL counterparts which we have already discussed, is necessarily conjectural. Moreover, studies of Arm1's translation technique in other books reveal a greater maleability in its form of expression, unrestricted by Gk's mor-phological and syntactic encodement.[21] At all events, this final table serves to reinforce the Lucianic orientation of Arm1, re-vealing further traits held in common with the pre-hexaplaric P and OL as well as opening up fresh examples of Antiochian bib-lical exegesis.

Arm 1's affinity to P and Luc: It is axiomatic not to proliferate the hypothetical stages a text has passed through without compelling evidence. Here on the contrary there are some posi-tive indications to suggest that Arm's contact with P and Luc belongs to the same early stratum of tradition.

While both P (ܠܗ, ܫܬ ܗ) and Th (τοῦ πότου αὐτοῦ) agree at 1:5 and 1:8, it is significant that Arm follows P's rendering in the first instance (զոր ինքն ումպէր) and Th in the second (ումպելոյ նորա). The same type of metaphrastic variety of expression is observable at 11:11,12 where P in both verses reads ܠܐ as Th evinces ὄχλος. Arm in contrast supports P in the first instance rendering զառ and Th in V.12 with ամբոխ.

The process of interweaving is more explicit at 10:9 where Th=MT reads καὶ τὸ πρόσωπόν μου ἐπὶ τὴν γῆν. P employs the more vivid verbal expression ܐܦܝ ܠܐ ܐܦ ܠܐ ܐܪܥܐ. Although not a direct translation of P, Arm's reading և երեսք իմ յերկիր խոնարհեալ seems to have been influenced by it.

The process is slightly more complicated in the following example. Perplexed by his visions, Daniel, turning to one of the visitants, seeks an explanation from him in similar terms at 7:16 and 19.

7:16 Th τὴν ἀκρίβειαν ἐζήτουν παρ' αὐτοῦ (+ μαθειν BᶜA''88 410
                                                590 Chr)

    P ܠܗ ܠܐ ܐܬܒܩܐ ܢܝܙܐ ܠܐ
v. 19 Th ἐζήτουν ἀκριβῶς

    P ܐܬܒܩܢܬ ܢܓܝ ܢܝܙܐ

Arm 7:16 զճշմարտութիւնն (կամէի M287' M178 կամեցայ
                         M4834: խնդրէի rel)
- 19 բնէի (ճշմարիտ M287 ճշմարտիւ rel)

The addition shared by certain Luc witnesses in V.16 which seems to be the result of a misplacement from V.19 (cf. P=MT) is obviously the source of Arm's reading ուսանէլ. However, the Armenian tradition is split over the identity of the verb on which that infinitive is dependent. A form from կամէլ commends itself as the reading of Arm1 both on grounds of manuscript authority and proximity to P in V.19 (ܢܓܝ). On the other hand խնդրէլ is Arm2's regular translation equivalent for ζητεῖν. Similarly, it is likely that the choice of Arm's verb բնէի in V.19 was influenced by that found in P in both instances (ܐܬܒ) which in addition to 'seek' can mean 'dispute, discuss'. However, there can be no doubt that Arm's continuation is based on Th which in common with some MT MSS, interpreted

ליצבא as 'truth' and not as the *pa'el* infinitive 'to ascertain' = P. It is difficult to conceive how Arm1's eclectic translation process could have been orchestrated without simultaneous resource to both P and Luc.

Montgomery's Textual Classification: Before treating in detail Arm2's affinities with Th witnesses, it is necessary to clarify the framework within which these relationships may be evaluated. Obviously the mere enumeration of agreements with isolated MSS would tell us little about Arm's textual complexion and consequent placing within the book's entire transmission history. Two attempts have been made to present a systematic picture of its textual development which, while sharing much of the general outline, diverge at points which are crucial to our understanding of the Armenian Version. It is therefore expedient to give a brief, critical account of their outline.

Montgomery,[22] whose reconstruction forms the reference point for the work of his pupils, Wyngarden and Gehman, espouses a two-tier theory according to which the primitive Th text evolved into three local texts, those of Egypt, Palestine and Syria. The second phase is marked by the dissemination of the Hexapla and its convergence with each of the local texts. The Lucianic recension was the fruit of this union in Syria, the Hesychian in Egypt and the Constantinopolitan in Palestine.

The Hexapla in its pristine Origenic form is best preserved by the group V62-147 to which Montgomery ascribes the siglum OR^P. In its more advanced form (Or^c) it is extant in AQ 106 35 230 42 followed by the Arabic and Bohairic versions (to which Gehman would add the Armenian version). After initial indecision about how to provide a historical setting for the second phase he came under the influence of Margolis' proposition for Joshua which ultimately rests on a hypothesis of Conybeare regarding the nature of the exemplar the Armenians brought from Constantinople. This was held to be one of the fifty copies prepared by Eusebius of Caesarea for Constantine.

Notwithstanding the elaborateness of the theory, Montgomery confesses that "we possess no detail about the Eusebian edition."[23] However, if he gives the impression towards the end that the proposed historical superstructure is expendable, he emphasizes the validity of the textual distinction between Pr^p and Or^c of which it is supposed to be the external expression.

Since Or^p evinces no Lucianic characteristics, agreements between these recensions imply Lucianic dependence. Moreover, the contention is that intersections between Lucian and the Or^c recension are not due to direct contact but since they are limited to material found in Or^p, such readings passed independently into the later streams from that source. The Hesychian recension is, on the contrary, the main device by which Q variations from the rest of Or^c are explained. Of the remainder the Arabic Version is felt to be the best representative owing to A's many solecisms. The whole may be portrayed diagramatically as follows:

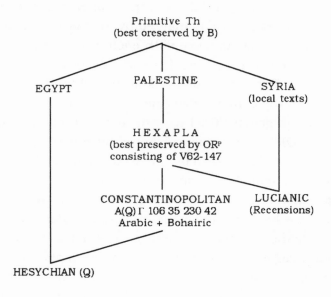

In the introduction to his edition Ziegler subjects the above *Gestalt* to methodical scrutiny which leads him to reject the handling of the Hexapla and Constantinopolitan recension. He questions whether Origen played any part in Th's textual evolution and, if so, how this might be recovered. Origen's main efforts had been expended on the OG text as indicated by the critical symbols retained by the Syrohexapla. By contrast MSS 62-147 which are classed as the best witnesses to the Origenic text of Th are completely lacking in both obelus and asterisk.[24]

Moreover, the type of changes towards MT do not seem to be in accord with Origen's usual practice, although in Montgomery's opinion,[25] "The Aquilianic earmarks are just such as we know were introduced by Origen in his revision." To Ziegler they appear too pedantic in points of detail to be ascribed unreservedly to Origen and therefore he countenances the possibility that they are the work of a later corrector.

While he agrees that these additions antedate the Lucianic recension which (with a certain amount of adaptation) makes use of them, he denies their effect on Q and raises the usual question as to what exactly constitutes the Hesychian recension. In his estimation Q is closely related to B and frequently reads the primitive text. Hexaplaric contacts as in the case of B are not particularly important.[26] The miniscule 230 which is Q's frequent satellite also has a strain of agreements with Hippolytus which are similarly prehexaplaric.

The unevenness of the components of Or^c for Ziegler disqualified it from being classed as a group. First he queries the extent to which A has been coloured by the Hexapla noting that A "[hat] ofter ohne Ruchsicht auf nach dem Sinn geändert; vielfach waren Parallelstellen massgebend."[27] The close relationship the uncial usually shared with the Arabic Version was likewise tenuous. The final linchpin in Montgomery's thesis concerning the exclusivity of Or^p as the locus for agreements between Lucian and the Constantinopolitan recension is also challenged by a series of cases where A and Q individually and jointly are dependent on the Lucianic reading where Or^p is absent and therefore cannot have acted as mediator.

Gehman's Treatment of Arm Affinities: As a result Ziegler abandons the neatness and simplicity of Montgomery's reconstruction in favour of a more cautious approach which does more justice to the complicated textual prehistory of most of the MSS. This obviously has immediate repercussions for our estimate of Gehman's conclusions particularly as his fundamental declaration that Arm belongs to Or^c is stated as a *fait accompli* at the commencement of his article without argument or illustration.[28] The main burden of his presentation is the proof that within the recension Arm's closest affinity is with the Egyptian group represented by Q-230. Ziegler's reassessment of the minor significance of hexaplaric influence in these MSS goes some way towards solving one of the problems facing Gehman's opening thesis. The latter proposes that "in a few cases the translator either removed the Hexaplaric additions or had a MS in which they were lacking.[29] However, the former alternative is as incompatible with Arm's translation technique as the latter is with the version's suggested affinity to Or^c.

The narrowness of Gehman's focus, giving significance only to members of Or^c and deliberately ignoring other support for a given reading, automatically prejudices his results. Thus in commenting on the absence of ὁ θεός from Armenian at 5:21 he remarks that this coincides with the reading of four Lucianic MSS whereas of Or^c only A and 230 are found in agreement. Yet such cases do not prompt him to reconsider the definitiveness of his opening statement concerning Arm's affinity. Similarly, variations between the 'Hesychian' and A branches of Or^c achieve larger than life proportions. Where the range of witnesses is limited to eight, Arm's stance over against anomalous readings of A, e.g. its plus προσευχομένου at 9:21 (a parallel from V.20) may be accorded a certain significance. But as evidence for Arm's special relationship with Q-230 this is hardly convincing when it is observed that it is shared at the same time by the overwhelming preponderance of the tradition of both Th and OG.

Another weakness in Gehman's treatment of Arm is his failure to take seriously the divergences within its manuscripts as revealed by Zohrab's apparatus and its possible impact on a unitary theory of translation and transmission. Recognizing disparate elements within the present texture of the version, Syriac and OG parallels, supposed hexaplaric affiliation and the absence of several of its additions as well as Or[P] and Lucianic agreements over Or[c], he makes no allowance for them in his overall assessment. Basing himself purely on material in print he nevertheless feels able to conclude: "No doubt Mesrop and Sahak's final recension is the prototype of all the Armenian MSS."[30]

With regard to the execution of his study it is also necessary to exercise care in checking the accuracy of Gehman's collations as there as several discrepancies between his presentation and that of Ziegler over the readings of MSS which are key to the issue the reading was chosen to illustrate.

Arm's Affinity with the Hexapla: Turning to the evidence collected during the present study we shall first try to determine Arm's orientation vis-à-vis the Hexapla, since in Gehman's opinion the version is to be classified in a group heavily dependent on Origen's *magnum opus,* a view frequently reiterated as a generalization for the whole OT in text critical introductions.[31] However, it is only fair to say at the outset that in some respects Daniel constitutes an exception to the rule. Ziegler's remarks upon the elusive nature of the recension and unusual character of the additions has been noted. To this we should add the break in patterns of textual affiliation observable in other witnesses, e.g. the miniscule 26, a regular satellite of A, here reads with B, while the Arabic Version is also estranged from A.

Of the twenty readings marked with an asterisk in Th Daniel,[32] Arm contains four, three of which could easily have been mediated by P and one of those most probably. Only the first instance is necessarily from Greek (failing direct contact with MT which is extremely unlikely) and that has the backing of the manuscript majority.

1)　　2:16 Δανιηλ B-26 Q-541 Aethp Hippol vid (=P)] εισηλθεν δαν. και　A Polychr (om και); intravit Bo; + εισηλθε(ν) (εξηλθε Chr) και rel=MT.

2)　　7:10 αὐτῷ various] εμπροσθεν αυτου Q L'' C' 106 233 393 407 534 584 590 La⁼ Sa Aethᴾ Arab Arm Eus Chr (=1.294ᴾ) Lucif =MT (=P)

3)　　11:36 θεόν B-26-130-239　La꜀ˢ Sa Hippol Consult] + και επι (> 764) τον θεον των θεων rel =MT (=P)

4)　　3:3 τῆς εἰκόνος　2˙ B-26-46' 239 Q 380 410 aethᴾ Hippol] + ης (pr. aureae Bo Aethᴾ) εστησε(ν) (+ ὁ 88) ναβουχοδονοσορ (+ ο βασιλευς V233 Bo Arm=P A'' V111 Zᵛⁱ C' 233' 393 407 534 588 verss = MT

Arm has few significant agreement with Ziegler's Q group since their convergence coincides with the mass of witnesses. Even when this is not the case there is usually outside support, while the Q group is incomplete, such readings being mainly found only in 62-147, e.g. 8:19 τῆς ὀργῆς] της γης 62'48 91ᵗˣᵗc 410 (ի վերայ երկրի Arm). Some examples of this type agree with MT: these usually comprise small points of grammatical interest, e.g. 7:8 τοῖς] pr. εν 62' La⁼ Arab Arm Lucif.=MT. This is not a real variant from an Armenian point of view since the Greek compound verb προσενόουν already contains a prepositional element within itself which Armenian has to express separately.[33] As a result it is unjustifiable to argue that Arm had a different *Vorlage.* Other MT agreements may have entered via P, e.g. 7:4 ἀνθρώπου 1˚] pr ως 62' = MT (=P ܠܗ). Moreover, other variants have no contact with MT and are likely pre-hexaplaric, e.g. 3:41 καρδία] + ημων 62' verss[P] *Cypr.* Fulg. p. 360. As Cyprian was an older contemporary of Origen his text was probably pre-recensional. Judging from the insignificance of both the number and calibre of Arm's agreements with the Q group, it must be assumed that the base text of its revision must have been of a different type.

Arm's Affinity with MT: This conclusion is fully justified by a scrutiny of the whole body of readings where Arm=Th=MT as noted in Ziegler's edition. Of some 80 cases listed 39 concern the presence or absence of the copula, 14 the addition of possessive pronouns with nouns and 3 the addition of objective pronouns after verbs. If we further exclude agreements over the singular/plural number of χεῖρ and the presence /absence of πᾶς, the remainder amounts to only 12 cases of which all but one could have emanated from P.

1)   2:3 ἠνυπνιάσθην] + ενυπνιον Q* -233' L' -88 Co Aeth Arm Tht cf. MT.   In fact Arm's reading is a direct translation of P ܠܡ ܚܠܡ

2)   2:34 om ἐξ ὄρους Q 233' 670 Arm Hippol p. 56, 18 et 68, 10 Ath. 111 968 Ir.[lat] p.118 395 = MT (=P).

3)   3:5 καὶ παντός B-26-46' Q-541 c 380 407 Aeth Hippol] + συμφωνιας C; pr και συμφωνιας rel = MT cf. 710 15 (=P).

4)   3:18 τῇ εἰκόνι B 87[txt] La[w] Spec. Aug.] + τη χρυση   rel (Cypr.) =MT (=P).

5)   6:27 ἐπὶ τῆς γῆς] εν τη γη 1l 230 La[ɇ] Cypr. = MT (=P).

6)   7:2 ἐθεώρουν B-26-46' La[ɇ] Aeth Hippol Cyr. V 253 Lucif. Prisc.] + εν οραματι (-μασι 233); ορασει 239 407 534 Tht; τη

ορασει L" 590 Chr) μου (>A" 541 Bo Arm) της νυκτος (+ ιδον 393) rel =MT (=P).

7)   7:10 εἰλκεν various] + εκπορευομενος Q L" C' 233 393 407 534 590 Bo Arab Arm Chrᴵᵉᵐ (= 1294 πορ.) PolyChr Tht = MT (=P).

8)   7:14 αυτω δουλευσουσιν (- σωσιν 62' 230) Q L -311-449 C 26 106 230' 393 (+ και υπακουονται :ex 27) 407 534 Arm Eus eccl. theol. etc. Marc. Chr (=1828) Cyr. VI 284 VII 656 VIII 648 1048 IX 933 X 309. Tht Aug. civ. 18, 34 = MT (=P).

9)   10:9 αὐτοῦ 2˙B-26-239 Laᶜˢʷ Sa] Q L'-³⁶ AethᴾChr Tht; pr φωνην (-νης 584; την φ. Q; της φ. των 36-88 c 230) ρηματων rel = MT (=P).

10)   10:10 fin.] + και ταρσους χειρων (pedum Arab) μου A" Q-230" Q C' 534 Arab Arm = MT (=P).

11)   12:1 ὁ γεγραμμένος B Q Lᴸ⁻³⁶ Laˢ Or. 1110 Cyr. Hieros. p. 893 Ambr. exc. Sat. 2, 66] pr ο ευρεθεις A" Q* 36; ο ευρεθεις γεγρ. rel. (Chr 1895 Aug. civ. 20, 23 et 22, 3 Fulg. p. 655) = MT (=P).

12)   12:7 γνώσονται B-26 Laˢ Aeth Hippol Cypr. Irᴵᵃᵗ] pr και 130 239; 46; pr χειρος (>A) λαου ηγιασμενου (αγιου 393? = o'; + καιA) A" Q-230" Q || C' 393 410 534 Bo Arab Arm = MT.

In fact MT reads שדק םע די while P renders ܠܒܝ ܪܩܚ ܠܒܐ ܐܡܪ ܠܝ . The presence of the participle սրբեցելոյ instead of the simple adjective սուրբ is clear proof that Arm was dependent on the Greek reading.

    Three further cases of Arm agreement with MT without Th support (2:26 om καί, 5:12 om σοι, 5:29 om περιέθηκαν Armᴾ)³⁴ are shared by P which, considering the extent of its influence on Arm1 and its regular parallelism of instances where Arm=Th=MT, must be considered the main source of MT readings in Arm. Thus such readings have an *a priori* claim to be regarded as a feature of the earliest phase of the version rather than its Greek revision.

The most serviceable type of variant for delineating the character of Arm2 is that where the Armenian tradition is bifurcated in such a way that when Arm1=P or Luc Arm2 supports a minority Greek reading. In very many cases where Arm1=P, Arm2 evinces the undivided Th reading and where Arm1=Luc, Arm2 is engulfed in the amorphous mass of Th witnesses. Nevertheless, examples of the kind required do occur and present a reasonably consistent picture of Arm2's exemplar, e.g.

a)   2:41 ի խեգոյ ... յերկաթոյ   =P =MT
        M287 M2585 M2627' M182'']   =Q-230' 449 ͼ 239
          tr. rel   Hippol[A]

b)   3:27 ӡշմարիտ են M2627]   =Q-541 <u>L</u>'-311 ͼ 407
                            Tht^P = <u>o</u>' [35]
        ӡշմարտութիւն rel   =B-46' A[36]V-62
                            Aeth Aug. ep. 111,
                            3 Fulg. p. 360

c)   4:14 տէր է M287' J1925']   = P
        տիրէ rel   =230'' 407 Tht^P

d)   4:19 յերկինս M287'' J1925']   =P (except 7a1)
        pr մինչև rel.   εἰς τὸν οὐρανόν]
                            εως τον ουρανον
                            230 712
                            εως του ουρανου
                            311 541

e)   4:28 ասեն M287]   = P
        ասեմ rel   = 106 584 Aeth^P

f) 7:9 իբրև գձիւնն/սպիտակ   =P=MT Clem.
    M287']tr rel   = tr. 538 87 230' verss
                                   Hippol^P Eus eccl. theol.
                                   Ps. Aeth. Bas IV380 Cyr
                                   Hieros p. 900 Chr^lem
                                   (=1 294 V776) PsChr IX
                                   736 Tht^cit Lucif Ps Vig

Just as OL readings continued to be copied in Vulgate MSS, so there are occasions where Arm1 seems to have made more impression on the manuscript tradition than the revised text.[37]

g) 11:15 ոչ 1˙ M287" M178-   =P=MT
    M346-WN11*-M2585 M182^mg-
    V1508^mg-M351
    om J1925' M2627' M182^txt-   =B 88 106
    V1508^txt-WN11^c

h) 12:2 ի հող M287' M178-M346'- =P=MT
    M2585 M9116-M2627' M182"
        ի հողոյ M4834 J1925   =231 91 26 230"
                                   534 594 Hippol^A
                                   Constit^P

lesser examples

i) 6:14 և վասն Դանիէլի ջանայր   =P=MT
    վ. Դ. և ջանայր M4834   =230
    J1925-M2627 M182"

j) 8:19 ի ժամանակս է վախճանն
    M287' M178-M346'-   =P=MT
    M2585 M9116-M2627'
    M182"
        ի ժամանակս է տեսիլ (-լ տ M4834) վախճանի
    M4834 J1925 =fin + η ορασις B-26 A' 62' 230" 534
    La^w Sa Arab Hippol

Although the minority variant adduced by M4834 and J1925 is not an exact reflection of the Greek reading set out below, it is very likely dependent upon it. The revisers, being uncertain about how to construe the addition, decided to alter the syntax in order to make better sense.

k)	9:20	զմեղս ժողովրդեան	τοῦ λαοῦ μου Ισραηλ]
		Իսրայէլի rel	
		զմեղս ժողովրդեան իմոյ	om μου 764* 233'
		M2627	Hippol⁵ Tht^P

As P agrees with the Th reading at this point and granted the conservative nature of MS M2627,[38] it is reasonable to suggest that Arm1 contained both elements (i.e. ժողովրդեան իմոյ Իսրայէլի). If so, the possessive adjective subsequently dropped out of the revised text under the influence of a Greek exemplar of the type cited above.

When we compute the number of times the same witness appears in the 13 examples the main results are as follows: 230 (8), 233 (7), 541 (5), Hippolytus (5), Theodoret (3), 106 (3), B (3). The first three MSS with the highest scores frequently read together and are classed as satellites of Q by Ziegler although the latter occurred only once.

Hippolytus' frequent occurrence with the group is illuminated by Ziegler's monograph[39] devoted to the commentary. There he lists a number of examples where Hippol=Q=B. In addition, out of 89 cases where Hippol=B, 44 also find support from Q, regularly accompanied by 230-233-541. Moreover, of 80 instances of agreement with minuscules only 230 scores (35), 541 (19), 584 (18), 239 (17), 233 (12). As a result, he concludes that while regularly a witness to the B text, Hippolytus has a close relationship with Q and 230. The implication is therefore that Arm2's exemplar most resembled MS 230 (with which the version shares readings without outside support) and, from a more generic perspective, belonged to the text type represented by the Q satellites.[40]

In order to test the general validity of this finding, we shall survey the version's affinities with Ziegler's remaining textual classifications, commencing with the Catena Group (C̲ 87-91-490: c̲ 49-90-405-764). As is immediately apparent, links between them are rather tenuous since the readings are mostly minor and frequently adduced by MSS of various textual types, so that no direct contact can be established.

1a) agreements with C̲ (+c̲)

Sus:14 om καί 3˙	C̲' 541 Co
3:94 δυνάσται]δυνατοι	C̲ 239 (=Arm զաւրաւորք)
7:25 παλαιώσει] πλανησει	36-770 C̲ 26 46" 239 410 590
	(մոլորեցուցէ)
	Aeth Arab Hippol Polychr
9:8 om ἐν	C̲' 26 239 584
Bel:1 ψευδόμενος]ψευσαμ.	AQV 36-11 C' 46" LaᵛBo (որ սուտ
	խաւսեցաւ)
-33 ἄρτους] αρτον	C̲ (hաg⁴¹)

1b) agreements with C MSS

Sus:52 եւ 1˙] om M2627' M182"-CHB5: om δέ 91ᶜ

2:23 μου] ημων 87ᵗˣᵗ 584 LaᶜAethᴾ (հարցն մերոց)

-28   αἱ ὁράσεις] η ορασις 538 87ᵗˣᵗ 584 verssᴾ Thtᴾ (տեսիլ)
                                                  (=P≠ MT)

5:29 περί 1˙] επι 490-405 230 Aethᴾ Arab (=P) (ի պարանոց)

8:19 καιροῦ] καιρους 87ᶜ-91   (ժամանակս)

1c) agreements with c

2:5 διαρπαγήσονται]   εις διαρπαγην (+ εσονται c̲ Arm)
                                      Qc Bo Arm (լինիցին)

3:1 εὖρος] pr. καιQ 62' L̲" c̲46 239 verss Chr Tht
                                      (և լայնութիւն: =P≠MT)

-31 ἡμῖν ἐπήγαγες] tr V 538-449 87-c̲ 106 239 534
                        verss Ps. Chr 111, 818
                        ածեր ի վերայ մեր
                        Aug ep. 111, 3. Fulg p. 360

(=P)10:14 om ἔτι   A'O̲ c̲46' 230 Aeth

1d)   agreements with c̲ MSS

3:40 ἐκτελέσαι] -λεσθαι   V 49-90-405 233   լինել կատարեալ

2a)   agreements with A and satellites 106-584

2:30 om τοῦτο A''

4:18 καί 1° Spec] > A'' 46' Bo Aeth^P (=P=MT)

6:20 φωνῇ ἰσχυρᾷ B-26-534 538 Laˢ (vid) Arab]

φωνη μεγαλη A'' 46' 230' 239 590 Bo Aeth (ի ձայն մեծ)

7:1 ἔτει πρώτῳ Bᵐᵍ A'' verssᴾ (=P=MT)]

τω πρωτω ετει rel.   (յամին առաջներորդի)

8:18 πίπτω] pr εθαμβηθην

A'' 538-449 26 46'' (om και 534)

Sa Aeth Arab Hippol (ex 17)   (յիմարեցա և անկա)

2b)   agreements with A-106

2:8 om καί 1° A' 46' Bo (=P=MT)

10:20 ἐπιστρέψω] -στρεφω A' 46'   (դառնամ)

12:7 ἥμίσυ] pr εις A'   (ի կէս)

2c)   agreements with A

Sus:10 ἀνήγγειλαν BL-311] ανηγγελλον AQ;   (շ)պատմեին

απηγγειλαν rel.

3:5 om τῇ χρυσῇ A^ᵗˣ¹ Tht^P

The conclusions formed about Arm's relation to the Catena Group apply here also. As the focus is broadened A's agreements with Arm increase, signifying that A type readings played little part in the composition of Arm2's exemplar.

3a)   agreements with 106-584

3:4 γλῶσσαι] pr και   106 233 584 verssᴾ (=P=MT)

(և լեզուք)

4:4 γαζαρηνοί, χαλδαῖοι]

γαζ. και χαλδ.   538 106 584 verssᴾ Hippolˢ (=P)

(եղձք և բաղդեայք)

11:40 καιροῦ] καιρω   106 534 584 Arab Tht^P (=P=MT)

(ի) ժամանակի

3b) **agreements with 106**

1:18 om ὦν   106 239 407ᶜ

4:32 om αὐτῷ   106

12:12 init] pr και   106   (և երանի)

3c) **agreements with 584**

Sus:18 εἶπε] + αυταις   584 588 verssᴾ   (ասաց ցնոսա =P)

2:23 μου] ημων   87ᵗˣᵗ 584 Laᶜ Aethᴾ cf. Table 1b

-28 αἱ ὁράσεις] η ορασις   538 87ᵗˣᵗ 584 verssᴾ Thtᴾ
                               cf. Table 1b

-35 ὁ χρυσός] pr και   584 verss (=P=MT) (և ոսկին)

-40 πάντα] tr post δαμάσει   584 Arab (=P)   (մալէ զամենայն)

3:15 om καί   584 =MT

-91 ἤκουσεν] pr ως   584   (իբրև լուաւ)

6:23 ἐπ᾽ αὐτῷ] εν αυτω   584   (յանձն իւր)

8:14 δισχίλιαι] χιλιαι   26 584 Hippol (հազար
                               M4834ᵐᵍ M346'-M2585 M182')

11:8 πᾶν] pr και   584 Bo Aeth Hippol (և զամենայն)

-26 κατακλύσει] κατακαυσει   130 239 534 584 (այրեսցեն)

Arm's agreements with the minuscules 106 and 584 are more numerous and important. However, the fact that they coincide with Arm when alone or in concert with other minuscules only serves to emphasize Arm's distance from A and proximity to the secondary witnesses of BQ.

4a) **agreements with B and satellites (26-46-130-239) La Sa Aeth Hippol**

2:39 βασιλεία] tr ἑτερα   B 538 verssᴾ(այլ թագաւորութիւն)

3:23 τῆς καμίνου B-26-46'-239 LaʷSa Hippol] + του πυρος rel
                               (հնոցն)   = MT

-70 πάχναι] παχνη   B 62 88 Co Arab (եղեմն)

5:17 καὶ εἶπε(ν) Δαν. B-25-46'239 Las Aeth] τοτε
     απεκριθη δαν. A; τοτε δαν. απεκριθη και ειπεν 11: τοτε
     απεκριθη δαν. και ειπεν rel (tr καὶ εἶπεν post βασιλέως
                               230 410 584) = MT
                               (և ասէ Դանիէլ)

9:2   init B-26-130-239 230 La^w Sa Aeth Hippol Eus dem
(vid) Tert 11 2276] pr εν ετει ενι (> 46; + επι L-311)
της βασιλειας αυτου rel (Tht = 11 857) = MT

-20   ἁγίου B-239 106 Hippol] + αυτου 490; + μου του θεου 91; +
του (> Q) θεου μου (ημων 36* 233 = OG) rel = MT

11:5   fin. B-26-130-239 La^w Aeth (=P)] + επ (επι 11; εκτος L'46
Tht; >87*) εξουσιας (- σιαν 147 87*) αυτου rel = MT

-14   τῶν λοιμῶν] των λοιπων B-26-130 534 230" Arab
                             (մնացելոց ng)

-23   αὐτοῦ] αυτους   B-26 La^{cs} Bo (նոցա)

-24   λογισμούς B-26-46'-239 La^{sw} Aeth^P] + αυτου
        rel = MT   (խորհուրդն)

-36   καὶ ὑψ. ὁ βασ. καὶ με. B-26-46'$^{'}$-239-233 La^{æs} Co.
Consult.]
    και υψ. και μεγ. ο βασ. A"; ο βασ.
    και μεγ. L-88 Tht = MT; και ο βασ. υψ.
    και μεγ. Q-230' Q11 - 770 C' 410 534 Aeth (vid.) Arab
    Chr I 895 (om ο βασ.). Polychr

-44   om καὶ τοῦ ἀναθεματίσαι   B-26-130-239 La^s Sa:
homoeotel.

12:10 ἄνομοι 2° B^{txt}-26-130 Aeth] παντες ασεβεις (ամնարտելիք)
L' 46 Chr (παντες οι ασ. cit) Tht;
δυνατοι 11; pr παντες rel = MT

The above instances are of greater value in delineating the character of Arm2's exemplar than those of any other manuscript group reviewed so far. The scope of the agreements extends beyond those where B probably contains the primitive text of Th to encompass examples where it evinces secondary scribal mistakes (e.g. the readings at 11:14 and 11:44). However those cases are particularly noteworthy where Arm supports B over against additions and other subsequent changes to bring Th closer to MT. This confirms our previous conclusion that most MT agreements were transmitted to Arm via P in the first phase of the translation. Similar examples may be offered where Q joins the B group.

3:4 λαοί B(λαοις) 26-130-239 Qᵗˣᵗ Aeth Hippol]
  > 410; pr εθνη rel (Chr 11 64) (աqqp)

-36 ἐλάλησας B-26-239 Q 449ᵐᵍ 233 410 Laʷ Arm Aug.
  ep. 111, 3 Ver] + προς αυτους A; + eis Sy Syp;
  + προς αυτους λεγων Q C' 46" 106 407 541 Bo Arab
  Thtᴾ: ex OG + αυτοις λεγων L" (449ᵗˣᵗ) Aeth
  Thtᴾ; + pollicens Laᵛ (խաւսեցար)

4:1 fin B-26-46 Q 590 Aeth HippolA] + εν τω θρονω
  μου 230" 584; + επι του θρονου μου και πιων εν
  τω λαω μου L' 588 Chr Tht; lect dupl.; + επι του
  θρονου μου rel. = OG cf. MT.

-5 ᾧ B-26-46' Q 410 Aeth Hippol] και το ενυπνιον
  ενωπιον (> 147) αυτου (αυτω pro ενωπιον αυτου
  230"; tr το ενυπνιον ενωπ. αυτου post ειπα 239)
  rel = MT (gnn)

7:20 τρία B-26-239 Q-230 Laˢ Hippol Lucif.]
  + και (> 410 541 Bo) το κερας εκεινο L' 46ᶜ 233'
  410 590 Bo Arab Chr Tht = MT; + κεπας εκεινο
  rel. (Aug. civ. 20, 23) (qերիսն)

8:5 κέρας B-26-130 Q Laˢʷ Aeth Hippol Or.]
  pr εθεωριτο (sic) 230; + εν (ex OG = Arm)
  θεωρητον L Tht; + θεωρητον rel. = MT (եղջևր)

-22 αὐτῶν B-130-239 Q* Laˢʷ Aeth (=P)] -του rel
  = MT (իրենանց)

In a fewer number of cases A joins the B group

8:27 ἐμαλακίσθην B-26 A 410 Laˢʷ Co Hippol] +
  επι (> 230) ημερας πολλας 230" Aethᴾ = OG:
  + ημερας rel = MT (խաւթացա)

11:39 ἀλλοτρίου B-26-239 A'Laᶜˢ Sa Aethᴾ] + ον
  (+ ουκ 88) εγνωρισε(ν) L'⁻³⁶ Tht; + ου (ους
  Q 584; ους 62) εαν (αν Q-541 62 410 584)
  επιγνω (επεγνω 541; + ον εγνωρισεν 36) rel = MT (աւտարի)

4b) **agreements with B**

2:30 τῷ βασιλεῖ / γνωρίσαι B] tr   (գուցանելոյ արքայի)
3:33 τὸ στόμα] + ημων B verss   (qբերանս մեր)

4:4   om εγω B Arab

-17   ἔφθασεν] εφθανεν B   (հասանէր)

12:11 δοθήσεται B Tht 11 1432ᵖ(=P≠MT) (տացի)

4c)   agreements with 26

3:10   ἔθηκας] εδωκας 26 380   (եդուր: but հրաման տալ is
                                                Armenian idiom)

5:19   om αὐτός 1˚ 26 verssᵖ

11:29 om καὶ ὡς 26

Bel:8 αὐτοῖς] + ο βασ. 26   (ցնոսա թագաւորն)

4d)   agreements with 46 (+130)

3:44   δυναστείας Aug. ep. 111, 8 Ver] +   (րնութենէ իւրեանց)
         αυτων 46' verssᵖ (=P)

5:16   ἐπὶ τὸν τράχηλον] εν τω τραχηλω 46'   (ի պարանոցի)
         verssᵖ (=P)

7:7   om αὐτοῦ 2˚ 46 Chrⁱᵉᵐ

4e)   agreements with 239

6:28   om ἐν τῇ βασιλείᾳ 2˚ 239

9:5   ἠδικήσαμεν, ἠνομήσαμεν B-26-46'   (անաւրինեցաք,
         584 Sa Hippolᴬ] tr 239 Laʷ Hippolᴮˢ   անիրաւեցաք)
         Aug ep 111, 4.

12:5   om ἕτεροι 239 Bo Hippolᴶ

Bel:8 δαπάνην] τραπεζαν   239   (զսեղանն)

-29   παράδος] δος   239   (տուր)

4f)   agreements with Hippolytus

2:45   τὸν σιδηρόν] pr. και   verssᵖ Hippolˢ Tht   (և զերկաթն)

3:23   om τῆς καιομένης   Hippol Or

-49   κυρίου] του θεου   Hippolᴬ (om Arm Աստուծոյ:
                                              om V280=P: reading of Arm1)

4:15   τὸ σύγκριμα 1˚] +αυτου   verssᵖ Hippol (=P=MT Qre)
                                              (զմեկնութիւն նորա)

-28   ἔτι] pr και 588 verssᵖ Hippolˢ (=P: om *waw* 6h21 8al*)
                                              (և մինչդեռ)

5:8 σύγκρισιν] + αυτης   742 verss[P] Hippol p. 152, 12

                                     (=P=MT Qre) (զմեկնութիւն նորա)

6:12 καί 2˚] η   48ᶜ Arab Hippol[met]   (կամ)

7:9 φλόξ] pr ως   La[s] Hippol[s] Ps. Ath.   (իբրև զբոց)

                                     cf. OG

9:4 om μου   Arm Hippol[s] = OG

The contrast between the importance of Arm's agreements with the B group and most of those with its individual members indicates that Arm2's connection is with the general text type rather than a particular representative of it. Nevertheless there were a few noteworthy readings shared especially with MS 239.[42]

5a) agreements with Q and satellites (230-233-541)

4:16 σύγκρισις 1˚] + αυτου   Q-230' 538 90 46 588 Bo Tht

                                    (=P=MT Qre) (մեկնութիւն նորա)

7:20 ῷ] ου   Q-230 590 Hippol[B] Lucif (որոյ)

11:4 ἀν στῇ] αναστη   Q*-230 46 Hippol[ABS] (յարիցէ)

5b) agreements with 230-233-541

5:13 ὁ βασ.] ναβουχ.   230'' Hippol (նաբուքոդոնոսոր)

7:9 om καί 2˚]   230' Hippol[s] Polychr Tht[cit]Lucif Ps.

                                     Vig fide Nic (=P=MT)

9:17 τὸ ἔρημον]το ερημωθεν 230''(pr 541) 393; quae deserta est

                                     Aug (=P) (որ աւերեցաւ)

5c) agreements with Q

2:29 ἐπὶ τῆς κοίτης σου/   tr Q   (առնեին զքեզ

      ἀνέβησαν   յանկողնի քում)

5:3 om αὐτοῦ ult.   Q[mg]

8:1 πρὸς μέ] μοι   Q verss   (իՆձ)

-3 πρό] επι   Q Hippol Tht   (հանդէպ)

11:33 ἐν φλογί] εν πυρι   Q[txt] (=P)   (հրով)

5d)   **agreements with 230**

Sus: 55 om παρὰ τοῦ θεοῦ

1:8   ἐν τῷ οἴνῳ] εκ του οινου (=P)   (ի գինոյ)

4:20   εἶδεν] ειδες   (տեսանէիր)

6:5   εὑρήσομεν] ευρισκομεν   (գտանեմք)

-12   αἰτήσῃ] + αιτησιν   (խնդրիցէ
                            խնդրուածու)

-20   Δαν.] pr. και ειπεν   230 Aeth   (և ասէ Դանիէլ)

7:15   αἱ ὁρ. τῆς κεφαλῆς μου 230 La⁵ Hippoƚ   (տեսիլ գլխոյ
        ἐτάρ. με] η ορασις της Ps. Chr IX 736   իմոյ խռովեցուցg
        κεφ. μου συνεταρασσεν με (συνεταραξε) Lucif   զիս)

8:4   στήσονται] ιστаντο   230; non stabant   (կային)
                            Spec; non poterant stare La⁵ Bo.

-4   ἐποίησε] εποιει   (առնէր)

-20   fin.] + εστιν   230 verss^P Hippol   (մարագ է)

11:14   ἐπαναστήσονται]   (=P)   (յարիցեն)
        αναστησονται

-36   om καί 4°   230 Chr^cit (=P=MT)

Bel:29 Init.- βασιλέα] και   (և իրրե եկին ասեն
        ελθοντες ειπον τω βασ.   gԹագաւորն)

-30   καὶ εἶδεν] ιδων   (իրրե տեսեն)

-37   λέγων] και ειπεν   (և ասէ)

-42   ἀνέσπασεν] ανηγαγεν   (առ զնա ի վեր

WO 4:3 δἰ ἐμοῦ ἐτέθη δόγμα]   (սուաւ հրաման յինէն)
        εξετεθη δογμα παρ εμου

-5   θεοῦ ἅγιον] tr   230 Bo Ps Vig.   (սուրբ Աստուծոյ)

-11   οὕτως εἶπεν] tr   230 588 verss^P   (ասէր այսպէս)

-33   ἐπεστράφησαν / ἐπ᾽ ἐμέ] tr   (առ իս դարձան)

6:16   ὁ βασ. / εἶπε] tr   230 verss^P (=P)   (ասէ արքայն)

5e)   **agreements with 233**

1:5   om καί 3°   233 239 670

5:1   χιλίοις] + ανδρασι   233 590 Arab   (hազար առն)

-11   θεοῦ] pr αγιον   233 Spec.   (սուրբ Աստուծոյ)

-16   om ἔσται   233 Aeth (=P=MT)
                            (+ լhgի M4834 M178-M346')

7:9 πῦρ] pr ωσει   233 (իրրև հուր)
10:8 τὴμ μεγάλην/ταύτην] tr 233 (զայն մեծ)

5f) **agreements with 541**

1:10 om ὑμῶν 2°   239 410 541
(Sus:46 ἐγώ] pr ειμι   233-541 Laˢ(vid.))   (եմ ես)
(8:26 fin] + εστιν   233-541)   (բաղումն է)

The most salient feature to arise from the last series of tables is the marked affinity Arm shows towards 230 which thus appears the one extant MS which most corresponds to Arm2 textually. This is indeed what we might have been led to expect from the results of our previous examination of variants illustrating the version's division into two phases. However, the finding should not impel us to a wholistic identification of their textual character.

According to Ziegler's classification, 230 joins 233-541 in providing not infrequent support for Q readings. Judging from that uncial's renowned idiosyncracy it is understandable that Arm should have little movement with it individually. In addition, it has little in common with that part of 230's compass where it gravitates to the Q group e.g.

4:15 σύγκριμα 2° Q-230' 62'] κριμα αυτου 534; + (զմեկնութիւն
      somnii mei Ps Vig. c. Var. 2.12; + αυτου rel.   նորա)
8:10 δυνάμεως 2° Qᵗˣᵗ 230' Q Lʼʼ⁻³⁶ 764 46 106   (զաւրութիւն
      393 410 Laˢʷ Bo Hippol Tht] +   երկնից)
      του ουρανου rel. (=P)

As we noted, 230 has an affinity to Hippolytus' commentary which betrays no rigid affiliation, but vacillates between B and Q as well as containing other minor elements. Examples of Arm's relation to the B group suggest that it is under a greater magnetism towards that standard than 230 which on the contrary reveals a higher percentage of additions towards the quantum of MT. Granted the pervasive influence of the Hexapla, it is hardly absurd that a 10-11th century MS should show more signs of its effect than a fifth century translation. However, they share several readings with B's satellites:

7:4   λέαινα] + εχουσα πτερα B^c-46''-239 A^* 230'   (առիծ
         Aeth Arab: ex OG   թեատր)
11:8   αὐτῶν 1°] + καταστρεψαι B^c-26-46''-239 A^*   (նոցա
         Aeth Arab PolyChr: կործանեցէ)
         ex OG
4:34   om οὖν   46' 230' 239
7:1   αἱ ὁρ.] η ορασις   230 239 584 Aeth   (տեսիլ)
         Hippol^s Tht^lemP
-19   πᾶν θηρίον Ιπαντα τα θηρια 26 46' 230 239 590 (զամե-
         La^s Aeth Lucif   նայն զազանս)
9:3   τὸν θεόν] + μου   26 46'' 230 239 584   (Աստուած
         Aeth Arab Hippol^A   իմ)
         Eus dem
-26   ἀφανισμοί B^*] αφανισμον 46'' 230 239 410 Arab.
                                             (զապականութիւնն)
11:30 ταπεινωθήσεται] -θησονται 46^* 230'' 410 Tht
                                             (խոնարհեցքին)

Moreover, if Arm2's exemplar further resembled 230 and its related minuscules in their agreements with Lucianic witnesses (and P), this may partially account for the preservation (in all the MSS of our edition) of Arm1 components which were held to have emanated from the Antiochian text type e.g.:

1:2   σενναρ]σενααρ   538-88 130 407 410   (Սեննար)
                                  534 590 Hippol^Met
-15   τά 1°] pr παντα   538-449 106 230'' 239   (զամենայն)
                                  380 407 410 584 Bo
                                  (=P=MT)
2:20   τοῦ θεοῦ (=MT)] κυριου Q-233 L-311 239 410 (Տեառն)
                                  590 verss^P Hippol (=P
                                  except 7a1)
3:17   θεός B^txt QV La^w Hippol^A Cypr. Greg. El.]   (մեր
         ο θεος ημων εν ουρανοις (-νω 88 584)   Աստուած

A"L'-36-88 26 130 233   յերկինս)
239ᶜ380 410 534 588
Chr 111 478 Tht

3:51 καὶ ἐδόξαζον / καὶ
εὐλόγουν   ] tr. V-147 22ᶜ-96-11-   (աւրհնեին
770 490-ᴄ 26 46 233'   գովեին)
239

5:23 ἤνεγκαν B-46'-239 62'L'-³⁶Laˢ Arab (=P)]   (բերին)
-κας rel (=MT)

6:7 om ὅς   147 L-449* C' 26 46
407 541 Hippolᴬ

9:27 θυσία Q L"46' 106 239 410 Co Aeth HippoIᴾ (զպատարագու)
Eus dem et ecl. Tht Irˡᵃᵗ Orˡᵃᵗ XI 78.80
(=P=MT)] θυμιαμα Chrᶜⁱᵗ; pr. θυμιαμα και
Chr; >230; pr μου rel.

12:5 om τοῦ χ. τοῦ ποταμοῦ 2˚   L'87* 130 239 Aethᴾ
Hippolᴮᴶ Tht (=P=OG)

-7 πάντα ταῦτα Cypr Irˡᵃᵗ] tr   62 11 87 230" 239 (զայս
393 410 584 verssᴾ   ամենայն⁴³)
Hippol Chr Thtᴾ (=P
=Geo)

Bel:6 ζῶν θεός] tr   L-88 106 230' 584   (աստուած
742 Laˢ Bo Arab.   կենդանի)

CONCLUSION

According to our initial probe, Arm's main affinity had been with the Greek tradition, with the result that the question arose whether Arm 1 had ever amounted to a complete translation from P.[44] Later versional variants where one reading was consistently Lucianic and the other of a different text type compelled us to postulate two stages in Arm's contact with Gk. That in all three stages (Syriac-based, Lucianic and secondary Gk) were not required was indicated by certain metaphrastic treatments which could best be explained on the assumption of simultaneous translation from P and Luc in Arm1.

As we have postulated that a Luc codex was employed by the original translator, where there is no evidence to the contrary, it is logical to suppose that Arm's Lucianic agreements stem from Arm1. If then the extant Greek witnesses closest to Arm2's projected *Vorlage* also contain several Lucianic readings, this may also be true of the MS on which the Armenian redactors based their revision. Finding no discrepancy between Arm1 and their new standard in such cases, it is understandable how they left the Arm1 reading unaltered in Arm2.

Several factors facilitated the establishment of a sound stratification in which priority was accorded to the Lucianic layer. Most of the readings were furnished by the same MSS which were rich in P agreements. Moreover, as the local text of Antioch and Syria it had already been partially incorporated into P Daniel with the result that it had historical verisimilitude to recommend it. Furthermore, like OL and P, Arm1 betrays a wide range of characteristic Lucianic features not extant in Greek. Where its readings are supported by OL, P and other pre-hexaplaric witnesses Arm1 testify to the proto-Lucianic stratum. One of the latter's notable characteristics in Daniel is its receptivity to OG readings of which Arm, like P, has a number without support from other Th witnesses. Arm's relation to MT is generally mediated by P: it has relatively little in common with the adaptations to MT introduced by Lucian himself but sometimes concurs with the text of the contemporary Syrian commentators. Such readings may therefore belong to the later stratum of the Lucianic tradition.

If the Lucianic phase was prior, how could the second stream be identified and its extent estimated? Where the variants consisted of a small group of MSS they consistently pointed to MS 230 as the nearest model for Arm2's *Vorlage,* in close conjunction with 233-541 Hippolytus. The conclusion was verified by an examination of Arm's affinities with the various groups outlined by Ziegler and their individual members.

Contrary to Gehman's view that Arm was dependent on a reworked version of the Hexapla, it was demonstrated that the version has little in common with the hexaplaric group either when it approximates to MT or otherwise. Indeed it frequently reads the shorter, more primitive text with B and satellites. In contrast, it is rather distant from the uncials A and Q, both of which have many unique readings. Yet often in the company of 230 Arm coincides with their minuscules, especially 584 and 233 and 239 of the B group. Together they exhibit several agreements with Lucianic witnesses. If these minuscules authentically reflect Arm2's *Vorlage* in this respect also, it helps explain how so much of the earlier translation has survived the process of revision.

NOTES

1. Aquila reads πραιτώριον (cf. Symmachus ἱπποστάσιον).

2. The Lucianic form αμελλασαρ at 1:11 to which Arm is related also seems to maintain the original vocalization.

3. For an Aramaic fragment possibly related to the Susanna episode see J.T. Milik, "Daniel et Susanne à Qumran", *De la Tôrah au Messie* M. Carrez *et al* (eds.), Paris: Desclée, 1981, pp.337-359.

4. Unless expressly specified to the contrary, J2558 is to be taken as seconding V280's reading.

5. Georgian evidence has been excluded from the investigation owing to lack of information regarding its textual composition. Although its witness to the antiquity of Syriac readings cannot be impugned, the likelihood that it contains elements of both Arm1 and Arm2 as well as a subsequent Greek revision renders hazardous its use in support of Greek readings until it has undergone detailed scrutiny.

6. As neither early citations nor versions are extant for these examples, they may reflect a more developed text type.

7. Ziegler, p.57.

8. J. Ziegler, *Duodecim prophetae* Septuaginta, vol.xiii, Göttingen: Vandenhoeck & Ruprecht, 1943, pp.90-91.

9. Ziegler classifies MS 311 in the Lucianic sub-group 111 of Isaiah (*Isaias* Septuaginta vol.xiv, 1939, p.75) as a secondary Lucianic witness to Jeremiah (*Jeremias, Baruch, Threni, Epistula Jeremiae* Septuaginta vol.xv, 1957, pp.80-83) and in the sub-group 11 of Ezekiel (*Ezechiel* Septuaginta vol.xvi/1, 1952, p.44).

10. See J. Ziegler, "Der Bibeltext im Daniel-Kommentar des Hippolyt von Rom", pp.163-199.

11. See Ziegler, p.55 for OG influence on the Lucianic text.

12. MSS appearing in brackets represent the Th text.

13. As the result of more extensive collations of Th and Arm witnesses and our findings regarding P contact in Arm1,

the bulk of the examples Gehman quotes under this heading on pp.93-94 of his srticle must be reclassified. Mostly they entered Arm via P or a Lucianic witness, while sometimes the reading is best viewed as an inner-Armenian corruption.

14. Cf. the interpretation of these as free renderings in Ziegler, p.43.

15. This form recurs at 6:23, 24 over against εἶπε in Th (=P) where OG is extremely divergent. These instances are probably the result of analogy with the examples in this table.

16. It is widely held that OG reflects an alternative semitic substratum in chapters three to six. See P. Grelot, "La septante de Daniel IV et son substrat semitique", *RB* 81 (1974), p.5 and cf. M. Delcor, "Un cas de traduction "targumique" de la LXX à propos de la statue en or de Dan III", *Textus* 7 (1969), pp.30-35. Koch goes so far as to suggest that OG in these chapters derives from a different hand than the one responsible for the rest of the book (*Das Buch Daniel,* p.19).

17. B. Fischer, "Lukian-Lesarten", p.176.

18. Examples of the first category, corrections to MT, are not forthcoming.

19. On a similar contrast between OG and Th in Daniel see Sh. Pace, "The Stratigraphy", p.27.

20. Where no witness is expressed V280-J2558 is to be understood.

21. See S.P. Cowe, "The Two Armenian Versions of Chronicles", and "Epistle of Jeremiah".

22. J.A. Montgomery, "The Hexaplaric Strata in the Greek texts of Daniel", pp.289-302. See further his discussion in the introduction to his commentary on Daniel.

23. Ibid., p.299.

24. In consequence, there is a corresponding dearth of hexaplaric signs adduced by Armenian witnesses to Daniel. See C.E. Cox, *Hexaplaric Materials Preserved by*

the Armenian Version.

25. J.A. Montgomery, "Hexaplaric Strata", p.296.

26. Ziegler, p.53.

27. Ibid., p.47.

28. No evidence is felt necessary since his investigation "proves that Arm beyond the shadow of a doubt belongs to the Or group." "The Armenian Version of the Book of Daniel", p.88.

29. Ibid., p.93.

30. Ibid., p.88.

31. For details see General Conclusion p.430 and notes 51-61.

32. Ziegler, pp.52-53.

33. Divergence in the position of the verb among those witnesses which adduce it underlines the secondary nature of the addition. Thus MSS M346'-M2585 M2627' set it before the accompanying phrase.

34. For the phenomenon see chapter four, pp.255-272.

35. As Ziegler notes on p.57 of his introduction, where Q agrees with Luc, this is because it is dependent on the recension.

36. Where A agrees with B its reading represents the prehexaplaric text.

37. For a similar observation on the text of the Armenian gospels see J. Alexanian, "The Armenian Gospel Text", p.386.

38. MS M2627 alone of the 15 MSS of the edition preserves the reading ս̔ար at 5:31 cf. the four instances where it supports the lectionary readings against the other biblical MSS.

39. "Der Bibeltext im Daniel-Kommentar des Hippolyt von Rom", *NAW Gott,* Phil-hist. Klasse, 1952, pp.166ff.

40. N.B. example k where Arm2 = 233' Hippols, whereas 230 transmits the majority reading.

41. This agreement may be more apparent than real since the Armenian term is hardly ever used in the plural, so that its Greek retroversion is not assured. See *NBH* vol.2, p.70.

42. Conversely, some agreements with Hippolytus which co-incide with P or OG may be vestiges of Arm1.

43. However, it should be noted that this sequence represents the regular order of these Armenian morphemes.

44. Nevertheless, it is clear that the P component in Daniel exceeds both quantitatively and qualitatively the level recorded in Chronicles and the Epistle of Jeremiah.

CHAPTER 6

TRANSLATION TECHNIQUE

From our textual analysis in chapters four and five it has emerged that Arm, as it is preserved in our MSS, is the product of two distinct phases of translation. In our attempt to distinguish them we have already remarked upon some of the metaphrastic features of the early stage, several of which correspond to Lyonnet's findings in the gospels. These have also been contrasted in summary fashion with the approach which characterizes Arm2.[1] It is now proposed to consider the question in greater detail, laying the emphasis on this later stage and the process by which it took shape from its Greek model.[2] The review will include those readings presumed to emanate from Arm1 which were retained in Arm2 since their very survival is a tacit acknowledgement of the reviser's approval and hence they form an integral part of his end product.

The main categories employed to classify translations are those of freedom and literalism. Although in the past their use as labels has been rather impressionistic, having to a greater or lesser extent been tinged with associations of praise or blame, within a more rigorously applied framework of sub-categories their descriptive content can be greatly refined.

The translator of necessity has to bridge the gap distancing his base texts from his intended readers. Depending on which of these fixed points he tends to emphasize in his work, his results can be gauged accordingly on a scale extending between the two poles. Pre-occupation with reproducing the formal minutiae of his exemplar would mean falling into excessive literalism, while single-minded obsession with an effective narrative, couched in an acceptable literary velure, results in a freedom that risks censure as licence.

Against such a scale, Arm rates somewhere between Th and OG. The former in places preserves a more or less one to one correspondence with MT, sometimes straining the limits of Greek grammar in an effort to maintain semitic idiom and WO. OG in contrast, even allowing for a difference in *Vorlage* from Th, appears to paraphrase the sense at several points with abbreviations and expansions to produce a smoother, more readable version.[3] Still, granted the accumulated experience of producing written translations after a prolonged period of oral rendition and deeper exposure to Greek grammatical instruction which the younger generation underwent at Constantinople and elsewhere,[4] it is natural that Arm2 displays more of the hallmarks of literalism than the early stratum. Consequently, although less pronounced, here too we can perceive something of the dynamism of the translation process exemplified by the range of developments from OG to Th.

Translation Unit: To evaluate the applicability of the foregoing generalisation let us consider in turn various categories for defining literalism which have been devised by Barr and Tov.[5] In this way a more precise impression can be formed about which aspects of the version are literal and which free. Arm's overall translation unit is fixed at the phrase level (though there are many instances of almost *verbatim* rendering). This can result in often minor rearrangement and modification of elements within the unit in an attempt to capture and re-create the semantic whole without doing despite gratuitously to Armenian usage; hence the following idiomatic renderings.

6:10 ἦν κάμπτων ἐπὶ τὰ γόνατα αὐτοῦ   դնէր ծունր
7:21 ἐποίει πόλεμον   տայր պատերազմ
8:7 τοῦ στῆναι ἐνώπιον αὐτοῦ   ունել զդէմ նորա (cf. 11:16)

(At 1:19 and 2:2 where the phrase refers to an audience with the king it is translated by կալ առաջի but here where the sense is 'to stand up to, to oppose' the translator remoulds the expression to bring out the hostile overtones.)

5:2 ἐν τῇ γεύσει τοῦ οἴνου   իբրև ընդ գինիս եմուտ

The translator is not satisfied with a bland, non-committal rendering although this is perfectly possible, but has decided to give his interpretation of Belshazzar's mental state when he called for the temple vessels to be brought to the banqueting hall (cf. 4 Kgdms. 20:12,13 ընդ գինի մտեալ էր և արբեալ.)

Similarly, he avoids a direct rendering of the phrase ἔδωκα τὸ πρόσωπον, preferring the expression more common in Daniel դարձուցի զերեսս (usually =ἐπιστρέφειν) at 9:3 and անկայ ի վերայ երեսաց իմոց at 10:15.

By drawing out the phrase οὗτοι διασωθήσονται at 11:41 he also provides a more effective introduction to the ensuing list of the countries to survive attack.

The phrase-long translation unit frees the translator from slavish subservience to his exemplar, and allows him to set about reshaping the semitic caste of Th's Greek in greater harmony with Armenian style, e.g.

Sus:13 ἕτερος τῷ ἑτέρῳ   գմիմեանս
-52 εἷς ἀπὸ τοῦ ἑνός   ի մ*ի*մեանց
2:11 μετὰ πάσης σαρκός   ի մէջ ամենայն մսեղեաց (contrast Bel:5)
4:31 εἰς γενεὰν καὶ γενεάν   յազգաց յազգս
6:4 πᾶσαν πρόφασιν   ամենևին պատճառս ... ոչ

6:23 πᾶσα διαφορά　　ամենևին ապականութիւն ոչ

9:18 ἐφ᾽ ἧς ἐπικέκληται τὸ　　յորոյ վերայ կոչեցեալ է
ὄνομά σου ἐπ᾽ αὐτῆς　　անուն քո

Bel:15 καὶ αἱ γυναῖκες καὶ τὰ　　կանամբք եւ որդուլք
τέκνα αὐτῶν　　իւրեանց
καὶ Δανιηλ μετ᾽ αὐτοῦ (re-　　Դանիէլիւ հանդերձ
placement of polysyndeton)

Nevertheless it is worth recalling that Arm2 adopts some of Th's semitic transliterations (8:13 փիլմոնիս 10:5 բադեան 12:7 բադէնն 11:45 յեփանդոն, contrast ιρ 4:10, 20, βειρα 8). As Arm conforms semitic features to its own idiom, it also accommodates other elements of Th often of a distinctly Greek order. In treating singular and plural number Arm usually follows its exemplar, however there is some interesting variation.[6] There are several cases where բանք renders λόγος (e.g. Sus: 27, 4:28). Similarly when something is attributed to more than one person, the plural form is often found probably on the principle that each individual had one, e.g. Sus: 61 ἐκ τοῦ στόματος αὐτῶν ի նոցին բերանոց 5:4 τοῦ πνεύματος αυτῶν ոգւոյ նոցա 3:41 ἐν ὅλῃ καρδίᾳ ամենայն սրտիւք. Although the first two cases may be regarded as the consequence of confusion of յ/ց which are similar in form, the third example establishes the existence of the phenomenon. Parallel logic perhaps informed the reading հրապարակքն և պարիսպքն 9:25. The rebuilt city of Jerusalem would require a whole network of walls and squares.

Three classes of nouns appearing in Greek in plural form are rendered by an Armenian singular.

a)　indefinite neuter pronouns

2:23 ἅ　　որ ինչ ... ինդրեցաք

-28　ἃ δεῖ γενέσθαι　　որ ինչ լինելոց է (=P)
　　　　　　　　　　(for the *participum*
　　　　　　　　　　necessitas see Jensen
　　　　　　　　　　§265, p.103)

8:19 ἃ δεῖ γενέσθαι τὰ ἐσσόμενα　որ ինչ լինելոց է　(=P)
Bel:6 ὅσα　որչափ
(cf τὰ προστεταγμένα αὐταῖς　զոր ինչ հրամայեաց նոցա V.18)

b)　αὐτά when used as a pronoun is rendered by զայն
(1:2, Bel: 9, 13)

c)　substantivized neuter plural of
2:38 κύριον πάντων　Տէր ամենայնի
7:16 πάντων τούτων　ամենայնի այնորիկ
(see further 3:27, 28, 29, 31, 4:9, 18, 12:7 and Jensen §240, p. 91.)

Infinitive: Greek prepositional phrases are usually translated exactly e.g.

Sus:15 ἐν τῷ παρατηρεῖν αὐτούς　ի սպասել ն նոցա
2:30 ἕνεκεν ... τοῦ γνωρίσαι　վասն ցուցանելոյ
10:9 ἐν τῷ ἀκοῦσαι με　ի լսել ն իմում
11:2 μετὰ τὸ κρατῆσαι αὐτόν　յետ զաւրանալոյ նորա
Bel:18 ἅμα τῷ ἀνοίξαι　ընդ բանալ

(contrast the use of իբրև at 6:19, 8:15 and մինչդեռ 8:18 and the rendering of διά by զի Sus:4 and բանզի in v.39). The negative articular form τοῦ μή cannot be paralleled and is therefore rendered by զի մի with the conjunctive. The positive form is always rendered by the infinitive; in 5:20, 7:26 τοῦ ἀφανίσαι 9:24, 25, 11:35 τοῦ πυρῶσαι the Armenian infinitive is preceded by the preposition ի of purpose.[7] In several other cases the question is complicated by manuscript variation in both Greek and Armenian.

　　The Armenian infinitive also renders Greek abstract verbal nouns.

Sus:42 πρὶν γενέσεως αὐτῶν　յառաջ քան զլինել նոցա
1:8 τοῦ πότου αὐτοῦ　ըմպելոյ նորա
8:17 ἐχόμενος τῆς στάσεώς μου　ուր եւն կայի (=P)

10:3 πληρώσεως	ի կատարել երից
	Նթներորդաց
10:16 ἐν τῇ ὀπτασίᾳ σου	յերևելդ քո
11:13 ἐπελεύσεται εἰσοδείᾳ	եկեսցէ մտանել
(cf. 11:8 μετὰ αἰχμαλωσίας	գերի առեալ

Future: Similarly tenses of the indicative mood are normally rendered by their direct equivalents. The following cases are worthy of comment. Three cases of the participium necessitatis were noted as representing a Greek simple future:

Sus:22 οὐκ ἐκφεύξομαι	չեմ ապրելոց
2:9 ἀναγγελεῖτε	պատմելոց էք
10:14 ἀπαντήσεται	անցանելոց իցեն

Imperfect: The forms κατεσκήνουν and κατῴκουν in 4:9, 18 are represented by the participal construction բնակեալ էին, հանգուցեալ էին as regularly with these verbs.[8] The only case of an imperfect being rendered by an Armenian aorist is խոնով եգն չg at 7:15 (=P)

Present:

8:17, 18 πίπτω (historic present)[9] անկայ (= P + OG)
6:20 λατρεύεις պաշտեիր (cf. 6:16) (=Geo[I]) and in a future context: Sus: 23 αἱρετὸν μοί ἐστιν լաւ լիցի ինձ
11:36 γίνεται լինելոց է; 11:45 οὐκ ἐστιν ὁ ῥυόμενος ոչ որ իցէ որ փրկիցէ.

Aorist: Arm tends to introduce direct speech by the present tense of ասել (e.g. Sus:13 εἶπαν ասեն) which is as much a convention in *grabar* as quotation marks are in modern dialogue. Among examples where Arm translates Gk aorist by imperfect in dreams and visions is ὁρᾶν in 2:41, 45, 8:4, 6, 7, 9:21. This may have been influenced to some extent by the imperfect of θεωρεῖν (e.g. 4:7, 5:5) which is rendered in the same way (e.g. 2:31 ἐθεώρεις տեսանեիր).[10]

In the earliest period of literary Armenian especially, the verb system was not as developed as in Greek. Thus in the case of denominatives, what Greek achieves by transmuting the substantive into verbal form, Arm renders by a noun and auxiliary verb, e.g.

προσεύχεσθαι	կալ յաղաւթս	(3:25, 6:10, 9:4)
καρποῦν	տալ երեխայրիս	(3:38)
ἀποκρίνεσθαι	տալ պատասխանի	(passim)
πολεμεῖν	տալ պատերազմ	(10:20, 11:11)
ἐνυπνιᾶσθαι	երազ տեսանել	(2:1, 2)
καταιαχύνειν	յամաւթ առնել	(3:42)
καταισχύνθαι	զամաւթի հարկանել	(Sus:27)
ἐντράπεσθαι	յամաւթ լինել	(3:44)

Phrases composed of a simple adjective and լինել are found as the quivalent of a finite verb at the following points:

3:29	ἀποστῆναι	ապստամբ լինել
7:23	ὑπερέξει	առաւել իցէ (քան)
-24	ὑπεροίσει	առաւել իցէ (քան)
Sus:14	ὡμολόγησαν	խոստովան ան եղեն
3:96	δυνήσεται	կարող իցէ
4:24	ἀρεσάτω σοι	հաճոյ թուեսցի քեզ (cf. 3:99)
3:19	ἐπλήσθη	լի եղև
6:27	ἀντιλαμβάνεται	աւգնական լինի

Three examples of a simple adjective assisted by առնել with factitive force can be cited:

(passim in chapter 3) ὑπερυψοῦτε բարձր արարէք
8:7 συνεπάτησεν կոխան արար
Bel:9 δείξητε յայտ առնիցէք

Another notable feature of Arm, probably consistent with the general tendency of the language, is its replacement of finite passive forms by those of a related active.[11]
Sus:44 ἀπαγομένης αὐτῆς մինչդեռ տանէին զնա

5:13 εἰσήχθη   ածին ի ներքս
6:9 γραφῆναι   գրել զհրաման
7:8 ἐξερριζώθη   ի բաց խլեին
Bel:32 οὐκ ἐδόθη αὐτοῖς   ոչ ինչ արկին նոցա

There are two cases of rendering by the verbal adjective in
-ի (Jensen §268, p.104):
3:39 προσδεχθείημεν   ընդունելի լիցուք
10:12 ἠκούσθησαν   լսելի եղեն

Participle: The bald statement that in contrast to the verbal
components we have treated so far Arm reveals a wide range of
renderings of the Greek participle might give the impression of
disproportionate freedom in its translation technique.
However, when we reflect on the various subtle nuances condensed in the participle which are indispensable for a full understanding of the sentence at large, it is rather the case that
the translator would be reneging on his duty if he were not to
make these explicit for his readers.

The most widespread rendering is by the appropriate
1)   finite form with or without the copula, e.g.
Sus:13 ἐξελθόντες διεχωρίσθησαν   ելին մեկնեցան
-23 μὴ πράξασαν ἐμπεσεῖν   չգործել զայդ և անկանել
3:5 πίπτοντες προσκυνεῖτε   անկանիցիք և երկրպա-
                                   գանիցիք
7:7 ἐσθίον καὶ λεπτῦνον   ուտէր և մանրէր

2)   sometimes it is rendered by the (aorist) participle, e.g.
3:52 ὑπερυψούμενος   առաւել բարձրացեալ
5:19 τρέμοντες καὶ φοβούμενοι   զարհուրեալ դողային
(cf. the reversal of the elements as in 7:10 յորդեալ ելանէր)

Bel:12 βεβρωμένα   կերեալ
-21 ὀργισθείς   բարկացեալ

3)   There are two examples of the instrumental of the infinitive where the two actions are regarded as contemporaneous.

Sus:35 κλαίουσα ἀνέβλεψεν   լալով հայեցաւ

Bel:7 εἶπε γέλασας   ասէ ... ծիծաղելով

4)   The articulated participle usually becomes a subordinate relative clause, with tense depending on the context.

1:15 τὰ ἐσθίοντα	որ ուտէին
5:25 ἡ ἐντεταγμένη	որ գրեալ է
7:20 τοῦ ἀναβάντος	որ ելանէր
9:26 τῷ ἐρχομένῳ	որ գայցէ
11:26 τά δέοντα αὐτοῦ	որ ինչ նմա անկ իցէ

5)   Where the articulated participle denotes a class of person or object it is rendered by a substantivised participle or other verbal adjective in -իչ or -ի.

Sus:60 τούς ἐλπίζοντας ἐπ᾽ αὐτόν	զյուսացեալս իւր (cf. 3:40)
3:35 τὸ ἠγαπημένον ὑπό σου	սիրելոյ քո
11:6 οἱ φέροντες αὐτήν	ածելիք իւր
-32 οἱ ἀνομοῦντες	ապականիչք
(cf. 12:3 οἱ συνιέντες	իմաստունք
Bel:13 κεκρυμμένην	անյայտ)

6)   Connotations of circumstance, cause or purpose are expressed by means of a subordinate clause; this applies particularly to the genitive absolute.

Sus:36 περιπατούντων ἡμῶν	մինչդեռ մեք զգնայաք
-39 ἰδόντες	իբրև տեսաք
-53 κρίνων	զի դատէիր
3:50 διασυρῖζον	որ շնչէ
8:22 τοῦ συντριβέντος	ի խորտակել նորա

7)   Where the participle accompanies the object of a verb of seeing or hearing it is regularly translated by զի and a finite verb.

Sus:8 ἐθεώρουν αὐτήν ... εἰσπο-   տեսանէին զնա զի մտանէր
ρευομένην

8:4 εἶδον τὸν κρίον κερατίζοντα   տեսանէի զխոյն զի ոգորէր

Sometimes it is expressed by other methods:

Sus:39 ἰδόντες συγγινομένους   տեսաք զլինել դոցա ընդ
αὐτούς   միմեանս

3:91 ἤκουσεν ὑμνούντων αὐτῶν (=P) լուաւ զաւրհնութիւն նոցա

Preposition: Even more than the participle the preposition is probably the grammatical category most dependent on the native language community for its function and significance, especially in idiomatic juxtaposition with certain verbs. As the rendering of the preposition cannot properly be detached from the phrase which surrounds it and is therefore contextually based, there is little that may be said by way of general comment. The most frequent preposition in Th is ἐν (mostly representing semitic ḅ), which is always rendered by the instrumental case, e.g.

4:34 ἐν ὑπερηφανίᾳ   անբարտաւանութեամբ

9:3 ἐν νηστείαις   պահաւք

11:33 ἐν ῥομφαίᾳ   սրով

(contrast 10:7 ἐν φόβῳ   զարհուրեալք)

As in these examples the preposition 'disappears', so there are others where the process is reversed, e.g.

6:10 τῆς ἡμέρας   յաւուր (=P)

7:7 τοῦ στερεώματος   ի հաստատութեան

Bel:18 φωνῇ μεγάλῃ   ի ձայն բարձր[12]

By the nature of things it is impossible to achieve a one to one relationship and Arm, construing the preposition within its phrase, produces better sense than if it were to enforce a system of rigid stereotyping.

9:7 διέσπειρας αὐτοὺς ἐκεῖ ἐν ἀθεσίᾳ αὐτῶν

գրուեցեր զնոսա անդր վասն անհնազանդութեան
իւրեանց

(cf. Montgomery, p.364 "Thou hast driven them for the treachery with which they betrayed Thee").

The most unsatisfactory case is ի տեղւոջէ իւրմէ which stands over against ἐπὶ τόπου αὐτοῦ at 11:38. Probably the translator found the form ἀπό in his *Vorlage* or read it as such.

Until now we have largely reflected upon how translation unit affects that part of the process which is determined by the nature of the base and receptor languages. Another area where the impact of the translator's personal input is even more immediate and decisive lies in the realm of exegesis. No instance of outright theological bias is discernible in Arm Daniel[13] but it is interesting to note the careful distinction in cultic terminology marked between the Jews and their captors, none of which is present in Th.[14] The terms applied to the Babylonian cult have been drawn from the contemporary polemic against Zoroastrianism practised (and periodically imposed by force) in eastern Armenia under Persian suzerainty. Thus the divinity of the former is given as Աստուած as opposed to դիք (2:11, 3:12,14,18), their temple is տաճար (3:53, 9:27) as opposed to մեհեան Bel:14,22 and their priests are քահանայք 3:84 over against քուրմք (Bel passim).[15]

Indeed the desire for clarity and intelligibility underlies several of Arm's inner-phrase modifications, e.g.
4:19 ἐμεγαλύνθη բարձրացաւ where the continuation indicates that the direction in which Nebuchadnezzar's greatness extended was up towards the sky. Yet when the verb ὑψώθης appears in 5:23 of Belshazzar's attitude before God, the metaphor is discarded in favour of the directness of հպարտացար.

10:16 τὰ ἐντός μου   փոր իմ
Bel:32 σώματα   մարդս which spells out the contrast with πρόβατα far more clearly.

10:14   ὅσα ἀπαντήσεται   npɔ̒ɯɯ̆ ḃḃɔ̒ ɯ̆ɑ̌gp ɯ̆ɑ̌gɯɑ̌ɑ̆hgɫɑ̆

As the translator is at pains to achieve clarity of expression, so he strives to present the material in a measured, symmetrical pattern. To this end he repeats certain elements of the text.

11:1   h hɯɯɯɯɯɑ̆ɑ̌nɣ̆θhɫɑ̆ ɫ /ʒ qɯɯnɣ̆θhɫɑ̆
-24   nɔ̒ ɯnɯnhɑ̆ hɯnp ɫɑ̆nɯ ɫ nɔ̒ hɯnp hɯng ɫɑ̆nɯ
or adds for balance

6:5   ɔ̒gɯɑ̆ɑ̆ɫɯ̆p nɯɯɫɣ̆p ... pɯjg ɫθɫ jɯɯnɣ̆ɫɑ̆ս Ɯɯɯɑ̆ɯɔ̒nj hɯnj
5:1ᵇ   Th: καὶ κατέναντι τῶν χιλίων ὁ οἶνος. 2 καὶ πίνων
Arm: ɫ nɯɯ hɯqɯnɯgɑ̆ ɑ̆njhɯjɣ̆ս ɫ qhɑ̆h
Note also the retention of *figura etymologica*[16]
12:10   οἱ νοήμονες συνήσουσι   hɯ̆ɯɯɯɑ̆ɯɑ̆ɑ̆ɫp hɯ̆ɯɯghɑ̆
          (νοήσουσιν 230" Thtᴵᵉᵐ)
and extension of its use
2:21   φρόνησιν τοῖς εἰδόσι σύνεσιν   ɣ̆nphɯɯnn ɣ̆nphnnɯɣ̆ɯɑ̆ɑ̆ɯg
(contrast 11:34 βοηθήσονται βοήθειαν   ɯɯqɑ̆ɯ̆ɯ̆ɯɑ̆ɑ̆ɯ̆nɯɣ̆θhɫɑ̆...

                                                    qɯɯgɫɑ̆
where avoidance of the passive may have been a greater priority.
cf.10:13   ἄλειμμα οὐκ ἠλειψάμην   hɯnnɯ nɔ̒ ɯɯɔ̒ɯɯj
          (cf. OG ἔλαιον)

Obviously the *locus classicus* in the book and one of the most formidable dilemmas of metaphrastic skill is the paronomasia of Sus:55-56 and 58-59 inculcating the lesson that the penalty should fit the crime. The solution adopted by the translator was to produce an artificial calque on the root of the verbs σχίζειν (hɫnɔ̒ɫp) and πρίειν (ɯnngɫp) in rendering the corresponding trees σχῖνος (hɫnɔ̒h) and πρῖνος (ɯnngh). The forms, designed solely to embody the Greek word-play, were destined quite understandably to remain *hapax legomena*.[17] However, the achievement becomes all the more laudable if, as R.A. Martin concludes from a syntactical survey[18] the OG version of the pun (retained exactly by Th) and the section enclosing it (vv.

50-59) constitute an original Greek composition and not a translation from a semitic substratum.

Compound Verbs: The translator's endeavour to give clear expression to the full semantic potential of Greek compound verbs is another hallmark of his work.[19] Preverbs were not an idiomatic feature of Armenian until the inception of the philo-Hellene school which devised a complex series of these to serve as direct equivalences for those of the Greek philosophical texts which it was their object to translate with the most rigorous literalism. Therefore the variant շրջապատէր shared by mss V280-J2558 at 3:48 obviously has less claim to originality since the first clearly datable citation of the term in *NBH* derives from after the end of the fifth century.

Nevertheless, Arm testifies to the ingenuity of the translators and the plasticity of the language to recapture the meaning required by the exemplar. Obviously the simplest examples involve directional preverbs used in their prime sense, which are represented

a) by adverbs or adverbial phrases, e.g.

Sus:39	ἐκπεπεδηκέναι	փախեաւ արտաքս
5:13	εἰσήχθη	ածին ի ներքս
10:20	ἐπιστρέφω	դառնամ անդրէն
11:2	ἐπαναστήσεται	յարիցէ ի վերայ

b) by the idiomatic classical construction of two verbs in juxtaposition[20] e.g.:

Sus:15	εἰσῆλθε	եկն եմուտ
3:47	διεχεῖτο	ելանէր դիզանէր
-49	συγκατέβη	էջ եկաց ընդ
cf. Sus:51	ἥκασιν	եկին հասին

On the other occasions the significance of the preverb is much more difficult to specify, but may represent some sort of emphasis or intensification of the simple form. Arm correspondingly does not render this type explicitly with the same frequency. However the following are worthy of note.

3:29	ἐξημάρτομεν	առաւել մեղաք
-52	ὑπερυψούμενος	առաւել բարձրացեալ
Bel:15	κατέφαγον πάντα καὶ	կերան զամենայն և արբին
	ἐξέπιον	և ոչ ինչ թողին
-42	κατεβρώθησαν	զէշ զէշ պատառեցան

Compound Adjectives: If Armenian was relatively poor in compound verbs, it was rich in compound adjectives and the translator knew how to use these to provide a neat equivalent for a longer Greek phrase, e.g.

4:12	ἐν δεσμῷ σιδηρῷ καὶ χαλκῷ	երկաթակապ և պղնձապատ
8:6	τοῦ τὰ κέρατα ἔχοντος	եղջերաւոր
(contrast 6:18	ἄδειπνος	առանց ընթրեաց)

Coupled with the auxiliary verbs լինել and առնել, as we noticed before, these compound adjectives were also employed to render Greek compound verbs or phrases[21] e.g.

1:10	καταδικάσητε τὴν κεφαλήν μου	առնիցիք զիս զլխապարտ
2:8	καιρὸν ὑμεῖς ἐξαγοράζετε	ժամանակաառ լինիք
3:8	διέβαλον	եղեն չարախաւս
11:40	συναχθήσεται	զաւրաժողով լինի

Another probable result of the translator's fascination with balance and symmetry is the way he has allowed himself to be influenced by the structure of parallel passages. Arguably, a number of such harmonizations may have already crystallized in his base text and the secondary nature of others is patent, yet the testimony of the Georgian Version corroborates the existence of at least a certain percentage at a very early date.

Sus:58	λέγε μοι	ասա
		(cf. the first question in v.54)
2:23	ἅ ἠξιάσαμεν	որ ինչ աղաւթիւք խնդրեցաք
		(cf. 9:3 խնդրել խնդրուածաք
		և աղաւթիւք)
3:56	ἐν τῷ στερεώματι	որ նստիս ի հաստատութեան
		(cf. v.54)

4:20 ἐν τῇ γῇ καὶ ἐν δεσμῷ   երկապակաապ և պղնծապատ
                                     (from v. 12)

5:23 τὸν κύριον θεὸν τοῦ οὐρανοῦ Աստուծոյ երկնից
                                       (cf. 2:18,19,37,44)

-29 ἐκήρυξε   քարոզ կարդայր (from 3:4)

6:12 κατὰ τὸ δόγμα Μήδων   զհրաման Մարաց և Պարսից
      καὶ Περσῶν   չէ արժէն շրջել

9:11 δούλου τοῦ θεοῦ   ծառայի քո (cf. 3:35 of Isaac)

-13 ἀδικίων ἡμῶν   յանիրաւութեանց հարցն
                                        մերոց

(cf. Jer. 11:10   դարձան յանիրաւութիւնս հարցն

        14:20   ծանեաա ... զանիրաւութիւնս հարցն մերոց

        Baruch 3:7 զամ. անիրաւութիւնս հարցն մերոց

-16 ὁ λαός (cf. 9:8,16) ամենայն ժողովլւրդ (cf. Sus:47,60, 9:6)

-19 καὶ ἐπὶ τὸν λαόν σου   om. (cf. v.18 where only the
                                       city is mentioned)

12:11 χίλιαι διακόσιαι ἐνενήκοντα հազար և երեք հարիւր և
                                        երեսուն և հինգ

Bel:9 αὐτά   զայն ամենայն (from v.12)

-21 τὰ ἐπὶ τῇ τραπέζῃ   զսեղանն (cf. 1:13,15)

Sectional Conclusion: Selection of a translation unit at the phrase length had profound consequences for Arm. It gave preference to the underlying meaning of a passage and granted the translator the freedom of movement to break down the sense packages and reparcel them in different ways. It thus favoured the removal of Semitic and Greek constructions and their replacement by idiomatic equivalents appropriate to the given context. Once again the phrase unit prevented the rendering from straying too far from its base and the evidence shows that such changes as were made were not capricious or generally motivated by the rhetorical device of *variatio*. Instead they embody the translator's aspirations towards greater clarity and comprehensibility of thought and balance of expression. In some cases the latter also involved the harmonization of parallel passages. Although few in number, they reveal the translator as a self-conscious craftsman, not afraid to leave his imprint on his work.

Quantitative Representation of Text: The second criterion concerns the referential approach adopted by the translator towards his exemplar. Literal renderings strive to remain faithful to the way their base text expresses itself and by adhering to a one-to-one unit preserve its full content. Free texts, on the contrary, may summarize a paragraph in a few sentences while expanding other sections where they feel it necessary to their purpose.

Minuses: Apart from those we have examined under previous headings (e.g. 9:18 ἐπ᾽ αὐτῆς and 9:19 καὶ ἐπὶ τὸν λαόν σου) and the ubiquitous variation in the copula which seems to permeate all textual witnesses, Arm has very few minuses. Some appear the result of the same deliberate policy of concisity and avoidance of semiticisms we have already encountered, e.g.

2:18 om ὑπὲρ τοῦ μυστηρίου τούτου

3:7 om τε καὶ κιθάρας

-10 om σαμβύκης

-10 om βασιλεῦ (probably regarded as redundant cf. 3:9)

5:2 հարճք և կանայք իւր (αἱ παλλακαὶ αὐτοῦ is strictly redundant)

6:13 արբայի (ἐνώπιον τοῦ βασιλέως)

9:8 om σοι ult. may have been influenced by other occurences of the same figure without an indirect object e.g. Jer 16:10 որ մեղք զոր մեղաք Ezek. 18:24ի մեղս իւր զոր մեղաւ 33:16 ամենայն մեղք իւր զոր մեղաւ

9:17 խնդրուածոց (τῶν δεησέων αὐτοῦ)

10:5 om καὶ εἶδον (probably regarded as redundant)

10:17   om τούτου   Apparently its deictic func-
                              tion in distinguishing the
                              visitant from the angel was
                              not appreciated and there
                              fore omitted in translation

Pluses: Arm's additions, though more numerous, carry about the same weight. They betray no vestige of any recondite exegetical traditions and the two examples where such a conclusion might be hazarded are more simply explained on textual grounds. As all the elements of 3:20 can be matched in sets of paired equivalents except εἶπε and հիﬓց, it seems logical to suppose that there is some connection between them and that Arm's reference to five men binding the three arises from a misreading of the Greek verb as πέντε in uncial script with the preceding ΥΙ doubling as Π (thus ΥΙΕΙΠΕ). Similarly, Arm's reading " *խաﬗաﬓձեﬗի և խնդրեին պատճառս զՂանիﬗել է*" (6:4) was likely brought about by a doublet translation[22] of ἐζήτουν first interpreting it as ἐζήλουν the regular equivalent of ﬓախաﬓձել and then in its own right, after which εὑρειν was left untranslated. The hope of finding inspires every search.

Armenian does not tolerate the absolute use of verbs to the same extent as Greek and therefore adds (a) direct and (b) indirect objects where appropriate.

a)   Sus:15 ի ապանել նոցա ﬓﬔա (=P)
        -23 ՀգործԾել զայդ

b)   1:10 որ կարգեացդ ձեզ
        -15 երևեցաւ երեսք նոցա ﬓﬔա
        4:15 աստ ինձ
        5:17 ցուցից քեզ
        11:32 աԾեն ի վերայ ﬕրեանց

A further source of multiple additions is the insertion of the copula verb where Th closely following its semitic model leaves it implicit e.g.

Sus:47 զինչ է բանդ

4:5 որում անուն էր Բաղտասար

More stylistically engendered is the addition of particles to enliven passages of dialogue:

Sus:58 բայց արդ *արդ է*

4:6 *արդ լուր դու*

5:15 արդ *ահաւասիկ*

The translator also seeks to improve the logical flow of the text, e.g. by the use of զի 3:33 and 11:21 where it provides a link between the future and aorist tenses where otherwise the transition is extremely abrupt in Greek. Similarly և *այս* at the beginning of 11:44 indicates both the next stage in the narrative and the king's change of fortune.

Sectional Conclusion: Arm's pluses and minuses, insignificant in comparison to the size of the whole work, are conditioned for the most part by the linguistic-interpretive role of the translator and do not fundamentally alter the nature of his presumed *Vorlage.*

Word Order: The category of WO is an almost self-evident gauge of freedom/literality as the exponent of the former method usually aims to retain the sequence obtaining in his exemplar in so far as this is practicable whereas his counterpart is free from this restraint but closely adheres to the idiom of the receptor language.[23] This investigation led to the isolation of 130 main examples of WO divergent from Th which can be analyzed according to the following groupings.

a) postposition of adjectives (27 cases) a semiticism of Th more easily tolerated by Greek than Armenian in general. Occasionally Arm saves WO by rendering the adjective by a dependent noun in the genitive, e.g. Sus:52 ἡμερῶν κακῶν աւուրբք չարութեան but this also renders prepositioned adjectives sometimes, e.g. Sus:63 ἄσχημον πρᾶγμα իրք գարշութեան.

b) Semitic WO involving a genitive: this cannot stand in Armenian.

3:52 τὸ ὄνομα τῆς δόξης σου τὸ ἅγιον   անուն սուրբ փառաց
                                        քոց
4:5 πνεῦμα θεοῦ ἅγιον   հոգի սուրբ Աստուծոյ

c) Greek constructions

5:2 βαλτ. εἶπεν ἐν τῇ   իբրև ընդ գինիս եմուտ
     γεύσει τοῦ οἴνου   Բաղտասար
                          հրամայեաց

Change in WO has been facilitated by the representation of a Greek phrase as a clause.

5:6 τοῦ βασιλέως ἡ μορφή   գոյնք Թագաւորին
                             (=P)

12:2 ἐν γῆς χόματι   ի հող երկրի
-6 τὸ πέρας ὧν εἰρήκας τῶν   վախճան աբանչելեացդ
     θαυμασίων   զոր ասեցեր

d) Armenian idiom.

2:28 Նաբուբողոնոսոր արքայի
      (cf. 6:9 and contrast 3:2,7) Titles usually follow personal names.

8:13 When not employed as the numeral, one follows the noun, (Jensen §174, p. 70). cf. 11:27 ἐπὶ τραπέζῃ μιᾷ ի միում սեղան

3:10 հրաման եաուր represents the usual order of this set phrase.

Sus:21 ἦν μετά σου νεανίσκος ոմն պատանի էր ընդ քեզ

The verb լինել in general and particularly in monosyllabic forms prefers enclitic WO (cf. Sus:18,37, 2:42, 4:24, 6:3, Bel:31).

Adverbs usually precede the verb they modify.

Bel:30 ἐπείγουσιν αὐτὸν σφόδρα կարի տագնապեն զնա (cf. 3:96, 6:20, 8:3)

Imperatives normally head their clause.

2:9 τὸ ἐνύπνιόν μου εἴπατέ μοι աասացէք ինձ զերազն իմ (cf. 4: 12,15, 6:8)

Infinitives dependent on finite verbs (modals, etc.) quite frequently come at the end of their clause.

Sus:14 αὐτὴν δυνήσονται εὑρεῖν μόνην կարասցեն զնա մ.իայն զտանել(cf. 7:25 and contrast 2:47, 5:16)

e) striving for balance and logical order

Sus:53 The translator undid the chiasmos to simplify the parallelism between the clauses (զանմեղս դատապարտեիր և զվնասակարս արձակեիր).

2:30 ἡ πρόσοψις αὐτῆς ὑπερφερής. ἑστῶσα πρὸ προσώπου σου, καὶ ἡ ὅρασις αὐτῆς φοβερά

Faced with this rather loose construction, the translator united the two parallel phrases before the participle to produce the following result: երեսք նորա և տեսիլ նորա ահագին յոյժ և կայր առաջի քո.

9: 17 ἐπίφανον τὸ πρόσωπόν σου ἐπὶ τὸ ἁγίασμά σου τὸ ἔρημον ἕνεκεν σου

As in all likelihood Arm followed the variant ἐρημωθέν 230 ' 541 393 the translator may have set his equivalent վ աստ քո in front of the phrase beginning ի սրբութիւն to avoid the possible interpretation that the temple was destroyed on God's account.

3:48 διώδευσε καὶ ἐνεπύρισεν οὓς εὗρε περὶ τὴν κάμινον τῶν χαλ–δαίων

The translator remoulds the sentence in his version so that it follows on more smoothly from the preceding verse. The flame has risen over forty-nine cubits above the furnace. It now *surrounds* the furnace (շրջէր պատէր զհնոցան) and burns anyone found in its path.

3:27-28ᵇ և իրաւունս ճշմարտութեան *արարեր* ըստ ամենայնի զոր *արարեր* մեզ

It seems that the translator transferred ἐπήγαγες to 3:27 in order to bring together the two occurrences of ἐποίησας (cf. 6:23, 7:23), thus creating an elaborate verbal chiasmus over the two verses.

Sectional Conclusion: In this way 64 examples (i.e. about half the total) can be shown to be either necessary or desirable linguistically or the result of sober exegesis and not mere *variatio* for its own sake. It is, however, more difficult to see what motivated the other transpositions.

Consistency: This category pertains to the extent to which the translator systematizes his translation equivalents. Literal units employ stereotyped equivalents which always represent the same word even if this means that, as no two words have identical semantic boundaries, contexts inevitably arise in which the calque will be manifestly out of place. Free units on the contrary, aim at producing a passable rendering of the immediate context and are thus less constrained to preserve some imprint of form of the base text in their work.

As is to be expected, everyday words with only one general meaning or used in one particular sense in the book receive a high degree of stereotyping from Arm. Thus մէջ always stands for μέσον սիրտ-καρδία (1:8 ἔθετο ἐπὶ τὴν καρδίαν ի մխին դնել is Armenian idiom) κάμινος -հնոց, τιμή-պատիւ, δόξα-փառք (11:20 շուրբ թագաւորութեան is probably *variatio* for փառք թագ. in 11:21) ἀναγγέλλειν -պատմել (2:4 ասացուր) κατευθύνειν-յաջողել (3:97 շբեղացոյց renders the only transitive example)   σφόδρα-յոյժ (Bel:30 կարի).

Another class of words may have two quite distinct meanings more or less distant from each other. In these cases the translator, aware of the semantic range of the original, varies his practice according to the requirements of the context. Should the word recur in the second sense, if nothing further prevents it, he repeats the equivalent used previously. Thus instead of being an arbitrary aberration from the

Vorlage, his method represents a more sophisticated approach to the elucidation of its content, e.g. σπέρμα 1:12,16 ունդ (=P) 'grain', զաւակ passim 'offspring',

πέρας   4:8,19 ձագ (territorial) վախճան passim (chronological)

σπουδή   Sus:50 վ ապվ ապակի
        3:91 տագնապաւ (trouble) (9:27, 11:44)
        2:25 փութապէս (haste)
        6:19 փութով

ὑπομένειν   Sus:57 կալ աւ յանձին (transitive: to bear, endure =P)
        12:12 համբերից (intransitive: be patient)

ταπεινός   3:37 տառապեալ p (abased, poor) (cf. Ezek.29:14)
        -87 խոնարհ (lowly, humble)

(cf. λαός: plural is rendered by ազգ p, singular ժողովուրդ (Sus:7 ժողով contextually based).

We can also gauge literalism by the extent to which a translator distinguishes between synonyms and words of related meaning. λόγος բան ῥῆμα բան (հրաման 2:15, 3:22 պատգամ 4:14)

δόγμα   հրաման ուխտ
ὁρισμός   ուխտ
ῥύεσθαι   փրկել   σῴζειν:active ապրեցուցանել
ἐξέλεσθαι   passive ապրել
οἰκτιρμός   գթութիւն(p)   (1:9. 4:24 ողորմութիւն)
ἐλεημοσύνη   ողորմութիւն
ἔλεος   ողորմութիւն   (3:89 ողորմ 9:20 գութp)
συμπατεῖν   կոխել   (8:7 կոխան արար
                7:7,19 կոտորէր)
συντρίβειν   խորտակել   (2:42 եղիցի շախշախին
                3:39 բեկելովp
                8:25 մանրեցէ =P
                11:4 փշրեցէ)

ἐξομολογεῖσθαι   գոհանալ
αἰνεῖν   աւրհնել   (4:31 գովlեցի)

εὐλογεῖν		where the translator has al ready used ապրնել to translate ἤνεσα.
κατασφάζειν	կոտորել	
κατασπᾶν	կործանել	
ἀποκτείνειν	սպանանել	(2:13, Bel:22 from կոտորել)
διαφθείρειν	ապականել	(2:9,44, 6:26 from եղծանել)
παράπτωμα	յանցանք	(6:22 վնաս where a more concrete sense is required)
ἁμαρτία	մեղք	
ἀδικία	անիրաւութիւն	(9:16 անաւրէն)

However on one occasion these established equivalencies are upset. Having used մեղք to represent ἁμαρτίαν (–ιας 230 etc.) the translator, rather than repeat with the Greek text, decided in favour of variation and paired անաւրէնութեանց with ἁμαρτίας. Also adducing the addition from OG, he then had to couple ἀνομίας (230, etc.) with անիրաւութեանց and supply ամբարշտութեանց to render ἀδικίας.

It is further characteristic of literal translators to group together words connected by root or stem and render them by equivalents which are linked by the same sort of etymological principle. In Arm ἰσχύς is stereotyped by զաւրութիւն and ἰσχύειν by զաւրանալ (Sus:39 բունն էր which may be influenced by OG βίαιος), ὑπερισχύειν by զաւրանալ ի վերայ 11:23 (3:22 սաստկանայր). ἔννοια մsimilar – ἐννοεῖσθαι ածել զմտաւ but προνοεῖν - հայել, πληροῦν 2:35 եւ ից, 5:26 վախճանեաց (=P), πλήρωσις կատարել συμπλήρωσις կատարումն 8:23 կատարել. γινώσκειν out of 22 occurrences 8 were rendered by գիտել, 9 by ճանաչել (forms based on the aorist stem only) 2 խելամուտ լինել, 2 իմանալ and one case of the imperative rendered by տես (Bel:19).

γνωστός		յայտնի		
γνώμη	2:14	խրատ	2:15 հրաման	
ἐπιγινώσκειν	Sus:48	հասանել ի վերայ		

συνιέναι : out of 21 occurrences 8 involved phrases with խելամտութ, 1 մխտ դնել, 4 ի մխտ առնուլ, 2 զմտաւ ածել, 1 խորհրդակ (8:23) 2 իմանալ, իմաստունք 2 (12:3) հանճարեղ (11:35) and (11:30) συνήσει ἐπὶ τοὺς καταλιπόντας διαθήκην զուսարեցի ի վերայ այնցիկ որ ... which is undoubtedly the result of contextual exegesis.[24]

συνετίζειν　2 cases of խելամտութ առնել, 1 իմացուցանել
σύνεσις　　 2 cases of իմաստութիւն, 3 հանճար, 2 phrases with խելամտութ.

It therefore appears that as a general rule the translator of Arm was not concerned systematically to encode into his version information on etymological relationships obtaining between terms in the present text.

If, as we have seen, certain Greek words may be translated by several Armenian variants, the opposite is equally true. անկանել mainly renders πίπτειν but also one example of ἀναπίπτειν (Sus:37) ἐμπίπτειν (Sus:23) εἰσπηδᾶν (Sus:26) καταφέρεσθαι (5:20) ῥίπτεσθαι (8:12) and ἐμβάλλεσθαι (3:11, 15, 6:7, 12)[25]. խորհուրդ generally renders διαλογισμός but also λογισμός (11:25) βουλή (2:14) φρόνισις (2:21) μυστήριον (2:27, 28, 29, 4:6); մերձենալ renders ἅπτεσθαι, ἐγγίζειν and also (although the usual equivalent is խաւսել) ὁμιλεῖν at Sus:57 on the conduct of the daughters of Israel towards the elders (contrast the use of խաւսել for Susanna and the youth vv 54 and 58) վախճան, a word of significant importance in the book stands 6 times for πέρας, 3 for τέλος, 3 for συντέλεια and twice for τὰ ἔσχατα.

Sectional Conclusion: Arm bears the stamp of someone experienced in the practical activity of translation, convinced of the primacy of meaning over form and confident that where he has employed a single Armenian word to do duty for several Greek ones his readers would grasp the sense appropriate to each context. As a result his work lacks the systematization and regularity of a fully literal technique which means that the critic must investigate his treatment of each word separately in attempting to decide which reading is supported by Armenian, and in the case of several synonyms, as already observed, caution is required in making any inference about the version's *Vorlage.*

Linguistic Adequacy: The final category is also the most difficult to apply since the criteria for measuring it are more subjective. A literal translation may be unsatisfactory because of the comprehensibility gap it causes by neglecting what the text actually means in an effort to express as closely as possible the letter of what is written. On the other hand, a free rendering may come in for censure for altering the tenor of the *Vorlage* by relegating certain features to parentheses, while over-emphasizing others by tendentious interpretation and introduction of extraneous material.

The knowledge of Greek possessed by Arm's translator was generally quite sufficient for his task. However, there are a few cases of words occurring once in the book or used once in an uncommon way which he represented either by the usual equivalent or by recourse to contextual interpretation. Thus (Sus:5) ἀπεδείχθησαν is rendered by երևեցան 'appeared' whereas the required sense is 'were appointed'. Similarly (Sus:15) ποτε is translated by երբեմն 'at some time or other' whereas the context demands 'at length', now'. Sus:18 κατὰ τὰς πλαγίας θύρας becomes ի կողմանէ դրացն 'from the side of the doors' and not 'by the side doors'. Ανέβησαν at 2:29 is rendered մտայոյզ առնէին.[26] Perhaps the translator did not grasp the sense 'occurred' and therefore rendered it as 'troubled, upset' which is what thoughts are generally described as doing in the book (cf. 4:16, 5:6,10). Σαμβύκη only occurs in chapter 3 of Daniel within the Old Testament according to *HR* and so does not seem to have been familiar to the translator. However, he was well-acquainted with another kind of instrument which sounded very similar, i.e. the թմբուկ (drum) which is substituted at 3:5. Likewise, παραβιβάζων only appears at 11:20 in Th where it refers to dispatching a foreign ambassador to win kingly power. Arm renders բռնադատիցէ 'he will force, oblige' obviously construing it from some compound of βιάζειν. Another word to occur once in the Greek Bible is θερισταί at Bel:33, which has been translated by մշակ the normal equivalent of γεωργός.[27]

It is hardly surprising that chapter 11's veiled, allusive language caused the translator some difficulty and this was compounded by the confusion of subsequent copyists. Indeed, it appears that the version was subject to primitive error which has affected most of the manuscript tradition apart from the text recently discovered at Union Theological Seinary, New York (NYU4)[28]. Hence, the course of the conflict between the two kingdoms is obfuscated by faulty identification of the combatants;[29] for the aggressor βασιλεὺς τοῦ βορρᾶ is rendered Թագաւորն հարաւոյ by the majority tradition at v.15, probably as a result of harmonization to the occurrence of the name of the defender later in the same verse. With the aid of NYU4 the original text may be restituted as Թագաւորն հիւսւսոյ. Similarly, at v.19 the king of the North's final unsuccessful rally in his own territory (ἐπιστρέψει εἰς τὴν ἰσχὺν τῆς αὐτοῦ) is depicted more as a triumphal progress by the majority text (դարձցի զաւրութեամբ յերկիր իւր) which renders his ultimate failure all the more paradoxical. The UTS MS adduces the variant զաւրութիւն which exactly parallels Th ἰσχύν. Moreover, the disappearance of the preposition which probably introduced it is easily explicable by haplography after դարձցի.[30]

Nevertheless, other *aporiai* still remain in this chapter, some of which may derive from the translator or his *Vorlage*.[31] In v.6 Th locates the signing of the treaty between the kingdoms of North and South after the interlude μετὰ τὰ ἔτη αὐτοῦ (i.e. εἶς τῶν ἀρχόντων) yet Arm dates it after the kings' deaths (յետ մահացն իրեանց). Moreover, in v.16 Arm fails to recognize ὁ εἰσπορευόμενος as the assailant (i.e. the king of the North) and by translating the participle as a circumstantial phrase (ի մտանել իւրում) leaves the sentence without any explicit subject. In v.17 Th's expression πάσης τῆς βασιλείας αὐτοῦ intensi-

fies the might of the king of the North, whereas Arm mistaken-
ly construes it as the direction in which the king will avance, i.e.
into his enemy's kingdom (մտանել ... յամենայն թագաւորութիւն նորա)   while relying on his own strength   (զաւրութեամբ իւրով).

In v.18 MT twice reads 'his insult'. Feeling uncomfortable
with Th's text where the first occasion is plural (in most witnesses) and the second singular, our translator appears to
have restored the balance by rendering both as plural, as he
does in v.23 where, reading αὐτούς with B, he translates the following αὐτοῦ by means of a plural pronoun (ի վերայ նոցա).
Moreover, noting the two occurrences of the form ἐπιστρέψει
following in quick succession at the end of v.18 and beginning
of v.19, he decided that the object of the second (τὸ πρόσωπον)
could be put to better use if construed with the first. Suitably
modified, the phrase provides a more fitting climax to the
king's prowess. Not only does he return the princes' insult but
hurls it back in their faces (զնախատանս նոցա դարձուցէ
յերեսս): The verb ἐπιστρέψει at the beginning of v.19 is then
taken as intransitive and rendered accordingly (դարձի).

Sectional Conclusion: In general Arm provides an adequate
rendering of its *Vorlage* which demonstrates easy familiarity
with Greek. However, the translator was sometimes unaware
of the meaning of unusual words or of everyday words used in
an uncharacteristic way. Whereas his understanding of the
text is commonly of a high standard it seems he is somewhat
thrown off his balance in places by the deliberately veiled nature of the language in chapter eleven. As a result, his regular
desire for clarity of expression prompts him to set about
emending his *Vorlage* in an attempt to make more sense of the
passage.

NOTES

1. For a fuller discussion of the contrasting profiles in translation technique between Arm1 and Arm2 see S.P. Cowe, "The Two Armenian Versions of Chronicles."

2. For a general introduction to the issues involved in translating from Greek into Armenian see E. Rhodes, "Limitations of Armenian in Representing Greek", in *The EarlyVersions of the New Testament.* B.M. Metzger (ed.), pp.171-181 and C.E. Cox, "The Use of the Armenian Version for the Textual Criticism of the Septuagint", *La Septuaginta en la investigación contemporánea*, N. Fernández Marcos (ed.), Madrid: TECC 34, 1985, pp.25-35, TECC 34 and for a more specific consideration S.P. Cowe, "La versión armenia" pp.1xxi-1xxix.

3. See Sh. Pace, "The Old Greek Translation of Daniel 7-12".

4. As Koriwn records, he himself along with Eznik, Yovsēpʻ and others studied Greek in the Byzantine capital. Thereafter, Łazar informs us in his letter (Patmagirkʻ Hayocʻ p.187) that he studied in Byzantine territory. See further chapter four, note 18, pp.291-2. Similar traditions concerning other contemporaries emphasize the importance ascribed to such studies by one of the most influential ecclesiastical circles in Armenia.

5. J. Barr, *The Typology of Literalism in Ancient Biblical Translations;* and E. Tov, *The Text-Critical Use of the Septuagint in Biblical Research*

6. See Rhodes, "Limitations of Armenian", p.173.

7. This represents an accommodation to Greek morphology on the part of the revisers, since Arm 1 reflects a tendency to render infinitives of purpose by a final clause. See S.P. Cowe, "The Two Armenian Versions of Chronicles".

8. Meillet, p.114, §130.

9. Jensen, p.120, §309.

10. A.A. Abrahamyan's observation that several occurrences of the imperfect in Koriwn's "Life of Maštocʻ" should be ren-

dered by the aorist in Modern Armenian (*Grabari Jeṙnark* [Handbook of Classical Armenian] Erevan: Luys, 1976, p.399, note 12) suggests that the semantic range of the imperfect in Classical Armenian was wider than the cases of continuous, inceptive and iterative activity usually associated with that tense.

11. Indeed, as the distinction between active and passive voice was not morphologically articulated in certain verbal forms, Armenian usage diverges palpably from Greek. One aspect of this is the greater tendency to present events in the active mode.

12. Jensen, p.130, §344 B.

13. For *Tendenz* in Arm 1 directed against idolatry see S.P. Cowe, "Epistle of Jeremiah".

14. For a consideration of the distinction between Θυσιαστήριον and Βωμός in rendering מזבח in the Greek pentateuch see S. Daniel *Recherches sur le vocabulaire du culte dans la sep - tante*, pp.15-32.

15. The same set of distinctions is maintained in Arm1 of Chronicles and the Epistle of Jeremiah. On the background to the various terms see J.R. Russell, *Zoroastrianism in Armenia*, HIS 5 Cambridge, Mass.: Harvard University Press, 1987.

16. For the retention of *figura etymologica* in Arm2 of Chronicles see S.P. Cowe, "The Two Armenian Versions of Chronicles".

17. That they also constituted a *crux interpretum* is manifest from the commentator Vardan Arewelc'i's enumeration of several previous hypotheses to penetrate the arboreal aenigma. See Arm B, vil.3, 1977, p.88.

18. See C.A. Moore, *Daniel, Esther and Jeremiah The Additions* 1977, pp.25 f. On the Greek origin of the paronomasia see also S.T. Lachs, "A Note on the Original Language of Susanna", *JQR* 69(1978), pp.52-54 and for the attempt to reconstruct a Hebrew *Vorlage* F. Zimmermann, "The Story of Susanna and its Original

Language", JQR 48(1957-1958), p.239. For a more recent study of the question see H. Engel, *Die Susanna-Erzählung. Einleitung, übersetzung und Kommentar zum Septuaginta-Text und zur Theodotion-Bearbeitung* OBO 61, 1985.

19. Meillet, pp.164 f, §134.
20. Meillet, pp.115 f, §132.
21. Jensen, pp.116 f, §299dd.
22. Cf. 6:17 այլագգք ինչ իրք շրջեացին where both այլագգք and the verb seem to be derived from the Greek verb ἀλλοιωθῇ.
23. There is a danger sometimes, especially when engaged in the study of ancient texts, to take up a rather abstract approach. Thus, although in absolute terms Wever's statement: "Da das Armenische eine im hohen Masse flektierende Sprache ist, ist die Wortfolge relativ bedeutungslos" (J.W. Wevers, *Septuaginta Vetus Testamentum Graecum Auctoritate Academiae Scientiarum Gottingensis editum* Vol.1 *Genesis* . Göttingen: Vandenhoeck & Ruprecht, 1974, p.46) is correct, it is probable that out of "x" number of theoretical arrangements, only a very few are really practical alternatives. Those in general currency within the speech community which acquire the status of an idiom are so basic to the way the receptor language expresses itself that it cannot be regarded as the result of the translator's caprice if he prefers such a formulation to the one found in the base text.
24. The concordance to the Armenian Bible indicates the occurrences of medio-passive forms of the verb գումարել follow no clear equivalency pattern. It may be that the translator confused the morpheme from συνιέναι with one from συνεἶναι.
25. Several of these entries do not appear in the Armenian concordance.
26. Significantly, this is the only occurrence of the phrase in the book.

27. Cf. հնձող in Ruth 2:3 etc. to render the cognate θερίζων.

28. This can be stated categorically since the passage falls within the third collation sample which was applied to all witnesses available to the present study.

29. For an investigation of the divergent OG text here see A. van der Kooij, "A Case of reinterpretation in the OG of Daniel 11, 72-80", *Tradition and Re-Interpretation in Jewish and Early-Christian Literature* SP-B 36, J.W. Henten et al (eds.), Leiden: E.J. Brill, 1986, pp.72-80.

30. As variation between the forms յերկիր and յերկրի is extremely common in Armenian manuscripts, as is confusion between երկիր and յերկիր, it may be that an original երկրի (= τῆς γῆς) became transformed into յերկրի → յերկիր in the course of copying, though the available MSS lack data which might confirm this.

31. MS NYU4 offers another valuable early reading at 11:30:
    ταπεινωθήσεται] -θησονται   46' 230'' 410 Tht
    խոնարհեսցին] -gh
    The likelihood is that it represents the Arm1 reading, while the majority text witnesses the revision in company with MS 230 *et al.*

CHAPTER 7

PATRISTIC AND LITURGICAL
CITATIONS

In chapter two an attempt was made to delineate in essentials the pattern traced by Arm's unfolding manuscript transmission. However, as even the oldest of the extant codices are closer to us by one century than they are to the autograph and granted the extensive transformations through which the text passed in the latter period where documentation exists, the question of the trustworthiness of the medieval witnesses is posed acutely. Excepting the discovery and decipherment of further palimpsests,[1] the only means of pursuing our examination behind MSS with the full text of Arm is that of lectionaries, commentaries[2] and citations woven into the fabric of works by pre-Cilician Armenian writers. The latter term is used advisedly since despite the advantage the method has of securing an approximate *terminus ante quem* for the text type, it cannot be immediately assumed that the quotation preserves unchanged the form of words directly extracted from a biblical codex.[3]

Without the facility of chapter and verse divisions, check-ing the precise formulation of a particular phrase would have been an arduous task. Moreover, this was not always what was required. Grammatical data especially are frequently expend-able in dovetailing a quotation into its new context. As citations were employed to evoke a certain mood or achieve an elevated style depending on the genre, as well as in closely-argued theo-logical discourses, the level of accuracy varies accordingly. In addition to the vagaries of the original author's memory we must also contend with the work's own textual transmission which may have suffered from the scribal tendency to harmo-nize biblical texts to the one with which they were familiar.

To these general remarks in an Armenian context it must be added that though there is a rich early tradition of historiog-raphy and hagiography, the works are not infrequently pre-served in MSS of the seventeenth century or later which, in cer-tain cases, reveal signs of stylistic redaction.[4] Moreover, not all are yet available in critical editions, hence impairing the accura-cy of any textual collation. With these caveats in mind let us proceed to an investigation of the evidence which has been se-lected mainly from fifth to seventh century writers. Of these Lazar P'arpec'i had to be excluded from the list of possible sources since the editors do not indicate any citations from Daniel.[5]

The procedure to be followed in the comparison is first to quote the citation by the section and page number of the edi-tion and underneath to set out the major variants abstracted from its apparatus. The text of MS 287 of the diplomatic edi-tion of Daniel is then given in parallel along with its variants. Sections of text where contact between the two documents is particularly close are italicized. A brief analysis rounds off the consideration of each case.

Chronologically the first author to be examined is the theologian, Eznik Kołbac'i,[6] whose life is generally accepted as straddling the break between the fourth and fifth centuries.

a) § 113 p. 43 ... եւ ոչ գազանք սպանանել յաւժարեն որպէս ոչ Դանիէլի գազանքն վնասեցին, եւ ոչ *երից մանկանցն հուր հնոցին*

   3:23 եւ *երեքին նորա* Սեդրաք, Միսաք եւ Աբեդնագով անկան ի մէջ *հնոցին* կապեալք.

   (3:21 b ... եւ ընկեցան ի մէջ *հրոյն* բորբոքելոյ)

   (3:49 եւ հրեշտակ Աստուծոյ . . . Թափափեաց զբոց *հրոյն ի հնոցէ* անտի)

   6:22 Աստուած իմ առաքեաց զհրեշտակ իւր եւ եխից զբերանս առեւծուցս, եւ ոչ ապականեցին զիս

The citation combines disparate elements from the book with extraneous material, indicating the responsibility of the theologian for its present form. As such it is more a reminiscence of the incidents of Daniel in the lions' den and the three young men in the fiery furnace. In the Bible the lions are always named expressly with the result that Eznik's term 'գազանք' appears a generalizing allusion. Similarly վնասեցին echoes the ապականեցին of 6:22, which seems a closer parallel to the theologian's words than 14:30 suggested by the editors, Mariès and Mercier. The reference to the three and the fire of the furnace show acquaintance with 3:23 and 3:21b/49 respectively.

b) § 283 p. 87 այլ եւ զվիշապս եւ *զգազանս* եւ *զխաւար* եւ *զխայյատակունս* զոր ի չարէ դնեն, ի նոյն փառատրութիւն նորին հոգւոյ կոչեցեալ, եւ Դաւթաւ եւ *երեք մանկամբքն ի հնոցի անդ ընծայեցուցանէ*

Eznik selects highlights from the species of the physical universe called to join in a paean of praise to their creator by the three in the furnace. The reference to the three again echoes 3:23 and v. 51 which also parallels 'ի հնոցի անդ' with 'ի մէջ հնոցին'. With regard to the specific items, 'գազանս' refers to v.81 ... 'ամենայն գազան եւ անասուն' where its plural form coincides with MSS M346-M2585 M9116-M2627' M182''=GK, 'խատար', is taken from v.72 and 'փայլատակունս' from v.73. The first item, 'վիշապս' seems roughly parallel to 'կետր' in v.79 in that it basically represents the class of reptiles over against land mammals (cf. v. 81).

c) § 255 p. 79 որպէս Յովսեփայ եւ *Դանիէլի* մեծամեծ իրաց տեսիլք յայտնեցան. The third citation is extremely general and contains no direct contact with the biblical text although it is similar to formulations such as at 7:1 երազ եւես Դանիէլ եւ տեսիլ գլխոյ նորա յանկողնի and 8:1 տեսիլ երեւեցաւ ինձ, եսԴանիէլ յետ տեսլեանն առաջնոյ

§ 118 p.45 եւ իւր իսկ երբեմն իբրեւ *զհիննարեայ*, երբեմն իբրեւ զմատաղաւրեայ, վասն այլ եւ այլ տեսչութեանց կերպարանեալ՝ *գանկալոյ առնն* երեւէր.

The final case also has only isolated words in common with Arm. The form 'զհիննարեայ' recalls 'հիննաւուրց' of 7:22, while 'գանկալոյ առնն' reflects the expression 'այր գանկալի' found at 9:23 and 10:11 (cf. Koriwn's citation to be discussed).

In sum, the references are allusive rather than precise, so that they do not offer a clear picture of the biblical text with which Eznik was familiar and thus cannot serve as a touchstone by which to assay the medieval MSS.

Only one citation from Daniel is noted in the "Life of Maštocʻ" by Eznik's younger colleague, the hagiographer Koriwn[7] composing in the mid 440's and that consists of only one word.

p.5 այլ եւ հոգեկան ազգին հրեշտակութեամբ գովեալ զարբրցն զաւրութիւն որ զԴանիէլ «*գանկալի*» քարոզեալ կոչէին.

(9:23; 10:11, 19) այր *գանկալի*

Third in chronological succession is the hagiographer Agathangelos who was active in the second half of the fifth century.

§ 393 p. 198 ... եւ յարուցեալ Թագաւոր համաշխարհական, զամենայն ազգս հնազանդելով եւ *զԹագաւորութիւն* իւր *ազգի այլում ոչ* փոխեալ ըստ ասեցելոյն Դանիէլի

qԹագ. –այլում] qԹագաւորութիւն նորա այլում ազգի Ա Բ
ազգի այլում] այլում ազգի b   փոխեալ] տացի g

2:44 յաւուրս Թագաւրացն այնոցիկ յարուսցէ Աստուած
երկնից Թագաւորութիւն որ յաւիտեան ն չ եղծանիցի *եւ
զԹագաւորութիւն* նորա *ազգի այլումոչ* մնասցէ.

As is indicated by the italics, there is a certain contact between the texts but Agathangelos' formulation seems to tele-
scope various passages into one. The reference to 'all peoples'
may derive from the continuation of the same verse: մանրեսցէ
եւ հոսեսցէ զամենայն Թագաւորութիւնս. The element 'com-
manding obedience' perhaps reflects 11:39 եւ յածախեսցէ
փառս եւ հնազանդեցուսցէ նոսա գրագումս. MS g's variant
'տացի' has probably been influenced by the phrase 'որէ
բարձրեալն Թագաւորութեան մարդկան եւ ում կամի տացէ
զնա' at 4:29 and parallels.

§ 179 p. 99. *Զու եւ* որ *փառաւորեալ* դ եւ *ի վերայ
ամենայն տիեզերաց*

3:45 *Զու եւ* Տէր Աստուած մ*իայն* *փառաւրեալ ի վերայ
ամենայն տիեզերաց*
Աստուած] + որ V280 M346'
փառաւորեալ] (-եալդ M178-M346') + եւ V280-M346'-
M2585 M2627

In contrast to the first quotation, this is far more exact.
One likely reason is the use of the Prayer of Azariah as a liturgical reading. In fact apart from the omission of the divine name
and the accompanying adverb մ*իայն* it agrees with both occurrences of the verse in the Jerusalem lectionary and MSS M345'
(and V280). It is, therefore, extremely plausible that their combined witness represents an earlier stage of Arm's textual history.

§ 502 p. 249. Նոյնպես եւ *Բաղտասար* ասաց գՂանիէլ Թէ
«Գիտեմք զի *հոգի սուրբ Աստուծոյ գոյ ի քեզ*»

4:6 *Բաղտասար իշխան գիտաց զոր ես գիտեմ թէ հոգի սուրբ*
Աստուծոյ գոյ ի քեզ
թէ] զի M178 M346-WN11*

Here it is evident that Agathangelos is quoting from
memory and has therefore confused Nebuchadnezzar's son
who appears in Chapter 6 with the Babylonian name given
Daniel. Here Nebuchadnezzar is addressing Balthasar (Daniel).
Thus the variation between first person singular/plural is of little consequence when the speaker is a king. Although թէ and
զի can both introduce an indirect statement, the latter is less
common and so the agreement with representatives of sub-
group B1 may be of some significance.

§ 179 p. 99 ... *փոխեալ զնա ի կերպարանս անասնոց եւ*
ընդ գազանս անապատի եղեր զբնակութիւն նորա եւ ընդ գիսս
վայրի զառոտ նորա
եւ 1*b] om rel

4:22 *եւ ընդ գազանս անապատի եղից բնակութիւն քո*
5:21 *եւ ընդ գիսս բնակութիւն նորա եւ խոտ իբրեւ զարջառոյ*
ջամբէին նմա

Here the author weaves an intricate tapestry from diverse
strands of Arm. կերպարանս perhaps finds an echo in the detail mentioned in 4:33 կերպարանք իմ առ իս դարձան. The
generic term անասնոց sums up the process by which (4:30)
վարաք նորա իբրեւ զառեւծուց մեծ. etc. Probably literary parallelism dictated the balance between անապատի and վայրի and
the reference to food by means of a noun in antithesis to
dwelling.

The final citation by Agathangelos (§475 p.235) which
corresponds to 9:26 will be dealt with in the General
Conclusion because of its association with P and the question
of an early Armenian translation from Syriac.

Then follows the historian traditionally referred to as P'awstos Buzand who wrote his account of events in the period 325-386 probably in 470s.[9]

Bk.IV.4, p.66[10] *զմեղս ձեր ողորմութեամբ պարտ է քաւել ձեզ.*

4:24 *զմեղս քո ողորմութեամբ քաւեսցիր*

 եւ զանօրէնութիւնս ձեր զթուութեամբ եւ *արօք* *աղքատաց:*

 եւ զանիրաւութիւնս քո   *արօք* *տնանկաց:*

արօք M287ᵐᵍ V280] om M287 ᵗˣᵗ զթով M178-M346' J1925-
        M2627'

    զթովքⱼ rel

The numerical variations are clearly an adaptation to the new context. Catholicos Nersēs has assumed Daniel's mantle and directs what had been discrete advice to Nebuchadnezzar to the populace at large at the inauguration of his primacy. The two forms for injustice are close synonyms and hence the variant may be the result of quotation from memory rather than a divergent manuscript reading. The same consideration applies to the substitution of the common counterpart աղքատ for the more unusual choice found in scripture. The most important datum from the verse is the historian's corroboration of the minority text 'alms' which is the probably to be assigned to Arm1. It may be that the form զթովութեամբ reflects knowledge of the Arm2 reading adduced by the majority of witnesses, but is more likely to have been inserted to achieve a rhetorical symmetry between the two halves of the sentence. The first part contains the primary elements sin, mercy and atonement, whereas the second is deficient, involving only injustice and poor relief. Hence զթովութեամբ balances ողորմութեամբ as the appropriate attitude to accompany the deed.[11]

Two rather passing references to chapter 3 are found in the history of the Armenian revolt of 451 led by Vardan Mamikonean to protest religious persecution instigated by the Sasanian monarch Yazdgard II.[12] Dating the author Ełišē is a subject of controversy, but the first decades of the sixth century seem to offer the most plausible setting.[13]

p.9 որք *կապեալ էին* ի կռապաշտութեանն անլուծելի հանգուցիւք, վառեալք եւ *ջեռեալք* իբրեւ *զհնոց* առ այրել զուխտ սուրբ եկեղեցւոյ:

3:19 *ջեռուցէք զհնոցն* եւԹնպատիկ

-23 անկան ի մէջ *հնոցին կապեալք*

p.13 զայս լսելով Թագաւորին` *բորբոքեցաւ* իբրեւ *զհուր հնոցին* ի Բաբիլոն, մինչեւ իւրքն իսկ անդէն դեռ եւս իբրեւ *զբաղձացիսն այրեցեալ* լինէին:

3:6 ընկեսցի ի *հնոցն հրոյն բորբոքելոյ*

-22 հրաման Թագաւորին սաստկանայր եւ *հնոցն բորբոքէր*

-48 (բոցն) շրջէր պատէր *զհնոցաւ ն* եւ *այրէր* զորս գտանէր ի *բաղձացւոց* անտի

Another passage likens the king to the ferocious beasts of Daniel's night vision in his uncontainable fury.[14] Several of the motifs are handled allusively, but the following example contains some concrete points of contact:

p.7 *յարձակեցաւ ի վերայ* աշխարհին Ցունաց, *եհար մինչ* ի քաղաքն Մծբին

եհար մինչ] եւ եհար մինչեւ MSS< Թ Ժ Ի Խ Կ Հ Ձ S[2]

8:6-7 *յարձակեցաւ ի վերայ* նորա զաւրութեամբ ուժոյ իւրոյ... զայրացաւ եւ *եհար* զխոյն

Nevertheless, the references are not sufficiently detailed to be of much assistance in assessing the text of Daniel the writer was familiar with.

Next in order we shall examine the seventh century historian Sebēos[15] whose work contains two sizeable quotations from chapter seven.

p.14 1Թափեցան վարագաթեւքն եւ ջնջեցաւ յերկրէ եւ եկաց

7:4 Թափեցան Թեւք նորա   եւ ջնջեցաւ յերկրէ եւ եկաց իբրեւ ի վերայ ոտից մարդոյ, եւ սիրտ մարդոյ տուաւ նմա:

-4 իբրեւ ի վերայ ոտից մարդոյ, եւ սիրտ մարդոյ տուաւ նմա:

ահա գազանն երկրորդ նման արջոյ, եւ եկաց ի կողմն մի

-5 եւ ահա երկրորդ գազանն նման արջոյ, եւ եկաց ի կողմն մի

եւ կողք երեք ի բերան ունելով ասէին ցնա արի, կեր գմարմինս

եւ կողք երեք ի բերան նորա   ասէին ցնա արի, կեր գմարմինս

բազմաց». գազանն երրորդ իբրեւ զինճ, եւ չորք թեւք թռչնոց

-6 բազմաց այլ գազան ելանէր իբրեւ զինճ, եւ չորք թեւ թռչնոց

ի վերայ նորա եւ չորք գլուխ գազանին.

ի վերայ նորա եւ չորք գլուխ գազանին (գազանն] գազան Ա)

ելանէր M287 WN11-M2585] էր M346; om rel = Jer 121 = Gk.

թեւ M287] թեւս WN11 թեւք rel

թռչնոց M287' M346 J1925] (-ն WN11) -նյ rel.

գազանն չորրորդ ահեղ եւ   զարմանալի   եւ ժանիք

-7 գազան   չորրորդ ահեղ եւ հզաւր առաւել եւ ժանիք
նորա երկաթիք եւ մագիլք նորա պղնձիք. ուտեր եւ
մանրէր եւ

-7 նորա երկաթիք եւ մագիլք նորա պղնձիք. ուտեր եւ
մանրեր եւ

գմնացուածսն առ ոտն կոտորէր.

-7 գմնացորդսն   առ ոտն կոտորէր.

գազան M287] -զանն rel = Jer 121.

եւ մագիլք նորա պղնձիք M287' M178-M346'] om rel.

ոտն] ոտանն V280 WN11 J1925

p.177 գազանն չորրորդ ահեղ եւ զարմանալի, եւ հզաւր յոյժ.
ժանիք նորա երկաթիք, եւ մագիլք նորա պղնձիք. ուտեր
եւ մանրէր եւ գմնացեալսն առ ոտն կոտորէր.

This case is particularly interesting in that it appears in two places in slightly different form. That the phrase եւ հզաւր առաւել is absent from the long citation on p. 141 does not imply that the author was unfamiliar with it though in quoting it on p. 177 he uses a positive adverb (յոյժ) instead of the comparative (առաւել). The fact that he employs different variants from the reading of the biblical MSS զմնացորդսն - a) զմնացուածսն b) զմնացեալսն suggests that he is quoting from memory. Far more significant is the support he gives to the reading եւ մագիլք նորա պղնձիք on both occasions since it is not found in the Jerusalem lectionary and has little outside backing (Hippol Thtᵖ Prisc).

p.141 գազանն չորրորդ Թագաւորութեանն*   կացցէ
7:23 գազանն չորրորդ Թագաւորութիւն չորրորդ կայցէ
        որ առաւել իցէ քան զամենայն Թագաւորութիւնս
-23 յերկրի որ առաւել իցէ քան զամենայն Թագաւորութիւնս

(* Թագաւորութեանն is the main reading of the MSS and edd. MS Ա reads Թագաւորութիւնն and the MS of 1852 Թագաւորութեան. The latest editor wishes to amend the historian's text to that preserved in the biblical MSS).

p.162 գազանն չորրորդ չորրորդ Թագաւորութիւն կացցէ ի վերայ երկրի.
    կայցէ M287 J1925-M2627] կացէ WN11* կացցէ rel.
    յերկրի] ի յերկրի M178 M2627   ի վերայ երկրի V280

Again the form of the quotation varies from section to section, though most of the text is preserved intact. The most important point is the agreement between Sebeos and MS V280 in reading ի վերայ երկրի (= OG) against the rest of the witnesses to the edition.

p.141 եւ   ժ   եղջիւրք   ժ   Թագաւորք յարիցեն, եւ զկնի
7:24 եւ տասն եղջերն որ տասն Թագաւորք յարիցեն, եւ զկնի
        նորա յարիցէ այլ որ առաւել է չարեաւք քան զամենայն
-24 նոցա յարիցէ այլ որ առաւել իցէ չարիք քան զամենայն
        առաջինսն
-24 առաջինսն

եղջերն] եղջիւրք M4114 M351

չարիւք M287] -րեաւք rel = Jer 121

նոցա] նորա M178-M346' J1925'-M4114 V1508 = Jer 121

իգէ] է J1925

p.162 որ առաւել է չարեաւք քան զամենայն թագաւորութիւնս

The singular/plural variation in the form of the personal pronoun is reflected in Th also (αὐτῶν] - του A' AethP ArmP Cyr Hieros). The present tense of the copula may imply familiarity with a text of the type witnessed by MS J1925. The possibility is heightened by its presence in both occurrences of the citation and the use of the future form in the parallel phrase of the preceding verse. In such cases secondary changes are normally harmonistic not dissimilating.

The final writer on whose work we are to focus attention is Movsēs Xorenaci.[16] He has been taken last because of the difficulty of arriving at a precise dating. Though there may be early elements in the book, it is likely that the overall texture of the history belongs to an era at some remove from the lament on the demise of the Arsacid royal house and Gregorid catholicate with which it concludes.[17]

As several of the references noted by Thomson feature in Bk.1,26 describing Aždahak's dream, it may be convenient to consider them together. In several of them the parallelism is so general that it is unclear how direct an influence Arm exercised on the precise formulation of Movsēs' account. Thus the situation of a king, disturbed by a dream, summoning his counselors (p.75 of the critical edition) recalls that of Nebuchadnezzar in 2:23. Moreover the phrase 'զիրս ահագին տեսլեանն' bears a resemblance to տեսիլ նորա ահագին յոյժ from Dan 2:31.

In the dream Aždahak visualizes himself honouring the gods 'զոհիւք եւ խնկովլ p' (p. 76), a phrase slightly reminiscent of Nebuchadnezzar's immediate response to Daniel's explanation of his vision at 2:46 'եւ զոհս եւ խունկս անոյշշութեան հրամայեաց մատուցանել.' However, if Movsēs was indeed dependent on the Bible at this point it is more likely to have been 1 Kgdms 3:4 where his exact phrase recurs. Nevertheless, as this was a customary expression of reverence towards deities in antiquity cf. 3 Kgdms 4:3, 11:8, etc., it is unnecessary to insist the detail was appropriated from Arm.

Aždahak, like Daniel, is perturbed by the approach of strange beasts. According to Movsēs (p. 76) 'առաջինն գերանան ած ... առիւծու ... եւ երկրորդն ի վերայ բծու'' cf. Dan 7:4 'առաջինն իբրեւ մատակ առիւծ v. 6 ահա այլ գազան ելանէր իբրեւ զինձ.

Yet there are notable differences between the two accounts: in the latter the visionary creatures are merely described as resembling the terrestrial variety while in Movsēs they are positively identified as such. In the biblical narrative the animals appear alone whereas the historian remarks that they are being ridden. Their order is also different: the second beast in Daniel is a bear, but a leopard in Movsēs. As such phenomena are part of the stock-in-trade of Near Eastern dream lore both incidents probably derive from this general source.

Later Aždahak intervened to oppose one of these fabulous riders who 'խորհէր կործանել զդիս', an intention actually to be carried out by the king of the South against his northern rival in Dan 11:8 'եւ զաստուածս նոցա կործանեսցէ.' However as կործանել is frequently employed in descriptions of the destruction of representations of deities (4 Kgdms 3:2, 10:27; 1 Macc 5:68, 6:7) or their altars (Judg 6:8 cf. the fate of Bel in Bel 22, 28) it is doubtful whether the phrase in point has any special relation to Dan 11:8.

The final two examples from Book 2 of the history share the same character. Movsēs' phrase 'գորս ոչ պատկառեմ ասել հետեւող լինել Անանիանց' in chapter 9 (p. 119) indicates his broad familiarity with the exploits of Daniel and the three in Dan, Chapter 3. In like vein the collapse of a marble statue crushing and killing those below in chapter 35 (p. 159) has a certain amount in common with the career of the stone dashing to pieces the metal statue of Dan 2:45. Yet neither of these could be said to be expressly based on the text of Daniel.

In conclusion, we may say that Movsēs' relation to the passages of Daniel referred to is not one of specific dependence but rather a general parallelism of motifs and situations. As this is not substantial enough to prove direct contact with Arm the historian yields little assistance in monitoring the version's transmission history.

In broaching liturgical evidence by first examining the *Čašoc* (lectionary) it is useful to note that in contrast to the *Žamagirk* (breviary) and *Maštoc'* (ritual), Lyonnet found no characteristically early readings in the lectionnaries he consulted at Venice, Vienna and Paris.[18] Subsequently, Renoux's detailed survey of the genre uncovered three manuscripts preserving the state of affairs which obtained at Jerusalem during the early part of the fifth century.[19]

In consequence, it was decided to compare Arm with the three readings contained in the codex of the Armenian Patriarchate of Jerusalem no. 121 which is a prime witness to this pre-recensional form. The first reading from Daniel, found on pp.22ff. and the third on pp.424ff. are taken from Chapter 3:1-90 while the second on pp.113ff. consists of Chapter 7:2-27.

The antiquity of the codex is evident from the fine uncial script and primitive orthography in which numbers are always written in full, abbreviations are restricted to *nomina sacra*, ɩ is regularly employed in imperfect indicative verbal forms and η represents 'l' in words of foreign origin, e.g. Դանիէդ, Բարեդացիք. Sometimes by hyper-correction the practice spreads to indigenous words, so that այլ appears as այդ etc., as in MS 178 of our diplomatic edition.[20]

Comparison of the two readings from Chapter 3 uncovered certain minor variations of orthography and substance (e.g. +/-copula) which lacked Arm support. The most notable case witnessed by the first reading is ազգս for ազգաց at 3:5. The third reading had ɩ before թմբկի at 3:5, but this has been erased. In the same verse it reads անկանիցիք for անկանիցիք.

At v. 7 it omits եւ 2° and transposes the order of արքայ նաբուքողոնոսոր at the end of the verse. Finally, it evinces the variant ի վերայ երկնից at v. 60 which appears a corruption of Arm's text ի վերոյ քան զերկինս.

In general, the two readings coincide and possess a number of variants in common which lack Arm support.

3:5	սրնկի	] +(եւ reading 3)	-26 գովեալ] om
		զբնարի	-32 եւ 2°] om
-25	մէջ	] միջոյ	-35 սրբոյ] ընտրելոյ

The above examples indicate that the base text of the two readings was similar but the following incidence of bifurcation in which they agree independently with various groups of Arm witnesses proves conclusively that their provenance was not identical.

Reading 1= Arm witnesses

3:7 արքայ ult] om V280 M2627
-15 լինիցիք] -չիք M4834 J1925-M2627
-15 թե] եթէ M4834
-18 այս M287] +ինչ rel.
-40 զբիւրաւորս] pr իբրեւ M4834 M2585 J1925'-M2627' M182"
-42 եւ 1°] om J1925
-47 դիզանէր] -նայր V280 M346 J1925-M2627' M182"
v. 55 tr ante 54 = V280 M346'-M2585 V1508-M351
-63 ամենայն] om V280
-81 գազան] -գանք M346-M2585 M9116-M2627' M182" (=Eznik)
-81 անասուն] -ունք M346-M2585 M2627 M351 (=Eznik)

Reading 3 = Arm witnesses

3:7 զարնգին] սրնգի (սրընգի M4834 J1925)
-12,18 պատկերիդ] -ին V280 M346' J1925

-14 պաշտիցէք]պաշտէք V280 M346' J1925'
-15 եւ 1˚] om V280'
-15 ամենայն] om V280 J1925' V1508-M351
-37 նուաղեցաք] +մեք V280 M178-M346'-M2585 M9116
-39 տառապանաց]-նաք V280
v.54 ante 55 = M287' M178 J1925'-M2627' M182

These independent agreements demonstrate that the antiquity of the lectionary's script is matched by that of its text
type. Where the readings diverge from the standard of MS
M287 they are mostly seen in the company of MSS V280
M346' J1925 which consistently adduce early variants.

The trend is corroborated by the much larger corpus of
agreements with Arm witnesses shared by both readings (R1 +
R3).

3:1 արբա M287] -այի rel
-5 պազանիշիք]-իցիք M2627
-5 ընկեցցի M287 M9116-M2627' M182" R1R3] անկցի rel
-8 նարբուբողոնոսոր (արբայ) M287 M2585]
-նոսորայ M4834 M9116-M4114 M182"
-11 պազգէ M287 M351] պազանիցէ rel
-15 թէ] om M2627
-15 նուլոյ M287' M2585 J1925] om rel
-15 է] իգէ M2627
-18 զի M287 WN11*] +մեք rel
-19 այբեսցին] -զի M346-WN11* J1925-M2627
-21 հրոյն M287 J1925] pr հնոցին rel
-23 անկան] -կանէին M2627
-25 Ազարիաս M287] -հայ rel
-29 եւ 1˚, 2˚] om M346' J1925
-32 եւ 1˚, 2˚] om M346
-32 անաւրինի] անիրաւի J1925'-M4114 M182"
-33 եղաք] եղեն V280 M9116
-33 եւ 6˚] om V280 M178-M346'-M2585 J1925'-M2627
-35 առնել M287] առներ rel

-35 զողորմութիւն M287 M178-M346] -թիւնս rel
-35 Սահակայ] խսահակայ V280 M346-M2585 M9116-
     M2627' M182"
-38 եւ 4˚] om V280'
-39 ոգւով M287] հոգւով p J1925' M182" (cf. V280' M2627)
-39 լիցուք] + մեք V280'
-40 իբրեւ] որպէս M4834 M178-M346'-M2585
-40 եղիցի] -ցին V280'
-40 զի] եւ M346'
-41 երկրնչիմք M287' WN11 M9116] + մեք rel
-42 քո] + տէր M4834 M346' J1925
-42 ընդ M287 J1925'] առ V280 WN11 M2627
-44 եւ 1˚] om M178 M346
-44 եւ 2˚] om J1925
-44 խորտակեցի M287 M2627' M182' R1R3] -ցին rel
-45 միայն] + որ V280 M346' (=Agathangelos)
-45 փառաւորեալ դ V280" M2585 J1925'-M2627' M182"
     R1R3 (=Agathangelos)] -եալ rel
-45 ի 1˚] pr ես V280 M178-M346'-M2585 M2627
     (=Agathangelos)
-50 որ ցաւդագին շնչից] ցաւդագին զի շնչից J1925
-51 երեքեան] + նոքա V280 (երեքին նորա J1925)
-52 եւ] + դու V280' M346' V1508-M351
-60 ամենայն] om V280 M346-WN11* M182
-61 ամենայն] om V280 WN11*
-62 լոյս M287] լուսին rel
-63 աստեղք M287] + երկնից rel
-65 հողմք M287 J1925] pr ամենայն rel
-66 տապ] չեր M4834 J1925-M2627'
vv 67-73 in consecutive order = MS 178
v. 77 ante 78 = M178-M346'-M2585 M182"
-78 ծովք] ծով M4834 M178-M346'-M2585 J1925 M182"
-80 ամենայն] om V280 M178-M346'-M2585 M4114 M182"
-81 ամենայն] om V280 M178-M346-WN11*-M2585
-84 քահանայք] + տեառն M178-M2585
-90 զի քաղցր է M287 M2585] om rel

Similar instances from Reading 2

7:6   ելանէր] om V280' J1925' M2627' M182'' (=Sebēos)

-6   թոչնոց M287' M346 J1925] -նոյ rel (=Sebēos)

-6   գլուխ M287' M2627 (=Sebēos)] գլուխք rel

-7   եւ մագիլք նորա պղնձ.] om M4834 M2585 J1925'-M2627' M182''

-8   որ M287 M4114 M182''-WN11ᶜ] նորա rel

-12   ժամանակ] -նակս V280 WN11 J1925

-16   կամէի M287' M178] կամեցայ M4834   խնդրէի rel (R2)

-17   արդ M287 M346-WN11* M4114] այդ rel

-19   ձշմարիտ M287] ձշմարտիւ rel

-19   գազանս]գազանն որ յառաջ քան զնա M2585 M2627 M178''

-20   առաւել M287'] + էր rel

-22   պարբայութիւն նորա M287'] -թիւնն rel

-24   նոցա] նորա M178-M346 J1925'-M4114 V1508 (=Sebēos)

-25   չարիք] -չարեաք M182'

-26   ժամանակ] -նակս (ras R2) V280

-26   ժամանակի M287 M2585] -կաց rel

-27   ամենայն 1˚] om M9116-M2627' M182''

The first major conclusion to emerge from this study is the non-existence of a distinctive lectionary text type which arose independently of Arm from a different *Vorlage*.[21] Nor do the readings evinced by Jer 121 antedate those of the biblical codices, but rather reinforce the significance of V280 as the bearer of an early text, often in conjunction with MSS 346' and J1925 and sometimes M2627. Their joint witness frequently calls into question MS M287's singular readings. Though some may attest early variants, they are regularly the product of secondary scribal development within that particular manuscript's transmission. The fact that the lectionary preserves more of the ancient stratum here than in Lyonnet's investigation of the Gospels is thus due probably to the greater latitude with which the revision was executed. At the same time, R2 seems to share a strain of secondary readings with later C witnesses along with representatives of groups DE.[22]

In addition, the canticle of Azariah (3:26-45) and song of the three youths (vv. 52-90) form part of divine worship in matins.[23] Moreover, the breviary text[24] differs in major respects from that of the lectionary, but is closely parallel to the long citation from the canticle found in P'awstos.[25] As a cleric, the latter would obviously have had an intimate acquaintance with this passage from his daily prayer cycle.

On the whole, agreements between the breviary and lectionary texts are negative, consisting of minuses of connectives which could easily be accounted for independently: v. 29 om զի, 38 om եւ 1՛, 64 om ամենայն (=Sy Aeth).   Much more important is the positive agreement at v. 36 խաւսեցար] խոստացար (=R1+R3). Though this might be construed as a secondary corruption of the reading of the biblical MSS, the Latin variant *in loco* (+ pollicens La[v]) suggests the possibility of a proto-Lucianic *Vorlage* or exegetical tradition.

P'awstos' text similarly witnesses a number of minor secondary minuses e.g. v. 34 om այլ, yet the one noteworthy instance v. 28 om եւ քաղաքի սրբոյ հարցն մերոյ երուսաղէմի is certainly redactional, as being too explicitly bound to the original context of the passage. It also evinces one case of harmonization to immediate context at v. 27: Ճշմարտութիւն] Ճշմարիտ են M346; արդար են Brev.; ուղիղ են P'awst. (cf. ուղիղ են Ճանապարհք քո in the next clause).

The breviary text also adduces a singular secondary minus at 3:60 om բան, but at v. 56 om որ նստիս probably maintains the original reading which has been obscured in the other witnesses by harmonization to v. 54. It can be corrected by P'awstos at vv. 28, 29 for its minus of the connective զի and of the pronoun subject դու at v. 27.

P'awstos' authority as a witness is established by three instances where he alone seems to preserve the Arm1 reading:

v. 28 եւ Arm MSS = Th + OG] զի P'awst. = P (, ܝܒܩ) : om Brev.

v. 29 ապատամբ լինել (-նիլ Brev.) Arm MSS + Brev.]

եւ ապատամբեցաք մեր P'awst.[26] = P (ܩܘܝ‌ܐܘ)

cf. αποσταντες A' Q 11-88-770 C'-405 26 Laᵛ Ps Chr III.818

V 587 Thtᴾ Fulg p.360

v. 43 տուր փառս անուան քում Arm MSS = Th + OG + P]

փառաւոր արա զանուն քո P'awst; փառաւորեցի անուն քո

յաւիտեան Brev.

The factitive combination of տնել with an adjective is characteristic of Arm's translation technique and the morphological freedom of the rendering is apposite to Arm1 in contrast to the greater literality observed by Arm2. The breviary text must have developed from the same matrix as that of P'awstos but was subsequently influenced by parallels e.g. v. 26 փառաւորեալ է անուն քո յաւիտեան and Isa 65:5 անուն տեառն փառաւորեցի.

Four later examples illustrate some of the stages in the process by which the Arm2 text contaminated different strands of the tradition, the original being maintained only by the breviary with occasional support.

v. 40 οὔτως γενέσθω θυσία ἡμῶν Th = P

    այնպէս ընդունելի լիցին պատարագք մեր Brev.

    այնպէս ընդունելի *լիցի* պատարագս մեր M346-M2585

    այնպէս եղիցին *պատարագք* մեր V280

    այնպէս ընդունելի եղիցի պատարագս մեր WN11* J1925

    այնպէս եղիցի պատարագս մեր rel = Th

The three variables of number, verbal form and complement afford us an insight into the pattern of corrections of Arm1 MSS to the standard of the revision. One tradition of the A group discards the epithet and verb, while retaining the plural numʮer (V280') whereas an early stratum of the B group alters only the number. Later the verb too was affected (WN11 J1925). The base of the majority tradition of groups C D E, in contrast, was already a text of the Arm2 standard.

v. 45 καὶ ἔνδοξοs (ο ενδ. 88) Th

որ փառաւորեալդ եւ Brev. = V280 R1 + R3 Agath
եւ փառաւորեալդ եւ M2585 M2627
եւ փառաւորեալդ   J1925' M4114 M182''
որ փառաւորեալ եւ M346'
եւ փառաւորեալ   M287

Arm1 probably derives from the reading preserved in the Lucianic minuscule 88 as articulated adjectives and participles are normally rendered by the relative clause. Articulation is further implied by the addition of the deictic suffix (-դ). The distribution of witnesses almost mirrors the first example.

v. 81 πάντα τὰ θηρία καὶ τὰ κτήνη Th
գազանք եւ անասունք Brev. = M346-M2585 M2627 R1
Eznik
գազան եւ անասունն V280 M178-WN11*
ամենայն գազանք եւ անասունք M351
ամենայն գազանք եւ անասուն M4114 M182'
ամենայն գազան եւ անասունն M287' J1925

The key criterion for differentiating the strata here must be the adjective which is also lacking from the breviary in the preceding verse. Variation in number is probably a secondary factor, as implied by the reading of M4114 M182' where the omission of final ք is likely to be a simple scribal error.

v. 44c καὶ ἡ ἰσχὺs αὐτῶν συντριβείη Th
եւ ամենայն զօրութիւնք նոցա խորտակեսցին Brev. =
P'awst. V280
եւ   զօրութիւնք նոցա խորտակեսցին M4834
M178-M346'- M2585 M9116
եւ   զօրութիւն նոցա խորտակեսցի rel

The evidence once again vindicates MS V280's textual witness as well as that of the B group over against the rest of the tradition. Nevertheless, only the breviary and P'awstos preserve what must be the Arm1 text of the previous clause (b) ամաչեցեալ լիցին բնութիւնք նոցա the formulation of which is modelled on the clause we have just discussed. In Th, in contrast, clause b is symmetrically balanced with a with which it shares a subject.

There are several further instances like the last where the Arm1 reading is only found in the breviary and P'awstos:

v.27 δίκαιος εἶ ἐπὶ πᾶσιν, οἷς ἐποίησας Th

> յիրաւունս անցուցեր (+ դու P'awst.) զայս ամենայն ընդմեզ Brev. + P'awst.

> արդար ես յամենայնի զոր արարեր ի վերայ մեր Arm MSS

Clearly Arm1 rests on a different *Vorlage:* it is plausible that the verb depends on a Syriac text. Only the diacritical point distinguishes the root ܒܕ witnessed by P here from ܒܕ which is the counterpart to the Armenian root անց. Hence the Armenian causative may derive (directly or indirectly) from the *aph'el* form of the Syriac verb. The inclusion of the pronoun subject by P'awstos is in harmony with Arm1's usage.

v. 28 κρίματα ἀληθείας Th

> դատաստան արդարութեան Brev. + P'awst.

> իրաւունս ճշմարտութեան Arm MSS

The Arm1 reading depends rather on P ܠܐܒ, ܘܘ ܠ,

v. 32 Βασιλεῖ ἀδίκῳ Th

> ի ձեռս թագաւորի անօրինի Brev. (ի ձեռն M2585)

> թագաւորի անօրինի M280'' M178-M346' M9116

> թագաւորի անիրաւի J1925-M2627' M182''

While the breviary plus may reflect harmonization to the previous clause, the parallel P reading ܠܐܒ, ܠܘܝܐ seems an abstract interpretation of the concrete form presupposed by the Armenian text.

v. 38 οὐ τόπος τοῦ καρτῶσαι Th

    ո չ տեղի պատարագս մատուցանելոյ Brev.

    ո չ տեղի տալոյ երախայրիս Arm MSS

Arm1 probably attained the true sense of καρποῦν [27] through the intermediary P (ܠܒ, ܐ ܠܚܝ ܡܣ, ܠܚܘ, ܝܘ). Arm2 arrived at an etymologizing rendering instead, cf. Deut 18:1 καρπώματα κυρίου - երախայրիք տեառն.

P'awstos and the breviary also evince a number of agreements with Lucianic witnesses (unparalleled by the biblical MSS) which likely derive from Arm1.

v. 27 ἀλήθειά] αληθιναι Q-541 L'-311 c 407 Tht[P] = OG

    ճշմարտութիւն] ճշմարիտ են 73; արդար են P'awst. + Brev. cf. P ܠܐܡܐ

v. 28 πάντα ταῦτα] + εφ ημας L'' c 233 239 588 Co Aeth[P] Arab Tht

    զայս ամենայն] + ի վերայ մեր P'awst. + Brev. (≠P)

v. 32 fin] + παρεδωκας ημας 88 Tht[P]

    երկիր] + մատնեցեր զմեզ Brev. (≠P)

v. 36 ἐλάλησας] + αυτοις λεγων L'' (449[txt]) Aeth Tht[P]

    խաւսեցար] + նոցա եւ ասացեր Brev.

    πληθῦναι τὸ σπ. αὐτῶν] πληθυνω το σπ. υμων L'' (449[txt]) 541 Tht[P]

    բազմացուցանել զզաւակ նորա] բազմացուցից զզաւակ ձեր Brev. (≠P)

Granted the antiquity of the breviary text type established by the preceding examples, its agreements with clusters of biblical MSS offers a useful guage of their relative importance. Significantly, there are none with MS M287, the collation base of the present edition, from which we may infer that it represents a pure, early type of Arm2 text innocent of the corruptions of Z's base text.[28] Hence those readings where the breviary is supported by MSS V280' must largely be designated an aberration from the group A norm towards an Arm1 standard. Stratigraphically expressed, they form a separate sub-stratum of the unrevised text which was not completely obliterated by the Arm2 overlay. This accounts for the intergroup alignments in which MS V280 finds itself when witnessing to Arm1, since group adherence is primarily conditioned by uniquely shared errors arising from the copying process which thus have no direct relation to the substratum e.g.

v. 33 մեզ] +զամ = V280 M346'
v. 37 նուադեցաթ]+մեթ=V280 M178-M346'-M2585 M9116 + R3
vv. 54/55 tr = V280 M346'-M2585 V1508-M351 R1 + R3
v. 54 հայիս յանդունդս / եւ նստիս] tr = V280 J1925
v. 63 արեւ]արեգակն = V280' J1925
v. 66 տաղ] չեր = M4834 J1925-M2627' R1 + R3

In contrast, the breviary adduces a number of agreements with most of the group B which would seem to indicate that corporately the latter has preserved more of Arm1 than the other groups, at least in this textual portion e.g.

v. 38 fin] +ի թէն = M178-M346-WN11*
v. 43 Sէր] om = M178-M346-M2585
v. 86 նգիթ] անձիւթ= M346-M2585
WO   vv. 77-78 = M178-M346-M2585 M182'' R1 + R3

The following example, however, suggests that the exemplar from which the breviary text was drawn had not escaped the revision entirely, but contained a certain Arm2 component.

v. 75 բարձունք] բլուրք = M178-M346'

The likelihood is that the variant renders the Th reading βουνοί, while the lemma reflects P ἰλώϳ, its etymological counterpart.

In addition, the breviary text illustrates several features of Arm1's style and translation technique, often uniquely, or with the sole support of P'awstos. Apart from the instance of pronoun subjects already cited one should note the idiomatic role of the indefinite particle (e.g. v.28 զոր] +ինչ Brev. + P'awst.) and avoidance of polysyndeton (e.g. v.31 եւ]արդ Brev. + P'awst. = R1 + R3). Furthermore, infinitives of purpose are rendered by a final clause (v.40 լիներ կատարեալ] զի կատարեալ զացուր Brev.). In comparison with Arm2 its mode of expression takes less account of the form of the Greek e.g.:

v. 30 εὖ ἡμῖν γένηται Th

բարի լինիցի մեզ] զբարիս զացուր (+ մեք P'awst.) ի քէն Brev. + P'awst.

Arm1 may have been influenced by parallels such as Exod 33:13 զտի շնորհս առաջի քո.

v.38 οὐδὲ ὁλοκαύτωσις οὐδὲ θυσία οὐδὲ προσφορά Th

ոչ ողջակէզք եւ ոչ զոհք եւ ոչ պատածագք] ոչ ողջակէզք պատարագաց Brev.

Possibly the second component dropped out by *para-blepsis* at some point in transmission.[29] More importantly, the final item has been characteristically subordinated to the first within a genitival relationship.

v. 39 ἐν ψυχῇ συντετριμμένῃ Th

անձամբք բեկելովք] անձ. խոնարհեալ Brev. + WN11*

The Arm1 translator has subtly changed the metaphor from contrition to abasement to provide a closer parallel to the following phrase հոգւով տառապանաց (Th πνεύματι ταπεινώσεως).

v. 44 ἐνδεικνύμενοι τοῖς δούλοις σου κακά Th

ցուցանեն չարիս ծառայից քոց] չարչարեն զծառայս քո Brev.

Here the translator has condensed the expression, selecting a simple verb to render the more periphrastic Greek. The reviser's intention has been rather to mirror more approximately the Greek syntactic configuration.

The breviary thus emerges as an important witness to the early Armenian text, its readings often supported (and on occasion corrected) by those of P'awstos. Its antiquity is marked by the paucity of Arm2 contamination and its confirmation of the various facets of Arm1's textual affinity and translation technique distinguished by examination of the biblical manuscripts. Its separate transmission process has preserved it intact from secondary attempts to assimilate it to the prevailing text and where it has suffered scribal corruption the pristine reading can usually be restored with facility.

The ritual (*mayr maštoc'*),[30] in contrast, offers a rather developed text of the passage 9:4-19 as the last reading in the rite of laying the foundations of a church. The indications given by the medieval forms լիսիլ[31] (v. 13) and եած[32] (v. 14) are reinforced by the pattern of its textual agreements. As one might expect, it supports the majority text against M287's solitary readings: om քո 1° (v. 4); երեսագ] + մերոց (v. 8); քո] + Տէր (v. 11); յամենար 10] յամեր rel (v. 19). However, it shares some secondary readings with MS M9116 of the C2 sub-group: om մեր (v. 11); զգուրս] զգուր M9116 M351 (v. 18) and more importantly աննու որպէս] աննու նոր որպ. M9116 (v. 15) which is patently the result of dittography. Further secondary readings agree with larger C groupings (om կոչեցեալ J1925' v. 17); էին] են J1925'-M4114 M351 (v. 16) as well as representatives of DE e.g. om որ V280' J1925'-M4114 M182'' (v. 11). Only one variant is of possible versional interest:

v. 8   ἡμάρτομεν] ημαρτοσαν 147;   ημαρτον 584 Bo Arm[p]
մեղաք] մեղան M346' = Rit.

A secondary (and largely unique) scribal characteristic of the ritual text is the consistent use of the plural relative pronoun (որք) throughout the passage, while Armenian idiom regularly tolerates the singular form.[33] Finally, the insertion of the divine name (այ) at the end of the passage is probably a liturgical addition to introduce the ensuing doxology.

CONCLUSION

The attempt to regulate the textual data of the biblical MSS of the thirteenth century and later by means of patristic and liturgical sources achieved some valuable results. The indirect nature of the type of evidence adduced by patristic citations predisposes one to caution in assessing the writer's context and purpose in referring to a scriptural passage as well as the possible intervention of later copysits to harmonize a given phrase to the form with which they were familiar. Four of the authors (Eznik, Koriwn, Ełišē, Movsēs) whose quotations from Arm were scrutinized adopted such an allusive stance towards the text that precluded any detailed comparison with the biblical codices. In contrast, the three remaining (Agathangelos, Pʻawstos, Sebēos) cited extended passages with such accuracy as to leave no doubt with regard to the latter two sources, that the main factor determining the length and accuracy of the quotations must be their regular occurrence in liturgical use.

Despite the independent transmission history of the readings from Daniel found in the lectionary, breviary and ritual, there are no distinctive liturgical text types. All derive from the biblical tradition and those of the first two afford ample indication of their early origin. In consequence, they frequently unite with Agathangelos and Pʻawstos confirming the readings of such MSS as V280, M346' and J1925 which were previously ascribed to Arm1. In addition to affiliation with both P and the Lucianic recension, these agreements also highlight features of Arm1's translation technique which clearly distinguish it from the greater literality to which the revisers adhered. At certain points it appears that all the biblical MSS collated offer the Arm2 variant and the original reading is adduced only by Pʻawstos and the breviary. Very occasionally these witnesses also reveal limited Arm2 influence which seems to result from early contamination between the two textual strata.

NOTES

1. M. van Esbroeck, "Leningradi M.E. Saltikov-Ščedrini anvan hanrayin gradarani hayerēn krknankarē" No.14" [The Armenian Palimpsest (New Series No.14) of the M.E. Saltikov-Ščedrini Public Library of Leningrad] *B Mat* 13 (1980), pp.271-274.

2. Unfortunately, indigenous commentary writing began rather late in Armenia and the oldest extant example on Daniel is that composed by Vardan Arewelci in 1268. That contains citations from a work of Step'annos Siwneci (d.735) which has not survived intact.

3. On this general problem see R.P. Casey, "The Patristic Evidence for the Text of the New Testament", *New Testament Manuscript Studies*, M.M. Parvis and A.P. Wikgren (eds.), Chicago: 1950, pp.69-80.

4. The best documented example of this phenomenon is the history of Lazar P'arpeci. For details see C.J.F. Dowsett, "The Newly Discovered Fragment of Lazar of P'arp's History", *Mus* 89 (1976), pp.97-122. For the discovery of an uncial folio which largely confirms the text of MS J1925 see S.P. Cowe, "An Armenian Job Fragment".

5. Lazar P'arpeci, *Patmagirk'Hayoc*, pp.213-214.

6. Eznik Kołbaci, *De Deo*.

7. Koriwn, *Vark Maštoci*.

8. Recent investigations suggest the work is composite and that particularly the large central section devoted to St. Gregory's teaching may have undergone expansion and revision during the sixth century as a result of the contemporary controversies on faith and order. See M. van Esbroeck, "Le résumé syriaque de l'Agathange et sa portée pour l'histoire du développement de la légende", *HA*, 90 (1976), cols. 493-510 and Agathangelos, *Patmut iwn Hayots'*, 1980, p.xiii.

9. On authorship and dating see N.G. Garsoïan, *The Epic Histories* pp.11-16 and 35-41. For biblical references see

pp.577-585.

10. P'awstos Buzandac'i, *Patmut'iwn Hayoc'*.

11. The long citation P'awstos makes of the canticle of Azariah will be considered later in conjunction with the breviary text with which it shows marked affinity. See pp.406-13.

12. E. Tēr-Minasean (ed.), *Eliśēi vasn Vardanay ew Hayocc' Paterazmin* [Eliśēs History on Vardan and the Armenian War], Erevan: Armenian Academy of Sciences, 1957.

13. For details of the debate see R.W. Thomson (trans.), *Elishē History of Vardan and the Armenian War*, p.22 ff and p.340 for scriptural citations. See also *Yeghishe: History of Vardan and the Armenian War*. A photographic reproduction of the Erevan edition with an introduction and select bibliography by S.P. Cowe. Delmar, NY: Caravan Books [in press].

14. Thomson cites a third allusion from the phrase ամենայն փափկութիւն հայոց (p.124) to the description of Susanna as փափուկ (Sus:31). However, as the noun is not at all uncommon and there is no more concrete datum to align the texts, the evidence is not compelling. For the significance of Yazdgard's portrayal as a beast by Eliśē see S.P. Cowe, op. cit. note 13.

15. G.V. Abgaryan (ed.), *Patmut'iwn Sebēosi* [The History of Sebēos], Erevan: Armenian Academy of Sciences, 1979.

16. See Movsēs Xorenac'i, *Patmut'iwn Hayoc'*. The table of biblical citations is taken from R.W. Thomson (trans.), *Mosēs Khorenats'i History of the Armenians*, 1978, p.407.

17. See the introduction to this work for background to the dispute on dating as well as C. Toumanoff, "On the date of the Pseudo-Moses of Chorene", *HA* 75 (1961), cols. 467-476.

18. *Les origines*, p.166.

19. A. Renoux, *Le codex arménien*, pp.155-161. These MSS are Armenian Patriarchate of Jerusalem MS no.121, pages 1-612 of which were copied in 1192, the remainder being added in 1318; Paris, Bibliothèque Nationale no.44 dated

to the tenth century, and Erevan, Maštoc̣ Matenadaran no.985 also regarded as from the tenth century.

20. For further details see N. Bogharian, *Grand Catalogue of St. James Manuscripts*, vol.1, pp.338-352.

21. Although in editing the rubrics of the Armenian lectionary of Jerusalem Renoux studiously avoids specific discussion of the textual origin of the lections, his remarks on the translation of the former directly from the Greek have sometimes been misconstrued as applying to the latter also. See *Le codex arménien*, p.162 and cf. K. Aland and B. Aland, *Der Text des Neuen Testaments*, Einführung in die wissenschaftlichen Ausgaben so wie in Theorie und Praxis der modernen Textkritik, Stuttgart: Deutsche Bibelgesellschaft, 1982, p.211 and also the English edition of the above, *The Text of the New Testament*, E.F. Rhodes (trans.), Grand Rapids: Eerdmans, 1987, p.201.
Similarly, Ter-Petrosyan rejects the hypothesis of a distinct text type for the liturgical psalter, arguing that one codex varies from another in the same manner as biblical witnesses. See A.S. Zeyt̕unyan, *Girk̕ Cnndoc̕*, p.53.

22. For similar conclusions in Deut see C.E. Cox, "The Use of Lectionary Manuscripts to Establish the Text of the Armenian Bible", pp.365-380.

23. For the structure of the office see the edition by Movsēs Erznka c̕i of Xosrov Anjewac̕i's *Meknut̕iwn Žamakargut̕ean*[Commentary on the Breviary] Istanbul, 1840.

24. The collation base utilized was *Žamagirk̕ Hayastaneayc̕ surb ekelecwoy*[Breviary of the Holy Armenian Church] seventh edition, Jerusalem: St. James Press, 1959, pp.212-218.

25. Dr. R. Ervine was first to note the affinity between P̕awstos text and the breviary. See Garsoïan, *The Epic Histories*, p.310. P̕awstos cites 3:27-31, inserting at that point a refrain from Ps 118:39 զի դատաստանք քո քաղցր են, before continuing with 3:34, 43-45. At the end of v.44 he adduces the addition զի մի երբէք ամաչեսցեն ոյք յուսացեալ լինին

ի քեզ which reverberates with echoes from a number of scriptural passages:

Ps 21:6 ի քեզ յուսացան եւ ոչ ամաչեցին

Ps 5:12 որք յուսացեալ են ի քեզ ուրախ լիցին

Sir 15:4 ի նա ապաստան լիցի, եւ ոչ ամաչեսցէ

26. The support of P and Lucianic witnesses (n.b. the translators' tendency to assimilate Greek participles to the form of accompanying finite verbs) suggests P'awstos preserves the early Armenian text. Although one might argue he simply accommodated the infinitive to the surrounding context, the fact that his text evinces so few secondary features militates against this interpretation.

27. See Daniel, "Le vocabulaire du culte", pp.364-366.

28. Nevertheless, as the tables in chapters four and five demonstrate, this MS is not devoid of unrevised Arm1 readings.

29. It is impossible to state categorically at which of the four main stages (*Vorlage,* translation, biblical exemplar, breviary copy) this occurred. Obviously, more light could be shed on the subject by attempting a critical edition of the liturgical text.

30. *Girk mec mastoc' koc'ec'eal*[The book called Great Maštoc'], Istanbul: Połos Yohannisean Press, 1807, pp.165-166.

31. Meillet, §105e, p.93.

32. Ibid., §106a, p.94.

33. Ibid., §154, p.128.

GENERAL CONCLUSION

Introduction: The present study has sought to analyze the manuscript evidence for the Armenian Version of Daniel in a more comprehensive way than hitherto essayed and, by subjecting the secondary literature and related scriptural versions to critical examination, to achieve a more exact appreciation of Arm's nature and value. Drawing together the various strands of the argument in this final section it is proposed to set out the major results attained in the course of our research and to outline some of their implications for further investigation of the Armenian Bible and related issues.

The Two Strata of the Version and P Component of Arm1: The prime fact to emerge was that the version is composed of two distinct phases, the original translation (Arm1) and a subsequent revision (Arm2). The distinction was established on the basis of recurrent variants in which both readings consistently supported contrasting external sources. Cases where Arm=P≠(MT+Gk) set out in the tables of chapter four, particularly those involving linguistic criteria, demonstrate Arm's direct Syriac contact. The priority of that contact (i.e. its presence in Arm1) became apparent from the combined testimony of MSS of the three groups of early text type A (MSS V280-

J2558), B (MSS M346-WN11) and C (MS J1925) over against the rest of the tradition. Further corroboration was provided by the Georgian Version which was shown to be dependent on Arm, by early liturgical texts and the presence of certain stylistic features shared with the corresponding early phase of the gospels, to which Lyonnet had already drawn attention.[1]

Character of Arm=P Readings: In addition to readings where P is the sole source, Arm contact was seen to include a number of instances where P=MT. Contrary to Gehman's thesis that Arm was based on a revision of the Hexapla, it was shown in chapter five that the version adduces extremely few of the hexaplaric additions to Th and that its overall agreement with the main Origenic group is not of great import. Therefore, it is likely that Arm=MT readings not found in the early Th text entered Arm not through the Greek recensions but via P. P may also have communicated to Arm certain readings characteristic of the local Antiochian variety of Th. In the appendix to chapter four it was argued that P came under the influence of the proto-Lucianic text both in the canonical and apocryphal sections of the book. As a consequence where Arm=P=Luc and linguistic considerations do not bear upon the problem, it is hard to identify Arm's exemplar.

Extent of Arm=P Contact: Arm=P agreement is such that it cannot be explained as contingent upon the translator's memory recall or occasional reference to a Syriac codex.[2] At the same time, the discovery of a series of Luc agreements in Arm's P-oriented MSS referred to above (where the remainder witnesses to another Greek standard) suggested that translation from Syriac never extended throughout the whole compass of the book thereby paralleling the situation in Ruth. Confirmation of this view was afforded by features of translation technique implying that P and Luc were consulted simultaneously in rendering Arm1 and are not to be apportioned to two separate stages in the process.[3] Nevertheless, it is surmised that Arm1's relation to P was originally more extensive than the instances presented in our tables, since agreements are preserved by Geo which are not reflected in the fifteen MSS of our edition of Arm. This naturally poses the question how far it is possible to reconstruct the first stratum of the version.[4]

Arm1's Testimony to P: In assessing the calibre of Arm's witness to P, the first factor to be considered is date. Arm precedes by fully a century P Daniel's earliest manuscript 6h10 with which it concurs several times against the rest of the P tradition. The quality of its text is indicated by cases of joint Arm-Geo readings which seem to presuppose a Syriac *Vorlage* that, though not represented in P's Leiden edition, is closer to MT on occasion than that of the extant P witnesses. In both these respects it resembles the citations of Afrahat and commentary of St. Efrem referred to by Wyngarden[5] and adds to the corpus of early Syriac readings preserved in Armenian .

Historical Aspect of Arm=P Relations: It was observed that traditions concerning the Armenian translation of the Bible are vague and contradictory. Nevertheless, it is clear from the testimony of Lazar P'arpec'i that prior to the invention of an indigenous alphabet Syriac liturgical texts were utilized in Persarmenia.[6] The same author also confirms that Armenian clergy received their formation at Syrian centres.[7] Paramount among these would have been Edessa and Samosata, the two foci of Maštoc's expedition, according to Koriwn.[8] The Syriac acts of the Latrocinium or "Robbers' Synod" of 449 actually include documents establishing the existence of an Armenian school in the former city alongside that of the Syrians and the more famous school of the Persians which had been founded by refugees from Nisibis.[9]

The greater familiarity with Syriac on the part of at least some of the translators is implied by Koriwn's narrative concerning Yovsēp' and Eznik. Their thorough knowledge of the language is presupposed by the commission to render patristic writings directly into Armenian. Their subsequent activity translating from Greek was preceded by a period of apprenticeship until they had sufficiently mastered the necessary skills.[10] The same impression is also left by the corpus of Greek works rendered into Armenian at around this time from a Syriac intermediary, e.g. St. Cyril of Jerusalem's catechetical lectures,[11] Eusebius' ecclesiastical history[12] and St. Basil's Hexaemeron[13] and Evagrius' ascetic and mystical treatises.[14] Consequently, the utilization of P by the Armenian translators of the Bible as a resource to facilitate their task becomes all the more plausible historically.

Luc Component of Arm1: The second important result was the discovery of a broad diffusion of Lucianic material in Arm1, thus rendering the latter a hybrid composition from both Greek and Syriac sources. Its presence was detected by monitoring repeated variants where one branch of Arm's tradition (especially MSS V280-J2558 M346-WN11 and J1925) supported Luc while the others attested another type of Th text. Cohesion of Luc and P elements within the same early stage of the translation, as stated above, was confirmed by their preponderance in the same few MSS and complementary role in Arm1's translation technique.

Nor is Lucianic affinity without precedent in the Armenian Bible. On the contrary, it has commended itself as the main component in the *Vorlage* of the Arm1 stratum of Ruth, 1-2 Kgdms and Chronicles.[15] Moreover, the possibility that it may perform a similar function in other OT books is plausibly suggested by a number of other studies which were mostly restricted to the data available in Z. Accordingly, Luc has been considered to provide Arm's primary textual colour in 2-3 Macc and the *Dodekapropheton.*[16] Subsidiary Luc influence has also been detected on Isa,[17] Ezek, Esth and 3-4 Kgdms. Thus, detailed scrutiny of more primitive text types may further enhance the status of the Lucianic component in the Armenian version.[18]

Character of Arm=Luc Readings: In comparison to B, Luc evinces a high proportion of OG-readings and was probably instrumental in introducing a number of these to Arm, despite the absence of some Arm=OG examples from extant Luc sources. Moreover, their pre-hexaplaric date is underlined by regular agreement with Chester Beatty Papyrus 967. Similarly, their concentration in MSS V280-J2558 suggests they formed part of Arm1, while their fragmentary and uneven dispersion militates against acceptance as remnants of a full translation from OG. In common with the other versions (e.g. OL and P) which have undergone Luc influence, Arm1 contains a variety of readings from different categories which typify the recension but are not reflected in Greek witnesses. Some of these may have existed in Greek, while others reveal the extent to which the translators were imbued with the same stylistic and exegetical principles.

Arm1's Testimony to Luc: Arm1, in keeping with OL and P, is mostly oriented towards the local Antiochian text which served as the raw material for Lucian's revision. In consequence, it evinces none of the major doublets which betray the latter's activity. However, as an interval of two centuries separates it from P, it is natural that Arm should also reveal signs of penetration by a later type of Syrian text in the shape of agreements with the roughly contemporary commentaries of St. Chrysostom and Theodoret of Cyrrhus. Arm's links with the sub-group constituted by MSS 311-538 are worthy of mention on the grounds of their persistence in other books and the early readings they preserve. Even more noteworthy is the resemblance Arm1's *Vorlage* must have had to MS 410 for whose Lucianic complexion we have argued in the appendix to chapter four.[19] From its affinities with P we may infer that 410 represents a variety of Antiochian text which circulated in Mesopotamia in the third and fourth centuries A.D. Granted the conservatism of scribal transmission it may be significant that the 13th century MS derives from the monastery of St. John the Baptist on the bank of the Jordan.[20]

Arm 1=Luc and Th Autograph: Estimation of Arm's value in the process of reconstructing the original text of Th is inevitably conditioned to some extent by the theory adopted of its origin and early history. The earlier opinion that it was a revision of OG by the second century figure Theodotion has long been modified by the observation of its incidence in NT and the Apostolic Fathers.[21] More recent research focusing on the text's linguistic features initiated by Ziegler and developed by Schmitt[22] has uncovered discrepancies of such magnitude from Theodotion's normal practice that his association with it has been rejected.

Th's dependence on the Alexandrian OG text has been re-emphasized by Schüpphaus.[23] Yet the difference in idiom marked by its more literal, semitic caste corresponds so neatly with its socio-political terminology[24] and provenance of its first witnesses that scholars are impelled to place its genesis in Syro-Palestine at about the turn of the eras. The fact that the proto-Lucianic text grew up in the same area suggests that it may have retained features of the original which were altered in the course of its transmission to other regions.[25]

Ziegler remarks that the convergence of B(Q) Luc generally signals the primitiveness of a reading, but like Montgomery, upholds the priority of B in cases where it diverges from Luc. Thus Luc's borrowings from OG are interpreted as the result of secondary conflation. That both texts circulated in close proximity is evident from the divided allegiance shown by Josephus and Cyprian in their scriptural citations. Moreover, the expansionist tendency of the Syrian text (familiar from NT also) could easily account for the procedure by which the early scribes enriched Th by inserting, among other extraneous details, elements from OG before it was largely supplanted by Th in the mid-third century A.D.[26]

Nevertheless, it does not automatically follow that the shorter text is always to be preferred. Some of the secondary instances in B were caused by homoeoteleuton arising from copyists' inattention. Others may have been created by the tradents' desire to reduce Th's form of expression to its essentials. Their recurrence in B's NT text cannot simply be ascribed to hazard and so reinforces the demand for a more systematic explanation. Moreover, Westcott and Hort's acceptance of the celebrated 'Western non-interpolations' with their negative implications for the shorter text may warrant a re-appraisal of some of B's readings in Daniel. This is further sanctioned by Carlini and Citi's estimation of the proto-Lucianic text as represented by Th's oldest witness, the Bodmer Papyri Nos. x1v and x1vi:

> "Ora, quando ad AQL [i.e. Luc] si associ Bodm. si deve rinunciare a credere che si tratti di innovazione normalizzatrice della redazione antiochena: Bodm. garantisce il valore tradizionale e non <<recensionale>> di quelle varianti e invita a riconsiderare attentamente il problema generale del deposito di lezioni prelucianee in Luciano." [27]

Despite the usual drawbacks of using versions to reconstruct the niceties of the morphology of a base text, Arm1, OL and P, antedating the main body of Lucianic minuscule evidence by some centuries, may be of service in illuminating the proto-Lucianic text and assessing its merits over against B.

Historical Aspect of Arm=Luc Relations: Due to the apparent lack of a semitic exemplar for the apocypha (except Sirach) P's translators had recourse to a Greek text of necessity, usually if not always of Lucianic type. That being the case, Arm1's counterparts laboured under no such constraint. Possessing a complete P text of Daniel, their decision to translate from Luc must have been motivated differently.

Syrians at Hellenized cities like Antioch had been engaged in the exegesis and textual criticism of the Greek Bible for over a century, and yet availed themselves of their native Syriac as a means of explicating the Greek version, because of its affinity to Hebrew. We have noted the possibility that Lucian (d.312) had been influenced by P in compiling his recension. Moreover, references to ὁ Σύρος abound in the works of Eusebius of Emesa (d.c.359) and are a feature of the commentaries of Diodore, Theodore and Theodoret of Cyrrhus also.[28] Although initially unreceptive to Greek culture, gradually the Syriac-speaking municipalities of the hinterland began to adopt its learning[29] and render it into their own idiom.[30] Emblematic of this tendency was the replacement of St. Efrem's commentaries by those of Theodore as the standard biblical textbook at the school of Edessa where lively interest was exhibited in ancient philosophy.[31] In light of the Armenian affiliations with the latter institution, it is perfectly natural that the Arm1 translators should have adhered to the same exegetical approach.

The plausibility of this procedure is heightened when we consider how pivotal the Antiochene role was in shaping Armenian scriptural interpretation. Apart from St. Efrem, St. Chrysostom provided the most diverse basis for commentary writing and frequently features in medieval *catenae.*[32] Granted the proscription of Theodore's works in Armenia through association with Nestorius' condemnation at Ephesus (431), it is hardly surprising that none of his works seem to survive in Armenian. Nevertheless, he had been in contact with ecclesiastics there and at some point had been commissioned to write a refutation of Persian magism. Thus Antiochene themes have also been discerned in the corresponding section of Eznik's treatise. Moreover, it has also been argued that Theodore's influence is to be felt in some of the discourses of the collection known as *yačaxapatum*[33] In addition, the Armenian version offers the most complete text available of Eusebius of Emesa's *quaestiones* on the Octateuch[34] as well as a number of homilies by Severian of Gabala (d.p. 408).[35] Theodoret likewise engaged in correspondence with Armenian churchmen[36] and has a commentary on the Psalter[37] and Ezekiel[38] in Armenian translation. The former was preserved through its ascription to Epiphanius while the latter, like that of Eusebius, was transmitted under the guise of his arch-opponent, Cyril of Alexandria. The writer Step'annos Siwneći (d.p. 735) also demonstrates familiarity with the views of Polychronius of Apamea.[39]

The actual effect of Antiochene exegesis is visible on Arm1 in several respects. A fundamental distinction is drawn between a literal reading of the text (κατὰ λέξιν) and its underlying meaning (διάνοια) which might then be stated by way of paraphrase. Comparison of different renderings was an integral part of this process[40] in which preference would be given to the most semantically apt. Consequently, Aquila was frequently upbraided for his extreme literality, as in the following citation from Eusebius of Emesa:

> "It would have been more appropriate to pass over the individual form of the lexemes in different languages and interpret the sense of the language and set that forth rather than impair the sense by rendering the individual characteristics of the lexemes." [41]

It is against this background that we are to view the greater freedom the Arm1 translator permits himself in representing Greek morphology and syntax. Thus his tendency to paraphrase which Marr characterized as "targum translation"[42] derived not only from the pre-existing oral liturgical tradition which has been postulated,[43] but from his desire to elucidate the book for his readers. Moreover, the comparison of versions embraced parallel passages relating the same events and there too the clearest would be employed as a paradigm for interpreting the others.[44] It is likely that this acted as a stimulus to the harmonization which is one of the translator's hallmarks. Far from the accidental instances adduced by copyists, his will have been a deliberate application of principle.

The exegetes' rhetorical training disposed them to elucidate the figures of speech encountered in the text. Thus in commenting on Ps 44:5c Diodore explicates "Ἡ δεξιά σου"

Τουτέστιν ἡ δύναμις σου.[45] In similar vein St. Chrysostom re-marks on Ps 43:3 "χεῖρα δὲ τὴν δύναμιν αὐτοῦ φησιν."[46] This exact interpretation emerges in Daniel at 4:32 where Th's τῇ χειρί is aligned with զաւրութեան adduced by V280 representing Arm1 in contrast to the literal rendering ձեռին in the majority tradition (Arm2). In like manner, Arm1 gives a psychologically apposite rendering of ἐν ψυχῇ συντετριμμένη (3:39) by անձամբք խոնարհեալ, while Arm2 reproduces the metaphor with անձամբք բեկելովք. Moreover, as Lucian was exercised to maintain his recension at a high linguistic register with due emphasis on Greek idiom, the Armenian translator also strives for symmetry and balance in his phraseology.[47] Consequently, although Koriwn dismisses Arm1 as *p'utana-ki*,[48] it is revealed as a responsible undertaking incorporating a lucid methodological framework which had been elaborated over several generations.

The Components of Arm2: The existence of a second phase within Arm was established by versional variants where the majority of the MS tradition in contrast to MSS V280 and its associates displayed affinities with another type of Th text. The latter was often read by the majority of Greek witnesses from which no conclusions could be drawn. However, in those cases where support was offered by a small group, this consistently comprised the satellites of B Q along with Hippolytus' commentary, out of which a closer affinity was seen to obtain with MS 230. The result was verified by an independent comparison of Arm with Ziegler's Origenic and Catena texts and the groups centering on the uncials B, A and Q. Its secondary nature, a logical necessity from our arguments about Arm1, was underlined by developments in translation technique. Its close adherence to the Greek *Vorlage* resembles the second stratum of a number of OT books investigated as well as the Gospels, indicating the likelihood that they all form part of the same translation process.

Extent of Arm2: Unlike Arm1 which, though of hybrid origin, represents in all likelihood a complete translation, the very fact that it is possible to discern so much of the early phase clearly indicates Arm2's dependence. Without evidence to the contrary it is therefore more economical to assume its status as a revision than try to explain its present condition as the product of conflation of two separate versions.[49]

Arm2's Testimony to Th: Although Gehman interpreted Arm as belonging to a hexaplaric recension, the present study has shown Arm2's decided inclination towards the B text. Its seviceability in recovering the Th autograph accordingly merits a higher evaluation. Its agreements with B are both generic, arising from preferred, early variants, and more particular, the result of conjunctive error. Indeed B is the uncial to which it is most closely related, as demonstrated by the tables in chapter five. MSS Q and A, conversely, rarely converge with Arm unless accompanied by B, in which case they attest the primitive text. Where they join the Th majority in admitting plusses in conformity to MT, Arm2 usually adheres to the B standard. In addition, it has some secondary readings with B alone and shares variants which evolved during the transmission of its branch of the tradition (e.g. λοιπῶν = ւՐհաղերլng for λοιμῶν at 11:14).

Despite its contacts with B, Arm2 sometimes evinces a more developed form of text which implies that its *Vorlage* should be categorized more specifically with the ancestors of the B and Q group minuscules. Nevertheless, their early basis is frequently vouched for by Hippolytus' commentary (c. 204 A.D.) which is especially close to MS 230.[50] The antiquity of the Biblical text of this Italo-byzantine *menologion* with which (apart from its leaning toward Q) Arm2 can be most readily identified is further indicated by its retention of the pre-seventh century system of lections.

Historical Aspect of Arm2=Th: Whereas the Lucianic component of Arm1 represented very much the local Greek text, the tradition is unanimous in attributing the revised standard to a type that had been brought from Constantinople. Scholars have generally regarded this type to be hexaplaric and so far this seems to have been confirmed by the conclusions of several studies. Thus it is considered a primary hexaplaric witness in Gen,[51] Lev,[52] 1-2 Kgdms,[53] Esther[54] and Job.[55] It is classified as a valuable secondary witness to the recension in Numb[56] and Deut[57] and Origenic affiliation has further been indicated in Chron,[58] Wisd[59] and the Bagratuni text of Sirach.[60] Its varying degrees of affiliation may also be monitored by the extent to which it evinces the critical signs which accompany the recension.[61] Yet Ruth's association with the pre-hexaplaric *R* group in adducing a *Kaige* texttype provides a valuable corrective to any premature tendency to generalize about Arm2's *Vorlage.*[62]

Moreover, Ziegler points out that other witnesses undergo a change in textual affiliation in Daniel, which may be partly explicable in terms of the transition from roll to codex. The former contained individual books with the result that, when their text was transferred to codices of larger capacity, the text of the final product obviously reflected the variety of the constitient documents. Anticipating the results of our codicological examination, there is a distinct possibility that the Arm2 *Vorlage* consisted of several part-Bibles rather than a single manuscript. This is also supported by Koriwn's account which relates that the revision was effected ճշմարիտ օրինակօք բերելովք (with the authentic exemplars they had brought).[63]

Translation Technique: Arm was analyzed from various perspectives to ascertain the translators' general practice and, where possible, to ascertain the principles which informed their activity. This was then applied to the grading of the examples selected to delineate the version's translation bases, since the certainty of Arm's retroversion and reconstruction of its contact with other texts varies according to the nature of the reading. In addition, the discovery of a difference in emphasis in translation technique aided the differentiation of the phases of the process, Arm1 and Arm2.[64]

Arm1: As befits the first undertaking to commit an Armenian translation to writing, Arm1 preserves continuity with the oral targums which must have preceded it. Its prime concern is the semantic content of the exemplar and the most simple, direct means of rendering it. The context-related interpretation and idiomatic mode of expression which result lead to variation in translation equivalents and independence from the syntactic make-up of the base text, reflecting the influence of Antiochene exegesis.[65]

Arm1-Arm2 Transition: The transformation in translation technique between the strata may be explained on the theological plane as a reaction against the School of Antioch which had fallen under considerable suspicion during the period in question.[66] Nevertheless, the development from a comparatively free mode of rendering to a more literal standard conforms to the regular pattern for such undertakings. It is exemplified by the methodological diversity between the original version of several books of the Greek OT, their revisions and later independent renderings. A similar process is to be observed between the Old Syriac and Harclean versions and the Old Latin and Vulgate.[67] The decision to retain certain facets of Arm1 unrevised must be confronted as a feature of Arm2's principles, yet the striking character of the agreements witnessed by MSS V280-J258 with P and Geo-P indicates that the most obtrusive elements of the original stratum were neutralized.[68]

Arm2: The progression is partly the fruit of practical experience. Repeated exposure to the same sort of problems led the practitioners to generalize and thus increase stereotyping of equivalents, basing these on the root meaning of the word, even where that was not the most appropriate in context.[69] The reviser's philological preoccupation is observable in the retention of *figura etymologica,* semitic transliterations and other linguistic features from his base text. At times he is even prepared to sacrifice aspects of the idiom of the target language in order to achieve this, though he is not always rigorously systematic in their application.[70] As such, his work is to be viewed as an intermediate point on a trajectory of literalizing translation technique extending from Arm1 through the later phase of patristic renderings from Greek to the highly developed system of calques devised by the Hellenophile school to capture the minute lexical nuances of scholarly and philosophical texts.[71] Here too the process is paralleled by a similar movement in Syriac which is roughly contemporaneous and may have acted as a stimulus to the Armenian trend. It is also reminiscent of the later evolution in Georgian translation technique from St. Euthymius Mt'ac'mideli in the 10th century to Ioanne Petric̣i in the early 12th.[72]

Where sense and form corresponded or were closely parallel in both languages, the reviser did not pursue variation for its own sake. Faithful in the quantitative representation of his exemplar, his veneration for scripture was not such as to deter active intervention when difficulties arose. Refusing to opt for a bland rendering which left the problem for the reader to puzzle over, his attempts to clarify the text and express it more intelligibly were generally successful. Unfortunately, these got out of hand in the predictions of chapter eleven where the result must be termed linguistically inadequate.

That exception apart, the version's profile is both textually reliable and sufficiently uniform that only two hands need be posited to account for all the data (i.e. one for each stratum). By re-applying the procedure they employed with a consistency defined by the above limits one can mostly ascertain their *Vorlage* with reasonable accuracy, thus reinforcing the version's significance for text criticism of Daniel which we established on the affinities of its readings with P and Gk.

Transmission History - Early Scribal Practice: Since the liturgical tradition is of some antiquity, it is understandable that some of these books preserve a valuable early text. Thus the breviary adduces a relatively pure form of Arm1 cited by P'awstos and the lectionary reads one only slightly more contaminated by the revision which is probably the source of Sebēos' quotations in the seventh century.[73] Lyonnet resorts to the same authorities to recover facets of Arm1 in the gospels. However, the closer proximity of the Greek parent texts of the strata of Daniel[74] implies that the revision itself will have been more moderately conducted.[75] Moreover, from what we can deduce, there was little attempt to suppress the earlier phase, so that even manuscripts of the fifteenth (V280) and early seventeenth century (J2558) evince an important Arm1 cache. Naturally, the contrast between Arm1's Syriac *Vorlage* in the gospels and the Greek standard of the revision will have induced a major textual transformation. The Diatessaronic affinities of the original version will also have rendered it theologically suspect as is evidenced by Theodoret's attempts to eliminate all the copies in his diocese.[76] Nevertheless, a minority group within the manuscript tradition of the Armenian gospels is found to retain certain Arm1 readings.[77]

As Arm1's more significant readings are attested by only a small group of MSS, it is evident that the majority normally witnesses to the revised text. Nevertheless, examples of the opposite phenomenon are encountered where the Arm2 reading is preserved by a minority of the tradition, a phenomenon also detected in the gospels[78] e.g. 3:25 Ազարիա MS 287=Gk] -հայ V280' M346' J1925-M2627 -հա rel=P. These indicate that a certain amount of conflation must have taken place, remnants of which are still to be found in the form of doublets.[79] Conservative tradents unwilling to make a choice between two readings, retained both. The practice pertains especially to instances where Arm2 adopts Th's transliteration of semitic terms which Arm1 had translated,[80] e.g.

10:5 բադեան M287]բադեն M346

բադեն (-դէն V280) փառս V280' M2585

փառս rel.

Confronted with the same issue, many scribes preferred the translation, presumably on the grounds that it was immediately intelligible whereas the transliteration was not. In consequence readings like մանզ WN11, մառզին V280' at 11:38 dropped out of the main tradition, while Arm1's rendering հզաւր continued to be copied. In such cases the reaction of the tradents was crucial for the survival of early readings.

Local Texts: Outlining the history of Arm's transmission from the thriteenth to the seventeenth centuries, the period from which most of our documentary evidence derives, is relatively straightforward. Retrojecting the situation 'on the ground' in this later era we have more tentatively suggested that, as the prevailing provenance of A group MSS is from S.W. Armenia, it may have been the local text of Vaspurakan, while the B group circulated in Siwnik' to the South-East and the early C group in the Bagratid domains of N and NW Armenia before becoming transplanted in Cilicia as a result of the migrations of the tenth and eleventh centuries.[81]

In order to verify the theory quotations from writers of greater chronological and geographical diversity must be collated to determine whether any consistent local affiliation emerges. If so, the known location of the writer will serve to anchor his text type as Theodore, Theodoret and Chrysostom do for the Lucianic Recension and Lucifer of Cagliari for the European OL. Apart from external details of provenance, few internal peculiarities, dialectal forms, etc. were observed to characterize the text of the three local groups. The most notable case is Group B's predilection for the form որպէս over իբրեւ.[82]

Despite the thoroughgoing *rapprochement* of the later Syriac and Georgian versions with the Greek there is no indica-

tion of this having affected the Armenian of Daniel and relatively minor incidence of secondary Greek influence on other parts
of scripture.[83] Certainly it is possible that learned *vardapets*
consulted Greek codices and introduced their own changes
into the text or left as marginal notes, yet this has had no appreciable effect on the extant MSS of this book.[84]

Documentary Types: As we have shown in chapter two, the
one volume Bible MS evolved in the medieval period and subsequently became the main unit in which Arm was transmitted.
A scribal colophon in a full Bible (M177) copied during the reign
of Lewon III (1269-89) attributes the initiative to Nersēs
Lambronaci (1153-98), one of the most prolific ecclesiastical
figures of the previous century:

> "May God in His love for mankind glorify the soul of the
> Lord Nersēs Lambronac'i who, in addition to all the other
> benefits he bestowed upon our people through translating
> and commenting upon many texts presented us with the
> comprehensive collection of biblical books. Thereby he
> stimulated everyone to emulation since it does not appear
> that such a thing had existed in our nation before him. In
> our time too we have only seen two or three which have been
> produced after him. See our nation's indolence: it is already
> a hundred years or more from his time to ours and only the
> number we stated has increased." [85]

Previously the various books circulated in a number of units, as
in surrounding cultures.[86] The most common division was into
two parts, the former containing the Pentateuch and historical
books while the latter was formed by the wisdom books and
prophets.[87] Thus it appears that the two halves of OT have independent transmission histories. For that reason it was impossible to compare the performance of many of the early witnesses in Arm with Deut and vice versa because their compass
was limited to one part of OT. Similarly the extreme variation in
textual quality which some Bible codices evince in the same two
books often stems from the diversity of the exemplars from
which the archetype of the codex was constructed.

Since anyone commissioning a MS usually provided the exemplar for copying, once a documentary type became established it was automatically propagated with only minor variations. Therefore since a number of the members of Arm's early groups A and B possess only the second half of OT, there are grounds for thinking that this arrangement is of early origin and may even remount to the translation itself.

If we can rely on the tradition that Maštoc̕ commenced his translation with Proverbs, then Conybeare's suggestion that he employed an exemplar containing the second half of OT may be correct.[88] Its plausibility is increased by the existence of Greek MSS which closely parallel that description, e.g. 147 (12th cent.) comprises catenae on Prov, Eccl, Cant, Job + the twelve minor and four major prophets; 311 (12th cent.) Prov, Eccl, Cant, Wis, Sir, the twelve minor and four major prophets, Esth, Jdt, Tob, 1-3 Macc; 613 (13th cent.) Ps, Od, Prov, Cant, Wis, Sir, Job, the twelve minor and four major prophets.[89]

Extant Peshitta MSS however are not so arranged. Moreover, the theory is corroborated by internal evidence of readings in a growing number of OT books, indicating that the principal Arm1 *Vorlage* was of a Lucianic complexion. The implication would seem to be that despite the overall similarity in translation technique, the renderings of the two testaments were discrete activities. In that case one might speculate about their relation to the division of labour among Maštoc̕'s disciples which Koriwn describes:[90]

> "fond of his pupils, the vardapet divided into two groups those whom he had brought with him, allocating some of them to Syriac learning in Edessa and the rest to Greek learning with him in Samosata."

Although requiring further elaboration, it is at least possible to surmise that Maštoc̕ entrusted the NT to the team in Edessa to translate from Syriac, while he personally undertook supervision of rendering the OT from Greek (with intermittent recurrence to P as we have seen).

Bearing in mind the copyist's complaint about the paucity of one volume Bibles and the scribe of J1925's ascription of
the initiative to produce one in Erznka to divine intervention,[91]
the question arises of how the format came to gain such
widespread popularity as to dominate the textual transmission
history from the fourteenth century onwards. This typological
unit became the paramount vehicle for the circulation of the
'Cilician Vulgate'. Yet, it is now clear that the latter's currency
is not primarily determined by its textual transformation to
that of Latin codices brought by Dominican friars invited by
the court. The latter may have been responsible for introducing
certain readings not traditionally represented in the Armenian
gospels and for the gradual acceptance of Vulgate chapter divisions. However, this can hardly be termed a revision.[92]

The characteristic arrangement of books in the one volume Bible is first observed in M345 of 1270, commissioned by
Yovhannēs Arkayełbayr, abbot of Gїner and younger brother of
Hetʿum I. Another feature typologically germane is the inclusion of synopses *(naxadrutʿiwnkʿ)* for each book and chapter
headings *(gluxk)* for the OT which we find in the MS M177 that
we have already encountered. The scribe, Movsēs Erznkacʿi, informs the reader that these were composed by his vardapet.[93]
A colophon in MS V841 stipulates the author's identity as
Gēorg Skewṙacʿi, while another source reports the synopses
had been commissioned by the future king Hetʿum II. This was
one of many royal commissions Gēorg was vouchsafed.[94]

Certainly, he had the appropriate connections to receive
such honour both through his uncle, Grigor Skewṙacʿi, who had
been a pupil of Nersēs Lambronacʿi and the very relation between the monastery of Skewṙay and the Hetʿumid house on
whose ancestral estate it was situated. Moreover, his uncle had
been a skillful scribe and given Gēorg a thorough apprenticeship in the art. So much so that he went on to write a number
of orthographical works of some importance for the transference of texts from the *scriptio continua* of uncial manuscripts
to the minuscule pattern with word division. His treatment of

syllabic division was of particular assistance in facilitating wordbreaks at the end of lines. Just as his many pupils almost monopolized Cilician Bible copying in the fourteenth century, so his writings became standard school texts which in turn were the subject of commentaries.[95] So much in awe were his exemplars held for their readers' aids, orthographical purity and consummate penmanship that subsequent scribes punctiliously reproduced them without change. Hence the prestige of the Cilician type resided far less in its textual antiquity than the fitness of its presentation.

Date: The limits of the original translation are fixed fairly precisely. Its pre-condition was the invention of the Armenian alphabet which is traditionally assigned to the early fifth century. Furthermore, it was completed before the arrival of the Constantinopolitan exemplars sometime after the Council of Ephesus in 431. At all events it must pre-date the following citation from Agathangelos:

§475 p. 235 uщшидh uлðбищ u = P Ł

The majority of Arm MSS read рарծgh uлðnıрhul WN 11 J 1925-M4114;   -рhull M178-M346-M2585   M2627-M9116 M182"   -рhulp M287

=Th ἐξολεθρευθήσεται χρῖσμα at 9:26

However V280'-M2558 adduce a doublet joining the former reading (Arm 1) to the latter (Arm2) by means of the copula. That Agathangelos' source was indeed Arm 1 is underlined by Wyngarden's observation[96] that it embodies the exegesis of P's Christian translators and the fact that uщшïшïhï in Arm is the more natural translation equivalent of Greek ἀποκτείνειν.

If Koriwn's reference to Catholicos Sahak's role in the revision is to be given credence,[97] then the bulk of the task must have been accomplished within a span beginning at some point after 431 until 438/9, the year of his death. Moreover, if, as seems plausible, the revision of OT and NT belong to one process, it is worth noting Lyonnet's finding[98] that the Georgian Version of the gospels derives from its mid-point and witnesses elements of both Arm1 and Arm2. As the Georgian Martyrdom of St. Šušanik ostensibly written c. 480 makes reference to the gospels, they must already have been in existence, and consequently provides secondary corroboration for dating the Armenian revision about mid-century or slightly before.

Diplomatic Edition: The present edition of Arm in several respects marks an advance on its most distinguished predecessor, the edition of Zohrab. Having distinguished itself in the tests formulated in chapter three to detect singular and secondary readings, its base text, MS 287, represents Arm's early text far more exactly than MS V1508 of Z.[99] The latter is classified in the D3 sub-group, an outgrowth of the more common Cilician group C which evinces a late, derivative text type which does not yield early variants independently of groups ABC.[100]

Its apparatus is also far more representative of Arm's manuscript tradition. Firstly, its composition is larger, being comprised of fourteen witnesses as opposed to Zohrab's eight. More importantly, the MSS were selected after a systematic analysis of all available extant witnesses due to their low rating in singular readings of substance and orthography.[101] On the whole, they preserve the norm of their sub-group and point back to the archetype from which all the members originate. Taken together, they give a reliable picture in miniature of the entire range of the manuscript tradition.

In contrast, the scope offered by Zohrab's apparatus is severely restricted. Although the editor neglects to cite his witnesses by library number, from the brief description he provides in his introduction we have been able to identify seven. (1) V1634; (2) V1006; (3) V623; (4) V229; (5) M188; (6) V1182; (7) K258.[102]

According to their classification in Daniel, we arrive at the following spread: one MS from each of B1[a] C2[a] C2[b] and two from D3 and E2. Granted the close affinity of groups D and E and their development from a C matrix, only MS V1258 presents any major variation from Z. Moreover, despite his realization of the fact, Zohrab's observation «բայց ոչ ինչ առաւելութիւն գուցանէր այնու»[103] (yet it evinced no advantage thereby) indicates he had failed to grasp its import. MS V1258's valuable textual potential is already indicated by its typological categorization as a part-Bible.[104] Hence it does not feature in Deut as it lacks the first half of OT: the low evaluation of the rest is largely upheld, one being ranked in CII and d and two in e1. The exception is MS V229 which belongs to a family whose archetype was of a composite origin such that the first half of OT is of a text type superior to that of the wisdom books and prophets. From the details Zohrab discloses it is difficult to trace his eighth MS. However, since he remarks that textually it resembled Oskan's edition based on MS M180, we are probably justified in assuming that it belonged to the C2[b] subgroup in Daniel and thus supports our previous conclusion on the poor range and quality of the editor's sources.

Similarly, the layout of the apparatus is more systematic and precise in accord with standard critical practice. In particular, the removal of orthographic variants (common to several MSS or specific to one) for special consideration both decongests the apparatus and affords an insight into the propensities of the various scribes which may be of value in determining the merits of their individual readings. If it is known that a MS frequently adduces the same unusual form, the chances of its being secondary are far higher than otherwise. In addition, such data may sometimes be of service in locating the provenance of a text by means of dialectal features.

Separating the Strata: Within the framework of our textual investigation Arm's complex origins have been established and their legacy, the variegated colouring of the extant witnesses has been revealed in the diverse character of the readings displayed by the base text and apparatus of the diplomatic edition. As it stands, Arm's textual condition resembles that of the Ethiopic Version which is also hybrid. Stemming from a Greek exemplar similar to MS B, it underwent a revision in the thirteenth century on the basis of Arabic MSS which had a definite connection with P. To allow such a version to make its optimum contribution to the text criticism of its translation bases it is therefore necessary to consider the possibility of separating the strata. Judging from the present study, prospects are favourable for proceeding towards this cautiously in Arm's case.

As Montgomery states that all Th MSS including B have been influenced by the Hexapla,[105] so no Arm MS escaped the effects of the revision. Even MS V280 sometimes evinces Arm2 readings as well as scribal errors arising from its particular transmission history (e.g. orthographical irregularities and homoeoteleuton). However, this can partly be rectified with the aid of MS J2558 with which it is closely related, while MSS M346' and M48 regularly augment V280's arsenal of Arm1 readings. Adopting the latter as the skeleton of Arm1 to be fleshed out by the above MSS along with appropriate liturgical and patristic material and performing a similar operation for Arm2 therefore seems to constitute the best line of advance, taking into consideration the issues of *Vorlage* and translation technique which have been the object of the present investigation.[106]

NOTES

1. For further corroboration of these features see S. P. Cowe, "The Two Armenian Versions of Chronicles".

2. For a positive statement of these views see E.L. Colwell, "Slandered or Ignored: the Armenian Gospels", JR xvii (1937), pp.48-61, and for a re-assessment S.P. Cowe, "Problematics".

3. Similarly, Johnson's contention that the first stratum of the Armenian version of 1 Sam derived completely from Syriac should probably be rejected on insufficient evidence. The same conclusion seems warranted in connection with Marr's conjecture on Chronicles recently revived by Ter-Petrosyan.

4. For an assessment of the extent to which the manuscripts witness to Arm1 see S.P. Cowe, "Canticle of Azariah", where the importance of the Georgian version is also underlined.

5. See Appendix to chapter four, pp.300-1. The theory, which seems corroborated by Arm evidence, that the original P text was closer to MT textually than that of the later majority is cogently argued against Vööbus' by hypothesis of a Targumic origin to the version by M.D. Koster in *The Peshitta of Exodus,* pp.198-212. See further A. Gelston, *The Peshitta of the Twelve Prophets,* pp.86-87 and Koster's more recent study "which came first: The Chicken or the Egg?" in *The Peshitta: Its Early Text and History,* P.B. Dirksen and M.J. Mulder (eds.), Leiden, E.J. Brill: 1988, pp.99-126.

6. Lazar Parpec̆i, *Patmagirk' hayoc̆,* §x, p.13.

7. Ibid.

8. Koriwn, *Vark̆ Maštoc̆i,* pp. 94, 96. There the author also mentions the city of Amida and it is interesting to note that that was the place of Lazar's refuge during a temporary fall from favour. See Lazar Parpec̆i, *Patmagirk' hayoc̆,* p.186.

9. See J. Fleming, *Akten der Ephesinischen Synode vom Jahre 449 Syrisch*, AKGW Gott Phil.-Hist. Kl. N.F. xv,1 Berlin, Weidmannsche Buchhandlung: 1917, p.25.

10. Koriwn, *Vark Maštoci*, p.122.

11. See G. Garitte, "Les catécheses de S. Cyrille de Jérusalem en arménien", *Mus* (1963), pp. 95-108.

12. On this translation see the notes by A. Merx in *The Ecclesiastical History of Eusebius in Syriac*, W. Wright and N. McLean (eds.), Cambridge, The University Press: 1898.

13. See L.H. Ter-Petrosyan, "Barsel kesara c̆u 'Vec̆oreanki' hayeren t'argmanu yan naxorinakë", *PBH* (1983) no.2-3, pp.264-278 [The Exemplar of the Armenian translation of Basil of Caesarea's Hexaemeron] (*pace* K. Muradyan (ed.), *Barsel kesaraci yalags vec'awreay ararc̆ut ean* [Basil of Caesarea's On the Six Days of Creation] Erevan, Armenian Academy of Sciences: 1984, pp.x-xi).

14. See I. Hausherr, "Les versions syriaques et arménienne d'Evagre le Pontique. Leur valeur, leur relation, leur utilization" *OC*xxii, 2 (1031), pp.65-118.

15. For details see the relevant section of chapter four.

16. R. Hanhart (ed.), *Maccabaeorum liber II*, Septuaginta ix, 2, Göttingen, Vandenhoeck & Ruprecht: 1976, pp.31-32 and Id., *Maccabaeorum liber III* Septuaginta ix, 3 Göttingen, Vandenhoeck & Ruprecht: 1960, pp.25-27. See also J. Ziegler (ed.), *Duodecim prophetae*, Septuaginta xiii, Göttingen, Vandenhoeck & Ruprecht: 1943, pp.80-81.

17. See M.E. Stone, "The Old Armenian Version of Isaiah: Towards the Choice of the Base Text for an Edition", *Textus*AHUBP, viii (1973), pp.107-125.

18. For a discussion of the possibility of there being a Lucianic text of the Pentateuch which concludes there is no evidence to support such a theory see J.W. Wevers, *Text History of the Greek Genesis*, Göttingen, Vandenhoeck & Ruprecht: 1974, pp.158-175. This probably explains the negative results obtained in *Deut.*

19. Among several instances of Arm=410 without outside support we may count the location of the heading "Third Vision" at 1:20. They concur with a wide selection of witnesses in placing the second, fourth and fifth visions, while Arm alone puts the sixth and seventh at the beginning of chapter 10 and Bel respectively.

20. See A. Rahlfs, *Verzeichnis der griechischen Handschriften,* p.85.

21. However, the resemblances noted between Daniel 9:5-19 and Baruch 1:15-2:1 have been demonstrated rather to be of a general character, reflecting a similar type of translation technique rather than direct dependence of one upon the other. See E. Tov, "The Relations between the Greek Versions of Baruch and Daniel", *Armenian and Biblical Studies,* M.E. Stone (ed.), pp.27-34. For the view (now generally rejected) that Th forms part of the pre-Theodotionic KAIGE revision process see D. Barthelemy, *Les Devanciers d'Aquila,* p.44.

22. A. Schmitt, *Stammt der sogenannte 'ɵ'-Text bei Daniel wirklich von Theodotion?* MSU IX Göttingen, Vandenhoeck & Ruprecht: 1966. For the theoretical issue of how to isolate Theodotionic material in connection with Daniel see R. Hanhart, "Die übersetzungstechnik der Septuaginta als Interpretation" (Dan 11:2 und die Aegyptenzüge des Antiochus Epiphanes) *Mélanges D. Barthélemy* OBO 38 (1981), p.150, note 5.

23. J. Schüpphaus, "Das Verhältnis von LXX - und Theodotion-Text in den apokryphen Zusätzen", *ZAW* 88 (1971), pp.4 ff.

24. K. Koch, "Die Herkunft der Proto-Theodotion-übersetzung des Danielbuches", *VT* 23 (1963), pp.362-365.

25. On the same grounds he argues that P-Th agreements do not imply the former's dependence on the latter, but rather their mutual dependence on a form of MT circulating in Syro-Mesopotamia. See K. Koch, *Das Buch Daniel,*

pp.20-21.

26. At the same time more recent studies have underlined the extent to which Th preserves OG unaltered. See Sh. Pace, "The Stratigraphy of the Text of Daniel", p.26.

27. A. Carlini and A. Citi, "Susanna e la prima visione di Daniele in due papiri inediti della Bibliotheca Bodmeriana: P. Bodm. XLV e P. Bodm. XLVI", *Museum Helveticum* Sonderdruck. Basel/Stuttgart, Schwahe Co. Ag. Verlag: 1981, p.91.

28. See H.J. Lehmann, "The Syriac Translation of the Old Testament as Evidenced around the Middle of the Fourth Century in Eusebius of Emesa", *SJOT* 1 (1987), pp.66-86.

29. For an overview see S. Brock, *Syriac Perspectives on Late Antiquity*, London, Variorum Reprints: 1984, pp.17-34. That some of the P translators also employed Gk intermittently in rendering the MT is demonstrated in A. Gelston, *The Peshitta of the Twelve Prophets*, pp.160-177.

30. On this point see W.S. McCullough, *A Short History*, p.62.

31. A. Vööbus, *History of the School of Nisibis*, CSCO Sub. 26 Louvain: 1965, pp.14-21. There the author also mentions the translations of the works of Diodore.

32. Extant in Armenian are commentaries on Isaiah, Psalms, Matthew, John, the Pauline Epistles and a few miscellanica.

33. On this see L. van Rompay, "Eznik de Kolb et Théodore de Mopsueste à propos d'une hypothèse de Louis Mariès", *OLP* 15 (1984), pp. 15-173. Van Rompay poses the possibility that the author of at least that part of the *Yačaxapatum* corpus was Maštoc. The complexity of the authorship of this collection is underlined by a more recent thesis that the compilation may derive from the early sixth century. See R. Darling Young, "The Depiction of Monasticism in the *Yačaxapatum č'aik*", *Abstract of Lectures* AIEA Fifth Biennial Conference, Bologna,

University of Bologna: 1990. On the difficulty of specifying any links betweeen Theodore and Maštoc̕ see most recently G. Winkler, "Die Spätere Überarbeitung", pp.146-147. In Daniel Arm is dependent on Antiochene exegesis for the reading 'Parthians' at 1:3 which is adduced by St. Chrysostom and Theodoret. For further details, see chapter four p.270.

34. V. Yohannesean (ed.), *Ewsebiosi Emesac̕woy meknut̕iwnk̕* [The Commentaries of Eusebius of Emesa] Venice, St. Lazar Press: 1980.

35. For these see H.J. Lehmann, *Per Piscatores* Studies in the Armenian version of a collection of homilies by Eusebius of Emesa and Severian of Gabala, Arhus, Odder: 1975.

36. See J.P. Migne (ed.), *PG* 83: 1864, col.1245-1252 for the letter to Bishop Eulalios and col.1252-1255 for that to Bishop Eusebius. It has been suggested that they succeeded one another in the same see. For a critical edition with French translation see Y. Azéma, *Théodoret de Cyr Correspondance II* , SC 98, Paris, Editions du Cerf: 1964, pp.166-183.

37. B. Outtier, "La version arménienne du commentaire des psaumes de Théodoret. premier bilan", *REA* N.S. 12 (1977), pp.169-180. It appears that this formed the basis for a Georgian translation by Dač̕i in the ninth/tenth century. See M. Tarchnišvili, *Geschichte der kirchlichen georgischen Literatur,* p.101

38. W.C.H. Driessen, "Un commentaire arménien d'Ezékiel faussement attribué à saint Cyrille d'Alexandrie", *RB* (1961), pp.251-261.

39. Ibid., p.260.

40. See the citation from the Psalter commentary quoted by M.F. Wiles in "Theodore of Mopsuestia as a Representative of the Antiochene School", *CHB* vol.1, P.R. Ackroyd and C.F. Evans (eds.), Cambridge, The University Press: 1970, p.496, note 12.

41. Op. cit. note 34, p.2.

42. N. Marr, "Echmiadzinskij fragment drevne-gruzinsko-jversii Vetkhago Zaveta" [The Ejmiacin Fragment of the Old Georgian Version of the Old Testament] *Khristianskij Vostok* ii (1913), p.387.

43. See S.P. Cowe, "The Two Armenian Versions of Chronicles".

44. For an example cited from Theodoret see op. cit. note 28, p.84.

45. J.-M. Olivier (ed.), *Diodori Tarsensis Commentarii in Psalmos 1-L* COSG 6, Turnhout, Brepols: 1980, p.271.

46. J.P. Migne (ed.), *PG* 55: 1859, col.174.

47. See S.P. Cowe, "The Canticle of Azariah".

48. See Koriwn, *Vark Mastoci*, p.124. Though the epithet is pejorative, it is probably a euphemism for the author's fear of its theological opprobrium as an embodiment of Antiochene exegesis.

49. See S.P. Cowe, "The Two Armenian Versions of Chronicles". Contrary to the norm Arm2 there constitutes an independent translation.

50. J. Ziegler, *Der Bibeltext im Daniel-Kommentar des Hippolyt von Rom*, NAW Gött. Phil-Hist. kl. 1 52, Göttingen, Vandenhoech & Ruprecht: 1952, p.180.

51. J.W. Wevers (ed.), *Genesis*, Septuaginta 1, Göttingen, Vandenhoeck & Ruprecht: 1974, pp.46-47.

52. Id., *Text History of the Greek Leviticus*, Göttingen, Vandenhoeck & Ruprecht: 1986, p.9.

53. See *1 Sam*, pp.158-160 for 1Kgdms and S.P. Cowe, "La versión armenia", p.lxxvi for 2Kgdms.

54. R. Hanhart (e.d), *Esther*, Septuaginta viii, 3, Göttingen, Vandenhoeck & Ruprecht: 1966, p.33.

55. J. Ziegler (ed.), *Iob*, Septuaginta xi, 4, Göttingen, Vandenhoeck & Ruprecht: 1982.

56. J.W. Wevers (ed.), *Numeri*, Septuaginta, Göttingen, Vandenhoeck & Ruprecht: 1982, p.26.

57. See *Deut*, p.294.

58. See L.C. Allen, *The Greek Chronicles:* The Relation of the Septuagint of I and II Chronicles to the Massoretic Text, 2 vols. Leiden, E.J. Brill: 1974, p.8 and S.P. Cowe, "The Two Armenian Versions of Chronicles".

59. J. Ziegler, *Sapientia Salomonis,* Septuaginta xii, 1, Göttingen, Vandenhoeck & Ruprecht: 1962, pp.32-35.

60. Id., *Sapienta Iesu Filli Sirach,* Septuaginta xii, 2, Göttingen, Vandenhoeck & Ruprecht: 1965, p.59.

61. See C.E. Cox, *Hexaplaric Materials. Preserved in the Armenian Version,* Atlanta, GA, Scholars Press: 1986.

62. See S.P. Cowe, "The Armenian Version of Ruth", p.197.

63. Koriwn, *Vark Maŝtoc'i,* §19, p.124.

64. See especially S.P. Cowe, "The Two Armenian Versions of Chronicles".

65. See chapter six, pp.358-72.

66. For an overview of the question see S.P. Cowe, "Tendentious Translation and the Evangelical Imperative".

67. See S.P. Brock, "The Phenomenon of Biblical Translation in Antiquity", *Studies in the Septuagint Origins, Recensions and Interpretations* Selected Essays with a prolegomenon by S. Jellicoe, New York, Ktav Publishing House, Inc.: 1974, p.551 as well as his "Aspects of Translation Technique in Antiquity" in *Syriac Perspectives on Late Antiquity,* III, pp.69-87 and his recent "Translating the Old Testament" in *It is Written: Scripture Citing Scripture,* D.A. Carson and H.G.M. Williamson (eds.), Cambridge, The University Press: 1988, pp.87-98. For further information on the character of these versions see the appropriate chapters of B.M. Metzger (ed.), *The Early Versions of the New Testament*

68. For a study of the revisers' procedure in one passage of the book see S.P. Cowe, "The Canticle of Azariah".

69. For examples of this see id., "The Two Armenian Versions of Chronicles".

70. Ibid.

71. For greater detail see S.P. Cowe, "Problematics".
72. For these authors and the development of Georgian translation technique see the relevant sections of M. Tarchnišvili, *Geschichte der kirchlichen georgischen Literatur.*
73. For details see chapter seven, pp.396-9, 406-13.
74. See chapter five, pp.349-50.
75. For details see S.P. Cowe, "The Chronicle of Azariah".
76. For the background see A. Vööbus, *Early Versions of the New Testament,*PETSE 6, Stockholm: 1954, p.26.
77. See S. Lyonnet, *Les origines,* pp.55-194 and J. Alexanian, "Armenian Version in Luke", pp.221-223.
78. See J. Alexanian, "The Armenian Gospel Text", p.386 and "Armenian Version in Luke", pp.221-223. Similarly Sh. Pace notes the preservation of OG readings by Th manuscripts of Daniel in "The Stratigraphy of the Text of Daniel", pp.18, 28.
79. For further reference to such doublets see W. Kappler (ed.), *Maccabaeorum liber I,* Septuaginta ix, 1, Göttingen, Vandenhoeck & Ruprecht: 1 67, p.21 and the bibliography cited there.
80. For a similar contrast in translation technique between the two strata of Greek Daniel see Sh. Pace, "The Stratigraphy of the Text of Daniel", p.27.
81. For the importance of an east-west division in the transmission history of the Armenian Gospels see J. Alexanian, "Armenian Version of Luke", pp.210-211.
82. Seventeen examples of the variation were collected where MS M287 reads իրրեւ; B Group members reading որպէս are cited in brackets after the verse number: 3:40 (M178-M346'-M2585 +M4834); 50 (M178-M346'-M2585); 51 (M178-M346'-M2585); 4:22 (M178-M346'-M2585); 2˚ (M178-M346'); 30 1˚ (M178-M346' M2585) 2˚ (M178) 3˚ (M178-M346'); 7:4 1˚ (M178) 2˚ (M346'-M2585); 9 1˚ (M178) 2˚ (M178 +V280) 3˚ (M178-M346') 4˚ (M346'º; 8:15 (M178); 25 (M178-M3466' + M351).

83. For secondary Greek influence on the Armenian gospels see J. Alexanian, "The Armenian Gospel Text", pp.384-386. The most extensive case of this is Nersēs Lambronac'i's revision of the text of Revelation in the second half of the twelfth century. For a detailed investigation of this see F. Murat, *Yaytnureann Yovhannu hin hay targmanuṛiwn* [The Ancient Armenian Translation of the Revelation of John] Jerusalem, St. James Press: 1911, pp.cxix-cxlv. Another area where the Greek Bible impinged on the Armenian appears to be the textual division into sections. On this see B. Johnson, "Armenian Biblical Tradition", pp.361-362. Finally, one might mention the impact of Byzantine lumination on the iconography and miniature style of several medieval Bible-related manuscripts.

84. An exception to this general rule is the incidence of variants from the three secondary Greek translators (Aquila, Theodotion and Symmachus) in certain books. See B. Johnson, "Some remarks on the Marginal Notes in Armenian 1 Samuel", *Armenian and Biblical Studies,* M.E. Stone (ed.), pp.17-20 and M.E. Stone, "Additional Note on the Marginalia in 4 Kingdoms", ibid., pp.21-22.

85. See O. Eganyan et al. (eds.), *Mayr Cucak hayeren jeṛagrac* vol.1, col.712.

86. For Gk see R.A. Kraft, "Earliest Greek Versions (Old Greek)", *IDB* Supplementary Volume, K. Crim (gen.ed.), Nashville, Abingdon Press: 1976, p.811.

87. For an overview of the question see S.P. Cowe, "A Typology of Armenian Biblical Manuscripts", pp.49-67.

88. See F.C. Conybeare, "Armenian Version of the OT", *A Dictionary of the Bible,* J. Hastings (ed.), New York, Charles Scribner's Sons: 1905, vol.1, p.152.

89. For further details see A. Rahlfs, op. cit. note 20.

90. Koriwn, *Vark' Maštoci,* §vii, p.94.

91. For details see S.P. Cowe, "A Typology of Armenian Biblical Manuscripts", p.57.

92. See J. Alexanian, "The Armenian Gospel Text", pp.388-389 and B. Johnson, "Armenian Biblical Tradition", pp.360-361. For the later introduction of Vulgate verse numeration see S.P. Cowe, "Armenian Sidelights on Torah Study in 17th Century Poland" *JJS* xxxvii (1986), pp.94-97.

93. See O. Eganyan et al (eds.), *Mayr Cucak hayeren jeṙagrac*, col.708.

94. See B. Sargisean, *Mayr Cucak hayeṙen jeṙagrac*, cols. 47-62. The significance of Georg Skewṙaci for the history of the Armenian Bible was first noted by the vardapet Sargis Malean while collating manuscripts in Jerusalem. See S.P. Cowe, "An 18th Century Armenian Textual Critic", p.538.

95. L. Xačeryan (ed.), *Grčutyan arvesti lezvakan-ker-akanakan tesutyunë mijnataryan Hayastanum* [The Linguistic and Grammatical Theory of the Scribal Art in Medieval Armenia], Erevan, Academy of Sciences: 1962.

96. M.J. Wyngarden, *The Syriac version of the book of Daniel*, p.31. Afrahat already cites the P reading in his nineteenth discourse. The early fifth century Armenian translation of this work articulates the Christian interpretation even more explicitly by rendering ապանցի Քրիստոսu. See L. Ter-Petrosyan, *"Danieli Margareutyan T glxi asorerenic katarvac dasakan hayeren targmanu-tune"* [The Classical Armenian Translation from Syriac of the Ninth Chapter of Daniel's Prophecy], *B Mat* 14 (1984), p.193.

97. Koriwn, *Vark' Maštoci*, §xix, p.124. For the proposal that the disciples returned from Constantinople in 435 see G. Winkler, "An Obscure Chapter", pp.111-115 and p.106, note 92 for the date of Sahak's death.

98. S. Lyonnet, *Les origines*, p.15.

99. As has been demonstrated, MS M287 witnesses mainly to a relatively pure form of Arm2 with comparatively few Arm1 readings in contrast to some members of the A group such as V280-J2558. The editors of the

Matenadaran catalogue are inclined to locate its copying in Hromklay, seat of the catholicate at this period. The plausibility of this ascription is supported by the statement in the colophon that the catholicos was especially helpful to the patron, the priest Petros (O. Eganyan et al. (eds.), *Mayr Cucak hayeren jeragrac,* col. 1200). There the latter refers to his father as Kostandin the priest and informs us he himself has sons. These data render it likely that he is to be identified with the scribe of a gospel of 1248 at Hromklay also styled Petros the priest, son of Kostandin the priest and father of two sons, Arakel and Kostandin (A.S. Matevosyan (ed.), *Hayeren jeragreri hisatakaranner ig dar*[Armenian Manuscript Colophons 13th Century] Erevan, Armenian Academy of Sciences: 1984, p.242, no.196). He may also be the Petros the priest who encouraged the scribe Kiwrakos while copying a gospel at Hromklay in the same year (ibid., p.241, no.195). In light of the view that certain centres sought to preserve an unadulterated Arm2 text (J. Alexanian, "Armenian Version in Luke", p.209) it is significant that the exemplar for M287 seems to have been provided from the catholicosal collection. Hence its text may well derive from just such a controlled environment.

100. For a similar assessment of the value of later witnesses to P see P.B. Dirksen, "The Relations Between the Ancient and the Younger Peshitta MSS in Judges", p.163.

101. See chapter three, pp.84-8, 91-2.

102. See Zohrab's introduction pp.5-7. For more detailed information concerning these witnesses consult B. Sargisean (ed.), *Mayr Cucak hayeren jeragrac* nos. 2, 6, 3, 7 and 14. These represent the totality of witnesses comprising OT available at the Mkhitarist Monastery in Venice at the time. See C.E. Cox, "Introduction", p.xi.

103. *Astuacasunc'hin ew nor ktakaranac,* p.7

104. For the significance of this see S.P. Cowe, "A Typology of Armenian Biblical Manuscripts", p.67.

105. J.A. Montgomery, *A Critical and Exegetical Commentary on the Book of Daniel,* p.51.

106. The tentative nature of any reconstruction of Arm1 in Daniel may be deduced from collating the breviary text of chapter three with that of the biblical manuscripts. On this see further S.P. Cowe, "The Canticle of Azariah". For a more circumstantial discussion of the transition from a diplomatic to critical edition see also id., "Problematics".

In proceeding towards an eclectic edition our present resources require supplementing by further manuscript collation throughout the book. From the profile of the whole tradition provided by chapter one it is evident where the emphasis should lie. Members of groups ABC on the whole present more inter-group variation which means that the possibility of large scale duplication of readings is reduced, while their generally early text type offers the promise of a richer harvest of primitive variants. In particular, full collation of M5809 is likely to be productive since its singular readings cited in chapter one bear a remarkable resemblance to the unsupported readings of V280 which exhibit Lucianic characteristics. Likewise M1500 whose high textual calibre has been vindicated by several studies should prove of significant value.

BIBLIOGRAPHY[1]

1. Editions of the Armenian Bible

Oskan Erevancʻi (ed.), *Astuacašunčʻ hnocʻ ew norocʻ ktakaranacʻ* [Bible of the Old and New Testaments] Amsterdam, St. Ejmiacin and S. Sargis Press: 1666.

Mxitʻar Abbay Sebastacʻi (ed.), *Astuacašunčʻ grabar* [Classical Armenian Bible] Venice, Antoni Bortoli Press: 1733.

Zohrapean, H. (ed.), *Astuacašunčʻ hin ew nor ktakaranacʻ* [Sacred Scriptures of the Old and New Testaments] Venice, St. Lazar Press: 1805.

Bagratuni, A. (ed.), *Girk Astuacašunčʻk hin ew nor ktakaranacʻ* [Holy Scriptures of the Old and New Testaments] Venice, St. Lazar Press: 1860.

2. Reference Works

a) Dictionaries

Awetikʻean, G. et al (eds.), *Nor Baṙgirkʻ haykazean lezui* [New Dictionary of Armenian] 2 vols. Venice, St. Lazar Press: 1836, 1837 (reprinted Erevan, Erevan State University: 1979, 1981.)

Künzle, B.O., *Das altarmenische Evangelium* vol.2, Lexikon, Bern, Peter Lang: 1984.

Liddell, H.G. and R. Scott (eds.), *A Greek-English Lexican* (H.S. Jones (rev.) Ninth edition. Oxford, Clarendon Press: 1940.

Payne Smith, R., *Thesaurus Syriacus* 2 vols. Oxford, Clarendon Press: 1879, 1901.

b) Concordances

Arapkertcʻi, T. and V. Astuacaturean (eds.), *Hamabarbaṙ hin ew nor ktakaranacʻ* [Concordance to the Old and New Testaments] Jerusalem, St. James Press: 1895.

---

[1] Works of major significance for the Armenian Version of Daniel cited by abbreviated title in the notes are given full reference here. Those adduced in connection with very specific questions are cited in full in the appropriate notes and excluded from the bibliography.

455

Hatch, E. and H.A. Redpath (eds.), *A Concordance of the Septuagint and the other Greek Versions of the OT* 1-111. Oxford, Clarendon Press: 1892-1906 (reprinted Graz, 1954.)

c) **Bibliographies**

Anasyan, H. (ed.), *Haykakan Matenagituṭiwn* [Armenian Bibliography] Erevan, Armenian Academy of Sciences: vol.1, 1959; vol.2, 1976.
Brock, S.P. et al (eds.), *A Classified Bibliography of the Septuagint* Leiden, E.J. Brill: 1973.
Dirksen, P.B. (ed.), *An Annotated Bibliography of the Peshitta of the Old Testament* Leiden, E.J. Brill: 1989.
Rahlfs, A., *Verzeichnis der griechischen Handschriften des Alten Testaments* MSUII Berlin, Weidmann: 1914.

2. **Manuscript Catalogues**

Akinian, N. (ed.), *Katalog der armenischen Handschriften des armenischen Hospitals zu S. Blasius in Rom und des Pont. Leoniano Collegio Armeno, Roma.* Vienna: Mxitarist Press, 1961.
Bogharian, N. (ed.), *Mayr Cucak jeṛagrac srboc Yakobeanc* [Grand Catalogue of St. James Press Manuscripts], vols.I-X. Jerusalem: St. James Press, 1966-91.
Conybeare, F.C., *A Catalogue of the Armenian Manuscripts in the British Museum.* London: 1913.
Dashian, J. (ed.), *Katalog der armenischen Handschriften in der K.K. Hofbibliothek zu Wien.* Vienna: Mxitarist Press, 1891.
— *Katalog der armenischen Handschriften in der Mechitaristen-Bibliothek zu Wien.* Vienna: Mxitarist Press, 1895.
Der Nersessian, S., *The Chester Beatty Library: A Catalogue of the Armenian Manuscripts,* Vol.1 (Text) Dublin: Hodges Figgis & Co. Ltd., 1958.
Eganyan, O. and K.H. Sukiasyan, *Cucak hayeren jeṛagrac arewelaget Ser Harold Valter Beylii* [A Catalogue of the Armenian Manuscripts of the Orientalist, Sir Harold Walter Bailey] *B Mat* 11 (1973), pp.357-376.
Eganyan, O. et al (eds.), *Mayr cucak hayeren jeṛagrac Maštoci anvan Matenadarani* [Grand Catalogue of the

Armenian Manuscripts in the Maštoc̕ Matenadaran] Erevan, Armenian Academy of Sciences: 1984.

Ismailova, T., "Армянские иллюстрированные рукописи Государственного эрмитажа" [Some Illuminated Armenian Manuscripts in the Hermitage Collection] *Trudy Gosudarstvennogo Ermitazha* 10 (1969), pp.110-141.

Johnson, B., "Fünf armenische Bibelhandschriften aus Erevan" *Wort, Lied und Gottesspruch,* Festschrift for Joseph Ziegler (ed.) J. Schreiner. Würzburg: Echter Verlag/Kathol. Bibelwerk, 1972.

Keschischian, M. (ed.), *Katalog der armenischen Handschriften in der Bibliothek des Klosters Bzommar.* Band 1. Vienna: Mxitarist Press, 1964.

Kurdian, H., *"Hamařot c̕uc̕ak hayeren grc̕agirneru K̕yurtyan havakacoyi i Vič̕ida, Kansas. A.M.N."* [Brief Catalogue of the Armenian MSS of the Kurdian Collection in Wichita, Kansas, U.S.A.] *B Mat* 11 (1973), pp.399-422.

Macler, Fr., "Rapport sur une mission scientifique en Belgique, Hollande, Danemark et Suede juillet-septembre 1922, Paris: 1924, pp.19-164. (*Nouvelles Archives des Missions scientifiques,* XXII, pp.295-440.)

Minassyan, L.G. and O.S. Eganyan (eds.), *Katalog der armenischen Handschriften in der Bibliothek der Losters in Neu-Djoulfa.* Band II. Vienna: Mxitarist Press, 1972.

Sargisean, B.V. (ed.) *Mayr c̕uc̕ak jeřagrac̕ matenadaranin Mxit̕arean c̕ i Venetik* [Grand Catalogue of Armenian MSS of the Mxitarist Library in Venice] Vol.1, Venice, St. Lazar Press: 1914.

Ter-Avetissian, S. (ed.), *Katalog der armenischen Handschriften in der Bibliothek des Klosters in Neu Djoulfa.* Band 1. Vienna: Mxitarist Press, 1970.

Tisserant, E. (ed.), *Codices Armeni Bibliothecae Vaticanae Borgiani Vaticani Barberiniani Chisiani.* Rome: Vatican Polygott Press, 1927.

Xač̕ikyan, L. and A. Mnac̕akanyan (eds.) *Cuc̕ak jeřagrac̕ Maštoc̕i anvan Matenadarani* [Manuscript Catalogue of the Maštoc̕i Library] 2 vols. Erevan: Academy of Sciences of the Armenian SSR, 1965, 1970.

4. Commentaries

Koch, K., *Das Buch Daniel,* Erträge der Forschung 144. Darmstadt, Wissenschaftliche Buchgesellschaft: 1980.

Montgomery, J.A., *A Critical and Exegetical Commentary on the Book of Daniel* (I.C.C.) New York, Charles Scribner's Sons: 1927.

Moore, C.A., Daniel, Esther and Jeremiah The Additions (The Anchor Bible) New York, Doubleday & Co.: 1977.

5. Texts and Translations

Agathangelos, *Patmut iwn Hayoc* [History of the Armenians] G. Ter-Mkrtčean and St. Kanayeanc (eds.), Tiflis, St. Martiroseanc Press: 1909 (reprinted with an introduction by R.W. Thomson, Delmar, NY, Caravan Books: 1980.

Blake, R.P. and M. Brière (eds.), *The Old Georgian Version of the Prophets* PO XXIX, fasc. 5, Paris, Firmin-Didot et Cie.: 1961 (Apparatus criticus PO XXX, fasc. 3, 1963.)

Eznik Kołbaci, *De Deo,* L. Mariès and Ch. Mercier (eds.), PO XXVIII, fasc.3-4, Paris, Firmin-Didot et Cie.: 1959.

Garsoïan, N.G. (trans.), *The Epic Histories Attributed to P'awstos Buzand,* Cambridge, MA, Harvard University Press: 1989.

Koriwn, *Vark Maštoci* [Life of Maštoc] M. Abełyan (ed.), Erevan, Erevan State University: 1981.

(Koriwn II), *Patmut iwn srboyn Mesrovbay* [The History of St. Mesrop] Soperk Haykakank II. Venice, St. Lazar Press: 1854, pp.1-37.

Lazar P'arpeci, *Patmagirk Hayoc* [History of the Armenians] G. Ter-Mkrt čean and St. Malxasean (eds.), Tiflis, Aragatip Mnacakan Martiroseanc: 1906 (reprinted with an introduction by D. Kouymjian, Delmar, NY, Caravan Book: 1985.)

Movses Xorenaci, *Patmut iwn Hayoc* [History of the Armenians] M. Abełean and S. Yarut iwnean (eds.) Tiflis, Elektratparan: 1913 (reprinted with an introduction by R.W. Thomson, Delmar, NY, Caravan Books: 1981.)

P'awstos (Buzandaci) *Patmut iwn Hayoc* [History of the Armenians] K.P.[atkanean] (ed.), St. Petersburg, Imperial Academy of Sciences: 1883 (reprinted with an introduction by N.G. Garsoïan, Delmar, NY, Caravan Books: 1984.)

Renoux, A. (ed.), *Le codex arménien Jérusalem* 121 PO XXXVI, fasc. 2, Turnhout/Belgique, Brepols: 1971.

Stone, M.E. (ed.), *The Testament of Levi,* St. James Press: 1969.

— *The Armenian Version of the Testament of Joseph* SBLTT6, Pseudepigrapha Series 5, Missoula, Scholars Press: 1975.

Thomson, R.W. (trans.), Agathangelos History of the Armenians. Albany, State University of New York Press: 1970.

— *ELISH₌History of Vartan and the Armenian War* Cambridge, MA, Harvard University Press: 1982.

— Moses Khorenats'i History of the Armenians. Cambridge, MA, Harvard University Press: 1978.

Xačikyan, L.A., *Že Dari hayeren jᶜagreri hišatakaranner* [Colophons of fifteenth century Armenian Manuscripts] Erevan, Armenian Academy of Sciences, vol.1, 1955; vol.2, 1958; vol.3, 1967.

Zeytᶜunyan, A.S. (ed.), *Girk Cnndoc* [The Book of Genesis] Erevan, Armenian Academy of Sciences: 1985.

6. Studies

Akinean, N., "Mxitᶜar Ayrivanecᶜwoy čaᵣₑntiri noragiwt yišatakaran e" [The Newly-found Colophon of Mxitᶜar Ayrivanecᶜi's Homiliary] *Akaws* 13 (1946), pp.120-126.

Alexanian, J.M., "The Armenian Version in Luke and the Question of the Caesarean Text" (Ph.D. dissertation, University of Chicago, 1982.)

— "The Armenian Gospel Text from the Fifth through the Fourteenth Centuries", T.J. Samuelian and M.E. Stone (eds.), *Medieval Armenian Culture,* UPATS 6, Chico, CA, Scholars Press: 1984, pp.381-394.

Barr, J., *Comparative Philology and the Text of the OT.* Oxford, Clarendon Press, 1968.

— *The Typology of Literalism in Ancient Biblical Translations,* NAW Gött, Phil.-Hist. kl. 1979, 11. Göttingen, Vandenhoeck & Ruprecht: 1979.

Barthélemy, D., *Les devanciers d'Aquila,* VT Suppl.10, Leiden, E.J. Brill: 1963.

Bogharian, N., *Hay Groïner* [Armenian Writers] Jerusalem, St. James Press: 1971.

Cox, C.E., "Introduction", H. Zohrapian (ed.), *Astuatsashunch' Matean Hin ew Nor Ktakarants'* (sic) [Scriptures of the Old and New Testaments]. A facsimile reproduction of the 1805 Venetian Edition, Delmar, NY, Caravan BooksL 1984, pp.v-xxvi.

— "The Use of Lectionary Manuscripts to Establish the Text of the Armenian Bible", *Medieval Armenian Culture,* (T.J. Samuelian and M.E. Stone (eds.) UPATS 6, Chico, CA, Scholars Press: 1984, pp.365-380.

— "Concerning a Cilician Revision of the Armenian Bible", *De Septuaginta.* A. Pietersma and C. Cox (eds.), Mississauga, Ontario, Benben Publications: 1984, pp.209-222.

— *Hexaplaric Materials Preserved by the Armenian Version* SCSS 21, Atlanta, GA, Scholars Press: 1986.

Cowe, S.P., "The Armenian Version of Daniel: Diplomatic Edition and Investigation of its Textual Affinities", (Ph.D. dissertation, Hebrew University of Jerusalem, 1983.)

— "A Typology of Armenian Biblical Manuscripts", *REA* NS 18 (1984), pp.49-67.

— "The Armenian Version of Ruth and its Textual Affinities", *La Septuaginta en la Investigación Contemporánea,* N. Fernández Marcos (ed.), Madrid, 1985, pp.183-197.

— "An 18th Century Armenian Textual Critic and His Continuing Significance", *REA* NS 20 (1986-87), pp.527-541.

— "La versión armenia", *El texto antioqueno de la Biblia griega,* N. Fernández Marcos and J.R. Busto Saiz (eds.), Madrid, TECC 50: 1989, pp.lxxi-lxxix.

— "Literary and Theological Considerations Governing the Strata of the Armenian Version of Scripture", *Translation of Scripture,* JQR Suppl. Philadelphia, PA, Annenberg Research Institute: 1990, pp.29-45.

— "The Armenian Version of the Epistle of Jeremiah: Parent Text and Translation Technique", *VII Congress IOSCS* C.E. Cox (ed.), Chico, CA, Scholars Press: (in press), pp.373-392.

— "The Two Armenian Versions of Chronicles", Their Origin and Translation Technique", *REA* 22 (forthcoming).

— "Tendentious Translation and the Evangelical

Imperatives: Religious Polemic in the Early Armenian Church", *REA* 22 (forthcoming).

— "Problematics of Edition of Armenian Biblical Texts", *Priorities, Problems and Techniques of Text Editions,* H. Lehman and J.J.S. Weitenberg (eds.), Aarhus (forthcoming).

— "An Armenian Job Fragment from Sinai and its Implications", *Or Chr* (1992) (forthcoming).

— "The Canticle of Azariah and its Two Armenian Versions" *JSAS* 5 (forthcoming).

Daniel, S., *Recherches sur le vocabulaire du culte dans la sep - tante,* Paris, Klincksieck: 1966.

Der Nersessian, S., *L'art arménien,* Paris, Arts et Métiers Graphiques: 1977.

Dirksen, P.B., "The Relation between the Ancient and the Younger Peshitta MSS in Judges", *Tradition and Re-Interpretation in Jewish and Early Christian Literature,* SP-B 36 J.W. van Henton et al (eds.), Leiden, E.J. Brill: 1986, pp.163-171.

Fischer, B., "Lukian-Lesarten in der VL der vier Königsbücher", *Miscellanea biblica et orientalia R.P. Athanasio Miller oblata* (Studia Anselmiana XXVII-XXVIII) Rome, 1951: pp.169-177.

Gehman, H.S., "The Armenian Version of the Book of Daniel and its Affinities", *ZAW* 48 (1930), pp.82-99.

Geissen, A., *Der Septuaginta—Text des Buches Daniel kap.5-12 zusammen mit Susanna, Bel et Draco nach dem Kölner Teil des Papyrus 967,* PTA 5, Bonn, Rudolf Habelt Verlag: 1968.

Gelston, A., *The Peshitta of the Twelve Prophets,* Oxford, Clarendon Press: 1987.

Grélot, P., "Les versions grecques de Daniel", *Bib* 47 (1966), pp.381-402.

Hamm, W., *Der Septuaginta—Text des Buches Daniel Kap.1-2 nach dem Kölner Teil des Papyrus 967,* PTA 10. Bonn, Rudolf Habelt Verlag: 1969.

— *Der Setuaginta—Text des Buches Daniel Kap.3-4 nach dem Kölner Teil des Papyrus 967,* PTA 21. Bonn, Rudolf Habelt Verlag: 1977.

Inglisian, V., "Die armenische Literatur", *Armenisch und Kaukasische Sprachen* HO 1/7. Leiden/Köln, E.J. Brill: 1963, pp.157-250.

Johnson, B., "Armenian Biblical Tradition in Comparison with the Vulgate and Septuagint", T.J. Samuelian and M.E. Stone (eds.) *Medieval Armenian Culture,* Chico, CA, Scholars Press: 1984, pp.357-364.

Kallarakkal, A.G., *The Peshitto Version of Daniel — A compari-
son with the Massoretic Text, the Septuagint and
Theodotion* (Ph.D. dissertation, University of
Hamburg, 1973.)

Leloir, L., "Orientales de la Bible (Versions): Arméniennes",
Supplement au Dictionnaire de la Bible, L. Pirot et
al (eds.), Paris, Librairie Letouzey et Ané: 1960,
vol.VI, cols.810-818 (géorgiennes: cols.829-834.)

McCrystall, A., "Studies in the Old Greek of Daniel" (D.Phil. dissertation, University of Oxford, 1980.)

McCullough, W.S., *A Short History of Syriac Christianity to
the Rise of Islam,* Chico, CA, Scholars Press: 1982.

Metzger, B.M., *The Early Versions of the New Testament,*
Oxford, Clarendon Press: 1977.

Montgomery, J.A., "Hexaplaric Strata in the Greek Texts of
Daniel", *JBL* 44 (1925), pp.289-302.

Muradyan, P., "Hay-Vra dakan grakan-mšakut'ayin p'ox-
haraberut'yunneri patmut'yunic' [From the History
of Armeno-Georgian literary-cultural Relations]
Ejm (1966) no.11-12, pp.51-58.

Oskanyan, N. et al, *Hay Girkё 1512-1800 t'vakannerin* [The
Armenian Book from 1512-1800], Erevan,
Myasnikyan State Library: 1988.

Pace, Sh., "The Old Greek Translation of Daniel 7-12" (Ph.D.
dissertation, University of Notre Dame, 1984.)
[CBQMS 19, Washington, D.C., Catholic Biblical
Association: 1988]

— "The Stratigraphy of the Text of Daniel and the
Question of *Tendenz* in the Old Greek", *BIOSCS*
17 (1984), pp.15-35.

Rhodes, E.F., "Limitations of Armenian in Representing
Greek", *The Early Versions of the New Testament,*
B.M. Metzger, Oxford, Clarendon Press: 1977,
pp.171-181.

Running, L.G., "The problems of mixed Syriac MSS of Susanna
in the seventeenth century", PICVIII, *VT* XIX
(1969), pp.377-383.

Šanize, M., "Remarques au sujet de la Bible Géorgienne", BK XLI
(1983), pp.105-122.

Saiz, J.R. Busto, "El texto Teodociónico de Daniel y la traducción
de Simaco", *Sef* XL (1980)1, pp.41-55.

Stone, M.E., "The Old Armenian Version of Isaiah: Towards the
Choice of the Base Text for an Edition", *Textus*
AHUBP viii (1973), pp.107-125.

Tarchni švili, M., *Geschichte der kirchlichen georgischen
Literatur SeT* 185, Vatican City, Biblioteca

Apostolica Vaticana: 1955.

Tĕr-Movsessian, M., *Istoriia Perevoda Biblii na Armianskii Yazyk*[History of the translation of the Bible into Armenian] St. Petersburg: Pushkinskaia Skoropechatnia, 1902.

Tĕr-Połosean, P., *Łazar V. Baberdaci ew Yovhannĕs T'lkurancwoy Tał kajn Liparti* [Łazar Baberdaci and Yovhannĕs T'lkuranci's poem on Brave Liparit] National Library 203, Vienna, Mxitarist Press: 1968.

Tov, E., *The Text-Critical Use of the Septuagint in Biblical Research,* JBS 3, Jerusalem, Simor Ltd.: 1981.

Winkler, G., "An Obscure Chapter in Armenian Church History (428-439)", *REA* XIX (1985), pp.85-180.

— Die spätere überarbeitung der armenischen Quellen zu den Ereignissen der Jahre von bis nach dem Ephesinum", *Or Chr* 70 (1986), pp.143-180.

Wyngarden, H.J., *The Syriac Version of the book of Daniel,* Leipzig, W. Dragulin: 1923.

Zeyt'unyan, A.S., "Astuacašnči hayeren t'argmanut'yan jeṙagrakan miaworneri dasakargman masin" [Concerning the Classification of Manuscript Sources of the Armenian Version of the Bible] *B Mat* 12 (1977), pp.295-304.

Ziegler, J., "Der Bibeltext in Daniel - Kommentar des Hippolyt von Rom", *NGW Gött,* 1952, pp.163-199.

INDEX OF PERSONS
Ancient and Patristic

Medieval

Modern

Toporaphical Index

Subject Index

INDEX OF BIBLICAL PASSAGES

-45   34, 39, 44, 259
-46   38, 270, 348
-47   30, 36, 45, 314, 374
-48   36, 38, 40, 43, 267, 305, 379
-49   34, 35, 38, 42, 43, 45, 89, 244
-50   35, 37, 89, 304, 306, 378
-51   32, 33, 37, 44, 255, 369
-52   35, 40, 43, 44, 102, 103, 244, 270, 274, 285, 340, 359, 374
-53   33, 34, 35, 36, 37, 40, 44, 45, 244, 269, 284, 365, 376
-54   35, 38, 45, 89, 120, 380
-55   30, 36, 38, 42, 89, 109, 347, 368
-56   32, 34, 43, 104, 270, 368
-57   32, 104, 111, 248, 255, 259, 378, 380
-58   32, 33, 35, 43, 90, 267, 368, 370, 374, 380
-59   34, 38, 43, 44, 45, 90, 111, 244, 249, 267, 270, 368
-60   32, 44, 270, 274, 365
-61   30, 32, 33, 34, 35, 36, 40, 45, 88, 89, 102, 110, 305, 319, 360
-62   38, 89, 270, 274, 306
-63   31, 44, 45, 88, 272, 274, 374
-64   105, 244, 267

1:2   251, 281, 316, 349, 361
-3   32, 270
-4   249, 259, 267, 270, 274, 324
-5   103, 241, 270, 277, 314, 327, 347
-6   314
-7   106
-8   107, 121, 259, 267, 282, 319, 327, 347, 361, 377
-9   121, 288, 378
-10   109, 121, 246, 324, 348, 370, 373
-11   121, 327, 353
-12   109, 111, 242, 270, 378
-13   258, 259, 270
-14   326
-15   107, 256, 259, 264, 349, 365, 373
-16   107, 109, 378
-17   100, 256, 322
-18   121, 267, 325, 326, 341, 342
-19   243, 359
-20   245
-21   104

2:1   249, 363
-2   108, 243, 359, 363
-3   335

-3   317, 334
-4   107, 271, 273, 341, 344
-5   107, 269, 319, 335, 341, 364, 381, 401, 402, 403
-6   103, 108, 260, 396
-7   106, 107, 108, 372, 375, 402
-8   370, 403
-10   108, 271, 273, 345, 372, 375
-11   107, 108, 380, 403
-12   107, 109, 380, 403
-13   254, 325
-14   107, 242, 270, 367, 403
-15   107, 108, 119, 120, 342, 380, 402, 403
-16   317
-17   105, 349
-18   107, 119, 120, 249, 271, 281, 335, 367, 402, 403
-19   260, 316, 363, 396, 403
-20   257, 373
-21   263, 305, 391, 403
-22   271, 323, 325, 378, 379, 396
-23   277, 342, 345, 391, 396, 403
-24   102, 271, 277, 307
-25   363, 402, 403, 435
-26   257, 402, 406, 407
-27   260, 315, 337, 363, 377, 406, 409, 410, 417
-28   260, 314, 361, 376, 406, 407, 409, 410, 412
-29   260, 361, 363, 365, 370, 403, 406, 407
-30   106, 243, 412
-31   107, 271, 340, 361, 412, 417
-32   244, 402, 403, 409, 410
-33   260, 319, 344, 374, 403, 404, 411
-34   110, 406, 417
-35   112, 268, 301, 307, 365, 404
-36   307, 344, 406, 410
-37   106, 243, 250, 378, 403, 409
-38   103, 307, 316, 317, 363, 404, 406, 409, 410, 411
-39   110, 243, 364, 378, 403, 404, 412, 428
-40   106, 244, 320, 341, 365, 402, 404, 407, 412, 449
-41   244, 257, 271, 317, 334, 360, 404
-42   110, 260, 308, 363, 402, 404
-43   308, 404, 407, 411, 417
-44   242, 345, 363, 404, 408, 413, 417
-45   108, 393, 404, 406, 408, 417
-46   104, 105
-47   369, 402
-48   109, 280, 302, 369, 376, 396

```
-2      121
-3      106, 347
-4      110, 341, 345
-5      106, 242, 250, 251, 261, 319, 344, 347, 371, 375
-6      119, 244, 246, 261, 374, 380, 394
-7      245, 362
-8      261, 267, 286, 317, 360, 378
-9      103, 107, 258, 261, 361, 362
-10     14, 106, 121, 261, 263, 360
-11     106, 258, 347
-12     13, 261, 268, 269, 271, 370, 376
-13     106
-14     14, 106, 120, 245, 337, 378
-15     105, 345, 348, 373, 376
-16     258, 271, 313, 346, 381
-17     38, 254, 269, 271, 345
-18     13, 103, 261, 271, 341, 361, 362
-19     268, 337, 278
-20     14, 106, 110, 246, 261, 268, 271, 317, 347, 360, 371
-21     326
-22     242, 269, 274, 327, 394, 449
-23     43, 271, 274, 319, 326, 349
-24     283, 363, 375, 378, 395
-26     242, 271, 319
-27     34, 38, 39, 40, 269
-28     31, 38, 45, 102, 246, 326, 337, 345, 360
-29     33, 36, 37, 320, 393
-30     31, 32, 34, 38, 314, 316, 394
-31     34, 45, 280, 313, 359, 378
-32     33, 37, 41, 242, 268, 284, 342, 428
-33     32, 33, 35, 36, 42, 45, 317, 347, 394
-34     33, 34, 38, 46, 349, 366

5:1     37, 39, 277, 327, 347, 368
-2      32, 33, 39, 40, 44, 102, 256, 271, 316, 320, 359, 372, 375
-3      31, 33, 39, 40, 41, 43, 107, 242, 271, 274, 313, 346
-4      31, 32, 33, 37, 39, 45, 102, 103, 107, 110, 323, 327, 360
-5      19, 31, 33, 36, 40, 271, 274, 362
-6      43, 107, 110, 271, 273, 375, 381
-7      33, 34, 41, 42, 43, 246, 316, 320
-8      318, 320, 346
-9      246
-10     381
-11     261, 347
-12     336
```

-5   397
-6   102, 104, 106, 110, 306, 325, 397, 405
-7   104, 110, 122, 243, 246, 247, 261, 315, 319, 320, 345, 364, 366, 378, 397, 405
-8   100, 102, 104, 262, 264, 271, 321, 334, 364, 405
-9   102, 108, 258, 268, 308, 338, 346, 348
-10   102, 334, 336
-11   104, 106
-12   106, 405
-13   102, 246
-14   106, 272, 274, 336
-15   347, 362
-16   318, 328, 361, 405
-17   258, 259, 322, 405
-19   122, 246, 325, 328, 334, 349, 378, 405
-20   103, 257, 272, 274, 318, 344, 346, 365, 405
-21   103, 252, 359
-22   340, 392, 405
-23   121, 318, 363, 377, 398
-24   104, 277, 363, 398, 405
-25   243, 340, 376, 405
-26   318, 361, 405
-27   106, 268, 280, 405
-28   110

8:1   104, 244, 261, 346, 392
-2   241, 251, 261, 263
-3   272, 346, 375
-4   322, 347, 362, 366
-5   102, 324, 344
-6   249, 261, 272, 362, 370, 396
-7   252, 280, 285, 319, 359, 362, 363, 378, 396
-8   322
-9   104
-10   108, 272, 348
-11   104, 267, 269
-12   106, 108, 380
-13   106, 109, 241, 245, 269, 273, 360, 375
-14   342
-15   102, 272, 361, 449
-16   243
-17   108, 110, 249, 272, 273, 277, 361, 362
-18   102, 108, 272, 341, 361, 362
-19   109, 110, 268, 277, 334, 338, 340, 361
-20   314, 347
-21   106

-14   340, 362, 368
-15   108, 359
-16   255, 362, 367
-17   120, 288, 373
-19   392
-20   120, 243, 341, 363, 369

11:1   244, 368
-2   272, 320, 325, 361, 369, 444
-4   272, 346, 378
-5   343
-6   103, 104, 245, 269, 272, 365, 382
-7   104, 253
-8   104, 110, 323, 342, 349, 362, 400
-11   30, 32, 104, 274, 328, 363
-12   33, 272, 328
-13   31, 104, 362
-14   35, 41, 44, 343, 347, 429
-15   36, 37, 40, 88, 109, 304, 325, 338, 382
-16   37, 45, 110, 276, 359, 382
-17   39, 42, 45, 272, 273, 274, 382
-18   31, 32, 40, 42, 45, 269, 314, 383
-19   108, 382, 383
-20   30,32, 33, 38, 39, 41, 42, 323, 377, 381
-21   42, 107, 319, 374, 377
-22   34
-23   36, 107, 272, 343, 379, 383
-24   30, 37, 40, 46, 245, 247, 325, 343, 368
-25   41, 42, 44, 245, 322, 380
-26   108, 342, 365
-27   31, 36, 42,46, 269, 288, 375
-28   41, 42, 45
-29   35, 247, 269, 273, 345
-30   31, 32, 34,36, 40, 41, 349, 380, 387
-31   30, 33, 39, 112
-32   32, 46, 107, 247, 249, 315, 322, 327, 365, 373
-33   31, 32, 245, 268, 327, 346, 366
-34   31, 36, 40, 107, 268, 368
-35   36, 40, 110, 272, 361, 380
-36   110, 334, 343,347, 362
-37   317
-38   104, 105, 253, 272, 274, 276, 287, 367
-39   253, 268, 272, 325, 344, 393
-40   104, 105, 247, 314, 341, 370
-41   272, 359